OXFORD READINGS IN CLASSICAL STUDIES

The series provides students and scholars with a representative selection of the best and most influential articles on a particular author, work, or subject. No single school or style of approach is privileged: the aim is to over a broad overview of scholarship, to cover a wide variety of topics, and to illustrate a diversity of critical methods. The collections are particularly valuable for their inclusion of many important essays which are normally difficult to obtain and for the first-ever translations of some of the pieces. Many articles are thoroughly revised and updated by their authors or are provided with addenda taking account of recent work. Each volume includes an authoritative and wide-ranging introduction by the editor surveying the scholarly tradition and considering alternative approaches. This pulls the individual articles together, setting all the pieces included in their historical and cultural contexts and exploring significant connections between them from the perspective of contemporary scholarship. All foreign languages (including Greek and Latin) are translated to make the texts easily accessible to those without detailed linguistic knowledge.

OXFORD READINGS IN CLASSICAL STUDIES

Aeschylus
Edited by Michael Lloyd

Ovid
Edited by Peter E. Knox

The Attic Orators
Edited by Edwin Carawan

Lucretius
Edited by Monica R. Gale

Catullus
Edited by Julia Haig Gaisser

Seneca
Edited by John G. Fitch

Vergil's *Eclogues*
Edited by Katharina Volk

Vergil's *Georgics*
Edited by Katharina Volk

Homer's *Odyssey*
Edited by Lillian E. Doherty

Livy
Edited by Jane D. Chaplin and Christina S. Kraus

Persius and Juvenal
Edited by Maria Plaza

Horace: *Odes* and *Epodes*
Edited by Michèle Lowrie

Horace: *Satires* and *Epistles*
Edited by Kirk Freudenburg

Thucydides
Edited by Jeffrey S. Rusten

Lucan
Edited by Charles Tesoriero, with Frances Muecke and Tamara Neal

Xenophon
Edited by Vivienne J. Gray

The Religious History of the Roman Empire
Pagans, Jews, and Christians
J. A. North, S. R. F. Price

Greek and Roman Historiography
Edited by John Marincola

Tacitus
Edited by Rhiannon Ash

All available in paperback

Oxford Readings in Classical Studies
Latin Panegyric

Edited by
ROGER REES

OXFORD
UNIVERSITY PRESS

OXFORD

UNIVERSITY PRESS

Great Clarendon Street, Oxford OX2 6DP

Oxford University Press is a department of the University of Oxford.
It furthers the University's objective of excellence in research, scholarship,
and education by publishing worldwide in

Oxford New York

Auckland Cape Town Dar es Salaam Hong Kong Karachi
Kuala Lumpur Madrid Melbourne Mexico City Nairobi
New Delhi Shanghai Taipei Toronto

With offices in

Argentina Austria Brazil Chile Czech Republic France Greece
Guatemala Hungary Italy Japan Poland Portugal Singapore
South Korea Switzerland Thailand Turkey Ukraine Vietnam

Oxford is a registered trade mark of Oxford University Press
in the UK and in certain other countries

Published in the United States
by Oxford University Press Inc., New York

© Oxford University Press 2012

The moral rights of the author have been asserted
Database right Oxford University Press (maker)

First published 2012

All rights reserved. No part of this publication may be reproduced,
stored in a retrieval system, or transmitted, in any form or by any means,
without the prior permission in writing of Oxford University Press,
or as expressly permitted by law, or under terms agreed with the appropriate
reprographics rights organization. Enquiries concerning reproduction
outside the scope of the above should be sent to the Rights Department,
Oxford University Press, at the address above

You must not circulate this book in any other binding or cover
and you must impose the same condition on any acquirer

British Library Cataloguing in Publication Data

Data available

Library of Congress Cataloging in Publication Data

Data available

Typeset by SPI Publisher Services, Pondicherry, India
Printed in Great Britain
on acid-free paper by
MPG Books Group, Bodmin and King's Lynn

ISBN 978-0-19-957671-5 (Hbk.)
978-0-19-957672-2 (Pbk.)

1 3 5 7 9 10 8 6 4 2

Preface

This book reproduces sixteen chapters or articles from the diverse body of modern scholarship on classical Latin political praise-giving. The book's focus is the *XII Panegyrici Latini* collection, but I have made an attempt in the introduction to combine some sense of the role of literary praise in Roman society (in verse as well as prose), with a survey of the major achievements and trends of modern scholarship on the material; I hope my introduction's range offers some consolation to those who rue its inconsistent coverage as to those who take issue with the omission from the volume of favourite scholarly 'classics' I might have included. On that score I might protest that I did not find the selection straightforward, and that I was determined that it should include studies on textual, literary, historical and ideological matters, as well as feature works from across the many decades of modern scholarship.

The book is arranged in three parts, 'Introductions', 'Pliny's *Panegyricus*' and 'The Gallic Panegyrics'. 'Introductions' opens with my survey chapter before moving to Roger Mynors' explanation of the state of the text of the *Panegyrici Latini*, (translated from the 1964 Latin preface to his OCT edition) and closing with the landmark discussion of the late antique creation of the *Panegyrici* anthology, by René Pichon (translated from the 1906 French original). The second part, 'Pliny's *Panegyricus*', features six works on the speech: the 1968 account by Betty Radice (the Loeb translator of Pliny the Younger) of the context of the speech's composition, with some stylistic observations; two works from the 1990s on Pliny's political intentions (Susanna Morton Braund and Mark Morford); from the same decade, Shadi Bartsch's consideration of the strategies Pliny employed to assert his sincerity and Elaine Fantham's discussion of the detail and aspirations in his revision and publication of the written version; and the book's most recent contribution, Stanley Hoffer's 2006 analysis of the relationship between the speech and the opening of Pliny's *Letters* book 10. This book's final part, 'The Gallic Panegyrics' consists of eight articles on the late antique panegyrics. Five of these each consider the panegyrics en masse, covering the relationship between orators and government (Ted Nixon, 1983); the speeches' frequent deployment of a marked visuality as a constituent of late antique ceremonial (Sabine MacCormack, 1975); also from 1975, Edmond Vereeke's discussion of suitable methodologies for study of the speeches' rhetorical and literary background (translated from the French original); William Maguinness' 1933 article on the rhetorical techniques employed in the speeches (including Pliny's); and Barbara Saylor Rodgers' 1986 survey of the religious lexis in the third and fourth century speeches. The final three articles are examples of scholarship focussing on one emperor or speech, selected here for the intrinsic importance of the research and for the prominence of those emperors in contemporary academic enquiry: Constantine (Brian Warmington, 1974), Julian (Roger Blockley, 1973) and Theodosius (Adolf Lippold, translated from the 1968 German original by David Richardson).

The articles are reprinted without authorial revision, although Susanna Morton Braund and Barbara Saylor Rodgers have taken the opportunity to provide brief postscripts to their work. I have taken some editorial liberties: historically, citation of the *Panegyrici Latini* has been complicated by the currency of two fundamentally different reference systems--throughout this book, references have been altered as necessary to conform to the system of manuscript sequence followed by chronological order in parenthesis (see below p. 24); where I thought it helped, original references to Spengel's *Menander Rhetor* have been replaced with references to Russell and Wilson (1981); similarly, most original notes are now presented as footnotes, and are numbered by article, not by page; as necessary, references to secondary literature have been modified to conform to a standard for this volume; there have been some minor alterations to original punctuation, and typos have been corrected; on a few occasions, full citation of the *Panegyrici* text has been replaced with detailed references instead; in every chapter, numbers in square brackets indicate the pagination of original publication; on occasion, square brackets denote the insertion of some new text, usually for the sake of clarity; similarly, there are a very few instances of minor omission of original material (essentially to avoid endless repetition within this collection, or to accommodate changes to the article's publication context); some of Mynors' more technical material has been relegated to the footnotes. Latin and Greek has been translated throughout; where they have been necessary, new translations of the *Panegyrici* are my own, informed at times by Nixon and Saylor

Rodgers (1994). Finally, *PanLat* X(2) and XI(3) are considered by some to have been the work of one orator, sometimes identified as 'Mamertinus'. The name is put in inverted commas throughout this book to remind readers of the controversy and to facilitate differentiation from (Claudius) Mamertinus, the author of *PanLat* III(11).

Editing a volume such as this incurs a number of debts, and it is a great pleasure to record my thanks to the contributors and/or their original editors and publishers for permission to reprint their work; and for various kind offices, to Felix Racine, Jon Hesk, Roy Gibson, Pilar Maria Ruiz, Catherine Ware, Diederik Burgersdijk, Anna Radons, David Richardson, David Scourfield, Petra Schierl, John Atkinson, Barbara Saylor Rodgers, Mark Humphries and the other OUP reader, and to the OUP editorial and production teams. My greatest thanks are reserved for Bruce Gibson, whose speedy and helpful replies to my various and sometimes onerous requests have gone far beyond the duties of friendship.

October 2010

Contents

PART III. THE GALLIC PANEGYRICS

Abbreviations

Anon.	
Epit. De Caes.	*Epitome de Caesaribus*
Chron. Pasch.	*Chronicon Paschale*
Coll. Avell.	*Collection Avellana*
Ad Her.	*Ad Herennium*
Ambros.	Ambrosius
Amm. Marc.	Ammianus Marcellinus
Apul.	Apuleius
de Mundo	*de Mundo*
Arist.	Aristotle
Rh.	*Rhetorica*
August.	Augustine
Civ. Dei.	*De civitate Dei*
Aur. Vict.	Aurelius Victor
Caes.	*Liber de Caesaribus*
Aus.	Ausonius
Ec.	*Eclogues*
Gr. Act.	*Gratiarum Actio*
Prof. Burd.	*Commemoratio Professorum Burdigalensium*
BMC	*British Museum Catalogue*
CAH	*Cambridge Ancient History*
Calpurn. Flacc.	Calpurnius Flaccus
Cic.	Cicero
Att.	*Epistulae ad Atticum*
Brut.	*Brutus*
Cael.	*Pro Caelio*
Cat.	*In Catilinam*
Cluent.	*Pro Cluentio*
De domo.	*De domo sua*
De Invent.	*De inventione*
De or.	*De oratore*
De Prov.	*De Provinciis consularibus*
De Sen.	*De Senectute*
Deiot.	*Pro Rege Deiotaro*
Div.	*De divinatione*
Fam.	*Epistulae ad familiares*

Fin.	*De finibus*
Harusp.	*De Haruspicum responsis*
In Piso.	*In Pisonem*
Leg.	*De legibus*
Man.	*Pro lege Manilia*
Mil.	*Pro Milone*
Nat. Deor.	*De natura deorum*
Offic.	*De officiis*
Orat.	*Orator ad M. Brutum*
Phil.	*Philippicae*
Pro Caec.	*Pro Caecina*
Pro Mar.	*Pro Marcello*
Rep.	*Republic*
Rosc. Am.	*Pro Sexto Roscio Amerino*
Tusc.	*Tusculanae Disputationes*
Verr.	*In Verrem*
CIL	*Corpus Inscriptionum Latinarum*
Claudian	
Carm.	*Carmina*
Cod. Iust.	*Codex Iustinianus*
Cod. Theod.	*Codex Theodosianus*
Demos.	Demosthenes
de cor.	*De corona*
Dio Chrys.	Dio Chrysostom
Or.	*Orationes*
Epict.	Epictetus
Erasmus	
Ep.	*Epistles*
Eunapius	
Vit. Soph.	*Vitae Sophistarum*
Euseb.	Eusebius
LC	*Laus Constantini*
Vita Con.	*Vita Constantini*
Eutrop.	Eutropius
FGH	F. Jacoby, *Fragmenta der griechischen Historiker* (1923-)
Gregory Nazanien	
Or.	*Orationes*
A. Gell.	Aulus Gellius
Hor.	Horace
Epist.	*Epistulae*
Sat.	*Satirae or Sermones*

Hydatius
  Chron.   *Chronica*
ILS   *Inscriptiones Latinae Selectae (1892-1916)*
Isidore
  Orig.   *Origines*
Isoc.   Isocrates
  Ages.   *Agesilaos*
  Archidam.   *Archidamus*
  Evag.   *Evagoras*
Jerome
  Chron.   *Chronica*
Julian
  Ep.   *Epistles*
  Ep. Ad Ath.   *Epistle to the Athenians*
  Ep. Ad Them.   *Epistle to Themistius*
Juv.   Juvenal
  Sat.   *Satires*
Lact.   Lactantius
  de Mort.   *De mortibus Persecutorum*
Lib.   Libanius
  Ep.   *Epistles*
  Or.   *Orationes*
Liv.   Livy
LSJ   Liddell, Scott and Jones, *A Greek-English Lexicon*

Lucian
  Hist. conscr.   *Quomodo historia conscribenda sit*
Lucr.   Lucretius
Macrobius
  Sat.   *Saturnalia*
Manil.   Manilius
M. Aur.   Marcus Aurelius
Mart.   Martial
  Epig.   *Epigrams*
Menand. Rhet.   Menander Rhetor
  OCT   *Oxford Classical Text*
  OLD   *Oxford Latin Dictionary*
Orosius
  Adv. Pag.   *Historia adversum paganos*
Ov.   Ovid
  Met.   *Metamorphoses*

Trist.	*Tristia*
Pont.	*Epistulae ex Ponto*
Pan. Lat.	*Panegyrici Latini*
Pan.	Pliny's *Panegyricus*
Petron.	Petronius
Pind.	Pindar
Pyth.	*Pythian Odes*
PIR	*Prosopographia Imperii Romani*
Pl.	Plato
Gorg.	*Gorgias*
Phdo.	*Phaedo*
Rep.	*Republic*
Symp.	*Symposium*
Tht.	*Theaetetus*
Plin.	Pliny the Elder
NH	*Naturalis Historia*
Plin.	Pliny the Younger
Ep.	*Epistulae*
Pan.	*Panegyricus*
Plut.	Plutarch
Polyb.	Polybius
Prosper Aquit.	Prosper of Aquitaine
Chron.	*Chronica*
Quint.	Quintilian
Inst.	*Institutiones Oratoricae*
RIC	*Roman Imperial Coinage* (1923-)
Sall.	Sallust
Iug.	*Bellum Iugurthinum*
Sen.	Seneca the Elder
Controv.	*Controversiae*
Sen.	Seneca the Younger
Suas.	*Suasoriae*
Apoc.	*Apocolocyntosis*
Ben.	*De Beneficiis*
Clem.	*De Clementia*
Const. Sap.	*De Constantia sapientis*
Helv.	*Ad Helviam de consolatione*
HF	*Hercules Furens*
Ira.	*De ira*
[Octav.	*Octavia]*
Prov.	*De Providentia*

Q. *Nat.*	*Quaestiones naturales*
Vit.	*De vita beata*
Servius Auctus	
Ad Aen.	*Ad Aeneidem*
SHA	Scriptores Historiae Augustae
Sid. Apoll.	Sidonius Apollinaris
Ep.	*Epistulae*
Sozom.	Sozomen
Hist. eccl.	*Historia ecclesiastica*
Stat.	Statius
Silv.	*Silvae*
Suet.	Suetonius
Aug.	*Divus Augustus*
Calig.	*Gaius Caligula*
Claud.	*Divus Claudius*
Dom.	*Domitianus*
Poet.	*De Poetis*
Tib.	*Tiberius*
Tit.	*Divus Titus*
Vesp.	*Divus Vespasianus*
Sulpicius Severus	
Chron.	*Chronica*
Dial.	*Diologues*
Vita. S. Mart.	*Vita Sancti Martini*
Symm.	Symmachus
Ep.	*Epistles*
Orat.	*Orationes*
Tac.	Tacitus
Agr.	*Agricola*
Ann.	*Annales*
Dial.	*Dialogus de oratoribus*
Germ.	*Germania*
Hist.	*Historiae*
Ter.	Terence
Eun.	*Eunuchus*
Tert.	Tertullian
De Anim.	*De anima*
Them.	Themistius
Or.	*Orationes*
Theodoret	Theodoret
Hist. eccl.	*Historia ecclesiastica*

Abbreviations

Thuc.	Thucydides
TLL	*Thesaurus Linguae Latinae*
Val. Max.	Valerius Maximus
Vell.	Velleius Paterculus
Virg.	Virgil
Aen.	*Aeneid*
G.	*Georgics*
Xen.	Xenophon
Mem.	*Memorabilia*
Zos.	Zosimus

Part I

Introductions

1

The Modern History of Latin Panegyric

Roger Rees

1 LATIN PANEGYRIC

The word 'panegyric' is Greek in origin, a noun derived from an adjective meaning 'relating to a public festival'.[1] Such festivals would have seen the delivery of speeches in honour of the occasion, and so in time 'panegyric' came to denote rhetorical discourse which offered praise. But literary praise-giving took many forms in Classical Greek and Hellenistic culture, ranging from the victory poems of Pindar and Bacchylides, to funeral orations such as Perikles' in praise of the dead in Thucydides book 2, to Theocritus' *Idyll* 17 in praise of Ptolemy. Much as contemporary rhetorical theory sought to organize and classify oratory by type, and to identify argumentational techniques and literary styles according to subject matter, nevertheless, 'panegyric' understood as 'praise-giving' seems to have remained a versatile discourse with many applications across prose and verse. And so, although in the taxonomies of classical rhetorical treatises, 'panegyric' (i.e. 'praise') is paired off with its antitype 'invective' (i.e. 'blame') under the heading 'Epideictic' (i.e. 'display oratory'), the third and last category of speech type after 'Deliberative' (i.e. 'political oratory') and 'Forensic' (i.e. 'legal oratory'), in practice praise-giving could be as much a part of free-flowing generic traffic as any other discourse, and similarly open to innovation and growth.[2] The most heralded

---

[1] Ziegler (1949); Russell (1998) 19–21 discusses the available terminology.
[2] For the tripartite division of oratory, see in Greek e.g. Aristotle *Rh.* 1.3 and in Latin e.g. *Rh. Ad Her.* 1.2; Clarke (1996[3]) 24. On Greek epideictic see Burgess (1902)

innovation was perhaps the one claimed by Isocrates for his *Evagoras* of 365 BC, which he insisted was the first work to praise an individual in prose (5–11); the accuracy of the claim is open to challenge, but the principle holds good that the discourse of praise-giving— 'panegyric'—could legitimately seek new direction.[3]

The phrase 'Latin panegyric' presupposes some sort of relationship between Greek praise-discourse and its Roman counterpart, but like many aspects of Greco-Roman cultural interaction, surviving sources present a complicated picture.[4] Cicero said 'we tend not to use speeches of praise much' (*De or.* 2.341), a differentiation between Roman and Greek practice that was echoed by Quintilian (*Inst.* 3.7.1–2) and could even be traced further forward to the pointedly racist edge of Juvenal's identification of praise-giving as a Greek cultural trait (3.86).[5] Claims such as these, and the survival record of Latin panegyric may fuel the prejudices of those who wish to see it as a Late Antique movement, symptomatic of courtly decadence and cultural decline, but the funeral speech (*laudatio funebris*) offers an example of an established format for rhetorical praise-giving in Roman culture;[6] and so too does the shorter-lived speech in praise of a defendant (*laudatio iudicalis*) in Roman courts.[7] Even so, in Roman society of the late Republic and early Empire, literary praise in honour of the highest politicians while still alive found conditions in which it could flourish, and it is with the pages of Cicero that histories of Latin panegyric begin, as Susanna Braund demonstrates below in chapter five.[8]

The earliest Ciceronian speech to be considered panegyrical is his *De Imperio Cn. Pompei*, also known as the *Pro lege Manilia* ('For the Manilian Law').[9] Cicero delivered this speech in 66 BC in support of Gaius Manilius' proposal to give Pompey unlimited military powers

---

and Carey (2007); the magisterial work of Pernot (1993) traces developments in classical literary praise-giving through to the 'Second Sophistic' in particular.

[3] Hardie (1983) 92–3; Braund (1998) and below pp. 85–7, (2009) 19–20.

[4] Rees (2010b) on the Roman lexicon of praise, including *panegyricus*.

[5] Hardie (1983) 101; Rees (2007).

[6] Vollmer (1891); Durry (1942); Kierdorf (1980); Fantham (1999) 227 and below pp. 115–16; Covino (2011).

[7] Rees (2011a).

[8] Nixon and Saylor Rodgers (1994) 1–3; Dewar (1996) xxi–xxix; Braund below pp. 87–8; Rees (2007); Manuwald (2011).

[9] Dewar (1996) xxiv; Braund below pp. 106–7; Rees (2007) 139–41; Braund (2009) 20–1.

in his campaign against Mithridates; in detail, style and technique, Cicero's characterization of Pompey became an exemplar for Latin panegyric for centuries to come.[10] Of particular importance here is the construction of the speech around a series of personal virtues identified in Pompey—his 'military knowledge, courage, authority and success' (*Man.* 28).[11] After Pompey's defeat in the civil war, during what was in effect Caesar's monarchy, Cicero delivered three works known collectively as the 'Caesarian speeches', dubbed by Braund 'the earliest Roman imperial panegyrics that survive'.[12] In each case, in his *Pro Marcello* ('For Marcellus'), *Pro Ligario* ('For Ligarius') and *Pro rege Deiotaro* ('For King Deiotarus'), Cicero makes representation on behalf of a former supporter of Pompey, in part by articulating the qualities of Caesar in panegyrical vein: in each speech, prominent place is given to Caesar's *clementia* ('clemency'); compared with some of Cicero's earlier oratory, there is restraint in the literary style, such as a general lack of periodicity, but also a neat elegance.[13] In structure, style and ambition, Cicero's four speeches were to influence Latin panegyric for centuries to come;[14] Braund argues that in their original contexts the Caesarean speeches can be seen as an attempt to influence government by panegyric.[15] This critical observation attributes a vital agency to praise discourse and makes sense of what seems the increasing importance of Latin panegyric in Roman imperial politics.

In the context of the Late Antique court poet Claudian, Michael Dewar observed that 'the history of panegyric is inseparable from the history of many other genres'.[16] In the Roman world this was true from at least the late Republic on, in both prose and verse literature, and in fact undermines understanding of panegyric as a distinct genre at all. Two fine illustrations of this in incomplete prose works of the early empire are the *Histories* of Velleius Paterculus and Seneca's *De Clementia* ('On Clemency'). Velleius' ambition was certainly great—his work begins with Greek myth-history from the aftermath of the Trojan War and draws to a close with Tiberius' reign up until

---

[10] See below 'Panegyric as literature'.   [11] Braund (1998) and below pp. 106–7.
[12] Braund (1998) and below p. 100.   [13] Gotoff (1993) xxx–xl.
[14] Suster (1890); Klotz (1911); Braund (2009) 21; cf. Morford (1992) and below chapter seven on some differences between Cicero's 'For Marcellus' and Pliny's *Panegyricus*.
[15] Braund (1998) and below p. 102; also Braund (2009) 79.
[16] Dewar (1996) xxii.

AD 29. As his subject matter neared his own time, so too it increased in detail and length. The closing chapters of the second book are emphatically panegyrical, towards Tiberius and, to a lesser extent, Sejanus.[17] The inclusion of a panegyrical mode in historiography drew stinging criticism in antiquity itself, such as from Tacitus (at the beginning of his *Annals* and *Histories*) and Lucian (*Hist. conscr.* 7) for being incompatible with appropriate historical integrity, and has contributed to modern disapproval of Velleius.[18] But Tony Woodman argued that condemnation of Velleius for his inclusion of panegyric fails to take account of the rhetorical nature of classical historiography.[19] Traffic in panegyric would be seen in Latin historiography of Late Antiquity too, as Ammianus Marcellinus freely admits (16.1.3).[20]

A generation after Velleius, Seneca the Younger incorporated panegyric in his *De Clementia* ('On Clemency').[21] This work also survives incomplete, but we have enough to be confident of its general scope. Picking up on Cicero's technique of both praising and urging upon Caesar the virtue of clemency in his attitude towards former political rivals, the 'On Clemency' was addressed to Seneca's pupil, Nero, early in his reign. The work resists neat generic classification, as it incorporates aspects of panegyrical oratory, kingship theory and moral philosophy, but it was clearly designed, amongst other things, to influence the young emperor in his new office.[22] Seneca's didactic method is to represent to Nero a praiseworthy mirror (*speculum*, 1.1.1) of kingship, modelled, he can claim, on Nero's actual practice, but which could also (tacitly, or even insidiously) function as an example to which Nero is in effect encouraged to aspire. When combined with kingship theory, and within the intimacy of a personal relationship, the panegyrical element loses some of the declamatory clangour of formal oratory; but it is there, seeking in effect to shape

---

[17] Elefante (1997) 32–9; Ramage (1982) 271, 'the eulogy of Tiberius that ends Book 2 is, so far as we know, the first panegyric of a living *princeps*'.

[18] Woodman (1977) 28–9, 51.

[19] Woodman (1977) 51–4.

[20] See Nixon (1983), reprinted in chapter ten below. Panegyrical topoi—and their opposites—were common in Roman imperial biography too; e.g. Wallace-Hadrill (1983) 142–74 on Suetonius.

[21] Edited with commentaries by Malaspina (2001) and Braund (2009).

[22] Adam (1970); Braund (1998) and below pp. 103–6 and (2009) 17–23 labels the 'On Clemency' a 'hybrid'. For the date of the 'On Clemency', and therefore, its political 'timing' see Braund (2009) 16–17, with bibliography.

government policy, and in its inventiveness, Seneca's 'On Clemency' was to be an important text in the Mediaeval and Renaissance eras.[23]

In addition to the *Panegyrici Latini* collection which forms the focal point of this book, several other complete and fragmentary Latin prose panegyrics survive from antiquity. Only tiny scraps survive from the oratory of Fronto, appointed tutor to Marcus Aurelius and Lucius Verus by Antoninus Pius, but from his correspondence, discovered in the nineteenth century, it is clear that he was prolific in writing prose panegyrics and was keen that they be viewed as literary achievements.[24] Fate has been more gentle with speeches from later antiquity. Among the fragmentary speeches by Symmachus, preserved in palimpsests, are panegyrics to Valentinian I (AD 369 and 1st January 370) and Gratian (368/9).[25] The speech of thanks for the consulship of 379 is the only oratory to survive by Ausonius, tutor to the same Gratian; it survives complete with Ausonius' other works.[26] The panegyric of Ennodius to Theodoric (c. AD 507) also survives complete, with others of his works.[27] In palimpsest are fragments of two panegyrics—one prose, one verse—by Merobaudes from the middle of the fifth century, addressed to Flavius Aetius, the de facto ruler of the west under Valentinian III;[28] and the fragments of panegyrics to Gothic kings by Cassiodorus in the early sixth century, the latest classical Latin prose panegyric to survive.[29] Although this survival record appears quite diverse, according to a passage of Ovid, quoted by Elaine Fantham below in chapter six, and remarks made by Seneca and Pliny, it seems that panegyrical addresses were a conventional aspect of the formal assumption of responsibilities by new office holders, such as consuls and governors.[30] If prose panegyric

[23] Stacey (2007); Braund (2009) 77–9.

[24] See below n. 89; on Fronto as panegyrical orator, see Champlin (1980), Van Den Hout (1999), Rees (2011b).

[25] Edited by Seeck (1883) and Pabst (1989, with German translation and commentary); Del Chicca (1984) treats the first speech to Valentinian.

[26] In Green (1991) 146–60 and 537–54.

[27] Vogel (1885) 203–14.

[28] Vollmer (1905) 7–10; Clover (1971a), (1971b) considers the fragments to be separate works. Bruzzone (1998) for the verse panegyric.

[29] Traube (1894) 465–84; and Janson (1979) 897–8; Janson's concordance includes the complete and fragmentary panegyrics of Symmachus, Ausonius, Ennodius, Merobaudes and Cassiodorus.

[30] Ovid *Ex Ponto* 4.4.25–42; Seneca *Q. Nat.* IVA Pref. 13; Pliny *Ep.* 3.13.2; Paladini (1960).

was a standard element in the rituals and protocols of Roman imperial government, the survival record is poor.

2 LATIN PANEGYRICAL POETRY, FROM THE
REPUBLIC TO DOMITIAN

The willingness to compose in both prose and verse was not a Late Antique phenomenon, but Merobaudes was perhaps atypical for writing panegyric in both forms. The relationship between prose and verse forms was an interesting aspect of Latin panegyric, over several centuries. By the time he wrote the 'On Clemency', Seneca had already indulged his taste for literary hybridity in his satirical *Apocolocyntosis*, including some panegyrical hexameters (*Apoc.* 4.1).[31] These lines, whose tone the context makes difficult to gauge, seem to assume of the reader some familiarity with genre and topoi, but early Latin panegyrical poetry is not well attested.[32] The relationship between epideictic prose and verse has been part of a wider enquiry into the techniques and aesthetics of 'rhetorical poetry' in general in Roman antiquity, and has most frequently been considered through comparison of poetry with recommendations of rhetorical treatises. As with Latin prose panegyric, research has tended to turn to Greek practice and theory to find its bearings, such as where Isocrates explicitly weighs the merits of prose and verse forms for literary praise-giving (*Evag.* 190–1), or Menander Rhetor's recommendations for the composition of epideictic oratory to suit specific occasions.[33] The attraction of this method is that some evaluation of a poet's originality and dexterity is made possible;[34] but a potential pitfall is the presupposition of a dialogue between two literary cultures and in cases such as the Late Antique Menander, some considerable discrepancy in dates.[35]

[31] See Braund (1998) and below, chapter five.
[32] Dewar (1996) xxii–xxiii.
[33] e.g. Du Quesnay (1976); Hardie (1983) 91–102; on Menander Rhetor, see Pernot (1986) and Heath (2004) and Vereeke below.
[34] The study of Latin verse panegyric by Cesareo (1936) begins with Greek precedents to include Catullus, pseudo-Vergil, Horace, Ovid, Propertius, Calpurnius, Statius and Martial.
[35] The classic study is Cairns (1972). On Menander Rhetor, see Russell and Wilson (1981), Heath (2004).

On the question of the relationship between Latin prose and verse panegyric, there has emerged a general consensus that prose distinguished more formal, public contexts, such as political, civic or royal ceremonial, and that praise in verse was reserved for more intimate, private contexts, and admitted more licence.[36] But this schema fails to accommodate the exigencies of particularities, such as an individual's inclination to literary innovation, or the pressures of sociopolitical circumstance.[37] Writing successful praise poetry was, in the words of Carole Newlands, 'a challenging enterprise'.[38]

In fact, the earliest surviving example of dedicated Latin verse panegyric is now rarely read: the *Panegyricus Messallae*, a hexameter poem, usually dated to 31 BC is preserved in the Tibullan corpus but is now accepted to be anonymous.[39] Ceri Davies sees this 'turgid piece, full of rhetorical embellishment and strained mythological reference' as illustrative of traditional poetic patronage from the mid-Republic on, in turn to influence the panegyrical pseudo-Vergilian *Catalepton* 9.[40] Horace quotes very briefly from what his later commentator Porphyrio calls the 'very well known panegyric of Augustus' by Varius (*notissimo ex panegyrico Augusti*), but the authenticity of the lines has been variously challenged and defended.[41] Another anonymous hexameter panegyric is the *Laus Pisonis*, also in hexameters.[42] Scholarly energies have tended to be directed to attempts to date this poem and to identify its addressee, Calpurnius Piso; after Ted Champlin, the orthodoxy has been to see the addressee as the eponymous figurehead of the Pisonian conspiracy against Nero in AD 65, but to date the poem to much earlier, to AD 39/40.[43] Without lasting conviction, Calpurnius Piso has sometimes been equated with

---

[36] e.g. Barr (1981) 17–20, Coleman (1988) 62–4, Dewar (1996) xxiii–xxiv, Geyssen (1996) 3–4, Newlands (2002) 22; Hardie (1983) 102 differentiates between Roman and Greek rather than prose and verse.

[37] Russell (1998) 40.

[38] Newlands (2002) 21.

[39] Text and commentary in Tränkle (1990); on its authorship, see Verdière (1954).

[40] Davies (1973) 29 and 26. See also Namia (1975), Schoonhoven (1983). Cameron (1995) 463–71 discusses the late Republican and Augustan panegyrical verse; at 463 he writes of 'the scant literary merits' of these two poems.

[41] Horace *Ep.* 1.16.27–9; Courtney (1959) 275; Doblhofer (1966) 52–66; Cameron (1995) 464; Hollis (2007) 273–5; Estefania Alvarez (1998).

[42] Amat (1991); the most recent edition, with full commentary, is Di Brazzano (2004).

[43] Champlin (1989); see also Reeve (1984); for a revival of a later date for the poem, Green (2010).

Calpurnius Siculus, the author of seven bucolic poems usually dated to the Neronian era, some of which have a panegyrical tendency;[44] but other identifications have been posited too.[45]

Like the *Panegyricus Messallae*, the *Laus Pisonis* has been considered valuable evidence for the efficacy of praise discourse within a patronal system, but is granted little respect as a work of literature. An interpretative reluctance to take seriously the merits of versified praise has touched much modern literary criticism, as the stock of Horace's *Carmen Saeculare* and *Odes IV* makes clear. In his *Life of Horace* (2.20–5), Suetonius claimed that Augustus 'coerced' (*coegerit*) Horace to add these works to the three books of lyrics he had published in 23 BC. Suetonius' reliability has been questioned by reference to the dating of some of the poems in *Odes IV*, but the remark that Horace's later lyrics were written to order seems to have allowed a critical attitude to take root;[46] that poems commissioned in praise of the political regime lack the poetic independence and integrity of *Odes I–III*, where Horace had denied he was able to sing the 'praises of outstanding Caesar' (1.6.11).[47] Recent criticism acknowledges a pivotal redirection after *Odes III*, but accommodates that within a greater representativeness of the poetic voice in and after the *Carmen*, commissioned for public performance in 17 BC.[48] In his introduction to his reading of each of the poems of the fourth book, Michael Putnam's delineation of 'the change from private to public voices' in *Odes IV* insists on the poet's (ongoing) independence and integrity;[49] and Timothy Johnson argued that 'Horatian panegyric depends on an invitation to community.'[50] Such attention to voice and context points to the greater ambition and versatility that were in the reach of Latin lyric in the hands of a politicized Horace;[51] at the same time it shows how brittle criticism's Augustan/anti-Augustan polarity was.

[44] *Ecl.* 1, 4 and 7; see Giarratano (1943), Amat (1991).

[45] Cesareo (1931); Champlin (1986).

[46] Fraenkel (1957) 354; Doblhofer (1966); White (1993) 124–7; Johnson (2004) 40–2.

[47] Putnam (1986) 21; Barchiesi (2002) 107.

[48] Putnam (2000).

[49] Putnam (1986) 28.

[50] Johnson (2004) xix. NB Hägg and Rousseau's claim, in relation to Late Antique Greek panegyric, 'not that panegyrics were necessarily performances, but that they pretended to be' (2000) 2.

[51] See also Barchiesi (1996).

Where traditional criticism of the *Odes* was hard-wired to see a drop in literary achievement at the point where the poet was assumed to have surrendered his independence from Augustan ideology, the literary critical response to panegyrical verse under a routinely demonized emperor has varied. Surviving sources make Domitian a valuable test case here. His bad reputation was immediate, and the panegyrical poetry to survive from his reign can be adduced as evidence of his tyranny, to be blown away by the welcome fresh air of Nerva and Trajan. Approached from this point of view, the panegyrical poetry of Martial, such as in books 8 and 9, and Statius, such as *Silvae* 1.1, 1.6, 4.1, 4.2, 4.3 needed no scholarly apologetics: simply explained as a product of the intolerant tyrant's regime, such poems could be set aside by literary critics as unworthy of notice.[52] But more progressive studies revealed the historical perspectives against which sensitive readings could take place. Alex Hardie emphasiszed the backdrop of Greek epideictic composition which underlay Statius' formative experiences; that is, his origins in the Greek culture of Naples and his exposure to a Greek rhetorical education prepared Statius for a successful career in epideictic poetry of various types, including imperial panegyric, where he could both conform and innovate.[53] Ruurd Nauta considered the power balances in the various patronal relationships which Statius' poems attest.[54] The commentaries of Kathleen Coleman (on *Silvae* 4) and John Geyssen (on *Silvae* 1.1) relate Statius' verse panegyrics variously backwards to Augustan poetry and forwards to Claudian and Sidonius.[55] Rather than a beleaguered lackey responding to coercion, Statius emerges from these studies as an adept and observant operator with serious literary credentials.

Statius' panegyrical poetry was one of the examples Frederick Ahl cited in his controversial article about 'safe criticism' in times of tyrannical rule in antiquity.[56] According to Ahl, some Greek and Latin rhetorical textbooks encouraged the use of 'figured speech'

---

[52] Scott (1933); Geyssen (1996) 6 collects some examples. Howell (2009) 63 quotes Mackail's caustic judgement.

[53] Hardie (1983); on the 'aetheticization of power' resulting from the transfer to Flavian autocracy of encomiastic poetry from Hellenistic monarchies, see Rosati (2006).

[54] Nauta (2002), esp. chapter 9.

[55] Coleman (1988) esp. 62–5; Geyssen (1996).

[56] Ahl (1984).

which could both play up safely to a self-delusional ruler and, at the same time, criticize him in the eyes of his underlings. Key to Ahl's argument here is the 'susceptibility to flattery' that could mark out a ruler who commits, for example, to an ideology of his own immortality; simultaneously, such a ruler both demands a rhetoric that promotes that ideology, and renders himself vulnerable to derision for that rhetoric's excess.[57] Among other things, Ahl ran the risk of equating all ancient monarchical politics, from classical Greek tyrannies to certain Roman imperial regimes, but his argument had the enduring virtue of rescuing court panegyrical poets and orators from the charge of exercising no independence or integrity. After Ahl, in the texts of ancient panegyric, the dishonesty of extravagant flattery and the speaker's sincerity could co-exist.[58]

Inevitably, not everyone has been persuaded. For example, Geyssen insisted on the danger supposedly 'safe' criticism courted;[59] Michael Dewar accepted the probability of the widespread use of 'figured speech' in the way Ahl discussed, but denied its presence in the panegyrical proem to Lucan's *Pharsalia*;[60] Shadi Bartsch, in the chapter on the *Panegyricus* in her book *Actors in the Audience*, reprinted as chapter eight below, extended the concept of 'double-speak' in panegyrical address and, in particular, used it to address the problematics of sincerity in flattery;[61] Pliny's gambit, according to Bartsch, is to insist from the speech's opening that the congruence between 'hidden' and 'public' transcripts attests the sincerity of both under Trajan; and using Statius' *Silvae*, Carole Newlands rejected the model of a static Roman imperial ideology on which panegyric simply passed comment, sincerely or ironically, and proposed instead a dynamic dialogue between ruler and writer, through negotiation of which political autocracy and literary independence could cohabit.[62]

---

[57] Ahl (1984) esp. 198–9 in discussion of Juvenal 4.

[58] Dyer (1990) asserts an example of 'safe criticism' in action, in Cicero's *Pro Marcello*, challenged by Levene (1997) esp. 68–9. Ahl and Dyer are followed by Morford (1992), reprinted below, chapter seven.

[59] e.g. Geyssen (1996) 6–7.

[60] Dewar (1994); on the proem, see also Martindale (1984).

[61] Bartsch (1994) and below chap. 8. For consideration of the sincerity of Martial's panegyrics, see Garthwaite (1993).

[62] Newlands (2002) esp.18–27.

The relatively low status epigram could command in a classical generic pecking order would limit the success Martial could enjoy for his panegyrical attitude towards the same emperor Domitian.[63] Epigram was neither the optimum medium for public display nor best known for its expressions of thoroughgoing approbation, and it seems that despite his considerable output, Martial did not secure Domitian's favourable attention as Statius did. William Fitzgerald prizes Martial's interplay of panegyric and invective, as the brevity and pointedness of epigram works a pinball dynamic across books. The collectivity and juxtaposition of opposing epideictic stances generate an energy across a book which cannot be encapsulated in one individual poem.[64] Drawing on Bartsch, Fitzgerald uses the juxtaposition of epigrams of praise and abuse, as well as their texts, to identify their 'nonsincerity';[65] the concept of 'nonsincerity' defuses the dilemma between 'sincere' and 'insincere' which in antiquity and the modern era has encouraged an essentially moralizing approach to panegyric.[66] But some ancient texts also indicate how persistent was the anxiety about the sincerity of the panegyrical voice: Martial's poem 10.72 (presumably written for a second edition which postdated Trajan's accession), with its denunciation of panegyrical practice under the Flavians, may resonate with some of the claims made by Pliny, discussed below by Bartsch and Mark Morford, but it too seems to confess the insincerity of his earlier panegyrics.[67]

3 LATIN PROSE PANEGYRICS

The earliest, longest and best known formal prose Latin panegyric is the only surviving speech by Pliny the Younger, now known as the *Panegyricus*, which is addressed to the emperor Trajan. Pliny's *Panegyricus* survives at the head of the collection known as the *Panegyrici Latini* ('Latin panegyrics'). This collection consists of twelve speeches addressed to various Roman emperors from Trajan in AD 100 to

---

[63] Garthwaite (1993).
[64] Fitzgerald (2007) 112–21; see also Rimell (2008) 7–14.
[65] Fitzgerald (2007) 4–7, 114.   [66] e.g. Levene (1997) 93–9; Rimell (2008) 13.
[67] Nauta (2002) 382–3.

Theodosius in 389.[68] The majority of the eleven speeches after Pliny's date to the Diocletianic and Constantinian eras of the late third and early fourth centuries. Many of these, but not all, are anonymous. This represents a considerable body of classical Latin oratory—the largest to survive, in fact, after Cicero's oratory, and with a few mainly fragmentary exceptions, the only Latin oratory to survive from the imperial period.

The modern history of the *Panegyrici Latini* has been mixed. As Mynors records in his introduction to his 1964 *Oxford Classical Texts* edition, reprinted in translation below, it seems it was a Late Antique manuscript of the speeches that Giovanni Aurispa found in the library of the Cathedral of Saint Martin in Mainz in the summer of 1433, on a break from a church council at Basle.[69] Although Aurispa is best known for his discovery of countless manuscripts of Greek classics, he seems to have been very pleased with his Latin find, especially that of Pliny the Younger's speech, which heads the collection.[70] He made a copy. At the same church council, and perhaps on the same trip to Mainz, was the Archbishop of Milan, Francesco Pizzolpasso who also made a copy.[71] From these copies, twenty-seven further Italian copies stem, plus more which include only Pliny's speech.[72] The enthusiastic welcome this immediate distribution suggests was underlined by the number of early print editions: the first was Puteolanus' Milan edition of c.1482, to be followed over the next three centuries by many others, including Cuspinianus (Vienna 1513), Livineius (Antwerp 1599), Gruterus (Frankfurt 1607) and Valpy (London 1828).[73] This appetite for classical Latin prose panegyrics no doubt owed much to the good reputation

---

[68] For bibliographies of scholarship on the collection, see Baehrens (1925), Lassandro (1989), Lassandro and Diviccaro (1998); for Pliny's *Panegyricus* alone, see Fedeli (1989).

[69] Below pp. 49 and 51. Also recorded in Baehrens (1874) viii, Durry (1938) 73, Galletier (1949) xxxix, and Garcia Ruiz (2006) 38–9, with bibliography. See also Rundle (1998) 150–1.

[70] Below p. 49. On Aurispa, Wilamowitz-Moellendorff (1982) 24, Pfeiffer (1976) 48. Pliny's *Letters* had survived by a separate transmission tradition, and given that in III.13 and 18, Pliny discusses his speech, Aurispa must have been particularly thrilled; Rundle (1998) 152.

[71] Below p. 50, Lassandro and Diviccaro (1998) 132 and Garcia Ruiz (2006) 39–41, with bibliography.

[72] Rundle (1998) 151–2.

[73] See Lassandro (1989) 228–31; (1992) xxix–xxxvii. According to Lassandro (1992) xxviii, Gruterus introduced the now orthodox chapter divisions.

enjoyed by Pliny the Younger and his addressee-emperor, Trajan; but so too it seems, the *Panegyrici Latini* had a role as distinguished examples of literary praise-giving to inform and refine contemporary rhetorical culture in the various royal courts of Europe.[74]

By contrast in the light of the twentieth century's emerging democracies and their mistrust of totalitarian regimes, rhetorically elaborated works in praise of Roman emperors were never likely to fare very well.[75] William Fitzgerald said in respect of Martial, 'It is often said, in a rather self-congratulatory way, that imperial panegyric is the aspect of Roman literary culture that is most difficult for us to appreciate, most alien to our tastes and experience, and it is certainly true that the hyperbolic deference of . . . panegyric is hardly suited to the sensibilities of a democratic society.'[76] No longer role models for respectable political discourse, the *Panegyrici* became relics once more, the exclusive preserve of academics, but in that context too, they were subject to scorn. In 1924 Harry Caplan wrote of the classification of panegyric by some scholars as 'the most worthless bequest of antiquity'.[77] Twenty years later, William Alexander attacked not only the speeches themselves but also their modern readers, who, he assumed were not many:

'It is safe to wager that the *Panegyrici* find few readers today, and perhaps reasonable to guess that anyone known to loiter in their neighbourhood is mentally suspect'.[78]

Even William Maguinness, a scholar who highlighted the important distinction between the literary dexterity of the orators and the ethical values which underpinned their subject matter began his 1932 article in an apologetic tone, writing of the speeches' 'attendant vices'.[79] And with the change in times came a change in aesthetic criticism, as

---

[74] Römer (1989); Rundle (1998); Bannister (2001); Stacey (2007) 191–2.

[75] Previale (1949) 72; Formisano (2008) 581 cites the French Revolution as the critical moment.

[76] Fitzgerald (2007) 115, with further references to Dewar (1994) and Coleman (1998); see also Saylor Rodgers, 'In the twentieth century, it is hard to imagine delivering a panegyric with a straight face' (1986) and below p. 328; Morford 'It is hard in modern and democratic societies to understand, much less sympathize with, such political role–playing' (1992) 592 and below p. 146.

[77] Caplan (1924) 41.

[78] Alexander (1944) 37.

[79] Maguinness (1932) 41; see also his introductory remarks in his review of Mynors' *OCT*, Maguinness (1966) 65.

responses to Pliny's *Panegyricus* amply demonstrate: in the fifteenth century Aurispa pronounced it 'the most delightful read I have ever had' and Peter Decembrius, acquaintance of Pizzolpasso and Humphrey, Duke of Gloucester, said 'there is nothing more perfect, more beautiful, more embellished';[80] by contrast, in the twentieth century, the same *Panegyricus* was said by Ronald Syme to have 'done no good to the reputation of the author or to the taste of the age', by A. N. Sherwin-White to be 'terrible... where every fact and point, every adjective and adverb is swollen and multiplied in series of turgid restatements' and by Robin Seager to be 'monotonous, repetitive and unimaginative'.[81] The panegyrics are now widely accessible, available in translation in French, English, Italian, German and Spanish and the subject of critical enquiries of various classical disciplines.[82] If the majority of most recent studies tend to reserve ethical and aesthetic judgements on this corpus of oratory, flattery, it seems, will always attract attention in one form or another.

Texts, manuscripts, and editions

The first critical edition of the *XII Panegyrici Latini* was that of Emil Baehrens, published by Teubner in 1874.[83] Scholars had already scrutinized several manuscripts as recently as a few years earlier, but, as Baehrens was quick to point out in the opening to his preface, had added little to the appreciation of the interrelationships between them.[84] His preface is wordy, with fulsome explanations, justifications and examples, but Baehrens was clearly pleased to have brought a greater thoroughness to the reconstruction of the text.[85] He had consulted various manuscripts himself, including A (Upsala), copied

---

[80] For Aurispa, see below p. 49; for Decembrius, Rundle (1998) 151.

[81] Syme (1958) 1, 114; Sherwin-White (1969) 77, 82; Seager (1983) 129; see Morford (1992) reprinted below, chapter seven.

[82] The Late Antique panegyrics are available in French, Galletier (1949–55), English, Nixon and Saylor Rodgers (1994), German, Müller-Rettig (2008), Italian, Lassandro and Micunco (2000); Ruiz (2006) gives a Spanish translation of III(11). Lassandro (1992) xxxii, xxxvi–vii gives other versions and details of translations of Pliny's *Panegyricus*.

[83] Baehrens (1872) published some critical remarks in advance of the edition.

[84] Baehrens (1874) v names Ruehl, whose dissertation had appeared in 1868 and Keil, whose Teuber edition of Pliny the Younger had appeared in 1870. For relevant references, see Lassandro (1989) 220–8, and 236.

[85] Baehrens (1874) v–xxv.

by Johannes Hergot in the 1450s; and Baehrens relied on the collations of manuscripts made by other scholars for several more. In his
application of the newly developed stemmatic method, he identified
as the archetype the now lost M (for Moguntinus, so-called after
Mainz where Aurispa had seen and copied it); from M, Baehrens
postulated, were derived two apographs, namely A and the lost copy
made by Aurispa, from which in turn were derived two separate
branches, which could be used to characterize Aurispa's lost copy.[86]
Baehrens considered A a better guide to the lost M than Aurispa's
copy, as his inclusion of a list of its variants and its prominence in his
apparatus confirm. Baehrens also had a high opinion of *w*, a corrector
of Vaticanus 1775. Although he accepted and offered many conjectures, Baehrens' edition signalled a new rigour and professionalism in
the reconstruction of the text.

But for all its merits, the 1874 edition was to be swept aside. Too
late to be taken into account in his edition, Baehrens found more
manuscripts, including the British Library's Harleianus 2480, known
as H, which he immediately realized was very important in recon-
structing the archetype; he concluded that H was younger than A, but
like it, directly descended from M, and that because of it he would be
able to produce a text of greater certainty in his second edition.[87] But
a revised edition was not published until 1911, this time by his son
William Baehrens who had been only three when his father died in
1888. In his lengthy introductions to his dissertation of 1910 and the
new edition of 1911, William Baehrens was quick to point out the
faults in his father's edition—published before discovery of H, and
too early to benefit from the great advances made in the field of
prose rhythm in the last two decades of the nineteenth century,
which were to expose many of his conjectures—but he was also
sure to criticize intervening scholars for failing to take due account
of his father's advertisement of the importance of H.[88] Baehrens the
Younger accepted his father's conclusion that A and H were sibling
apographs from M, along with Aurispa's lost exemplar.

---

[86] Now known as X_1 and X_2; see below in this section and Mynors (1964) and
below pp. 49–50.

[87] Baehrens (1875); Sachs (1885) 5.

[88] (1911) iii–xi; see also Baehrens (1910) 5–8; Suster (1888) and Novák (1902) are
singled out for their oversights and weaknesses. Chruzander (1897) 2 also seems to
have been unaware of H. Pichon (1906a) 292–6 discusses prose rhythm and the
problems of some of Baehrens' 1874 conjectures.

Four French publications marked the next significant step in the modern history of the text of the *Panegyrici*. In 1938, Marcel Durry published his magisterial edition of Pliny's *Panegyricus*, with a wide-ranging introduction including historical, literary and textual matters, and a text with brief critical apparatus and detailed commentary. Like Keil and Kukula, earlier editors of Pliny, and the elder and younger Baehrens before him, Durry too took advantage of some superior readings preserved in an antique palimpsest, (Mediolanensis Ambrosianus E 147, known as R), discovered in 1815 by Angelus Maio and preserving several chapters of Pliny's *Panegyricus*, along with works of Fronto and Symmachus.[89] Other manuscripts too preserve Pliny's speech without the Late Antique eleven.[90] Durry's text rarely departs from the younger Baehrens'; it is essentially for his introduction and commentary that his publication has been considered a landmark ever since.[91]

Similarly enduring has been the excellent reputation of the three-volume edition of the eleven Late Antique *Panegyrici*, with introduction, text with facing French translation and brief notes, by Edouard Galletier (1949, 1952, 1955). The first volume has a lengthy introduction of essentially literary and textual matters, with useful sketches of the scholarly controversies and advances of the previous sixty years. The three volumes then present the eleven speeches, each with short discussions of its author, the historical circumstances and context of its original delivery, its historical value, and its literary character. The brief notes vary in coverage: some provide specific historical or geographical orientation, others cross-refer within the collection, and others again identify literary hypotexts and parallels. Galletier knew of, but had not consulted in full, two manuscripts which had come to light in recent years; one of these, from the Cathedral Library at Blaj in Romania, now at Cluj and known as Napocensis (N), Galletier identified as being in a tradition from A, but it does not appear in his stemma.[92] Like Durry, Galletier valued highly the text of younger Baehrens, mirroring his stemma in most respects.[93]

---

[89] See Mynors (1964) and below, p. 52. On the manuscript, see Lassandro (1992) xvi–xvii, Lassandro and Diviccaro (1998) 135.
[90] Listed in Lassandro (1988) 107–8 and (1992) xvi–xx; see also Mynors (1964) x and below p. 54.
[91] Reviewed by Syme (1938).
[92] Galletier (1949) xli n. 1, lv.   [93] Galletier (1949) lv.

Much more heterodox was Willem Lubbe, who proposed a radical and complicated stemma in the preface to his 1955 edition of the panegyric to Constantine of 313 AD, based upon his collation of twenty-five of the twenty-seven manuscripts to contain that speech.[94] Lubbe accepted that A and H were siblings, but granted them much less authority than earlier editors had, relegating them to being merely the latest witnesses to one of three lengthy branches to stem from the archetype. (Lubbe was to complicate this stemma further in a short note in 1957, written after consultation of the elusive N;[95] Lubbe related N to A and H, which he no longer thought siblings.) The effect of the challenge to convention raised by his stemma was to validate Lubbe's frequent turns to manuscript readings rejected by earlier editors on grounds of reliability. But as Galletier pointed out in his courteous review, Lubbe's rewriting of the manuscript tradition was based on his research of the material for one speech only.[96] Certainly, Lubbe's radical stemma seems an over-ambitious extrapolation from his collations. In addition, the decision to write his introduction in Latin, a very brief summary in English, and his translation and commentary in Afrikaans, probably further served to isolate his work.

Of more lasting reputation, on the other hand, has proved Roger Mynors' *Oxford Classical Texts* edition of the twelve *Panegyrici*.[97] Broadly speaking, Mynors' edition marked a return to the traditions of young Baehrens, Durry and Galletier. Like Lubbe, Mynors had been able to consult N (Napocensis) and in his characteristically crisp preface concluded that it derived from H (Harleianus), and A (Upsaliensis) from N.[98] This was an important hypothesis and on its basis Mynors rarely featured N or A in his apparatus; variant readings from the two Italian branches appear in his apparatus subsumed (after younger Baehrens and Galletier) under the generic identifiers X_1 and X_2, or where they are in agreement, simply X, thought to derive directly from M (Moguntinus). The effect of these decisions is to present an abbreviated critical apparatus, where few codices appear and H is assumed the surest guide.[99] Indeed, so tidy is Mynors'

---

[94] Lubbe (1955), with the radical stemma at p. 31.
[95] Lubbe (1957).   [96] Galletier (1957).
[97] Mynors (1964).   [98] vii; see below p. 51.
[99] Maguinness (1966) 65 'nobody would expect Mynors to gabble'; Paladini and Fedeli (1976) xxiii and Winterbottom (1979) 234 also mention Mynors' brevity.

reconstruction of the textual transmission that he felt no need to provide a stemma. On the other hand, he admits some emendations, offers his own conjectures, and even revives some made by the elder Baehrens.[100] But reviewers objected that in his decisiveness in the fundamental questions of transmission and in individual readings, Mynors suppresses the detail on which any dissenting voice would rely.[101] In fact, time has served Mynors' *OCT* edition well. In 1967 Domenico Lassandro published the results of his examination of H, N and A; his painstaking research collated the individual and shared errors across all twelve of the panegyrics in the three related manuscripts, and his conclusions confirmed Mynors' belief about their stemmatic relationship. Thirty years after Mynors' publication, Ted Nixon and Barbara Saylor Rodgers reprinted his text and apparatus, together with an English translation, as the subject of their historical commentary on the eleven Late Antique panegyrics.[102] Nixon and Saylor Rodgers depart very rarely from his text, and helpfully include a stemma.[103] Mynors' 1964 Latin preface to his OCT edition is translated below as chapter two; a model of succinct authority on the manuscript tradition, with occasional glimpses of its author's humour, it is well to make it available to readers of Nixon and Saylor Rodgers, who use Mynors' text but omit the preface.

There have been two Italian editions of the *Panegyrici* since Mynors. Vergilio Paladini died in 1971 and the edition he had begun was completed by Paulo Fedeli, and published in 1976. Although Pliny's *Panegyricus* is not included, in other respects the volume makes Mynors' look a little parsimonious:[104] the introductory history of the textual transmission and modern editions is full, manuscripts are listed, the apparatus disaggregates X into its various constituents, and both a stemma and a bibliography are included. It is elegantly

---

[100] Usefully listed by Maguinness (1966) 66.

[101] Beaujeu (1965) 565 and Maguinness (1966) 65, although on the question of Mynors' *Bagaudicae rebellionis* ('Bagaudan rebellion') for *Batavicae* ('Batavian rebellion') at IX(5)4.1 see Nixon and Saylor Rodgers (1994) 154 n. 12. See also Schetter (1967=1994).

[102] Nixon and Saylor Rodgers (1994) 37.

[103] The most notable textual departures are openly discussed by Nixon and Saylor Rodgers (1994) at 81, 154, 454, and 517–19. The stemma appears at 37, but does not feature Pizzolpasso, whom Mynors (1964) vi, below p. 50, suspected was the origin of the X_2 branch of Italian codices.

[104] Winterbottom (1979) 235 describes the book as 'a useful supplement to Mynors'.

produced too. The text itself broadly reprises the orthodoxy of the pre-eminence of H.

After his 1967 article, Lassandro's fresh examination of the manuscripts continued, resulting in a full inventory and, in 1992, a new edition.[105] This publication includes description of the manuscripts, a by now conventional account of the textual transmission together with useful references, and the text of all twelve speeches with a critical apparatus which reverts to reference to X.[106] The text is in broad agreement with Mynors and Paladini-Fedeli.[107] Lassandro includes a second apparatus which cites references for literary parallels, without comment, both within and beyond the *Panegyrici Latini* collection.[108] There are also plates of sixteen manuscripts.

Eight years later, in collaboration with Guiseppe Micunco, Lassandro published an Italian translation of his own text of the speeches, with introduction, some plates of relevant visual material such as manuscripts, early editions, art and architecture, and very brief notes.[109] Most recently, Brigitte Müller-Rettig published, in two volumes, editions of the Latin panegyrics, with facing German translation and very brief notes: some pages are devoted to the major textual controversies.[110]

In addition to the works of Durry and Lubbe, there have been other editions of and commentaries on individual speeches.[111] In terms of selection of speeches for attention, there has been a distinct tendency towards panegyrics by named authors. Most popular have been Pliny's *Panegyricus* to Trajan, where Durry's 1938 edition was followed by Enrica Malcovati (1952, with Italian translation), Alvaro D'Ors (1955, with Spanish translation) and Werner Kühn (1985, with German translation);[112] and Claudius Mamertinus' speech to the

---

[105] Lassandro (1992a). Lassandro's inventory (1988) describes each of the thirty-five manuscripts and gives the text of the *incipit* ('title' or 'lead in') for each speech; Lassandro also reproduces a plate from each manuscript. For a briefer account see Lassandro and Diviccaro (1998) 134–44; and 152–5 for a bibliography of the textual criticism of the speeches.

[106] Winterbottom (1995) was scathing in review of Lassandro's critical apparatus. Lassandro reprises his account of the textual transmission and editorial history of the collection in (2000) 25–32.

[107] Lassandro (1992) xxvi.

[108] Winterbottom (1995) 561 noted the value of this.

[109] Micunco and Lassandro (2000), reviewed by Hostein (2004).

[110] Müller-Rettig (2008) and forthcoming.

[111] Lassandro gives a full list of editions from Puteolanus, (1992) xxix–xxxvii.

[112] Pliny's *Panegyricus* has also appeared with his *Letters* in Radice (1969, with English translation) and Trisoglio (1973).

emperor Julian, given in thanks for the consulship of 362, with a commentary by E. Strömberg (1902, with Swedish translation) and editions by Hans Gutzwiller (1942, with German translation), Giuseppina Barabino (1965, with Italian translation) and Pilar García Ruiz (2006, with Spanish translation).[113] The number of editions (and translations) of these two speeches in particular might be thought to provide an index of the interest in Trajan and Julian in the twentieth century, particularly among ancient historians, but it would be wrong to downplay the attention paid by historians in the same decades to other addressees of imperial panegyrics, especially Diocletian, Constantine and Theodosius. Editions of or commentaries on any of the other individual speeches have been less common. Exceptions are Oskar Schaefer who included 37 sides of densely annotated commentary on very selective features of the two speeches addressed to Maximian as part of his 1914 dissertation; Friedrich Grinda, whose 1916 dissertation on the speech to Theodosius included a brief survey of relevant scholarship to date and a commentary aimed primarily at elucidation of historical points; A. Marsili, whose 1965 book on the speech by Eumenius included Italian translation and commentary; and Brigitte Müller-Rettig, who published a German translation with full notes on the speech to Constantine of 310. In 2009 Maria Stella De Trizio's commentary on the speech of 289 was the first to be published as part of an ongoing project based in Bari under the guidance of Lassandro, whose characteristically learned and detailed publications since 1967 on the text, scholarly history and critical interpretation of the collection have done much to consolidate the place of the *Panegyrici* in academic consciousness.[114]

Whether working on all twelve speeches or one in isolation, modern scholars have reached a wide consensus that the text of the *Panegyrici Latini* is best recovered from Harleianus 2480 against the X family of Italian manuscripts. Apart from the value of readings where H is in error, or occasional conjectures, the most controversial issue in establishing the text is the appropriate status to be granted to lost manuscripts which seem to have informed two sixteenth-century editions of the collection. Cuspinianus' edition, published in Vienna in 1513, contains readings which are otherwise unattested. Some are only one word in length; the longest runs to thirteen. In many other

---

[113] The speech is also translated into English, with historical notes, in Lieu (1989).
[114] De Trizio (2009) uses Lassandro's 1992 text.

places, Cuspinianus' edition is in agreement with H against X. If the unique readings in Cuspinianus should be thought of as conjectures, or if not, and they should be attributed to a manuscript (or manuscripts) Cuspinianus had consulted, what relation it (or they) had to the Mainz archetype, are questions that have found no consensus among critics and editors.[115] Less controversial has proved the codex known as Bertiniensis (so named after the abbey of St Bertin at Saint-Omer) from which Franciscus Modius made notes which he then made available to Livineius, who included them as variants in the marginalia of his 1599 Antwerp edition.[116]

The collection

According to a reconstruction of the Moguntinus archetype from H and X, it seems that the manuscript tradition did not preserve the *Panegyrici* in their chronological order.[117] Different editors of the collection have not adopted the same practice in sequencing the texts: Baehrens the Elder, Galletier, Nixon and Saylor Rodgers, Lassandro and Mincunco, and Müller-Rettig presented the speeches in chronological sequence; Baehrens the Younger, Mynors, Paladini and Fedeli, and Lassandro in the sequence preserved in the manuscripts. Given that some of the speeches are anonymous and most do not have distinctive titles in the manuscripts, scholarly convention has evolved a system of abbreviated reference to enable identification of individual speeches, essentially by combining position in 'manuscript sequence' with position in date. For clarity's sake, many extended discussions of the *Panegyrici* present the speeches in tabular format.[118]

---

[115] e.g. Ruehl (1868) 16, Mynors (1964) p. viii and below p. 52. Mynors was generally inclined to accept Cuspinianus' readings. His comment in his apparatus on XI(3)7.6, 'I do not envy a man his nose if he thinks these words smell of a gloss' (1964) 262 is a combative response to Baehrens (1911) 281 'these words . . . should not be accepted because they smell of a gloss', reprised by Galletier (1949) 57. See also Klotz (1911b) 45; Galletier (1949) lii–liii, Winterbottom (1979); Thomas (1979); Lassandro (1992) xv–xvi; Nixon and Saylor Rodgers (1994) 36–7.

[116] Mynors (1964) p. viii and below p. 52; Lassandro (1992) xv, with bibliography; Nixon and Saylor Rodgers (1994) 36; Lassandro and Diviccaro (1998) 144.

[117] Mynors (1964) vii–viii and below p. 51 observes that M might have been ancient itself or descended from antiquity via few intermediaries.

[118] The convention of a tabular format seems to have originated with Galletier (1949) x–xi.

Orator	Manuscript Order	Date	Chronological Order
Pliny the Younger	I	1/9/100	1
Pacatus	II	389	12
Claudius Mamertinus	III	1/1/362	11
Nazarius	IV	March 321	10
Anonymous	V	311	8
Anonymous	VI	310	7
Anonymous	VII	September 307	6
Anonymous	VIII	297	4
Eumenius	IX	298	5
Anonymous	X	289	2
Anonymous	XI	291	3
Anonymous	XII	313	9

Unfortunately, the attempt to create a clear reference system has not been entirely successful, partly because of controversies about the dates of certain speeches—most notably the relative chronology of the two speeches dated above to 297 and 298[119]—and partly because of inconsistencies about which of the two references, chronological or manuscript, has priority. For example, the speech delivered in 313 is numbered simply IX by Baehrens the Elder and IX(12) by Galletier, who give priority to chronological order, and XII(IX) by Baehrens the Younger and Mynors, who indicate the 'manuscript sequence' first.[120] Tore Janson's concordance to the speeches refers to the *Panegyrici Latini* by manuscript sequence only.[121] Throughout this book, where necessary, original references have been adjusted to a system of citation by manuscript sequence in Roman numerals and in parenthesis, chronological order in Arabic numerals. According to this system, the anonymous speech of 313 is cited XII(9).[122]

---

[119] See below 'Dates, authors and addressees'.

[120] I am passing over the inconsistencies in use of Arabic and Roman numerals. Inevitably, in published work confusion has been particularly common between the speeches dated above to 307 and 310, variously cited as VII(6) and VI(7); and between the speech of 311 and that of 297 but which has sometimes been dated to 298 [see previous note], giving rise to V(8) and VIII(5).

[121] Janson (1979) uses Mynors' *OCT* text. On the other prose panegyrics in Janson, see above.

[122] Exceptionally, it has become a scholarly convention to refer to *Pan. Lat.* I(1) simply as Pliny *Panegyricus*.

Where we have the name of the author for a panegyric, the evidence comes from the manuscripts, although in a few cases, these attributions can be sensibly corroborated by other sources: Pliny, for example, discusses his speech to Trajan in two of his letters (*Ep.* 3.13 and 3.18). Apart from in the manuscript titles, the name Claudius Mamertinus appears in the text of his speech (III(11) 17.4);[123] similarly, Eumenius' name appears in the text of his speech (IX(5)14.5); the names Nazarius and Pacatus appear in the manuscript titles but not in their speeches, but both are named in contemporary texts.[124] The manuscript titles preserve one more name: speech XI(3) is introduced in H as 'the birthday address to Augustus Maximianus by the same teacher Mamertinus'.[125] The possibility that this orator was the 'same Mamertinus' who addressed Julian in III(11) has been dismissed on grounds of age, as he would have to have been a centenarian by 362.[126] But the coincidence in name has led some to posit a relationship—parental or grandparental—between the two.[127] More attractive has proved the theory that the phrase 'the same Mamertinus' indicates that speech X(2)—its immediate predecessor within the collection in both chronological and manuscript sequence—was by the same author.[128] Certain stylistic and thematic similarities between the two speeches can lend weight to the theory.[129] But doubts have been expressed about the reliability of the manuscript titles, and scholarship is divided in the attribution of both

---

[123] Claudius Mamertinus, known as Mamertinus, appears several times in the pages of Ammianus Marcellinus; see e.g. Galletier (1955) 4–5; Nixon and Saylor Rodgers (1994) 386–9.

[124] Nazarius is mentioned by Ausonius (*Prof. Burd.* 14.9) and Jerome (*Chron.* 324), and Pacatus, a correspondent with Symmachus, by Ausonius (*Ec.*1.10–14) and Sidonius (*Ep.* 8.11.1–2). All the manuscript titles are reproduced in Lassandro (1988).

[125] Lassandro (1988) 151.

[126] Galletier (1955) 3; this does not fit with Claudius Mamertinus' occasional autobiographical remarks III(11)17.2, 18.1, 18.5. Lassandro (1988) 149 reports that manuscript Guelferbytus Gud. Lat. II 45 attributes III(11), X(2) and XI(3) to Claudius Mamertinus.

[127] Schaefer (1914) 6, Galletier (1955) 3, Barabino (1965) 17–18, recorded by Nixon and Saylor Rodgers (1994) 388 who argue that the coincidence is more probably a scribal error.

[128] Some manuscripts of lesser reputation name Mamertinus in the title of X(2): Lassandro (1988) 117, 119–20, 153.

[129] Ruehl (1868) 18–31; Stadler (1912) 20; Galletier (1949) 5; D'Elia (1960/1) 130–2; Rees (2002) 198–204.

or either of the speeches to 'Mamertinus' (about whom no other sources provide any information).[130]

The greatest disregard for the manuscript titles was shown by Otto Seeck, who in his radical discussion of how the collection of twelve speeches came into being, dismissed 'the same Mamertinus' and focused exclusively on the author of IX(5), named in its text as Eumenius, who identifies himself as the Professor of Rhetoric at the school at Autun, known as the Maenianae. In 1882, Samuel Brandt had placed his confidence in the manuscripts' attribution of this speech alone to Eumenius and challenged some earlier scholars, including Livineius, who had identified Eumenius as author of two or more speeches.[131] Brandt's position was in turn assaulted, first in review by Gaston Boissier, then by Arminius Sachs, whose 1885 dissertation concluded that V(8) was also by Eumenius, and then again in 1888 by Seeck's bold proposal of a *corpus Eumenianum* which extended to all eight of the collection's speeches except those of Pliny, Nazarius, Claudius Mamertinus and Pacatus.[132] These different conclusions depended variously on prosopographical, lexical, stylistic, syntactical and historical data from both within the speeches and related sources. While today the impulse of scholarship in the wake of the publication of the first critical edition by Baehrens the Elder looks quaintly obsessed in its concern to attribute speeches to names, the controversy did have lasting value;[133] in addition to generating some valuable philological research, it prompted consideration about how the collection of panegyrics had come together in the first instance. According to Seeck's hypothesis, the *corpus Eumenianum* could have been adopted wholesale in later antiquity to contribute the majority of the twelve to the collection.

Brandt's position was reprised a decade later by Richard Götze, but decisive demolition of Seeck's *corpus Eumenianum* waited until the

---

[130] e.g. Baehrens (1874), Baehrens (1911), Galletier (1949), Mynors (1964), Rodríguez Gervás (1991), Lassandro (1992, 2000), Lassandro and Micunco (2000) and Stella de Trizio (2009) accept the attribution; Pichon (1906a) and below p. 55, Stadler (1912), Schaefer (1914), D'Elia (1960/1), Nixon and Saylor Rodgers (1994) and Rees (2002) are more diffident.

[131] Brandt (1882); for an earlier critic, see Kilian (1868–9).

[132] Boissier (1884); Sachs (1885); Seeck (1888).

[133] Russell notes the *Panegyrici* collection as exceptional for containing anonymous speeches. Generally, surviving panegyrics are 'the work of noted authors' (1998) 17.

new century, when René Pichon published *Les Derniers Écrivains Profanes* ('The Last Pagan Authors'), part of a multi-volume project on Gallic Latin.[134] *Les Derniers Écrivains Profanes* has two chapters on the panegyrics, then one each on Ausonius, the *Querolus* and Rutilius Namatianus. In chapters one (on rhetorical education in Late Antique Gaul) and two (on the speeches' engagement with imperial politics) Pichon's collation of evidence from the full range of the collection differentiates his work from most earlier research into the *Panegyrici*. His thematic, historical and ideological criticism pioneered a new methodological approach, one which has rarely been out of vogue since; but perhaps his most enduring detailed argument was saved for appendix 1, also published separately as an article in 1906, and translated as chapter three below.[135] Here Pichon locks horns with the predominantly German scholarship of the late nineteenth century, and most directly with Seeck.[136] Notwithstanding Pichon's insistence that his objections to Seeck's theory rest on historical data, his argument covers wide ground, including literary critical and palaeographical matters. His manner is trenchant, his conclusions forceful: that the collection was not dominated by Eumenius but included the work of many different Gallic authors, and that Pacatus himself edited the collection which he made up to a 'sacred' twelve in number, putting his own speech second to Pliny's.[137]

Since Pichon, discussion of the 'collectivity' of the twelve panegyrics has been rare, although certain observations have a significant bearing:[138] for example, that on the evidence of close verbal reminiscence, Pacatus seems to have known the speech of 313 although it has

---

[134] Götze (1892); Pichon (1906a).

[135] Pichon's appendix 2 considers prose-rhythm. See above n. 88.

[136] Franco-Prussian and -German relations of the late nineteenth and early twentieth centuries provided the tense political backdrop to the pioneering studies of the *Panegyrici Latini*, several of which were originally delivered in Trier, close to the border between Germany and France, disputed in Late Antiquity as in the decades that saw this scholarship published. At times, to greater and lesser extents, this scholarship seems informed by nationalist posturing, e.g. Boissier (1884) 5 in response to Brandt (1882); the introduction to Pichon (1906a) is subtitled '*Les origines de l'ésprit français*' ('the origins of the French spirit').

[137] (1906a) 290–1, see below pp. 73–4. Pichon's rejection of Seeck's conclusions was accepted by German scholars such as Klotz (1911) and Stadler (1912).

[138] Faure (1961) esp. 4–24; L'Huillier (1992) 21–48; Lassandro and Diviccaro (1998) 156 list only MacCormack's (1975) 144 reprisal of Pichon's hypothesis.

been argued it was unknown to the two other orators whose works post-date it;[139] and the radical suggestion that on the evidence of his vocative addresses to Theodosius, Pacatus never actually delivered his speech.[140] On the question of the ambition of the collection itself, the circumstances of the original contexts of delivery seem to rule out certain possibilities—for example, the imperial constitutions prevailing when the twelve speeches were delivered range from the adoptive monarchy of Trajan to the non-dynastic collegiate rule of Diocletian (see below 'Dates, authors and addressees'), and the official religious dispensations include the Tetrarchy's 'Great' Persecution, Julian's apostasy and Theodosius' Nicene Christianity (see below pp. 36ff). Nixon and Saylor Rodgers conclude 'the rationale for the collection was clearly literary'.[141] In every case except for Pliny's speech, the location of delivery or the orator's apparent origin was in Gaul (see below); from this consistent focus, Rees hypothesized a more politicized function for the collection—that, suitably expressed in elegant and authentic Latin rhetoric, it could serve as an index of Gallic loyalty to the central empire.[142] Traditionally scholars have understood Pliny's *Panegyricus* to have been some sort of 'model' for the eleven later speeches with which it was collected;[143] questions of the role/s of Pliny's *Panegyricus* within the collection and his work more generally in Late Antiquity are discussed in forthcoming publications.[144] The related questions of the identification, authorship, motivation, transmission and circulation of an earlier collection or collections, which might have formed the kernel of Pacatus' anthology, currently seem intractable.

Dates, authors and addressees

The manuscripts themselves do not preserve the original dates of delivery of the panegyrics, but with their general riches of detailed historical information, some speeches have been easy to pin down to

---

[139] Nixon and Saylor Rodgers (1994) 6, cf. 345 n. 9 and Saylor Rodgers (1989a) 244–5.

[140] L'Huillier (1992) 169. The conventional assumption is that with the exception of Pliny's *Panegyricus* (see below pp. 226–7) the speeches were delivered as they survive.

[141] (1994) 7, in part accepted by Rees (2002) 21.

[142] (2002) 23, taken further in (2012).

[143] e.g. Durry (1947) 89.

[144] Rees (2011b), and Gibson and Rees (forthcoming).

a specific date, in certain cases to the very day. Others have proved more elusive, and have been the subject of lengthy scholarly disagreement. The arguments fuelling these controversies have generally drawn on references in the speeches to events datable from elsewhere, such as other texts, but the early debates about the authorship of individual speeches also encouraged attempts to situate speeches in a relative chronology. Orthodoxies have been slow to emerge, but can be summarised as follows (with the speeches in chronological sequence):[145]

I(1) is a revised version of the speech delivered by Pliny the Younger to the Emperor Trajan in thanks for the suffect consulship, in Rome on 1st September 100.[146]

X(2) was delivered on Rome's birthday, 21 April 289, to Maximian, probably in Trier.[147] Maximian ruled jointly with Diocletian in an imperial college now known as the 'Dyarchy'.[148]

XI(3) was delivered in 291 to Maximian, probably in Trier.[149] The occasion was an imperial birthday.[150] The 'Dyarchy' of Diocletian and Maximian still ruled the Empire. The orator knew the speech of 289 and may have written it.[151]

In 293 the 'Dyarchy' was expanded to the 'Tetrarchy' of Diocletian, Maximian, Constantius and Galerius.[152] VIII(4) dates to spring 297.[153] It was delivered to Constantius by an orator from Autun, probably in Trier, perhaps as part of the celebrations of Constantius' recovery of Britain from separatist rule in 296.

---

[145] L'Huillier (1992) 29–39.

[146] Durry (1938) appendix 4; Paladini (1961); Radice (1968) 166 and below p. 77.

[147] e.g. Schaefer (1914) 16; Galletier (1949) 7–8; D'Elia (1960/1) 256; Nixon and Saylor Rodgers (1994) 42–3; Rees (2002) 27–34; De Trizio (2009) 10–11.

[148] Schaefer (1914) 32–76; D'Elia (1960/1); Kuhoff (2001) 28–106; Leadbetter (2004); De Trizio (2009) 8.

[149] Schaefer (1914) 15–16; Galletier (1949) 9–12, 41–4; Seston (1950); D'Elia (1960/1); Nixon and Saylor Rodgers (1994) 76–9.

[150] Arguments for a date of 21 July have not been universally accepted. The nature of the birthday hinges on the reading and interpretation of a textual crux *genuinus* ('genuine') or *geminus* ('twin') Schaefer (1914) 5, Galletier (1949) 11, Wistrand (1964), Nixon (1981a).

[151] Rees (2002) 193–204; De Trizio (2009) 11–13.

[152] Kuhoff (2001) 107–219.

[153] Pichon (1906a) 279–82 and below pp. 62–5; Galletier (1949) 73; Nixon and Saylor Rodgers (1994) 106 reject the precise dating of 1st March; Barnes (1996) 540; Rees (2002) 101.

IX(5) was delivered by Eumenius in 298, to a provincial governor, perhaps of Lugdunensis, in Autun or Trier or Lyons.[154] This is the only speech in the collection not to have an imperial addressee. The 'Tetrarchy' still ruled the Empire. Eumenius was the Professor of the School of Rhetoric at Autun known as the Maenianae, and asks for permission in his speech to use his own salary to help to redevelop the School.[155]

Diocletian and Maximian retired from imperial office in 305, the 'Second Tetrarchy' made up by Constantius, Galerius, Severus and Maximinus Daia. Usurpations, deaths and power struggles characterized the next few years of imperial college history.[156] VII(6) was delivered in Trier in July or September or December 307 to Maximian and Constantine on the occasion of Constantine's marriage to Maximian's daughter Fausta.[157]

Maximian died soon before VI(7) was delivered in Trier, probably in 310.[158] It is addressed to Constantine on the anniversary of the city's foundation.

V(8) was delivered to Constantine in Trier in 311, as a speech of thanks for granting the city of Autun a tax relief.[159]

In 312 Constantine defeated the usurper Maxentius at the Battle of the Milvian Bridge at Rome.[160] XII(9) was delivered to Constantine in Trier in 313 in celebration of that victory.[161]

Nazarius, who is usually assumed to have been Gallic, delivered IV (10) in Rome in 321 to celebrate the fifth anniversary of the accession of the Caesars Crispus and Constantinus; Constantine was absent but his sons were perhaps in attendance.[162]

---

[154] Pichon (1906a); Galletier (1949) 106–9; Saylor Rodgers (1989b) 262–6; Nixon and Saylor Rodgers (1994) 146–8; Barnes (1996).

[155] Alexander (1944); Maguinness (1952); Saylor Rodgers (1989b); Corcoran (1996, 2000²) 132–3.

[156] Kuhoff (2001) 784–840.

[157] Galletier (1952) 3–4; Nixon and Saylor Rodgers (1994) 179–85; Grunewald (1990) 26, 163; Nixon (1993); Rees (2002) 165.

[158] Galletier (1952) 34–5; Müller-Rettig (1990) 10–11; Nixon and Saylor Rodgers (1994) 212–14.

[159] Nixon (1980) and Nixon and Saylor Rodgers (1994) 255–6, with bibliography, against the claim for 31 March 312 supported by Galletier (1952) 77–8; Ronning (2007) 200–9.

[160] See e.g. Barnes (1981) and (1982) 12–13.

[161] Galletier (1952) 105–6; Lubbe (1955) 49–50; Nixon and Saylor Rodgers (1994) 289–90.

[162] IV(10)3.1, Galletier (1952) 149; Nixon and Saylor Rodgers (1994) 334–8.

III(11) was delivered in Constantinople to Julian on 1st January 362 by the Gaul Claudius Mamertinus, in thanks for his consulship.[163] Julian was the sole emperor.

II(12) was delivered in Rome by the Gaul Pacatus to Theodosius in the summer of 389, at a time when Theodosius and Valentinian II ruled the Empire uneasily.[164] The speech celebrates Theodosius' victory the year before over the usurper Magnus Maximus.

The speeches themselves yield very little information about the circumstances of their composition or survival; in the Late Antique speeches there are occasional details (such as XI(3)1.2–3 and II(12) 47.5–6), but the fullest account of the process of writing is provided in the case of the *Panegyricus* in two of Pliny's *Letters* (3.13 and 3.18).[165] Here Pliny discusses his revision of the speech for publication, as Betty Radice discusses in the introductory article she wrote in 1968 for *Greece and Rome*, reproduced below as chapter four.[166] If Radice's tone now seems a little lukewarm towards Pliny's speech, it ought to be noted that in the context of the publication of her own 1963 Penguin translation of and Sherwin-White's 1966 commentary on the *Letters*, the *Panegyricus* had been relatively neglected, at least in Anglophone scholarship; Radice covers much ground in only a few sides, raising many of the issues that were to be further explored in the succeeding generation, including historical, rhetorical and stylistic matters, and the 'new side of Pliny' that familiarity with the *Panegyricus* makes available to readers of his *Letters*. Other Latin authors whose prose panegyrics survive or are known to have existed in addition to work in different genres—thus allowing appreciation of the contribution of panegyrical composition to their wider literary profile—are Fronto, Symmachus, Ausonius and Pacatus.[167]

Despite Pliny's frank discussion of the process of revision of his speech, the published version sustains an affectation of 'live' performance.[168] The transformation of the *actio* ('delivery') of Pliny's

---

[163] Gutzwiller (1942) 17, Galletier (1955) 6; Nixon and Saylor Rodgers (1994) 389; Ruiz (2006) 19–22.

[164] Galletier (1955) 51–2; Nixon and Saylor Rodgers (1994) 443–4.

[165] Sherwin-White (1966) 245–6, 250–3.

[166] The translations were for Penguin (1963) and the Loeb library (1969).

[167] NB Russell (1998) 17; Turcan-Verkerk (2003) attributes a Christian poem to Pacatus.

[168] The revisions are discussed in Mesk (1910).

Panegyricus to a text is the subject of Elaine Fantham's contribution to a conference on oral traditions in Greco-Roman society, reproduced in chapter five. Fantham's purpose is not simply to identify in the *oratio* material that post-dates the original delivery, but to discuss Pliny's use of 'ritualistic' formulae to add a solemnity which ultimately authorizes a speech that might otherwise be dismissed. Whereas Pliny is particularly helpfully forthcoming about his act of revision, many details of which would be easily detectable anyway since they refer to events which must post-date the original delivery, no comparable evidence survives in the case of the later speeches. In a conference paper published in 1983, and reproduced below as chapter ten, Ted Nixon expresses his doubts that these speeches were subjected to a process of revision after their delivery and bases his discussion of the orators' relationship with the powerbrokers of the central empire from the Dyarchic, Tetrarchic and Constantinian periods on that assumption. Nixon's article bypassed the debates concerning attribution of speeches to individual authors, to set the various authorial-prosopographical details embedded in those nine speeches against the practicalities and ideologies of the contemporary imperial court. This includes consideration of the likely audiences in attendance at the speeches' delivery. Nixon uses prosopography to address the question of the degree of political independence the orators enjoyed: specifically this demands assessment of the function of the speeches in the mechanics of imperial propaganda, an issue which had had ethical implications for modern scholarship (see below, 'Panegyrics as historical sources'). A frequent reference point for Nixon is the Schools of Gaul, best exemplified by Eumenius' Maenianae, and the subject of many studies from Pichon to the current century;[169] the Schools of Rhetoric are seen by Nixon as the breeding grounds for orators who then use their skills in the service of the government; this model of a reciprocal dynamic between pedagogy and state offers a flexible alternative to the traditional image of orator as governmental mouthpiece (see below 'Panegyrics as historical sources').

In addition to Pliny in 100, Claudius Mamertinus in Constantinople in 362 and Ausonius in Trier in 379 both delivered their surviving imperial panegyric as a *gratiarum actio* ('speech of thanksgiving') for

---

[169] Pichon (1906a) 36–85; Haarhoff (1920, 1958²); Van Sickle (1934); Marrou (1948); Chadwick (1955); Russell (1998); Ronning (2007) 137–88.

the consulship; and in his letters, Fronto refers to his *gratiarum actio* in 143, delivered in Rome.[170] Clearly, the inauguration of the consul was a regular occasion for the delivery of a *gratiarum actio*.[171] In the list above, other occasions marked by delivery of a panegyric include imperial-family events such as accession anniversaries, marriages, and birthdays, military victory celebrations, and instances of local significance. Clearly the civic calendar would be busy, as Sabine MacCormack noted: 'Those panegyrics which survive are no more than fragments of a continuous frieze of imperial occasions';[172] in her ground-breaking monograph, anticipated by a long article of 1975 which still serve as excellent introductions to the culture of Late Antique court oratory, MacCormack demonstrated how (Greek and Latin) panegyrical orators were able to take the often mundane starting point for their own speech and elaborate in suitable style grand expressions of imperial power.[173] Since MacCormack, as much as imperial occasions such as arrivals, funerals and accessions, oratory itself has been firmly established as a key component in the imperial ceremonial of Late Antiquity.

Panegyrics as historical sources

As sources for a discourse conducted in direct contact with imperial power, the Latin panegyrics have offered manifold opportunities for historical enquiry far beyond the establishment of the date and place of delivery and, where possible, the identification of the orator.[174] The introductory pages to each speech in the commentaries by Galletier and Nixon and Saylor Rodgers generally dedicate several paragraphs or more to the broad significance of each panegyric. In certain instances a speech is the best surviving evidence for a particular historical episode or phenomenon, without which our knowledge would be significantly shallower.[175] Given the nature of the Roman

---

[170] For Pliny, Paladini (1961); for Ausonius, Green (1991); for Fronto, see Den Hout (1999) 44–6, 61 and 382–3.

[171] Pliny *Letters* 6.27; Nixon and Saylor Rodgers (1994) 3; Fantham (1999) 228 and below p. 117.

[172] (1981) 9.

[173] MacCormack (1975), reprised in (1976).

[174] 'They are priceless historical documents', Nixon and Saylor Rodgers (1994) 34.

[175] e.g. Passerini (1948).

principate, a conspicuous example is military matters: sections of panegyrics where campaigns and battles are narrated in celebratory fashion, often in close detail, have been invaluable to military and political history, such as the recovery of Britain from the separatist regime of Carausius and Allectus, narrated in VIII(4), Constantine's campaign against Maxentius culminating in the Battle of the Milvian Bridge, narrated in both XII(9) and IV(10), and Theodosius' victory over Magnus Maximus in 388, as told in II(12).[176] Outside such rhetorical set pieces, details within the speeches that might be termed 'incidental' furnish useful evidence, for example, for the emperors' military careers;[177] frontier strategies and troop movements;[178] specific campaigns;[179] barbarians;[180] the composition and size of the armies;[181] battle tactics and armour.[182] Naturally, career summaries of individual emperors or isolated details within the speeches have proved useful to modern biographers.[183] The peculiar preoccupations of the speeches have also rendered them useful sources for economic subjects such as taxation, land use and imperial investment, or other administrative topics, such as constitutional reform or law.[184]

In the above examples, the speeches have been seen to yield a type of evidence which, with only minor reservations, can be taken at face value as essentially unproblematic; typically, the speeches have contributed in specific and often very isolated ways to the wider ambition of such enquiries. In comparison, the speeches have held centre stage

[176] e.g. on VIII(4) and the recovery of Britain, see Eichholz (1953), Shiel (1977), Casey (1994); on Constantine's campaign, see Levi (1934); on Theodosius' campaign against Maximus, Baldus (1984), Nixon and Saylor Rodgers (1994) 443.

[177] e.g. Sydenham (1934); Durry (1938) 107; Hanson (1974); Barnes (1976), (1982), (1996); Nixon and Saylor Rodgers (1994) 172–7, 517–19.

[178] e.g. Asche (1983); Nixon and Saylor Rodgers (1994) 64–5; Lassandro (1998), (2000) 33–47, 59–90.

[179] Lassandro (1981–2), (1993), (2000).

[180] Lassandro (1980), (1986).

[181] e.g. Simpson (1977); Lippold (1981); Nixon and Saylor Rodgers (1994) 141–3, 499.

[182] e.g. Nixon and Saylor Rodgers(1994) 367–8, 503.

[183] e.g. Paribeni (1927); Piganiol (1932); Bennett (1997); Pasqualini (1979); Leadbetter (2009); Piganiol (1932); MacMullen (1971); Odahl (2004); Grünewald (1990); Nixon (1993); Cullhed (1994); Castritius (1969); Bidez (1930); Ricciotti (1962); Browning (1975); Bowersock (1978); Athanassiadi-Fowden (1981); Lippold (1968b).

[184] e.g. Piganiol (1935); Häfele (1958); Faure (1961b); Jones (1964); Whittaker (1976); Messina (1980); Barnes (1982); Spagnuola Vigorita (1984); Corcoran (1996, 2000²); Gonzales (2000); Lassandro (2000) 51–8; see above on Eumenius for references to the restoration of the Maenianae under Constantius.

in historical enquiries which treat them as representations of or responses to aspects of contemporary ideologies. A particular case in point is Werner Portmann's comparative survey of the use of history in Greek and Latin panegyric of the later imperial period.[185] Studies of the nature of imperial power have been numerous, with various political, ethical and religious focuses, often overlapping.[186]

Given its distance in time from the panegyrics from Late Antiquity, the various ideologies of Pliny's *Panegyricus*—explicit and implied— have usually been discussed in dedicated studies. The key factors for most examples of this historicizing approach to Pliny's speech are the newness of Trajan to the throne in 100, and the contrast of his reign with that of Domitian.[187] In his article from 1992, reproduced as chapter seven below, Mark Morford argues that the speech attempted to negotiate a relationship between Trajan and the senate: in contrast to Domitian, Trajan is characterized by Pliny as observant of the laws, a citizen amongst citizens, rather than a *dominus* ('lord'), one who encourages *libertas* ('freedom'). Morford's interpretation of the *Panegyricus* recalls the broader scheme for imperial conduct set out by Andrew Wallace-Hadrill ten years previously, which itself frequently draws upon the *Panegyricus*.[188] Similar lines on Pliny's presentation of Trajan as non-tyrannical are taken by Braund, on imperial feasting practice, and Rees, on imperial private conduct.[189] Stanley Hoffer, in the only article reproduced in this book from the current century, identifies similar rhetorical tropes in the *Panegyricus* and in certain of Pliny's *Letters*—both an important, literary case for the cohesiveness of Pliny's surviving works, and from an ideological perspective, an insistence on the centrality of the theme of imperial legitimacy at a time of a new reign.[190] Hoffer's 'intersecting axes of ideology' return to the *Panegyricus* the status of official propaganda without sacrificing

---

[185] Portmann (1988), ranging from Pliny to the sixth century in Latin, and covering Eusebius, Libanius, Themistius, Julian and Procopius in Greek. See also Nixon (1990) and Ramelli (1999).

[186] e.g. Barabino (1965); Baglivi (1984); Lassandro (1992c), (1995); Ramelli (1999).

[187] Häfele (1958); Soverini (1989).

[188] Wallace-Hadrill (1982).

[189] Braund (1996); Rees (1998). See also Barbu-Moravová (2000). Rees also argues for Pliny's presentation of a paradoxical range of virtues in Trajan which allowed him to be both a peer and a superior (2001).

[190] Hoffer (2006).

or even castigating Pliny's integrity, in a move that would barely have
been thought possible in the mid twentieth century.[191]

The religious content of the *Panegyricus* has perhaps featured less
than might have been expected in discussions of Roman religion in
general or of the Imperial Cult in particular.[192] The fullest discussion
is by Daniel Schowalter, in his monograph about Trajan.[193] Kenneth
Scott's often-cited article concluded that the speech reveals the Imperial Cult under Trajan as a political institution rather than one
based on 'belief'.[194] By contrast, with its frequent turns to ethical
virtues, Yanir Shochat sees the speech as indicative of a move in
Roman religion under Trajan away from a ritualistic system towards
a moralizing code.[195] Ittai Gradel draws attention to Pliny's explicit
comparison between Trajan's conduct within the Imperial Cult and
Domitian's—in keeping with the senatorial approval the speech articulates through the movement of its rhetoric in other respects.[196]
David Levene highlights the consistent problematics of divinity in
Latin panegyrical texts from Cicero's *Pro Marcello* to Pliny, at the
centre of which is the difficult issue of the speaker's sincerity.[197]

Two particular focal points have dominated survey studies of ideological material: imperial ethics and religion. Within this scholarship,
it has been the norm for Pliny's speech to be addressed only cursorily
or be divorced completely from the later panegyrics.[198] Opportunity
for comparison with the rhetoric and political ideology of the *Panegyricus* is offered by the so-called 'kingship orations' of Pliny's contemporary Dio of Prusa;[199] with his emphatically more philosophical
foundation, Dio provides the best extant example of a Greek reaction
to Trajan's reign, and thus a 'Second Sophistic' comparandum for
Pliny's work.[200] In a short article, Lester Born collates details which
characterize emperors by their virtues in prose and verse works from
Pliny to the sixth century;[201] Michael Mause surveys presentation of
the emperor in the full range of Latin panegyrical texts from Statius to
Sidonius.[202] By tracing common themes such as the emperor's career,

[191] e.g. Syme (1958) 754.
[192] e.g. Beaujeu (1955); Liebeschuetz (1979); Beard, North, and Price (1998).
[193] Schowalter (1993).   [194] Scott (1932).   [195] Shochat (1985).
[196] Gradel (2002) 191–2, 227–8.
[197] Levene (1997). Levene does not discuss the later speeches.
[198] e.g. Molin (1989).   [199] Jones (1978); Moles (1990).
[200] e.g. Trisoglio (1972); Fedeli (1989); Moles (1990).
[201] Born (1934); shorter still is Storch (1972).   [202] Mause (1994).

family relationships, civil and military achievements, Mause high-lighted ideological continuities across the various surviving works.[203] Several other long studies of ideological phenomena across the *Panegyrici* effectively or explicitly exclude Pliny's: François Burdeau's wide-ranging study considers religious, civil and charismatic material in the eleven Late Antique speeches;[204] Robin Seager's influential discussion of the virtues in the Late Antique panegyrics is chronologically orga-nized, tracing the themes of *virtus* ('virtue'), *victoria* (victory'), *pietas* (piety'), *clementia* ('clemency'), *felicitas* ('good luck') and the emper-ors' relationship with the divine;[205] Manuel Rodríguez Gervás surveys imperial virtues in the speeches in chronological sequence, in each case interpreting the ethical content as a means of justifying imperial authority;[206] Marie-Claude L'Huillier's wide ranging monograph in-cludes tabulation of virtues.[207] Other studies on ethics and virtues include Lassandro on usurpers, L'Huillier on the relationship between imperial virtues and the grandeur of state, Lolli on imperial speed, and Cecconi on luxury.[208] Epideictic oratory contributes to Michael Mac-Cormick's picture of the political ideologies of imperialism in Late Antiquity and beyond.[209]

Levene observes that in their various recommendations about panegyrical oratory, the Latin rhetorical treatises of the late Republic and early Empire do not mention religious matters.[210] Menander Rhetor's *Basilikos Logos*, usually dated to the late third century, is more forthcoming, but still stops short of urging orators to expatiate on the nature of a relationship between imperial addressee and the divine realm.[211] Nonetheless, the Late Antique panegyrics contain much religious material, and given the sea changes in religious culture of the fourth century in particular, this has been the subject of several studies, with various approaches. Treatments of specific aspects of

---

[203] Fox (1996) pointed out ways in which continuity itself was a function of panegyrical practice.

[204] Burdeau (1964). See also Chambers (1968).

[205] Seager (1983). NB Charlesworth (1936), (1943); Fears (1981); Wallace-Hadrill (1981), (1982).

[206] (1991) 77–110, following Rodríguez Gervás (1984–5).

[207] L'Huillier (1992) 321–60.

[208] Lassandro (1981); L'Huillier (1986); Cecconi (1991). Rees (1998), Lolli (1999), Castello (1975) and Lassandro (2000) 91–102 consider Constantine.

[209] MacCormick (1986).

[210] Levene (1997) 92.

[211] Russell and Wilson (1981). See below 'Panegyrics as literature'.

'Dyarchic' and 'Tetrarchic' religion often draw on the speeches of 289, 291, 297 and 298, such as Seston (1950), Mattingly (1952), Kolb (1987), Rees (2005), and Brosch (2006). The survival of five speeches over fourteen crucial years (307–321) in the history of the Church, has made Constantine a particular focus of interest.[212] The vision of Apollo that Constantine is said to have had in 310 (VI(7)21) has been variously interpreted;[213] it has also been a perennial stopping point in studies which contemplate an evolution in religious attitudes across the Constantinian speeches in particular or the whole collection in general.[214] Pichon noted a trajectory towards monotheism in the speeches from the speeches of the late third century up to Nazarius in 321.[215] In his survey of the twelve speeches, Jean Beranger related the speeches' rhetorical and lexical continuities to the evolving religious climate, and concluded that the monotheistic speeches of the fourth century were attempting to reconcile pagan and Christian interests.[216] Wolf Liebeschuetz's similar review situates the 'neutral monotheism' of the speeches from the panegyrics of Constantine onwards in the conventional expression of fourth century literature, pagan and Christian alike, and closes with the suggestion that the suppression of paganism at the fourth century's end necessarily changes panegyrical discourse.[217] The basis of Barbara Saylor Rodgers' article, reproduced below as chapter fourteen, is a survey of religious vocabulary in the eleven Late Antique speeches, from which more discursive analysis is possible. Saylor Rodgers tabulates frequencies of the terms *divinus, caelestis, divinitas, maiestas,* and *numen,* in each case suggesting the semantic significance from its particular context. Saylor Rodgers' closing words, 'There is no system and there never was. There is circumstance, preference, and ambiguity', challenges research which subsumes the speeches into one monolithic category and that which organizes them into strict linear progressions.

---

[212] For a specific study, see Odahl (1990).

[213] e.g. Grégoire (1931); Galletier (1950); Moreau (1953); Enenkel (2000); Turcan (1964); Saylor Rodgers (1980) and Lassando and Diviccaro (1998) 191–4 have full bibliography. See also Müller-Rettig (1990) and Nixon and Saylor Rodgers (1994) ad locc.

[214] e.g. Starbatty (2007).

[215] (1906a) 86–108; see also Maurice (1909); Kolb (2004) extends into the Constantinian period.

[216] Beranger (1970).

[217] Liebeschuetz (1981, reprinted 1990).

Without seeking to define specific signification, L'Huillier also establishes lexical frequencies as the data for analysis, and points out the role religious discourse fulfils in imperial ceremonial.[218] The orators' politicized ideologies of virtues and religion have also been central to studies concerned to relate a speech or speeches to the specific contexts of delivery. Susanna Morton Braund, Gunnar Seelentag and Christian Ronning situate Pliny's *Panegyricus* within its senatorial context in the city of Rome: Seelentag sets the speech within a canvas of narrative history, congruent with Trajan's architectural and numismatic art;[219] Ronning examines the various Trajanic characteristics and functions within the speech.[220] Paul Roche relates the speech to contemporary monuments such as the Circus Maximus and the Domus Flavia.[221] Rees considers the local, Gallic loyalties, as articulated in the speeches from 289 to 307.[222] Ronning's monograph traces continuities and changes in imperial and rhetorical practices by moving from Pliny's *Panegyricus* to the speeches of 311 (V(8)) and 313 (XII(9)), in both cases addressed to a 'post-Tetrarchic' Constantine.[223] Three articles from a six-year period from 1968, focusing on a single emperor each, and reproduced below, exemplify the durability of closely contextualized readings of oratory in recent decades. Brian Warmington's study of the presentation of Constantine in the speeches of 307, 310 and 313, reproduced as chapter fifteen ties the evidence of the panegyrics closely to the contemporary political context; in large part this is achieved through cross referencing to another medium—coinage. In Constantine, Warmington argues for a shrewdly versatile political operator, able to adapt to a shifting political landscape without over-committing himself to any long-term political policy or creed. Roger Blockley's article dedicated to the speech to Julian illustrates both the confidence and tact Claudius Mamertinus exercised in 362; his confidence is seen in his critical attitude towards the previous emperor Constantius II, and his tact in approaching religious matters with considerable restraint. And chapter seventeen reproduces Adolf Lippold's 1968 article on Theodosius,

---

[218] L'Huillier (1992) 360–96; see also L'Huillier (1986) 545–61.
[219] Braund (1998) and below, chapter five; Seelentag (2004) 214–96.
[220] Ronning (2007) 24–136.
[221] Roche (2011a).
[222] Rees (2002), reviewed by Hostein (2004); Rees (2003).
[223] Ronning (2007) 189–380; see also Castello (1975), Rodríguez Gervás (1986), Saylor Rodgers (1989a), Grünewald (1990).

in which Pacatus' commitment to a traditional form of imperial rule is emphasized.

Directly or otherwise, many readings of ancient panegyrics raise the question of the status of the works as propaganda (or not).[224] A particularly strong line was taken by Johannes Straub, writing in Nazi Germany, who in his study of the Late Antique principate, saw panegyrics as publicity channels for official messages.[225] A classic example in support of the view that the Latin panegyrics formed part of an orchestrated government message is the descent from Claudius Gothicus claimed for Constantine in the speech of 310 (VI(7)2).[226] The orator presents this detail of family lineage as news, and it has been generally accepted that he and the imperial court must have communicated before the delivery. Similar cases could be made for some of the more explicit religious positions adopted across the collection. Scholars to have taken such a 'propagandistic' line to some extent, include Galletier, Burdeau, MacCormack, Franzi, Lomas, Grünewald, Rodríguez Gervás and Méthy.[227] The findings of studies which compare panegyrics with other media can also be used in the service of the 'propagandistic' argument: inscriptions and coins have been particularly common here as official documents employed in the advertisement of imperial virtues and achievements, such as those which feature in the speeches.[228] Against this, Nixon's 1983 article showed that the orators were not in the pay of the court.[229] Mary Whitby's collection of articles on Late Antique panegyric raises the debate precisely: 'What is the role of the panegyrist, that of mediator, adviser, propagandist or (most likely) some variable intermediate admixture?'[230] Inspired by Vereeke's challenge

---

[224] Perelli (1999); Veyne (2002), cited in Hostein (2004); Enenkel and Pfeijffer (2005).

[225] Straub (1939) chapter three.

[226] Nixon and Saylor Rodgers (1994) 28–9.

[227] Galletier (1949–55); Burdeau (1964); MacCormack (1975), (1976); Franzi (1981); Lomas (1988); Grünewald (1990); Rodríguez Gervás (1991); Méthy (2000). See also MacCormack (1975) 177–86, reprinted below as chapter eleven, and (1981) 2–3, Elliot (1990). Within this volume see also Warmington and Blockley.

[228] e.g. D'Elia (1960/1); Andreotti (1964); L'Huillier (1976); Christol (1976), (1980), (2000); Bastien (1978); Belloni (1981); Lassandro (1987b); Smith (1997); Tantillo (1999); Perassi (2000); Rees (2002); Hostein (2003); Roche (2011a).

[229] See above, 'Dates, authors and addressees', and chapter ten. See also Nixon (1993), a response to Grünewald (1990).

[230] Whitby (1998) 1; Hostein (2004) 382.

to find new ways to conceive of panegyric (see below, 'Panegyrics as literature'), Guy Sabbah proposed a two-way dynamic for the speeches, consisting of *communication descendante* by which officially sponsored messages (such as Constantine's descent) could be advertised to the audience, and *communication ascendante* by which local concerns (such as Eumenius' request concerning the Maenianae) could be articulated.[231] Sabbah's influential model accommodates a range of motivations and functions for praise-giving; its versatility encourages as wide a reconstruction of the circumstances—geographical, political, ideological, religious, and so on—of delivery of individual speeches as possible.[232]

Panegyrics as literature

Despite Aurispa's enthusiastic reaction to his discovery of the manuscript at Mainz or the knowledge that the orators were acclaimed men of letters, modern literary critics have paid the *Panegyrici Latini* less attention than historians.[233] Galletier has prefatory paragraphs on the literary character of each speech; Nixon and Saylor Rodgers devote a section of the main introduction to literary matters; and commentaries on individual speeches, such as Grinda, Durry and Garcia Ruiz include more lemmata on lexical, stylistic, rhetorical and intertextual details. But the speeches have never belonged to the literary canon of Latin prose 'classics', dominated by Cicero, Livy, Sallust and Tacitus. Furthermore, two of the main critical approaches to the speeches have contributed to their marginalization as works of literary merit, according to Edmund Vereeke in his article of 1975, translated below in chapter twelve. Vereeke identifies as polarities in criticism two 'problems of imitation': one, presents Late Antique panegyrics as essentially modelled upon the works of Cicero and Pliny; the second sees the speeches' inspiration in the theory and recommendations of rhetorical treatises, best exemplified by Menander Rhetor's *Basilikos Logos*.[234] This Greek text, usually dated to the late third century, instructs the

---

[231] Sabbah (1984).

[232] Sabbah's model is accepted by Rees (2002) 23–6; Ronning (2007) 12; on communication in panegyric, Seelentag (2004) 30–4.

[233] See Aurispa quoted by Mynors (1964), below pp. 49. On the literary pedigree of surviving orators, see Russell (1998).

[234] For the *Basilikos Logos* with English translation and notes, see Russell and Wilson (1981); Bursian (1882); Pernot (1986).

reader in what to say, and in what sequence, when delivering a panegyric to the emperor. With its date and subject matter, it has been a
regular *comparandum* for the speeches—to varying extents and with
different speeches, Kehding, Pohlschmidt, Parravicini, Mesk, Schaefer,
Cesareo, Galletier and Gutzwiller, for example, have identified the
Basilikos Logos as a model.[235] Against this 'textbook' approach, Vereeke
sets the 'Latin intertextualist' approach, exemplified in the work of
Boissier, Suster, Pichon, Parravicini, Klotz and Maguinness.[236] Vereeke
does not condemn either approach but questions the balance that can be
achieved by an exclusive commitment to either. Vereeke's analysis
illustrated how literary criticism of the speeches has been dominated
by two competing schools of *Quellenforschung* which in combination
created the axiom that the speeches were derivative in nature and
fundamentally similar to each other.

One scholar Vereeke singled out for praise for his approach to the
rhetorical techniques in the speeches was William Maguinness, who
wrote two articles in *Hermathena*, one of which is reproduced below
as chapter thirteen. In the article of 1932, Maguinness illustrates the
widespread use in the speeches of the rhetorical figure technique of
comparison, before noting too the orators' interest in personification,
imperial virtues and occasional philosophical reflection.[237] In the
article of the following year, as part of the same project, Maguinness
adopts a similarly panoramic vantage to discuss the phrasing and
lexical formulae which characterize the speeches, especially at moments of contradiction.[238] Maguinness makes almost no reference to
material such as historical context or literary precedent; the 'insular'
character of his research limited its significance, even for scholars of
Latin prose. However, the importance of his non-judgemental focus
on rhetorical strategies has been recognized by specialists in panegyric ever since, and his approach stands as a forerunner to the more
historicized studies of recent decades.[239]

---

[235] Kehding (1899); Pohlschmidt (1908); Parravicini (1909); Mesk (1912); Schaefer
(1914); Cesareo (1936); Galletier (1949–55) and Gutzwiller (1942). See Del Chicca
(1985). Nixon and Saylor Rodgers (1994) 11 and De Trizio (2009) 26 demonstrate the
close similarity between the *Basilikos Logos* schema and X(2).
[236] Ruehl (1868); Boissier (1884); Suster (1890); Pichon (1906a); Parravicini
(1909); Klotz (1911) and Maguinness (1932).
[237] Maguinness (1932).
[238] Maguinness (1933).
[239] del Chicca (1985), Gruber (1997).

Pliny's *Panegyricus* has attracted more literary studies than the later speeches. Durry devotes sections of his introduction to consideration of the speech's literary characteristics.[240] Etienne Aubrion discusses Pliny's use of hyperbole, repetition, amplification, antithesis, preciousness and spontaneity as components of Pliny's 'rhetoric of affirmation' in his *Letters* and *Panegyricus*.[241] C. Hofacker applied new discoveries in prose rhythm to address Pliny's clausulae.[242] G. Picone considers the evidence for Pliny's eloquence.[243] Frederico Gamberini's stylistic analysis of Pliny's work includes the diction and rhetoric of the *Panegyricus*.[244] Morford treats the speech in relation to discussions of style in Cicero, Quintilian and Pliny himself.[245] Bartsch applies the contemporary discourse theory of James Scott to the speech in her contention that Pliny employs 'counter-strategies' (of performance and transcription) as he dances around the problem that his audience expected public praise-giving to be insincere.[246] Bruce Gibson looks at Flavian rhetorical techniques as *comparanda* for Pliny's in his analysis of the authenticity of Pliny's claim to be practising a new rhetoric under Trajan.[247] Eleni Manolaraki considers sea imagery in the speech;[248] Gregory Hutchinson its stylistic sublimity;[249] Rees its antithesis;[250] Lassandro the rhetoric of universal acclamation;[251] Bruce Gibson the rhetoric of the speech's great length.[252] Alain Gowing and John Henderson discuss aspects of cultural memory and historical exemplarity in the speech, from the recent to the Republican.[253] In addition to Durry's commentary, research to address the relationship between the *Panegyricus* and other texts includes R.T. Bruyère, Rudolf Güngerich and E. Woytek.[254] Recent and current work dedicated to the speech and to Pliny's Late Antique reception attest contemporary criticism's ongoing interest in the *Panegyricus* as a considerable literary achievement.[255]

---

[240] Durry (1938). [241] Aubrion (1975). [242] Hofacker (1903).
[243] Picone (1978). [244] Gamberini (1983); see also Fedeli (1989).
[245] Morford (1992) reprinted below, chapter seven.
[246] Bartsch (1994), above ('Latin panegyrical poetry, from the Republic to Domitian') and below chapter eight.
[247] Gibson (2011). [248] Manolaraki (2008).
[249] Hutchinson (2011); see also Armisen-Marchetti (1990).
[250] Rees (2001). [251] Lassandro (2003). [252] Gibson (2010).
[253] Gowing (2005), Henderson (2011).
[254] Bruyère (1954), Güngerich (1956), and Woytek (2006).
[255] Roche (2011b) and Gibson and Rees (forthcoming).

As was mentioned above, much modern literary criticism of the Late Antique panegyrics was concerned with establishing the role of treatises and the literary 'models' of Cicero and Pliny in the composition of the speeches.[256] This has certainly furthered appreciation of the crucial importance of the Schools in aristocratic culture, and has led in recent decades to the consensus that the Schools and the Imperial Court existed in a happy symbiosis, where the Schools prepared young men for careers such as imperial administration while the court, of course, created the circumstances in which the Schools could thrive.[257] But focus on the speeches' possible sources and inspiration has overshadowed analysis of the literary, rhetorical and linguistic character of the texts themselves, with the notable exception of Maguinness' pendant articles mentioned above. From the late nineteenth century, Chruzander compiled a deal of information on the vocabulary and syntax of the speeches.[258] From the same era is R. Novák's broad research into grammatical details.[259] Understanding of clausulae is now much firmer than before, and the use throughout the collection of the *cursus mixtus*—a combination of metrical and accentual rhythms—is accepted.[260] Maguinness highlighted a usage of the gerundive.[261] The Gallic orators' awareness of their own Latinity has been discussed by Jim Adams.[262] Burkhard treated contracted forms and the particle *dein/deinde* ('next').[263] Rees considers some uses of vocative address,[264] and narrativity.[265] La Bua sees the origins of some rhetorical structures in laudatory hymns to gods.[266] A more expansive intertextuality can also be gleaned from various studies, extending, for example, to the orators' evocations of poets such as Homer, Ennius, Horace, Lucan, Statius and Vergil.[267]

---

[256] See Vereeke below, chapter twelve. For Cicero and Pliny, e.g. Ruehl (1868) 21–3; Klotz (1911a).
[257] Russell (1998); Ronning (2007).
[258] Chruzander (1897).
[259] Novák (1901).
[260] This understanding emerged in the late nineteenth century. See Oberhelman and Hall (1984 and 1985) and Oberhelman (1988a, 1988b, and 2003).
[261] Maguinness (1935).
[262] Adams (2007).
[263] Burkhard (1886) and (1903).
[264] Rees (2003).
[265] Rees (2010a).
[266] La Bua (2009).
[267] See the various commentaries ad loc.; Bonaria (1958); La Penna (1963); Lassandro (1998); Lagioia (2004); Rees (2004); De Trizio (2005), (2006), (2009) 26–30;

Some studies have also identified relationships between panegyrics and contemporary texts.[268] Once identified, the richness of this literary profile can begin to be accommodated within a broader conception of the literary culture of the Late Antique West;[269] the literary and the ideological are inseparable when panegyrical parole is interpreted as a construction of and a participant in imperial power.[270]

Panegyric's contribution to imperial ceremonial was brought out by Sabine MacCormack in *Art and Ceremony in Late Antiquity*.[271] Mac-Cormack explores the congruence between oratorical and visual images of imperial power across three particular ceremonies: imperial arrival (*adventus*), accession and funerals (*consecratio*). The context of the delivery—the architectural setting, the individuals involved and their status—and an insistence on the heightened visuality of much panegyrical discourse are central to MacCormack's argument. The study grew out of MacCormack's discursive articles of a few years before, a section of which is reprinted here as chapter eleven.[272] Here, MacCormack proposes that through a mode of discourse that has much in common with formal ecphrasis, panegyrical orators of the third and early fourth centuries in particular, elevated description to a symbolic realm which resonated clearly with contemporary imperial visual art.

4 LATE LATIN PANEGYRICAL POETRY

A panegyrical curiosity from the reign of Constantine is the collection of twenty poems by Optatianus Porfyrius.[273] It seems the poems earned Optatianus a recall from exile;[274] the poems themselves are

Baglivi (2002). See above, 'The Collection' and Pichon (1906b), below chapter three for intertextual relationships within the collection.

[268] e.g. Sordi (1988); Lovino (1989); Ruiz (2008b); Kehding (1897) on the *Panegyrici* and Claudian, Pohlschmidt (1908) on the *Panegyrici* and Themistius; Paschoud (2002) on the *Historia Augusta*.

[269] For Late Antique literary culture, see e.g. Glover (1901) or the collections by Binns (1974), Rees (2004), and Scourfield (2007); Roberts (1989) is a celebrated analysis of Late Antique Latin verse poetics.

[270] e.g. L'Huillier (1992); Rees (2002); Ronning (2007); and Formisano (2008).

[271] MacCormack (1981), reviewed by Hunt (1983).

[272] MacCormack (1975), reprised in (1976).

[273] Kluge (1926) and Polara (1973), the latter with commentary.

[274] Barnes (1975) reconstructs a possible career for Optatianus.

difficult to categorize, but are characterized by ingenious textual
devices such as acrostics, related inscriptional conceits and graphic
forms for verses, such as the outline of an altar.[275] Seen as acutely
idiosyncratic and experimental, Optatianus is hardly accommodated
in broad schemas of Latin panegyric or even Latin poetry generally.
More central to modern scholarship on late Latin panegyrical poetry
have been questions of the wide cultural and political preoccupations
played out in surviving texts. Prominent here has been the possibility
of an influence from Menander Rhetor on Latin panegyric—as part of
the wider question of the interrelationship between Greek and Latin
literary cultures, particularly towards the end of the fourth century,
and the political split between Eastern and Western empires.[276] Eumenius speaks of his Athenian ancestry; and Claudius Mamertinus
addressed the hellenophile Julian in Constantinople.[277] The Greek-
Latin matrix has been a dominant interest in criticism of Claudian, a
native Greek speaker who effectively became the court poet of the
western empire under Honorius.[278] Claudian wrote six surviving
Latin hexameter panegyrics, including three to the emperor Honorius.[279] Claudian's panegyrics form part of a poetic oeuvre which includes invective, narrative and occasional verse.[280] Kehding's image of
him as man who rendered efficiently the precepts of the *Basilikos Logos*
in a Vergilian style has endured, but advances in intertextual theory in
particular have enabled recent studies, including commentaries, to
identify different influences too.[281] Claudian, it seems, knew Pacatus'
speech to Theodosius, but his deployment in panegyric of hexameters of
a Vergilian style marks a new turn in the aesthetics of praise discourse,
one which for all the popularity of Silver poetry in Late Antiquity,

[275] Levitan (1985).
[276] Nissen (1940); Schindler (2009) considers Latin verse panegyric from Claudian
to Corippus.
[277] e.g. Ruiz (2008a and b).
[278] Cameron (1970) is a pioneering study; see also Romano (1958), Cameron
(1974) and (2000).
[279] Available in the Loeb series, Platnauer (1922), the Bude, Charlet (1991, 2001),
and Teubner (Hall (1985)); the concordance to Claudian is by Christiansen (1988).
[280] Levy (1958); Schmidt (1976).
[281] Kehding (1899); Parravicini (1905), (1909); Struthers (1919) cf. Fargues (1933);
Christiansen (1969); Schmidt (1976); Fo (1982); Lehner (1984); Wilfried (1987);
Gruzelier (1990); Cameron (2000); Ware (2004); Wheeler (2007); modern commentaries include Fargues (1939); Simon (1975); Barr (1981); Lehner (1984); Taegert
(1988); Dewar (1996); Ware (forthcoming). This scholarly pattern duplicates that
identified and decried by Vereeke (1975).

differentiates Claudian's verse panegyrics from Statius'—the elevation of a rhetorical form by epic colour.[282]

A Janus-like Claudian emerges from modern scholarship's landscape of late Latin poetry—he is characterized as both the last great classical Latin poet and as the inspiration for a revival of Latin verse panegyric of the fifth century and beyond, in Sidonius, Merobaudes, Priscian and Corippus. Sidonius Apollinaris, the Bishop of Clermont in Gaul, included three verse panegyrics amongst his diverse output.[283] His work is available in French and English translations, but dedicated literary and philological studies had been few until very recent decades.[284] Also from the fifth century are the fragments of Merobaudes.[285] In addition to Merobaudes' career, the relationship between the literary and political character of his work has been a focus of discussions, and the fragmentary verse panegyric to Aetius was the subject of a commentary by Antonella Bruzzone, who paid particular attention to the text's literary character, such as the allusions to Vergil, Silver epic and Claudian.[286] A hexameter panegyric to the emperor Anastasius is one of the less well known works by Priscian, better known for his eighteen-book work on Latin grammar.[287] The final Latin panegyrics to survive from antiquity are the hexameter poems by Corippus, the *Iohannis* and the *In Laudem Iustini Augusti Minoris*.[288] The eight-book *Iohannis*—also known as the *De Bellis Libycis* ('On the Libyan War')—dates to the middle of the sixth century and narrates the campaign of John Troglita against

---

[282] On hexameter epic-panegyric as a distinct genre, see Hofmann (1988) and Schindler (2009) 12–60. On Claudian and the *Panegyrici*, Kehding (1899); Barr (1981); on his epic poetry, Nissen (1940); Schindler (2004) and (2009) 60–172.

[283] Stevens (1933); Loyen (1942); Harrison (1983); Harries (1994).

[284] Luetjohann (1887). The Teubner is by Mohr (1895), the Bude is by Loyen (1960), the Loeb by Anderson (1936–1965); Watson (1997); on Sidonius' Latinity, see Bitschofsky (1881); Müller (1888); on his metrics Condorelli (2001). See also Semple (1930); Bonjour (1982); Brodka (1997), (1998); Watson (1998); Colton (2000); Schindler (2009) 181–212; a concordance to Sidonius' poems was published by Christiansen and Holland (1993).

[285] Vollmer (1905); Clover (1971a).

[286] See above p. 18; See e.g. Gennaro (1959), Mazza (1984) and Bodelòn (1998–9); Bruzzone (1999), reviewed by Clover (2004); Schindler (2009) 173–81; Bruzzone also published the concordance to Merobaudes (1999).

[287] Baehrens (1883); Chauvot (1986); Coyne (1991); Schindler (2009) 216–26; for the date see Cameron (1974b).

[288] Partsch (1879); for details of Corippus' biography, see Baldwin (1978) and Cameron (1980); Estefania Alvarez (1972).

the Moors.[289] The four-book poem in praise of the emperor Justin II also combines epic narrative technique and panegyrical rhetoric.[290] Meantime, the poetry of Corippus' contemporary Venantius Fortunatus demonstrates that the traditions of Latin panegyric continued to be redeployed in the post-Roman society of Merovingian Gaul.[291]

[289] For the text, see Diggle and Goodyear (1970); for an English translation, see Shea (1998), for French Teurfs and Didderen (2007). For commentaries on individual books, see Vinchesi (1983) and Moreschini (2001). For Corippus' epic-panegyric artistry, see Romano (1968), Ehlers (1980) and Zarini (1997a), (1997b) and (2003), and Schindler (2009) 228–73. For a concordance, see Andrews (1993).

[290] Text by Romano (1970); text, commentary and English translation by Cameron (1976); the same year saw the commentary by Stache. A French edition and translation was published by Antès (1981) and a Spanish edition and translation by Ramirez de Verger (1985); on epic continuities, see also Welzel (1908).

[291] Leo (1881); selected translations in George (1996), who also published discursive interpretations in (1992) and (1998); Roberts (2009).

2

Preface to the *OCT* Edition of the XII
Panegyrici Latini

R. A. B. Mynors

1. The first in the modern era to have discovered Pliny's speech in praise of the emperor Trajan, together with the others that are called the 'Panegyrics' seems to have been Johannes Aurispa, at Mainz in 1433; for, while he was at a council in Basle, he wrote to a certain Florentine friend, 'In a library at Mainz I have found a codex in which there is a panegyric by Pliny addressed to Trajan—I have never read anything more delightful—and in the same codex are panegyrics by other authors to various Caesars.'[1] From that codex at Mainz, now lost, there can be little doubt that twenty-seven Italian books derive their origin with a further twelve which transmit Pliny's speech and leave out the rest. Following the work of scholars, it is generally agreed that these separate into two families, X_1 and X_2.[2] The best witnesses for these are as follows:

X_1: Parisinus lat. 8556, Venetus Marcianus lat. xi 12 (4082), Vaticanus lat. 1775, Londinensis Additicius 16983, all of which I could hardly believe were written after the middle of the fifteenth century.

---

[1] Sabbadini (1931) 82.
[2] In particular I must mention Keil in his edition of Pliny Secundus (1870); A. Baehrens and his son W. Baehrens, who published the Teubner (Leipzig) editions, the former in 1874, the latter in 1911. To these are added Suster (1888) and Lubbe (1955). To all these I gratefully acknowledge my considerable debt, and also to Galletier, whose editions were published in Paris (1949–55).

X_2: Parisinus 7805, Venetus Marcianus Z 436 (1706), Bruxellensis 10026-32, and (as Lubbe testifies) Budapestinensis University Library 12.[3]

[vi] When these are in agreement, what existed in the common source X is rarely left in doubt; that this was nothing other than the copy of the codex at Mainz made for the use of Aurispa anyone can work out. Furthermore, I suspect that the X_2 family stems from Francisco Pizzolpasso, Archbishop of Milan (1435–1443) who was at the same council as Aurispa. For a man of immortal memory in my country, Humphrey Duke of Gloucester, gifted Parisinus 7805 to Oxford, his old university, in about 1442; at that time, Duke Humphrey used to search for codices with the help of Peter Candidus Decembrius, and Peter admitted that all his familiarity with the panegyrics came from Francisco.[4] But today we know nothing about Francisco's text beyond some excerpts of the said Peter, which are in codex Ambrosianus R.88 sup.[5]

2. Besides the Italian codices, we have Londinensis Harleianus 2480, (mid fifteenth century) well written on paper in a German hand (H), which is derived from the same source as the others, but has its own particular qualities. (A hand from the same time, known as h, makes several corrections). [vii] Another German codex stands alongside this, Napocensis University Library; but because it preserves no true reading that is not already in Harleianus, beyond perhaps twelve instances where it corrects the slightest errors without direction from elsewhere, and has added many errors of its own, it does

---

[3] I could believe that Oxoniensis Balliol College 315 was copied from Parisinus 7805 in about 1442; and that Vaticanus 1776 was copied from Marcianus Z 436 (1706) (at least decorated by the same artist), since the latter belonged to Iohannes Bessarion, Cardinal of the Holy Church of Rome (1435–72), and the former, unless I am mistaken, to Niccolò Perotti, who was his guest from about 1447. From one or other of these, Caesenas Malatestianus S. xvii descends, and from it Vaticanus Ottobonianus 1303 (thus W. Baehrens (1911) xxv). Related to Bruxellensis 10026-32 are Vindobonensis 48 (dated to 1468), the Vaticani Reginensis 1475 and Urbinas 314, Monacenses 309 and 756 (written in 1495 by Peter Crinitus; Pliny's speech is missing), and (as Lubbe testifies) Matritensis Biblioteca Nacional 8251, which I have not seen.

[4] Suster (1888) 511; Borsa (1904) 517.

[5] Published by Sabbadini (1903) 263–7; I sought in vain for more on this matter in Paredi (1961).

not deserve uninterrupted admiration.[6] After some missing pages it begins at I(1)45.6 *opus est* ('there is a need').

But I see nothing to counter the conclusion that Napocensis descends from Harleianus, especially since after *momentoque* ('at that time') at II(12)18.3 the words which it inserts, from *ut illi* ('just as, to that') to *assistere* ('to sit'), fill up precisely one line in Harleianus. Several mistakes teach us that from Napocensis is derived Upsaliensis C 917 (when this codex was written is not preserved; Iohannes Hergot wrote sections variously at Mainz and Turin between 1455 and 1460); unless the origin of these mistakes is not in the rather frequent misreadings of the Napocensis, with its very long lines here and there, it can hardly be from elsewhere.[7] Therefore, it is of no weight.

3. The relationship between these witnesses is that when there is agreement, as there very often is, between *H* and *X*, or *HX₁* against *X₂*, or *HX₂* against *X₁*, it becomes clear what there had been in their common source (*M*), which in all likelihood was the Mainz codex itself. But when *H* and *X* do not agree, wherever we can make a judgement based on sense, language or prose-rhythm, it is clear that most often of all the correct reading is preserved by *H*; from this, at other points where we cannot make such a judgement, it is wise to prefer *H*. But if someone were to ask about the nature [viii] of the Mainz codex, it was either an ancient book itself or derived from an ancient one with few intermediaries; for the errors arising from the script they call 'continuous', that one encounters on almost every page, teach us that the distinction between [the endings and beginnings of] words had not yet been mastered. However, such was the carelessness of scribes in interchanging letters (for example *cl* and *d* at II(12)20.1 and 31.1) that I believe it was written rather in semi-uncial (as it is called) or miniscule script. In addition the text had been corrected or supplemented here and there between lines (as at IV(10)

---

[6] Colonia Napocensis is modern Cluj. Lubbe first used the codex [(1957) 247] when it was kept in the library of the Greek-Catholic bishop in the town of Blaj. I am very grateful to Aemilius Condurachi who kindly oversaw the preparation of excellent photographs of the codex for my use.

[7] e.g. II(12)6.3 *dignum dignum,* III(XI)8.1 *tum isti,* III(11)18.4 *prestit,* IV(10)23.3 *oportites,* XII(9)9.3 *de te,* and others. With her characteristic experience in these matters, Elisabeth Pellegrin (1955) has written on the Upsaliensis which A. Baehrens rated highly (as was appropriate before the discovery of Harleianus); I have only glanced at it.

19.3, *tenerabas*), and more frequently in the margins (as at VII(6) 12.7, IX(5)7.3, X(2)8.2, 12.6 and more often).

4. There are also some less reliable witnesses. Selections by Franciscus Modius from a now lost Bertinensis codex had been made available to Livineius as he prepared his edition of 1599. Just as this codex was closely related to the Mainz one (although it seems to have missed out Pliny's speech; otherwise Modius would have not kept silent about it), so it was spoiled with many mistakes, unless these are rather to be imputed to Modius; however, it has some good readings such as II(12)1.1 *iure*, 11.1 *nec id ad*, and others. It could have been a twin of the Mainz codex rather than a descendant from it; our ignorance makes it most difficult to say what it really was. There is testimony of similar weight from a most unexpected quarter—Johannes Cuspinianus, a tireless investigator of codices, whose edition was published in Vienna in 1513. Cuspinianus agrees on twelve of the seventeen occasions in Pliny's speech where the genuine words preserved in the German branch of the family (which was not yet known) perished in *X*; and also on four occasions where *H* and *X* are lacunose (*Pan.* 2.5, 24.2, 34.1, 59.6), Cuspinianus supplies readings which correspond with Pliny's not only in thought but also in prose-rhythm—something which is not generally the case with scholars of the modern era. I conclude from this that Cuspinianus used here and there in his deliberations a codex unknown to us, very closely related to our *M*, but more accurately transcribed.[8]

5. [ix] The rescripted Bobiensis codex (*R*)—today the Mediolanensis Ambrosianus E 147 sup.—also contains the speech in praise of Trajan. Underneath the Acts of the first Synod of Chalcedon, written in the seventh century, this codex preserves fragments of several older books, including speeches by Pliny (entitled the '*Panegyricus*') and Symmachus, written in semi-uncial letters in the sixth century. We do not know if it also contained others; but perhaps it is apposite to mention that the *genus dicendi pingue et floridum* ('the rich and florid genre of speaking') is exemplified by two names in Macrobius (*Saturnalia* 5.1.7)—of course, those of Pliny the Younger and Symmachus.

---

[8] I have not been able to bring myself to believe that at the beginning of the sixteenth century a Viennese doctor, although very skilled, made up the words *dext(e) rae verecundia* ('the modesty in your hand gestures'), which seem authentically Plinian, at I(1)24.2 where there was no reason why anyone would suspect there was a lacuna, without direction from elsewhere.

Two double folia survive from Pliny's text: in the first, the first side (pp. 367–8) is empty, the second (pp. 361–2) contains c.7.4 *uterque* to 8.5 *fuisset*; the other double folium (pp. 27–8) has c.78.4 *verecundiae* to 80.3 *atque* and, after two lost sides, (pp. 21–2) c. 85.6 *amicos* to 86.6 *ille qui-* (or *quidem*). It seems that this codex, which was reused, had almost twice as many errors as our archetype *M*; however, it should not be scorned, as it has preserved on twelve occasions genuine words, of which there is no trace or track in *M*.[9]

Finally Isidore the Bishop of Seville, who died in 636 wrote out some sections from our speech in his book entitled the *Institutionum Disciplinae*.[10]

6. Therefore after the words of the panegyrics have been recovered from these sources, there remain several places where, for the reasons given above, where the archetype seems corrupt or has been read without due accuracy, the text that has been handed down is unsatisfactory and must be restored by emendation. [x] I would not always dare to confirm who first made what correction; but I have indicated what I could, so that my well-deserving predecessors do not lie hidden beneath the usual notations *dett.* and *edd.* and ç. Learned Italians first practised correction of this sort in the later codices in the fifteenth century; I have tried to indicate whence their emendations are known to me, with short abbreviations:

I have already said what X_1 and X_2 signify.

w is the corrector of codex Vaticanus 1775, whose name I am ashamed not to know; rather often he agrees with X_2, but he emended much more with admirable skill.

p the corrector of codex Parisinus 8556 has much in common with *w*, and makes some additions for himself.

c Bruxellensis 10026-32 with its adherents mentioned above. (It is C in W. Baehrens, δ in Lubbe.)

d indicates the descendants of the corrected Vaticanus 1775, the twinned Vaticanus 3461 (perhaps belonging to Bishop Marcus Barbò, who died in 1473) and Parisinus 7840 (once belonging to Antonello Petrucci who was secretary to King Ferdinand of Naples; he died in

---

[9] Lowe (1938) 20 n. 29 discusses this. I consulted the codex afresh with some profit, but I do not report all the text's rejected readings.

[10] The most recent edition is by Pascal (1957); some Plinian sentences had been detected by Beeson (1913).

1487), the Veneti Marciani xi 2 (3924) and xiii 119 (3922) which only
contains panegyrics IX(5), XI(3), VI(7) and VII(6), Guelferbytanus
Gudianus 2° 45 (Keil collated it amongst his Plinian material), with
which codices Parisini 7807 (which lacks Pliny's speech) and 7841
sometimes agree.[11]

There are also codices which contain Pliny's speech and not the rest,
namely:

b   that is, three codices written very beautifully by the same scribe [xi]
(unless I am mistaken), Vaticani Barberinianus 88 and Urbinas 1156
with Placentinus Com. 100;[12]

g   is Londinensis Additicius 12008, unlikely to have been written by
the hand of Guarinus Veronensis himself (1374–1460), together with
Vaticanus Ottobonianus 1215 which Suster believed belonged to his
pupil Blondus Forliuiensis (1392–1463);[13] with these are four codices
which join Pliny's speech to his letters, namely Augustanus 2° 118 of the
year 1466 with its twin Londinensis Arundelianus 154 (once belonging
to Bilibaldus Pirckheimer), Caesena Malatestianus S.xx. 2 and Vindobonensis 141 (corrected in 1464 at Buda);

Med.   The Mediolanensis Library Braidensis AD xiv 40, once belonging
to the Paduan Monastery of St Justina, and Londinensis Regius 15 B. 5,
written at Papia in 1473 which itself belonged to Antonello Petrucci.

In addition, editors of printed books have made many corrections: at
their head Franciscus Puteolanus, who is believed to have published
the first edition, at Milan, around 1482, and Iohannes Livineius in
1599. But I intended to prepare a new text based on fidelity to the
codices, not to compose a history of the text; reader, at this point, let
me bid you farewell and entreat your kindness towards my mistakes.

R.A.B.M
Corpus Christi College, Oxford

---

[11] Between Pliny's speech and the rest in this [last] codex is inserted a speech
attributed to Metius Voconius', [derived] from Vopiscus. You have the same speech in
Caroliruhensis 457 (Durlach 36) and Florentinus Riccardianus 619 as well as in
Vaticanus Ottobonianus 1303, thus corrected as it now is.
[12] Each one bears its ancestry at its head: the Barberinianus belonged to one of the
cardinals of the Piccolomini papacies, whom Suster believed was Jacobus Ammanati
(1461–1479); the Urbinas belonged to Federico Duke of Montefeltro (1422–1482); the
Placentinus belonged to a family named after St Severinus. It is characteristic of the
scribe not to put the usual Explicit or Finit at the end, but Exiit.
[13] From which Suster (p. 516) likewise saw that the codex Florentinus Mediceo-
Laurentianus Ashburnham 1017 was copied.

3

The Origin of the *Panegyrici Latini* Collection

René Pichon

The attribution of the *Panegyrici Latini* has often been discussed, in particular in the last twenty years; but it seems to me that the approach the critics involved have employed has been a little unsystematic, making it necessary to question their assertions and to examine afresh this rather difficult question.

The question would be very easy—and to put it better, would not be posed at all—if we could attend to the evidence of the manuscripts. After the panegyrics of Trajan by Pliny, of Theodosius by Drepanius Pacatus, of Julian by Mamertinus and of Constantine by Nazarius, the manuscripts have the following notice: *incipiunt panegyrici diversorum septem* ('seven panegyrics by various authors begin'),[1] and effectively the speeches which follow are all designated by their order of sequence, without their authors' names. Only one is titled *eiusdem magistri memet genethliacus Maximiani Augusti* [XI (3)] ('the same teacher's "memet" birthday address to Maximianus Augustus'):[2] we can see from this that this panegyric has the same author as the one before it [X(2)] and that this author is an imperial

---

[1] In reality, there are eight panegyrics from this point and not seven; I will return to this slight difficulty.

[2] Upsaliensis (A) has this. Marcianus (B) has mistakenly corrected the altered text to 'the same teacher Mamertinus'. Vaticanus (W) simply has 'the birthday address by the same.'

secretary, [271] the *magister memoriae*.[3] On the other hand, in the text of the speech composed for the occasion of the restoration of the School of Autun [IX(5)], we can read the name of the author, Eumenius, and we learn that this Eumenius was *magister memoriae*.[4] For the other speeches, the manuscripts give us no information about the identity of the author.

Without doubt, this is little to go on; and as it comes up often, this very lack of information has pricked curiosity and provoked hypotheses. Many critics have noted a certain number of analogies between these different speeches, either in thought or in expression; and without considering the possibility that these analogies can be explained by the similarity in subjects, the shared provenance, time, social milieu, and lastly, rhetorical habits, they have grouped under Eumenius' name some of the anonymous panegyrics, sometimes more, sometimes fewer, and principally those which, in chronological sequence follow the *Oration for the Restoration of the School*, [VIII(4), VII(6), VI(7) and V(8)]. These are the ones which, for example, the 'classic' histories of Latin literature—that of Teuffel and those of Schanz, attribute to Eumenius.[5] On the other hand, struck very much by several differences in tone between the speech on the School and the panegyrics (properly called), Brandt judged that only the former was Eumenius'.[6] Boissier's ingenious objection to this was that it was not necessary to exaggerate the seriousness of these differences—that, for [272] example, if speech IX(5) had a more daring dignity, and was less adulatory, this perhaps came about because the situation was not the same in the two cases.[7] Naturally, Brandt's trenchant hypothesis gave birth to an opposing one no less intransigent, and Seeck attributed to Eumenius not only panegyrics VIII(4), VII(6), VI(7) and V(8), but XII(9) in honour of Constantine, and X

---

[3] The archetype must have had *the same* (followed by the author's name), and in the next line *magistri mem. et* (then another title). [The *magister memoriae* was an emperor's legal advisor.]

[4] IX(5)14.8 (a letter from Constantius to the author): 'Farewell Eumenius, most dear to us'—IX(5)11.2: 'those three hundred sesterces which I has received as *magister sacrae memoriae*'.

[5] In 1599, Livineius attributed speeches VIII(4), VI(7) and V(8) to Eumenius (almost nothing is known of the author of VII(6); the opinion of Tillemont, Gibbon and Burckhardt is the same. Arntzen only makes a case for VI(7), Bernhardy and Sachs (1885) for V(8).

[6] Brandt (1882). Brandt's opinion was reprised by Götze (1892).

[7] Boissier (1884).

(2) and XI(3) in honour of Maximian. In a word, the whole collection of eight speeches taken chronologically between the panegyric of Trajan by Pliny and that of Constantine by Nazarius was the work of one and the same orator.[8] This is an interesting opinion in that it attributes to Eumenius a considerable productivity and, accordingly, an important personality. That opinion has for itself the prestige which the name of its author and his great knowledge of Roman history of the fourth century give it. It is, moreover, cleverly asserted; nothing is more skilful, more enticing than the argumentation by which Seeck, advancing step by step, successively increases Eumenius' portion of all the speeches he meets; there is there as much dialectical finesse as erudition. For all that, his theory strikes me as more specious than true, and because it does not seem to me to have been subjected to very thorough discussion until now, I would like to point out its weaknesses.

There would be much to say on the general considerations at which Seeck believed it was necessary to close his argument. According to him, all the speeches which he claimed were Eumenius' from VIII(4) to XII(9) had the double character of resembling each other a great deal and differing a great deal from those of Nazarius, Mamertinus and Pacatus. I have already said what I think about these resemblances: they are inevitable in works which came into being in the same country at the same time and under the same circumstances. As for the differences which Seeck shows between the eight earlier addresses [273] and the three later ones, they are real. We could reveal another difference, striking enough, which unless I am mistaken Seeck failed to note: that is that the earlier speeches are much shorter than the others; they are only from twelve to twenty pages in Baehrens' 1874 edition, while the address of Nazarius is thirty-one and a half, that of Mamertinus more than twenty-six, and that of Pacatus just reaches to forty-four. But what conclusion do we draw from that if not that these later speeches are from a more recent period, where taste had changed, where orators' customs had transformed, where longer amplifications were supported more willingly? It is the same, I believe, with all the comparisons we could make between the two groups of panegyrics. If the earlier ones differ from the later ones, it is perhaps simply because they are older, without for

---

[8] Seeck (1888).

that deriving from one hand only. Seeck also notes that the later speeches of the first group carefully omit certain themes from developments used in the preceding addresses: we can see there, he claims, an orator who avoids repeating himself. Maybe, but perhaps we can just as well see here different orators who are looking to rejuvenate a banal tradition, both leaving out of their selection that which has been said too many times, and above all adapting their amplifications to their actual circumstances as closely as possible. For these circumstances vary without cease: at one time, it is the emperor's birthday,[9] at another it is the town's,[10] now the orator gives thanks for a favour granted,[11] now he celebrates a prince's visit,[12] or a victory,[13] or a marriage.[14] There are then elements of novelty which impose so forcefully on the eloquence that this eloquence could be that of one or of several orators. At heart, these general arguments can be bent in every direction. It is necessary to come to a detailed examination of the panegyrics [274]—an examination on which moreover, Seeck has insisted a very great deal.

Among these panegyrics, there are two—VII(6) and XII(9)—about which he confesses nothing can be asserted because they contain next to no personal detail. The author of XII(9) declares only at the start that he has often given speeches of praise of Constantine:[15] that, says Seeck, could well relate to the speeches we have. Why not to other ones? The chances are the same for both sides. The major reason he invokes to have these two panegyrics included in his *corpus Eumenianum* is that with all the other speeches of this part of the collection being Eumenius', it is likely that these also are likewise. The argument could be turned against itself: if it were demonstrated that speeches X (2), XI(3), VIII(4), VI(7) and V(8) were not by Eumenius, VII(6) and XII(9) would naturally follow the same fate.

Let's leave these aside for now and come to VI(7) and V(8). For V (8), Seeck's reasoning is completely hypothetical. The author of this

---

[9] Maximian's birthday XI(3).

[10] Anniversary of Rome's foundation X(2); that of Trier VI(7).

[11] Thanks for the restoration of the School of Autun IX(5), and for the tax exemptions for inhabitants of Autun V(8).

[12] That is probably the case for VIII(4), delivered to Constantius as he stood, (4.4).

[13] The victory of Constantine over Maxentius XII(9).

[14] The marriage of Constantine and Maximian's daughter VII(6).

[15] XII(9)1.1 *is qui semper res a numine tuo gestas praedicare essem*, 'I, who have always been accustomed to praise your achievements'.

speech, he says, originates from Autun; he had been a rhetor; he must have been fairly well known, and fairly well looked upon by the court, for without such it would be incomprehensible that he had been appointed to convey to the emperor the thanks of the people of Autun; Eumenius fulfilled all these conditions, hence he must be the man. Not so, I would reply; it could be him, but nothing is less certain. The School of Autun, like all the Empire's universities included several teachers of rhetoric and all these teachers were generally well considered; one could, without offending the emperor, assign to him any one of them. Had the orator of V(8) already delivered official addresses? He makes no allusions, and he even seems to indicate the contrary since he is pleased to have become 'the spokesperson not of private literary studies but that of public thanksgiving'.[16] In any case, it seems doubtful to me that he was the same as the orator [275] of VI(7). At the end of this speech, the orator invites Constantine to visit Autun.[17] This visit, which happened in between the two addresses, is recounted in V(8) without mention of the earlier invitation. If these two speeches had been by one author, there is no doubt that he would have publicly boasted to have seen his request granted, to have had procured by means of his entreaties for his hometown the honour of the imperial visit, etc. For all these reasons, I do not believe that panegyric V(8) is by the same hand as VI(7), or any of the earlier speeches.

On VI(7) Seeck reasoned a little like he did with V(8), but with more force. The author, there again, is a native of Autun;[18] he is a retired rhetor;[19] he is a retired functionary of the palace;[20] he has a son already grown-up, who has reached the position of counsel to the fisc.[21] All that accords well with what we know of Eumenius from his speech *For the Restoration of the School*. Of these correspondences, some are real but prove nothing substantial; others are less well founded. Eumenius is not the only rhetor native to Autun, nor the only one to have fulfilled administrative functions close to the emperor: we know that it was from the world of the schools that the imperial bureaucracy habitually recruited.[22] Eumenius is by no means the only one to have had a son and to have wished to place him

---

[16] V(8)1.2, *ut essem iam non privati studii litterarum, sed publicae gratulationis orator.*

[17] VI(7)22.   [18] VI(7)22.   [19] VI(7)23.2.
[20] VI(7)23.1.   [21] VI(7)23.1.   [22] IX(5)5.4; cf. VI(7)23.2.

advantageously near the emperor, without considering that in IX(5) there is the question of only one son, and here five.[23] Such vague analogies do not allow the two authors to be assimilated. And a reasonable challenge can be made to this assimilation. [276] In his speech *For the Restoration of the School* Eumenius says explicitly that he has never been a lawyer.[24] The author of VI(7) seems to have been a lawyer, if we accept Baehrens' very plausible conjecture, *hanc meam qualemcumque uocem diuersis fori et palatii officiis exercitam* ('this voice of mine, such as it is, practised in the forum and the palace', 23.1), instead of *otii et palatii* ('in leisure and the palace') which the manuscripts have. Seeck, it is true, rejects Baehrens' correction to return to the text of the manuscripts. By *otium*, he understands 'tuition in rhetoric' which could therefore be named such because it is a municipal not an imperial activity. But far from the possibility that *otium* could designate a rhetor's profession, it is often opposed to words which qualify that profession.[25] By complete contrast, *forum* is often placed in antithesis with *palatium*.[26] The proposed correction is perfectly explicable palaeographically. Everything then converges to render it likely; only in that case, it is necessary to renounce the assimilation of the orator of VI(7) with Eumenius.

On the other hand, I see a quite obvious difference between VI(7) and VIII(4). In both, Constantius' naval expedition to Britain is narrated, but not in the same way. In VIII(4) it is presented as rather difficult, hampered by the wind, rain and fog.[27] On the contrary, in terms less likely and more emphatic, VI(7) speaks of a peaceful sea, of an ocean astonished to see itself crossed by such a hero.[28] This contradiction is easily explained if we admit two orators, with one well informed of the facts, the other more vaguely informed and inclined to substitute [277] eloquence for precision; it is less well understood if we admit a sole orator. Finally, if we add that at no point does the orator of VI(7) seem to have already delivered other official addresses—rather he seems to lack self-confidence as if this

---

[23] IX(5)6.2; VI(7)23.2.   [24] IX(5)1.1.

[25] IX(5).15.1; VIII(4)1.4 *quies* ('quiet', an equivalent to *otium*) is opposed wholesale to tuition in rhetoric and to the exercise of administrative functions.

[26] See IX(5)5.4 and VI(7)23.2.

[27] VIII(4)14–15. Moreover, the fog was more useful than harmful to the Roman fleet's manoeuvres; but this is far removed from the details of the description outlined in VI(7).

[28] VI(7)5.4.

were his first experience of formal eloquence[29]—I believe we will be carried to the conclusion that, just like V(8), this panegyric is independent of IX(5) and VIII(4) and in general of all those to precede it.

We come now to the heart of the discussion: it is, in effect, to prove the common origin of X(2), XI(3), VIII(4) and IX(5) that Seeck dedicated his most urgent efforts and his most subtle arguments. I cannot reproduce or likewise summarize his demonstration; I will only indicate the results at which he arrived. According to him, after X(2) and on Constantius' recommendation, Eumenius would have been named *magister memoriae* by Maximian, about 290. In this capacity, he would have delivered XI(3). Then he would have retired to the countryside. In about the middle of 297, in the name of the town of Autun he would have left his retirement to come to greet the emperor on his return from Italy, and on this occasion would have delivered VIII(4). That would have brought him back into view, and from there Constantius took the decision to entrust to him the directorship of the School at Autun, a decision for which Eumenius thanked him in IX(5). All this history connects up very well; it almost wins recognition for itself by its logical and natural appearance. However, let us see if it raises serious objections.

One of the arguments Seeck employs to assimilate VIII(4) with the three others is that, like them, it is the work of a *magister memoriae*. But that is not certain; the author says only that he fulfilled a position of trust in the imperial bureaucracy.[30] He could have been [278] *a memoria*, but he could just as well have been *ab epistulis* or *a libellis*.[31] If we admit that he was *a memoria*, who is to say that between 290 and 297 there was only one *magister memoriae*? We do not know for how long functionaries of this type usually held their posts. In short, from this perspective, the question remains open.

There is some data of greater precision. The author of VIII(4) says that he had previously spoken before Maximian, who had received

---

[29] The whole exordium is of a modesty which surpasses that of all the other introductions. At the end the orator dreads that he has fallen short of what he ought, and finds consolation in thinking of the numerous civil servants he has educated for the imperial administration (23.2). He is pleased to have been able to *consacrare* ('devote') his eloquence while speaking before the emperor (23.1), which seems to prove that this was his first such occasion.

[30] VIII(4)1.4.

[31] Different legal offices within the imperial court.

favourable notice of him from Constantius.[32] If we accept Seeck's hypothesis, this could correspond with X(2). But this speech was pronounced in 289 (or at the latest in 290): well, at that date, how could Constantius have known Eumenius? At that time Constantius was only a simple general, and it was not until three or four years later that he was promoted to imperial power. From the fact that the author of VIII(4) was a personal protégé of Constantius, I believe we can infer that he was not the same as the author of X(2) and XI(3). A more important difference distinguishes him from Eumenius. He outlines for himself very neatly three periods in his life; that when he was a rhetor, that when he was a functionary of the palace, and that when he retired to the country.[33] By contrast, Eumenius has not known the leisure of retirement. If he speaks of *otium*, it is while dreaming of his former profession as an orator;[34] but he passed without break from the office of *magister memoriae* to that of the director of the School of Autun. Brandt had already noted this, and Seeck believed the assertion could be undermined by saying that Constantius' letter did not in any way prove that Eumenius was already the director when he received it. In effect, the imperial letter, with its periphrasis *salvo privilegio dignitatis tuae* ('with the privilege of your rank intact'[35]) could [279] be as well addressed to a former secretary as to one still in office. But there is another passage where Eumenius explicitly declares that he had been sought to fulfil his new employment in the palace of Maximian himself, and that he had been moved from the imperial bureaucracy to the sanctuary of the Muses.[36] This testimony is too formal to assimilate the retired functionary who gave panegyric VIII(4) with Eumenius, called upon at Autun to leave the emperor's secretariat.

That is not all. To justify his opinion, Seeck was obliged to invert the chronological order which custom has established for IX(5) and VIII(4). If VIII(4) is later than IX(5), as almost all critics have believed, it is impossible to attribute them to one author, for not only does the author of VIII(4) make no allusion to IX(5), but he says in distinctive terms that he is breaking a long silence.[37] He could not say this if, several months before (for the two addresses are separated by a very short interval) he had given the *Oration for the Restoration of the School*. Seeck understood that well and it is for that reason that

---

[32] VIII(4)1.5–6. [33] VIII(4)1.4. [34] IX(5)15.1.
[35] IX(5)14.4. [36] IX(5)6.1–2. [37] VIII(4)1.1.

he was forced to show that VIII(4) is the older of the speeches—that is, dates to the middle of 297 and IX(5) to the end of the same year.

To tell the truth, the difficulty is not totally resolved in this manner, for it is no more a question of [allusions to] VIII(4) in IX(5) than of [allusions to] IX(5) in VIII(4). And still, if Seeck's hypothesis were correct, when enumerating the tokens of the emperors' prodigious kindness to the city of Autun,[38] Eumenius would have to have mentioned the welcome given to the embassy entrusted to him by the same city, that same year, to give thanks to Constantius.[39] [280] Without being as unbelievable as in the case which we will explore shortly, his silence is not automatic. Nor is it any more automatic that these two panegyrics were delivered in an order other than that which the manuscript tradition shows. I'll explain: between the panegyric of Theodosius (inclusively) and the two panegyrics of Maximian, the order followed by the manuscripts is precisely the inverse of their chronological order. We could conclude, without being too rash, that since VIII(4) precedes IX(5) in the manuscripts, it is VIII(4) that is the later in the order of dates.

What arguments does Seeck invoke against this presumption? He insists principally on the manner in which relations between the Roman Empire, the Persians and the Moors are represented in the two speeches. Galerius' expedition against the Persians in 297 is mentioned in the *Oration for the Restoration of the School.*[40] By contrast, in VIII(4) not only is it not in question, but the orator speaks several times of the peace treaty imposed beforehand on the Persians by Diocletian, and he speaks as if this treaty had not been broken. Seeck says this shows that this peace had not been violated and that Galerius' expedition began after VIII(4) and before IX(5). But in reality, the silence observed in VIII(4) on the campaign of 297 in no way proves that the campaign had not already been undertaken. As Brandt remarked, the early stages had been quite unsuccessful for the Roman army, which explains why an official orator could not make mention of it. Galerius had hoped to triumph over the rebellious Persians, and it is to this hope that the phrase from IX(5) refers, which could just as well suit an anticipated victory as one already won. When these bright visions were disappointed [281] in the first contact between the Roman and Persian armies, the most sensible

---

[38] IX(5)4.   [39] VIII(4)21.2.   [40] IX(5)21.2.

course—the one which conforms to the panegyrists' courtly norms—
was to leave this detail of imperial politics in the shade. And this is
why the author of VIII(4) takes care not to summon the embarrassing
memory of the Persians in the passage where he lists the victories won
against the Sarmatians, Egyptians, Carpi and Moors.[41] But, Seeck
objects that in that case, he ought never to mention their name or
to recall their earlier submission in a manner which would urge the
belief that this submission would always endure. I think Seeck exaggerates the import of the two phrases which mention the old treaty
with the Persians. Both refer to the past not the present. In one, the
orator describes the state of the Empire four years beforehand, at the
moment when Diocletian and Maximian decided to add two Caesars
to their number;[42] and what proves clearly that he considers this state
from a position of hindsight is that he presents as an intention the
recovery of Batavia and Britain, a recovery which had been effected by
the time he spoke.[43] The other phrase likewise indicates a look back:
the author lists the successes which Rome had brought from all
quarters up until the time when Britain alone remained rebellious,
and amongst these successes he signals the suppliant embassy of the
Persian king.[44] From these two passages an unbiased reader infers
only that between Rome and Persia a peace had been signed after long
hostilities. The orator does not say that this peace was holding good,
that it would be a sham; he no more says the opposite, because he had
to confess that the break had not been favourable to Rome until that
point. He hides in a vagueness which suits his own national pride as
much as the exigencies of an address to the court.

As for the war against the Moors, Seeck claims that the *Oration for
the Restoration of the School* shows the Moors utterly [282] defeated,[45] whereas VIII(4) depicts them only under attack from Maximian.[46] That is, I think, to interpret the sense of the words beyond

---

[41] VIII(4)5.

[42] VIII(4)3.3, *Partho ultra Tigrim redacto*, 'when the Parthian had been driven
back beyond the Tigris'.

[43] VIII(4)3.3, *destinata Bataviae Britanniaeque vindicta*, 'the intention to recover
Batavia and Britain'.

[44] VIII(4)10.

[45] IX(5)21.1 *aut te, Maximiane invicte, perculsa Maurorum agmina fulminantem*,
'or you, invincible Maximian, striking the battle-lines of Moors with lightning'.

[46] VIII(4)5.2 *reservetur nuntiis iam iamque venientibus Mauris immissa vastatio*,
'Let the devastation inflicted on the Moors be left for the messengers who are making
their way here right now'.

proportion. 'Striking the battle-lines of Moors with lightning' and 'the devastation inflicted on the Moors' seem to me to be two clearly synonymous phrases. And if the author of VIII(4) speaks of leaving the eulogy of Maximian until the arrival of fresh reports, it is simply because on that day there, in the circumstances where he found himself, he only wanted to dedicate his praises to Constantius. The two passages give us a similar idea of a war that has begun—begun well, not yet finished, and the next stage of which is awaited with confidence. It is impossible to affirm that one was written before the other.

In this way, the reasons on which Seeck depends for the identification of the author of VIII(4) with Eumenius disappear bit by bit. There remains a final problem to consider: ought speeches X(2) and XI(3), addressed to Maximian, be attributed to Eumenius? Seeck of course answers in the affirmative, without otherwise giving his very characteristic arguments. To my mind, there is nothing in the contents of these three speeches to prevent belief in a common origin; nor anything else to force it. In support of Seeck's hypothesis, we could assert that the panegyrist of Maximian fulfilled the functions of *magister memoriae*, like Eumenius. He seems to have received this title between the two speeches, very probably as payment for the first one, in approximately 290.[47] On the other hand, Eumenius left his post as *magister memoriae* at the time he was appointed director of the school at Autun, in 296, as I demonstrated above. From 290 to 296, there might have been only one *magister memoriae* at the chancellery of Trier, and if so, the identification would be sure; but it is quite possible that there were two. From another point of view, if Eumenius is indeed [283] the author of X(2) and XI(3), it is perhaps a little surprising that he does not speak at all about his beloved hometown of Autun, as Schanz remarks. I will add that not only does he not mention Autun, but he even seems to ignore the situation the town found itself in. While he carries off his official bearing as fully as one could want, we cannot but be surprised to see so cheerful a picture of the empire drawn by a man whose home country was still in ruins after a recent war—devastated, taken apart, and crushed

---

[47] XI(3)1.2 *voveram longe infra spem honoris eius quem in me contulisti*, 'I had prayed and hoped for something far short of the honour you have bestowed on me'.

by poverty.[48] This would be all the more extraordinary because not only Eumenius but all the other panegyrists have a very burning local patriotism. As a result, I find it difficult to believe that the eulogies of Maximian could be the work of an orator from Autun. But this position is not irrefutable, and in sum, I consider the question undetermined.

From all that has preceded, it results in my view that it is possible—but not necessary—to attribute X(2) and XI(3) to Eumenius; that it is almost impossible to attribute to him VIII(4), VI(7) and V(8); and that it is useless to pose the question for VII(6) and XII(9). But, to overlook nothing, we must discuss an argument Seeck proposed about the way in which, according to him, the collection of panegyrics came into being. Moreover, the question is important enough of itself to warrant discussion.

Seeck claims, then, that the intention of the editor who collected the speeches from X(2) [AD 289] to XII(9) [AD 313] was to gather together the addresses of one single author, to form a *corpus Eumenianum*. The proof, he says, is that the *Oration for the Restoration of the School* which features in this *corpus* is not a panegyric and as a result has no right to feature amongst eulogies of emperors other than a common origin. I think that Seeck exaggerates the distance which can separate this *Oration for the Restoration of the School* from its neighbouring addresses. It is not a eulogy proper [284]: so be it, yet eulogy plays a major role; VIII(4) is purely laudatory to no greater extent, but is a speech of thanksgiving (*gratiarum actio*) whose design has some analogy with that of the *Oration for the Restoration of the School*. Will we mention that the speech about the school was not delivered before the emperors? It was at least delivered before their representative, the governor of Lyonnaise I, and questions are directed to them at every opportunity;[49] and finally the text is to be given to them.[50] We could, then, reconcile this work of official eloquence with the others, whether or not it was by the same author. But if we

---

[48] IX(5)4.1 *civitatem ... gravissima clade perculsam; ... pro miseratione casuum ...* 'the city ... struck by most heavy disaster; ... in pity for its misfortunes'. Cf. V(8)6 and 7.

[49] IX(5)4, 5, 6, 8, 10, 11, 13, 15, 16, 17, 18, 19, 20, 21.

[50] IX(5)21.4 *habes, vir perfectissime, studii ac voti mei professionem. abs te peto ut eam litteris tuis apud sacras aures prosequi non graveris* ('you have had an expression of my enthusiasm and prayers, Your Excellency. I ask you not to be slow to advance its cause in your letters to the sacred ears').

accept the hypothesis of a *corpus Eumenianum*, there are two aspects which it is very difficult to explain. First, there is the very heading of the manuscripts: *incipiunt panegyrici diversorum* ('panegyrics by various authors begin'). A collection which was put together precisely to reunite the works of one sole author and has for its title 'The Works of Various Authors' is certainly a bizarre anomaly! Besides, we do not understand the order followed in this collection. When the ancients collected their own works or those of another, they generally adopted an order by date or by genre (as is the case for the poems of Catullus, for example). I do not see why Eumenius' editor would have chosen an inverted chronological sequence, with this situation made worse by the fact that for two speeches, X(2) and XI(3), he would have returned to a plainly chronological sequence. However, if we were to accept Seeck's conclusions, it would be necessary to admit not just one exception to the firm principle but two, since Seeck believes IX(5) is later than VIII(4). And finally, that he wants to extend the *corpus Eumenianum* up to XII(9), which is at once the most recent of the group and the last in the manuscripts, further complicates matters. By accepting as correct all of Seeck's assertions, we reach the following conclusion: [285]

> The first in the manuscripts is the seventh in date [i.e. V(8)].
> The second in the manuscripts is the sixth in date [i.e. VI(7)].
> The third in the manuscripts is the fifth in date [i.e. VII(6)].
> The fourth in the manuscripts is the third in date [i.e. VIII(4)].
> The fifth in the manuscripts is the fourth in date [i.e. IX(5)].
> The sixth in the manuscripts is the first in date [i.e. X(2)].
> The seventh in the manuscripts is the second in date [i.e. XI(3)].
> The eighth in the manuscripts is the eighth in date [i.e. XII(9)].

One can hardly fete the hypothesized editor of the *corpus Eumenianum* for having chosen a simple and logical arrangement!

While professing an opinion radically opposed to that of Seeck on the attribution of the speeches, Brandt had set out a hypothesis on the formation of the collection bordering on the one I am coming to discuss. To his eyes also, the first nucleus of the series which we have would have been a collection put together a little while after 311, consisting of X(2), IX(5), VIII(4), VII(6), VI(7) and V(8), placed in reverse chronological order. This collection would have been extended later while consistently following the same reverse order, by the addition of the speeches of Nazarius, Mamertinus and Pacatus (or rather, according to the manuscripts, Pacatus, Mamertinus and Nazarius), transcribed in front of the first collection. Finally, the panegyric of Trajan would have been put at the front, and XI(3) and XII(9) at the end. This theory is still a little complicated and does not pass without raising several objections. It does not explain why the first group would have had the heading 'seven panegyrics by various authors begin' when, according to Brandt, it ought to have contained only six addresses. The reason for the reverse chronological order cannot be seen. Finally, the reason for the addition of Pliny's speech is not clear, and even less for the addition of XI(3) and XII(9), which have no affinity between them.

If I were to dare to offer a hypothesis in my turn, in the first place I would lay stress upon a clear characteristic that the speech of Pacatus shows amongst all the others. It is the last in date, and it is this one which offers the most striking similarities with the others. Certain of its developments produce a very strong impression of *déjà vu*. For example [286], the manner in which he recounts the journey through the Alps made by the soldiers of Theodosius (II(12)39), a journey which he pronounces miraculous in the strict sense of the word, recalls the account Nazarius gives of the heavenly army supporting Constantine (IV(10)14–15); the memory of the legend of the Dioscuri further indicates the desired analogy. Pacatus likewise borrows from Mamertinus his satirical amplification on the luxurious dining of former emperors, opposed to the sobriety, in Mamertinus' case of Julian, in Pacatus' of Theodosius (II(12)13–14 and III(11)11); and moreover in this case, the mention of 'winter roses' (*hibernae rosae*) and 'summer ice' (*aestiva glacies*) is like an acknowledgement of the borrowing (II(12)14.1 and III(11)11.3). The same Mamertinus supplies his successor a very beautiful image of Philosophy raised from obscurity by Julian and placed beside him on the highest throne—it will suffice to compare the two texts.

> *tu Amicitiam, nomen ante priuatum, non solum intra aulam uocasti, sed indutam purpura, auro gemmisque redimitam solio recepisti*

Not only did you summon inside the palace Friendship—formerly a word used by private citizens—but you even welcomed it to the throne clothed in purple and garlanded with gold and jewels (II(12)16.2)

*tu Philosophiam paulo ante suspectam ac non solum spoliatam honor-
ibus sed accusatam ac ream non modo iudicio liberasti, sed amictam
purpura, auro gemmisque redimitam in regali solio conlocasti*

Not only did you set free Philosophy from judgement—only recently
considered suspect, stripped of honours, accused and held on
charge—but you even placed it on the throne cloaked in purple and
garlanded with gold and jewels (III(11)23.4).

Pliny had feted Trajan for having triumphed not over the patience
of his subjects but over the arrogance of his predecessors;[51] in similar
terms, Pacatus praises Theodosius for having triumphed over arrogance.[52] When talking of the death of Maximian, the author of
panegyric VI(7) had found this ingenious formula to compliment
Constantine, 'the gods avenge you even against your will' (*di te
vindicant et invitum,* 20.4). Changing only one word, Pacatus trans-
fers it to Theodosius' soldiers who 'avenge you even against your will'
(*tui te vindicant et invitum,* II(12)44.2). Elsewhere, [287] concerning
the inferiority of Gallic to Roman eloquence, he takes up an idea
already expressed little differently in XII(9).[53] Of Theodosius' ceaseless activity, he says that truly divine spirits cannot take rest; the
magister memoriae of Maximian Herculius had said the same thing.[54]
Against the victories won in ancient civil wars by Marius, Sulla, and
Cinna he opposes that of Theodosius, more forgiving and more

---

[51] I(1)22.2 *non de patientia nostra quemdam triumphum sed de superbia principum egisti* ('you performed a triumph not over our patience but over emperors'
arrogance').
[52] II(12)47.3 *de superbia triumpharis* ('you triumphed over arrogance').
[53] II(12)1.3 *absurdae sinistraeque iactantiae possit uideri his ostentare facundiam,
quam de eorum fonte manantem in nostros usque usus deriuatio sera traduxit* ('It
could seem an absurd and strange conceitedness to show off my oratory to these men,
when only recently has a side channel from their spring brought it flowing for our use
too'); XII(9)1.2 *latine et diserte loqui illis ingeneratum est, nobis elaboratum et, si quid
forte commode dicimus, ex illo fonte et capite [et] facundiae imitatio nostra deriuat*
('speaking Latin, and well, is innate in them, but for us it is through hard work and if
by chance we say something stylish, our imitation derives from that spring and source
of oratory').
[54] II(12)10.1 *gaudent profecto perpetuo diuina motu, et iugi agitatione se uegetat
aeternitas, et quidquid homines uocamus laborem uestra natura est* ('The divine
certainly enjoy perpetual motion, and eternity keeps itself awake by everlasting
activity, and whatever we mortals call "work" is your nature'); XI(3)3.2 *quicquid
immortale est stare nescit, sempiternoque motu se seruat aeternitas* ('Whatever is
immortal does not know how to stand still, and eternity preserves itself by everlasting
movement').

blessed;[55] a similar parallel is found in XII(9) on the occasion of Constantine's victory over Maxentius.[56] He fetes Theodosius for having sought his own safety in the affection of his subjects rather than in the protection of his bodyguards;[57] this idea, indicated for the first time by Pliny the Younger,[58] had been reprised by Mamertinus;[59] in this way, Theodosius inherits from the praises of Trajan and Julian, and his panegyrist from the expressions of his two predecessors. The prosopopeia which he puts in the mouth of the state to force Theodosius to accept power (II(12)11.4–7) recalls that which one of his predecessors has attributed to Rome to implore Maximian to take up control of the empire.[60] Often it is not only imitation, but almost servile transcription: [288]

qui consilium tuum participant (II(12)1.1 and III(11)1.1)

'who share your council'

det igitur mihi sermonis huius auspicium ille felicitatis publicae auspex dies qui te primus inaugurauit imperio (II(12)3.1)

'Therefore let that auspicious day of public felicity which first inaugurated you in power give me the starting-point of my speech'

det igitur mihi . . . hodiernae gratulationis exordium diuinus ille uestrae maiestatis ortus (VIII(4)2.2)

'Therefore let that divine rising of your majesty give me the introduction to today's rejoicing'

aut boni consulit ut quiescat aut laetatur quasi amica si seruiat (II(12)22.4)

'it thinks it sensible to be quiet or rejoices like a friend if it is enslaved'

aut boni consulit ut quiescat aut laetatur quasi amica si pareat (VII(6) 8.5)

'it thinks it sensible to be quiet or rejoices like a friend if it obeys'

---

[55] II(12)46.1 *Cinnanos furores et Marium post exsilia crudelem at Sullam tua clade felicem* ('Cinna's rages, Marius cruel after his exile, Sulla "Fortunate" because of your destruction [Rome]').

[56] XII(9)20.3–4 *Cinna furiosus et Marius iratus . . . Sulla, felix si se parcius vindicasset* ('Raging Cinna and angry Marius . . . Sulla, "Fortunate" if he had avenged himself more sparingly').

[57] II(12)47.3 *remota custodia militari tutior publici amoris excubiis* ('with your armed guard removed, safer under the watch of your public's love').

[58] I(1)49.2 *non crudelitatis sed amoris excubiis . . . defenditur* ('He is not defended by the watch of cruelty, but of love').

[59] III(11)24.4 *quid istis (= gladiis atque pilis) opus est cum firmissimo sis muro civici amoris obsaeptus?* ('What need is there for these [swords and spears] when you are surrounded by the most solid wall of citizens' love?').

[60] VII(6)11.1–4.

rex eius dedignatus antea confiteri hominem iam fatetur timorem (II(12)
22.5)
'her king who previously thought it beneath him to confess his humanity now admits his fear'

*rex ille Persarum, numquam se ante dignatus hominem confiteri, fratri
tuo supplicat* (X(2)10.6)
'that king of the Persians, previously thinking it beneath him to confess
his humanity, is a suppliant to your brother'

qui nihil magis timuerat quam timeri (II(12)35.2)
'who had feared nothing more than being feared'

nil magis timuisti quam ne timereris (IV(10)18.2)
'you feared nothing more than being feared'.

Finally, there is a striking similarity between the comparison of
Constantine and Maxentius in XII(9) and that of Theodosius and
Maximus in Pacatus:

> . . . *te esse triumphalis uiri filium, se patris incertum; te heredem nobi-*
> *lissimae familiae, se clientem; te omni retro tempore Romani exercitus*
> *ducem, libertatis patronum, se orbis extorrem patriaeque fugitiuum? iam*
> *uero te principem in medio rei publicae sinu, omnium suffragio militum,*
> *consensu prouinciarum, ipsius denique ambitu imperatoris optatum; se*
> *in ultimo terrarum recessu, legionibus nesciis, aduersis prouinciarum*
> *studiis, nullis denique auspiciis in illud tyrannici nominis adspirasse*
> *furtum? postremo tecum fidem, secum perfidiam; tecum fas, secum*
> *nefas; tecum ius, secum iniuriam; tecum clementiam pudicitiam religio-*
> *nem, secum impietatem libidinem crudelitatem et omnium scelerum*
> *postremorumque uitiorum stare collegium?* (II(12)31.1–3)

' . . . that you are the son of a triumphant man, but he was unsure of his
father's identity; you were heir of the most noble family, he was a client;
you led the Roman army all this time, the champion of freedom, he was
an exile from the world, a fugitive from his country? Now indeed that in
the middle of the state's lap you had been chosen emperor by the vote of
all the troops, the consent of the provinces, finally the canvassing of the
emperor himself; that he had aspired to that theft of the title of tyrant in
the world's furthest recess, with the legions unaware, against the wishes
of the provinces, and finally no auspices? Finally, that trust was with
you, with him treachery; with you right, with him wrong; with you law,
with him injustice; with you forgiveness, respect, piety, with him impiety, lust, cruelty and a collection of all crimes and the worst vices'.

*ille Maximiani suppositus tu Constantii Pii filius; ille despectissimae
paruitatis, detortis solutisque membris, nomine ipso abusiua appellatione
mutilato, tu (quod sufficit dicere) tantus ac talis; ut haec, inquam,
omittam, te, Constantine, paterna pietas sequebatur, illum, ut falso generi
non inuideamus, impietas; te clementia, illum crudelitas; te pudicitia soli
dicata coniugio, illum libido stupris omnibus contaminata; te diuina
praecepta, illum superstitiosa maleficia; illum denique spoliatorum tem-
plorum, trucidati senatus, plebis Romanae fame necatae piacula, te
abolitarum calumniarum, te prohibitarum delationum, te conseruati
usque homicidarum sanguinis gratulatio* (XII(9)4.3–4)

He was Maximian's changeling, you the son of Constantius Pius; he was
of a despicably small stature, with twisted and weakened limbs, with his
name itself mutilated by a misapplied addition, you (it is enough to say)
as you are in size and character; to leave these things aside, Constantine
I say, your father's piety followed you; impiety followed him, so that we
do not deny him his paternity, although false; clemency followed you,
cruelty him; you, the respect devoted to a single spouse, him, a lust
stained by all foul acts; you, divine commands, him, superstitious
misdeeds; finally, him the punishment for despoiling temples, slaugh-
tering the senate, killing the Roman plebs by starvation, you the thanks
for abolishing calumnies, prohibiting delation, the protection even of
murderers' blood. [289]

The process is plain to see and there can be no doubt that Pacatus had
a very precise knowledge of the earlier panegyrics, and made a very
submissive imitation of them, not to say a very servile one. To
suppose from there that he took on himself the editorship is perhaps
not a great step. Let us accept it provisionally and see how, in that
case, the collection could have formed.

Pliny's panegyric of Trajan is encountered first: that is not cause for
surprise. Besides that it is the first model of the genre, Pliny was quite
well thought of in the Theodosian period. It was by him that Symmachus was guided in his correspondence, and the very arrangement
of this correspondence, published by the author's son, replicated that
of Pliny's *Letters*, with letters to the emperor reserved for the tenth
book. There would be nothing surprising, then, that Pacatus, an
admirer himself of Pliny the Younger, had the idea to edit the
panegyric of Trajan and to make follow it his own one, which his
vanity would easily have made him judge worthy of that honour.

Next, to connect these two extreme points, Pacatus would have
conceived of establishing a series of panegyrics, and he would have

looked for elements amongst the speeches which he knew, tracing the passage of the years and enriching his collection with discoveries which seemed to him the most important. And so from the outset he would have met the speech of Mamertinus, then that of Nazarius, and finally the 'seven panegyrics by various authors', the two last (those which are addressed to Maximian [X(2) and XI(3)]) being reunited together, which would explain at once both that they were placed in direct chronological order and not reversed, and that the second of the two [XI(3)] bears the label *eiusdem magistri*, etc. ('by the same *magister*'). I say 'seven panegyrics by various authors' because I am convinced that this part of the collection could originally only contain seven speeches and not eight. In finding eight, Seeck asks himself if he must impute the error to the collection's redactor who would have counted incorrectly or to a copyist who would have missed out a downstroke in the figure VIII. It was neither one nor the other, in my view. These seven speeches are all in reverse chronological order (with [290] the exception which I am coming to explain); the eighth speech, XII(9), is not. The seven are numbered; the eighth is not. In short, it seems to me difficult that it featured from the very first in the group of anonymous panegyrics. It was added later, either by the same editor of the collection, who would have corrected his first design too late, or by another editor. And it must have been added for a motive which today can seem rather pitiful, but which was quite powerful at the time: I want to suggest the wish to arrive at the sacred number twelve. Let us suppose that at that period a considerable value was attached to certain numbers; that one of our panegyrists saw a providential purpose in the fact that Maxentius had exercised exactly six years of power and was overthrown immediately afterwards, so as not to contaminate the sacred number seven;[61] that Ausonius, a contemporary and friend of Pacatus,[62] gives much attention to these juvenile symmetries, as can be judged from his poem

---

[61] XII(9)16.2 *diuina mens et ipsius urbis aeterna maiestas nefario homini eripuere consilium . . . ne septenarium illum numerum sacrum et religiosum uel inchoando uiolaret* ('the divine mind and the eternal majesty of the city itself took sense away from the wicked man . . . so that he would not violate that sacred and holy number seven even by beginning it').

[62] Ausonius dedicated several of his works to Pacatus, notably the *Ludus septem sapientum* ('The game of seven sages') and one of the two editions of his *Technopaegnion*. These are only two works in which the symmetrical character is particularly remarkable.

Griphus ternarii numeri ('The riddle of the number three'). The designs which I am coming to expound are hypothetical and must remain as such. What I want to hold on to is that nothing, either in the formation of the collection or in the content of its speeches, gives authority to the attribution of panegyrics [in chronological order] X (2) to XII(9) to Eumenius alone, but that on the contrary, everything invites us to view these as works of different authors.

This is not a new conclusion, since Brandt already reached it. However, perhaps it was right to defend it against the arguments by which Seeck had tried to weaken it. Above all, it was necessary to insist exclusively, as I have tried to do, on historical reasons without involving, as [291] Brandt did, considerations related to the moral character which the panegyrics disclose, or to their language and style, or to the imitation of earlier writers. For I am not saying that it is of no consequence that in truth there are more reminiscences of Pliny in the *Oration for the Restoration of the School* than in VIII(4) and fewer than in VI(7), that *statim atque* ('as soon as') is found in VIII(4) [at 7.3, 13.1, 15.2, 19.1] and *ilico atque* ('as soon as') in VI(7) [at 8.2], and other observations accumulated at length by Brandt— nothing is of no consequence—but other differences like this as much as the similarities which can be invoked on the other side can be the work of chance and as a result prove nothing. And in the same way that IX(5) has a more spirited and noble tone than the others—to suppose that this is true—could be attributed simply to the circumstance in which it was delivered. Here, only historical arguments seem to me to offer something solid; I have tried to show that they are more against than for the hypothesis of a shared origin and that from that we have in the first group of panegyrics not the works of a single author, but examples of the whole of Gallo-Roman rhetoric.

Part II

Pliny's *Panegyricus*

4

Pliny and the *Panegyricus*

Betty Radice

The younger Pliny was *consul suffectus* from September to October, AD 100, and delivered in the senate his official *gratiarum actio* ('speech of thanksgiving') to the emperor Trajan for his appointment. This practice went back to the days of Augustus, according to Ovid (*Pont.* iv. 4. 35), though nothing is known of the senatorial decree which made it obligatory. Nor do we know if *both* consuls made speeches, or whether Pliny was following normal practice when he spoke on behalf of his colleague, Cornutus Tertullus. In *Letters* 2.1.5 he tells us that Verginius Rufus was rehearsing a similar speech (to be addressed to Nerva) at the time of his fatal accident, and elsewhere (3.13) he writes of the boredom of having to listen to speeches of this kind, brief though they could be, and the distasteful duty of addressing words of insincere flattery to an emperor (Domitian) under whom freedom of speech was impossible. The custom of the official vote of thanks continued; M. Cornelius Fronto was suffect consul in July–August 143, and delivered his speech to Antoninus Pius on 13 August (Fronto, *Letters* 2.1).

Pliny then revised his speech, according to his usual practice, and considerably enlarged it for publication. Durry points out that September and October were months of vacation for the senate (cf. Suet., *Augustus* 35), so he may have wished to reach a wider audience.[1] The result was the *Panegyricus*, though the name was never used by Pliny: the written as well as the spoken version for him is always *gratiarum actio* (*Letters* 3.13. 1; 18. 1; *Pan.* 1. 6; 90. 3). The word *Panegyricus*

---

[1] Durry (1938) 5.

seems to have been used first by Sidonius Apollinaris (*Letters* 8.10.3).
Pliny sent this enlarged version to his Spanish friend, Voconius
Romanus (3.13. 1); and to Vibius Severus, a literary friend probably
from Milan, he wrote a letter describing the appreciative reception of
the speech by the friends invited to hear it read aloud in instalments
on three successive days (3.18). The length of these sessions is disputed; Durry thinks that they were one hour each and that the
Panegyricus was at least trebled in length, and Syme evidently agrees.[2]
Sherwin-White thinks that each session was one and a half to two
hours as it would take all of that time to read the whole: *experto crede*
('trust one who knows from experience').[3] But he also rightly points
out that in *Letters* 3.18.4 Pliny says that he had intended to stop the
reading after two days, so he may have been reading extracts rather
than going straight through. And of course we have no idea how
much of each session was taken up by applause. [**167**]

    There is no further mention of the speech, and at some point it
became detached from Pliny's letters and survived in manuscript as
the first of the collection known as the *XII Panegyrici Latini*, though it
antedates the other speeches by some 200 years. In the early editions
it was sometimes printed with the *Letters*, notably by Beroaldus
(1501), Aldus (1508) and Catanaeus (1506 and 1533); and sometimes
with the *XII Panegyrici*, notably by Puteolanus (1482), Cuspinianus
(1513) and Livineius (1599). This dual treatment has continued to the
present day. German editors (Kukula and Schuster in the Teubner
texts) have put it with the *Letters*; the French Budé edition is divided
between the Private Correspondence (Guillemin 1927–1947) and
the Correspondence with Trajan plus the *Panegyricus* in a single
volume (Durry 1947). English editors have kept it apart from the
Letters. The *Oxford Classical Text* of Pliny and the *XII Panegyrici*
are two separate volumes; the major commentary on Pliny by A. N.
Sherwin-White does not include the *Panegyricus*, nor does the 1915
Loeb edition, and it does not feature in any of the Selections designed
to give a general picture of Pliny and his background (e.g. those of
Merrill (1903), Allen (1915), or Sherwin-White (1967)). The standard
Commentary on the *Panegyricus* alone is still that of Durry (1938),
who acknowledges his debt to Schwarz (1746) and Baehrens (1910);
that of Malcovati (1952) I have not been able to see.

---

[2] Durry (1938) 8; Syme (1958) 94.
[3] Sherwin-White (1966) 251.

Durry writes fully about Pliny's style and syntax, his vocabulary and debt to Virgil, and his affinities with Tacitus. The question of style is taken up in a valuable article by Bruyère in which Pliny's debt to Tacitus' early works is balanced against Tacitus' echoes of the *Panegyricus* in the *Histories* and the *Annals*, which were written after the speech was published.[4] But on the whole it has been left for the historians to sift the grain from the chaff and to use its evidence for the reigns of Nerva and Trajan in the absence of other literary sources—Suetonius ends with Domitian, what we have of Tacitus breaks off in the reign of Vespasian, the *Historia Augusta* starts with Hadrian. Durry of course deals fully with the historical and political importance of the speech in his introduction, notes, and appendices, and Syme quotes it frequently, as do the authors of the relevant chapters in volume 11 of the *Cambridge Ancient History*. Its view of Domitian is distorted, and consistent with what Pliny says in the *Letters*, though charged with even stronger emotional feeling—he will concede nothing to what Mommsen called the 'sombre but intelligent despotism' of Domitian, who is not even given credit for suppressing the mimes (*Pan*. 46. 3) or allowed to join his armies at the time of the revolt of Saturninus (*Pan*. 14. 3). But it confirms what Dio Cassius says about the state of the country just before the adoption [168] of Trajan by Nerva, when the praetorian guard mutinied and *concussa respublica ruensque imperium* ('the state had been struck and the empire was collapsing', *Pan*. 6. 3; Dio. 68.3.3), and skilfully conveys the uneasy atmosphere of those crucial moments. It supplies what scraps of information we have about Trajan's career before his accession (*Pan*. 14–15), though Pliny chooses to say nothing about Trajan's Spanish origin and glosses over his military service under Domitian, as he does over the part played by the army in bringing about his adoption. It gives a good deal of specific information about electoral procedure, the circumstances of Trajan's adoption and accession, and his acclamation by senate and people. Moreover, the speech goes much further than offering factual information or an uncritical encomium of Trajan.

Historians have recognized that Pliny's avowed intention was that *boni principes quae facerent recognoscerent, mali quae facere deberent* ('good rulers shall recognize their own deeds and bad ones learn what

[4] (1954).

theirs should be', *Pan.* 4. 1). This, then, is no idle flattery in conventional form; it is rather a sort of manifesto of the senate's ideal of a constitutional ruler, one chosen to rule because he is qualified to do so, with emphasis on his *obsequium* ('obedience') to the people's will and his sense of service to his country. He is the *optimus princeps* ('best emperor')—an expression which has supplied the title for a 350-page book on Trajan by Paribeni.[5] This political message has inspired several articles, notably Born's 'The Perfect Prince' and Hammond's 'Pliny the Younger's views on government', and its connection with the coin-legends of the period with their emphasis on Security, Liberty Restored, and Good Fortune is explicitly noted by H. Mattingly in his introduction to the *Coins of the Roman Empire in the British Museum* (vol. 3, Nerva–Trajan).[6] Pliny draws the contrast between the *dominatio* ('Dominate') of the past and *principatus* ('Principate') of the present, with the recurrent refrain that if the *princeps* will continue as he has started, he will provide a model for his successors for all time. This is skilful propaganda, a subtle blend of fact and 'wishful thinking', a tactful way of telling Trajan what his grateful subjects would have him be, and our chief regret is that we do not know how much of it was conveyed in the senate in the original version. If its message was clear from the start, it is perhaps understandable that Pliny's senatorial friends were eager to hear more. The opening paragraphs of the *Panegyricus* contrast the distasteful duty of pouring out the flattering words which were expected by the emperor who was the senate's enemy with the pleasure of expressing genuine appreciation of a truly virtuous ruler (1–3). If Pliny then pronounced the opening sentence of the next paragraph he would have surprised his more attentive hearers: 'But now I must bow to the decree of the senate which in the public interest [169] has declared that under the form of a vote of thanks delivered by the voice of the consul, good rulers shall recognize their own deeds and bad ones learn what theirs should be.' As Durry remarks, 'the intention of making the speech of thanksgiving serve the edification of emperors belongs not to the senate's decree but to Pliny'—as he makes clear himself in his second letter on the subject (*Letters* 3.18).[7] There he contrasts the speech delivered in the senate 'in the customary manner, befitting time and

[5] Paribeni (1927).
[6] Born (1934); Hammond (1938); Mattingly (1950).
[7] Durry (1938) 89.

place' with the fuller and more elaborate written version prepared 'first, to commend our emperor in sincere praise of his virtues, and secondly so to show future emperors how to strive towards the same glory most effectively, not learned from teacher but from his example'. This implies that Pliny's imagination had been fired by the possibilities of what could be made of an obligatory speech now that a new spirit was abroad in the person of a new type of ruler, and a new freedom of speech was an encouragement to enlarge on the theme. He must have given a great deal of time and thought to the development of the political theme, and to publish the results seems to have been without precedent at the time.

However, its recognized importance has not persuaded many that the *Panegyricus* is enjoyable reading. There is a delightful story of Alfieri (quoted by Bruyère) whose enjoyment of the *Letters* led him on to read the *Panegyricus* with pleasurable expectations—only to be disgusted with what he found. He then set about composing a more worthy tribute to Trajan of his own, a literary curiosity which survives in his complete works. From F. A. Wolff's acid comment 'if he spoke as he wrote, the new consul would have offended the emperor' down to Syme's uncompromising judgement that the speech 'has done no good to the reputation of the author or the taste of the age', the general view is the same:[8] the *Panegyricus* is indispensable but unreadable, and only a historian's sense of duty towards his sources can make him keep on until the last, ninety-fifth chapter. Is this fair judgement on 'the solitary specimen of Latin eloquence from the century and a half that had elapsed since the death of Cicero'? Is it fair to Pliny, who was so proud of it, to ignore it as if it added nothing to what we know of him from the *Letters*?

The faults of the *Panegyricus* are obvious. It is much too long, and some of its topics are laboured to the point of obscurity or hidden behind a façade of elaborate rhetoric. A simpler treatment in chapters 36–40 would make it much easier to grasp the details of Trajan's tax concessions. The scene described in chapter 22 of Trajan's entry into Rome is ludicrous in its artificial detail and defies intelligible translation. The constant straining after antithesis can be tedious and obscure; from a wealth of examples one can suffice: *duces porro nostri non tam regum exterorum quam suorum principum insidias, nec tam*

---

[8] Syme (1958) 114.

hostium **[170]** *quam commilitonum manus ferrumque metuebant* (18.
3). The hard-pressed translator is tempted to cheat or at any rate to
offer an alternative rhetorical figure: 'Thus our generals had less to
fear from foreign foes than from their masters' treachery, and more
from the swords their own men held than from their enemies'. Every
trick of rhetoric is there—chiasmus (10. 3), zeugma (14. 3), anaphora
(17. 1)—all of which Durry examines in detail. And what are we to
make of a sentence like 60. 3, (*quod enim interesset rei publicae, si
privatus esses, consulem te haberet tantum an et senatorem, hoc nunc
scito interesse, principem te habeat tantum an et consulem*)? It must
mean something like 'Rest assured that your country's present interest in wanting to see you consul as well as emperor is simply what it
would be if you were an ordinary citizen and could be senator and
consul as well.' Durry remarks: 'a complicated thought, but the text is
sound. The consulship to the principate is as the title of senator to the
consulship. In both cases, the inferior title adds to the superior title.
An emperor is more than a consul yet while holding consular office
he acquires new prerogatives'.[9]

   One's admiration for the stamina of the invited audience grows as
the stunning effect of the speech's fervour makes itself felt, and it is
difficult not to remember Pliny's own strictures on the flamboyant
Asian style of Regulus, or the volubility of Bithynian advocates: *est
plerisque Graecorum, ut illi, pro copia volubilitas: tam longas tamque
frigidas periodos uno spiritu quasi torrente contorquent* ('Like them,
most of the Greeks have volubility rather than copiousness; they hurl
such long and such cold sentences in one breath, like a torrent',
Letters. 5. 20. 4).

   On the credit side there are many passages which provide a fine
example of rhetorical virtuosity, when a theme is stated in a forceful
opening sentence and then expanded logically with great technical
skill. The main points are not withheld until the climax of the
paragraphs, and so the style is quite different from that of Cicero;
though the prototype for the treatment of the subject is that of Cicero
in the *Pro Marcello* ('For Marcellus'). Seneca in the *De Clementia* ('On
Clemency') dedicated to Nero may also have been an influence, and
certainly Tacitus in the *Agricola*, but it was Pliny who created out of

[9] Durry (1938) 176.

the official, often brief votes of thanks something which was to serve as a model for many less talented imitators.

Though some of the later additions are quite obvious, as when Pliny looks forward to Trajan's triumph after the first Dacian War in chapter 17, or in the more lurid passages on Domitian (48–9), the drought in Egypt (30–2), or the fate of the *delatores* ('informers', 34–5), in general the elaborations are artfully integrated into the main text. There are some striking scenes where the atmosphere created is as sombre as anything in Tacitus—chapter 76 for example, the senate under Domitian—and some equally Tacitean pregnant epithets and *sententiae*, collected and discussed by Durry. Moreover the whole concept does surely bring to [171] light something in Pliny which is not easily discernible in his letters. He rarely appears there to be interested in abstract thinking (he mentions Plato twice but never Aristotle, and apart from an occasional quotation, his detailed knowledge of Greek authors is confined to Homer and the Greek orators) or in political theorizing. His interest in the Stoic opponents of the emperors is personal—nowhere does he discuss the basis for their views—and he may have found it easy to accept offices from Domitian simply because he was not politically minded. He romanticizes neither the past nor the rural scene, his generalizations are rarely more than conventional, and though he is unfailingly considerate towards individuals and tolerant of superstition or simple piety despite his own scepticism, he appears as a rather unimaginative man, with his interests largely centred in legal and professional questions or in practical problems of all kinds. He is, of course, always conscious of the senate's dignity, and more than once he regrets its loss of effective power, but only the *Panegyricus* and the two letters which refer to it indicate that he had ever thought deeply about the necessary co-operation between senate and emperor and the possibility of constitutional rule by someone who was fitted to be stronger than Nerva and less autocratic than Domitian.

Yet though the *Panegyricus* shows a new side of Pliny, it is not inconsistent with what we know of him; its head may sometimes be in the clouds of verbiage, but its feet are firmly planted on earth. Its advice to Trajan is far more direct than anything in Dio Chrysostom's addresses—Trajan is to provide a model for the ideal ruler by practical example, and Pliny's observant eye notes all the details of his appearance and habits which serve to illustrate his theme. He mixes well with all classes, he shares camp-life with his armies, he keeps himself fit with out-of-door exercise, his good looks are enhanced by the impressiveness of his prematurely grey hair; his wife is never ostentatiously dressed and goes about Rome on foot. Were these the 'least elaborate passages' (*severissima quaeque*) which, Pliny noticed (*Letters* 3.18. 8), pleased his invited audience most? In his earlier letter (3.13, evidently written before the reading) he had drawn especial attention to the rhetorical devices in the speech which were to compensate for the lack of novelty in a *gratiarum actio*. In *Letters* 3.18 he admits that he wrote the revised speech *hilarius et quasi exultantius* ('rather cheerfully and exultantly, as it were'—he was carried away by it at the time, and still defends a more florid style (*laetior stilus*, 'richer style') as the right one, though now that the excitement of the reading is over he seems to be aware that something plainer suits him best, and ends the letter by hoping that one day audiences will expect no more than strict simplicity. Perhaps his appreciative listeners were in fact a little critical of the speech's exuberance and made him feel that this was not his natural [172] style. This is in keeping with his views on oratory expressed in the two long letters (1.20 and 9.26) which compare the Attic and Asian styles; the mixed style described by Quintilian (*Inst.* 12.10) is the one which fits him best.

There is no further mention of the *Panegyricus* and no indication that Pliny ever expressed himself in this way again. His legal work and several public trials in which he appeared were to occupy his time, and forensic oratory was a more lasting interest than any other form of writing, apart from his letters. He rejected the suggestion that he should write history: it was incompatible with oratory. ('Oratory deals largely with the humble and trivial details of everyday life, history is concerned with profound truths and the glory of great deeds' (*Letters* 5.8.9).) Then came Bithynia, and a new life as a practical adminis-trator. He retained his admiration for Trajan, and their relations were always friendly. Whether Trajan actually ever read or heard the full *Panegyricus* cannot be known.

5

Praise and Protreptic in Early Imperial Panegyric: Cicero, Seneca, Pliny

Susanna Morton Braund

No other way of correcting a prince is so efficacious as presenting, in the guise of flattery, the pattern of a really good prince.
Thus do you instil virtues and remove faults in such a manner
that you seem to urge the prince to the former and restrain him
from the latter.

(Erasmus *Ep.* 179.42–5)

PROSE PANEGYRIC: ORIGINS

Unlike most genres of classical literature, prose panegyric appears to
have an originary moment. Isocrates claims that his *Evagoras* (365 BC)
is innovative (5–11) in that it offers an encomium in prose of a
man of contemporary times (5). 'I realise that what I intend to do is
difficult—to eulogize a man's virtues in prose . . . No one has ever
attempted to write on such a theme' (8). The central difficulty is that
the resources of poetry are not available to him (8–11).[1] Despite these
(alleged) obstacles, the speech that he produced was taken as a model
by later writers of panegyric and clearly played a significant part
in establishing the 'rules' of the genre. But can we accept his claim
of innovation? Such claims of primacy occur throughout classical

---

[1] Cf. Russell (1998) 24.

literature. For example, both Lucretius and Virgil use the imagery of treading untrodden mountain paths,[2] yet it seems clear that Lucretius' poem is breaking new ground in a [54] way in which Virgil is not in his *Georgics*, a poem which is heavily indebted to Lucretius in both language and ideas. Claims of innovation and primacy are designed to prepare the audience for something daring and unexpected and to protect the author against the risk of failure. By announcing the novelty and audacity of the undertaking, the author raises the audience's expectations and promises an experience deserving of attention.

It is just possible that before Isocrates no one had produced such a panegyric in prose. Yet there are clear congeners. *Evagoras* seems to combine the hymning of the (very much alive) victorious athlete in poetry such as Pindar's with the collective and anonymous Athenian funeral oration, such as Pericles' *epitaphios logos* ('funeral speech'), represented by Thucydides (2.35–46).[3] Like Pindar in his epinician hymns, Isocrates praises an individual; as in the funeral oration, his subject is dead. His subject is Evagoras, king of Salamis in Cyprus, and this may constitute the innovation: whereas in democratic Athens no individual receives the spotlight of attention, in a monarchical context, Isocrates is free to elevate one individual above the rest. The speech is addressed to his son and heir, Nicocles, who is described in the opening sentence as honouring his father's tomb with offerings and activities which suggest a commemorative festival (1, cf. 73–7), possibly several years after Evagoras' death in 374 BC. The originality of Isocrates' composition may be the fusion of these two traditions.

Isocrates' oration was clearly immediately influential. Its effect can be seen in Xenophon's *Agesilaus*, an encomium on the king of Sparta (398–*c*.361/60 BC) written soon after his death and explicitly described as an Ἐγκώμιον ('encomium') not a 'funeral dirge' (θρίνον, 10.3), and more generally in the *logoi epitaphioi* incorporated into

---

[2] Lucr. 1.922–30 e.g. *auia Pieridum peragro loca nullius ante | trita solo* ('I traverse the pathless places of the Pierides, not yet trodden by any foot'); Virg. *G.* 3.291–3 e.g. *iuuat ire iugis qua nulla priorum | Castaliam molli deuertitur orbita cliuo* ('I delight in walking on the heights where no forerunner's track turns down to Castalia on a gentle slope').

[3] The hallmark of the Athenian funeral oration was collective civic celebration: see Loraux (1986) 1–76, esp. 1–3 and 42–3 (contrast with the individualistic Roman funeral oration). For other, literary, encomia see Russell (1998) 18 ff.

historiography,[4] in Velleius' miniature panegyric of Tiberius in his history[5] and ultimately in Tacitus' *Agricola*.[6] [55]

ROMAN PROSE PANEGYRIC

It might be expected that Roman prose panegyric emerged from the highly developed tradition of funeral orations, significantly different from the Athenian practice, in that funerals were occasions for panegyric of individuals. Similarly, Roman gravestones bore encomia of the dead. But these orations and epitaphs do not constitute or even belong to the genre of Latin panegyric. The chief differentiation is that Latin panegyric takes as its subject someone living. Moreover, it is characteristically rooted in highly specific sociopolitical occasions. These characteristics will emerge from the classic case of Pliny's *Panegyricus*, Pliny's expanded version of the vote of thanks (*gratiarum actio*) delivered to the emperor Trajan in the senate on 1 September AD 100, which heads the collection of the twelve *Panegyrici Latini* and indeed served as a model for the later speeches.[7]

In what follows, I shall refrain from generalizations about Latin panegyric of the early period, chiefly because every panegyric makes its own adaptation of the Greek framework to its specific context, often a context of inauguration. I shall use that context to illuminate Pliny's mammoth oration and the Caesarian speeches of Cicero which I shall style proto-panegyrics. The marked protreptic element in these works will lead to a consideration of Seneca's treatise to the young emperor Nero, *On Clemency*, modelled on Hellenistic kingship treatises, another inaugurative text with similar concerns and material. The resulting illumination of the practices of early imperial Latin panegyric as instantiated in Cicero, Seneca and Pliny will respect the

---

[4] Seneca the Elder mentions Sallust's penchant for incorporating *epitaphia* (obituaries) into his works and preserves a number of obituaries of Cicero at *Suas.* 6.21–7.
[5] Velleius 126: see Woodman (1977) 234–5 for discussion of this miniature panegyric.
[6] Quintilian's prescriptions for panegyric (*laus hominum*) envisage as models of organization the chronological account of a man's life and deeds and sections on the different virtues with deeds included under these headings (3.7.10–18, esp.15).
[7] For an overview of Pliny's *Panegyricus*, which we should properly refer to as his *gratiarum actio* (*Pan.* 1.6, 90.3), see Radice (1968, reproduced above); Fedeli (1989).

very significant differences of each panegyrist's situation and relationship with his subject.[8] [56]

PANEGYRIC AND VIRTUES ACCORDING TO ISOCRATES AND MENANDER RHETOR

First, I shall briefly consider the panegyrical framework established by Isocrates' exemplar and the theoretical prescriptions of Menander Rhetor for the *Basilikos Logos*. Isocrates starts with Evagoras' illustrious descent (13–18), then moves to his birth (19–21). His description of Evagoras' youth indicates that he was destined for greatness (22) and the catalogue of his adult qualities confirms this ἀνδρεῖα, σοφία, δικαιοσύνη 'courage, wisdom, justice', (23). As proof of his greatness Isocrates describes how Evagoras seized Salamis from the usurper with a band of only fifty followers (28–32) and compares him with a great man from the past, Cyrus (33–9). He proceeds to depict Evagoras' characteristic virtues as king: energy, impartiality, humanity, fairness, consistency, self-sacrifice (40–6). After details about Evagoras' Hellenization of Salamis and the political and military consequences of that Hellenization, especially the assistance he gave to Conon of Athens (47–57), he asserts that Evagoras surpasses the heroes who waged war on Troy: 'they, accompanied by all Greece, captured only Troy while Evagoras, with only one city, made war on all Asia' (65). He finally claims that Evagoras deserves immortality as much as anyone (70–2) and concludes by offering his depiction of Evagoras as a model for future emulation, in particular by Evagoras' son, Nicocles (73–7). He exhorts Nicocles to prove himself worthy of his father and encourages him by suggesting that to do so he only has

---

[8] For a brief general overview of Latin panegyric, prose and verse, see Born (1934) 20–35, supplemented by Coleman (1988) 62–5 (introduction to *Silv.* 4.1). Mause (1994) is a comprehensive compilation of prose and verse panegyric in Latin. On the sources of particular ideas and phrases in Pliny's *Panegyricus* see the detailed compilation of Mesk (1911), followed broadly by Durry (1938), 27–33, including Isocrates, *Evagoras*, Xenophon, *Agesilaus*, Cicero, Velleius, Seneca, *De clementia* and Tacitus, *Agricola*. On Velleius' miniature panegyric for Tiberius see Ramage (1982). For the connection between Cicero, Seneca and Pliny see Syme (1958) 95. On the later panegyrists' development see MacCormack (1975). On their inventiveness and ingenuity see Seager (1983).

to maintain his present conduct (78–81). We find a remarkable similarity in the prescriptions for the 'Imperial Oration' or, better, 'King Speech', the *Basilikos Logos*, in the school handbook attributed to Menander Rhetor and probably written in the late third century AD.[9] Significantly, the treatise starts by recommending that the [57] orator assert his inability to tackle the theme by claiming to be at a loss where to start or how to do justice to his subject: elements which feature prominently at the start and close of Isocrates' oration. A central feature of Isocrates' speech is his praise of Evagoras' 'virtues'. This feature reappears in Menander Rhetor's prescription in a more codified catalogue of the four classic virtues of a ruler, derived ultimately from Plato: courage, justice, temperance and wisdom ἀνδρεία, δικαιοσύνη, σωφροσύνη, φρόνησις (elsewhere σοφία) Menand. Rhet. 373). It seems that during the Hellenistic period a canon or, better, pool of virtues of the ruler developed, described in what we can call 'kingship treatises',[10] which was in turn adopted by the Romans (*fortitudo, temperantia/continentia, iustitia* and *prudentia/ sapientia* are Cicero's terms) and adapted to Roman ideology.[11] An eloquent example is the Golden Shield (*Clipeus Virtutis*) presented to Augustus in 27 BC by the SPQR which proclaimed his 'courage, clemency, justice and piety' (*uirtus, clementia, iustitia* and *pietas: Achievements* 34.2), a significant variation on the classic quartet of virtues.[12] The pool of virtues provided an instant template against which any ruler, including an emperor, could readily be measured. But of course,

---

[9] Durry 1938, 27 n.2 rightly mentions other theoreticians too, including Aphthonius and Theon, and rhetoricians, including Pliny's contemporary Dio Chrysostom and Aelius Aristides, whose orations on kingship continue the tradition of the Hellenistic kingship treatises. On Menander Rhetor see Russell (1998) 29–33, and for translation and commentary on the *Basilikos Logos* see Russell and Wilson (1981), with summary 271.

[10] See Goodenough (1928). The central texts are the pseudo-Pythagorean tracts preserved by Stobaeus, which may date from the third century BC or from considerably later. See Delatte (1942). Plutarch draws heavily on Hellenistic writings in his discussions of kings and kingship.

[11] On the Platonic-Stoic 'fundamental canon' see North, (1966) 166–7; on Hellenistic canons of virtue ibid. 174–5. On the problems associated with 'canons' see Wallace-Hadrill (1981) 300–7. On Hellenistic 'kingship treatises' cf. Adam (1970).

[12] See Ryberg (1966) 234 'not the orthodox Greek list of wisdom, justice, fortitude, and moderation'. Wallace-Hadrill, while conceding that Augustus' Golden Shield may be a variation on the Hellenistic philosophical canon of virtues, prefers to set it in the tradition of Hellenistic honorific presentations to kings and other benefactors (1981) 300–7.

different rulers had different strengths and preferred to emphasize some virtues and to play down others.[13] [58]

This emerges through the different media of self-representation available to emperors, which include celebration by poets and imagery offered in cult contexts, in inscriptions and particularly in the minting of coins. Coins readily carried a single word and image—and that image could readily be the personification of an imperial virtue, such as *pietas* ('piety'), *iustitia* ('justice'), *liberalitas* ('generosity') or *clementia* ('clemency').[14] This focus upon specific virtues selected from the pool will emerge as an important feature in the early imperial panegyrical texts under scrutiny here.

PLINY ON TRAJAN'S VIRTUES

Pliny in his *Panegyricus* reproduces all the standard topics and adopts the standard chronological sequence, although he plays down aspects of Trajan's origin and early years, presumably because Trajan's adoption by Nerva complicates the situation. The bulk of the speech is Pliny's celebration of Trajan's virtues as emperor, which have an impressively wide range, given that he had only been emperor for two years and had spent only half of that time in Rome, which reduces the material available (although Pliny claims, of course, that this is no impediment: 56.2). Pliny closes with intimations of Trajan's divinity and with invitations to his adoptive father and his natural father (the only place Trajan senior is actually named in the speech) to take pleasure in their son's success (89). Finally he addresses a classic prayer to the gods and especially to Capitoline Jupiter for the 'emperor's preservation' (*salus principis*, 94.1–2). Against the background of the conventions of panegyric and the pool of imperial virtues, it emerges that Pliny makes significant adaptations to accommodate and articulate (his view of) Trajan's uniqueness. Particularly important are the comparisons with Trajan's predecessors embedded

---

[13] The classic discussion is Charlesworth (1937). See now Wallace-Hadrill (1981) and Fears (1981).

[14] On virtues on imperial coinage see Wallace-Hadrill (1981), esp. the appendix with a chart of the personifications which appear on Roman coinage (319–23); of these thirty-six personifications he defines twelve as virtues (309–10).

throughout the speech, above all the contrast with Domitian. This is a salutary [59] reminder that panegyrics are rooted in specific contexts, a point to which I shall return later.[15]

At the beginning of the speech, Pliny faces a potential difficulty over Trajan's origin, as the prescriptions of Menander Rhetor warn may happen. He refrains from naming Trajan's natural father, M. Ulpius Traianus, and Trajan's Spanish birthplace (Italica, in Baetica).[16] Instead, he asserts that Trajan is an emperor created by the gods (5.1–2) and he celebrates his adoption by Nerva, complimenting Nerva on the wisdom of his choice and Trajan on the qualities that merited that choice (6–8). That is, he turns a potential difficulty to his rhetorical advantage by portraying Trajan's *electio* as meeting unanimous approval (7.5–6).[17] He then dwells upon the deification of Nerva (11) which, of course, renders Trajan 'the son of the god', *diui filius* (although Pliny does not use the phrase). That is, the relationship between Nerva and Trajan and in particular the deification of Nerva takes the place of the usual praise of the subject's origins by neatly asserting superhuman status right at the start.[18] This is underlined by the fact that Pliny nowhere uses the name *Traianus*, which could act as a reminder of his human origins, except at the very close (88.6).

After this, Pliny proceeds in a more conventional fashion by describing Trajan's early years (14.1). He alludes to early military successes Trajan achieved with his father (14.1) and to later exploits under Domitian. He claims that Trajan had ten years' experience as military tribune (15.3: probably an exaggeration), which is designed as proof of his expertise. By picturing a future triumph Pliny moves closer to the time of Trajan's accession and return to Rome while maintaining the military emphasis.

Pliny has so far neatly combined the requirement to describe the subject's early years with a celebration of one of the chief qualities of a ruler: his military courage and excellence (*uirtus*). He has also incorporated many of the other classic, conventional virtues [60] into

---

[15] As MacCormack (1975) argues for the later Latin panegyrics.

[16] The mention of Trajan's descent from a father who was a patrician, a consular and awarded a triumph (9.2) is deeply embedded in a discussion of Nerva's adoption of Trajan.

[17] On Trajan's suitability for power see Hammond (1938) 122 and 139 and Syme (1958) 58.

[18] For the analogy with Tiberius' adoption by Augustus see Ramage (1982).

these opening sections.[19] Trajan is praised for his 'devotion to duty, self-restraint and sense of pity' (*pietatem abstinentiam mansuetudi-nem*, 2.6), his 'humanity, self-control and accessibility' (*humanitatem temperantiam facilitatem*, 2.7) and his 'modesty and moderation' (*modestiam . . . moderationemque*, 3.2). By presenting himself pondering the qualities needed in the Roman emperor, Pliny compliments Trajan as exceeding his highest ideal (4.4). He alone, claims Pliny, has virtues unsullied by faults (4.5). He proceeds to celebrate Trajan's qualities: 'How wonderful! His sternness (*seueritas*) is not at all diminished by his sense of humour (*hilaritas*) or his authority (*grauitas*) by his openness (*simplicitas*) or his grandeur (*maiestas*) by his sense of humanity (*humanitas*). What is more, his robustness and height, his fine head and noble face and the unbent strength of his maturity along with his hair adorned with the early signs of old age, the gift of the gods designed to enhance his grandeur—are these not the marks, far and wide, of our ruler?' (4.6–7).

Pliny records Trajan's rapturous reception in Rome early in AD 99 on his first arrival there since becoming emperor (his *aduentus*) and proceeds to work through his actions and achievements in broadly chronological sequence from that point, using his behaviour to demonstrate his virtues. Standard items from the pool are named throughout: his seriousness, moral excellence and self-control (*grauitate sanctitate temperantia*, 82.8), his generosity (*benignitas*, 25.3, 39.3, 60.7; *munificentia*, 25.5; *liberalitas*, 25.5, 27.3, 33.2, 38.2), his freedom from guilt (*innocentia*, 49.3) and his consequent freedom from fear (*securitas*, 68.4). 'Justice' (*iustitia*) is a canonical virtue. Pliny highlights Trajan's *iustitia* in his restoration of the rule of law to the treasury (36.1–3); and his *iustitia* is first mentioned in the form of the fairness he demonstrates in his management of a show (33.2). In court he exhibits 'how strictness (*seueritas*) need not be cruel and how mercy (*clementia*) need not be weak' (80.1). He is also credited with mercy (*clementia*) for the way he entrusts the punishment of informers to the gods (35.1) and with pity (*mansuetudo*) for his alleviations of bereavement (38.5). [61]

---

[19] Wallace-Hadrill finds twenty in sections 2–4 and a further fifteen in the rest of the speech (1981) 312 n. 67.

TRAJAN'S UNIQUENESS

In all this, there is nothing startling. But there is one specific cluster of qualities which recurs throughout the oration and which seems to be singled out as characteristic of Trajan. Pliny goes out of his way from the beginning to emphasize that Trajan is and indeed considers himself 'one of us' (*unum ille se ex nobis ... putat*, 2.4). The seeds are there from the start. In his years of active military service before becoming emperor, Trajan's position as *imperator* did not prevent him behaving as one of his men (10.3) and 'you regarded yourself as an ordinary citizen' (*priuatus*, 10.4). Pliny goes so far as to call him a 'fellow-soldier', *commilito* (15.5, cf. 19.3).[20] Trajan continues this behaviour. Hence he is praised for his accessibility (*facilitas*) which he demonstrates at his accession (23.2) and thereafter by his adoption or even extension of Nerva's 'open house' policy (47.4) and by his personal approachability (*humanitas* 'humanity', 48.1; *suauitas* 'charm', 49.5; and *iucunditas* 'delightfulness', 49.7). It is to Trajan's credit that he adopts no airs and graces but retains his former 'sense of respect' (*humanitas* and *uerecundia*, 24.2). According to Pliny, he brings the perspective of a *priuatus* ('private citizen') to the position of emperor (44.1–2), even to the extent of offering accountability in court (36.4), of attending his proclamation as consul (described as *moderatio* 'moderation' and *sanctitas* 'reverence', 63.8) and taking the consul's oath (64.1), of submitting himself to the jurisdiction of law in the forum (65.1) and of behaving as an equal of the candidates nominated for office (71.3, another sign of his *humanitas*, 71.5). In short, 'a ruler behaved the same as a citizen, an emperor the same as one of his subjects' (64.4). Similarly, he is said to conduct his private life like an ordinary citizen (83–4). This behaviour is best captured in the quality Pliny calls *humanitas* and in the concept of *ciuilitas*: courtesy.[21]

This *ciuilitas* emerges more generally throughout Trajan's conduct of politics (87.1), in particular, for example, in his not seeking, or

---

[20] On Trajan as *priuatus* see Rees (1998) and (2001).

[21] Pliny's use of the adjective (2.7) and adverb (29.2) in this sense anticipates the coining of *ciuilitas*, which first appears in Suet. *Aug.* 51. See Wallace-Hadrill (1982) for a full exploration of the ambivalence of the 'citizen-emperor ideal' and the rituals of 'deference' and 'condescension'.

reluctance to accept, honours and high office. This motif gains prominence from repetition. Early in the speech, Pliny describes [62] the
omen by which Trajan was acclaimed *Imperator*, which Trajan alone
was unwilling to acknowledge (5.2–5). The same point recurs in the
award of the title 'Father of his Country', *Pater patriae*, over which a
battle was fought with Trajan's modesty (*modestia*) (21.1). Then there
is the question of Trajan's third consulship (56–60). He could have
followed precedent and held this in 99 (57.1), but declined to do so
until the following year (60.4). Later, Pliny raises the prospect of
a fourth consulship (78–9). Another battle is in prospect between
the senate's loyalty (*pietati . . . senatus*) and the ruler's moderation
(*modestia principis*) (79.4). This picture of Trajan's reluctance deftly
characterizes his *moderatio* and demonstrates his suitability to be
emperor (5.5).

This is Trajan's personal manifestation of the classic trait of self-
control.[22] Pliny has made it the mainstay of his oration.[23] That is, he
has adapted the standard material to Trajan's particular configuration
of virtue. Pliny cleverly blends panegyric and protreptic to his senatorial perspective: hence the respect with which the emperor treats the
senate is absolutely critical (76.1–6) and hence the speech is, techni-
cally, addressed to the senate (*patres conscripti*, e.g. 1.1, 90.1, 95.1) in a
framework which encloses apostrophe to Trajan.[24]

Pliny also capitalizes upon two of the titles granted to Trajan. He
develops the title of *Pater patriae* into an image of Trajan as father to
his people: 'How generous and kind you are in fulfilment of this title!
You conduct yourself towards your citizens as a father towards his

---

[22] In essence *moderatio* (54.5, 56.3, 63.8; also *modestia*, 58.2, 79.4 and *temperantia*,
82.8): see Wallace-Hadrill (1982) 41–2 and on the links with *humanitas* and *ciuilitas*
43–4.
[23] The virtue of *ciuilitas* will be not praised again in the panegyrical corpus until
Mamertinus' *gratiarum actio* for the consulship to Julian in 362 (*Pan.* III (XI)): see
Rees (1998).
[24] Cf. Syme (1958) 58 on 'Trajan's career of service—and subordination . . . The
word is *obsequium*'; Wallace-Hadrill (1981) 316 says: 'The focus is not on the
possession of power, but on the control of it in deference to other members of society.'
On imperial deference to the senate see Wallace-Hadrill (1982) 37–8 and on the link
between *ciuilitas* and respect for the senate ibid. 45. On the *Panegyricus* as 'écrit
senatorial' ('senatorial script') see Durry (1938) 21–4 and Gamberini (1983) 393 on
address and apostrophe in the speech. Bartsch (1994), reproduced as chapter eight
below, also recognizes Pliny's senatorial perspective (e.g. 186 = pp. 191–2) but highlights other perspectives which present Trajan—and Pliny—in a less complimentary
light (166–7).

children!' (21.4), evoking this emotive imagery by twice describing Trajan as *parens publicus* ('public parent' 26:3, 87.1) and suggesting that [63] his benign protection encourages people to raise children again (27). The climax of the oration is Pliny's fulsome justification of Trajan's title 'The Best', *Optimus* (88.4–10, developing the brief mention at 2.7).[25] Pliny insists upon its appositeness: 'It may seem ready-made and commonplace, but actually it is an innovation. You could know of no one who deserved it previously' (88.4). This is because it embraces all the virtues (88.6). Pliny proceeds to draw an analogy with Jupiter who is worshipped as *Optimus Maximus* (88.8). He even suggests that the title *Optimus* will always be associated with Trajan in the same way as the title *Augustus* is always a reminder of the first Augustus (88.10).

PLINY: HAVING IT BOTH WAYS[26]

Pliny insists from the outset upon Trajan's being what we might call 'an ordinary bloke' or 'a regular guy' (*ciuilitas*) yet cannot resist intimations of immortality throughout the speech. This is his programmatic statement: 'Nowhere should we flatter him as a god and a divinity: we are talking of a fellow-citizen, not a tyrant, a father not a master' (2.3). Not surprisingly, Pliny attributes Trajan's election as emperor to divine agency (e.g. 5.1–2, 10.4, 72 and 74). But early in the speech, when describing Nerva's search for a suitable heir, Pliny asserts that the essential requirement is for the person who is 'the best and most like the gods' (*optimum . . . dis simillimum*, 7.5). Later, when praising Trajan's solution of the crisis caused by a shortage of

---

[25] On the title *Optimus* see Durry (1938) App. 1 (231–2) for a survey of the evidence. He concludes that Trajan was known as *Optimus* throughout his reign, although the point at which this became official is unclear. There are coins with dedications OPTIMI PRINCIPI from 103 and in the summer of 114 Trajan took the agnomen *Optimus* (Dio Chrys. 68.23.1).

[26] A panegyrist's trait: see Syme's remark quoting *Pan.* 46.3 *utrumque recte* (1938) 224 and the excellent discussion by Maguinness (1933), reproduced as chapter thirteen below, (117–24= pp. 265–73). Pliny's exploitation of antithesis and paradox is central to Rees (2001). Bartsch (1994) esp. 149, 183 (= below pp. 149–50, 188–9) offers a provocative interpretation of Pliny's use of antithesis in her reading of the *Panegyricus* as 'an obsessive attempt to prove its own sincerity' (149 = 149) which at the same time 'names itself clearly as a study in moderation' (158 = 159).

grain in Egypt, Pliny describes his transferring of natural resources from one part of the world to another [64] in terms of superhuman powers (32.1–2).[27] When commending his changes in inheritance tax Pliny suggests that Trajan has outdone even the gods through his retrospective legislation (40.3). He becomes bolder when, in praise of Trajan's sharing his consulship with two third-time consuls, he implies that this is the act of someone more than human (61.9). More explicit still is his description of Trajan's third consulship in which he was 'a candidate not only for the consulship but for immortality' (63.1). Again, Trajan is set on a par with divinity in his role as arbitrator of disputes: 'These are the real concerns of a ruler and even of a god, to reconcile states in rivalry ... finally, like a swift-moving star, to see and hear everything and to be there to help right away wherever you are called for' (80.3). Pliny implies that Trajan is the chosen deputy of Jupiter (80.4).

Pliny is concerned to avoid calling Trajan a god by presenting a rationalizing picture of him, yet evokes a charismatic kind of divinity nonetheless.[28] He mentions the 'divinity of our leader' (2.7) but immediately turns the focus on to his human qualities. This is designed as a stark contrast with Domitian's insistence on being addressed as 'master and god', *dominus et deus*.[29] This antithesis with Domitian pervades the oration,[30] but is perhaps most developed at the centre of the speech in an extended passage on the ways in which the two emperors deal with people (48–9).[31] Pliny praises Trajan for his accessibility and for setting people at their ease (48.1–2). In contrast, Domitian is depicted as a terrifying monster lurking in a cave licking up the blood of relatives he has murdered or emerging to slaughter the most illustrious citizens [65] (48.3). Pliny emphasizes that walls are no protection against vengeance (49.1) and praises Trajan

---

[27] See Scott (1932) 164.

[28] The antithesis is taken from Wallace-Hadrill (1981) 317 who, however, underestimates the evocations of divinity in the *Panegyricus*. See Bartsch (1994) 163–4 (= below 164–7).

[29] See e.g. Suet. *Dom.* 13.2, Mart., 5.8.1, 7.34.8.

[30] e.g. 16.3, 20.4, 33.4, 45, 46, 47, 48, 49, 50.5, 52.3, 53.4, 54, 55.7, 62.3, 66.2–3, 72.2, 76 and cf. Molin (1989) 787 n. 34 and Fedeli (1989) 439–44 on Domitian's demerits. The negative picture of Domitian is one of the features shared with Tacitus' *Agricola*, with which Pliny was clearly familiar: see Bruyère (1954) on the reciprocal relationship between Tacitus and Pliny; on *Agricola* specifically see 162–4. On the antithesis with Domitian see Bartsch (1994) 154, 159–60 (= below 154–5, 160–1).

[31] See Braund (1996).

for surrounding himself with his subjects instead of seeking solitude (49.2). These stark differentiations are explicitly justified as a demonstration of how Trajan is reforming the character of the principate, which had become corrupted (53). Comparison, he asserts, is central to panegyric because 'the person who does not detest bad rulers enough cannot adore good rulers enough' (53.2).[32]

PANEGYRIC FOR A NEW REIGN

The contrast with Domitian is a reminder that the *Panegyricus* dates from the early years of Trajan's reign. Domitian died in 96 and after Nerva's short reign Trajan became emperor early in 98 and arrived in Rome for the first time early in 99. Pliny's speech in the Senate in September 100 can therefore plausibly be regarded as part of the optimistic outpouring of literature which typically greeted a new emperor on his accession.[33] Although such speeches of gratitude had long been obligatory,[34] they were usually brief—and tedious, as Pliny himself observes (*Letters* 3.18.6). Pliny has taken a duty (explicitly, the *senatus consultum* 'decree of the senate' prescribing the *gratiarum actio*, 'speech of thanksgiving', *Pan.* 4.1) as an opportunity to celebrate the new emperor.

Panegyric which participates in what we might call 'accession literature' has a difficult task to fulfil. Of course it needs to deliver praise of actual achievements and behaviour—and yet at or soon after the accession there may not be much material available. Pliny turns this potential difficulty to his advantage in his [66] rhetorical exhortation to Trajan to accept his third consulship—rhetorical because

---

[32] Hence panegyric and satire are complementary genres: see Braund (1993). On comparison as a central element of panegyric see Maguinness (1932) 45–51, a feature which he rightly connects with assertions of superhuman or divine status. Maguinness observes that Pliny even compares Trajan with future emperors at *Pan.* 73.6 (*onerasti futuros principes*, 'you have burdened future emperors'). Bartsch (1994) 170 (= below 173) attempts to dissolve the distinctions between eulogy and satire by appealing to the gap between the 'public transcipt' and the 'hidden transcript'.

[33] In this respect, the *Panegyricus* resembles the later panegyrics tied to occasions of *aduentus* (arrival), as discussed by MacCormack (1975) 157–8.

[34] On *gratiarum actiones* see Radice (1968) 166 and above pp. 77–8, Durry (1938) 3–5, Hammond (1938) 120, with Fedeli's caution about the date of the establishment of this practice (1989) 400–4.

Pliny knows all along that Trajan has accepted it (60.4). He argues that rumour reports Trajan's conduct of his second consulship (held when Trajan was abroad) to have shown him to be 'the essence of justice, kindness and tolerance' but insists that he requires actual proof instead of rumour and that this can only come from a third consulship (59.3)! And despite its length (on which see below), the oration actually is relatively thin on material points, for which it compensates in generalizations.[35]

Panegyric produced so early in the reign can serve another function besides praise: it can reflect or even prescribe a programme of behaviour to the new emperor. In the *Panegyricus*, the key theme, as I have argued above, is *humanitas* and *ciuilitas*. These are the qualities that Trajan is urged to (continue to) exhibit. Of course, the panegyrist has to exercise considerable tact in offering such a protreptic. Pliny's tact and persuasion emerges in his assertion that Trajan is 'the one man who relishes the ancestral traditions and excellence, who strives and competes with himself, with no other rival or role model' (13.5). The idea that the new emperor is already perfect and therefore already supplies his own model is a successful means of argument. And the role of the panegyrist in this relationship readily resembles that of adviser to a king, reminiscent of Seneca's relationship with Nero.[36]

I have emphasized that Pliny's oration is tied to a particular moment and context. In fact, we need to distinguish between the original delivery of the speech and its subsequent expansion for publication. Pliny delivered the original version as his thanks for his suffect consulship of the months of September and October in the Senate on 1st September 100. This accounts for his focus upon the inauguration of Trajan's reign, especially his reception in Rome (22–3), for his praise of Trajan's civility in his dealings with senators and the Senate (e.g. 76.1–6) and for the section at the very end in which Pliny talks about himself as consul and about his relationship with the emperor (95, cf. 90.3). Topical details fit the [67] moment for which

---

[35] Syme (1958) 31–42, 57–8 supplements the *Panegyricus* by reading between the lines. See too Fedeli (1989) 461–97 and 511–13 on Trajan's programme as glimpsed behind the *Panegyricus*.

[36] See Molin (1989) esp. 792–7 on the relationship between panegyrist and ruler. But his argument that the virtues Pliny mentions articulate a neo-Stoic programme perhaps underestimates the extent to which Stoic ideas had entered the mainstream of Roman élite thought by this period.

the speech was written, for example, the elaborate dramatization of Trajan's eventual acceptance of his third consulship (59–60) in 99. More significantly, Pliny suggests an analogy between Trajan and Hercules (explicitly at 14.5, hinted at at 82.6–7), which Trajan evidently encouraged. Coins of 100 showing Hercules Gaditanus make the connection with Trajan's southern Spanish provenance.[37] Dio Chrysostom's first oration *On Kingship*, probably delivered in Rome early in Trajan's reign, presents Hercules as Trajan's 'prototype and avatar' in the extended climax to the speech (*Or.* 1.56–84).[38] And at about this time, a new legion, the Second Traiana, took Hercules as its emblem.

Pliny later expanded the speech substantially, perhaps by a factor of two or three, for publication.[39] He states his purposes in publishing this expanded version: 'Firstly, to recommend his virtues to our emperor with genuine praise, secondly to advise future rulers of the most effective way to attain the same renown, not by offering instruction but by presenting a role model' (*Letters* 3.18.2). The risk of seeming presumptuous in offering advice to the emperor is thereby palliated (3.18.3). The expanded version of the speech evidently reflects events subsequent to September 100. For example, when Pliny anticipates Trajan's celebration of a triumph (*Pan.* 16.3–17.4) he may have had in mind Trajan's First Dacian War which began in March 101 and, perhaps, the consequent triumph celebrated in 102/3.[40] A key point which undoubtedly reflects the general context, without being definitively connected with either the original oration or the expanded version, is Pliny's praise of Trajan as *Optimus* (2.7, 88.4–10): as noted above, this appellation was in currency from the start of Trajan's reign and [68] coins bearing the legend

---

[37] On the parallel with Hercules see Syme (1958) 58. On the new coin type of 100 see Strack (1931) 95–104.

[38] Jones (1978) 117; see 115–23 on Dio Chrys. and Trajan, including 116–20 on the similar ideology of Pliny and Dio Chrys.'s first oration.

[39] See *Letters* 3.13 on the difficulties in composing such a speech, because the content is utterly familiar to everyone already, and 3.18 on his expansion of the original for publication. For speculation on the extent and nature of the expansion see Radice (1968) 166 (= above pp. 77–8), Gamberini (1983) 381, Fedeli (1989) 405–11.

[40] See Durry (1938) 13–14 for the debate about whether or not this is prediction after the event. Syme (1938) 218 concurs with Durry (9–15) in seeing no reason to date publication later than 101 (for a view that it may date from up to three years later see Fedeli (1989) 405–11.

OPTIMVS appeared from 103 onwards.[41] The *Panegyricus* is, then, rooted in its context(s).

Yet Pliny was also seizing the opportunity offered by an obligatory speech of thanks to express a broader political vision for the future.[42] This was a kind of innovation. But Pliny was not working in a vacuum. Besides the Greek models and the prescriptions of rhetorical theory mentioned above, there were earlier Roman sources of inspiration. In particular, the themes and presentation of Pliny's oration are illuminated by a comparison with Cicero's ideas on how to address the man with absolute power and by juxtaposition with the model presented in Seneca's inaugurative protreptic to the young emperor Nero, *On Clemency.*

CICERO'S PANEGYRICS OF CAESAR

Cicero's 'Caesarian' speeches dating from 46–5 BC undoubtedly provided a model for later panegyrists. The three speeches—*For Marcellus, For Ligarius* and *For King Deiotarus*—have much in common. They were all delivered before Caesar, and in effect to Caesar, in the Senate, in the forum, and in Caesar's house respectively. They all address some of the circumstances and consequences of power being vested (for the first time) in one man. That is, the speeches mark the inauguration of Caesar's one-man rule. These, then, are the earliest Roman imperial panegyrics that survive. The three speeches are rooted in specific contexts, yet those contexts are used by Cicero to praise Caesar and, perhaps, to proffer a programme for the future.

For Marcellus is perhaps the most obviously panegyrical of the three speeches. It is Cicero's articulation of thanks to Caesar for his demonstration of mercy (*clementia*) towards M. Claudius Marcellus, who had supported Pompey in the civil war, in response to an appeal for his pardon which was supported by the entire Senate. Cicero's speech of gratitude (*gratiarum actio*, 33) in the Senate in 46 BC marked the breaking of a long, determined silence (cf. *Fam.* 4.4.4) since his return to Rome after his own pardon by Caesar. Cicero's opening sentence claims that his panegyric of Caesar will be delivered

---

[41] See n. 25.
[42] Cf. Radice (1968) 169 = above p.w.

in what he claims to be his old (i.e. frank) way of [69] speaking: 'It is absolutely impossible for me to refrain from remarking on this amazing leniency, this unusual and unprecedented clemency, this consistent restraint in a position of supreme power, this unbelievable and virtually divine wisdom' (1). He declares the impossibility of adequately representing Caesar's achievements in words yet asserts that this day is the day of highest praise (4–5): Caesar's military conquests are less significant than the self-control he has demonstrated in his act of *clementia*, which provokes Cicero to classify him as 'most resembling god' (8–9).[43] One reason is that unlike his other achievements, which were shared with others, 'this is entirely his own' (11). Cicero prophesies that his other monuments will fade 'but this justice (*iustitia*) and merciful disposition (*lenitas animi*) of yours will flourish more and more daily' (12). The competitiveness of the leading players which we associate with the Republic has now given way to the kind of competition we noticed in Pliny (*Pan.* 13.5), competition with oneself: Caesar is declared to have already surpassed all others 'in fairness (*aequitas*) and pity (*misericordia*)': 'today you have actually surpassed yourself' (12).

Cicero now begins to shift from praise to programme by introducing into the speech prospects for the future. He asserts that the gods have conferred 'all hopes of safety/prosperity (*salutis*)' upon Caesar's clemency (*clementia*) and wisdom (*sapientia*) (18) and lays out a programme of action for him: 'setting up courts of law, restoring confidence, controlling passions, promoting population growth, binding together with stern laws everything that has disintegrated and been dismantled' (23). He calls on Caesar to heal the wounds of war, wounds which only he can heal (24). Complaining of the brief span of Caesar's life so far (25) he attributes 'divine excellence' to Caesar (26) and looks towards an immortality beyond the body (28). The speech, in short, attributes to Caesar many items from the standard pool of virtues—*sapientia, iustitia, aequitas, liberalitas, bonitas*, ('wisdom, justice, equity, generosity, goodness') but all presented in a way in which they complement the central focus of the speech, Caesar's *clementia*. Like Pliny's *Panegyricus*, this is a speech which exhibits most of the standard features of the *Basilikos Logos* but which is at the same time firmly rooted in a particular ideological

---

[43] Perhaps echoed by Pliny at 7.5 *dis simillimum*.

moment. Cicero is concerned to establish Caesar's *clementia* and thereby encourage him to [70] maintain that quality, just as Pliny's priority is to praise and encourage Trajan's *humanitas* and *ciuilitas*. And, like Pliny, Cicero closes his speech by asserting the personal relationship between panegyrist and his subject. The climax to Cicero's praise is his declaration of personal devotion to Caesar (32), after which he delivers an elaborate closing expression of gratitude asserting that Caesar has outdone his generosity to Cicero by pardoning Marcellus (33–4).

For *Ligarius* (46 BC) and For *King Deiotarus* (45 BC) exhibit many of the same features. In For *Ligarius* Cicero is working to extend Caesar's recent pardon of Marcellus (to which he refers at 37) to Ligarius, another Pompeian supporter. IIis central tactic is to appeal to Caesar's *misericordia* (1) and he does this by celebrating Caesar's *clementia* in emotive language (6). Besides his *clementia* (10, 15, 19, 30), he praises Caesar's 'generosity' (*liberalitas*, 6, 23) and 'wisdom' (*sapientia*, 6), his 'humanity' (*humanitas*, 13) and 'mildness' (*lenitas*, 15) and 'goodness' (*bonitas*, 37), which all come down to a single heading which consists of Caesar's *uel humanitatis uel clementiae uel misericordiae* (29, cf. 37). In a passage which resembles Pliny's emphasis upon Trajan's role as father of his people, Cicero claims to be pleading for Ligarius as if before a father, not a judge (30). And in the climax to the speech Cicero asserts that to show pity to other men is to approach most closely to the status of divinity (38). Although For *Ligarius* is, of course, a forensic speech, it borrows many of the regular tropes of panegyric and evokes topics treated in For *Marcellus*.

For *King Deiotarus* exhibits the same concerns again. Deiotarus, king of Armenia Minor, had been another active supporter of Pompey during the civil war but had secured a pardon from Caesar in 47; Cicero is defending him against a subsequent accusation of treachery. Accordingly, the speech is lavish with praise of the king, but it focuses still more upon Caesar's 'outstanding and unique character' (4). He declares that 'we have seen you as far from being a tyrant but rather as a leader of unsurpassed clemency in his victory' (34) and closes the speech with a series of appeals to Caesar's *clementia*: 'many are the memorials of your clemency, but none greater than the amnesty you have granted to those who owe their lives to you' (40). Significantly, the speech ends with the words *clementiae tuae* ('your mercy', 43).

The three speeches present a substantial corpus of panegyrical [71] material rehearsing many of the standard features of the genre, in particular, a combination of praise of proven virtues with a programme or expression of hopes for the future. In Caesar's case, the outstanding virtue which is attributed to him is *clementia*, a term which suddenly entered political discourse at this time not only in these speeches but also with the senate's decree in 45 BC to build a temple to the *Clementia Caesaris* ('Mercy of Caesar') with the statues of Clementia and Caesar clasping hands (although this temple was never built).[44] The balance between programme and prescription is, again, a fine one.[45] And all three speeches are rooted in specific contexts early in Caesar's rule and, especially in the case of *For Marcellus*, can be regarded as performing the inaugurative function of imperial accession literature. These speeches, then, may be regarded as prototypes of Roman imperial panegyric.

PANEGYRIC AND PROTREPTIC: SENECA, ON CLEMENCY

Cicero's Caesarian speeches commending and encouraging *clementia* ('mercy') provided important models for all later panegyrists. Many later emperors would lay claim to *clementia*. This is most memorable in the panegyrical work which Seneca wrote to his pupil, the young emperor Nero, early in his reign, the treatise *On Clemency*.[46] Ostensibly this treatise, which was planned in three books,[47] although only the first and the beginning of the second survive, resembles other Senecan treatises, most obviously *On Anger*, also in three books. In fact, the two works do in many ways form a complementary pair, since, as we have seen above, anger and pity are readily contrasted with one another (Cic. *Deiot.* 40). But Seneca [72] goes to considerable

---

[44] See Weinstock (1971) 233–43.

[45] Weinstock (1971) 238 sees Cicero as the initiator of *clementia* as a political term where I would prefer to see Cicero as one of several organs of Caesar's political self-representation, which can be seen in part at least as an attempt at self-definition through antithesis with the cruelty of Sulla.

[46] *On Clemency* was written shortly after Nero's accession, in AD 55 or perhaps 56. The date of composition, especially whether or not it precedes the murder of Britannicus early in 55, is hotly disputed among scholars. See e.g. Giancotti (1954); Grimal (1978) 119–31; Griffin (1976) 133–4 and appendix A, 3.

[47] This is implied by the programmatic statement at *Clem.* 1.3.1.

trouble to distinguish clemency (*clementia*) from pity (*misericordia*). In Cicero's day, it seems, the two words could be used interchangeably, but from Seneca's Stoic perspective, it was important to distinguish the virtue of *clementia* from the weakness of *misericordia* (2.3.1–7.5 = end of extant text).

To understand *On Clemency*, it is crucial to set it in context. Along with other compositions by Seneca and by others,[48] it is part of the inauguration of Nero's reign and in that respect may be seen as closely analogous to Cicero's *For Marcellus* and to Pliny's *Panegyricus* and, doubtless, to other panegyrics which have not survived. Seneca deploys markedly similar tactics to those used in other panegyrics, as I shall indicate briefly.

He starts with praise of Nero as he is now, at the moment of his accession: 'I have undertaken, Nero Caesar, to write on the subject of clemency "to serve as a mirror" (*ut quodam modo speculi uice fungerer*) and reveal you to yourself as one destined to reach the greatest of all pleasures' (1.1.1). That is, he is asking Nero to continue behaving as he now does. This compliment combines the panegyrical motifs of praise and programme observed elsewhere. Seneca continues even more explicitly: 'no one looks for any model for you to copy except yourself' (1.1.6). Nero is so perfect that he must be his own role model.[49] Seneca's central idea is that the emperor needs to be a *sapiens* (wise man), in this respect building on Plato's ideal of philosopher-kings and on ideas first formulated in Latin by Cicero in his (fragmentary) *On the Republic* and harnessed in (for example) Augustus' self-representation in his *Achievements* and in the Golden Shield. Nero's perfection consists of his *innocentia* (1.1.5), 'freedom from guilt' of civil war, in contrast with the civil conflict that marred the opening of Claudius' reign,[50] and above all his *clementia*, which is claimed as the essence of *humanitas* (*Clem.* 1.3.2). Seneca is praising Nero for the *clementia* he has so far exercised and promoting *clementia* as a key element in his conduct for the future.

Three features in particular evoke the other panegyrical texts we have already considered: imagery of fatherhood, comparisons [73] with predecessors and analogy with divinity. Seneca uses many

---

[48] Seneca composed several key speeches for Nero, including a funeral speech for Claudius and accession speeches to the praetorian guard and to the senate: see Griffin (1976) 133.
[49] Cf. Plin. *Pan.* 13.5.   [50] See Wiseman (1982).

strands of imagery in *On Clemency* to articulate his vision of the relationship between emperor and state as mutually dependent and as one organic whole. Central to this is the mind/soul and body (1.3.5, 1.5.1) analogy, supplemented by head and body (2.2.1), with imagery of doctor/surgeon and patient (1.5.1, 1.9.6, 1.17.1–2), rider and horse (1.24.2), farmer and trees (2.7.4), king bee (*sic*) and hive (1.19.2–3) and so on, tending in the same direction of mutual need and benefit. The image of the emperor as father is one of those strands (1.14, 1.16.2–3) and it is hardly surprising that Seneca 'cashes' this image in the title *Pater patriae* (1.14.2). Seneca does not load his treatise with lengthy comparisons between Nero and his predecessors to the extent that Pliny contrasts Trajan with Domitian (discussed above), but the entire treatise invokes a contrast with his immediate predecessor Claudius. Moreover, it does incorporate an explicit contrast with the young Octavian who had blood on his hands, the antithesis of Nero's claimed *innocentia* (1.1.5, 1.9.1, 1.11.1–3). Finally, Seneca throughout suggests the emperor's superhuman status (e.g. in the image of the bright and beneficent star, 1.3.3) and at 1.7.1–2 presents a sustained analogy between the emperor and the divinity.

On Clemency is not a classic panegyric but it participates in the genre's conventions enough for it to deserve this as one of its labels. The work is, in short, a hybrid: a philosophical disquisition on one of the classic virtues of a ruler and a didactic treatise addressed to the new ruler.[51] In this, Seneca has incorporated many of the tropes of panegyric associated with literature celebrating an accession and inaugurating a new reign. It is one of several works composed at the beginning of Nero's reign which welcome the new emperor with a reflection or articulation of his self-representation and programme, often through antithesis with his predecessor Claudius. It is therefore rewarding to situate *On Clemency* alongside Seneca's political satire of Claudius, *Apocolocyntosis*, as well as the *Eclogues* of Calpurnius Siculus and the proem to Lucan's epic poem, *Civil War* (1.33–66). Seneca devotes most of his brief prose satire *Apocolocyntosis* to a savage attack on Claudius' faults and vices. But [74] he does incorporate a verse

---

[51] There is not space here to pursue a detailed comparison with Isocrates' speech of advice to Nicocles, Evagoras' son and successor. Isocrates' focus in *To Nicocles* is essentially similar to Seneca's in *On Clemency*, although Seneca not surprisingly prioritizes *clementia* above the other virtues he mentions.

panegyric of the new emperor Nero in 32 hexameters.[52] In this epic-style insertion, Nero's origin and superhuman life expectancy are described in elevated phrases. Seneca introduces Phoebus to complement Nero on his beauty and artistry and his bringing of justice and happiness to the world and to compare Nero with the Morning Star, the Evening Star and the sun (*Apoc.* 4.1). That is, Seneca suggests an association if not an assimilation between Nero and Phoebus: an intimation of immortality.

PROTO-IMPERIAL PANEGYRIC: CICERO'S PRAISE OF POMPEY

Yet panegyric is not exclusively an imperial phenomenon. This is suggested by a consideration of Cicero's oration before the people in 66 BC arguing that Pompey be given command of the war in Asia against Mithridates, *On Pompey's Command*. Much of this speech is devoted to praise of Pompey in a prefiguring of imperial panegyric. Early in the speech he declares his theme: 'the unique and extraordinary qualities of Pompey' (3). Accordingly, he endows Pompey with a wide range of virtues. Of course, this speech has its specific context which demands that Cicero emphasize Pompey's military expertise. So he organises his material around the four qualities necessary in a general: 'military knowledge, courage, authority, good fortune' (*scientiam rei militaris, uirtutem, auctoritatem, felicitatem,* 28, cf. 49). First he deals briefly with Pompey's knowledge and experience (28), covering here the standard topic of the subject's early years and formation, in Pompey's case in school and then in his father's army where he gained military knowledge not from others' instructions but from holding commands himself. Then Cicero expands upon his ability in 29–35 adding to his definition 'hard work, endurance, application, swiftness and deliberation' (*labor, fortitudo, industria, celeritas* and *consilium*). Twice in close succession he uses the words 'unbelievable and divine excellence' (*incredibilis ac*

---

[52] We can only speculate on the relation of these verses to the lost *laudes Neronis* that Lucan composed for the Neronia in 60. The proem to Lucan's *Civil War* is clearly a reprise of the proem to Virgil's *Georgics* (1.1–38) in which Octavian/Augustus is treated on a par with the gods praised there.

diuina uirtus, 33, echoed at 36 and cf. 'fallen from heaven', *de caelo delapsum*, 41) and as proof of this he asserts that Pompey has other qualities necessary in a great [75] general: 'freedom from guilt, self-control, loyalty, accessibility, talent and humanity' (*innocentia, temperantia, fides, facilitas, ingenium* and *humanitas*, 36), qualities which he proceeds to demonstrate. Then he illustrates Pompey's *auctoritas* ('authority', 43–6) and *felicitas* ('good luck', 47–8). As in the later panegyrics, comparison features prominently. In his introductory words about the general, Cicero asserts Pompey's uniqueness. He surpasses contemporaries and predecessors: 'He stands alone as a man, one who in his excellence has surpassed the glory not only of his contemporaries but even the record of ancient times' (27). Later, after saying that he would demonstrate Pompey's qualities by comparison with others (36), he refrains from doing that because Pompey himself provides 'examples of every kind of distinction' (44).[53]

Towards the end of the speech, after his panegyric of Pompey, Cicero refers to the objections raised against vesting power in one man (59–62). Cicero's arguments centre upon the nature of the crisis and above all upon the uniqueness of Pompey to meet that crisis. 'One and only' (*unus*) is Cicero's key note (e.g. *in uno Cn. Pompeio* 'in Gnaeus Pompey alone', 59; *unius adulescentis uirtuti* 'the bravery of one young man', 62; *in hoc uno homine* 'in this one man', 62). That is, Cicero singles Pompey out in terms which make him a proto-*princeps* and which consequently lay the groundwork for later imperial panegyrics. Cicero was later to rue the precedent that he helped to set by vesting so much power in one individual, a precedent that ultimately contributed to the weakening of the Republican constitution and the rise of the Principate.[54] *On Pompey's Command* raises one man head and shoulders above the rest on to a virtually divine level. It presents a proto-imperial panegyric. Later, Cicero, Seneca and Pliny develop and elaborate the prose panegyric to articulate combinations of praise and prescription in a process of subtle persuasion to the autocrat to accommodate the wishes of his subjects.[55]

---

[53] Cf. Plin. *Pan.* 13.5 and the mirror image at Sen. *Clem.* 1.1.1.

[54] Cicero realises that Pompey would have acted as Caesar did in the same position: *Fam.* 4.9.2.

[55] I have benefited enormously from seeing Rees (2001) and from Mary Whitby's astute editorial comments. I have only just seen Levene (1997), a useful discussion of religious themes and in particular the divine/human axis or antithesis in Cicero's *For Marcellus* and Pliny's *Panegyricus*.

Postscript

Since writing the essay on Pliny's *Panegyricus* I have published a large-scale commentary on one of the other key panegyrical texts from the early Principate, Seneca's *De Clementia* (2009). In my introduction I discuss the panegyrical tendencies of the work, particularly in relation to kingship treatises (17–23), along with discussion of Greco-Roman kingship theory (24–30). For a valuable overview of the political role of *clementia* see Griffin (2003) and in more depth Dowling (2006). Other recent publications which discuss Roman praise and panegyric include Flower (1996) 159–84 and appendix B on encomia on epitaphs. On the highly relevant topic of ancient kingship theory see now Murray (2007) who rightly refers to two useful older German studies, Barner (1889) and Kaerst (1898), chapters 2–4. The mirror image with which Seneca opens *De Clementia*, as a way of both praising and exhorting Nero, provides a seminal image for European political thought, as discussed by Stacey (2007) 37–41; see also my edition of *De Clementia* 77–9. The ubiquity and importance of father imagery in Greco-Roman political thought is ably discussed by Stevenson(1992). Finally, no study of the early Principate should neglect the excellent book by Roller (2001), especially chapter three, on the emperor's authority, and chapter four, on the prevailing paradigms for the emperor in the early Principate.

6

Two Levels of Orality in the Genesis
of Pliny's *Panegyricus*

Elaine Fantham

It may seem paradoxical to bring to a conference on the transformation of orality a paper dealing with an elaborately wrought literary text from Trajan's Rome, for certainly Rome in the first century of our era was a highly literate and literary society. However, there are significant ways in which both the age of Pliny the Younger and this particular text return to and depend upon a greater stress on orality. So it will be useful first to set the interpretation of Pliny's only surviving speech into context, beginning with a more general survey of oral performance and the reception of literature in the last years of the first century and during Pliny's later years.

What does the student of literature after the Homeric age associate with orality? First comes Homer's heroic narrative, initially composed without the aid of writing, and relying on the prefabricated components of a rich formulaic vocabulary; epic heard and recalled (more or less) as it was heard; then perhaps distichs of elegy or short lyrics improvised and sung from the couch, of the symposion by archaic Greek nobles flushed with wine. In the public assembly of Athens or elsewhere, speeches oral in the simple sense were also oral in the more interesting sense of *ex tempore*: either improvised responses to unforeseen or only half-foreseen challenges, or simulated improvisation, to add credibility to drafted decrees or prepared policy statements. Greek court briefs for prosecution and defence were prepared, but would also require improvisatory elements: again, oratory at its most artificial, witty and stylised, offering epideictic displays in praise of everything from love to garlic or bumble bees, might be spoken by

Isocrates or a member of his school from carefully composed and memorised texts, or might answer a challenge to display spontaneous eloquence, as was the boast of Gorgias or his follower Alcidamas. [222]

At Rome oral performance developed new forms: as early as 13 BC Horace speaks regretfully of old men and boys alike declaiming verse at the dinner table, and deplores an increasing flock of casual and prolific amateur poets.[1] Besides improvised poetry, improvised declamation was the main form of rhetorical training in the Augustan age, practised by adults as well as adolescent pupils, and attended as literary entertainment by the historians Asinius Pollio and Livy, and even by the emperor Augustus and his right-hand men Maecenas and Agrippa.[2] While this kind of declamation may have lost its appeal by the end of the first century, recitation of verse and prose texts proliferated: the practices of improvisation and recitation include almost every literary form in the age of Statius, Martial and Pliny. These social activities dominated the cultured city man's passive experience of verbal art.[3] However, the same man as author saw his social performance not as an end so much as a means of transition to the written text; for this written text would reach those outside the city, in villas or provincial communities, and was expected to spread the work of literary art beyond its immediate place and time. Improvisation and recitation are the most frequent modes of poetry, while recitation seems to replace the exercise of declamation as the dominant medium of spoken prose, and as a secondary form even of oratory itself.

When Cicero praised the poet Archias in 66 BC for his skill at improvising verse on a given theme and producing instant variations on his own settings,[4] he was praising a Greek poet, who could either compose by improvisation in small genres, or produce longer narrative texts to celebrate victorious campaigns in the epic form: composed for a coterie, such verse was probably not intended to circulate in writing beyond perhaps a copy to the dedicatee. But a century later

---

[1] Hor. *Epist.* 2.1.109–10: *pueri patresque severi/fronde comas vincti cenant et carmina dictant*, ('boys and stern old men, their hair bound with leaves, dine and recite poems'); cf. 117 *scribimus indocti doctique poemata passim* ('learned and unlearned, we write poems everywhere').

[2] For a fuller account see Fantham (1996) 90–4, and Bonner (1969) and (1977) ch. 6.

[3] See Fantham (1996) 220–1.   [4] Cicero *pro Archia* 18.

the Neapolitan Greek Papinius Statius both improvised his sympotic and occasional verse, and published it. Alex Hardie's fine study provides the best survey of the range of such improvisation in Greece and Rome, and its development in prose and verse.[5] Hellenistic poetry saw an increasing growth of [223] praise poetry in hexameters, and this metre formed the bulk of Statius' occasional poetry, recited and often composed, as he insists, in immediate admiration of or emotional response to the tables of his hosts. The preface to his first collection of *Silvae* claims one poem was written over dinner *intra moram cenae* ('in the pauses at dinner'). Other occasional poems celebrating a statue or a wedding, if not improvised, were written in one or two days and baptised in oral performance: always these poems are seen as speech acts, of praise, consolation, congratulation or worship.[6] Poetry was its performance. Very often Statius describes the scene around him as his poem unfolds: a conspicuous example is his speech of thanks to Domitian (*Silv.* 4.3) for being invited to his feast in the new palace, detailing in the continuous present tense the exotic decorations of the dining hall and the radiance of the emperor's presence.

The smaller compass of the epigram makes it less surprising that not only Martial but also Pliny and Suetonius should write about improvising poems at the table. The situation is encapsulated in Martial's two liner:

> *Lege nimis dura convivam scribere versus*
>   *Cogis, Stella. 'Licet scribere nempe malos.'*[7]
> Stella, your law of dining is too harsh, forcing your guests to write verses!
> 'But you can always write bad verse'.

Diners who did not have to sing for their supper were regularly entertained by poetic, dramatic or musical performance, whether comic scenes or readings, or a *lyristes*, perhaps as likely to be a singer as a plain instrumentalist. By day the lectures and diatribes of an

---

[5] Hardie (1983).

[6] Compare the preface to *Silv* 3: *Hercules Surrentinus . . . quem in litore tuo consecratum, statim ut videram, his versibus adoravi*, ('your [statue of] Hercules at Sorrento, whom I immediately worshipped with these verses as soon as I had seen him dedicated on your shore').

[7] Martial 9.89. See also Pliny *Letters* 4.7.4; 4.14.2 and 7.9.9, Suetonius *Titus* 3.2 and *de Grammaticis* 23.3.

Isaeus or a Euphrates in quiet corners of the Forum were ostensibly impromptu,[8] and even the more elaborate speeches of Dio Chrysostom were first delivered and only afterwards published in writing. If the recitation was usually of a previously composed work, the audience at least experienced the new work by hearing, however inattentively; at home too, in view of elderly eyesight and cramped, [224] unpunctuated manuscripts, they listened to slave readers rather than reading for themselves. The public recitation was first practised as a social activity by Asinius Pollio more than a century earlier. Pollio's interests were as much in preserving the literary texts as in the audience experience. He also founded the first public library at Rome, a decade before Augustus' Palatine library, and both hosted and attended displays of declamation, that is, improvised oratory on a set theme.[9] Originally a form of training of adolescents for political and judicial oratory, declamation developed in the age of Augustus into an *ex tempore* art form practised by adult experts. The declaimer either constructed speeches of persuasion for a historical character at a time of crisis and decision-making, or argued the defence of imaginary clients in the context of some lurid family crime. Quintilian, Pliny's own teacher, denounced declamation as a teaching method, for its remoteness from the real world of law and policy, and although it survived in the schools it would seem that by Pliny's generation it was no longer a diversion for adult performers or audience.[10]

In contrast, composing and reciting verse became such a disease of the leisured class in Pliny's day that Juvenal professes to have taken up satire purely in order to take revenge. Yet as Juvenal complains of the boredom of listening to amateur epic and tragedy, he thinks in terms of the written texts, and the generic *Telephus* or *Orestes* of his first *Satire* is written right up to the margin and the last space on the final column of the scroll.[11]

Pliny is more polite. Himself an indefatigable composer, he regrets openly the indifference and impatience of audiences coerced into

---

[8] For Isaeus see Pliny *Ep.* 2.3, for Euphrates, *Ep.* 1.10.
[9] See Dalzell (1955) 20–8.
[10] For Quintilian's strictures on declamation see *Inst.* 2.10.3–12 and 5.12.17–23.
[11] Juvenal 1.1–6, especially 4–6: *impune diem consumpserit ingens/Telephus aut summi plena iam margine libri/scriptus et in tergo necdum finitus Orestes?* ('Shall the outsize *Telephus* waste the whole day unpunished, or *Orestes*, written up to the margin of the end of the scroll and not yet finished on its reverse?')

attendance by social duty. Among his many letters involving recitations, two in particular measure the extent to which such readings dominated his social life. In the first (7.17) Pliny responds to apparent criticism for giving readings of his speeches, with a dialogue formulating both sides of the question.

sua cuique ratio recitandi; mihi quod saepe iam dixi, ut si quid me fugit ut certe fugit admonear. quo magis miror, quod scribis fuisse quosdam qui [225] reprehenderent quod orationes omnino recitarem; nisi vero has solas non putant emendandas. a quibus libenter requisierim, cur concedant si concedunt tamen historiam debere recitari, quae non ostentationi sed fidei veritatique componitur; cur tragoediam, quae non auditorium sed scaenam et actores; cur lyrica, quae non lectorem sed chorum et lyram poscunt. at horum recitatio usu iam recepta est. Num ergo culpandus est ille qui coepit? quamquam orationes quoque et nostri quidam et Graeci lectitaverunt. supervacuum tamen est recitare quae dixeris. etiam, si eadem omnia, si isdem omnibus, si statim recites; si uero multa inseras, multa commutes, si quosdam novos quosdam eosdem sed post tempus adsumas, cur minus probabilis sit causa recitandi quae dixeris quam edendi?

Each man has his own reason for giving readings; mine, as I have often said, is to be pulled up if I make a mistake—as I certainly do. I am all the more amazed, therefore, that you mention in your letter that there were some people who criticized me for reading out speeches at all; unless of course they think that speeches are the only kind of writing that is not in need of correction. I should very much like to have asked them why they grant (if they do still grant) that history ought to be recited, which is not a genre of display but of truthful representation of fact [i.e. like speeches?]; that tragedy should be recited, though it requires not an auditorium but a stage and real actors? or lyric poetry that needs not a reader but a chorus and accompanying lyre? It is now an accepted practice to recite these genres. Surely then the person who began the practice should not be blamed? And also, both Roman and Greek orators have regularly read their speeches aloud. Well, is it not superfluous to recite something you have already delivered? Only if the speech is unchanged, if the audience is unchanged, and the occasion follows close on the original event. But if the author makes many expansions and changes, if he adds new listeners or addresses the old ones, but after a lapse of time, why is there any less reason to recite one's speech than to publish it?

The whole letter, and the last sentence above in particular, is highly relevant to the genesis of the *Panegyricus*.

The other letter comes late in Pliny's collection (9.43) and concerns only his verses. Apparently Pliny often reads his short verses in public, and someone has told him he does not read them well. So he proposes to have a freedman read them for him, although the freedman himself is new to recitation. But then what is Pliny to do while the man reads? Sit by, nodding and gesturing approval? Mime his text alongside? We do not know how his correspondent, Suetonius, answered this delicate query: my point is only to stress how far Pliny went in assuming that he *must* read his works aloud, despite his evident commitment to editing and producing a final, written version. [226]

The focus has now been concentrated on Pliny, and his attitude to reciting his own works. From this point we will consider only his speeches, and the three phases of their existence that Pliny discusses: firstly on the occasion of their public performance, the *actio* or delivered speech; then in subsequent recitation to friends; and finally in the written form or *oratio*.[12] But already in distinguishing between live *actio* and published *oratio*, Pliny is differing in usage and perhaps also in emphasis from Cicero, for whom *actio* was strictly the manner of delivery and *oratio* the style or form of language, whether in the spoken or written text. Pliny seems to have given all his speeches the further stages of recitation and publication, and the early letter 1.20.9, discussing the relationship between an orator's spoken and published texts, indicates his own views on the proper development through the three phases.

A good performance, he declares, is different from a good written speech; it can excel purely as a performance, and fail as a text, but there is no way a good written speech could not be a good performance—it serves as the model ἀρχέτυπον of the performance, even including 'spontaneous' figures like jokes and self-corrections that evoke a 'live' presentation.[13] 'In this way the most perfect

---

[12] Pliny articulates this distinction first in *Letters* 1.20.9. The best discussion of Pliny's new approach in this letter to the spoken and written text is Picone (1978) 122–3.

[13] *at aliud est actio bona, aliud oratio. . . . persuasum habeo posse fieri ut sit actio bona quae non sit bona oratio, non posse non bonam actionem esse quae sit bona oratio. est enim oratio actionis exemplar et quasi* ἀρχέτυπον ('But a live speech is one thing, a published speech another . . . I am persuaded that a live speech may be good which is not good when published, [but] a speech which is good when published cannot be bad when delivered. For the written version is the exemplar and "model" for

performance will be the one that most resembles the written version'—*sequitur ergo ut actio absolutissima, quae orationis similitudinem expresserit*—provided there are no constraints of time. Clearly then, the *oratio* in this reference has been written down before and for the performance. On the other hand, Pliny more often speaks of *oratio* in the sense of a subsequent edition; only this is compatible with his claim that an *oratio* should be as full as possible, and satisfy in its written form the full potential of the case, which may have been cramped in the context of delivery.

Two private speeches that Pliny prepared for later publication were his address on presenting the library to his home town of Novum Comum and his funeral *laudatio* of his friend Spurinna's son. The speech at Comum was not even an *oratio*, but a *sermo* to the town council. The word suggests informality, but is normally used by Pliny for his [227] speeches at a political meeting.[14] Certainly he takes this one seriously, asking Pompeius Saturninus in a letter to review it and send criticisms, and writes sending a second, revised, version for further criticism that will determine whether he publishes it or holds it back. In this case he is further inhibited by the fear that publication, while it will serve the purpose of stimulating others to compete in generosity, may seem to be blowing his own trumpet (*privatae iactantiae*).

The other case is more complex. It was a long-standing Roman custom for the next of kin to deliver a *laudatio* of the dead at their funeral, and from this gradually sprang the notion of others composing written *laudationes* as their personal tribute. Cicero, for example, composed *laudationes* for written circulation of both the republican suicide Cato of Utica and his sister Porcia.[15] But in the age of Pliny these eulogies could be recited after the funeral itself. According to a letter to Spurinna (*Letters* 3.10), Pliny composed a brief life of Spurinna's son without any request from the grieving parents, and did not even inform them before reciting the tribute to others, in case it might renew their grief. He admits that while he is forwarding the text, he is

---

the performance' *Letters* 1.20.9) The reference to spontaneous figures (*figuras extemporales*) follows in 1.20.10.

[14] See Sherwin-White (1966) 105 on *Letters* 1.8.16. The distinction reflects not the deliberative political genre but the context of a meeting, whether of the Roman senate or an Italian or provincial council.

[15] Cf. Cicero *ad Atticum* 12.4 (the *laudatio* of Cato) and 13.48 (of Porcia).

beginning to doubt whether he should send it in its present form, or wait to add the material he proposes to include in a second scroll (*volumen*). The motive he gives is desire to broadcast and perpetuate the young man's memory, and his letter itself urges Spurinna to read the text and advise him, as he would a portrait artist or a sculptor, on any adjustments he should make to the written portrait. Here we see, as with Aquilius Regulus' *laudatio* for his dead son so mocked by Pliny,[16] that private texts were first performed in recitation, then published or privately circulated to publicise an occasion or memorialize the deceased, moving through successive revisions towards their final, written form.

With the *gratiarum actio* to Trajan, preserved from antiquity as the *Panegyricus*, we come to a highly public speech, but still one that is neither judicial nor deliberative: formally Pliny's *gratiarum actio* is an [228] epideictic text.[17] Thanks and praise often go together ἐπαινεῖν is both, and Latin *laudare* is often used of thanking). Despite a lack of models for the *Panegyricus*, one can usefully compare Pliny's address to Trajan with Cicero's *Pro Marcello*, a speech of thanks to Caesar for agreeing to the return of his antagonist, the old republican Marcellus. In fact the *Pro Marcello* is a double precedent, being both a speech of thanks given in and for the senate, and the first such speech to an autocrat. One of Ovid's letters from exile shows that it was already an established practice for consuls to thank the emperor for their office in AD 13: the poet's brief imaginative account of Pompeius' entry into office reconstructs the context of his *gratiarum actio*:

> *purpura Pompeium summi velabit honoris,*
>   *ne titulis quicquam debeat ille suis. . . .*
> *templaque Tarpeiae primum tibi sedis adiri*
>   *et fieri faciles in tua vota deos, . . .*
> *cumque deos omnes, tum quos inpensius aequos*
>   *esse tibi cupias, cum Iove Caesar erunt.*
> *Curia te excipiet, patresque e more vocati*
>   *intendent aures ad tua verba suas.*
> *hos ubi facundo tua vox hilaraverit ore,*

---

[16] *Ep.* 4.7. Regulus is an extreme case. Pliny reports that Regulus first recited this composition, then had it multiplied in a thousand copies and circulated to the cities of Italy and the provinces with instructions that it be read aloud.

[17] The best short general introduction to the *Panegyricus* is Radice (1968) 166–72 and above chapter four.

*utque solet, **tulerit prospera verba dies***
egeris et meritas superis cum Caesare grates
(qui causam, facias cur ita saepe, dabit),
inde domum repetes toto comitante senatu,
officium populi vix capiente domo.[18]

'The purple of the highest office will cloak Pompeius, so that he lacks nothing from his honours. . . . [I see] you first approaching the temple of Tarpeia's hill, and the gods show themselves assenting to your vows. . . . and while you wish all the gods to be well disposed, you will more urgently wish Caesar and Jupiter to favour you. The senate will welcome you and the fathers, duly summoned, will offer their ears to your words. When your voice has cheered them with its eloquence and the day has brought favourable words, as is its wont, and you have given due thanks to the gods along with Caesar (who will often give you cause to do so again) then you will return home escorted by all the senate, as your home scarcely contains the homage of the people'. [229]

Since Julius Caesar first designated consuls for three years ahead in 46 BC, it was increasingly the case that consuls owed their 'election' to nomination by Rome's *princeps*, her first citizen. Trajan himself had been twice consul before becoming emperor, but on his return to Rome as emperor inaugurated the year AD 100 by taking the consulship for January and February. He later marked his approval of Pliny by approving his election with his friend Cornutus Tertullus as the fourth pair of consuls for the same year. If every consul gave a vote of thanks (and there were up to twelve every year), we can see that such speeches would be formalities—brief and predictable. Pliny was not even the first consul to give thanks to Trajan in this first year of his presence as emperor at Rome, but it was he who converted this piece of etiquette into something more, and began an entirely new genre.

The rest of this paper considers two aspects of the *gratiarum actio*: first, in line with the discussion above, our evidence for Pliny's equal concern for the occasion of the oral performance and the subsequent recitation, circulation and final draft of the written text; secondly, and more significantly, the role played by oral utterance, by formal ritual language, in constituting the solemnity of the speech as we have it.

Three of Pliny's letters discuss his procedure, first in composing this speech, then in refining it after delivery, and each letter brings out

---

[18] Ovid, *Pont.* 4.4.25–42. I have highlighted the references to formal vows and thanks that will recur in Pliny's account of the occasion.

a new aspect of the speech. In 3.13 Pliny sends the text (*librum quo nuper optimo principi consul gratias egi*, 'the text by which as consul I recently gave thanks to our excellent emperor') to Voconius, and comments on the difficulties he experienced.

in ceteris enim lectorem novitas ipsa intentum habet, in hac nota vulgata dicta sunt omnia; quo fit ut quasi otiosus securusque lector tantum elocutioni vacet, in qua satisfacere difficilius est cum sola aestimatur. atque utinam ordo saltem et transitus et figurae simul spectarentur! nam ... disponere apte, figurare varie nisi eruditis negatum est. nec vero adfectanda sunt semper elata et excelsa. nam ut in pictura lumen non alia res magis quam umbra commendat, ita orationem tam summittere quam attollere decet.

In other speeches the very novelty holds the reader's attention, but in this the subject matter is noble but too familiar; everything has been said before; it is known and commonplace, leaving the listener free to pay attention to the diction, and all the more demanding because of it. I would wish him at any rate also to examine the arrangement, the transitions and the figures of speech. For only well educated speakers can control ... appropriate arrangement and varied ornament; even so there is a danger in continuous loftiness and exaltation of tone; for just as in a painting shadow [230] best enhances the impression of light, so in a speech there must be quieter passages as a relief for brilliance.

A little later a fuller letter to Vibius Severus (3.18) contrasts the scale of the original speech, adapted to its place and time and customary form, with his aim of expansion in written form. Pliny sees it as a patriotic duty both to give the emperor proper praise and to provide an example from which future emperors would learn the path to glory. He reports how he invited his friends to a recitation of the written version, and was amazed at their eagerness, when they even requested a third sitting. And yet, he adds, men are usually reluctant even to sit through the actual speech in the senate.[19]

To Vibius he claims that people welcomed his speech because it was free and gladly offered: instead of offending by its falsehood, it

---

[19] Here the key elements are the expansion of the written version *bono civi convenientissumum credidi eadem illa spatiosius et uberius volumine amplecti* ('I considered it only appropriate, as a loyal citizen, to give the same subject a more expansive and elaborate treatment in a written version'), and the description of the theme as *[materia] quam in senatu quoque, ubi perpeti necesse erat, gravari ... vel puncto temporis solebamus* ('[a subject] which we used to resent after the first minute even in the senate, where we had to endure it'). See also Picone (1978) 129–32.

delighted by its truthfulness. What is more, he has confidently used a richer style to avoid the effect of artificiality that more restrained speech would have had in these circumstances.

The speech, then, is substantially expanded, and scholars have devoted scrupulous care to distinguishing the supplementary material from what must have been its original content: while Sherwin-White[20] argues that Pliny simply expanded his praise of each separate item as he moved through Trajan's career, others have excluded material such as Trajan's early military record or his domestic harmony from the original performance as irrelevant to the occasion.[21] It was, in fact, very much a senatorial occasion, and examination of the speech has convinced me that the core of Pliny's actual vote of thanks must have been the strictly senate-related material that occupies the last 35 sections of the speech. Here the new consul speaks before Trajan and the senate of Trajan's own behaviour and respectful treatment of the senate in canvassing for his third consulship and holding that office. And Trajan as consul [231] showed he considered himself the representative of the senate, even as Pliny now identifies himself with the senate of which he had long been a member.[22] Pliny's entire audience had taken part in the ceremonies that the speaker is now reinterpreting so as to put moral pressure on both the emperor and senate. If it was potentially boring for Pliny's senatorial audience and later his personal friends to listen to enumerations of Trajan's virtues, even enlivened by contrasting abuse of his near predecessor Domitian, must it not have been supremely wearisome for them to listen to Pliny's recapitulation of recent events, most of them formalised procedure?

But the political complexity of these chapters justifies their seeming monotony: their ostensibly descriptive purpose of honouring the emperor's behaviour by recording his actions and the senate's

---

[20] Sherwin-White (1966) on 3.18.

[21] On the *Panegyricus* see especially the edition of Durry (1938) and comments on the added material in the review by Syme (1938). For a survey of more recent scholarship see Fedeli (1989) 513–14.

[22] Mause (1994) is largely focused on the later panegyrics; hence perhaps his stress on the facts of power underestimates the formal or psychological importance of the senate in this context: 'Even in the *gratiarum actio* of Pliny, which was given in the senate and in which is probably contained a senatorial programme, there is the one and only function of the senators–to approve the reign which Nerva had ordained concerning his succession', 112).

response was in fact prescriptive. And the language of public formulae carried an authority all the greater because the words were fixed
and could not easily be devalued, as were the 'original compliments
and flatteries of orators'; for we should not pass over the other
challenge in this form of speech, which has now been so splendidly
investigated by Shadi Bartsch[23]—the problem of restoring meaning to
courtly cliché and credibility to praises that had for so long been
forced and insincere. The very words were stale before Pliny could
use them.

For students of the later Roman panegyrics there is much to note
even in the early sections of the written speech: I cannot pass over,
because it is to become so central a part of future panegyrics, Pliny's
highly successful description of Trajan's *adventus*, his first appearance as emperor in Rome—a completely convincing and fresh
scene of public rejoicing whose only precedents known to me are in
Horatian lyric: 3.14 *Herculis ritu*, ('in the manner of Hercules') his
celebration of Augustus' return in 24 BC, and the anticipatory 4.5,
divis orte bonis ('descended from the great gods').

Yet this delightful passage can hardly have been part of the original
core *actio*. It is the consulate, not Trajan's record as *imperator*, that is
the overt theme of Pliny's speech. This entails a preliminary [232]
embarrassment in addressing Trajan's refusal as consul in 98 to be re-
elected to a third consulate for 99, but Pliny does equal honour to the
man and to the office by attributing this refusal (*Pan.* 60) to Trajan's
recognition that he could not exercise the consulship while he was
campaigning away from Rome. Rome, then, is where the consulship
realises its value, at Rome and in dialogue with the senate who is the
other half of Pliny's audience.

Pliny hits his stride when he surveys the record of Trajan's acts
since his return to Rome. Study of these sections reveals that each
major moment of constitutional procedure is marked by recall of
public speech, and what is more, in most cases recall of formulaic
ritual utterance in antiphony between the emperor-consul and his
senate. Initially Pliny opens with gestures and symbols of the newly
significant office—Trajan's inaugural act as consul for the third time,
with a colleague also holding his third consulship, as he turned to ask
the *sententia* ('opinion') of his designated successor (61.1), also about

---

[23] Bartsch (1994), reprinted below, chapter eight.

to hold his third consulship; then the ritual actions of his colleagues and their successors, putting off and resuming the honorific *praetexta* (purple-bordered toga) and the escort of lictors (61.7). He adds sound to vision as he simultaneously evokes the people's pride as they see the new emperor attending the election in person, patiently enduring the long sequence of formulae during the formal announcement (*longum illud carmen comitiorum*, 'that lengthy announcement of the assemblies' 63.2).

Apostrophizing Trajan, Pliny recalls how he actually 'swore obedience to the laws in words unfamiliar to former emperors' (*adigendum te praebes in verba principibus ignota*, 64.1), standing before the presiding consul who recited the words of the oath. Then turning to the senate, Pliny repeats and elaborates this record of oral utterance: the emperor himself enunciated (*iuravit expressit explanavitque*, 'he swore, expressed and stated' 64.3) the words by which he devoted his own person and family to the anger of the gods if he should knowingly violate his oath. With the same alternating apostrophe to emperor and senate, Pliny first recalls to Trajan how again on the Rostra he swore obedience to the laws with the gods as his witness (65.1), then interprets the significance to the senate. This procedural act on entry into office is answered in the same paragraph by Trajan's oath on departure from office that he had committed no acts contrary to the law. Though the words (*te nihil contra leges fecisse*, 'that you had done nothing against the law' 65.2) are constructed as indirect statement, the actual form of the oath emerges clearly. [233]

At the same time that Pliny exalts and celebrates Trajan's legality, he reminds the emperor, and the written text will survive to remind him, in later years when he might be tempted to autocracy, that Trajan has sworn obedience to the law.

Even more momentous is Trajan's entry into the senate as consul and his exhortation to the senate to take up its liberty and undertake with him the care over the empire common to both senate and emperor. This too, if not a formula, is recognised as a gesture made by every emperor before Trajan, but never before believed. Pliny strives with descriptive language to reconstitute Trajan's words, intonation, expression, eyes, stance, gesture, the sincerity of his whole bodily presence at this crucial moment.[24]

---

[24] 67.1: *quam inadfectata veritas verborum, quae adseveratio in voce, quae adfirmatio in vultu, quanta in oculis, habitu, gestu, toto denique corpore fides!* ('the

The ritual *nuncupatio votorum* (declaration of vows) for the emperor's safety, forms another topos binding his double audience (67.3). Pliny repeats the familiar words to his senatorial audience, asking them to note the language of their vows wishing the emperor continuing health 'if he has directed the state well and to the common interests of all' (*si bene rem publicam et ex utilitate omnium rexerit*, 67.4) before again turning to Trajan himself and reinterpreting these words as a pact made with the gods. In a third variation on the theme, the actual vow, the oral formula, is recast for the senate in direct speech to represent the emperor's own thoughts (67.8). In return Pliny conjures up the reverberation of the vows for the beloved emperor offered up all over the empire in response to the oath he has made (68).

This citation of ritual language is not unprecedented as a device to lend solemnity and respect to a political utterance: I think above all of Cicero's speech for Murena, which opens with the prayer Cicero himself had offered to the immortal gods as consul and presiding officer at Murena's election to the consulship. Cicero recites the prayer in order to argue that the fulfilment of his oath for the safety of the state depends upon upholding the validity of Murena's election to the same office.[25] In both cases the stress is on the reciprocity of pious prayer and divine sanction. Again the citation of an autocrat's words to remind him and bind him by them is exploited by Cicero in his thanks to Caesar for [234] permitting the return of Marcellus as an act of respect to the senate:[26] Cicero not only repeats and responds to Caesar's official speech at the relevant session; he quotes and answers a spontaneous reaction by Caesar to the senate's eager offer to give him official protection: 'I have lived long enough for either my natural life or my glory.'[27]

---

unaffected honesty of his words, the conviction in his voice, the candour of his expression, the complete sincerity of his gaze, his posture, his gestures, in short of his entire demeanour!')

[25] Cicero *Pro Murena* 1.

[26] Cicero *Pro Marcello* 3: *intellectum est . . . paulo ante omnibus, cum M. Marcellum senatui reique publicae concessisti . . . te auctoritatem huius ordinis dignitatemque rei publicae tuis vel doloribus vel suspicionibus anteferre.* ('It became clear . . . to everyone a little earlier, when for the sake of the senate and the Republic you allowed M. Marcellus to return . . . that you put the authority of this order and the dignity of the Republic before your own private resentment and suspicion.')

[27] *satis diu vel naturae vixi vel gloriae* (*Pro Marcello* 25).

The same device helps Pliny through his over-elaborate recapitulation of Trajan's actions and words as consul: standing to greet the candidates at the next consular elections, receiving the senate's acclamations 'so much more noble and revered!' (*tanto maior, quanto augustior*, 71.4); praying as presiding officer 'that the actual conduct of the election would result well and favourably for us, the state, and yourself' (*nobis rei publicae tibi*, 72.1). In Pliny's rendering Trajan's invocation is answered chiastically by the silent prayers of all the senate, that every action of the emperor might result favourably 'for yourself, the state, and us' (*tibi rei publicae nobis*). He even suggests that Trajan himself, if he could, would have added to the formula a wish that the gods might heed his prayers only if he continued to merit the senate's loyalty (72.3).

Pliny would have his listeners and readers believe that this climax inspired the senate to an ardour and enthusiasm that even Trajan could not control. But if Pliny is to convince Trajan himself that in these manifestations he witnessed true loyalty from his senate, he must deal with the shameful memory common to all his peers that they had uttered the same words to the hated Domitian. To this the only appeal is from the words to their actual intonation and utterance: the onlooker can tell, as Trajan did, the tone of true love from that of suppressed hate and fear. Through Trajan's alleged memory (*testis ipse es*, 'you yourself are witness' 73.1) Pliny recalls these demonstrations of loyalty, and the senators' cries 'O blessed man' (*o te felicem*, 74.1), 'have faith in us; have faith in yourself' (*crede nobis crede tibi*, 74.2) and prayers that the gods might love Trajan as he loved the senate (74). Pliny will dare one further step 'is it true' he asks 'that we also cried out "o blessed are we!"' (*estne verum quod inter ista clamavimus 'o nos felices'*? 74.4). [235]

Pliny could risk this hyperbole because he and his audience knew this was no invention. It was on written record, as he shows even while he pleads his inadequacy, doubting whether speech could encompass or memory recall 'the words that you, senators, to protect them from loss of memory, decreed should be committed to the public record and incised in bronze' (*et in publica acta mittenda et incidenda in aere censuistis*, 75.1). So the oral components that add such solemnity to Pliny's claims of harmony between emperor and senate before the gods themselves are confirmed in two kinds of writing, indeed may owe their presence in Pliny's speech to his consultation of this tedious senatorial record on parchment and in bronze.

But Pliny has not finished with extracting the juice from these formulaic utterances. He returns for the last time to the theme of oaths, honouring Trajan for announcing the newly elected consuls and reciting for them the oath of office that he himself had sworn only shortly before.[28]

Much is achieved by this cumulative reiteration of formulaic oaths to and by the gods, to and by the emperor: most of all, that these words still carry a solemnity that can override their past abuse in swearing loyalty to bad emperors.[29] The words must have resounded as the general confession or marriage ceremony does today to members of the church, and the invocation of the gods will have reinforced the familiar formulae. When Pliny returns in the written text from a eulogistic account of Trajan's impeccable private life, it is to define his own speech, expressing the twofold nature of his own *actio* as both a public declaration of thanks to the emperor and a personal one. Here too the ritual utterances performed by Trajan at the joint election of Pliny and his old friend Cornutus are given prominence: 'you deigned to preside over our election and rehearse that most reverend formula for us (*sanctissimum illud carmen praeire*, 92.3), we were elected by your judgement, and announced by your voice, as both nominator in the senate and herald on the field' (*suffragator . . . declarator*, 92.3). But I have again deliberately glossed over Pliny's stress on the written commemoration of his moment of glory: 'no other page will record us as consul but the one [236] that records your name as consul, and our names too will be added to the *fasti* (the inscribed magisterial calendar) which are headed by your name!'

Despite the sanction that ritual oral utterance has given to Pliny's affirmations of mutual loyalty, the written public record now has equal authority, if not the greater authority of its endurance as a *monumentum*.[30] Unfortunately the constitutional significance of all

---

[28] 77.2: *stabant candidati . . . adigebanturque in verba in quae paulo ante ipse iuraverat princeps* ('The candidates stood . . . and were requested to take the same oath sworn by the Emperor himself a little earlier').

[29] On the role of the gods as an authority superior to both senate and emperor see Schowalter (1993) ch. 3.

[30] Let me add here the last such reference: in 95 Pliny reports that his debt to the Senate is conveyed in *monumenta*, that is the *Acta Senatus*: can this be yet another speech of thanks?

this dwindles as the speaker praises Trajan's affability in allowing him and his colleague Cornutus the glory of remembering that they were actual consuls, and *his* consuls *(nos . . . consules fuisse et consules tuos,* 'that we were consuls and *your* consuls', 93.3): Pliny seems to have blinded himself to this paradox of autocracy.

Only the peroration is not addressed to Trajan, because Pliny invokes a higher audience: he turns to the gods as guardians of empire, and above all to Jupiter Capitolinus, reducing the plurality of possible prayers and vows to a single vow for the emperor that will contain and entail all other objects of prayers. Now Pliny himself performs the vow, uttering on his own account the prayers in the modified form that Trajan himself once bade men offer, that the gods should preserve the emperor 'if he rules the state well and in the interests of all' (*si bene rem publicam, si ex utilitate omnium regit,* 94.5): he cannot forebear to amplify and so he amplifies even this with a fuller prayer to Jupiter for Trajan's longevity and desired succession.

primum ut illum nepotibus nostris ac pronepotibus serves, deinde ut quandoque successorem ei tribuas, quem genuerit quem formaverit similemque fecerit adoptato, aut si hoc fato negatur, in consilio sis eligenti monstresque aliquem, quem adoptari in Capitolio deceat.

First preserve him for our grandsons and great-grandsons, then grant him one day a successor born of him and formed by him in the image of the adopted son he is, or if fate denies him this, guide and direct his choice to someone worthy to be adopted in your temple on the Capitol.[31]

Is it all over? Can the senators go home, or the reader end his recital, or the slave *anagnostes* ('reader') close the *volumen* ('volume')? NO! Pliny must renew his pledge to the senate and draw them into this magic circle of new hopes and promises; they too are reminded of an oral event—their [237] acclamations of his election that have inspired him to serve them and earn their approval (95.2). This transformation of a simple act of thanks into a lasting eulogy has also taken the fixed oral formulae of government and elevated them into quasi-biblical texts on which Pliny erects his sermon—a sermon first delivered, then given recitation, then finally embalmed as a model text that would have many descendants.

---

[31] Radice's translation (1969).

7

iubes esse liberos: Pliny's *Panegyricus* and Liberty

Mark Morford

Pliny's *Panegyricus* has been harshly treated in recent decades. The opinion of Frank Goodyear is typical: 'It has fallen, not undeservedly, into almost universal contempt.'[1] Sir Ronald Syme is hardly more subtle: 'The *Panegyricus* survives as the solitary specimen of Latin eloquence from the century and a half that had elapsed since the death of Cicero. It has done no good to the reputation of the author or the taste of the age.'[2] Such opinions from eminent scholars show how far removed our age of scholarship is from an understanding of the *genos epideiktikon*, and they express impatience with the conventions of ceremonial rhetoric, an important category of rhetoric under a monarchy.[3] I propose to show that within these conventions Pliny was offering to Trajan and to his fellow senators a serious statement

---

[1] Goodyear (1982) 660 (paperback ed., II.4 164). For a survey of scholarship on the *Panegyricus* see Fedeli (1989). For the structure and purpose of the *Panegyricus* see Feurstein (1979). I have used the text of Kühn (1985), and the commentary of Durry (1938). Useful also are Durry (1947), and Radice (1969).

[2] Syme (1958a) 114; cf. also 94–5. For a more balanced assessment see Syme (1938).

[3] For epideictic oratory see Kennedy (1963) 152–4; Kennedy (1972) 21–3, 428–30, 510, 634–7. Quintilian (*Inst.* 3.7) does not deal with the type represented by Pliny's *gratiarum actio*. The two essays on epideictic attributed to Menander, while much later than Pliny's speech, usefully summarize the rules for epideictic: see Spengler (1856) III 329–67, 368–446. In the second essay only § 229 (pp. 376.31–377.9 Sp.) is at all close to Pliny's speech: the topic is comparison of the recipient of praise with his predecessor. In the chapters on the *Technē peri tōn Panegyrikōn* attributed to Dionysius of Halicarnassus, see Usener and Radermacher (1965) 255–60; only § 8 (on *boulēsis*) is relevant to Pliny. See also MacCormack (1975).

on the relationship between the *princeps* ('emperor') and his colleagues after the autocracy of Domitian. Central to this statement is the
attempt to define *libertas* ('freedom') under a [576] monarchy, and it
will be shown that Pliny's definition displayed the vice of *adulatio*
('adulation') principally insofar as it was required by convention. The
necessary attributes of *libertas* ('freedom') for him, as for his friend
Tacitus, were *obsequium* ('obedience') and *modestia* ('modesty')
which could be displayed without falling into the extremes of *adulatio*
('adulation') or *ferocia* ('spirit').[4] I will further show that the choice of
an appropriate style for the political content of the speech was
important to Pliny and his hearers.[5]

The occasion for the speech was the *gratiarum actio* delivered by
the incoming *consules suffecti* on 1 September AD 100.[6] The published
version may be as much as three times the length of the version
delivered in the Curia.[7] Three of Pliny's letters (3.13, 3.18, 6.27) give
important information about the rhetorical and political problems
involved in composing and revising the speech. In 3.18.4 he records
how he recited the revised version to his *amici* ('friends') over a
period of three days, extended, at the request of the audience, from
the two days originally planned. He probably read the whole speech
in these sessions (rather than just the [577] 'lengthy extracts' that
Sherwin-White suggests). Attending a recitation was generally a
burdensome duty (as Pliny observes in 3.18.4), and busy men

---

[4] For these components of *libertas* see Vielberg (1987). Cf. Fedeli (1989) 497 'the
senate satisfied itself in respect of its status and *securitas*—even if a *securitas* guaranteed by obedience'. For relations between senate and *princeps* see further Morford
(1991) esp. 3440–2; Shotter (1991) esp. 3314–27; Soverini (1989).

[5] For the connection between rhetorical style and political content see Ahl (1984);
Ahl does not discuss Pliny's *Panegyricus*. For discussion of the relationship between
rhetoric and politics in Pliny see Picone (1978) esp. 159–90 (173ff. for *Pan.*). See also
Kennedy (1972) 543–6, who concludes (548) that 'it was possible . . . to use the art of
persuasion in a speech to the emperor'. Further references for style and language
appear in Fedeli (1989) 417–21.

[6] See Talbert (1984) 227–8, for the *gratiarum actio* as part of senatorial procedure.
Cf. Radice (1968), reprinted above, chapter four, who emphasizes Pliny's originality in
using the *gratiarum actio* for substantive political discussion.

[7] Sherwin-White (1966) 251–2 (on *Pan.* 4) estimates three sessions of one and
one–half hours each: cf. Durry (1938) and (1947) 87. Syme (1958a) 94 estimates about
three to four times the length (one hour) of the original. Both estimates are dismissed
by Fedeli (1989) 405 as '*semplici ipotesi*' ('simply guesses'). Pliny could speak for even
longer: see *Ep.* 2.11.14 (five hours) and 4.16.3 (seven hours). For the relationship
between the *Panegyricus* and *Ep.* 3.18 see Fedeli (1989) 405–11. Still useful is Mesk
(1910).

would not have given up three days to the recitation if all he had to offer was flattery of Trajan.

In Pliny's view the expanded speech was an example of *studiis* . . . *quae prope exstincta refoventur* ('literature . . . which almost extinct is now being revived', *Ep.* 3.18.5). He wished it to mark the revival of political oratory whose content might make a difference in the political decisions of the *princeps* ('emperor'). Syme has correctly observed that 'the speech is not merely an encomium of Trajan—it is a kind of senatorial manifesto in favour of constitutional monarchy.'[8] Pliny's views are like those of Tacitus in the introduction to the *Agricola*. Neither Tacitus nor Pliny for a moment would have welcomed a return to the oratory of the Republic, which Tacitus in the *Dialogus* explicitly describes as a recipe for anarchy.[9] But Pliny believed that his speech represented a break with its predecessors in the genre, in style, content, and significance.[10]

Pliny emphasizes that both the style and the *materia* ('substance') of the speech led his friends to give up so much time to his recitation:

> *at cui materiae hanc sedulitatem praestiterunt? nempe quam in senatu quoque, ubi perpeti necesse erat, gravari tamen vel puncto temporis solebamus, eandem nunc et qui recitare et qui audire triduo velint inveniuntur, non quia eloquentius quam prius, sed quia liberius ideoque etiam libentius scribitur. accedet ergo hoc quoque laudibus principis nostri, quod res antea tam invisa quam falsa, nunc ut vera ita amabilis facta est.*

But to what did they give their attention? What used to bore us at the first minute, when we had to endure it in the senate, can now discover readers and audiences for three successive days, not because its is written more eloquently than before, but more freely and so with greater pleasure. This also adds to our emperor's praise, that what was previously so hated and false has now been made both true and popular. (*Letters* 3.18.6–7)

---

[8] Syme (1938) 223; cf. Fedeli (1989) 492–7.

[9] *Dial.* 38.2. Although Maternus is the speaker, the views are those of Tacitus. *Letters* 9.13 appears to show that Pliny spoke more freely than Tacitus, but that letter refers to a debate that took place before Trajan's accession (indeed, probably before his adoption). In a speech given in the presence of the *princeps* Pliny was as circumspect as Tacitus. For the relationship of the *Panegyricus* to Tacitus in matters of style, see Bruyère (1954).

[10] For a negative view of Pliny's optimism see Syme (1938) 224.

Pliny thus claims that he has transformed the conventional *gratiarum actio* ('speech of thanksgiving') into a statement welcome to the *princeps* ('emperor') and deserving of the thoughtful attention of his fellow senators. The ultimate audience for the expanded speech, moreover, was not restricted to the group of *amici* ('friends') who heard the recitation but included all who would read the published [578] version: *memini quidem, me non multis recitasse quod omnibus scripsi* ('I remember I recited for a few what I wrote for everyone' 3.18.9).

The *Panegyricus* represented a new type of oratory at Rome. It was the first time that a living *princeps* ('emperor') had been eulogized in his presence by means of a speech that was designed to persuade rather than to flatter.[11] Cicero's *Pro Marcello* at first sight appears to be a model for Pliny, for there are many similarities in style and vocabulary.[12] Nevertheless, it is not a valid analogy. Unlike Pliny, Cicero was in an ambiguous situation, and there were grave political uncertainties in a Republic that to many people, including Cicero, still appeared capable of revival in some form. Caesar's position, moreover, was very different from that of Trajan in AD 100. He had defeated his enemies in a civil war, and the sign of his power was the exercise of *clementia* ('mercy'), a cause of resentment to the survivors among his enemies and of ambiguous rhetoric to politicians like Cicero. Thus what was outwardly a *gratiarum actio* was also a vehicle for scarcely concealed satire and, as has recently been suggested, possibly even for a call for the removal of Caesar.[13] In two letters written shortly after the original *Pro Marcello* was delivered in the senate, Cicero revealed more of his intentions. To Servius Sulpicius, writing in the early autumn of 46, he says: [579]

itaque pluribus verbis egi Caesari gratias . . . sed tamen, quoniam effugi eius offensionem, qui fortasse arbitraretur me hanc rem publicam non

---

[11] Cf. Durry (1947) 88–9: 'Pliny creates a genre . . . for the first time, praise of a living emperor forms the subject of a complete book'. For details of Pliny's style see Gamberini (1983) 377–448 (for the *Panegyricus*), 393–9 ('Devices of Eulogy' for the use of rhetorical figures in praising Trajan). For the limitations of Gamberini's approach see Pitkäranta (1987).

[12] See Suster (1890).

[13] See Dyer (1990) 30 'it issues, under the veil of figures, a clear summons to tyrannicide'. For an example of Cicero's satire see *Mar.* 5, with its fulsome hyperbole and extravagant figures.

putare, si perpetuo tacerem. modice hoc faciam aut etiam intra modum, ut et illius voluntati et meis studiis serviam.

And so I gave thanks to Caesar in many words . . . but because I avoided giving offence to him, who might think I do not consider this matter constitutional, if I kept perpetual silence. I will do this with moderation or even on the right side of moderation, to serve both his will and my interests. (*Fam.* 4.4.4)

Writing to Papirius Paetus during the summer of 46 he says:

ergo in officio boni civis non sum reprehendendus. reliquum est, ne quid stulte, ne quid temere dicam aut faciam contra potentes.

And so I am not to be reprimanded in the office of a good citizen; it remains for me to say nothing stupid or rash, or to act against the powerful (*Fam.* 9.16.5)

The *Pro Marcello*, therefore, is not a true forerunner of the *Panegyr icus*, except insofar as Cicero's cautious attitude towards the *potentes* ('powerful') is similar to that of Pliny, or of any politician who seeks to discharge the *officium boni civis* ('duty of a good citizen') under an autocracy.

A truer model is to be found in the *Evagoras* of Isocrates, where the author points out the difficulty of eulogizing a living person in prose. The poets, he says, are free to use language, imagery, and associative techniques that are denied to the political orator, whose use of language must be precise and factual.[14] Pliny set out to solve the same problems as those defined by Isocrates. He had first to develop an appropriate style as the vehicle for his message, and, second, he had to speak *in honorem principis* ('in the emperor's honour') without flattery or excessive frankness, that is, without falling into the extremes of *adulatio* ('adulation') or *contumacia* ('insolence'). His language had to be precise and based upon fact. These were Pliny's goals, we must emphasize: how successful he was in achieving them is not our primary concern here.

Sometime before the recitation described in *Letters* 3.18 Pliny sent a copy of the *Panegyricus* to his friend Voconius Romanus.[15] In the

---

[14] Isoc. *Ev.* 8–10. Xenophon imitated Isocrates in his *Agesilaos*. See Mesk (1911) esp. 78–9 (for *Ev.*) and 80 (for *Ages.*). Mesk (1910) 82–4 overvalues *Pro Marcello* as a model for the *Panegyricus*.

[15] *Letters* 3.13. Sherwin-White (1966) 245 suggests that the letter was written 'a good while after his delivery of the *Panegyricus* . . . and before his recitation of the final version'.

covering letter he emphasizes the difficulty of dealing with a subject on which there was little to be said that was new: *in hac* [*materia*] *nota vulgata dicta sunt omnia* ('in this [subject], everything is well known, understood and said before'). The choice of an appropriate style, however, was especially difficult. Even philistines, he said, can manage *inventio* ('imagination') and *enuntiatio* ('expression') but it takes careful research to be successful in arrangement and ornamentation: *nam invenire praeclare, enuntiare magnifice interdum etiam barbari solent, disponere apte, figurare varie nisi eruditis negatum est* ('for barbarians are used to employing strong imagination and grand expression from time to time, but suitable arrangement and varied figures are only available to the educated' *Ep.* 3.13.3).[16] [580]

He chose the intermediate style, that is, between the *genus subtile* ('plain') and the *genus grande atque robustum* ('grand and forceful') as defined by Quintilian.[17] This style allowed for variety and flexibility in figures of speech:

> *medius hic modus et translationibus crebrior et figuris erit iucundior, egressionibus amoenus, compositione aptus, sententiis dulcis, lenior tamen ut amnis et lucidus quidem sed virentibus utrimque silvis inumbratus.*

> This intermediate style turns more frequently to metaphor and employs figures more happily, charming in its digressions, suitable in its arrangement, pleasing in its thoughts, but rather gentle—like a clear river, shaded by green trees on either bank. (Quint. *Inst.* 12.10.60)[18]

The metaphor of light and shade refers to Quintilian's analogy of painting and rhetoric explained earlier in *Inst.* 12.10. Just as Zeuxis '[is said to have] discovered the system of using light and shade'— *luminum umbrarumque invenisse rationem . . . traditur*—so the orators of the intermediate style used light and shade in their figures.[19] This also was Pliny's principle in the *Panegyricus: nec vero adfectanda*

---

[16] For the antithesis of *eruditi* and *barbari* cf. Velleius 2.73.1, of Sextus Pompeius: *hic adulescens erat studiis rudis, sermone barbarus* 'as a young man he was unrefined in his studies and barbaric in speech'.

[17] Quint. *Inst.* 12.10.58.

[18] Austin (1972) 201 suggests that Quintilian is combining two passages from Cicero. *Orat.* 21 and 96. The latter passage, especially, with its metaphors of flowers and colour is a likely model.

[19] Quint. *Inst.* 12.10.1–9. For perceptive commentary see Austin (1972) 135–52. Zeuxis' system is referred to in 12.10.4. The analogy of the visual arts and oratory is used by Cicero (*Brut.* 70 and, most explicitly, *De or.* 3.26).

132   *Mark Morford*

sunt semper elata et excelsa. nam ut in pictura lumen non alia res magis quam umbra commendat, ita orationem tam summittere quam attollere decet ('we should not always affect the lofty and elevated. For just as nothing commends light in a picture as much as shade does, so too it is right to lower and raise a speech', *Letters* 3.13.4).

Pliny's careful attention to the intermediate style has been overlooked by those critics who are offended by his 'woolly repetitiveness' (Goodyear) and 'exuberant redundance' (Syme).[20] The evidence clearly indicates that he chose the varied style because it would best combine the rhetorical functions of pleasure and persuasion, exactly as Quintilian had defined its purpose: *tertium illud . . . delectandi sive, ut alii dicunt, conciliandi praestare videatur officium* ('that third style . . . seems to fulfil the task of pleasing or, as others say, conciliating [the audience]', *Inst.* 12.10.59).[21] The intermediate style was distinguished by variety and figures. The importance of figured speech in situations where tact and indirection are necessary has been shown by Ahl and Dyer.[22] Its appropriateness to Pliny's situation is well expressed by the words of Demetrius: 'To [581] flatter is disgraceful, to censure is dangerous. Best is the intermediate style, that is, the figured style (*to eschēmatizomenon*).'[23]

The idea of the mean goes back to Aristotle and is expressed by Cicero, for example, in the *Orator*:[24]

[20] See notes 1 and 2 above for references. Gamberini (1983) 402–3, 496, more accurately points out the lack of variety in the 'long continuum of figures'.

[21] The function of *conciliandi* ('conciliating') is a prerequisite for persuasion and is achieved by the modesty of the speaker (see *Inst.* 11.3.161) as well as by the attractiveness of his style.

[22] Ahl (1984) 185–97; Dyer (1990) 26–30.

[23] *On Style* 294, quoted by Dyer (1990) 27. Demetrius is specifically discussing figured speech in a democracy, but the passage is part of a general discussion of indirect criticism beginning (289) with criticism of 'a tyrant or any other violent person.' The precise translation of *schēma, to schēmatizomenon*, etc., is harder to achieve in English than in Latin, where *oratio figurata* better indicates the connotations of art and indirection than Grube's 'innuendo' and Robert's 'covert hint' (quoted by Dyer (1990) n. 57). For the Peripatetic origins of the doctrines of Demetrius see Solmsen (1931).

[24] Cf. Arist. *Rh.* 1404b 3–4. In *Fam.* 1.9.23 (Dec. 54) Cicero acknowledges his debt to Aristotle in the *De oratore*. For the relationship between Roman rhetoric and the Peripatetic tradition see Solmsen (1941). For the Aristotelian *mesotēs* see Hendrickson (1904). See also Solmsen (1931); Kennedy (1963) 272–84.

itaque neque humilem et abiectam orationem nec nimis altam et ex-
aggeratam probat [sc., Aristoteles], plenam tamen eam vult esse gravita-
tis, ut eos qui audient ad maiorem admirationem possit traducere.

And so [Aristotle] approves of neither a low and abject style nor one too
lofty and exaggerated, but wishes it to be full of gravity, so that it can
win its audience over to greater admiration. (*Orat.* 192)

Cicero discusses the intermediate style in *Orator* 91–96, and a few
quotations will illustrate the close connection between his doctrine
and the style chosen by Pliny:

(91) uberius est aliud aliquantoque robustius quam hoc humile de quo
dictum est, summissius autem quam illud de quo iam dicetur amplissi-
mum. hoc in genere nervorum vel minimum, suavitatis autem est vel
plurimum.... (92) huic omnia dicendi ornamenta conveniunt pluri-
mumque est in hac orationis forma suavitatis.... (95) in idem genus
orationis—loquor enim de illa modica ac temperata—verborum cadunt
lumina omnia, multa etiam sententiarum.... (96) est enim quoddam
etiam insigne et florens orationis pictum et expolitum genus, in quo
omnes verborum, omnes sententiarum inligantur lepores.

(91) The second style is richer and somewhat more forceful than this
low style just discussed, but plainer than the fullest style which will be
discussed shortly. In this style there is a minimum of vigour and a
maximum of charm.... (92) All the ornaments of speech suit this style,
and there is much charm in this form of oratory.... (95) Into the same
style of oratory—for I speak of that moderate and tempered type—all
ornaments of vocabulary fall, and many of thought.... (96) It is a
distinctive, florid, painted and polished form in which all the pleasant-
nesses of words and thoughts are intertwined.

The student of the *Panegyricus* cannot consider its political purpose
without understanding the significance of Pliny's choice of style. Style
and purpose are inseparable, as Pliny shows in his description of the
reworking of the speech in *Letters* 3.18. The intermediate style, with
its [582] *figurae*, was the only choice for the orator who wished to
make policy suggestions that might also imply criticism of the *prin-*
ceps. Cicero is quite clear about the modest expectations (and therefore modest risks for the orator) of this style:[25]

medius ille [sc., orator] autem, quem modicum et temperatum voco ...
non extimescet ancipites dicendi incertosque casus; etiam si quando

---

[25] Cf. Quint. *Inst.* 9.2.67–9.

minus succedet, ut saepe fit, magnum tamen periculum non adibit: alte enim cadere non potest.

That orator of the middle style, which I call moderate and tempered . . . will not fear the doubtful and uncertain fortunes of speaking; even if he underachieves a little, as often happens, he will not risk much danger, for he cannot fall far. (*Orat.* 98)

It is true that Cicero is here concerned primarily with style, but he also is considering its effect on the audience. In Pliny's case the effect on the audience (that is, primarily Trajan) was his principal concern, and the choice of style was therefore as much a political as an aesthetic decision.

Finally, the choice of style was influenced by the importance of knowing what was appropriate, *to prepon* in Greek, in Latin, *decorum* ('propiety').[26] Quintilian points out that Thersites' criticism of Agamemnon aroused contempt: put the words in Diomedes' mouth and everyone will find *magnum animum* ('great soul') in them.[27] He recognizes the dangers faced by the orator: *nec tamen quis et pro quo, sed etiam apud quem dicas interest: facit enim fortuna discrimen et potestas, nec eadem apud principem . . . ratio est* ('it matters not only who speaks and for whom, but also amongst whom: for their power and rank make a difference, and there is not the same principle with an emperor as with . . .' *Inst.* 11.1.43). Pliny's style, therefore, is a part of his political message. Those (and this includes nearly all modern critics) who are quick to dismiss the *Panegyricus* as mere flattery ignore an essential part of Pliny's technique and purpose.

Once he had chosen the appropriate style, Pliny was faced by a greater problem, that is, how to praise the *princeps* ('emperor') in his presence with moderation and credibility. Quintilian again is a guide for understanding Pliny's approach. In giving rules for praising human beings he focuses upon the moral qualities of the recipient of praise: *animi semper vera laus*, he says, *sed non una per hoc opus* [sc. *laudationem*] *via ducitur.* ('Praise of the mind is always true, but derives in a speech by more than one way').[28] Quintilian was follow-

---

[26] Discussed by Cicero at *Orat.* 69–74.

[27] *Inst.* 11.1.37.

[28] Quint. *Inst.* 3.7.10–18: § 15 is quoted. The fullest exposition of the rules for *laudationes* is that of Cic. *De or.* 2.341–9.

ing Cicero, who gives the primary position to *laudes virtutis* ('praise of virtue').[29] [583]

Cicero also had distinguished between the *naturae et fortunae bona* ('the benefits of nature and fortune'), which Quintilian specifies as the education of the recipient, the early evidence of his good character, and his mature virtues, as shown by his *facta et dicta* ('deeds and sayings').[30] Quintilian adds that the chance of praising the living is unusual: *rara haec occasio est* ('opportunity for this is rare', *Inst.* 3.10.17). This point, in fact, is further evidence for the originality of Pliny's speech. Indeed, Cicero introduces his discussion of *laudationes* by pointing out that they are a Greek genre, developed more to give pleasure to the audience and to compliment the recipient of praise.[31] Roman *laudationes*, however, are most often funeral eulogies marked by brevity and simplicity.[32] Cicero does admit that *laudationes* in the Greek fashion are sometimes necessary, but rarely. They do not seem to have become any more frequent in the 150 years after the writing of the *De oratore*, so that Pliny's originality can confidently be assumed.[33]

While Pliny observes the rules laid down by Cicero and Quintilian, they do not address his particular dilemma. A professor writing a textbook does not have to be as circumspect as a consul addressing the *princeps* ('emperor'). Pliny analyzes the problem in connection with a speech earlier than the *Panegyricus*:[34]

omni hac, etsi non adulatione, specie tamen adulationis abstinui, non tamquam liber et constans, sed tamquam intellegens principis nostri, cuius videbam hanc esse praecipuam laudem, si nihil quasi ex necessitate decernerem.

---

[29] *De or.* 2.343. Cicero divides the *virtutes* into several categories in 2.343–5.
[30] Cic. *De or.* 2.342, 346–7; Quint. *Inst.* 3.7.15.
[31] Cic. *De or.* 2.341–9 (341 quoted).
[32] *De or.* 2.341.
[33] *Encomium* was a regular part of the *progymnasmata* in the schools; see Quint. *Inst.* 2.4.20. Cf. Bonner (1977) 264–6; Kennedy (1972) 636–7; and see n. 3 above for the *basilikoi logoi* of Menander. Fedeli (1989) 411–16 denies the independence of Pliny and concludes (416) 'Pliny depends strictly on the schema of the *basilikos logos*'.
[34] Sherwin-White (1966) 387 suggests that Pliny is referring to the session of the senate described in *Pan.* 78, at which senators urged Trajan to take a fourth consulship. He was *Cos. IV* in Jan. 101, so that this session would have taken place not long before Pliny's *gratiarum actio*. The words *omni hac . . . abstinui* are appropriately translated by Guillemin 'I renounced this usage which, without being flattery, resembles flattery'.

> In all of this I abstained, if not from adulation, then from the appearance of adulation, not as if I were free and firm, but as one who understands our emperor. I saw it as his special praise if I showed none of it was compulsory. (*Letters.* 6.27.2)

He counsels matching the words to the occasion, but does not provide an adequate answer to the charge of indulging in flattery. Both in this [584] letter, however, and in the exordium to the *Panegyricus*, he claims to have avoided even the appearance of flattery.[35] In other words, his praise of the *princeps* (so he would have us believe) is based on facts and on the circumstances of the speech, and is not therefore just a repetition of empty formulae. Secondly, he maintains that his views are given voluntarily, which supports his claim to be speaking with *fides* ('honesty') and *veritas* ('truth'). For a tyrant demands praise, which is freely given to a *princeps* whose character welcomes freedom of speech. Such praise, spoken in the senate, may attempt also to define *libertas* ('liberty') restored.

The central political theme of the *Panegyricus* is the relationship between the *princeps* and the senate, which defines *libertas*. We have seen that Pliny sought to avoid the appearance of *adulatio* ('adulation') and he says very clearly in the letter to Severus that he equally avoided *contumacia* ('insolence'): he spoke, he says, *non tamquam liber et constans* ('not as if I were free and firm' *Letters* 6.27.2). The attributes of *libertas* ('freedom', in speech) and *constantia* ('constancy') are those of the Stoic opponents of *principes* ('emperors'), Thrasea or the younger Helvidius Priscus, whose execution seven years earlier was still a vivid memory.[36] Pliny, like Tacitus, did not choose the noble but politically ineffectual path of *contumacia* ('insolence') leading to martyrdom.[37]

Serious attempts to define *libertas* ('freedom') under the Principate began with Seneca. His hopes for a workable relationship between the princeps and his senatorial colleagues were expressed in the *De Clementia* and in the policy speech at the beginning of Nero's

---

[35] *Pan.* 1.6. [he prays] *utque omnibus quae dicentur a me, libertas fides veritas constet, tantumque a specie adulationis absit gratiarum actio mea quantum abest a necessitate* ('so that liberty, honesty and truth be in everything I say, and my speech of thanksgiving be as far from the appearance of adulation as it is from compulsion').

[36] Tac. *Agr.* 45.1, *mox nostrae duxere Helvidium in carcerem manus* ('soon, our hands dragged Helvidius into prison'). For senatorial feeling in the aftermath of the execution of Helvidius see Pliny *Letters* 9.13 (cf. n. 9 above).

[37] Tac. *Agr.* 42.4.

reign.[38] Central to Seneca's definition were the separation of the *domus* ('house') of the *princeps* ('emperor') from the public business of the state and the collegial assumption of responsibilities by senate and *princeps* ('emperor') in their separate spheres. But Seneca's vision was impractical and gave way to a personal concern with *otium* ('leisure') and withdrawal from political activity.[39] A more flexible definition of *libertas* ('freedom') emerged after the executions of Stoics and other critics of the regime under Nero and the Flavians. This is the definition of Tacitus and Pliny: by it a good man could obtain high office and perform [585] significant service to the *res publica* even under a bad *princeps* ('emperor') like Domitian. This is expressed in the *Agricola*, when Tacitus contrasts those who pursued their view of liberty even to death with men like Agricola:

> *Domitiani vero natura . . . moderatione tamen prudentiaque Agricolae leniebatur, quia non contumacia neque inani iactatione libertatis famam fatumque provocabat. sciant, quibus moris est inlicita mirari, posse etiam sub malis principibus magnos viros esse, obsequiumque ac modestiam, si industria ac vigor adsint, eo laudis excedere, quo plerique per abrupta sed in nullum rei publicae usum ambitiosa morte inclaruerunt.*

But indeed, Domitian's character was softened by Agricola's moderation and prudence because he did not invite renown and death by insolence or a show of empty liberty. Let those whose habit it is to admire what is forbidden know that great men can live under bad emperors, and that if industriousness and energy are in attendance, obedience and modesty can achieve the same height of praise as many who by precipitous measures, have been made famous by a showy death of no public benefit. (*Agr.* 42.3–4)

Under Trajan, *optimo principe* ('the excellent emperor'), *libertas* ('freedom') was still defined by inequalities of power. No one (least of all Pliny) could deny that the autocratic power of Domitian was still wielded by Trajan.[40] Therefore the practical mode of displaying

---

[38] Tac. *Ann.* 13.4.2, *discretam domum et rem publicam; teneret antiqua munia senatus* ('[I will keep] personal and public matters separate; let the senate maintain its ancient duties'.

[39] As expressed, for example, in *De Otio. De Tranquillitate* 3–5, *Letters* 19.

[40] See Waters (1969) 'the two emperors were in fact committed to an almost identical policy. That policy was one of increasing autocracy.' Waters does refer to Pliny's letter about Helvidius (391, where 9.13 should be read for 9.3), but he does not have time for the style and purpose of the *Panegyricus* (398, 'arrant compost of wishful thinking,' etc.).

libertas ('freedom') was that of *obsequium* ('obedience') and *moderatio* ('moderation'), as opposed to *adulatio* ('adulation') or *contumacia* ('insolence'). This is precisely the formula developed by Tacitus in his estimate of the public career of Agricola.

The *Panegyricus*, therefore, for all its ceremonial rhetoric, was a serious attempt to define a working relationship between senate and *princeps* ('emperor'). Pliny was trying to show *obsequium* ('obedience') with dignity towards a ruler who held overwhelming power, since the *Lex de Imperio Vespasiani* [586] had already defined the constitutional limits of senatorial *libertas* ('freedom').[41] His purpose in speaking was explicitly to outline a course of action for the princeps: *ut consulis voce sub titulo gratiarum agendarum boni principes quae facerent recognoscerent, mali quae facere deberent* ('so that in the voice of a consul, under the title of a speech of thanksgiving, good emperors may recognize what they do and bad emperors what they ought to do', *Pan.* 4.1).[42] Fundamental to this policy was the subordination of the *princeps* to the laws, whose supremacy had been affirmed by the *Lex de Imperio Vespasiani*:

> *utique quaecunque ex usu reipublicae maiestate divinarum humanarum publicarum privatarumque rerum esse censebit, ei agere ius potestasque sit, ita ut divo Aug. Tiberioque Iulio Caesari Aug. Tiberioque Claudio Caesari Aug. Germanico fuit.*

> And that whatever he considers is in the interests of the state, by the majesty of divine, human, public and private affairs, let him have the right and power to act, as it was so for Augustus, and Tiberius Julius Caesar Augustus, and Tiberius Claudius Caesar Augustus Germanicus. (*ILS* 244, 17–21)

The *princeps* ('emperor') had the same power to act *legibus solutus* ('free from the law') as his predecessors:[43]

> *utique quibus legibus plebeive scitis scriptum fuit, ne divus Aug. [etc.] tenerentur, iis legibus plebisque scitis imp. Caesar Vespasianus solutus sit.*

---

[41] *ILS* 244; McCrum and Woodhead (1966) I. Discussion by Brunt (1977).

[42] Cf. Sen. *Clem.* 1.1, *scribere de clementia, Nero Caesar, institui, ut quodam modo speculi vice fungerer et te tibi ostenderem* ('I have undertaken to write about mercy, Nero Caesar, so that I can function like a sort of mirror and show you to yourself'). The function of being 'a mirror for princes' is closely related to that of giving advice.

[43] As Brunt (1977) 109 has pointed out, this chapter is superfluous, since the previous one (*ILS* 244, 17–21) has already given the same legal power to the *princeps*.

And that from whatever laws and plebiscites it has been written that Augustus [etc.] should not be restricted, Caesar Vespasianus should be exempted. (*ILS* 244, 23–25)

This power was exercised so insensitively by Domitian that he aroused the bitter resentment of many moderate senators, including those, like Tacitus and Pliny, whose political careers had been advanced under him. Trajan was less blunt, even though the inequalities of power between princeps and senate were the same. To gain the cooperation of the senate, which he must have seen as necessary to the stability of his regime, he needed to clothe his legal authority to act *legibus solutus* ('free from the law') in the appearance of acting as if he were *legibus subiectus* ('subject to the law'). In the end the power of the *princeps* ('emperor') was the same, since by law (that is, the *Lex de Imperio Vespasiani*) he had as much power as he needed to pursue whatever policy he wished to implement. His power would not have been diminished if he were (as Pliny suggests) subject to the law, since the law did not limit his power. Yet the appearance of subjection to the law showed *moderatio* ('moderation') on the part of the *princeps* ('emperor'), and the act of taking the oath to obey the laws guaranteed the favour of the gods. Therefore Pliny could meaningfully say: *non est princeps super leges sed leges super principem, idemque Caesari consuli quod ceteris non licet. iurat in leges attendentibus dis* ('It is not that the emperor is above the law, but that the laws are above the emperor, and the same restrictions apply to Caesar when consul as apply to other consuls. With gods attending as witnesses, he swears obedience to the laws' *Pan.* 65.1).

The position of Trajan vis-à-vis the laws is central to Pliny's effort to define *libertas* ('freedom'). As the *Pan.* 65.1 shows, Trajan's consulship was the political context in which the issue of senatorial liberty was most delicate. When the *Panegyricus* was delivered in the senate, Trajan had been consul three times. Pliny passes over his first consulship in silence (except for a passing mention at 64.4); he devotes one chapter (56) to his second consulship, and thirty-four (57–80) to his third. The imbalance [587] reflects the relative importance of each consulship to Pliny's design. He ignores the first, because it was held (in 91) under Domitian, and to acknowledge Trajan's adherence to the Flavians would have been embarrassing in a speech which repeatedly criticized Domitian.[44] The second consulship was held in 98. It began on 1 January, when Trajan was already in Germany as *legatus Augusti* ('legate of Augustus'). After the death of Nerva on 27 January, Trajan, who was at Cologne at the time, stayed in Germany, and he did not return to Rome until October 99. He spent the whole of his second consulship (which he held until the end of April) campaigning and inspecting the armies on the Rhine and Danube.[45] Pliny, therefore, praises this consulship briefly, since Trajan's *acta* ('deeds') did not directly concern the topics upon which the speech is primarily focused, that is, liberty and the relationship of senate and *princeps*.

Trajan returned to Rome in October 99 and held his third consulship during the first two months of 100, the year of Pliny's suffect consulship, the trial of Marius Priscus, and the delivery of the *Panegyricus*.[46] It was a specially important year for Pliny, and therefore he devotes one-third of the speech to Trajan's third consulship, which he makes the context for his most significant remarks about senatorial liberty. Chapters 60–77 deal directly with the consulship: three preliminary chapters (57–59) lead up to Trajan's acceptance of the third consulship, and three concluding chapters (78–80) anticipate a fourth consulship (actually held in January 101) and end with a comparison of Trajan to Jupiter himself:

> *talia esse crediderim, quae ille mundi parens temperat nutu, si quando oculos demisit in terras, et fata mortalium inter divina opera numerare dignatus est; qua nunc parte liber solutusque tantum caelo vacat, postquam te dedit, qui erga hominum genus vice sua fungereris. fungeris enim sufficisque mandanti, cum tibi dies omnis summa cum utilitate nostra, summa cum tua laude condatur.* [588]
>
> I would believe they are such that that parent of the world controls with his nod, if ever he casts his eyes down to earth, and deigns to count the

---

[44] See Syme (1958a) 33–5; Hanslik (1965) 1037.

[45] *Pan.* 56.4, *gestum non in hoc urbis otio et intimo sinu pacis, sed iuxta barbaras gentes* '[the consulship] not held in the tranquillity of the city and the comforting embrace of peace, but next to barbarian peoples'. Earlier allusions to the campaigns of 97–9 were made at *Pan.* 9.5, 10.3, 12.3–4, 16.2. Cf. Tac. *Germ.* 37.2; Syme (1958a) 16–18, 46–9, 642–3, 648; Hanslik (1965) 1044–9. See also Syme (1958b).

[46] Cf. *Pan.* 92.2, *quid, quod eundem in annum consulatum nostrum <in quem tuum> contulisti?* 'am I not to mention that you conferred on us our consulship in the same year that you took yours?' See Hanslik (1965) 1053; Syme (1958a) 18; Durry (1938) 237–8, who prefers the end of April for the term of Trajan's consulship, relying on *Pan.* 61.6.

fates of humans among his divine duties; now set free from this task and at liberty he is available for heaven alone, after he gave you, to fulfil his role towards humankind. For you fulfil it and meet his instructions, since with you each day brings greatest benefit to us and greatest praise to you. (80.4-5)

This statement should be considered in the context of Jupiter's importance in imperial ideology.[47] It finds its visual expression in the attic of the Trajanic arch at Beneventum.[48] Although it appears to be one of the most extreme examples of flattery in the speech, its placement, as the concluding flourish to chapters 57–80, is an indication of the importance which Pliny attached to the third consulship.[49]

The central part of the review of the consulship occupies chapters 63–77, beginning with *praevertor iam ad consulatum tuum* ('I turn now to your consulate').[50] Its unity is marked by the two *renuntiationes* ('announcements') respectively for the ordinary and suffect consulships of 100.[51] Pliny's rhetorical *color* focuses upon the collegiality of the *princeps* ('emperor'). Thus at the first *renuntiatio* Trajan's *civilitas* ('civility') was shown in his personal attendance, an example for his successors and a contrast with his predecessors, notably Domitian (63.1). By attending he acted as an ordinary candidate of senatorial rank, *unus ex nobis* ('one from among us' 63.2). His predecessors' absence from their *renuntiatio* was an indication of their contempt for the forms of the political process in the *res publica* (63.4-6), whereas Trajan's attendance displayed his *moderatio* ('moderation') and *sanctitas* ('moral purity') (63.8).

[47] Fears (1981) 80–5 for Trajan.

[48] See Fears (1981) 83–5, with plate XI, nos. 70a and b (bibl. on 83). Cf. Strong (1976) 87–8 and plates 90–1. There are verbal echoes in Pliny of Lucan *BC* 1.56–9 (part of the *laudes Neronis*, 1.33–66); other references are noted by Durry (1938) 204–5.

[49] Trajan is likened to Hercules at *Pan.* 14.5 and 82.7; see Syme (1958a) 57; Hanslik (1965) 1055; Durry (1938) 108.

[50] For *praevertor* cf. *Ep.* 5.14.7 and Durry (1938) 181, where 7 should be read for 17.

[51] The *renuntiatio* 'announcement' of chapter 63 must have taken place after Trajan's return to Rome in October 99, that of chapter 77 probably before the trial of Priscus in the senate, perhaps on 12 January 100. See Talbert (1984) 204–5; Durry (1938) 244–5. For elections in the early Empire see Talbert (1984) 341–5, with bibl. on 341, n. 1; Durry (1938) 241–2; Levick (1967); and further references in Fedeli (1989) 435–8. For a description of electoral procedure in the senate see Pliny *Letters* 3.20 (cf. Talbert (1984) 205, 343).

In the next chapter (64.1–3) Pliny recalls how Trajan stood before the seated consul and took the oath to perform the duties of office faithfully:

> *peracta erant sollemnia comitiorum, si principem cogitares, iamque se omnis turba commoverat, cum tu mirantibus cunctis accedis ad consulis* [589] *sellam, adigendum te praebes in verba principibus ignota, nisi cum iurare cogerent alios. . . . Imperator ergo et Caesar et Augustus <et> pontifex maximus stetit ante gremium consulis, seditque consul principe ante se stante. . . . quin etiam sedens stanti praeiit ius iurandum, et ille iuravit, expressit explanavitque verba quibus caput suum domum suam, si scienter fefellisset, deorum irae consecraret.*

The election ceremonies had finished (if you think that you were emperor) and the whole crowd had already moved when to everyone's amazement you approached the consular chair, presented yourself to take the oath in words unknown to emperors except for when forcing others to take the oath. . . . Therefore the Emperor and Caesar and Augustus and Pontifex Maximus stood before the seated consul, and the consul sat with the emperor standing before him. . . . Furthermore, he who sat prompted the man who stood with the words of the oath, and the latter swore, pronounced and articulated words by which he committed his own life and family to the gods' anger if he knowingly lied.

The *renuntiatio* 'announcement' of 99 is especially significant for Pliny's definition of senatorial *libertas* ('freedom'). He does not conceal that the ritual of *renuntiatio* was mostly symbolic: the spoken formulae were *longum illud carmen comitiorum* 'that lengthy announcement of the assemblies' (63.2), and the procedure was but the *liberae civitatis simulatio* ('appearance of a free state' 63.5).[52] What was important was that the *princeps* had publicly shown himself as a senator among senators, a citizen among citizens. His power was superior to all, but he still shared the rank and duties of his colleagues. Thus the antithesis between *dominus* ('despot') and *princeps* ('emperor') is significant (63.6): *haec persuasio superbissimis*

---

[52] The truth is also revealed at *Pan*, 72.1 (*uni tibi in quo et res publica et nos sumus*, 'to you alone, on whom the state and we depend'), *Letters* 3.20.12 (*sunt quidem cuncta sub unius arbitrio* 'indeed everything is under the judgement of one'), and 4.25.5. For difficulties in interpreting Pliny's evidence for Trajan's role in the elections see Levick (1967) 219–28, and cf. *Pan*. 92.3.

dominis erat, ut sibi viderentur principes esse desinere, si quid facerent tamquam senatores 'this was the belief of the most arrogant despots, that they would appear to cease being emperors if they did anything as senators'. A *dominus* ('despot') orders the *renuntiatio* of his election (*renuntiareque te consulem iussisse contentus,* 'happy to give the command that he was proclaimed consul', 63.5), but a constitutional *princeps* ('emperor') orders his fellow senators to act as free citizens (66.4, *iubes esse liberos,* 'you order us to be free'). Finally, the sincerity of Trajan's words and actions was proved by the symbolism of his standing to take the oath administered by the seated consul.

The virtues of such a *princeps* ('emperor') are *moderatio* ('moderation') and *sanctitas* ('moral purity') (63.8), the former being the counterpart of the *obsequium* ('obedience') shown by his fellow citizens. In 64.4 Trajan acts as a citizen subject to the laws, even though he has the power to act as a *dominus* ('despot'): *idem tertio consulem fecisse quod primo, idem principem quod privatum, idem imperatorem quod sub imperatore* ('a consul for the third time acted as he had on his first time, a *princeps* acted as an ordinary citizen, a emperor as someone subject to an emperor'). Pliny then shows Trajan's display of the same *moderatio* ('moderation') on taking office on 1 January 100. This was the occasion for showing to the *populus* that he would observe the laws: *ipse te legibus subiecisti* ('you subjected yourself to the laws', 65.1). As has been shown above, the laws in fact gave Trajan all the power he needed; nevertheless, to show publicly that he was subject to them was to display *moderatio* ('moderation') and *sanctitas* ('moral purity'). Thus the Roman republican tradition of the supremacy of law and the establishment of the *pax deorum* ('peace of the gods') [590] continued under Trajan. Pliny shows in chapters 63–5 how the essential legal, moral, and religious foundations of the *res publica* were maintained by the new *princeps* ('emperor').

With this lengthy preparation, Pliny is now in a position to approach the heart of his discussion of the relationship of the princeps to the senate. He describes Trajan's attendance in the senate on 1 January 100:

inluxerat primus consulatus tui dies, quo tu curiam ingressus nunc singulos, nunc universos adhortatus es resumere libertatem, capessere quasi communis imperii curas, invigilare publicis utilitatibus et insurgere....[53] *iubes esse liberos: erimus; iubes quae sentimus promere in medium: proferemus.*

The first day of your consulate had dawned when you entered the senate house and encouraged now individuals, now everyone together, to resume their liberty, to take up, as it were, the concerns of a shared power, to watch over the public interest, and to act.... You order us to be free: we will be; you order us to bring into the open what we think: we shall. (66.2–4)

These words, which on a superficial reading might seem to be ironic or ridiculous, attempt to express a definition of *libertas* ('freedom') within the confines of the unequal relationship of *princeps* and senate. Pliny has elaborately shown how the *princeps* observes the laws. His *moderatio* ('moderation') is reciprocated by senatorial *obsequium* ('obedience') which is a virtue if joined to *vigor et industria* ('energy and industriousness') and exercised *ex usu rei publicae* ('in the public interest'). Thus Pliny treads the narrow path between flattery and independence. He recalls (no doubt with some exaggeration, given his own successful career) that under Domitian senators had been reluctant to cooperate with the *princeps*.[54] By respecting the laws and the dignity of the senate, Pliny suggests, Trajan will be sure of the energetic (*insurgere*, 'to act') cooperation of the senate in administering the state. It is notable that this chapter (66) is the only one (other than 80) in the whole passage dealing with the third consulship, in which Pliny makes prominent use of tropes.[55] The metaphors of the sea, shipwreck, and storm serve several purposes. They allow Pliny to veil a delicate topic in allegorical language, for both he and Trajan had been among those who had successfully navigated the political seas [591] of cooperation with Domitian. They recall well-known passages in Seneca and Lucretius, where the same metaphors had been used for the tranquil *otium* ('leisure') of the virtuous man who avoids or retires

---

[53] The words *invigilare* and *insurgere* express the same ideas as Tacitus' phrase (*Agr*, 42.4) *si industria ac vigor adsint* ('if industriousness and energy are in attendance').

[54] *Pan.* 62.3–5; cf. 66.3.

[55] For the limited use of tropes in *Pan.* 61–80 see Gamberini (1983) 444. 'Trope' is defined by Quintilian as *verbi vel sermonis a propria significatione in aliam cum virtute mutatio* ('a change of word or phrase from its proper meaning to another, to advantage', *Inst.* 8.6.1). The special *virtus* ('advantage') of the metaphors of the storm and shipwreck at 66.3 is that they allow Pliny to speak *decentius* 'more fittingly' (see *Inst.* 8.6.6) on a delicate topic. Cf. Pliny's choice of the word *decet* at *Letters* 3.13.4.

from political activity.[56] They illuminate a comparatively unfigured section of the speech so as to contrast light and shade at a point where stylistic *variatio* can be most effective.[57] Finally, they draw attention to the most significant statements in the speech, where Pliny seeks to define senatorial liberty. Thus Pliny chooses stylistic *variatio* exactly where he needs it.

After dealing with Trajan's activities in connection with the *comitia* ('elections') (67–75), Pliny turns to an example of cooperation between Trajan and the senate during Trajan's third consulship (76). The trial of Marius Priscus is delayed until the end of the review of the consulship so as to appear in an especially prominent place.[58] Since Pliny himself took a leading part in the trial, he does not need to draw particular attention to his own part.[59] Instead he focusses upon the *princeps* ('emperor').[60] Trajan attends the senate in person on three successive days: he presides as consul, and asks senators to express their opinions openly. Thus Pliny shows how the senate responded to the command of 66.4 (*iubes esse liberos* 'you command us to be free'), and he does not need to remind his hearers that he had taken the leading part in speaking as a senator before the *princeps* in his role as consul:[61]

> *iam quam antiquum, quam consulare quod triduum totum senatus sub exemplo patientiae tuae sedit, cum interea nihil praeter consulem ageres! interrogatus censuit quisque quod placuit; <licuit> dissentire discedere, et copiam iudicii sui rei publicae facere; consulti omnes atque etiam dinumerati sumus, vicitque sententia non prima sed melior.* [592]

Now how old-fashioned, how consular that for three whole days the senate sat following your example of patience, and during which time you did nothing beyond the capacity of a consul. When asked, each man

---

[56] Seneca *De Otio* 8.4; *Letters* 19.2; Lucretius *DRN* 2.1–13.

[57] See Pliny *Letters* 3.13.4, and cf. n. 19 above and related remarks in the text.

[58] See Sherwin-White (1966) 166 ('the trial is placed out of order in *Pan.* 76'), 168, and (for the chronology of the trial) 56–2.

[59] He does this fully in *Letters* 2.11, esp. 2.11.4–6, where he is careful to note Trajan's special concern for his well-being.

[60] See Talbert (1984) 183; and Durry (1938) 198–9, for the presence of *principes* ('emperors') in the senate.

[61] Cf. *princeps praesidebat (erat enim consul)* ('the emperor presided, for he was consul' *Letters* 2.11.10) and *imaginare quae sollicitudo nobis, qui metus, quibus super tanta re in illo coetu praesente Caesare dicendum erat.* 'picture what concern we had, what fear, when we had to speak on such a matter in that gathering, with the Caesar present', *Letters.* 2.11.11).

gave his opinion as he wanted; each man was free to disagree, to vote against, and to offer the state his own judgement; we were all consulted and even counted, and it was not the first opinion which won, but the better one. (*Pan.* 76.1–2)

The chapter on the trial of Marius exhibits senatorial *libertas* ('freedom') in action. It shows the *moderatio* ('moderation') of the *princeps*, and it displays senate and consul acting according to the ancient traditions of the Roman Republic. Its purpose is to show that senatorial *libertas* ('freedom') can still be practiced. Limited as such liberty is, it is nevertheless meaningful in a context where the lesser partner in an unequal relationship of power still has significant administrative responsibilities. In this context senators were still motivated by a tradition of public service and personal dignity. These are significant attributes of liberty under a constitutional monarch, for under a tyrant (which is the *color* repeatedly used by Pliny for Domitian, not least in this very chapter) even their limited display was suppressed.[62]

It is hard in modern and democratic societies to understand, much less sympathize with, such political role-playing. Nevertheless, it is irresponsible to dismiss the *Panegyricus* without an effort to understand how the political circumstances of Rome in AD 100 compelled Pliny to choose the style and material displayed in the speech. Perhaps some understanding can be gained from an episode during the Renaissance. In November 1599 the archdukes Albert and Isabella, governors of the Spanish Netherlands, visited the University of Leuven. Its leading professor, Lipsius, addressed them on a passage from Seneca's *De Clementia*.[63] Later he dedicated his commentary on the *Panegyricus* to them, remarking in the preface that he had not been

---

[62] *at quis antea loqui, quis hiscere audebat praeter miseros illos qui primi interrogabantur?* ('but who dared to speak before, who dared to open his mouth, except for those wretches who were questioned first?' *Pan.* 76.3). The usual view of modern scholars is expressed by Wickert (1954) s.v. *princeps*, that *libertas* in Pliny's time was but 'the peaceful comfort of dependents' (col. 2098). Cf. Wirszubski (1950) 167, defining it as 'merely the courage to keep one's *dignitas* alive.' But see Morford (1991) 3440–2.

[63] *Clem.* 1.3.3, from *illius demum magnitudo stabilis fundataque est* ('his greatness is stable and firm...' to *se opponent* 'they put themselves in the way'. The passage expresses the necessity of harmony between ruler and subjects for the stability of the state. The same passage is quoted by Mesk (1911), without mention of Lipsius, as a model for *Pan.* 48. Lipsius' extemporaneous address was published together with his commentary on the *Panegyricus*, (Antwerp 1600).

interested in *schemata & ornatus illos floridae orationis* ('those schemes and ornaments of the florid speech') These he found to be trivial and pedantic.[64] What concerned him, and should concern us, was the substance [593] of the speech, which focuses upon the political relationship between the ruler and those whose cooperation is necessary for the effective government of the state.

---

[64] Lipsius, *Ad Lectorem Panegyrici: quid quod nec schemata & ornatus illos floridae orationis tango? nam visum mihi pertenuia haec & scholastica esse, quae didicisse oporteat magis quam discere, aut alio certe doctore discere, neque 'Aquila' ut in proverbio est, 'captat muscas'* ('To the reader of the Panegyric: what is it that I do not touch upon the schemes and ornaments of that florid style? For it seems to me that they are trivial and pedantic which ought to have learnt more than it learns, or certainly to learn with a different teacher. It is not that "the eagle catches the flies", as in the proverb').

8

The Art of Sincerity: Pliny's *Panegyricus*

Shadi Bartsch

Pliny survived an unpleasant encounter with Regulus in the centumviral court and a brief foray into political doublespeak to see the assassination of the hated Domitian in September of AD 96.[1] Four years later to the month, we find him before his assembled peers in the senate, delivering a lavish speech of thanks to the emperor Trajan. The occasion was Trajan's award of a suffect consulship for the next two months of AD 100 to Pliny and his friend Cornutus Tertullus;[2] Pliny, as he himself notes, was emulating consuls before him in reciprocating with this *gratiarum actio* addressed to the emperor.[3] But the suffect consul also took the unusual step of publishing his speech. This is the version that has come down to us as the *Panegyricus*, an expanded edition of Pliny's original expression of gratitude and praise. Leaving aside unprofitable speculation on the seams between the oral version and written additions, I here treat the published *Panegyricus* as to all intents reproducing the concerns of the original rendition and including the emperor among its projected

---

[1] For this episode, see the beginning of Bartsch (1994) ch. 3.

[2] For Cornutus, see Pliny *Letters* 5.14 and *Pan.* 90–92. For the dating, see Hammond (1938) 120 n. 1.

[3] Cf. Pliny's comments at *Pan.* 2.2–3 and 4.1–3; *Letters* 2.1.5, 6.27. See also Hammond (1938), 120. For a history of this little-known custom see Durry (1938) 3–5; Fedeli (1989) 400–16; MacCormack (1975); Radice (1968) 166, reprinted above ch. 4, and her comments in the Loeb edition at *Pan.* 4.1, 328 n. 1; Talbert (1984) 227–78; Ziegler (1949). *In brevi*, 'the custom whereby the consuls thanked the emperor for their office in a speech in the senate became established under Augustus . . . Pliny's *gratiarum actio* therefore had many antecedents, of which, however, none survive', MacCormack (1975) 149.

audience. Indeed, Pliny seems to attest to the fact at *Letters* 3.18.2, where he claims the expanded version is meant to 'recommend to our emperor his virtues'.[4]

Yet it is not the idea of a *speculum principis*, or 'mirror for princes', that makes the *Panegyricus* a document fascinating beyond the extravagant play of its rhetorical figures, which assail the reader so mercilessly as to suggest that the author's goal was to stupefy his audience into acquiescence.[5] The workings of this imperial address [149] are more complicated and more revelatory than this, its final design more elusive: for, in large part, the *Panegyricus* is an obsessive attempt to prove its own sincerity. This is the end to which Pliny deploys the speech's most pervasive organizing device, an antithesis that gives it shape both at the immediate level of the rhetorical figure and at the larger one of general structure.[6] Working as if the formulation of a contrast in which one alternative is corrupt lends credence in and of itself to the remaining member of the pair, the speaker uses as his informing comparisons antitheses that powerfully mark the end of an era of dissimulation: against the theatricality of a bygone era is set the masklessness of the present, against the false flattery of Domitianic days the true praise of the living ruler, against the once hollow language of public life a new discourse that retains its validity even behind the walls of private homes. True of a new reign, these new conditions for self-expression in political life are to be true also of the speech that proclaims them. But the *Panegyricus'* obsession with the techniques of sincerity only provides testimony, in its own despite, to a widespread consciousness that the time when sincerity was possible is itself a lost feature of the more distant past.

---

[4] Pliny discusses the two versions in *Letters* 3.18. For speculation on the extent and content of the revision, see Durry (1938) 6–8; Fedeli (1989) 405–8; Picone (1978) 135; bibliography in Hammond (1938) 120 n. 1. I have not been able to see Feurstein (1979). On the final date of publication, again Durry (1938) 9–15, and Fedeli (1989) 408–11.

[5] For speculation on the purpose of the *Panegyricus*—often polarized into a manifesto of senatorial prerogatives *or* an act of imperial fawning—see the summation of the scholarship in Fedeli (1989) 492–7, and discussion in Moles (1990) 302–3. Linked to the first alternative is the notion of a *speculum principis*, a didactic piece meant to serve as a model for the ruler, supported by, e.g. Picone (1978).

[6] Aubrion (1975) 120–2, offers general observations on antithesis in the *Letters* and *Panegyricus*. See also Gamberini (1983) 393–9, on 'devices of eulogy', and Ramage (1989) 640–4, on Pliny's main antithesis: Trajan vs. Domitian.

I

The *Panegyricus* has hardly begun when Pliny sounds a theme that becomes a leitmotif throughout the work. In a prelude that does double duty as a description of the coming speech and an instruction on how to read it, he characterizes his tribute to the emperor as one that should reflect the changed conditions under Trajan and that therefore bears an obligation to differ from expressions of praise once elicited by fear:

> For my part, I think that not only the consul but all the citizens should strive not to say anything about our *princeps* in such a way that the same thing could have been said about another ruler. So may those expressions that fear kept extorting from us take their leave and retreat. Let us say nothing of the sort we did before, for [150] we suffer nothing as we did before; nor let us make the same remarks in open praise of the *princeps* as we did before, for neither do we say the same things in secret as we did before. (2.1–2)

Acknowledging that the payment of thanks and praise is in itself no new phenomenon, Pliny nonetheless would draw a distinction between the content of the *Panegyricus* and all prior praises of an emperor (with a special glance in the direction of Domitian). Why? Because experience and expression both can and should be linked: since present life bears no resemblance to the sufferings of the senatorial class under Domitian, so too what they utter now must be different; since private discourse about the emperor bears no resemblance to what was once said of Domitian, so too public praise should flaunt this happy distinction. In claiming that a change for the better in what is said privately can bring about a change in what is said publicly, Pliny would forge a link between the public and private discourse of the emperor's subjects, or (in J. C. Scott's terms) between the 'public transcript' and the 'hidden transcript' of his times.

Scott's terminology, which proves a particularly useful tool for understanding the *Panegyricus*, deserves some elucidation here. As he explains it, the term *public transcript* characterizes language shaped by the ideology and propaganda of the ruler or ruling class of a given society. As such its production by subordinate members of that society reflects conditions of discourse that are public (in the presence of, or accessible to, the ruler) or subject to some other constraint from above.

With rare, but significant, exceptions the public performance of the subordinate will, out of prudence, fear, and the desire to curry favor, be shaped to appeal to the expectations of the powerful. I shall use the term *public transcript* as a shorthand way of describing the open interaction between subordinates and those who dominate. The public transcript, where it is not positively misleading, is unlikely to tell the whole story about power relations . . . [It] is an [151] indifferent guide to the opinion of subordinates. (Scott [1990] 2–3)

As Scott points out, this public transcript not only represents the values of the dominant element that controls its utterance, but also suggests that the other representatives of society happily accede to these values; indeed, they are values cast by the public transcript in so positive a mold, and in such apparent conformity to the merit scale common to all members of that society, that there is little reason to question their appeal to those who endorse them with such enthusiasm.

The public transcript is—barring a crisis—systematically skewed in the direction of the libretto, the discourse, represented by the dominant. In ideological terms the public transcript will typically, by its accommodationist tone, provide convincing evidence for the hegemony of dominant values, for the hegemony of dominant discourse. It is precisely this public domain where the effects of power relations are most manifest, and any analysis based exclusively on the public transcript is likely to conclude that subordinate groups endorse the terms of their subordination and are willing, even enthusiastic, partners in that subordination. (Ibid. 4)

On the other hand, when the 'libretto' (or scripted 'truth' of the dominant) no longer dictates the content of what is said, the resulting discourse constitutes the *hidden transcript*, a communication that has been liberated from the constraints otherwise imposed by hierarchies of power, self-interest, caution, and so on.[7] This kind of discourse, as

---

[7] Scott (1990) 5 justly emphasizes that it is not a simple question of false versus true discourse, as if the hidden transcript represented the truth of a political situation veiled by the propaganda of the powerful: 'We do not wish to prejudge, by definition, the relation between what is said in the face of power and what is said behind its back. Power relations are not, alas, so straightforward that we can call what is said in power-laden contexts false and what is said offstage true. Nor can we simplistically describe the former as a realm of necessity and the latter as a realm of freedom.' (Consider, say, Tacitus' *Annals*, which issues an implicit claim to provide the hidden transcript behind the theatricalizing effects of imperial power: it is an immensely effective and persuasive claim and a brilliant rhetorical strategy, but offers us no less skewed a perspective for all that.)

Scott defines it, 'takes place "offstage," beyond direct observation by powerholders. The hidden transcript is thus derivative in the sense that it consists of those offstage speeches, gestures, and practices that confirm, contradict, or inflect what appears in the public transcript' (ibid. 4–5). As such, the hidden transcript represents what Pliny designates when he talks of 'the things we say in secret,' while we may usefully see in his depiction of 'those expressions which fear [152] kept extorting from us' (*Pan.* 2.2) a reference to the public transcript in place during the dangerous years of Domitian's reign.

In fact, when we return to the passage from the *Panegyricus* quoted above we can see that Pliny would dictate the interpretation to be tendered his speech precisely by invoking the new connection of the public and hidden transcripts, which, he would claim, must change *together*. Since the hidden transcript is no longer the same as it was under Domitian, so too the *Panegyricus*, that most public of documents, should constitute a statement that is qualitatively different from the encomia of prior rulers; Pliny exhorts, 'let us not make the same remarks in open praise of the *princeps* as we did before, for neither do we say the same things in secret as we did before' (2.2). This nonintuitive connection between the previously severed public and hidden transcripts is a tactic to lend strength to Pliny's intended differentiation of his own very public speech from similar and insincere productions of the past: the public transcript, no longer a sham discourse independent of the secret mutterings of the discontent, will shift into authenticity as these mutterings, too, meld into private panegyric. Moreover, both transcripts, and not just the hidden one, are linked back to the reality of experience, as if a new public transcript cannot now be lies independent of reality; 'let us say nothing of the sort we did before, for we suffer nothing as we did before' (2.2). Making a proleptic gambit to fix his language against the ravages of cynicism, Pliny tries to prove that his praise may be public, but it is for all this no less a testimony to lived experience. In short, he tries to ensure that the *Panegyricus* will *not* be read as were prior manifestos of the public transcript, *not* be interpreted as rote repetition of imperial ideology and contrasted to words spoken in private.[8]

---

[8] This is not, of course, to make claims about that elusive quality, sincerity itself; Solari (1950) goes to one extreme when he claims Pliny's speech is actually hostile to Trajan, and (for example) Trisoglio (1972) to the other—a more popular camp.

A moment's further reflection reveals that Pliny is making an even more important claim than this for his speech. In saying that public praise is different from what it was in the past, he is of course characterizing the present eulogy of Trajan—no longer extorted by fear—as *genuine* praise over and against the fake praise of Domitianic days. [153] And in saying that the hidden transcript too has undergone a change, he implies that it has shifted from obloquy and aspersion (genuine, since secret) to praise (likewise genuine and still secret; in this speech, the hidden transcript of the once oppressed *always* stands for the true discourse of Pliny's senatorial peers). On both counts, then, we are left with genuine praise as the marker of contemporary discourse about the emperor, whether public or private. In other words, during these blissful times the hidden and public transcripts have become one, and by a simple enough inference the *Panegyricus* is nothing but a public version of *quae secreto loquimur* ('what we say in private'). This early inference is taken up and made explicit as the speech goes on: public and hidden transcripts repeatedly emerge through the filter of Pliny's rhetoric as one and the same thing, even to the degree that he wishes Trajan *would* violate the privacy of his subjects:

> One might justly complain that no rulers inquire into our private lives except those whom we hate. For if good and bad had the same concerns, what admiration for yourself you would find everywhere, what joy and exultation, what conversations we all have with our wives and children, and even with the altars and hearths of our homes! You would understand then that I am being sparing of those most gentle ears of yours [with my praise]. (68.6–7)

Pliny's panegyric, it seems, actually pales by comparison to these household cries of rapture. And again, speaking of the present happiness and the sufferings of the past, he exhorts, 'Let this be the topic of our secret talk, this the topic of our conversations, this the topic of our very speeches of thanks' (53.6). It is certainly the topic of *his* 'speech of thanks' (*gratiarum actio*), which, though public, is thereby linked once again to a transcript of an entirely different sort.[9] Yet it is clear

---

[9] Cf. also 'may liberty, good faith, and truth be consistent with everything I shall say' (*Pan.* 1.6). Possibly falling into this category is Pliny's request to Trajan at 62.9: 'Believe us to be such . . . as vouchsafe our reputations. To this bend your ears, here direct your eyes: have no regard for furtive opinions and whispers that lay their traps most effectively for ears that listen to them.' But Pliny is not so much asking Trajan to

that all Pliny's protestations are undermined—as his very repetition of them might suggest to the skeptical—by the frame in which they are offered: a public panegyric is the most obvious site for the reproduction of the public transcript, and by dint of this fact any statement in it has but a tenuous hold on disinterestedness.[10] **[154]** This problem and similar ones with which the speaker is presented by his medium, his audiences both senatorial and imperial, and even his situation in history are topics to which I will return below (see section II).

Proclaiming the identity of public and hidden transcripts is one obsession of this speech; two others exist, likewise meant to be applied to their own oratorical context and equally relevant to the Plinian 'proof' of sincerity. For one, Pliny announces the end of all role-playing imposed by the hierarchies of power. No longer, he claims, do the emperor's terrified subjects (in a very Tacitean formula) need to know the *actual* truth of a given situation in order to respond accordingly to the *fake* truth that constitutes the script written by the emperor alone. 'We obey you in this,' says Pliny, 'that we do not gather in the senate for a contest of flattery but for the practice and service of justice, intending to pay this debt of gratitude to your frankness and truthfulness; that we trust that you want what you say and you do not want what you say you don't' (54.5).[11] Trajan (Pliny claims) lays no traps in his interactions with the senators; they can trust that his words reflect his intentions truthfully, that to take him at face value will not be fatal. All this is very much in contrast to Domitian, that prince of feigning; 'what sea was there so treacherous as the oily words of former rulers, whose fickleness and deceitfulness were so great that it was easier to guard against them when they were

believe that public and hidden transcripts are the same under his reign as demanding that he not listen to (false) reports against senators.

[10] A point that had little impact in times when cynicism was less modish than in our own; Scott (1932) 157, calls the man a 'distinguished and talented Roman' who was 'under no necessity to indulge in flattery, but [was] free to express [his] true convictions.' He is followed in this opinion by a veritable host of later commentators.

[11] I have supplied the auxiliary verb of speaking in the translation. The Latin translates literally: 'we trust that you want what you want and you do not want what you do not want.' I trust that my own readers will agree that the point here is one about the treachery of believing in imperial lies (especially in view of *simplicitati tuae veritatique,* 'your frankness and truthfulness') rather than the chance of being led astray by imperial indecision or the ruler's sad alienation from his 'inner child' (as we say in California). Cf. also *Pan.* 77.4.

angry than when benevolent?' (66.3). In Domitian's day, senators mouthed a despairing and dissimulated acquiescence to a public transcript in which they did not believe: none dared to speak in the senate but sat stunned in the face of the compulsion to agree (*adsentiendi necessitas*); all expressed approval of proposals of which the very sponsors could not approve (*Pan.* 76.3–4).[12] So great was the disparity between what was said and what men felt; indeed, 'nothing is more unpleasant for everybody than measures that are passed as if everyone approves of them' (76.4).[13]

In fact, the role-playing that prevailed in those times extended even to the stage itself, where real actors repeated a propaganda and praise [155] that was marked by the locus of its production and the degeneracy of the performers:

> And what site remained any longer unacquainted with wretched adulation, since the praises of the emperors were celebrated at shows and in competition pieces [*commissionibus*],[14] were danced out and effeminized by emasculated voices, rhythms, and gestures into every form of mockery? But this indeed was unworthy, that they were praised at the same time in the senate and on the stage, by an actor and by the consul. You, however, drove far from your worship theatrical practices. (54.1–2)

Here in fact we have two stages: the literal one, where transpired the praises that Pliny criticizes as insufficiently masculine in style and execution, and the metaphorical one supplied by the senate house, where the senators themselves acted out their roles as eager encomiasts. Stage and senate, actor and consul (*scaena/senatus, histrio/consul*) supply a dismal pair of equations to characterize the prevalence of role-playing under Domitian. Consul and actor alike praised the emperor, and in doing so the former was as much an actor as the latter. When Pliny asserts, then, that Trajan 'drove far from [his] worship theatrical practices,' his statement has meaning beyond the literal. The accession of this man signalled the end of role-playing *tout court*; his senatorial interlocutors have stepped down from their own 'stage' and their praise no longer entails 'theatrical practices,'

---

[12] Pliny writes in a similar vein in *Letters* 8.14.8: 'We too gazed upon the senate, but it was a senate fearful and tongue-tied, when it was dangerous to say what you wanted, but pathetic to do the opposite.'

[13] On the parallels to Tacitus here, see Bruyère (1954) 175–6.

[14] On the translation of *commissio*, see Bartsch (1994) ch. 4, n. 115.

ludicrae artes.[15] And again Pliny's comments—words of praise by a
senator and consul—are conveniently pertinent to the speech that
contains them. The *Panegyricus'* version of the truth endows the
Panegyricus itself with the validity of sincerity.[16]

The third topic too in this trio of concerns is, like the demise of
role-playing, a corollary of making the public and hidden transcripts
identical. Pliny notifies his audience of the end of political doublespeak, and begins by refusing the potential for such an interpretation
of his own words: [156]

> It is easy to thank one who deserves it, senators. There is no risk that
> when I speak of his civility, he will think his arrogance is being
> reproached; his profligacy, when I talk of his frugality; his cruelty,
> when I speak of his clemency; his greed, when I speak of his generosity;
> his malice, when I speak of his kindness; his lust, when I speak of his
> self-control; his laziness, when I speak of his work; his cowardice, when
> I speak of his courage. (3.4)

This pre-emptive attempt to control the possible interpretations of
his own panegyric must be the product of Pliny's awareness that
praise can in fact signal the presence of its opposite, that the same
words can carry different meanings for their different audiences. As
Charles E. Murgia observes, 'the implication is clear that bad emperors were praised as having virtues which they lacked, and for doing
what they did not do but should have done; the implication is also
there that the audience knew how to understand their praise' (1980,
123). It is this 'understanding' that Pliny would stave off (or at least
would seem to wish to stave off; indeed, we are dealing throughout
with the appearance of intention rather than intention proper);
the application of his proleptic denial is both local and global. Most
immediately, the pairs Pliny here posits are pure antitheses—civility/

---

[15] Even imperial triumphs and wild animal hunts change from theatre to true
representation: cf. *Pan.* 16.3 and 81.3.

[16] On the end of role-playing, see also *Pan.* 73.4: 'You yourself, too, bore out the
sincerity of our acclamations by the truth of your tears.' Another, striking, Plinian
indication of this situation is the new status of the imperial gaze at the circus, which is
now characterized as a sign of equality, not oppression: the new circus is a sight to be
seen not only for its beauty but also because the place of the princeps is now on a level
with that of the people, so *'he can be watched by the citizens as he too watches them'*
(*Pan.* 51.4–5; my emphasis). It is unclear what, if any, real changes in the seating
arrangment Pliny is talking about; perhaps Trajan just 'did away with or at least did
not use the pulvinar,' as Alan Cameron (1976) 177 says.

arrogance, frugality/profligacy, clemency/cruelty, and so on—of which one alternative is to be systematically excluded from possible interpretations of his list of imperial virtues. In the wider context of the *Panegyricus* itself, Pliny would thus enforce a reading of his speech that does not have access to the hermeneutic key provided by doublespeak, and this (of course unenforceable) 'rule' that he imposes on his audience is an extension of the alleged demise of the two transcripts. For one important trait of doublespeak, as we saw in chapter three [Bartsch 1994], is precisely its capacity to engage both the public and the hidden transcripts *at the same time and with the same words*. To praise the emperor using the terms and values of imperial propaganda, as Pliny does in this aretalogy of Trajan, is potentially to criticize the ruler to another audience who will read such terms as [157] their semantic opposites. It is the existence of this possibility—the existence of what I discuss below as the *praise/blame axis* (section II)—that keeps Pliny reaching for public control mechanisms such as the claim (which puts an end to all doublespeak) that the two transcripts are no longer at variance.[17]

   Up to this point we have considered three of Pliny's themes in the *Panegyricus* that, besides contributing to the pervasive antithesis between the false public performances of Domitianic days and the true happiness of the present, also reflect upon the official speech that is their context. Other such devices are more flagrantly presented as interpretive tools, or rather rules, for the audience. Brought in by the speaker to establish his sincerity in praising Trajan, they set guidelines for understanding which, when applied to the *Panegyricus* itself, invariably produce results that conform to Pliny's open statements of intention. One such tactic is to confront the issue of flattery head on by insisting that praise that is true (his own) and flattery that is false (the sort directed at Domitian) are in fact qualitatively different in a

---

[17] It should be noted that the public transcript is itself never without some appeal to subordinates, as Scott (1990) 18, emphasizes; and while Pliny's effusions may be slightly ridiculous, they must have found some resonance with their audience. If the public transcript of a ruler 'is to have any rhetorical force among subordinates, it necessarily involves some concessions to their presumed interests. That is, rulers who aspire to hegemony in the Gramscian sense of that term must make out an ideological case that they rule, to some degree, on behalf of their subjects. This claim, in turn, is always highly tendentious but seldom completely without resonance among subordinates.' It is this resonance that makes doublespeak possible, for if it did not exist there could be no 'he meant it sincerely' option for interpretation, and praise would be *merely* ironic.

way that does not elude the notice of the audience. We have seen how at *Panegyricus* 2.1 Pliny exhorts all fellow citizens 'not to say anything about our *princeps* in such a way that the same thing could have been said about another ruler.' A few words later he repeats the idea that such a distinction is possible, now in senatorial expressions of praise: 'let the difference in the times be discerned from our speeches, and let it be understood, *by the very nature of the thanks rendered*, to whom they were spoken and when' (2.3; my emphasis).[18] The *Panegyricus* itself stands here as the paradigm of a new and unadulterated praise; it is from the speeches of the liberated senators (such as the *Panegyricus* itself) that we are meant to discern the difference between true and false panegyric—as indeed will all future rulers. As Pliny remarks to Trajan, 'Let rulers too learn to distinguish true and false acclamations, and let them consider it your gift that they can no longer be deceived [by false praise]. They will not have to lay the road to a good reputation, only not to abandon it; they will not have to banish adulation, only not to recall it' (75.5). [158]

But wherein lies the difference which Pliny would establish? Apparently it issues from the fact that the flattery spawned by fear and the praise arising from true admiration are simply two different species, and whereas the former must appear far-fetched and contrived to its audience, the latter has the ring of simplicity that marks it as true.[19] When Trajan offered prayers to the gods at the recent elections, the senators in turn responded with acclamations;[20] of these cries, Pliny observes:

---

[18] Pliny likewise attributes changes to the cries of the populace at the theatres and circus: instead of shouting praise of the emperor's beauty or voice (referring to Domitian and Nero respectively), they now praise his bravery, dutifulness, self-restraint, and gentleness (*Pan.* 2.6). So praise is a constant, but the implication is that somehow the worth of the qualities praised have some bearing on their truth-content; any emperor who would want to hear he was a handsome fellow does himself discredit. Of course this point loses much of whatever efficacy it had when Pliny praises *Trajan* for his looks at *Pan.* 4.7: such vigour, such height, such glorious hair, so noble a face, etc. On the dissociation of eulogy from flattery, see further Ramage (1989) 644–6.

[19] Cizek (1983) 24, finds himself quite convinced: 'The glorification of Trajan's era clearly distinguishes itself from the praise of certain prior regimes. There is no feeling that a great effort is necessary to convince one's listener that one is talking about an era of perfect happiness. The authors refer to this period as if to a natural fact, as if to a concept accepted by everybody and deeply rooted in the public conscience.'

[20] On acclamation in the technical sense, see also Roueché (1984), who comments on its increasing frequency under the empire as a new means of communication between ruler and ruled and a venue for the expression of political opinion.

Those were expressions that came not from our ingenuity, Caesar, but from your virtue and your merits—expressions such as no adulation ever contrived, no terror ever expressed. Whom did we so fear as to invent these words? Whom did we so love as to avow these words? You know the compulsion imposed by slavery: did you ever hear or say anything the like? Fear devises many things, to be sure, but they seem strained and those who speak them, unwilling. Anxiety has its own ingenuity, security has another one altogether; the inspiration of the glum is different from that of the joyful: faking will reproduce neither. The unhappy have their own words, the happy theirs, and no matter to what degree the same things are said by both, they are said differently. (72.5–7)

While both the oppressed and the liberated have occasion to launch into imperial panegyric, the *way* they express themselves will be different. Pliny opposes truth and ingenuity as spurs to speech and then opposes their products as well: 'fear devises many things,' but these things seem stilted; the style if not the content of a speech produced by terror gives it away.

Naturally enough, then, Pliny is careful to characterize his own style as the right sort. As he says of both his own and senatorial attempts at praise, 'if we should wish to compete with the compulsion of former times, we will be defeated; for pretence is more ingenious at invention than truth, slavery more so than freedom, fear more so than love' (55.2). The implication is that the *Panegyricus* itself is no such attempt. Indeed, it is not only the product of liberty, truth, and love, but names itself clearly as a study in moderation. 'As [159] concerns myself,' Pliny announces, 'I will labour to bring down my speech to the level of modesty and moderation of the *princeps*, and I will consider what his ears can bear no less than what his virtues deserve' (3.3). After all, even the gods themselves prefer innocence to prayers well-honed and rehearsed (3.5)[21]—so we are now to believe that the far-fetched praises of the *Panegyricus* are no such thing.[22] It is

---

[21] Güngerich (1956) 148 complains that while Pliny clearly means the prioritizing of *casta mens* ('pure mind') over *meditatum carmen* ('studied incantation') at *Pan.* 3.5 to reflect upon his own situation, he uses the same term, *meditatus*, to characterize his own authorship at 3.1. (The same scholar, not very persuasively, suggests clumsy borrowing from the *Dialogus de Oratoribus* as the reason.)

[22] A belief that Pliny asks us to hold only in the context of the *Panegyricus* itself. In *Letters* 3.18, in which he discusses the revised version of this speech (that is, the one we have), he generally sticks to his public transcript theme in the *Panegyricus* that the speeches of praise that were so hated in Domitian's day are popular today, thanks to

interesting to note here the discrepancy between what Pliny does and what he says he does; he seems little perturbed by those of his statements that strain credulity to the point of being comic (at least for us modern readers), perhaps for reasons that will become clearer by the end of this chapter.

Another manifestation of what we might call Pliny's would-be performative language, which tries to influence the nature of what he says by the simple act of defining it, occurs in his contrast between the kind of criticism allowed by good emperors but forbidden by bad. Claiming that only good emperors allow the denigration of the bad emperors of the past, Pliny uses the discredited figures of Nero and then Domitian as a litmus test to prove Domitian's depravity, Trajan's benevolence, and his own sincerity:

> Moreover, no other act of our emperor deserves gratitude more gener-
> ous and widespread than the fact that it is safe to inveigh against bad
> rulers. Or has the recent avengement of Nero faded from our grieving
> memories? I suppose the ruler who avenged Nero's death would allow
> Nero's *life* and reputation to be criticized? I suppose he made it possible
> for what was said about one so similar *not* to be understood as an attack
> on himself? . . . Let [our speeches] remember that an emperor who is
> still living is most highly praised thus, if his predecessors are censured as
> they deserve. For when later generations keep their silence about a bad
> ruler [of the past], it is obvious that the present one is doing the same
> things. (53.3–6)

Domitian punished all criticism of his predecessor Nero, Pliny claims, because he knew himself to be 'doing the same things' and saw in such criticism a veiled attack upon his own person—or at least [160] knew that it would so be *interpreted* by its audience, who presumably were well aware of the similarities. But Pliny's technique throughout the *Panegyricus*, as he points out in words that frame the passage quoted above, has been to contrast Trajan to his own evil precursor Domitian: 'this is the first duty of good citizens toward an excellent emperor, to inveigh against those unlike him . . . let our very speeches

Trajan's stellar qualities (3.18.7). Yet, quite in contrast to what he says in the *Panegyricus* proper, he also congratulates himself at 3.18.10 on his florid style and opines that a terser and simpler version would seem stilted and less appropriate than what he wrote in his more exuberant state. The time for simplicity has not yet come; Leach (1990) 28 has interesting comments on how Pliny, in the *Letters* seems an actor contemplating his mask. See also *Letters* 3.13.3; and on the question of style, Gamber-ini (1983) 377–80; Guillemin (1928) 153–4; Sherwin-White (1966) 252–3.

of thanks treat this topic' (53.2, 6). By the simplest of steps Trajan's goodness stands revealed: neither does he suppress criticism of Domitian (as Pliny's fearless delivery of the *Panegyricus* proves) nor can it be that he and Pliny are nervous lest the senatorial audience will read into one diatribe the existence of another. Once again, Pliny safeguards the integrity of his speech by rules he lays down for its interpretation *within* the speech, and if the closed meaning-system of the world of the *Panegyricus* is accepted as valid, the hermeneutic freedom of its audience is channeled into the results required by its speaker. Contrasting Trajan to Domitian, Pliny makes the very existence of the contrast 'prove' the truth of its content.[23]

A final controlling tactic of the *Panegyricus* is, paradoxically enough, that of relinquishing control altogether and making the *recipient* responsible for the interpretation he imposes on what he hears. In commenting on the recent elections and the senate's emotional acclamation of Trajan in response to the prayers he pronounced on that occasion, Pliny claims that this act of senatorial praise found belief precisely because the emperor *could* believe in it: 'the very

---

[23] Even as he lies—for once again, what Pliny would have his audience accept in the *Panegyricus* does not bear a very satisfactory relation to what seems to have taken place outside its bounds. As Bardon (1940) 372 wryly notes, 'neither the past nor the present excuses his lies: he courts Trajan in the same way Martial courted Domitian, or Seneca Nero: he slanders. Now, the only liberty that Roman emperors had always tolerated was the liberty to abuse their predecessors. Trajan, who did not hesitate to criticize his precursors, found profit in this too. Illusion of words! In the epoch of Trajanic liberty, Pliny behaves toward Domitian as Martial toward Nero, and in the worst years of the Domitianic tyranny!' See similarly Flach (1972) 168; Syme (1958a) 12. And indeed there is plenty of literary evidence for criticism of Nero under Domitian; cf. Martial *Epig.* 4.63, 7.21, 7.34; Statius *Silv.* 2.7.100, 118–19; and the satirist Turnus, as cited in the corrupt lines in the scholia to Juv. *Sat.* 1.71 (on Turnus, see Coffey (1979) 89 who suggests he used a Neronian setting for his work; we know at least that he addressed the topic of Britannicus' poisoning at Nero's hands; cf., from the scholia, *ex quo Caesareas suboles Lucusta cecidit*, 'following whom Lucusta killed the Caesarian offspring'). There are discussions of this anti-Plinian evidence in Bardon (1940) 371; Coleman (1986) 3102; Hartman (1916) 367; Rudd (1986) 74 (Rudd adds to the list the satirist Turnus, who 'recalled'). However, Domitian's death did bring with it open equations with Nero (cf. Martial *Epig.* 11.33; Juv. *Sat.* 4.38, where Domitian is labeled *calvus Nero;* and Ausonius *De XII Caesaribus Monosticha* 2.12, cited in Szelest (1974) 110), a fact which suggests that the allusive quality of Nero's name may have been part of the hidden transcript under Domitian but not did not necessarily incur the risk of punishment. After all, even if Domitian were aware of—or cared about—the connection, to take umbrage would be to acknowledge its truth. Szelest (1974) 110 sides with Pliny's perspective, suggesting that Domitian was hostile to Martial precisely because he did make negative comments about Nero.

circumstance that used to detract from the credibility of our words
with bad emperors gave credibility to them with you, the best of
emperors; for although we used to act as do loving subjects, those
emperors would not believe they were loved' (74.4). Pliny here admits
that the senators' behaviour toward Domitian was outwardly that of
loving partisans, much as it is now under Trajan; similarly at *Panegyricus* 85.1 his emphasis is on the façade of adoration, the *amoris
simulatio*, which the senators presented to the tyrant in former times.
It seems that the difference between past and present lies not so much
in the nature of how the senators act as in the psychology and [161]
self-awareness of the respective rulers: since Domitian was well aware
of the discrepancy between his fiendish nature and the blandishments
of his flatterers, he suspected their sincerity; since Trajan is pure at
heart, he believes in the praise of his admirers. There is a sense, then,
in which Trajan has to accept the outré flattery of senatorial panegyric
as sincere; to do otherwise, to see it, for example, as an instance of
doublespeak is to condemn himself. It is up to the emperor to
mandate the sincerity of the speaker. Similar too is the working of a
passage we have already considered. When Pliny announces of Trajan
that 'there is no risk that when I speak of his civility, he will think his
arrogance is being reproached; his profligacy, when I talk of his
frugality; his cruelty, when I speak of his clemency; his greed, when
I speak of his generosity; his malice . . . ' (3.4), he is, to be sure, trying
to dictate the interpretation of this list, but he is also setting into play
an eternal verity that Dio and Tacitus would later apply to Tiberius: to
see a slur is to prove it true.[24]

   These strategies for interpretive control are intended to contribute
to the truth-value of the particular claims of the *Panegyricus* sketched
out at the beginning of this chapter: the insistence on the identical
content of the public and hidden transcripts, the proclamation of the
end of role-playing and doublespeak, the proof of the speaker's
sincerity.[25] For to argue that real and dissimulating eulogies are

---

[24] 'For what is disdained falls out of memory; if you become angry, the slurs appear
acknowledged as true' Tac. *Ann.* 4.34.5; '[Tiberius] in scrutinizing in great detail and
accuracy everything that people were accused of having said about him slanderously,
reviled *himself* with all the bad things people were saying,' Dio Cassius 57.23.1.

[25] Perhaps another interpretation-controlling strategy we could include here is
Pliny's tactic of forestalling the question of whether flattery is going on by mentioning
and repudiating that very possibility, e.g. at *Pan.* 78.1: the senate, he says, has spoken
with authority, not adulation, thanks to Trajan's deferent nature.

perceptibly different, that criticism of bad emperors is permitted only by good ones, that only a tyrant doubts the appearance of devotion, is to insist that the sincerity of the eulogist can be proved and should be trusted. But of course the sincerity of the speaker cannot be proved; the topos of praise swallows up all such devices intended to bridge the chasm between public and private discourse, frankness and feint. 'Such is your magnificence, O Emperor, that what might seem flattery before a tyrant is in your case only authentic praise'—this is a statement that sets to rest no qualms whatsoever about the acting, coercion, or self-interest of the speaker, but does fit in wonderfully with the public transcript of that reign. Hence Pliny cannot really prove that he is sincere, and his tactics must take their origin not [162] in any belief that he can, but as a response, however futile, to the modes of interpretation which he knows are already in place among his audiences senatorial and imperial. It is these pre-existent models for understanding which, as I argue below, impel our eulogist to adopt the counterstrategies we find in the *Panegyricus*.

II

The *Panegyricus* is of course a document of the public transcript, not only by dint of its content but also necessarily so through the addressee and the occasion. Pliny is attempting to reverse the instantly grasped *priority* of these 'transcript markers' in how we apprehend the speech;[26] over the indubitable facts of occasion, addressee, and panegyric he would give priority, in their claim on our attention, to his interpretive controls, his proclamation of the end of doublespeak and role-playing, the new unity of hidden and public transcripts. Considered through the frame of these self-fixing statements in the speech itself, the *Panegyricus* is a powerful, if numbing, testimony to his subjects' affection for Trajan; approached as a product of the

---

[26] The problem is that we all understand intuitively what Scott (1990) 4 spells out: 'The theatrical imperatives that normally prevail in situations of domination produce a public transcript in close conformity with how the dominant group would wish to have things appear. The dominant never control the stage absolutely, but their wishes normally prevail. In the short run, it is in the interest of the subordinate to produce a more or less credible performance, speaking the lines and making the gestures he knows are expected of him'.

public transcript, it falls apart at the seams, undone by the echoes of the public transcripts of the past. For the *Panegyricus* not only reproduces the imperial propaganda of its own, Trajanic, era;[27] it also—and this is far more destructive of its aims—reproduces the public transcripts of the very past reigns from which Pliny is so eager to distance himself and his praise.[28] 'Let us say nothing of the sort we did before, for we suffer nothing as we did before,' Pliny has said at *Panegyricus* 2.2; but over and over we find the particulars of the praise he does deliver anticipated in places where, according to his own depiction of the prior years of dissembling, they can stand only as a tribute to the power of the emperor to exact encomium, and the power of *this* power to render praise meaningless. Here, then, is one way of interpreting praise that lurks in the background to Pliny's speech and against whose ghoulish presence he so often raises the cross of sincerity.

'Let us never flatter you as a god or as a divinity; for we are [163] speaking not about a tyrant but about a citizen, not about a master [*dominus*] but about a father' exults Pliny (*Pan*. 2.3)—and echoes Statius' praise to Domitian for protesting against the same usage of *dominus*: at the festival of the Saturnalia, the people

> raise innumerable voices to the stars
> acclaiming the *princeps'* Saturnalia
> and they shout *dominus* with sweet affection:
> this title alone has Caesar refused to allow. (*Silv*. 1.6.81–84)

The refusal of titles openly monarchical or excessively honorific had been a line in the imperial script since the days of Julius Caesar; in the cases of both Domitian and Trajan it had little practical effect on the

---

[27] Documentation is hardly needed; see similar expressions of the public transcript in Tacitus' brief but requisite praise passages at *Agr*. 2.3 and 3.1 (the former probably borrowed by Pliny at *Pan*. 66.5; see Bruyère (1954) 162); Tac. *Hist*. 1.1; Pliny himself in *Letters* 8.14.2–10; Martial *Epig*. 10.72, trying to do much the same as Pliny in the *Panegyricus*; cf. esp. lines 13–14, about Trajan: 'Under this ruler, if you are wise, forbear/O Rome, to speak with the words you used before.' See also the sections on Trajanic propaganda in Cizek (1983) 100ff., and Fedeli (1989) 459–60 (on *Traianus optimus princeps*). None of this, of course, is intended to suggest that Trajan's rule was no different from Domitian's, just that expressing an appreciation of that difference was a difficult task.

[28] In *Letters* 6.27.3, Pliny links these flattering public statements to the worst among previous rulers.

everyday workings of the language of flattery and caution.[29] Even
Pliny, despite his reminder to himself not to praise Trajan as a god,
does not eschew flattering comparisons of the emperor to divinities
and demigods of all shapes and sizes. A few paragraphs after the
passage denouncing such extravagances, he is already announcing
that 'when I was trying to imagine and picture a *princeps* for whom
this power rivaling the immortal gods' would be appropriate, I never
had the good fortune to conceive even in my wishes of such a man as
we see here' (4.4).[30] Later still, Trajan has all but metamorphosed into
Jupiter himself; he hears everything, he oversees everything, and once
invoked he is present in an instant; as Pliny continues, 'such, I
imagine, is the realm which that father of the world controls with
his nod, whenever he has cast down his eyes upon the earth and
deigned to include mortal fates among his divine works' (80.4). This
semi-divine figure then evolves into Jupiter's regent on earth, freeing
the ruler of the gods from concern over that realm: 'so much time has
he free for the heavens, after he gave us you to fulfill his function
toward every race of man' (80.5). It is hardly surprising to find *this*
sentiment anticipated in the court poetry of the Domitianic period,
now in words spoken of that emperor by Statius' prescient Sibyl:
'Look! he is a god, Jupiter bids him rule/over the blessed earth in
his stead' (Stat. *Silv.* 4.3.128–129).[31] And there are other comparisons:
[164] to Hercules (*Pan.* 14.5); to the husbands of goddesses and the
sons of gods (82.7); to the gods (1.3, 4.4); the stars (19.1); the sun

[29] On the title *dominus*, see further Hammond (1938) 123–4 n. 1; Scott (1936)
102ff.; Waters (1964) 67. Scott, on the basis of Martial *Epig.* 5.8.1, 7.34.8–9, argues that
Domitian came to be called *dominus et deus* ('master and god') at a later point than
the festival described by Statius, and adduces Suet. *Dom.* 13.2. But the *Silvae* are
already late (books 1–3 'are clustered into the period 90/1', Hardie (1983) 64), and it is
more likely that the title was used from an early date by those who had anything to
gain by flattery; similarly, pointing out the emperor's resistance to the usage would
work equally well, since it would suggest that the public transcript ('our emperor is
our master, our divinity') was so true that it found utterance despite, not because of,
the wishes of the powerholder. For Pliny's use of *dominus* to Trajan, see below, n. 41.
[30] Juvenal, writing some fifteen years later, uses language like Pliny's but does so to
satirize the flattery lavished on Domitian; see *Sat.* 4.70–1 and the comments of Gérard
(1976) 320. Identical expressions of praise can easily cross the divide into satire and
back again into sincerity; see discussion of the praise/blame axis later in this chapter.
[31] See Fedeli (1989) 433–4; Hartman (1916) 1367 n. 1; Syme (1938) 218. Scott
(1936) 133–40, collects similar comparisons of Domitian to Jupiter by Statius and
Martial.

(35.5).[32] In large measure, Pliny's effusions are different from prior ones only in that their author announces their absence before he unveils their presence.[33]

A few more examples are particularly resonant with past praise. 'You modestly refused a third consulship, but finally heeded the senate's pleas and prayers,' Pliny commends with lengthy admiration (*Pan.* 56.3–60.7)—and willy-nilly evokes Statius' lines lauding Domitian for turning down the consulships oft proffered by an importunate senate; exclaims the poet,

> . . . How many you refuse,
> how many you forbid them offer! Still, you will be moved
> and will promise this day often to the senate's prayers. (*Silv.* 4.1.33–35)

This topic too is a frequent motif of the public transcript; Tacitus borrows it for Tiberius and cynically 'uncovers' the layers of deceit and dissimulation behind his reluctance to assume office (Tac. *Ann.* 1.7.3 ff., 1.10.7 ff.).[34] Its point lies in the fact that, like all comments on the reluctance of a ruler to accept or wield power, it places the will for his rule with the people, who then have reason neither for dissatisfaction nor for a hidden transcript. And discussing not the third but the first consulship of Trajan, Pliny touches upon another form of praise long since emptied of effective meaning; he hails the return of *libertas*. 'You exhorted all men alike to resume their freedom, to undertake the business of empire as if it were shared', he marvels to the ruler (66.2). But what else would one say about the status of *libertas* even to an emperor who abused the freedom and rights of his subjects (if such was Domitian)? Martial provides the answer with a rhetorical question: 'Under what other *princeps* was there so much freedom?' (*Epig.*

---

[32] See similar lists in Bardon (1940) 375–6 (for echoes of the past praises of Domitian), and Durry (1938) 35 ff. (for the *lieux communs* that display the conventionality of these compliments). At *Pan.* 6.2 there is also a striking evocation of the flattering proem of Lucan's *Bellum Civile* ('it was worth all the suffering if your rule was the result'), unfortunate given that Nero, like Domitian, is in Pliny's scheme a recipient of false flattery rather than true praise.

[33] Bardon (1940) 374 contrasts the references to Trajan in *Letters* books 2–9: 'Dignity is not lacking here; one feels that Domitian is no longer in power. But the *Panegyric* does not confirm this excellent impression.'

[34] The fact that Tacitus also takes Pliny's comments on the imperial adoption (*Pan.* 7.1ff.) and places them in the mouth of Galba at *Hist.* 1.15.1ff. is an interesting confirmation that the Plinian transcript *is* the imperial one. On this, see Bruyère (1954) 170–6; Fedeli (1989) 426–32, with bibliography.

5.19.6). And we can see Pliny, as if recalling prior praises of the free rein Domitian gave to freedom, trying to head off the inevitable undermining of his words by the addition of a phrase [165] to counteract scepticism: 'All rulers before you said the same things; but none before you was believed' (*Pan.* 66.3). Pliny's praise is marked by this self-consciousness, the attempt to frame and colour content through interpretive rules, and most of all the tacit acknowledgment that his eulogy is annulled by its very models, that other ways of interpreting imperial praise are familiar to his senatorial audience.[35]

In fact the problem Pliny encounters is that there *is* no new way to praise the emperor.[36] He can say that praise should be rendered anew, even claim that he *is* doing it and not repeating the gestures of the past ('let the difference in the times be discerned from our speeches, and let it be understood, by the very nature of the thanks rendered, to whom they were spoken and when,' *Pan.* 2.3), but the *Panegyricus* cannot escape the resonance of recent eulogies of Domitian—the resonance, that is, of a public transcript Pliny has tried to transform into the antithesis of the present one.[37] The interpretive lens that Pliny holds up to our eyes—'see, my praise is new, different, *real*'— itself has meaning only as a gesture; in this gesture alone, perhaps (given the absence of other examples; there is no certainty here), the *Panegyricus* distinguishes itself from its predecessors. But it is the gesture of a man who is no stranger to the rituals of praise and who knows all too well that his words are not new. If we are to believe Pliny's own claim, official business in the senate only a few years earlier was frequently punctuated by digressions in praise of Domitian (*Pan.* 54.3).[38] Elsewhere Pliny openly acknowledges the problem

---

[35] For a further catalogue of the imperial virtues praised in Martial and Statius for which parallels may easily be found in the *Panegyricus*, see Heuvel (1937) 304–5, who lists such topics as the peace, the prosperity, the moral probity of the age, the founding of a new *saeculum*, comparisons of Domitian to Hercules and Jupiter, etc.

[36] Compare the senate's difficulty in front of Otho, new emperor and recent senator, at Tac. *Hist.* 1.85.3: 'flattery was familiar to Otho, recently a private citizen and wont to say the same things'.

[37] Bardon (1940) 376, puts it well: 'Pliny's sincerity is not in question. And *yet it seems suspect*, since Pliny treats Trajan as Martial treats Domitian' (my emphasis). Soverini (1989) 540 finds the fault to be in the excessive ornamentation overlaying an essentially sincere statement.

[38] Of course, Pliny represents as the product of fear and coercion what may well have been voluntary and spurred by self-interest. Note also that what he says here will

of a praise that is always already pre-empted by the flatteries of the
past.[39] About the difficulties he encountered while writing his *Panegyricus*, he complains in *Letters* 3.13.2 that 'here everything is familiar, hackneyed, already said'; in *Letters* 6.27.3 he comments of another
occasion calling for compliments to the emperor that praise was
problematic because 'I remembered the numerous honorific speeches
delivered to all his worst predecessors.'[40] And for the benefit of Trajan
himself, this theme returns in the speech in the fancier dressing of
paradox, a Plinian favorite: as confesses encomiast to [166] emperor,
'since all innovation has long since been used up by adulation, no
other new honour remains to be paid you than that we should dare at
times to be silent before you' (*Pan.* 55.3). Anxiety over the problem of
sincerity makes sense in a context in which the speaker himself has
redefined his models as paradigms of insincerity and in which the
audience may apply *this* understanding of praise to the present
exemplum as well.

As it happens, Pliny has other reasons for anxiety over the issue of
credibility. His contribution to the public transcript contains much in
the way of factual misrepresentation that may have raised the eye-
brows of his audience. The question of the title *dominus*, which is in
notoriously frequent evidence in the vocative in Pliny's letters to
Trajan from Bithynia,[41] can perhaps be evaded on grounds of

be contradicted by his own later claim that Domitian was too evil to believe in the
senators who (supposedly) feigned their love, *Pan.* 74.4, while here the recipients 'are
gladdened, as if they deserved it' (54.4).

[39] As Kennedy (1972) 544 remarks, Trajan 'had begun well as emperor in the view
of Pliny and his friends, but so had other emperors including Nero and Domitian,
who had both ended badly. Enough time had elapsed so that some uneasiness had
begun to build up about the difficulty of maintaining the felicity of the times'.
Similarly MacCormack (1975) 150.

[40] Cited above, n. 28. As Syme (1958) 95 comments, 'in the *Panegyricus* the type of
discourse devoted to flattering the supreme power has come to perfection, with few
tricks left for later practitioners to learn. . . . Pliny is aware that his theme is far from
novel—*nota vulgata dicta sunt omnia* ('everything is known, broadcast, spoken').
Eloquent consuls there had been before, artists in adulation, managing an identical
technique whether the Emperor was good or bad; Pliny had listened to the thanks-
givings of senators in the days of Domitian; and he may have helped, as a proper and
pious duty, to compose the speech delivered by Verginius Rufus in his third consulate
under Nerva'.

[41] As noted by many scholars; see, e.g. Bardon (1940) 377; Cizek (1983) 235. But
contra see Sherwin-White (1966) 557–8 ('the title *dominus* by itself remained in
social, if not official, use. It was a common form of polite address between inferiors
and superiors of free birth, not only between masters and slaves'). He is followed by

chronology (the letters date, at the earliest, from AD 109), although it seems unlikely that Trajan's professed dislike for the title would have had any effect on its use by subordinates. Pliny's trouncing of the Capitoline Games instituted by Domitian, on the other hand, suggests that they did not continue under Trajan and certainly that his praises were not a topic of competition among the performers (*Pan.* 54.1–2). But they were; if, as seems the case, oratory had been excised as a category, not so the verse eulogies of the emperor,[42] and a letter of Pliny's reveals that to denounce Trajan's *gymnicus agon* ('gymnastic games') at Vienne and his games at Rome could be dangerous enough to be construed as an act of free speech—and win admiration (*Letters* 4.22.1–4).[43] Yet another letter encourages one Caninius Rufus to write his epic on Trajan's Dacian wars; Pliny advises him to begin with an invocation of the gods, as is a poet's wont, and to include among them Trajan himself (*Letters* 8.4.5).[44] More weighty than this are the political and electoral issues Pliny misrepresents or chooses not to address; among these, scholars have variously pointed out the influence of the army in Trajan's adoption by Nerva,[45] Trajan's apparently direct control of the candidates selected for office (*Pan.* 71),[46] the continuing influence of many powerful figures from Domitian's reign in Trajan's own administration,[47] Trajan's lack of [**167**]

Jones (1978) 193 n. 17 ('the use of *dominus* . . . in private intercourse, as in Pliny's letters to Trajan, is another matter'). See also Robert (1974) 242 n. 403, cited in Jones, loc. cit.; Williams (1978) 166–7.

[42] See Coleman (1986) 3098; Tandoi (1968) 141; and Bartsch (1994) ch. 4, nn. 115, 116, 135. On verse eulogy of Trajan in general, see the evidence collected in Bardon (1940) 372–3. Pliny's praise of Trajan at *Pan.* 54.2 for discouraging flattering verse, just as he 'discouraged' the use of *dominus*, probably has little relevance for the actual practice of poets.

[43] Iunius Mauricus wishes in Trajan's presence that the games at Rome could be abolished; 'he did so resolutely, you will say, and bravely; and why not?' is Pliny's comment to his correspondent. See Waters (1970) 74 and Thiele (1916) 247. On Trajan's taste for the stage, and his recall of the pantomimes which Pliny here praises him for banishing, see André (1975) 478.

[44] Pliny, like Tacitus, acts as if all literature had died in Domitian's reign; see *Pan.* 47.1ff, where Pliny hails the 'restoration' of the liberal arts, and *Agr.* 39.2, where Tacitus notes their silencing under Domitian. Martial, Statius, et al. merit no mention and, apparently, no thought.

[45] Hammond (1938) 122 with n. 5, has important documentation. Contrast Pliny in *Pan.* 7.5.

[46] See Bardon (1940) 364; Durry (1938) 21: 'as to the consulate, he distributes it'; also Radice in the Loeb edition, 490 n. 2.

[47] Discussed in Cizek (1983) 168 ff., and Waters (1969). See also Scott (1936) 111.

concern for senatorial protocol upon his accession,[48] and of course
the issue of *libertas* itself, which for all Pliny's rhapsodizing may have
amounted to little other than the check inflicted on the informers.[49]

Nor were the only problems those of subject matter. The speaker
himself must have provided a disabling handicap in the areas of
gratitude and sincerity, for Pliny was no victim of Domitian's régime,
pose among the liberated though he might. Our encomiast was in the
uncomfortable position of owing his career to the man he designated
monster: his official advancement was rapid and marked by signs of
imperial favor.[50] Pliny reached the quaestorship (probably in AD 89)
through imperial commendation, not election, and was one of the two
such officials whose task it was to communicate Domitian's desires to
the senate. Syme paints a vivid picture of the hypocrisies of this
situation:

> When the quaestor recited the imperial dispatches to the sad submissive
> senators, they endured the hollow phrases of deference, the dishonest
> asseveration of their collective loyalty and patriotism . . . Pliny has not
> chosen to tell how he fared during his uncomfortable apprenticeship in
> the arts and hypocrisies of public life. It was no bad training for one who
> hoped in due course to compose and deliver his own speech of thanks-
> giving to Caesar. (Syme 1958, 76)

This office was followed by the tribunate of the plebs, and then,
probably in AD 93, the praetorship—unusually rapid progress, thanks
to imperial dispensation.[51] Yet the year 93 also saw the deaths of

---

[48] Cf. Syme (1958) 16: 'Trajan made no haste to show himself to senate and People,
the ostensible and legal sources of the imperial authority'; he did not arrive in Rome
until about a year later. Cizek (1983) 195 makes little of this.

[49] As argued by Allain (1901–2), I.267–8, cited in Hammond (1938) 128. See also
Syme (1958) 12 n. 5, on the contradiction of the literary and numismatic evidence,
one touting *libertas*, the other *imperium*. Gianotti (1979) 76 is likewise sceptical about
the quality of the new *libertas*.

[50] In general, see Orentzel (1980); Sherwin-White (1966) 72–82; Soverini (1989)
522–35; Syme (1958) 72–82 with apps. 17 and 19. The brief summary of Pliny's career
that follows leans heavily on Syme's discussion at 76–7. Orentzel (1980) 51 sums up
Pliny's progress as follows: 'Pliny enjoyed Domitian's favour, since he was rapidly
advanced in the *cursus honorum* and participated in the one known extortion trial of
Domitian's reign [*Letters* 7.33].' Sherwin-White (1966) 74 likewise emphasizes the
crucial role of imperial favour in Pliny's rise: 'The exceptional circumstance in Pliny's
case was the continuous *suffragatio* of Domitian. Hence the rapidity of his rise from
quaestorship to praetorship, after a late start for reasons unknown.'

[51] The date of the praetorship has implications for the truth of Pliny's claim that
his career was halted late in Domitian's reign. See Soverini's discussion of the

several members of the senatorial opposition and the banishment of the professional philosophers, and Pliny transforms this year into the watershed of his career. It is a period during which (he claims) he narrowly escaped the imperial thunderbolts that heaped up around him the corpses of his friends (*Pan.* 90.5); it was a period which brought home to him the cost of further office. And thus he skirts the issue of his advancement by imposing on it a temporal limit. Admitting that he was helped in his career 'by that most [168] treacherous *princeps*, before he avowed his hatred of decent men' (95.3), he claims that after the emperor took a turn for the vicious in AD 93, he voluntarily put a stop to advancement and disdained foul shortcuts to status.[52] After this, there was only the struggle for survival and a narrow escape thanks to Domitian's assassination in September of AD 96, for in his desk was found information laid against Pliny that would surely have caused his death (*Letters* 4.24.4–5, 7.27.14).[53] And now that the tyrant is dead and gone, Pliny confesses as the *Panegyricus* draws to a close that 'I love the best of emperors as much as I was hated by the worst' (95.4).

Yet Pliny's distinction between his situations of pre- and post-AD 93 is not only artificial; it is false. True, he evaded the thunderbolts of an enraged despot, but he not only *evaded* them; as Syme observes, 'in fact, he prospered. With scarcely any delay, Pliny is discovered in possession of a fresh office, as one of the three prefects in charge of the *aerarium militare* (not a word about this anywhere in his letters). The post was praetorian in rank, triennial in nature. Few senators were fortunate enough to obtain it straight from the praetorship (1958, 77). Pliny was one of the fortunate few, a fact that wreaks irreparable harm on his narrative of sorrow and disfavour after

---

scholarship in (1989) 524–33; Soverini himself agrees with Mommsen's (1868–9) date of AD 93, also supported by Syme (1958) 656, and Sherwin-White (1966) 763 ff. For Pliny's cooperation with so tainted a Domitianic figure as Regulus, see Sherwin-White (1966) 96, on Pliny *Letters* 1.5.4 and 1.20.14.

[52] Bruyère (1954) 168 thinks these words refer to the prosecution of Baebius Massa, proconsul of Baetica, in AD 93 and not to the fall of Herennius Senecio, Helvidius Priscus, Iunius Rusticus, et al. It is difficult to see why, since Pliny was the *prosecutor* in Massa's case and also protested against his retaliatory impeachment of Pliny's co-prosecutor Senecio. See Pliny *Letters* 7.33.4 ff.

[53] Cizek (1983) 152 n. 107, believes in Pliny's danger and thinks his participation in the prosecution of Baebius Massa may have contributed; Hammond (1938) 129 suggests Pliny's support of the exiled philosopher Artemidorus but is somewhat sceptical; Syme (1958) 82 justly doubts the very existence of the letter in the drawer.

AD 93.[54] It is a rewriting of the recent past of which Adalberto Giovannini makes short work:

> [Pliny] admits in his *Letters* (7.16.2) and in the *Panegyricus* (95.3) that he advanced in his career under Domitian, but he claims at the same time that he put a halt to it once the emperor had revealed his hatred of good men ... But we know that in this respect [Pliny's 'danger' in the last years of Domitian], at any rate, Pliny is not speaking the truth: on his own telling [*Letters* 3.11.2–3], the Stoic opposition was condemned before or during his praetorship—a fact that did not hinder him from afterward assuming the very respectable office of prefect of the *aerarium militare*, a favor that he is careful not to mention to us. The fact is that Domitian backed Pliny's career right to the end and that Pliny did nothing, even in the final years, to evade it. (Giovaninni 1987, 233) [**169**]

Giovannini goes on to point out that Pliny would have good reasons to gloss over this appointment in subsequent years (238–9). As prefect of the military treasury, Pliny would have certified the legality of wills and received fiscal delations, so that if Domitian did persecute the upper classes out of personal hostility and for infusions into the treasury, Pliny is concealing the distinct smear of his complicity.[55] His vehement denigration of one emperor, his eagerness to praise the other, the claim that earlier adulation was role-playing, present adulation truth, all take on the discoloured patina of a situation compromised not only by the public transcripts of the past but also by personal history.[56]

---

[54] Syme (1958) 82 observes that 'the chance survival of authentic evidence, disclosing the prefecture of the *aerarium militare*, blows away the orator's assertion that he called a halt in his career'.

[55] Bowersock confirms and comments upon this perspective in the discussion following Giovannini's paper; see Giovannini (1987) 241.

[56] See Waters (1970) 63 'Pliny, who like Tacitus owed his earlier advancement in his public career to the Domitianic administration, and his later elevation to Trajan, with brazen shamelessness sang the praises of Trajan by the method of inversion, contrasting everywhere the vices and inadequacies he attributed to Domitian with their shining counterparts in the new *princeps*'. Giovannini (1987) 240 supplies similar commentary. And the observations of Syme (1958) 541 on the Pliny of the 'carefully contrived' *Letters* are apposite indeed: 'Parading candour, and not loath to be thought guileless, the author plays down that alert ambition which brought success swift and resplendent'. On this topic, see also the excellent article of Shelton (1987). Is it possible that the strong reaction against Pliny in the senate which he describes in *Letters* 9.13 could be a response to this hypocrisy—Pliny acts as turncoat, while others live and let live? On his self-avowed opportunism, see 9.13.2: 'Upon Domitian's

If Pliny's complicity in events of the recent past contributes to the particular concerns of this work and to the speaker's efforts to establish the sincerity of his content, other factors that are more directly the product of its history and of all prior praises of emperor play into the undermining effect exerted by this history and this past and illuminate, like Pliny's defence against the déjà vu of encomium, further modes of interpretation available to his contemporaries. Particularly important here is the familiarity of Pliny's senatorial and imperial audience with a discourse that plays on the slippery slope of praise and blame, namely, what we have been calling doublespeak. This doublespeak historically can appear under two guises; in both cases, it involves language taken over from imperial ideology or from the public transcript that lends itself to interpretation in a negative as well as a positive light. This may result because specific terms of praise encourage interpretation as their literal opposites (this is Pliny's fear, that generosity will stand in for meanness) or because such terms hint at a critical twist on their normal meaning, with the result that the positive term *generosity* stands in for the negative term *profligacy*, or *frugality* for *meanness*. The difference here, to be sure, is not great, for the crucial point remains the same: *terms of praise lend themselves to interpretation as blame.* Doublespeak in both cases is the use of the public (imperial) transcript in a way that destabilizes the positive content of that transcript.

This potential oscillation between the positive and the negative is [170] a factor I have referred to already in a kind of shorthand as the existence of the praise/blame axis: that is, the tendency for terms of praise and blame to be liable to slippage and thus to mean their opposites or their negative counterparts on one or another evaluative axis separating good qualities from bad. The praise/blame axis is thus characterized by the potential for coalescence into unity of contrasting value-terms, so that eulogy and satire can appear in the same garb, displacing the distinction between the two into a realm that is *interpretive* and not lexical. And when Pliny denies his deployment of doublespeak and appeals to his audience to confirm that denial, his words reveal precisely this semantic indeterminacy. I quote again the crucial passage at the beginning of the *Panegyricus*:

murder, I decided with some thought that this was a great and fine opportunity for attacking the guilty, avenging the wretched, and advancing myself'.

> There is no risk that when I speak of [Trajan's] civility, he will think his
> arrogance is being reproached; his profligacy, when I talk of his frug-
> ality; his cruelty, when I speak of his clemency; his greed, when I speak
> of his generosity; his malice, when I speak of his kindness; his lust, when
> I speak of his self-control; his laziness, when I speak of his work; his
> cowardice, when I speak of his courage. (3.4)

We have here a performative attempt to deny the risk of slippage and
a response to the existence of the praise/blame axis as an interpretive
tool among the community of listeners. Saying, in effect, that 'there is
no danger that Trajan will see my language as veiled, my signifiers as
having dual signifieds,' Pliny illustrates that danger and discloses the
potential for his praise to be understood as its opposite.

If we look for external evidence of this praise/blame axis in the
literary testimony of Greek and Roman culture, we find that a similar
feature had been a topic of rhetorical theory since the days of Aristotle
(most often in its guise as a slippage between positive qualities and
their negative correlates rather than their opposites). The discussions
of the technique for praise and blame that occur at Aristotle *Rhetoric*
1367a33–b3, Anon. *Ad Herennium* 3.3.6, and Quintilian *Institutio
oratoria* 3.7.25 all demonstrate an awareness that the terms [171] of
flattery and slander are closely related and can substitute for each
other depending on the speaker's immediate goal: it is possible to
blacken a man's character by transforming laudatory character traits
into their negative versions, and to whitewash it in turn by renaming
his vices as the corresponding virtues. In Aristotle's formulation,

> Assume that the characteristics close to the actual characteristics [of the
> person described] are the same for the purpose of praise and blame
> both; for example, that a cautious person is 'indifferent and calculating',
> a simple-minded one 'good-hearted', or an unemotional person 'gentle';
> and [when praising] use in each case a term from those that are
> adjacent, always according to the best sense; for example, call an
> irascible and impassioned man 'frank' and an arrogant one 'great-
> hearted' and 'noble' and treat those with excessive qualities as having
> virtues, so that the foolhardy man is 'brave' and the profligate one
> 'generous'. (*Rh.* 1367a33–63)

The flexibility of this kind of language depends on the positive or
negative portrayal of a *single* characteristic, while Pliny's practice
deals with praise terms that conceal their literal opposites. Yet both
practices share the feature that concerns us here: the possibility for a

term of praise to represent a term of blame. Both Quintilian and the author of the *Ad Herennium* offer a version that is derivative of Aristotlc's, although Quintilian is quick to add that this is not a technique for adoption by the morally impeccable orator who is his ideal: '[Aristotle] also teaches . . . that since there is a certain proximity between virtues and vices, we must exploit the close divergence in the sense of words so as to call a man "brave" instead of rash, "generous" instead of profligate, "sparing" instead of stingy; and these [critical] words can also have the opposite force. An orator (that is, a good man), will never do this unless he is led to by the common good' (*Inst.* 3.7.25).[57] Elsewhere in Quintilian we find the tactic named: it is *distinctio*, or, in Greek, *paradiastole*, a technique 'by which similar items are distinguished [as in this phrase]: "when you [172] call yourself wise instead of cunning, brave instead of rash, mindful instead of stingy"' (9.3.65).[58]

However, these rhetorical guidelines for praising the blameworthy and slandering the meritorious differ from the *Panegyricus* in a more important respect, that of how the audience's role and the relation of audience to speaker are understood. Pliny expresses a fear that the audience, *despite* his praise of the emperor, will interpret the approbative terms he uses as their opposites along that axis of corresponding virtues and vices, precisely as if secretly complicit in an act of doublespeak; or that his other audience, Trajan himself, will believe his intention is to encourage such a reading. His effort to stabilize the meaning of his praise-terms is a response to this possibility. On the other hand, the passages in Aristotle, Quintilian, and the *Ad Herennium* imply not the audience's complicity at the level of an underlying meaning but their deception at the level of the literal meaning, and the point here is to win belief for one's spoken misrepresentation of the positive or negative qualities inherent in the person praised or

---

[57] The treatment at *Ad Her.* 3.3.6 is slightly different from that of Aristotle and Quintilian, since it emphasizes the overturning of the language of one's court opponent, albeit by the same process of supplying synonyms with negative connotation: 'Likewise, we will show (if at all possible) that what our opponent calls "justice" is actually idleness and sloth and misguided generosity; we will say that what he calls "good sense" is a silly, garrulous, and despicable cleverness; we will say that what he calls "self-restraint" is sloth, and dissolute carelessness; we will call what he identifies as "bravery," a thuggish and injudicious rashness'.

[58] Further on *distinctio*, see *Inst.* 9.3.82. Practice rather than theory is famously illustrated by Thuc. 3.82.

blamed. The distinction between the two situations thus lies partly in the speaker's control over his audience: whereas praise and blame are understood in both cases to be closely related and easily transformed into their opposites, in Pliny's situation those with the power to effect this transformation are in the audience, and his denial of this possibility is performative rather than descriptive (it tries to control what happens by saying it); in the rhetorical treatments, on the other hand, it is the speaker who is the manipulator of representation.

This distinction changes when we turn to Quintilian's contemporary, Plutarch. In an essay on the dangers of flattery, Plutarch too addresses the topic of the proximity of terms of praise and blame, but he does so from the perspective not of the orator transforming the traits of his subject but rather of the recipient of flattery himself, who should be on guard against a praise that can only blind him to his weaknesses and foster a harmful self-indulgence. Beware those who would transform your faults into virtues, Plutarch urges: 'In [173] the case of flattery, one must look out and guard against profligacy called "generosity," and cowardice called "caution," capriciousness called "sharpness of wit," stinginess called "prudence," the lustful man called "companionable and affectionate," the irascible and arrogant man called "brave," and the worthless and humble one "kindly"' (*De adulatore et amico* 56C). Plutarch in fact closely describes what Pliny claims he is *not* doing. We can almost imagine Pliny unnerved before his speech by a chance sighting of Plutarch's essay in the emperor's hands: the essayist warns against flatterers who out of self-interest redesignate the recipient's vices as virtues, and Pliny appeals to Trajan to reject this interpretation of his own praise. Significantly enough, Plutarch's examples here are set in the context of subordinates interacting with emperors and tyrants—Dionysius II of Sicily, Ptolemy Philopator of Egypt, and Nero at Rome, among others. Here, then, the cultural background to Pliny's anxieties once again emerges, woven as it is out of a discourse about rulers and eulogists that strips bare the shifting mechanisms of praise and blame;[59] and we can see the makings of a situation in which these mechanisms spiral out of

---

[59] It is interesting that Suetonius' *Lives* are organized around a similar conception of corresponding virtues and vices. 'Each virtue/vice category applies as it were a litmus test. A good emperor will show up positively on the tests of clemency, civility, liberality and continence, a tyrant negatively on the same test', Wallace-Hadrill (1983) 144. With such an understanding of the relationship of specific virtues and vices, movement between the two becomes a simple step.

177 The Art of Sincerity: Pliny's Panegyricus

control, in which the best efforts of the praiser are always already suspect in the eyes of the imperial recipient. Under such circumstances, as Frank Whigham notes, 'the harder an individual tries to turn the system to his own advantage, the more quickly he undercuts its power. The kaleidoscopic relations between praise and blame, flattery and slander finally shift uncontrollably at every turn'.[60]

Further testimony comes from Dio Chrysostomus, rhetorician and orator, contemporary of Pliny, and a fellow eulogist—not only are the first four of his *Discourses* entitled *On Kingship* but the first and third are addressed like the *Panegyricus* to Trajan himself and are equally fulsome. Like Pliny, Dio flatters Trajan and vilifies Domitian;[61] perhaps Dio's banishment by the latter had some hand here, and indeed, it is interesting to note that the man's boast, unlike Pliny's, is that he never flattered the hated tyrant (*Or.* 13.12–13, 45.1, 50.8).[62] Reading his speech *Diogenes, or On Tyranny*, in which the [174] figure of the Persian king Darius Codomannus stands as an allegory for Domitian

---

[60] Whigham (1984) 42. This quotation is taken from a passage worth quoting in full for its insightful analysis of the instability of the praise/blame axis once both emperor and panegyricist are aware of its existence: 'As the theoretical force of the audience response becomes increasingly valorized, so the need grows for reactive and self-protective (and paranoid) interpretation. Self-judgement is undercut, but so too is audience response, when both audience and performer are ruled by the self-serving prescriptions of courtesy. When all audience members are also performers, [audience] judgements become performances and are subject to reinterpretive pressures. The result is an inversely proportionate relation between the intensity of self-projection and the reliability of audience reaction. The harder an individual tries to turn the system to his own advantage, the more quickly he undercuts its power. The kaleidoscopic relations between praise and blame, flattery and slander finally shift uncontrollably at every turn.' There is also a sense in which this phenomenon corresponds to what Goffman (1969) 69 has called 'the degeneration of assessment,' a 'demoralizing oscillation of interpretation' that results when the speaker knows his words may be examined with distrust by his audience but cannot try to counter this suspicion without increasing the appearance of guilt. As Whigham (1984) 60 adds, 'in such a universe of interpretation, the decision as to where to stop will be based not on rigorous epistemological concerns but on political affiliations'.

[61] Jones (1978) 118, notes the similarities between the speeches of the two and observes that 'these coincidences between Pliny and . . . [Dio] suggest that they are prompted by more than common friendship with Trajan. There is no evidence that one influenced the other; rather, they express the ideology of a particular time'. This is exactly right: both are mouthpieces for the public transcript. See further Fedeli (1989) 433 and Moles (1990) 301 ff. Whether or not Dio Chrysostomus' first and third speeches really were delivered in front of Trajan, as they purport to have been, is impossible to ascertain. On the *Orations on Kingship* in general, see Moles (1990).

[62] But Jones (1978) 50 points out that 'either this claim is grossly exaggerated or almost all of these works [critical of Domitian] have perished'.

himself, we encounter a passage that is telling for the prevalence of
the praise/blame axis as an interpretive construct in Pliny's own
culture and times; Diogenes, describing the bind that traps all who
have dealings with a tyrant (for flattery and frankness alike are
dangerous in such a situation), points out that the danger of praise
lies in the interpretation tendered it by the imperial interlocutor: 'If
someone should converse with him boldly, he gets angry and fears
such frankness. But if they do so flattering and fawning, he is suspicious of the flattery. And he thinks he is being insulted by those who
approach him freely, but deceived by those who approach him humbly . . . And when he is praised he does not take pleasure in it. For he
thinks that the speakers do not really mean it' (6.57–59). Dio's tyrant
cannot accept words of praise because he sees in them their opposites:
suspecting that all flattery is really deception, he cannot believe in the
sincerity of the speaker, who is left with precious little recourse for
any safe interchange at all. As Dio recognizes, to praise and to deceive
by praise are closely related activities.[63] It seems they oscillate along
an axis that must find fixity, if at all, through its extratextual context
rather than through its own content.

Nor is it only in the *Panegyricus* that Pliny himself shows his
awareness of the subordinate's access to a language that mocks and
denies even as it seems to praise.[64] In *Letters* 8.6 he denounces with

---

[63] As Martindale (1984) 67–8 rightly observes in an article on the flattering proem
to Lucan's *Bellum Civile*, 'there is a narrow dividing line between extravagant praise
and satire, a fact recognized in the eighteenth century, an age more attuned to
panegyric than our own . . . Lucan might have taken advantage of this doubleness,
which was widely recognized in antiquity'. In fact Lucan's praise of Nero in the
opening lines of the poem is exactly a praise that does double duty as blame, and
like other examples of doublespeak it can function as such (1) through its invocation
of *quinquennium* propaganda (cf. Heldmann (1982) 280: 'An essential means of irony
is, as has long been recognized, the uncritical and often exaggerated use of the languge
of state ideology') and (2) through its own context. As Due (1967) 102 notes, 'taken
together with the rest of the poem the Nero-proem is an absurdity, and that is the
point'. On the proem and the (misleading) question of its sincerity, see especially Due
(1967) and the bibliography in Bartsch (1994) ch. 3, n. 13.

[64] Mockery leaves the praiser with some measure of power, some distance from
engrossment in the public transcript that he reproduces. In an age in which *maiestas*
extended to language, the praise/blame axis, and doublespeak in general, thus provided an attractive safeguard of personal integrity—as emperors also knew. The
remarks of Goffman (1967) 58, are pertinent: 'By easily showing a regard that he
does not have, the actor can feel that he is preserving a kind of inner autonomy,
holding off the ceremonial order by the very act of upholding it'. Along these lines, cf.
Juvenal *Sat.* 4.69–71: a fisherman bearing a gift flatters Domitian by claiming that the

great indignation the excessive honours once voted to Claudius' secretary *a rationibus*, a freedman called Pallas, by a cowardly and fawning senate and thereafter recorded for posterity's scorn. Not content to offer Pallas a large sum of money and the *ornamenta praetoria*, the senators even thanked the emperor for allowing them to demonstrate their appreciation and went on to bestow upon that ex-slave—'most faithful, most abstemious custodian of the imperial finances,' in the words of their own decree (8.6.7)—a public commemoration for his loyalty and industry. Pliny, who has just consulted this senatorial decree, finds such praise too much to swallow and asks his correspondent in rhetorical umbrage, 'should I consider the men who [175] decreed these measures witty or wretched? I would say witty, if wit suited the senate' (8.6.3). Of course, we are meant to understand that the senate was all too far from mockery in the guise of praise. More important here, however, is Pliny's proposal of this unstable contrast of *urbanitas/miseria*, where the same language of praise can fall on either side of the divide between wit and degradation:[65] it is a configuration in which blame follows as the corollary of wit even as degradation attends upon praise.

In the instability of the praise/blame axis, then, we find another counter to Pliny's efforts at semantic determinism.[66] As Whigham notes of the workings of this contamination of opposites, which he

---

fish itself wanted to be caught; the satirist's comment is 'What could be more obvious? and yet/his crest rose up like a rooster's. There's nothing/that power equal to the gods won't believe of itself when praised'. Dio Cassius notes that if anyone bestows great praise on a trivial exploit, the individual praised suspects his exploit is being mocked (59.25.2). In Tacitus' works, on the other hand, the subordinate's flattery is almost always a sign of compulsion and fear, not of a language that reserves some power still for itself. See Bartsch (1994) ch. 3, n. 4.

[65] Pliny goes on to pose another rhetorical question about the senators' motivation, suggesting ambition and the desire for advancement as reasons for such excess, and thus demonstrating that flattery of a ruler need not always be represented as an act of coercion. 'Was it ambition, then, and the lust for advancement? But who is so deranged as to want to advance by means of personal and public disgrace, in a state in which exalted rank provided the privilege of being able to be the first to praise Pallas in the senate?'

[66] Important rhetorical testimony about the praise/blame axis also comes from Demetrius *On Style* (for the dating of this work, see Bartsch (1994) ch. 3, n. 74): 'Often, however, words say the opposite thing at the same time, and if anyone should wish to reproduce this effect and have his censure appear accidental, there is the model of what Aeschines says against Telauges. For almost all of his narration about Telauges *leaves one at a loss as to whether it is admiration or mockery*. This ambiguous usage, although it is not irony, nonetheless has a certain hint of irony in it' (291).

names (not quite accurately) by Quintilian's term *paradiastole*, 'this master trope governs evaluation, positing a matrix in which praise and blame, flattery and slander, interpenetrate absolutely...The matrix throws all such questions into a realm of politically determined textuality'.[67] In the case of the *Panegyricus*, the imbrication of the languages of praise and blame, already in place among the interpretive strategies of the imperial audience, displaces the burden of sincerity from the speaker and his words (including all his efforts to control the location of this burden) and transforms it into a question dependent on political context: do the participants *know* that this occasion can bear the weight of its clichéd and repetitious language and rise beyond it into a communication that inspires belief? It is a difficult question to answer; the context already bears the stigma of unequal power relations not only past but present, the stigma of the speaker's complicity in that past, the stigma of a praise that comes too early in the ruler's career to be able to be more than a wish. True, the pointlessness of a panegyric that does not announce itself as sincere spurs Pliny's attempt to drive a stake between the antitheses that are potentially synonyms. But he cannot control the fact that this scission itself enters into the play of the trope—that is, that protestations of frankness are themselves a form of flattery—and that his grand divide emerges framed by its context as a gesture that could, like all the other ones, point to its reverse.

Nor can Pliny control two other paradigms for interpretation that [176] are already in place in the minds of his audience in the senate house. One would make them conscious of a cardinal sign of despotic

---

Demetrius thus acknowledges that the same description can be taken as either admiration or mockery—praise or blame.

[67] Whigham (1984) 40–1. For further theoretical discussion, again on praise and blame in Elizabethan England, see Mullaney (1988) on 'amphibology'; also 107 with n. 49 in the same volume, where he notes the way the language of the law was appropriated by Elizabethan miscreants who turned it to their own use. This is 'the logic of Elizabethan thieves' cant, which customarily appropriated and inverted the official terms of authority in order to create an unauthorized but useful counterlanguage, one that could be spoken openly to hatch plots and devise stratagems without raising... suspicions' (I owe thanks to C. A. Gales [personal communication, June 1992] for this reference). Of some relevance here are also modern treatments of 'anti-language', the discourse of dissident subsets of a given society, such as the criminal class: 'Reversing the normal meanings of the words, the users of anti-language address the norm society dialectically. The rogues' *law*...works, semantically, [only] if the original meaning is not completely erased...Such words become the sites of dialogue between society and anti-society'; Fowler (1981) 149 and Halliday (1978).

power: the tyrant can measure his strength by his very ability to compel acts of praise from subordinates. Seen this way, praise involuntarily functions as a sign of the omnipotence of its addressee; and the more lavish the praise, the more the despot is marked as such. Such is the understanding of the workings of power that we find reproduced in Seneca's *Thyestes*. This is, not incidentally, a play whose author explicitly asserts the relationship between literary treatments of myth and the political conditions that produce them: Nero's erstwhile tutor comments of a line in Accius' tragedy *Atreus*—'Let them hate, so long as they fear'—that 'you would know it was written in the time of Sulla' (Sen. *De ira*, 1.20.4).[68] For his own play he offers a different formulation, as if to suggest, in an overturning of the public transcript of his own day, that 'you would know it was written in the time of *Nero*': the wish of Seneca's Atreus is to let them hate, so long as they *praise*. Plotting grisly revenge against Thyestes, he overrules a hireling's protests about public disapproval with a starker perspective on power:

> The greatest benefit of autocracy is this:
> the populace is forced equally to bear and to praise
> the actions of their ruler. (*Thyestes* 205–8)

The fact that fear induces hatred means little: as Atreus continues, 'true praise often befalls the lowly man too,/feigned praise only the powerful. Let them like what they don't!' (211–2). For this tyrant, then, praise works literally as the measure of power—especially false praise, for it marks the compulsion of the praiser and thereby the extent of the ruler's total control. Seneca anticipates Scott, who notes that 'ritual subservience reliably extracted from inferiors signals quite literally that there is no realistic choice other than compliance (Scott 1990, 66). And similarly, the tyrant of Epictetus' *Discourses* 1.19, titled *How to Behave to a Tyrant*, identifies his power by the volume of flattery he elicits from his subjects: when asked [177] 'What is the nature of your power?' he rejoins simply, 'All men flatter me' (1.19.4).

Lucan and Tacitus supply further examples of an understanding of praise that transforms it into a sign of the power of the recipient. The laments of the future captives of war in Lucan's *Bellum civile* expose the workings of flattery from the perspective of those who know what

---

[68] See Ahl (1976) 27, and Bartsch (1994) ch. 3, n. 53.

force will soon require of them. Lucan's Roman matrons know that once the victor has dictated the content of the public transcript, praise of the ruler becomes a necessary result of the 'truth' of that public transcript; it is a natural correlative of the 'fact' that the better man, the one worthy of praise, has won control.

> 'Now beat your breasts, wretched mothers', she said,
> 'Now tear your hair; do not put off this sorrow
> nor save it for the crowning ills. Now is there opportunity
> to weep, while the fate of the leaders is unsure; once either
> has won, you will have to rejoice.' (*Bellum civile* 2.38–42)

We find even a sense that flattery and insincerity are proportionate. Tacitus comments of the reaction to Galba's murder at the hands of the praetorians in January of AD 69, 'you would think it a different senate, a different populace . . . They inveighed against Galba, praised the soldiers' decision, kissed Otho's hand; and the more fake these actions were, the more they did them' (*Hist.* 1.45.1). As Paul Plass observes of this passage, 'the values that political hypocrisy reverses can safely be read backward: official zeal is a sign of dishonesty' (Plass 1988, 48). The frenzy to be sincere undermines itself, and effusive praise is a testimony to despotism despite the intentions of the speaker, which cannot have enough effect on the mien of his praise to counteract this problem of interpretation; as Scott puts it: 'one may curse such domination—in this case preferably offstage—but one will nevertheless have to accommodate oneself to its hard reality. The effect of reinforcing power relations in this way may be, behaviourally, nearly indistinguishable from behaviour that arises from willing consent'.[69] The imperial eulogist is at an impasse. [178]

The final interpretive paradigm that Pliny cannot control and that yet seems well ensconced in the culture of his audience is the retort from which frankness itself, and all reflexive references to frankness, emerge as a distillation of flattery. As one would expect, Pliny draws attention to his own frankness as speaker and claims at the outset of the *Panegyricus* that he is taking the path of free speech and

---

[69] Scott (1990) 67. Pliny determinedly underplays this spin on audience response when describing the reaction to his own recitations—at his readings of the revised *Panegyricus* attendance is high not through considerations of social hierarchy (or the subject matter!) but for sheer love of oratory. See *Letters* 3.18.4–7, where Pliny further uses this response to 'prove' that panegyric, 'once as hated as it was false, has now become as popular as it is true'.

truthfulness; in a formal opening invocation of Jupiter, he prays that 'everything I say be in accordance with freedom of speech, sincerity, and truth, and that my speech of thanks be as far from the appearance of flattery as it is from compulsion' (1.6).[70] The focus on frankness and the specific denial of flattery are attempts to fix the framework of his discourse by explicitly forestalling the possibility of flattery; such a focus, we may note, finds a parallel in Pliny's contemporary Dio Chrysostomus, who uses the topos in the third of his discourses on kingship addressed (like the *Panegyricus*) to Trajan himself. Early in this speech Dio praises the emperor for preferring frankness and truth over flattery and deceit (*Or.* 3.2) and, like Pliny, shows an obsession with 'proving' this frankness by comparative arguments based on the contrast of past and present.[71] As Dio argues, false flattery was a necessity under Domitian, but he spoke the truth even then and at the risk of his life; why would he engage in deceit now, when the truth is finally safe?[72]

> But there is no risk that I should appear to be speaking at all in flattery. For it is no small proof of outspokenness that I have given, nor a fleeting one. But if I alone dared to speak the truth in the past, when everyone thought it necessary to lie because of fear, and that at risk of my life, but now, when it is possible for all to speak the truth, I lie even though no danger is to hand, then I grasp the right occasion for neither frankness nor for flattery. (*Or.* 3.12–13)

Yet the different situations of the two eulogists makes Pliny's proof the more difficult: Dio has banishment to use as ballast, while Pliny can only claim that past praises of Domitian in which he too bears

---

[70] As Bardon (1940) 372, notes cynically of Pliny's freedom of speech, 'in the end, *libertas* is nothing but the right to flatter the ruler'.

[71] Dio Chrysostomus offers other elaborate 'proofs' that he is not engaging in flattery; for example, since the recipient of flattery is the one who best knows that what he hears are lies, what eulogist would be so stupid as to try to deceive his addressee on the topic of his own character? (*Or.* 3.19). This, of course, is an attempt to obliterate the very questions of power and self-interest that make flattery so suspect, and as Jones (1978) 119 notes with suitable scepticism, by Pliny and Dio's 'coincidences, among them their coinciding claims to frankness and spontaneity, they are revealed as the servants of his wishes'. On Dio's attitude toward flattery in this speech, see Moles (1990) 353–4. On the correspondences between the *Panegyricus* and the *Orations on Kingship* see Fedeli (1989) 433–5 and Trisoglio (1972).

[72] Jones (1978) 120 suggests that Dio's defensive tone in this eulogy has been spurred by criticisms of his earlier praises as precisely the false flattery he denies. See *Or.* 3.12–25 and 57.10.

[179] complicity were false, but this one is true. Under such circumstances the need to prove he is finally being frank becomes the more pressing and the goal more elusive: while the eulogist talks of frankness, the literary evidence of his contemporaries testifies to their sense that frankness *is* a species of flattery. Plutarch, for one, devotes a large portion of his essay *How to Tell a Flatterer from a Friend* to this subject, warning against the clever technique of flatterers who apply to their victims 'a frankness neither genuine nor helpful but one that winks from its scowl, so to speak, and merely titillates' (51D). These men flatter by using painless forms of criticism and so reap the benefits of frankness without applying its sting; observes Plutarch, 'understanding that frankness is a big help with respect to flattery, the wretches flatter by means of frankness itself' (61C).[73] Likewise, Tacitus in the *Annals* allows the 'frankness' that Plutarch warns against in daily life to reveal itself as corrupt in the political past, offering on this issue as on others a perspective whose persuasiveness lies in its unstated claim to strip from the public transcript its protective veils. When Valerius Messala suggests in the senate that the oath of allegiance to Tiberius be repeated annually, the emperor asks him 'whether he had made the proposal on Tiberius' instructions. He replied that he had spoken of his own accord and that in matters pertaining to the state he would rely only on his own opinion, even at the risk of giving offence. This was the sole form of flattery left' (*Ann.* 1.8.4).[74] 'Frankness' is merely the last development of an age saturated with flattery.[75]

And Pliny himself admits the paradox of such protestations. Giving advice to Vettenius Severus about the honorific measure on Trajan's behalf which, as consul-designate, he was expected to propose, Pliny describes his own course of action on an earlier similar occasion[76] as marked by a frankness aforethought:

---

[73] See also 59A ff. for a further exposé of the flatterer's crafty tactics and simulated severity.

[74] On talk of frankness as a form of flattery, see also Tac. *Ann.* 2.35.2.

[75] Lucan performs a similar operation on his subordinates' 'frank' reactions to Julius Caesar: pretending to rejoice over Pompey's death despite Caesar's 'grief', they 'dare' to be frank (that is, to disagree with Caesar's public reaction): 'They dare to gaze on bloody horror with happy mien/though Caesar mourns—O gracious freedom!' *Bellum civile* 9.1107–8. Note Lucan's sarcastic comment on this outspokenness: *o bona libertas* 'o great liberty'.

[76] 'This occasion was different from the *gratiarum actio* or Panegyric delivered on the day on which he entered office. It should be the session of *Pan.* 78, at which others urged Trajan to take a fourth consulship' Sherwin-White (1966) 387.

I wonder whether I should advise you to do the same as I. As consul-designate, I abstained from all appearance of flattery (even if it was not really flattery), not as if I were free-spoken and resolute, [180] but as if I understood our ruler's wishes: I saw that highest praise of him would be to say nothing as if through compulsion. I also remembered the numerous honorific speeches delivered to all his worst predecessors, from whom this best of rulers could be better separated in no other way than by the difference in my speech; which fact itself I did not pass over in dissimulation and silence, lest by chance it did not seem my decision but my forgetfulness [that was the cause]. (*Letters* 6.27.1–3)[77]

Pliny himself acknowledges here that the highest form of flattery is to appear to be frank. But if he avoids the appearance of flattery, *species adulationis*, it is to adopt instead the appearance of out-spokenness, *species libertatis*, as a specific stratagem for praise; he admits that his *libertas* is not real, that he does not speak 'as if I were free-spoken and resolute'. Moreover, he takes care to inform the recipient of his praise about his intentions in adopting this specious frankness: what a calamity if Trajan should misunderstand the fake frankness for the real thing and this modulation of more obvious methods should go unappreciated or cause offence! It seems that Pliny must remark on his abstention from flattery even as he abstains from it, lest such abstention be misunderstood as abstention rather than seen for the flattery it is. And yet this very letter is also a public document, and Pliny's revelations about the technique of 'frankness' come couched deep in the language of the *Panegyricus* itself—the 'best of rulers' is still to be separated from his predeces-sors, and the *Panegyricus* is still true because it is supposedly differ-ent—at the same time as he confesses to the concerns that dictate his interpretive controls in that document and admits the shadow cast by the spectre of praises past. In this letter we hear Pliny's own voice protest against the jaded understanding of the long-suffering sena-torial audience.

---

[77] The language of this passage is very strange; Pliny seems to say 'I abstained from all appearance of flattery, even if not from flattery itself'—certainly a more accurate description of the *Panegyricus*' technique, although it can scarcely be credible that we are meant to so understand it. See the interesting comment of Aubrion (1975) 108 n. 49.

III

The existence of these interpretive paradigms, and in particular of the problem of the praise/blame axis, has important consequences [181] for the language of the *Panegyricus*, replete as it is with moral and evaluative terms that so easily suffer slippage and corruption when uttered by an imperial eulogist. The result is that Pliny speaks in a language already, to the ears of his audience, whittled thin and stripped of the potential to make moral distinctions that have any credibility or resonance. But this is a linguistic bankruptcy that extends beyond the bounds of panegyric proper; it is a disease of the political discourse of the late first century, brought to its crisis point not only by the empty onslaughts of one wave of imperial ideology after another, but also by the merciless observations of those among the senatorial class who documented its progress— writers like Lucan and Tacitus, whose works constitute prolonged expositions of the loss of meaning suffered by value-terms through their usage in the ideology of the victors.[78] In the mouths of their historical figures, political rhetoric is repeatedly stripped bare, and once-idealistic words stand revealed as the manipulative tools of deception which they really are. As the legate Caesius Rufus Cerialis remarks in the *Histories* of the ethical vocabulary of the aggressor Germans, when they invade the Gallic provinces 'liberty and specious expressions serve as excuses; but no one has ever lusted to enslave others and win domination for himself without appropriating those same words' (*Hist.* 4.73.3). Similarly, Tacitus' Otho will denounce the self-serving moral terminology of the emperor Galba's public transcript: 'for what others call crimes, this man calls cures, while with false terms he names savagery severity, avarice frugality, punishment and insult discipline' (*Hist.* 1.37.4).[79] As Plass notes, Tacitus thus

[78] Henderson (1989) 173 on Tacitus: 'there is opened here the question whether in the shift from the Age of Kings to the Augustan Principate there is a place left for *libertas* and for *consulatus* to bear meaning or whether their future role in Imperial History is to be that of screens at the disposal of court protocol'.

[79] For a similar sense of the equation of ethical opposites, but in the author's own voice, see, e.g. Tac. *Hist.* 1.2.3, with a glance at Thuc. 3.82.2: 'Greater savagery took place in the capital: nobility, wealth, offices held or passed by were counted as a crime, and death was the most certain return for virtue'. On Tacitus' exposition of such 'fake political language' and further examples from the texts, see Plass (1988) 41–5 with nn. 31 and 33; Henderson (1989) 173 with n. 38; and Syme (1939) 149–61.

'quotes public language to bare its illusion', and when, for example, Otho 'appeals to his unruly soldiers to check their "bravery" and "virtue," both words are transparent and probably current euphemisms for "mutinous violence" (*Hist.* 1.83.2).'[80] Indeed, Plass persuasively argues that Tacitus' antithetical style is itself testimony to an awareness of the way political language masks its negative counterpart, since this style exposes the appropriation of positive terms to gloss over the abuse of power: 'because antitheses run in two directions, they [182] formally embody the historian's task of unmasking officially masked falsehood' (Plass 1988, 44). Political discourse thus loses its one essential trait, its ability to appeal to ideals larger than those who invoke them and that transform the structures of authority into institutions that seem both bearable and necessary.[81]

Nor must we rely only on Tacitus' late testimony for the sense that the self-justification of empire is hopelessly corrupted by the pliancy of ethical antitheses demonstrated in the public transcript of the rulers. Lucan's *Bellum civile* in its entirety is *about*, as well as reproduces, the oxymoronic equation of value-terms by the victors of war. Announcing its subject from the beginning as 'legality granted to crime' (2),[82] it consistently exploits paradox and antithesis to expose a world in which law and transgression are equated, thus making of its own rhetorical figures a comment on its subject matter. In Lucan's world, the world of civil war, Scaeva 'did not know how great a *crime* was *virtue/valour* in civil strife' (*qui nesciret, in armis/quam magnum virtus crimen civilibus esset*, 6.147–48), and the worst *punishment* is to be *pardoned* for defending your country (2.519–21), just as Tacitus' *Histories* expose the prevalence of a twisted language by which men can be 'convicted' of loyalty (*Hist.* 1.59.1, 1.71.2; compared by Plass (1988, 47)). As John Henderson points out in his difficult but brilliant essay on the *Bellum civile*, 'All Caesar's victories over Roman discourse . . . are warped *pari passu* with their narration by Lucan's catachresis, turning *virtus* to *crimen* and *nefas*, satirically exposing the appropriation of war as "Justice" (*iudice bello*, 1.227) in a

---

[80] Plass (1988) 46. Malissard (1990) 218 comments suggestively of the *Annals'* characters that 'they live, then, in a universe where fundamental notions such as liberty, love, or truth serve as a paper-maché stage set and are reduced to *simulacra*'.

[81] See especially Rodgers (1987) 5.

[82] Cf. Henderson (1987) 134 'the epic must despite its own best efforts tell of a *virtus* it knows to be *crimen* and *scelus*.'

totalising push toward a general subversion of cultural values, of *greatness* and *goodness*' (1987, 139). Such catachresis reduces opposites to synonyms, makes meaning dependent on the self-serving dictates of political power; it is exactly right to say, as does W. R. Johnson, that in Lucan's world—as in Tacitus'—'the condition of the *humanum genus* has become so debased that words such as *freedom* and *slavery* have become irrelevant and meaningless', and that his antithetical and epigrammatic style—like Tacitus'—is suited to, reproduces, and thereby exposes, 'the world of official imperial [183] history... where truths are decomposed (synthesized) into their opposites, into that identity of opposites where masters become slaves and slaves become masters, where freedom becomes slavery and slavery becomes freedom'.[83]

Even so brief a glance at two works of senatorial hand, one produced in the generation before that of Pliny, one written by his contemporary a decade after the publication of the *Panegyricus*, illuminates the existence of a strain of thinking that is well aware of how terms of value judgment usually designating opposites along a moral scale can be collapsed into single words, so that legality and crime are equated, liberty is a specious name for oppression, virtue deserves punishment. This is an approach intent on exposing the warping effect of political power on ethical language: exposé as act of resistance and counterideology. We can now see that Pliny's mission in the *Panegyricus* is, quite to the contrary, to *reinstall the differences* between such terms, to make antonyms of concepts merged by the linguistic distortions of power. And he appeals for our collaboration in his project: 'You are aware that just as tyranny and principate are different by nature, so too a *princeps* is most gratifying to those who chafe most under a tyrant' (*Pan.* 45.3). Principate and tyranny, Tacitean synonyms, are carefully peeled apart, in language if not in fact. Likewise senators and *delatores* ('informers') are carefully placed in opposite camps. Describing the punishment of the latter at 35.2, Pliny sets up a mutually exclusive contrast between the two groups, the one rejoicing as the other meets its just deserts: 'a throng of [exiled] informers filled all the islands that recently the throng of [exiled] senators had filled'. Yet many informers of the recent past

---

[83] Johnson (1987) 55. On the appropriation of the same ideology by opposing sides in the civil wars at Rome (esp. of AD 68–9), see Jal (1963).

were senators[84]—an uncomfortable truth that Pliny glosses over, choosing instead to set up a false antithesis that renders black and white the grey world of senatorial complicity. Likewise, when he specifies of Trajan that 'we are not discussing a tyrant, but a fellow citizen, not a master, but a father' (*Pan.* 2.3), Pliny tries to transform into antonyms terms that the propaganda of the public transcript had been allowing (despite itself) to be stripped of their difference since [184] the days of Augustus, that *pater patriae* ('father of the country');[85] and our much-quoted list of Trajanic qualities at 3.4 is a similar series of separations. Even when Trajan actually duplicates a policy of Domitian's, Pliny must as it were insert a difference. Domitian banished the pantomimes; recalled by Nerva, they were banished yet again by Trajan. So Pliny observes, '[Nerva and Trajan] acted rightly in both cases: for it was correct to restore those whom a bad ruler had banished and to banish those who had been restored' (46.3).[86] Our eulogist is constantly making such distinctions; to separate terms shown up as too synonymous by the discourse of political cynicism, he imposes false splits and opposed categories wherever he can. And as I have noted, the *Panegyricus* itself rests on the foundation of such a separating move: past and present are firmly, even obsessively severed, kept apart so that in their distance they may safely be invested with meanings immune to merging.[87]

---

[84] As Radice comments in the Loeb edition, naming Catullus Messalinus, Aquilius Regulus, and Mettius Carus; Fabricius Veiento is another example.
[85] *Pater patriae*, of course, is applied in Statius and Martial to Domitian; once parent, now tyrant.
[86] Cf. Syme (1938) 223–4: 'To sharpen the necessary contrast between good emperors and bad, no device was too trivial, no sophistry too transparent. Domitian abolished pantomimes: permitted again by Nerva, they were forbidden by Trajan. Pliny was equal to the theme—*utrumque recte; nam et restitui oportebat, quos sustulerat malus princeps et tolli restitutos* ('both right; for it was right for what a bad emperor had suppressed to be restored and for had been restored to be suppressed', *Pan.* 46.3). The government is always right. It is indeed fitting that Pliny should stand at the head of the *Panegyrici veteres*. They even surpass him in the technique of *utrumque recte* or 'having things both ways'.' One is inclined here to sympathize with the indignant protest of Hartman (1916) 367: 'Doesn't it occur to those who read such things to wonder which other of Domitian's many good policies were twisted into bad ones by those who criticized him and praised Trajan?'
[87] Many of these distinctions are collected in Fedeli (1989); see, e.g. 482–4 on *princeps* vs. *dominus* (an antithesis also used by Dio Chrysostomus in the Hercules myth of the first *Oration on Kingship*). Exactly as Aubrion (1975) 108 remarks, 'Pliny [in contrast to Tacitus] contrasts *humanitas* and *superbia, frugalitas* and *luxuria,*

If this feature of the *Panegyricus* is at all an antidote to some sense, on the part of both speaker and audiences, that 'the power of language to normalize by naming' has been abrogated forever by the distorting pull of ideology,[88] Pliny claims to be able to retrieve this determinacy of terms; he claims that it *is* retrievable given the *libertas* of the times. But of course it is *libertas* itself, that most value-laden of political shibboleths, that has been so thoroughly emptied of normalized meaning by prior usage; and so it seems the problem of the *Panegyricus* remains unaltered. For all its effort, it is a self-defeating exercise, 'You cannot order men to love you', says Pliny; he might well have said of frankness, 'you cannot order men to speak sincerely'. Yet we might note that Pliny has no difficulty with similar utterances that seem entirely paradoxical in their contradiction of this commonsense position: 'You order us to be free, and—we will!' he exults (*Pan.* 66.4).[89] This promise can be read in two ways: as a stark indictment of Pliny's speech, which betrays itself as that most paradoxical of projects, a strategy for sincerity; or else as an indication of why the problem of the *Panegyricus* really is not a problem. It is possible that the modern impulse to write off the *Panegyricus* as [185] not only excessive but also ineffectual in the manifest gulf between what it says it does and what it actually does is misguided; that our own interpretive lens is focused too sharply on issues that would win less attention on the occasion of its delivery; that it is not the doing but the saying which counts.

Pliny, we recall, lives in a world in which the perspectives of a Tacitus and a Lucan are possible, where it is just conceivable that the familiar ethical terms and the words upon which rest a whole

---

clementia and *crudelitas*, etc. only in order to affirm the perfect coincidence of language and reality'.

[88] The phrase is Henderson's comment on the style, and indeed the effect, of the *Bellum civile*; (1987) 135.

[89] Similarly at *Pan.* 67.2: 'And every time we make trial of the liberty he has given us, he will know that we obey him.' On the thematic contrast of *libertas/dominatio* see Fedeli (1989) 480–2 (suitably sceptical). See also Epictetus *Discourses* 4.1.14, who reproduces this paradox to show up men who are still slaves: 'By Caesar's fortune, we are free.' Morford (1992) 590, reprinted above ch. 7, tries to salvage the situation: 'These words, which on a superficial reading might seem to be ironic or ridiculous, attempt to express a definition of *libertas* within the confines of the unequal relationship of *princeps* and senate'.

culture's concept of political morality no longer have a fixed signifier-signified relation to the values they used to represent but now provide an empty nomenclature for ideas largely devoid of meaning; terms like *libertas* ('liberty'), *servitium* ('slavery'), *ius* ('law'), *crimen* ('crime'), *princeps* ('emperor'), *dominus* ('master') all supply a linguistic shroud for the slow corruption of their own content—and finally, for the absence of that content. Repeated in the public transcript of one regime after another, they become meaningless as the supremely good ruler too often reveals himself supremely corrupt, but official reality remains fixed nonetheless in the discourse of moral approbation. As I have argued, Pliny's own discourse, his efforts at authenticity, are in part a response to this evolution; rejecting or resolutely ignoring the instability of ethical language, our senatorial panegyricist, like other 'ideologists of representation' (the term is that of Dolan 1991), offers reassurance 'that the recovery of representation, the equation of sign and thing, of public and private, is still possible'. Pliny responds to what Jean Baudrillard has called the hallmark of an era of simulation: 'Simulation ... takes its departure from *the radical negation of the sign as value*, from the sign as inversion and assassination of all references' (1981, 16; original emphasis). For such an era inspires strategies to re-establish the real, to prove the sincerity of one's intentions, to demonstrate the authenticity of discourse and one's meaning. 'Once the real is no longer what it was, nostalgia takes on its full meaning. Ever-increasing myths of origin and of signs of reality; ever-increasing bids for truth, and for objectivity and authenticity next ... A crazed production of the real and the referential ... such does simulation [186] appear in the phase that concerns us—as a strategy of the real, of the neo-real and of the hyper-real' (Baudrillard 1981, 17). And indeed, Pliny's response to his times engages all manner of strategies to deny this collapse of signification—at least for the limited arena of his own speech—and to reunite 'sign and thing' and the public and private transcripts.[90] Given this intention on the part of the speaker, perhaps we should

---

[90] We might say Pliny suffers from 'fear of simulation': 'a concern that the outward appearances do not correspond to inner essences, and it generates strategies to distinguish the apparent from the genuine, simulations from representations. Taken to an extreme, it is a fear that no judgment, no distinction, is any longer possible'; Dolan (1991) 20.

read the *Panegyricus* as such a gesture pure and simple. That Pliny does so respond, that we come away from his encomium with this sense at all, reinvests the speech as a whole with something of what its figures fail to do.

Finally, this way of reading finds support in some oddly jarring observations of the *Panegyricus* itself. Occasionally, but always in an apparently complimentary sense, Pliny privileges simulation over reality as the defining characteristic both of his subject matter and of his speech itself. Offering a descriptive frame for his own speech, he reminds his audience that the thanks that *imitate* spontaneity are the most gratifying to the hearer: 'Therefore, let us maintain individually the same moderation in our planned speeches which we all preserve in that sudden heat of affection, and let us acknowledge that there is no sort of thanks more sincere or welcome than that which imitates those acclamations which have no time for pretence' (3.1). The obvious objection that to go to the trouble of simulating spontaneity involves a considerable degree of lack of spontaneity appears of little concern here. Pliny's *species libertatis* ('appearance of freedom') is enough; the appearance of spontaneity is acceptable in lieu of the real thing. The same emphasis on simulation occasionally emerges in the praises of Trajan's own role as emperor: what matters is that he keep up the appearance of senatorial participation and the illusion of free speech. Pliny praises 'the first day of your consulate, on which you entered the senate house and exhorted us now individually, now as a group, to take back freedom, to handle the business of state as if we shared it' (66.2)—it is the *as if* that is telling here—and praises Trajan too for preserving the 'simulation' of a 'free state' (63.5).[91] Moreover, these isolated comments seem the explicit expression of a much more [187] widespread but unspoken tendency of the *Panegyricus*. As we have seen on several separate occasions, Pliny repeatedly makes statements that seem patently untrue or unduly vulnerable to audience scepticism, such as his comments about Trajan's aversion to the title *dominus*, the impossibility of criticizing bad emperors of the past

---

[91] Durry (1938) 23 raises and then drops the possibility that Pliny realizes what he is saying. 'The *as if* inserted by Pliny is already telling; above all, what is one to say of this *liberae civitatis simulatio* with which he was satisfied—a phrase worthy of a Tacitus—one of the most sad and accurate in the speech but one about which its very author cannot have realized the distressing element it admitted'.

under those of the present, the difference between his praise and prior ones. It is as if the saying itself is enough, as if meaning lies in the assertion rather than in the facts, as if a world in which values are only surface deep will suffice even—or especially—when all acknowledge that this is so.[92]

---

[92] Lucan cries that even the simulation of freedom, *ficta libertas*, died with Pompey (*Bell. civ.* 9.204–7); as Due (1967) 112 comments, 'Liberty has long been dead but after all the stripped trunk has been reverenced; after Pompey, Tyranny will appear without wearing the mask of Liberty; he was the last who could and would wear it, but even with him it was a mask only'. Here too even the mask, the simulation, is better than the emptiness it shields; even *ficta libertas* is better than what is left when the word becomes meaningless altogether. And Pliny tries to bring *ficta libertas* back.

9

Divine Comedy? Accession Propaganda in Pliny *Epistles* 10.1–2 and the Panegyric

Stanley Hoffer

INTRODUCTION: THE 'SURPRISED-BY-PROVIDENCE' THEME IN IMPERIAL PROPAGANDA

The accession of a new emperor was not only the decisive political event in imperial Rome, but also the cardinal moment around which clustered the major elements of imperial propaganda and ritual, such as funeral and inauguration, deification and/or denigration of the predecessor, and the proclamation of a new age of ideal government under the ideal ruler. It was endlessly re-celebrated and re-enacted through such means as official visual art and monuments, annual oath ceremonies, and official speeches.[1] Pliny's letter of congratulations to Trajan on his accession (10.1) is therefore of supreme interest as a primary document of official accession propaganda in the guise of a private letter, and the rhetorical trope upon which it is built merits special investigation as a basic trope of imperial propaganda: Trajan wished to become emperor as late as possible, but the gods hastened his accession (10.1.1). This could be variously called the 'fortunate fall' *(felix culpa)* theme, or the 'divine comedy' theme, or perhaps the 'surprised-by-providence' theme.

This trope, which recurs in Pliny's letter on receiving the *ius trium liberorum* ('privileges for parents of three children', 10.2) and in the accession narrative of the speech (*Pan.* 5–6, 10), has a dynamic and

---

[1] e.g. Pliny *Letters* 10.35, 52, 100, 102, *Pan.* 5–11, 24; Herrmann (1968) 99–108.

paradoxical quality which allows it to deal with some of the basic paradoxes in imperial propaganda, in particular the problem of evil in imperial government. On the one hand, the present world is an ideal world governed by an ideal and divinely qualified ruler. But the existence of evil in the form of the bad emperor was not simply an unfortunate though unavoidable fact. Rather, it was a leading element of official ideology, enshrined through the widespread topic of denigration of the preceding emperor. Indeed, we also find denigration of future emperors, and even the potential denigration of the present emperor who may turn out bad.[2] This was primarily because imperial ideology controlled the anti-tyrannical and republican heritage of Greek and Roman political thought not by suppressing it but by co-opting it.[3] Indeed, even the possibility of tyrannicide of the *current* emperor was elevated by Trajan into a propaganda topic for legitimizing his reign (*Pan.* 67.4, 67.8, Dio Chrys. 68.16.1–2). Thus, an investigation into the panegyric trope of the fortunate fall can help us understand how the practitioners of imperial propaganda dealt with some of its main fault lines: between divine perfection and human fallibility, between republic and monarchy, and between the ideal of a providentially well-ordered world and the grim reality of past, future, and perhaps present tyranny. The ultimate goal of these conceptual efforts, as of most imperial propaganda, was the difficult task of generating legitimacy for a regime which had comparatively weak legitimacy.

The phrase *felix culpa* is known from the Christian description of the sin of Adam and Eve, fortunate in that it led to redemption through Christ.[4] This idea joins two related [74] elements, first, that a seemingly unfortunate event is actually for the best, and second, that the event seemed to be unfortunate only because of the limits of human wisdom in comparison with divine wisdom. These two elements are both prominent in the trope that Pliny uses. In *Letters* 10.2 Pliny refers to his limited understanding in not knowing that the bad emperor Domitian would be replaced by the good emperor Trajan, under whom it would be better to have children, and in 10.1 he refers to the limited understanding of Trajan in not knowing that he would be an ideal emperor in place of the imperfect Nerva. The phrase

---

[2] Durry (1938) 23; Kennedy (1972) 544.
[3] Whitmarsh (2001) 217.
[4] Its patristic origins are given by Lovejoy (1937); Milton *Paradise Lost* 12.469–78.

'surprised by providence' emphasizes this contrast between human and divine knowledge, and indeed the term *providentia* was a cardinal imperial virtue, combining imperial ritual (for example, the *Ara Providentiae*), philosophic doctrine (the divine providential governance of the universe), and the intimation of divine qualities in the living emperor (*suggestio divini*) who embodied the divine care of the universe.[5] On the other hand, I use the phrase 'divine comedy' to suggest how imperial panegyric is situated on the generic axis between the 'tragic' and the 'comic' (or 'anti-tragic') modes. Pliny's insistent use of the *felix culpa* motif highlights the anti-tragic tendencies of imperial panegyric (noticeable, for example, in the rarity of the 'tragic mode' from Pliny's private letters), although because of its strong anti-tyrannical element a tragic undertone remains.

THE ACCESSION LETTER: PHILOSOPHIC JUSTIFICATION, SUGGESTIO DIVINI, AND THE FORTUNATE FALL

Pliny's first letter to Trajan (10.1) exemplifies accession propaganda for a relatively smooth succession. Pliny discreetly balances joy for the accession of Trajan, the ideal emperor, without too much criticism of Nerva or celebration of his death, since he has just been canonized as a good emperor and as a god, and since it was his choice of Trajan as heir that gives the latter legitimacy.[6]

---

[5] The republican virtue *providentia* ('foresight') of a magistrate or commander, e.g. Cic. *Cat.* 3.14, Caesar BC 3.76.4) was joined to the philosophic term πρόνοια (divine 'superintendence' of the universe) to become a canonical imperial virtue (e.g. Pliny *Letters* 6.19.4, 8.17.2, 10.54.1, 10.108.2). On the explicit analogy between the superintendence by the emperor and by the gods, see e.g. Quint. *Inst.* 12.2.21, Dio Chrysostom 1.42; on the imperial sacrificial cult to *Providentia*, see RE Supp. 14.562–65 s.v. The philosophic-Stoic tradition, to be sure, had a more arduous approach to cosmic governance, fully recognizing the existence of 'ordinary' evils in the world, but asserting that they are lesser evils or not evils at all (e.g. Pl. *Crito* 44D, Sen. *Prov.* 2.1, Epict. 4.1.133, M. Aur. 2.11, and, on divine providence, e.g. Pl. *Rep.* 379, *Tht.* 176C, Sen. *Prov.* 2, Epict. 1.6.26–43, [Plut.] *de Fato* 573, A. Gell. 7.1.1).

[6] It is interesting to consider whether Pliny privately shared the plausible view of some recent scholars, that the 'choice' of Trajan as heir was forced on Nerva, and even that Trajan may have contributed towards pressuring Nerva to choose him (e.g. Syme (1958a) 13, 35; Bennett (1997) 46; Berriman and Todd (2001) 328; Eck (2002); Grainger (2003) 99.

C. Plinivs Traiano Imperatori

1 tua quidem pietas, imperator sanctissime, optaverat, ut quam tardissime succederes patri; sed di immortales festinaverunt virtutes tuas ad gubernacula rei publicae quam susceperas admovere. 2 precor ergo ut tibi et per te generi humano prospera omnia, id est digna saeculo tuo contingant. fortem te et hilarem, imperator optime, et privatim et publice opto.

1 Although your pious nature, most venerable Commander, had wished to take your father's place as late as possible, the immortal gods hastened to bring your excellent qualities to the steering wheel of the government, and indeed you had already taken up the government to yourself. 2 I pray, therefore, that everything that is favourable may fall to your lot, and through you to the lot of the human race—that is, everything that is worthy of your era. In both my private and my public capacity, most excellent Commander, I wish that you may be of good strength and good spirit. [75]

Pliny manages both to express joy at Trajan's accession and to restrain the tone of satisfaction at Nerva's death by using a subtle form of the fortunate fall motif. Trajan wanted to succeed to the place of his 'father' Nerva as late as possible, but the gods (in their greater wisdom) hurried his accession. We shall find almost every element of this trope reused and elaborated in the *Panegyric*, but for now we may note several peculiarities in its use here. First, at this moment of transition, the reigning emperor is cast on the side of the fallible humans whose 'misguided' wishes are overruled by the gods. The letter then shifts in mid-course to the conventional panegyric scenario which implicitly associates the reigning emperor with the providential gods who take care of the 'human race'.[7] The portrayal

---

[7] As coins and inscriptions (e.g. *CIL* 6.2042a14, 6.2044d3) show, official commemoration of the *providentia* of the emperor and the gods centres around 'providing' for the continuity of the current (ideal) government through suppressing conspiracies and especially through choosing a (good) successor; see e.g. Ovid *Met.* 15.834–36, Vell. 2.103.4–5, [Sen.] *Octav.* 279–81, 488, Josephus *BJ* 4.622 δαιμονίου προνοίας. Epictetus reports an amusing parody of *providentia* propaganda at Nero's death and Galba's accession: 'Someone said to [Musonius] Rufus after Galba had been slain, "is the universe being governed by Providence now?" And Rufus said, "did I ever use Galba even as an accessory support for the argument that the universe is governed by Providence?"' (3.15.14). Trajan's accession was marked by coins with the legend *providentia*, *BMC* III.53–5; Roche (2002) 53.

of a clean and sudden transition, however, is blurred by the complicating factor that Trajan was officially a (lesser) co-emperor already,
and in reality probably the dominant of the two co-emperors.[8] This
complication is dealt with by the slightly paradoxical intrusion *quam
susceperas*. Trajan had already 'taken up' the *res publica* (as adopted
co-emperor); now the gods have brought his virtues to the helm.
Trajan both was and was not emperor already; he had 'taken up' the
republic as a task, but he was not yet at the 'helm' as the true
emperor.[9] Pliny politely reflects, or helps create, the official propaganda, inverting the actual power relation between the old and weak
Nerva, who had barely survived a praetorian uprising, and the young
and dominant Trajan supported by the legions of Germany.

By the time of the accession-day letters 10.52 and 10.102 more than
10 years later, the paradox has disappeared: Trajan saved the *imperium* (imperial power/Roman empire) in taking it up.[10] The grey area
of co-emperorship before the *dies imperii* ('accession day') has no
place in this official provincial and military celebration of the day. On
the other hand, the plan of the *Panegyric* depends on the lengthy
recounting of the stages of Trajan's accession from before the adoption to the climactic entry to Rome (*Pan.* 5–24), so the ambiguity of
the co-emperorship gets a full rhetorical workup.

Pliny combines the 'fortunate fall' motif with the *recusatio* motif.
The good emperor generates legitimacy by making a show of unwillingness to accept titles, powers, and if possible, the imperial position
itself. This modest refusal acts against the best interest of the human
race, so it must be overcome, here by the providential action of the
gods. Pliny has fabricated this scenario of Trajan's pious unwillingness and the gods' superior superintendence, out of the raw fact of
Nerva's death soon after the adoption. This element is also suppressed in the later accession-day letters but elaborated in the

---

[8] Grainger (2003) 104; cf. Tac. *Hist.* 1.16 on Piso, *Galba . . . tamquam principem
faceret, ceteri tamquam cum facto loquebantur* 'Galba spoke . . . as if creating an
emperor, the rest as if to one already made emperor'. See also *Pan.* 57.3 on Trajan
as subordinate co-emperor.

[9] *suscipio* is a standard word for accession, as at 10.52 *diem . . . quo servasti
imperium dum suscipis,* ('the day . . . on which you saved the empire as you took
power'), *Pan.* 5.6, 7.3, Fronto *ad Antoninum Pium* 1.6.1, Suet. *Tib.* 17.2, *Claud.* 38.3,
Otho 7.1, *Vesp.* 1.1, *Dom.* 13.6, Tac. *Hist.* 2.1, *Ann.* 1.13, 4.9, 13.6, 13.14.

[10] 10.52 see n. 9; cf. *obstinatum enim tibi non suscipere imperium, nisi servandum
fuisset,* 'for you were determined not to take up power unless it had to be saved' *Pan.*
5.6; Durry (1938) ad loc. 'double sense'.

Panegyric, where the elaboration reveals its roots in Plato's *Republic* (345E–347D = Cic. *Offic.* 1.28). A good person gets no benefit, but only loss, out of holding power, so he will only rule under compulsion, under the threat of being ruled by someone worse. Pliny explains that Trajan wanted to remain in 'second place' (10.4) as co-emperor, since he had the 'more blessed' lot of being a 'private citizen under a good emperor' (*felicius . . . sub bono principe privatus esse . . . 7.2*). The near collapse of the state was the only way to 'force' Trajan to [76] accept Nerva's choice of him as heir.[11] The Platonic hints supply the philosophic backing of the 'philosopher-king' to the Roman panegyric of the ideal emperor, just as the motif of the emperor's providence adds the Stoic-philosophic idea that the world is governed by divine Providence. The 'pilot' metaphor ('to bring your virtues to the helm') also goes back to Plato, who used the image to show that the ideal ruler rules for the benefit of the citizens, and should be chosen for his ability.[12] In its many appearances in Latin texts, it always keeps its overtones of meritocracy, of rule by the best.[13]

We should note that it is not Trajan's ignorance but his piety that causes him to wish for Nerva's late death. Here we find the only faint reminder that, in principle, the situation calls not only for congratulations for Trajan's accession, but also for a *consolatio* for the death of

---

[11] *recusabas, quod erat bene imperaturi. igitur cogendus fuisti. cogi porro non poteras nisi periculo patriae et nutatione rei publicae*, 'you refused, which was a sign you would rule well. And so, you had to be forced. Then, you could not be forced except by danger to the country and by the faltering state' 5.6. Compare, for example, *quasi coactus*, 'as if forced' Suet. *Tib.* 24.2; *quasi . . . vi coactus*, 'as if driven by force' *Otho* 7.1, Vell. 2.124.2; Wallace-Hadrill (1982); Henderson (1998) 294.
[12] e.g. Pl. *Rep.* 342E; *Rep.* 488 = Cic *Offic.* 1.87; *Politicus* 298E = Arist. *Rh.* 1393B7 = Cic. *Rep.* 1.51.1; Xen. *Mem.* 1.2.9; cf. Theognis 675–6.
[13] e.g. Cic. *Dom.* 130, *in Piso.* 20, *Phil.* 2.92, *Rep.* 1.45.2, 2.51.1, *Div.* 2.3, *Offic.* 1.77, *Att.* 4.18.2, *Brut.* 2.1.2, *Fam.* 16.27.1 by Quintus, Liv. 4.3.17, 24.8.12, Val. Max. 9.15.5. The other standard use of the 'pilot' metaphor is to describe the gods' rule of the world; this may add to the divine overtones of the letter, e.g. Pind. *Pyth.* 4.274, Pl. *Symp.* 197B; Ter. *Eun.* 1044, Lucr. 1.21, Cic. *Cat.* 3.18, *Har. resp.* 19, Ovid *Trist.* 5.14.29, Val. Max. 9.12 pr., Manil. 1.247, 494, Sen. *HF* 459, A. Gell. 7.1.1, Apul. *De mundo* 35. The superhuman ruler is the highest form of meritocracy. Cicero provides a proto-imperial example of this topic of ruler-divinity: it takes an 'almost divine' man to be an ideal ruler-helmsman (*Rep.* 1.45.2, compare Pliny's divine orator-helmsman 'nearest to the gods of the sea', 9.26.4). The topic of the unity of the virtues at *Pan.* 59.5 adds another philosophical element to the portrayal of the 'philosopher-king'.

his 'father'.[14] We cannot know whether Trajan was unaware that he would be a better emperor than Nerva, because piety to the emperor is sufficient reason for anyone to wish for Nerva's long life; indeed, Trajan along with other upper-class subjects has been regularly making vows and prayers with *pietas* ('piety') for the emperor's long-lasting *salus* ('well-being') and *incolumitas* ('safety') (cf. 10.35, 52, 100, 102; see 10.52, 100 *pietate*, 10.35 *semper* ('always')). The (adopted) son has all the more reason to show *pietas* in wishing for his 'father's' well-being.

Furthermore, we might wonder about the implied portrayal of Pliny. Where is Pliny, the representative citizen, situated in relation to the comedy of divine providence and human piety or ignorance? Pliny recognizes now that Nerva's death was for the best, and not merely because whatever the gods do is done with providence; the meritocratic diction of 'bringing your *virtues* to the *helm*' shows why it was for the best. Trajan's pious wishes parallel those of Pliny the loyal courtier, who also piously wishes and makes vows for the well-being of the less-than-ideal Nerva. Indeed, since Pliny is not constrained by the imperial virtue of modesty that prevents Trajan from recognizing his own superior virtues, he can share the gods' omniscience even before Nerva's death.[15] The rule of the ideal emperor gives perfect security to his citizens, who are free from both the tragic irony of unexpected ruin and even from the comic irony of unexpected good fortune. The one area of dissonance or irony in the cosmic comedy of praise is the shadow of the worse emperor, either the imperfect Nerva (10.1) or the bad emperor Domitian (10.2), or in the *Panegyric,* the possibility that Trajan will be succeeded by a bad emperor, or become one.

After the accession (10.1.2), the diction suggests an association between the providential ruler and the providential gods: Pliny prays for good fortune for Trajan, and through [77] Trajan for the

---

[14] In the *Panegyric,* Pliny provides an appropriate though perfunctory scene of tears, 11.1. For a new emperor's show of grief, see Suet. *Tib.* 23.1, *Calig.* 15.1. The closing wish for Trajan to be of 'good strength and good spirits' may have a consolatory hint; in the second miscarriage letter, Pliny's wife has recovered her good spirits (8.11.2 *iam hilaris*). But the closing salutation to Fabatus (4.1.7 *fortes . . . hilares*) suggests that the combination was a fixed, though rarely attested, combination.

[15] On Trajan's 'imperial' modesty, see e.g. *beneficiorum tuorum parcissimus aestimator,* 'you gave the most grudging judgement of your kindnesses', *Pan.* 21.2.

human race.[16] The term 'human race' conveys not only the propaganda of a worldwide empire but also *suggestio divini*, a hint that the emperor is the vice-regent of the gods in tending for humanity.[17] The association between Trajan and the gods in bringing good fortune to humanity is explicated in the *Panegyric*: Jupiter has delegated the function of caring for the 'human race' to Trajan, and so he is freed up to take care of the heavens (80.5).[18]

This letter with its panegyric 'comedy' of imperial governance elegantly shows how to extract the maximum of providential good fortune at the cardinal imperial moment, the accession of an emperor. There is no need for a pretence of grief and consolation, and scarcely a hint of death. After all, the emperor has hardly died, but rather 'left the earth for you, you to the earth' (*Pan*. 10.6) and been 'claimed by the gods for heaven' (10.5). Trajan's 'reign/(golden) age' (*saeculum*) has begun, and the citizen needs only to pray for the 'best' emperor's good fortune to be in keeping with the new era (*digna saeculo tuo*); the well-being of humanity will automatically follow (e.g. *Pan*. 23.5, 67.3, 94.2). Behind this prayer, however, lurks the only tragic note, the death of the ideal emperor, possibly followed by the accession of a bad emperor.

THE REPRESENTATIVE CITIZEN'S ENCOUNTER WITH THE DIVINE COMEDY OF ACCESSION

Letter 10.2, also from the start of Trajan's reign, uses this surprised-by-providence motif in thanking him for the grant of the *ius trium liberorum* ('privileges for parents of three children'). Pliny desired children 'even in that very grim era (of Domitian) . . . but the gods

[16] A three-level continuous analogy (the gods are to the emperor as the emperor is to humans) is persistent in the *Panegyric* (5.1, 24.4–5, 52.2, 52.6, 74.4; Domitian failed in this analogical role, 33.4). See Fears (1977) 232.

[17] For the phrase *genus humanum* to describe the emperor's (divine) superintendence of the entire world, see Ovid *Met*. 15.759, Sen. *Clem*. 1.1.4; Fears (1977) 16, 130, 150; Brunt (1990) 298–302. Compare Greek adulation on Republican Rome's divine superintendence of the human race at Livy 37.45.9; Levene (1997) 83. Levene argues that the divinity of the emperor is often restricted to ambiguous hints in panegyric texts, and suppressed entirely in second-order descriptions of panegyric in rhetorical or historical texts.

[18] Fears (1977) 148; Bartsch (1994) 163 and above p. 165.

(ordained) better', in keeping him childless so that he could receive the grant, and become a father, under Trajan instead.[19] The appearance of this rather uncommon motif in both letters could be seen as a verbal-logical tic, something that lodged in Pliny's memory for reuse shortly afterwards. But if we consider the conceptual pose of the two letters, we shall find that similar situational and propagandistic demands underlie both passages—the need to manoeuvre among the forces of good and bad fortune, divine and human wishes and powers, and to situate the ideal and 'divine' emperor in this complex of forces.

There is a certain tension between the main body of the letter, in which Pliny expresses his thanks with unspeakable joy, and the final section, in which Pliny speaks of his continuing (and therefore unfulfilled) wish for children. The elaboration of the wish for children, to be sure, appears to be conventional, to preserve the appearances that the grant of the *ius trium liberorum* ('privileges for parents of three children') was not a tool for avoiding the law, but a rectification for those whose failure to have children was due to natural infertility.[20]

The 'gods willed for the better' motif enters the letter to deal with this dissonance between the obligatory expression of joy and the equally obligatory reference to the personal misfortune that led to the imperial favour. To smooth over this friction, Pliny has [78] imbued the entire letter with joyous tones. His joy is beyond his abilities to express it, and he appears to have achieved the sum of his wishes (*videor ergo summam voti mei consecutus*, 'Therefore I seem to have reached the height of my wish', 2).[21] And how does the childless Pliny reach inexpressible joy over a technical grant of

---

[19] *eoque magis liberos concupisco, quos habere etiam illo tristissimo saeculo volui, sicut potes duobus matrimoniis meis credere. sed di melius, qui omnia integra bonitati tuae reservarunt; malui hoc potius tempore me patrem fieri, quo futurus essem et securus et felix* ('all the more I long to have children–I wanted them even in that most grim age, as you can be sure from my two marriages. But the gods knew better when they held everything back for your kindness; I much preferred to become a father at this time when I am to be secure and blessed', *Letters*. 10.2.2–3).

[20] Cf. the apparently conventional mention of Suetonius' 'unfortunate' (infertile) marriage in the request for the *ius III liberorum*, 10.94.2. The satiric poet, on the other hand, must (casually) dismiss his wife so as not to ruin Domitian's gift with real children: *valebis, uxor./non debet domini perire munus*, ('farewell, my wife. A master's gift should not perish', Mart. 2.92.3–4).

[21] Inexpressible joy (or sorrow) is a conventional device for augmentation: Plin. *Letters* 5.14.2, 5.16.7, 7.8.1, 9.23.3; Fronto *ad M. Caesarem* 1.7.3, *ad M. Antoninum* 1.2.2.

inheritance rights and political seniority? First, the essence of what he has received is not privilege and profit, but rather, a sign of imperial favour. He thanks Trajan not for the rights, but for being *thought* worthy of them, as shown both by the grant itself and by the document explaining that Trajan granted it *not* just as a perfunctory favour to Servianus but because it was for Pliny (*quia pro me rogabat*, 'because he asked on my behalf', 1 cf. 10.13). Second, the expression of imperial favour makes him want children even more; the *Panegyric* develops this topic in full (27–28). Under a good emperor, parents no longer need to fear that the emperor will kill their children (*nec inter insanabiles morbos principis ira numerator*, 'nor is anger counted among the emperor's insane illnesses' 27.1); and more importantly, the *sign* of the emperor's favour, as shown by the *congiarium* grant, in itself increases the birthrate by making people more eager for children (28.7).[22] Therefore the grant of the *ius trium liberorum* ('privileges for parents of three children') will actually make it more likely for Pliny to have children. The logical reverse of this idea, the possibility that Pliny did not 'try' to have children as much as he could have, almost emerges from the rhetoric. He goes so far as to say that (even in those grim days?) he 'preferred'/'would have preferred' to have children now instead of then.[23] But his prior childlessness was 'actually' caused not by his weaker desire but by the provident gods, who ordained that it would be better to keep Pliny childless for Trajan's 'goodness', specifically the grant, but also by means of the grant (as a sign of Trajan's favour) greater desire for children and therefore fatherhood in the ideal reign. Whether by Pliny's greater desire or by the gods' providence, Trajan's ideal reign, as signified by the grant, has increased Pliny's chances for fertility. Thus, a pseudo-logical chain leads from the technical grant to the 'blessed' future when he will be both secure (under Trajan) and blessed (as a father); and the logical hinge is the superior wisdom of the gods, whose apparent curse of childlessness turned out to be a blessing in disguise.

---

[22] For the trope of imperial favour or disfavour being more desired or feared than actual grants and punishments, see *Pan.* 80.2.

[23] If the text is correct, that is (*malui* a, Mynors; *maluerunt* Keil, Müller). Sherwin-White wrongly renders *di . . . reservarunt; malui hoc potius tempore me patrem fieri* as 'the gods have acted thus, but my preference was for real paternity' (1966) 560. His preference was not for real over fictitious paternity, but for paternity (first fictitious, and then real) under Trajan over paternity under Domitian.

In contrast with the previous letter, here the emperor is not a recipient of the gods' surprising providence but a co-giver. Whereas previously Pliny readjusted Trajan's status over the course of the letter as he moved from half-private citizen to emperor, here we can observe Pliny's art of *suggestio divini* ('intimation of divine qualities') from the start, in the placement of Trajan in the network of *beneficia* (patronage) that spans from the gods through Trajan and Servianus to Pliny.[24] Again he uses ambiguous terms, *precibus* ('prayers') and *voti* ('something prayed for'), which can be used in either divine or human contexts. On the other hand, the favourite Plinian-imperial term 'indulgence' (1 *indulseris,* 2 *peculiarem indulgentiam tuam*) describes a human superior who forgoes the right of severity, and especially for the emperor's favour.[25] Trajan, at the summit of the human patronage pyramid, answers [79] prayers and fulfils 'vows' for things that are humanly possible. The gods, to be sure, have control over basic life conditions such as birth, sickness, and death, but Pliny imagines their efforts as being coordinated with or guided by the emperor: they decide to keep Pliny childless, and to kill off Nerva quickly, when they see the ideal emperor Trajan in the wings. Thus the 'blessedness' of Trajan's 'period of leadership' (2 *felicissimi principatus*) returns as the final word (3 *securus et felix*, 'secure and blessed'), to describe Pliny's blessed state as father. The cooperative favour of Trajan and the gods (or among the gods) makes his citizens blessed despite seeming misfortune.[26]

It may seem striking how casually one childless man announces to another his expectation of becoming a father, but then again the protestations of wanting children may be partly perfunctory, since

[24] See n. 16 on the three-level analogy from the gods to the emperor, and the emperor to humans.

[25] *indulgentia* is extraordinarily frequent in book 10, used not only by Pliny but also by Trajan (10.24.1, and rather negatively at 10.40.2) and by Nerva (10.58.8). The 34 uses in book 10 far outnumber the relative frequency of use in any other text, and equal the number in all of Cicero. In pre-imperial texts, *indulgentia* tends not to be used of the gods, but it *is* used of fortune (or Fortune—*fortuna, fata, sors*), presumably because fortune is often thought to be naturally unfavourable. When we find it applied to the gods, we might suspect that imperial diction is penetrating the divine sphere rather than vice versa (*Pan.* 74.5 *deorum indulgentiam*).

[26] On the reciprocal *felicitas* of the ruler and his citizens, see *Pan.* 2.8, 72.2, 74.4. In 10.94, Trajan's 'goodness' is imagined as making up for the 'badness' of fortune simply by the grant, without any reference to future children (*impetrandumque a bonitate tua ... habet quod illi fortunae malignitas denegavit,* 'he must look to your goodness ... to have what the cruelty of fortune has denied him').

childlessness probably aided one's safety and promotion at the dizzying heights of imperial power. Trajan probably owed the throne, and Pliny possibly his success, to childlessness.[27] L. Julius Ursus Servianus, husband of Hadrian's sister, is the only father among the principals here, with a daughter (6.26.2), and he may have owed his death, along with that of her son, to that fact, which made him a threat to Hadrian at age 90.[28] The fortunate fall motif appears in several other letters to Trajan. Its rarity in books 1–9 is therefore noteworthy: I have not found a single clear instance. We are clearly dealing not with a Plinian trope but a Plinian-imperial trope in his official, ceremonial mode. The misfortunes that Pliny occasionally admits into books 1–9 must provide the proper tragic shading to the idealized portrait of his private world, and not be swallowed up in rhetorical foil. Also, the divinity of the emperor is de-emphasized in the private letters.[29] In the official letters, echoes of the motif appear in 10.4 (the favour to Voconius Romanus was postponed to Trajan's reign) and 10.6 (ignorance of Arpocras' citizen status allows an additional favour). Here the motif adds not rhetorical celebration of past 'fortunate misfortunes', but rather, rhetorical leverage for extracting future favours. In 10.4, Pliny suggests that the problems in obtaining senatorial rank for Voconius were providentially fortunate. Pliny had requested from Trajan's 'divine father' to advance Voconius to senatorial rank, but this wish/prayer (*votum*) of his has been saved for Trajan's goodness.[30] The technical problem of a legal delay (in Voconius' mother's transfer of property) is subsumed under the familiar topos that Nerva's death was for the best for the representative citizen, since it saved this favour for Trajan to perform in his (superior) goodness. The rhetorical leverage (or blackmail) strengthens the request by

---

[27] On the advantages of childlessness see Hoffer (1999) 12, 230, and for Trajan, Grainger (2003) 127.

[28] Dio 69.17; SHA *Hadr.* 15.8, 23.2, 23.8, 25.8; *PIR*[2] J631; Birley (1997) 291. Cf. *Pan.* 94.5 on hopes for Trajan to have a son, like Martial's similar hopes for Domitian (6.3).

[29] The exceptions are mitigated by being marked as generic interference from philosophy (4.25.5 = Pl. *Phdo.* 95b) and poetry (8.4.5–6 *poetice*); see also 5.14.5 *voto*, 6.5.5 *propitium*. In books 1–9, even the gods themselves appear more in tentative prayers and hopes than in confident descriptions of their providence.

[30] *et a divo patre tuo petieram, ut illum in amplissimum ordinem promoveret; sed hoc votum meum bonitati tuae reservatum est, quia . . .* ('I had petitioned your father to raise him to the highest rank; but this my wish was reserved for your goodness, because . . .' 10.4.2).

hinting that a good emperor such as Trajan will naturally grant the favour. The fact that the request was apparently not fulfilled[31] accords with the rhetorical strengthening here and elsewhere in the letter (e.g. the *suggestio divini*, 'intimation of divine qualities' in the opening *votum* 'wish' and closing *compotem* 'able' and in the superlative *exoptatissimae* 'most desired'): we can sometimes gauge how much Pliny wants the favour and how big a favour he thinks it is by the level of importunity in his letters. By contrast, for example, 10.87, 104, and 106 are perfunctory or tentative requests.

In 10.6, Pliny similarly strengthens a request with the fortunate fall motif. He has no complaints about not having known that Egyptians need Alexandrian citizenship before [80] they can get Roman citizenship, since that was the ground for being obliged to Trajan more than once for the same person.[32] Trajan's *indulgentia* makes human errors harmless—if, that is, he will accede to the request. Here the motif functions not merely as rhetorical strengthening, but also as an apology: Pliny's own misdeed can be providentially advantageous if it is annulled by the ideal emperor.[33] Finally, we might detect an echo of the motif in 10.17A, where he tells Trajan that despite travel delays he 'cannot complain' since he made it in time to celebrate Trajan's birthday (10.17A.2 *non possum de mora queri* 'I cannot complain about the delay'; cf. 10.6.2 *de qua . . . non queror* 'I don't complain about this'). The rigours of travel (duly predicted at 10.15) are made void since they caused him to enter the province 'most auspiciously' on Trajan's birthday.

SUGGESTIO DIVINI AND THE DENIGRATION OF PREDECESSORS IN THE ACCESSION NARRATIVE OF THE PANEGYRIC

Let us look now at the use of *suggestio divini* ('intimation of divine qualities') and the fortunate fall motif in the accession narrative of the

---

[31] Syme (1958) 83.

[32] *de qua ignorantia mea non queror, per quam stetit ut tibi pro eodem homine saepius obligarer* ('I do not complain about my ignorance through which it means I am more frequently obliged to you on account of the same man', 10.6.2).

[33] One wonders whether the apology is covering up deceit. Did neither Pliny nor Arpocras know the rules about Alexandrian citizenship? Is Pliny tricking Trajan by asking for the easy favour first, or is Arpocras tricking Trajan through Pliny?

Panegyric. The accession sequence occupies the first main section (5–10) after the introductory material (1–4) of prayers to Jupiter (1), a programmatic promise to offer sincere and moderate praise (2–4.3), and a flourish of general compliments (4.4–4.7). The accession narrative follows a chronological sequence from (a) Trajan's departure to his province of Upper Germany (5.2–5.5), (b) the praetorian uprising (5.6–6.3), (c) the adoption (6.4–8.6) along with (d) Trajan's response (9.1–10.2), (e) the period of the co-emperorship (10.3–10.4), and (f) Nerva's death (10.5–10.6).

In explaining why he begins with a prayer to Jupiter, Pliny explicitly establishes the religious framework of his imperial praise: Trajan the ideal emperor is a gift from the gods (*munus deorum*), indeed the outstanding example that rulers are given to the world not by fortune and chance but by some divine will,[34] since he is himself 'most similar to the gods' in his purity and sanctity (1.3–4), and omens proved the divine election (1.5). On the one hand, the counterfactual *si adhuc dubium fuisset* ('if it were still in doubt', 1.4) implies that it is *not* in doubt that rulers are given to the world by divine will, and not by chance. But the constant denigration of prior emperors makes it clear why it might have been in doubt: were Domitian and Nero also divinely appointed? These problematic alternatives encapsulate the religious background of the speech, both the laudatory surface and the grim subtext. The virtues of the ideal emperor extend to the providentially perfect good fortune of the entire world; but the spectre of the bad emperor reminds us that we might be driven to doubt the existence of divine providence, or to understand it in a more arduous sense (as in the philosophic tradition). The accession narrative echoes this opening formula, again in reference to imperial omens: Trajan is an emperor of the sort that one should be who was 'given to the earth' not by civil war, but by peace, adoption, and *divinities* that were *finally* won over by prayers (5.1 *et tandem exorata terris numina dedissent*): divine providence *finally* answered our prayers [*not* as under Domitian].[35]

---

[34] *ac si adhuc dubium fuisset, forte casuque rectores terris an aliquo numine darentur* ('if it were still in doubt whether rulers were given to the earth by chance or fate, or by some divine power', 1.4).

[35] A standard motif is that others did the bloody job and so the *laudandus* came to power with clean hands, Isoc. *Evagoras* 25, Tac. *Ann.* 13.4; Wiseman (1982) 67; Braund (1998) 72 and above p. 104; *CAH*² 11.153. The motif is often used to hide the actual involvement of the ruler. Accordingly, scholars have wondered whether

The first step towards accession was the prophetic scene marking Trajan's departure to Upper Germany: a crowd shouted *Imperator* to *Iuppiter Imperator,* 'as they thought' [81] (5.4).[36] As we saw, this introduces the *recusatio* theme: the entire crowd understood the omen, but you yourself were *unwilling* to understand it—you refused to rule, a sign of someone who will rule well (5.5 *nam ipse intellegere nolebas; recusabas enim imperare...quod erat bene imperaturi*). Therefore you had to be compelled (by the 'collapse of the republic', 5.6, 6.3). Pliny could almost 'shout out' that it was worth so great a price, if this was the only way to bring Trajan to the helm (6.2 *si tamen haec sola erat ratio, quae te publicae salutis gubernaculis admoveret, prope est ut exclamem tanti fuisse*). Pliny alternates between diminishing the disorder (to suggest the peaceful, rational choice of the ideal ruler, 5.1) and highlighting it (to emphasize the compulsion needed to overcome the ideal candidate's modest refusal, 5.6–6.2).[37] If Trajan had understood, if he had been readily willing to rule, the country could have been spared the near 'collapse', but he was *unwilling* to understand. We might compare letter 10.1, where the co-emperor Trajan resists the divine plan due to *pietas.* Here, Trajan's resistance to the divine comedy comes from ignorance, but not simple human ignorance, but rather wilful ignorance due to the imperial virtue *modestia* (5.7); otherwise he could have understood as well as everyone else.

Another reflective passage on the mysteries of divine providence (5.8–9) interrupts the description of the praetorian uprising (5.6–6.3), and here both kinds of divine irony are explicit, unexpected

Trajan was involved in the praetorian uprising in 97 (n. 6), and one could also imagine that Trajan knew about the conspiracy against Domitian.

[36] Grainger calls it 'political theatre' (2003) 36. If Pliny's report is correct, it may indicate plans for Trajan's adoption from the start of Nerva's reign. But the motif of pre-accession omens is so well-worked that it is hard to put much trust in it. We could compare the report of a pre-accession crowd shout for Pertinax, Dio 73.4.2, *CAH*[2] 11.193. Menander Rhetor recommends inventing omens if necessary, 371.11–12.

[37] Lucan also uses the cautious conditional and the financial metaphor to say paradoxically that the wicked crimes of civil war were worth it if that was the only way for Nero to rule (*quod si non aliam venturo fata Neroni/invenere viam......scelera ipsa nefasque/hac mercede placent...* 'but if Fate found no other way for Nero who was yet to come...these crimes and evil are acceptable for this reward', 1.33–8), Durry (1938) 93; contrast 2.62–63, where an unnamed Roman says that civil war is scarcely worth it in order that neither Caesar nor Pompey will rule, that is, in order to preserve Republican government (*vix tanti fuerat civilia bella movere/ut neuter,* 'it had scarcely been worthwhile to stir up civil war for neither [to rule]').

misfortune as well as unexpected good fortune. 'Good fortune arises from bad fortune, and bad from good; God hides the seeds of each, and often the causes of good and evil lurk under the opposite appearance.' In this context of accession, it is natural to give a political meaning to both sides, both a deceptively strife-filled accession resulting in a good emperor, and a deceptively smooth accession leading to a bad emperor. The reigns of bad emperors are also part of the divine plan.

Pliny then subjects the idea of compulsion (*cogendus*, 5.6) to rhetorical-logical amplification. The essence of the bad situation which 'compelled' Trajan to accept the throne, was that Nerva himself was 'under compulsion' (*cogitur*, 6.1)—the antithesis of the emperor's role.[38] An emperor was 'compelled' to kill people, in order to produce an emperor who could not be compelled (6.2). The paradox highlights the opposition between private citizen and emperor. The ideal candidate must be forced to rule; the ideal ruler is omnipotent and cannot be forced. This opposition brings out the human nature of the impotent Nerva and the divine nature of the omnipotent Trajan. Thus Pliny uses the panegyric topic of 'parent of the human race' ironically, precisely at the moment that Nerva has lost the essential feature of the emperorship, power, and has virtually become a 'captive'.[39] Only through 'the divine and immortal deed' of adopting Trajan (10.5 *divinum et immortale factum*) does Nerva gain the divine aura of a 'good emperor' worthy of deification.[40] In accordance with the emphasis on Nerva's impotence the panegyric relation between the gods and the emperor is reversed: Nerva is an agent of the gods, but not as an authoritative co-worker in tending to humanity, as Trajan is (80.5). He is their helpless pawn, their attendant; he obeyed them in adopting as much as Trajan [82] did in being adopted (8.2); and they have laid claim to the glory of the deed, the glory is

---

[38] The imperial system was indeed not well equipped to balance independent sources of power without collapsing into assassination or civil war (Grainger (2003) 72).

[39] *imperator et parens generis humani obsessus captus inclusus* ('the emperor and parent of the human race was besieged, seized, shut in', 6.1).

[40] In the letters, which present the side of the private citizen, the only 'divine and immortal' deeds are Arria's suicide (3.16.6) and Verginius Rufus' declining the emperorship (6.10.4). Under the empire, a private citizen can win 'immortal' fame only through words (3.7.14), or through acts of renunciation, especially imperial renunciation.

theirs, not Nerva's (8.2 *sibi ... gloriam ... di vindicaverunt*). Nerva is imagined as having called into his advisory council the judgment not only of people but even of the gods (8.1).[41] By contrast, in the imaginary scene of Trajan adopting his successor, only a god (Jupiter) is explicitly invited to the consultation (*in consilio sis eligenti* 'may you assist him in his choice', 94.5).

The idea of human consultation for the consummate power-decision can be problematic, since the despotic power structure makes it almost inevitable that 'advice' on such a topic will take the form of flattery, undue influence, intimidation, or deceit.[42] It would be indelicate to urge the reigning emperor to consult with others on choosing an heir.

The adoption scene is presented by split screen, since Trajan is in Upper Germany. In cutting to Trajan's response, Pliny uses the time lag of ancient travel to play on the human ignorance of a subject as opposed to the divine omniscience of the ideal emperor. The period of co-emperorship itself is an awkward liminal zone (10.3–4), but rather than downplay it, Pliny heightens it by rhetorical paradox. It would be remarkable enough to say that Trajan did not know that he would be emperor, but in fact, he did not know that he *was* emperor (*magnum videretur, si dicerem* 'nescisti te imperatorem futurum': *eras imperator et esse te nesciebas*, 9.4). The rhetorical heightening deflects attention from the unseemly question to what degree Trajan did know about, or influence, Nerva's 'choice'. The paradox of ignorance in the all-provident emperor is matched by the paradox of obedience in the all-powerful 'commander'.[43] The flawed emperor Nerva was demoted to the merely citizen/human level in suffering compulsion and in obeying (8.2), whereas Trajan became emperor through the

---

[41] Cf. *hominum deorumque consensus* ('the consent of men and gods'), Val. Max. 1 praef. 1, Tac. *Hist.* 1.15; Fears (1977) 133.

[42] For example, Tacitus maliciously contrasts Galba's edifying comment on Piso being chosen by *consensus* and without prior constraints with the sinister string-pulling behind the scenes by Laco and Icelus against Vinius, *Hist.* 1.13 *Vinius pro M. Othone, Laco atque Icelus consensu . . .* ('Vinius was for Otho, Laco and Icelus were in agreement'), 1.15 *deorum hominumque consensus* ('the agreement of gods and men'), 1.16 *adoptandi iudicium integrum et, si velis eligere, consensu monstratur* ('[there is] a free choice in adoption and, if you wish to choose, it is made clear by agreement'); Damon (2003) 137, 140. Compare the insidious influences of step-mothers, *Pan.* 7.4, Tac. *Ann.* 1.3, 12.25.

[43] *ut imperator fieret . . . meruit et paruit . . . principatum obsequio pervenisti* ('to become emperor . . . he deserved and obeyed . . . you reached the principate by obedience', 9.2–3).

private citizen's virtue, obedience. The paradox of obedience/command allows even more rhetorical play than the paradox of knowledge/ignorance, since it continues past the moment that the information arrives: the citizen Trajan obeys his commander Nerva in accepting the role of commander.[44] At the moment of transition, the split screen is within Trajan himself, as it were. Trajan the citizen obeys and allows Trajan the imperator to take over. Indeed, Trajan the citizen virtually obeys Trajan the imperator, since Nerva had already lost his grasp on the supreme power, and only got it back because of having Trajan as co-commander (e.g. 8.6).

The brief account of the co-emperorship emphasizes Trajan's continuing subservience to Nerva (10.3–4). At this point Pliny gives a fuller rendition of the accession letter 10.1. Despite the titulature of imperial power, Trajan laid no claim for anything from the adoption but the piety and obedience of a son, and prayed that 'this name' ('son') would have a 'long perpetuity and long glory' (*cum . . . tuas aquilas . . . anteires, neque aliud tibi ex illa adoptione quam filii pietatem filii obsequium adsereres, longamque huic nomini aetatem, longam gloriam precarere*, 10.3). 'The providence of the gods had already brought you to the first rank, but you still wanted to remain, and even grow old, in the second rank' (*iam te providentia deorum primum in locum provexerat; tu adhuc in secundo resistere atque etiam senescere optabas*, 10.4). The echoes of the accession letter are clear, as is the elaboration. Again we have Trajan's 'piety' to his 'father', his 'wishes' to remain the imperial understudy, and the pluperfect indicating that he was already emperor in a sense (10.4 *provexerat*; 10.1.1 *quam susceperas*). Here Trajan the mortal pre-emperor not only 'wishes' but even 'prays', apparently to the gods, to remain (as if) Nerva's 'subject' (10.4 *privatus tibi videbaris*). And here the providential action of the gods in opposing Trajan's mortal wishes is explicit; only here does Pliny use the traditional phrase *providentia deorum* [83] ('providence of the gods').[45] The action of the gods must be emphasized to cover the virtual vacancy on the throne: Trajan sees himself as if a private citizen, while Nerva's mystique of power has been fatally impaired by the all-too-human

---

[44] *an non obsequereris principi civis, legatus imperatori, filius patri?* ('Did you not obey as citizen to the emperor, legate to the emperor, son to a father?', 9.4).

[45] First in Cicero, e.g. *Nat. Deor.* 2.73; πρόνοια θεῶν is from the fifth century, LSJ s. v. πρόνοια.

compulsion, obedience, and even *regret* (7.3 *paenitebat*) that he has undergone; indeed, to share power is almost to reliquish it.[46] The dissonance between Trajan's human *modestia* and the gods' providential care is softened, or perhaps emphasized, by a rhetorical surprise. 'You prayed to remain merely as Nerva's son . . . the gods *heard* your prayers—but only so far as was in the interest of that best and most venerable old man' (*audita sunt tua vota, sed in quantum optimo illi et sanctissimo seni utile fuit*, 10.4).[47] Trajan's prayers for Nerva's long life were *answered* by Nerva's early death; having fulfilled his function as the vehicle for the transmission of imperial power, his early death was in his *own* best interest, not Trajan's.

Only at Nerva's death does Pliny emphasize his providence: the gods claimed him for heaven, so that he would not do a mortal deed after that divine and immortal one. The one 'divine' deed of the all-too-mortal emperor Nerva was the adoption; any further action would be back on the mortal level of his prior emperorship. Therefore they decided that he must 'be deified' (die) at once, so that one day people would ask if he was already a god when he adopted Trajan (*ut quandoque inter posteros quaereretur, an illud iam deus fecisset*, 10.5). In this *suggestio divini* ('intimation of divine qualities') Pliny applies Nerva's official deification retroactively back to the final period of his life, in a blurring of status between Nerva as god-emperor (virtually already dead/deified) and Trajan as emperor-private citizen. The concluding *sententia* plays on an etymological variant of providence, *prospexerat*: Nerva was all the more missed, because he 'had the foresight'/'made provision' that he would not be missed (*eo ipso carus omnibus ac desiderandus, quod prospexerat ne desideraretur*, 10.6).[48] In sum, the early death of Nerva is a fortunate fall not only for the human race but for Nerva himself (*illi* utile *fuit*, 10.4).

Once the ideal emperor is installed in power, the fortunate fall motif is relatively uncommon, since under the ideal emperor there is neither misfortune nor even seeming misfortune. Even his judicial activities are presented not as punishing wicked deeds but as making people eager to become better through his inspiring example and the

---

[46] *nam quantulum refert, deponas an partiaris imperium?* ('for there is little difference between resigning and sharing power', 8.4).

[47] The shocking exaggeration led Schnelle to conjecture *audita <non> sunt vota tua.*

[48] See Cic. *Rep.* 1.45.2; Zetzel (1995) 135 on *prospicere.*

desire for his good opinion (80.2–3; cf. 46.5–6).[49] The main shadow
over the reign, the spectre of bad emperors past and future, can hardly
be treated as a fortunate fall in the manner of 5.8 ('bad weather makes
us appreciate good weather'), since the basic plan of denigration
requires making the past as bad as possible. Therefore we have to
turn to a natural disaster, drought in Egypt (30–32), to find a full use
of the motif, just as the (possibly) natural misfortune of Pliny's
childlessness was turned to similar use in letter 10.2. Not only was
Egypt's misfortune quickly remedied by the emperor's speedy assistance, but the misfortune was even for the best in allowing us to see
his greatness, and in restraining Egypt's pride. 'Although you deserve
good fortune everywhere, clearly if any misfortune should befall, it is
spread forth as material, as a field for your merits and excellences'
(*nam cum omnia ubique secunda merearis, nonne manifestum est, si
quid adversi cadat, tuis laudibus tuisque virtutibus materiam cam-
pumque praesterni . . .* 31.1; cf. 31.6). And until now, it had long been
believed that our city could not be fed without Egypt's resources
(31.2). The tone that all is for the best broadens into a justification
for Rome's empire, which this misfortune has shown is for the best.
'. . . we can do without Egypt, but Egypt cannot do without us; the
most fertile nation was finished, if she had been free' (. . . *ut . . . pro-
baretur et nos Aegypto posse et nobis Aegyptum carere non posse.
actum erat de* [84] *fecundissima gente, si libera fuisset*, 31.5–6). By
spreading out the risk of crop failure, the ideal emperor makes it
beneficial for the provinces to have come under Roman sway (32.1).
The ideal emperor has greater *benignitas* ('kindness') than the sky,
since it never enriches all lands at the same time, whereas he can
bring, if not fertility, then the benefits of fertility.[50] The term *caelum*
(sky/weather), often used for 'gods' (e.g. 10.4, 35.4, 89.3), adds a
suggestio divini ('intimation of divine qualities'), as in the earlier
description of Egypt 'invoking' not its river but Caesar's help
(30.5).[51] But the notion that drought and famine can be for the best

---

[49] This is taken seriously at *CAH*² 11.79. We observed the opposite idea, that
rewards are valued as a sign of his favour, at 10.2.1–2; cf. 10.13, Durry (1938) 204.

[50] *caelo . . . numquam benignitas tanta, ut omnes simul terras uberet foueatque: hic
omnibus pariter . . . hic si non fecunditatem, at bona fecunditatis importat* ('there is
never so much kindness in heaven that it enriches and favours all lands at the same
time; if not fertility, he can bring the benefits of fertility to all countries alike', 32.2).

[51] Méthy (2000) 399; Braund (1998) 64 and above p. 96; compare 32.3 on praying
to rivers. See *TLL* 7.2.256.5–9 s.v. *invoco* for prefatory invocations of emperors with

is so shocking that Pliny needs to soften it before and after with a prayer for fertility for the future (31.1, 32.3).

THE THEORY OF TYRANNICIDE AS A
METHOD OF GENERATING LEGITIMACY

Finally, let us turn to the one great evil in Pliny's ideal panegyric world that is never for the best: the bad emperor. At one point, to be sure, Pliny goes so far as to suggest that the evil done by a bad emperor (concerning the inheritance tax) can be corrected retroactively. 'You made it so that we *did not have bad emperors*' (*effecisti ne malos principes habuissemus*, 40.3). But the finality of death quickly cuts off this cheerful wish of undoing the past: 'In this spirit, if nature would allow it, how willingly *would* you *have* poured back their property and blood into so many people who were plundered, who were slaughtered' (*quo ingenio, si natura pateretur, quam libenter tot spoliatis tot trucidatis bona et sanguinem refudisses!* 40.4). At best, Pliny can suggest that it was 'useful' (for Trajan) to reach the enjoyment of good fortune through misfortune, since it enables him to take up the 'role' of the emperor with the understanding of a private citizen who used to complain and pray about the bad emperor (44.1–2).[52]

Alongside the denigration of prior emperors we find the denigration of future emperors, and even potential denigration of the present emperor. The exaggerated praise of the current emperor as 'the best' implies that future emperors too will be worse (or at most, equal, 88.9). Right after a 'bad' reign, senators are especially aware of future dangers. Tacitus has both the *delator* ('informer') Eprius Marcellus

---

suggestio divini ('intimation of divine qualities': Val. Max. 1 pr. 1, Stat. *Silv.* 4 pr., Quint. *Inst.* 4 pr. 4, Pliny *Letters* 8.4.5.

[52] *quam utile est ad usum secundorum per adversa venisse!* ... *meministi quae optare nobiscum, quae sis queri solitus. nam privato iudicio principem geris* ('How useful it is to have reached success through adversity! ... you remember what you used to hope for with us, and what you complained about, for you conduct your principate with a citizen's attitude', 44.1–2). Cf. 'we have *learned from* experience that an emperor's innocence is his trustiest guard', 49.3). In reality, of course, Trajan, like Nerva and Pliny, was outstandingly loyal to Domitian (*Pan.* 14.2–3); Grainger (2003) 36; Bennett (1997) 42–3—or at least until the plot to kill Domitian.

and the anti-*delator* Curtius Montanus tell the senators in the first days of Vespasian's reign that they should act with the possibility of future bad emperors in mind (*Hist.* 4.8 'I pray for good emperors, but I endure them however they are'; 4.42 'do you think Nero was the last of the *domini?*'). And at 9.13.11 Pliny describes terrified senators warning him that he will be marked out by future (bad) emperors. Throughout the *Panegyric*, Trajan is imagined as an example or benchmark for future emperors to follow *or not* (44.3–4). Future emperors will have to choose between Trajan's frugal travels with publicized accounts and Domitian's opposite example (20.6). Trajan's swearing the oath as consul-elect gives him equal glory whether or not future emperors do the same (64.3). The name *optimus* will always be recognized as Trajan's: in good emperors the name will be someone else's, in bad, it will be false (88.9). Until now Pliny never dared to hope for more than 'better than the worst', so grim were the expectations established by prior emperors (44.2). Pliny asks Trajan to hold the consulship in order to teach future emperors to give up their laziness and postpone their luxuries for a little while (59.2). Here it is presumed that (all) future emperors will have at least the second-order imperial vices of laziness and luxury, if not the first-order vices of arrogance and cruelty. Only occasionally do we find a general positive reference to future emperors: [85] they merely have to stay on the road to glory established by Trajan (by keeping adulation away), they do not have to build the road themselves (by removing adulation, 75.5).

One of the passages above (59.4) has a striking allusion to the all-too-familiar prospect of the current emperor *becoming* 'bad' through holding power. 'Let us be allowed to experience whether that second consulship gave you any haughtiness.' Though it is only a rhetorical fancy shielded off by the implied contrafactual mode (Trajan had *already* held his third consulship), it is remarkable that Pliny should venture to suggest that Trajan could acquire the canonical imperial vice *superbia* in mid-reign.[53] We can compare Trajan's addition to the senate's annual vows for the eternity of the *imperium* and the well-being of the emperor (67.3): '*if* he shall <govern> the republic well and in the interest of everyone' (*si bene rem publicam et ex*

---

[53] On *superbia* as a characteristic mark of a bad emperor, see e.g. 7.6 *superbum . . . et regium* ('arrogant and kingly'), 63.6 *superbissimis dominis* ('most arrogant masters').

utilitate omnium <*rexerit*>67.4). Pliny goes on to explain the subtext: death, or even tyrannicide ('that the gods should abandon you to vows that are *not* taken publicly', 67.5).[54] Later sources report that when appointing the praetorian prefect, Trajan said 'take this sword, to use for me if I rule well, but against me if I rule badly'.[55] Pliny reports similar words as Trajan's inner thoughts.[56] Whether Trajan actually said this, or whether this historical tradition was created out of this depiction of Trajan's thoughts, Pliny's use show that it was an acceptable topic for legitimizing the current regime.

I use the term 'tyrannicide' with its ancient connotation, to refer not merely to the killing of a tyrant but to the assertion that it is justifiable and legitimate (and accordingly I refrain from speaking of the 'murder', or even of the 'assassination' of emperors so as not to prejudge the issue). The well-known tradition in praise of tyrant-killing went back to Harmodios and Aristogeiton (e.g. Cic. *Mil.* 80, Sen. *Ben.* 7.15.2), and the philosophical tradition claimed further justification for it by saying it was in the (unredeemable) tyrant's own interest.[57] Furthermore, the frequent use of laws supporting tyrannicide in the declamatory tradition made the theoretical justification of tyrant-killing a basic element in rhetorical education.[58] To Cicero, Caesar was a tyrant simply for having illegally seized sole power (e.g. *Att.* 14.6.2, *Fam.* 12.22.2, *Offic.* 3.19; also *rex*, e.g. *Att.* 10.7.1, 14.21.3; cf. Suet. *Tib.* 4.1). But within a few generations, widespread acquiescence to the imperial system gave rise to the distinction between good and bad emperors, of which only the latter were tyrants.[59] Free states can have laws against trying to *become* a tyrant,

---

[54] Cf. Sen. *Clem.* 1.19.7 *vota non sub custode nuncupantibus* ('expressing prayers without being guarded'). Durry (1938) 187.

[55] Dio 68.16.1–2, Aur. Victor 13.9; Brunt (1979) 172.

[56] 67.8...*in me, si omnium utilitas ita posceret, etiam praefecti manum armavi* ('I have even armed the hand of the prefect against me, should public interest so demand').

[57] In the tyrant's interest, Pl. *Gorg.* 473–80, 525B, Cic. *Fin.* 4.56, or in both his own and the world's interest, Sen. *Ben.* 7.20.3.

[58] e.g. Cic. *de Invent.* 2.144, *Att.* 9.4.2, Sen. *Controv.* 1.7, Petron. 1.3, Quint. *Inst.* 3.6.25, Calpurn. Flacc. 1, Dio 67.12.5 (Maternus under Domitian).

[59] e.g. Tiberius, Tac. *Ann.* 6.6.2, Suet. *Tib.* 75.3; Nero, [Sen.] *Octav.* 83, Juv. 8.223, Suet. *Poet.* fr. 47 Lucan; Domitian, Plin. *Letters* 4.11.6; Seneca approves of the killing of Caligula (*Const. Sap.* 18) but not of Caesar (*Ira.* 3.30.4, *Ben.* 2.20; Griffin (1984) 173–4). On the distinction between the good monarch and the tyrant see e.g. Plato *Rep.* 562–9, *P* 291E, Polyb. 5.11.6, 6.7.8, Cic. *Rep.* 1.50.2, 1.65.2, Sen. *Clem.* 1.11.4, Dio Chrys. 1.67; Wirszubski (1950) 145; Whitmarsh (2001) 206–7.

but since there is rarely a non-violent or legal way to remove a tyrant, tyrannicide acquires justification as the only available method. And with no orderly way of evaluating who is a 'bad' emperor, almost any attempt to kill the emperor might be claimed to be justified tyrannicide; the main question is the practical one of whether it will improve the government, and whether it will result in further deaths or civil war.[60] Imperial Rome was trapped in a system of government with a low level of legitimacy, but no clear way to change it to a more legitimate system. [86]

We can understand the various panegyric motifs as attempts to generate this much-needed legitimacy in the ruler by emphasizing his virtues, his good government, his military success, and especially the authority of the senate and people. For example, the motif of divine election is sometimes favoured by rulers whose claim to power is particularly weak.[61] It might appear surprising, given the slippery nature of defining who is a tyrant, for Trajan and his panegyrist to tell people that he should die (or be killed) if he becomes a 'tyrant'. But Pliny (and Trajan) are confronting one of the strongest challenges to imperial legitimacy, the theory of justified tyrannicide, not by rejecting it, but by incorporating it into their ideological system; this approach is the inevitable result of the denigration of prior emperors that underlies the speech, especially of the slain Domitian. Pliny exults over Domitian's death (52.4–5; cf. Suet. *Dom.* 23.1), and implies approval of tyrannicide by deploring the punishment of the 'emperor-killers' Petronius Secundus and Parthenius, and Epaphroditus.[62] The approval of, and even complicity with the killing of Domitian, may seem to conflict with the oaths of loyalty that senators swore to all emperors, good or bad; but the principle of tyrannicide implies that forced oaths of loyalty to a 'tyrant' are non-binding. Thus, Pliny imagines Trajan as making this explicit, praying privately that the Republic may never have to take vows for him against its will, or if it does, that it not be obliged by them (. . . *obtestor ne umquam pro me vota res publica invita suscipiat, aut si susceperit, ne debeat,* 67.8). Pliny and Trajan are attempting to add validity to a

---

[60] Cic. *Att.* 9.4.2; Rawson (1991) 492.

[61] Fears (1977) 317–21. Compare Menand. Rhet. 370.21–8, 371.1–2 on using divine motifs for rulers of lowly family background; Kienast (1968) 65 n. 69.

[62] *Pan.* 6.2, Dio Chrys. 68.3.3, *epit. de Caesaribus* 12.6–8; *Pan.* 53.4, Dio Chrys. 67.14.4.

meaningless oath ritual by making the oath conditional on the emperor's not being a tyrant: 'if he should rule the republic well and in everyone's best interest' (67.4).

But the tyrannicide theme has a risky and subversive edge, and is suitable only for temporary propaganda among the upper class in a period of intense denigration of prior emperors. The emperor does *not* invite the armies and provinces to evaluate from year to year whether he has become a tyrant; the precedents of New Year's army revolts are bad enough without encouraging them.[63] The conditional oath formula never reached the provinces, and it was probably just a temporary publicity stunt in the senate.[64] Only from the gods does Trajan ask for an annual evaluation (67.6-7). It is a slight *suggestio falsi* ('intimation of a falsehood') when Pliny implies that it is because the armies use this conditional oath formula that Trajan feels no anxiety to hear about the New Years' vows throughout the empire (68.1-4); the 'correct' explanation for Trajan's calm is that since he is fulfilling his part of the condition by ruling well, he knows that the gods will preserve him.

The tyrannicide theory of legitimacy sits uneasily with the divine-election theory of legitimacy.[65] Yet Pliny does his best to join them: the fact that Trajan has not been killed proves that he is divinely protected, and therefore not a tyrant but rather a good emperor, ruling for the benefit of the state (67.5, 68.1, 72.4). This join is possible because unlike near-Eastern and other monarchical traditions, the Roman tradition used the divine-election theme for the person of the emperor and not for the office.[66] The current emperor was divinely chosen, but not all emperors were (*Pan.* 1.4), and though people said the same of Domitian during his reign, it turned out that this was false adulation.[67] Still, the prominence that Pliny gives to this potentially subversive motif is striking; the closing prayer to Jupiter is built around the tyrannicide motif (94.5) just as the opening prayer is built around the divine-election motif (1.4). Precisely in the closing prayer for 'perpetuity' does Pliny go back to Trajan's conditional formula with the spectre of tyranny and the [87] instability of

---

[63] Vitellius in 69 is the definitive example, Tac. *Hist.* 1.12, 1.55; for Saturninus in 89, see *CIL* 6.2066, *CAH^1* 172.

[64] *Letters* 10.35, 52, 100, 102; Herrmann (1968) 99-108.

[65] Brunt (1979) 172.

[66] Fears (1977) 187.

[67] e.g. *Pan.* 72.5-7, 74.3; Bartsch (1994) 162-4 and above pp. 163-7.

tyrannicide. This shows the strength of the traditional philosophical-Republican opposition between good government and tyranny, which had been incorporated into imperial ideology in the form of the denigration of predecessors. It is unnecessary to ask whether this is imperial flattery or hidden senatorial criticism, since the official imperial policy itself flaunted senatorial independence, along with the attendant philosophical-Republican baggage.[68]

CONCLUSION

Several useful oppositions have been suggested for categorizing types of panegyric works—for example, the 'charismatic'/'rational' opposition, with the 'charismatic' aspect emphasizing the benefits of autocracy (power, victory, stability, prosperity) and the 'rational' aspect emphasizing the liberty and authority of the senate and the good ruler's restraint from exercising arbitrary power;[69] the 'constitutional'/'theocratic' opposition;[70] and the 'official-ceremonial'/ 'private-informal' opposition.[71] I have tried to show that these oppositions should be seen as intersecting axes of ideology, each with its spectrum of possibilities, rather than exclusive dichotomies. For example, Wallace-Hadrill says that the 'charismatic' imperial virtues such as *aeternitas* or *providentia,* familiar from the coinage, predominate in the letters of book 10 but are absent from the *Panegyric.* It would be better, though, to say that the 'charismatic' voice alternates with the 'rational' voice, emerging especially at moments of oaths (67.3 *aeternitate*) and prayers (94.1 *perpetuitatem*), and even blending with it, when the imperial oath is joined to the tyrannicide theme (67.4).[72] It should also be clear that both 'constitutional' and 'theocratic' aspects abound in the speech. The constitutional aspect, to be sure, like the 'rational' aspect, is expressed by the dominant voice, and the theocratic aspect tends to be expressed through innuendo (*suggestio divini,* 'intimation of divinity'),

---

[68] 'The two views are not mutually exclusive', Fears (1977), 152–3; Méthy (2000) 371.
[69] Wallace-Hadrill (1981) 317–9; Syme (1958) 12.
[70] Brunt (1979) 172; Kienast (1968) 69; Cotton and Yakobson (2002) 206–9.
[71] Fears (1977) 151, 190; Gamberini (1983) 375.
[72] Wallace-Hadrill (1981) 317; contra, see Braund (1998) 64, reprinted above p. 96.

metaphor, or outright denial, though that does not necessarily make it the weaker voice.[73] As we have seen, the surprised-by-providence motif portrays the human persona of the emperor encountering his divine context. Gamberini draws from both book 10 and the *Panegyric* for examples of 'ceremonial' language as opposed to books 1–9, whereas Fears contrasts letter 10.1, a 'personal declaration', with the *Panegyric*, an 'official announcement'.[74] As I have shown, there is both a great deal of overlap and significant differences among the panegyric strategies used in Pliny's surviving works: books 1–9, the various parts of book 10, and the *Panegyric*. I would prefer to locate them all along a continuum between informal and public (or ceremonial) poles, with all of them being representatives of official propaganda in various generic settings. I would also suggest that we can consider the ceremonial writings of Pliny the expert orator as just as authentic a source of Trajanic propaganda as Trajan himself, if not more so. If the letters of book 10 do tend to give a more straightforward version of the imperial voice, this is partly due to the extreme rhetorical elaboration of encomiastic themes in the *Panegyric*, which makes it the paradigmatic example of literary imperial propaganda of its time.

[73] Even Menander Rhetor introduces divine topics through innuendo; see 371.5–12, 377.20, 28, 369.5–7. The disparity between Menander and the *Panegyric* is generally over-stated, e.g. Russell (1998) 45.

[74] Fears (1977) 151.

Part III

The Gallic Panegyrics

10

Latin Panegyric in the Tetrarchic and Constantinian Period

C. E. V. Nixon

his laudationibus historia rerum nostrarum est facta mendosior
'Speeches of praise have made our history more mendacious'
(Cicero, *Brutus* 16.62)

in summa meae res gestae tantae sunt, quantae sunt scilicet, quoiquoimodi sunt: tantae autem videbuntur, quantas tu eas videri voles
'In sum, such are my achievements, how great, and of whatever sort: but they will seem to be as great as you want them to seem'
(Lucius Verus Imperator to M. Cornelius Fronto, ed. Haines II, 196)

It was long before Late Antiquity that panegyric first infected history, and thereafter the two genres were seldom if ever completely distinct. As critical an historian as Ammianus Marcellinus appears to have had no compunction about using panegyrical techniques, or indeed an actual panegyric, in describing Julian and his exploits.[1]

It is not my brief to demonstrate either that my genre is 'old' or that its Late Antique manifestations are replete with traditional elements. Therefore I shall not mention *laudationes funebres* ('funerary speeches of praise'), nor the progress from praise of the dead to praise of the living (*Pro lege Manilia, Pro Marcello*, which influenced late

---

[1] Cf. MacCormack (1975) 153, n. 70 and the works there cited.

Latin panegyric), nor the fact that, while critics such as Lucian (*How to Write History* esp. 7, 13, 30f. and 61) identified and dramatised the problem illustrated in Lucius Verus' letter to Fronto, cited above, they did little to solve it.

But perhaps I should stress the enormous number of panegyrics that were delivered in the early Roman Empire, not just to princes and potentates but to *privati* ('private individuals') such as one's literary patron (for example the pseudo-Tibullan *Panegyricus Messallae*). The accident of survival and a certain prejudice against the post-classical age has sometimes led to an association of panegyric with the Late Antique period which is quite misleading. For example it is clear that the *gratiarum actio* ('speech of thanksgiving') became panegyrical at a very early stage. In the Republic, a speech of thanks would be delivered to the *senatus populusque Romanus* ('senate and people of Rome') for one's consulship. Ovid describes the change: the incumbent now thanks the gods—and Caesar (*Pont.* 4.4.35–9; there is the procession to the Capitol and the speech to the senate, *ubi . . . egeris et meritas superis cum Caesare grates* ('when you have given due thanks to the gods along with Caesar')). Had we all the *gratiarum actiones* of all the *novus homo* consuls of the Augustan era we might not sneer so much at Pliny the Younger.

Pliny's speech of thanks to Trajan heads the co-called 'Gallic corpus' which is my main subject here, but the fact that the next earliest speech is dated to *c.*289 of course does not imply a long gap in the genre. Fronto, for one, was active in the Antonine period (panegyric on Antoninus' victory in Britain, *Pan. Lat.* VIII(4)14.2; cf. Fronto, ed. Haines, I, 130, §1; 134, §4), as was Eumenius' grandfather, at the height of the disturbances in the mid third century, until the sack of Autun in the late 260s closed the Maenian schools (*Pan. Lat.* IX(5)17.3).

[89] How, then, do we account for the composition of the Gallic corpus which, in addition to the speech of Pliny's, is made up of nine speeches dating from *c.*289 to 321, plus speeches of AD 362 and 389? The contents of the corpus are said to reflect pride in the revival of the Gallic schools of Late Antiquity, and, as we shall see, there is much to suggest a literary motive for the collection.

The occasions on which the late Latin panegyrics were delivered— the foundation day of a city (*Pan. Lat.* X(2), VI(7)); the birthday of a ruler (XI(3)))[2]; the anniversary of an accession (VIII(4), V(8); Constantine's Quinquennalia ('fifth anniversary of accession', 25 July 311 (*Pan. Lat.* V(8)))[3]; the arrival of an important official (IX(5)); an imperial marriage (VII(6)); the return of the Emperor from a successful campaign (XII(9), II(12)); and the receipt of a consulship (*Pan. Lat.* III(11))—these occasions were traditional ones for such speeches, as the handbooks of rhetoric make clear. By and large, our panegyrics are traditional, too, in structure, theme and style. The more skilful speakers adapt the handbook rules to suit their requirements (as Mesk, amongst others, has shown[4]) but the conventional basic structure is usually preserved intact.

In style, the panegyrics are remarkably 'classical', indeed Ciceronian, for their time and place. The goals for which the panegyrists strove are clear, even if they did not always attain them; one speaker complains of the unfair advantages enjoyed by the 'real' Romans (in all likelihood he was from Trier):

> *neque enim ignoro quanto inferiora nostra sint ingenia Romanis, siqui-dem latine et diserte loqui illis ingeneratum est, nobis elaboratum. et, si quid forte commode dicimus, ex illo fonte et capite facundiae imitatio nostra derivat.*

> Nor am I ignorant how greatly inferior my talent is in comparison with the Romans, since indeed it is inborn among them to speak in Latin and eloquently, while for us it is a product of much labour, and, if perchance we should speak with any elegance at all, our simulation of fluency derives from that very font and source. (XII(9)1.2)

Klotz and others have traced, not always convincingly, the borrowings of the panegyrists from previous writers.[5] Cicero is prominent in their tables, but there is considerable variation between speakers. The reminiscences of Eumenius, for instance, are only of Cicero's *Oratorica*; 'Mamertinus' (= the supposed author of X(2) and XI(3)) is more learned, drawing (allegedly) on the *Philosophica*, and on much more. Some panegyrists seem to copy the phrases of others, the significance of which I shall comment upon in a moment. There are Vergilian quotations and tags, and occasionally what looks like a piece of personal research or autopsy. For example, in speaking of the cult

---

[2] For the occasion, Nixon (1981a).
[3] Not 312, as Galletier would have it; cf. Nixon (1980).
[4] Mesk (1912).   [5] Klotz (1911a).

of Hercules at Rome, 'Mamertinus' remarks that 'it is no fable stemming from poetic licence, nor mere belief based on the assertion of
by-gone eras, but a manifest and confirmed fact, as the great altar of
Hercules attests even today—*sicut hodieque testatur Herculis ara
maxima*—together with the Pinarian family, guardian of the cult of
Hercules,' that Hercules was received as a guest within the *Pallantea
moenia* . . . (X(2)1.3). But this is borrowed knowledge—note Servius
Auctus, *ad Aen.* VIII 271: *ingens enim est ara Herculis sicut videmus
hodieque* ('this is the great altar of Hercules, as we see today'). Elsewhere, 'Mamertinus' locates the rostra in the Circus Maximus (XI(3)
19.5)! Evidently he picked up the phrase via a chain of earlier
Vergilian commentators—Julius Hyginus, Suetonius, Aemilius
Asper et al. who repeat each other just as modern [90] scholars do,
and who are repeated in turn by Donatus, Servius and the later
commentators.[6]

I do not wish to speak at length of the content of the panegyrics,
which again is traditional and predictable: praise of rulers for time-
honoured virtues, martial and moral—for *pietas* and *felicitas* (XI(3)),
for *clementia* or *severitas*, as the occasion demands. Our skilful
orators are for the most part unruffled by delicate political matters
or abrupt imperial tergiversations; they respond with the gamut of
familiar techniques—rationalization, explication, exculpation, gloss,
silence or what have you: their conventions see them through.

A moment ago I said the panegyrics are, or purport to be, occasional. Scholars have sometimes suggested that they are 'school products, that the speeches we have were not actually delivered'.[7] Yet
there is a wealth of evidence to confirm that speeches were given on
such occasions—for example the Letters of Fronto (Haines, I, 130 § 1;
134, §4); indeed there is a reference to a panegyric of his on Antoninus' victory in Britain in one of our panegyrics (VIII(4)14.2). The

---

[6] Further on (X(2)13.5) 'Mamertinus' pointedly tells the story of Hercules' acquisition of the cognomen Victor; it was given to him by a merchant who defeated pirates
with Hercules' help. *adeo, sacratissime imperator, multis iam saeculis inter officia est
numinis tui superare piratas* ('thus for many centuries now it has been among the
duties of your godhead to overcome pirates, most sacred emperor'). Well might
Carausius quail! The same story turns up in Macrobius, *Sat.* II 6.11, who cites the
Julio-Claudian jurist Masurius Sabinus. Macrobius then cites (Aemilius) Asper the
Vergilian commentator. The world of Macrobius and that of our panegyrist are
similar: we are among schoolmen.
[7] e.g. Durry (1938) 4 n. 6.

panegyrists refer to the speeches of others celebrating imperial exploits (III(11)5.1; XII(9)1.1) and introduce circumstantial details about the occasions on which they themselves spoke—the presence of the emperor (for example VIII(4)1.1, 1.4), and on one occasion his absence (IV(10)3.1), the nature of the audience (V(8)2.1; see below, pp. 233–4) and so on. I think there is no real reason to suspect their authenticity in this respect; that would be to postulate a very elaborate charade, as we shall see.

I even doubt whether they were polished up or amplified after delivery, which was what Pliny did with his panegyric (*Letters* 3.18, 1–2; cf. 3.13, 7.17.5ff., 1.20). Our panegyrics, unlike Pliny's, are short (with one exception, II(12), to Theodosius); they would seem not to have been elaborated. Why believe that they had rough edges when delivered before such an august audience, and that they needed subsequent revision? Let us assume, then, and it is important to my case, that our corpus is a collection of speeches actually delivered, substantially in their present form. With a couple of exceptions they will have been delivered at the imperial court at Trier, as internal references make clear.

I have now set the stage for the main topic of my paper, namely the relationship of panegyric and panegyrist to the imperial Court. The period of the Tetrarchy and the early years of Constantine is a shadowy one. In the absence of a detailed narrative history the Gallic panegyrics, along with Lactantius' *De mortibus persecutorum*, loom larger than such sources normally would. It is of some importance, then, to try to establish the status of the panegyrics and the relationship of their authors to the imperial government. How dependent upon the court are the panegyrists, and what is the function of their speeches?

A sensitive student of the panegyrists, René Pichon, whose *Les derniers écrivains profanes* is still one of the best treatments of the subject, has suggested that the late Latin panegyrics were purely ceremonial without political aim, unlike earlier panegyrics.[8] On the other hand Johannes Straub bases an argument on their quasi-official character and political significance.[9] A more recent writer, none more aware of the ceremonial importance of the genre, Sabine MacCormack, avers that 'these panegyrics were all used as a medium to

---

[8] Pichon (1906a) 42–3.   [9] Straub (1955) 298.

announce imperial programmes and policies',[10] and frequently refers to them as an instrument of propaganda.[11] None of these statements in my opinion, does justice to the significance of the corpus. Without denying the immediacy of the political message of some of our panegyrics, I should like to emphasise that they have a public and political life which transcends this, that they are not merely occasional, [91] nor merely ephemeral pieces of propaganda (when, indeed, they are that at all). They have a 'hidden audience' of which more later on. I shall also explore as far as possible the individual circumstances of the panegyrists, and their careers, in order to determine the sense in which the label 'official' or 'quasi-official' may be attached to their products.

To generalise about the corpus is perhaps admirable in principle, but it is to do less than justice to the very real differences between individual panegyrics. Let us look more closely at specific panegyrics. If we were to take VI(7) of 310 as typical we might well subscribe to MacCormack's view. It is hard to believe that a panegyrist would dare to publicise a previously all but unknown and surely fictitious genealogy for a reigning emperor (Constantine) without some kind of encouragement from the court, nor that he would deal with such a delicate matter as the downfall of Maximian without first 'clearing' his version with it. Indeed, rather than to postulate such boldness and imagination from an independent speaker it would seem more reasonable to conclude that he had been primed by the court. On the other hand it is equally hard to believe that the imperial government would be much concerned with the details of a speech, delivered in Rome in 321 in the absence of the emperor (IV(10)), which largely consisted of a narrative of Constantine's invasion of Italy in 312, or with the details of the way in which Constantine was thanked for relieving the city of Autun of some of its tax burden (V(8)). But much depends on one's preconceptions, as a perusal of scholarly debate reveals.

In order to test the proposition that panegyric was a medium selected by the imperial government to *announce* imperial programmes and policies one might proceed by looking at individual panegyrists and attempting to determine their relationship with the court, the circumstances of the delivery of their speeches, and, if

---

[10] MacCormack (1975) 160.
[11] MacCormack (1975) 154 and 159–66 and (1981), 5; cf. too, Galletier (1952) 114.

possible, the procedure of selection of speakers for official occasions. It has to be conceded that this is a difficult project. Most of our speakers are anonymous, and while some divulge information about themselves, others are pertinaciously reticent. In the period under scrutiny, the Tetrarchic and Constantinian period, we have eight speakers and nine panegyrics. Let us tabulate and review them in chronological order:

1. 'Mamertinus' (X(2), XI(3)); refers in XI(3)1.2 to an *honor* received from Maximian which far exceeds his expectations; the incipit of XI(3) reads *eiusdem magistri* ('of the same teacher'); 'Mamertinus' has spoken before Maximian previously (XI(3) 1.2, 5.1) and confidently expects to again, five years hence (XI(3) 1.3); he is probably from Trier (X(2)12.6 and Galletier (1949) 6–7).

2. Anon. (VIII(4)). The speaker has come out of retirement (1.1; 1.4); he once taught youths (1.2); a considerable time ago he was introduced to the Court of Maximian by Constantius and delivered a speech on Maximian's exploits *qui me in lucem primus eduxit* ('which first brought into view', 1.5); that is, it led to a court post, apparently as some kind of secretary (1.4 and Galletier (1949) 71–2); he participated in an expedition of Maximian against the Alemanni (2.1); in this speech he conveys the congratulations of Autun to Constantius for his anniversary and victory in Britain (21.2).

3. Eumenius (IX(5)): grandson of an Athenian who taught rhetoric at Rome and then at Autun (17.2–3); a teacher of rhetoric himself (1.1, 2.2–5), but who had not spoken *in foro* before (1.1, 3.1); now speaks there at Autun, in the presence of the governor of Lugdunensis; formerly *magister memoriae* of Constantius (11.2; cf. 6.2); recently appointed by him director (*praeceptor moderatorque*) of the Maenian schools (5.3, 14 and *passim*). [92]

4. Anon. (VII(6)): no personal information discoverable; aware of the panegyrics of 'Mamertinus' (cf. Galletier (1952) 10).

5. Anon. (VI(7)): *mediae aetatis* ('of middle age', 1.1), he has had considerable experience employed in *diversis otii et palatii officiis* ('various duties in leisure and in court', 23.1); he commends his children to the Emperor Constantine, and especially his

eldest son, *summa fisci patrocinia tractantem* ('exercising the highest interests of the revenue'); he has numerous protégés *quos provexi ad tutelam fori, ad officia palatii* ('whom I have brought to the guardianship of the forum, to the offices of the court'); he is now engaged by *privatorum studiorum ignobiles curae* ('the ignoble concerns of private interests') but hopes for another court post (23.3); he is from Autun (22, esp. 22.7).

6. Anon. (V(8)): a rhetorician from the Schools (*iam non privati studii litterarum . . . orator*, 'an orator now not from the private study of literature', 1.2); a local senator (1, 3; 9.4) from Autun (4.2) who volunteered to convey the city's thanks to Constantine for tax cuts (1.1–3).

7. Anon. (XII(9)): A Gaul (1.2), and a rhetor, one *qui semper res a numine tuo gestas praedicare solitus essem* ('who was always accustomed to proclaim the achievements of your divinity' 1.1), but in the Schools or at court? He doesn't mention any imperial post.

8. Nazarius (IV(10)): speaking in Rome (1–3.1, with 38.6); a distinguished professor of rhetoric in the School of Bordeaux (Ausonius, *Prof. Burd.* XIV); his daughter a Christian? (Prosper Aquit., *Chron.* I, 452; cf. Jerome, *Chron.* s.a. 336).

So of the seven speakers for whom some biographical information is recoverable, four (numbers 1, 2, 3 and 5) have been in imperial service. But with the probable exception of 'Mamertinus' and only in the case of his second speech, none of them was *currently* engaged in such service at the time of delivery of his panegyric.[12] Number 2 (VIII(4)) speaks of *otium* ('retirement' or 'leisure'); he was called out of retirement to convey the felicitations of Autun to Constantius. Eumenius (no. 3) has moved from his post as *magister memoriae* to a new appointment as director of the Schools of Autun. The panegyrist of 310 (no. 5), while angling for a job at court, is currently engaged in private studies (VI(7)23.3). Clearly they are not imperial 'press secretaries', indeed they are not part of the imperial administration at all, and so their speeches are not *formally* official pronouncements on imperial policies or events of the day.

---

[12] They are not 'functionaries of the Empire', Pichon (1906c) 289, but former 'functionaries'.

In fact many of the speakers seem to be (nos. 3, 5, 6, 8 and perhaps 7), or to have been (no. 2), professors of rhetoric (or law, in the case of no. 5?) at Autun, Trier (?) and Bordeaux. But they are speaking at court in formal surroundings on important ceremonial occasions. How did they get there, seeing that they were not already employed at court? How independent were they? One might still be able to argue that 'these panegyrics were all used as a medium to announce imperial programmes and policies' despite the observations I have made. I shall return in a moment to these questions, noting only—at this point—that there is very little direct evidence on the subject of selection and briefing of speakers.[13]

I wish to turn now to a test case, which I regard as a salutary warning to exponents of the 'propaganda' argument in its extreme form, and which incidentally also raises other relevant questions. In 321 Nazarius spoke in Rome on the occasion of the Quinquennalia

---

[13] VI(7)1.1 gives us some information about a specific instance: *facerem, sacratissime imperator, quod paulo ante mihi plerique suaserunt ut, quoniam maiestas tua hunc mediocritati meae diem in ista civitate celeberrimum ad dicendum dedisset, de eo ipso ducerem sermonis exordium, nisi me ab hoc duplex ratio revocaret, considerantem neque mediae aetatis hominem ostentare debere subitam dicendi facultatem [dicendi] neque ad aures tanti numinis quicquam nisi diu scriptum et saepe tractatum adferri oportere* ('I would do, O most hallowed emperor, what a great number of people have been advising me just now (*paulo ante*) to do, namely, since your majesty has allotted to my modest talents a day so celebrated in this city for my speech [he speaks of the foundation-day of the city of Trier], derive the introduction to my discourse from that very circumstance, did a double reason not dissuade me from this procedure. I consider first that a man of mature age has no business making a display of his talent for extempore speaking, and secondly, that nothing should be brought to the ears of such a great divinity which has not been composed over a period of time and frequently revised.') From this one may deduce, that the emperor himself, or his representative, put the speaker on the programme, and perhaps it was normal for speeches to be prepared carefully in advance. Both these deductions are reinforced by XI(3); at 5.1 the speaker comments that he has celebrated the expeditions and victories of the emperor 'whenever your divine estimation has accorded me the favour of your audience' (*cum mihi auditionis tuae divina dignatio eam copiam tribuit*), and in the exordium he reveals that he had prepared a panegyric for Maximian's Quinquennalia, but for some reason or other (presumably the unexpected absence of the emperor) had been unable to deliver it—he now, in its stead, delivers a speech celebrating Maximian's birthday. But can we also deduce from the passage of *Pan. Lat.* VI(7) cited above that the speaker had no idea when, i.e. on what occasion, he was going to speak? Surely not. In this case it looks to me as if the panegyrist was not told exactly what day he was 'on' until his arrival at court. The festival in question lasted several days (2.1 and esp. 3.7: 'these days on which the origin of [Hercules'] immortality is celebrated'), and the reference in 1.1 would then be to his luck in being chosen to orate on the very foundation day of Trier, as distinct from the day before or after.

('fifth anniversary of accession') of the Caesars Crispus and Constantine II, but in the absence of Constantine himself. His speech, in essence, centres on the expedition of 312 against Maxentius (IV(10) 6–35), after brief praise of the young Caesars. Subsequent events are dismissed in a few lines (38.4 on recent legislation, Constantine's 'moral revival'). This is disappointing for us, for Nazarius adds comparatively little to the panegyric of 313; we have a 'lost decade'. Especially if your expectation is 'propaganda' or an 'official line', Nazarius seems obviously 'out-of-date'. [93]

What is the explanation? Was there really nothing of interest to say about recent events? Or is it the absence of the emperor that is crucial—the emperor was not there to brief him? But surely someone at court could have? Or did Constantine or his ministers choose not to have the events of 312–21 aired? A show-down with Licinius was obviously looming. In 320 Constantine had held a (sixth) consulship with Constantine Junior, out of turn, and in 321 when Crispus and Constantine II (again) were consuls, Licinius refused to permit the publication of their names in the East. On the other hand, one might argue the reverse case—now was the time for propaganda! As I remarked earlier, it would seem to depend on one's preconceptions.

But something may be learned from our example if we put it beside its 'parallel', the panegyric of 313. The latter panegyric was delivered in the imperial presence, and in its narrative of the invasion of Italy seems altogether 'up-to-date'. The juxtaposition might seem to illustrate graphically the difference between being 'briefed' and not being 'briefed'. But it is delusive, for the panegyric of 313 is *not* 'up-to-date' at all. The panegyrist himself refers to the speeches of *disertissimi* ('most eloquent men') which the emperor has already heard, both at Rome *and in Trier*, (*in urbe sacra et hic rursus*, 1.1), but cannot refrain from adding his feeble (and non-Roman) voice *inter tantos sonitus disertorum* ('among such great sounds of eloquent men'). In other words, panegyrics on the defeat of Maxentius were already 'old hat'. Even at Trier, their news value or impact as political messages must have been slight. This is a clear warning. It is hazardous to assume that any speech that happens to be preserved in our corpus is the first on its subject, and therefore announcing for the first time an imperial programme or policy. Imperial programmes and policies may have been announced 'publicly' in this fashion, but we cannot *assume* that there is any such announcement in our collection. I do not know, nor does Seston,[14] the date, occasion or manner of announcement of Diocletian and Maximian's relationship to Iuppiter and Hercules, but I wager it was not first announced by 'Mamertinus' in Trier on 21 April, 289 (*Pan. Lat.* X(2)).

A better candidate for really 'hot' news items is Panegyric VI(7) of 310, with its avowedly novel Constantinian genealogy *quod plerique adhuc fortasse nesciunt* ('which most people, perhaps, still don't know', 2.1), its undeniably local 'Vision of Apollo' (21.3ff.), and an account of the downfall of Maximian for which the orator awaits the approval of Constantine himself (*de nutu* 'from your nod', 14.1) before proceeding. But even here the apparent novelty may be misleading, and the 'boldness' arises not because the panegyrist has been briefed, but because he is an experienced old professional (see 'biography' above) and 'knows the ropes'.

Let me revert to Nazarius. Surely the key to our mystery is the venue—Rome—and the audience, which is bound to have included senators. Constantine, despite his appointment of aristocrats to important imperial posts[15] had scarcely given unequivocal support and comfort to the pagan aristocracy of Rome: the best political mileage for the panegyrist was obviously to concentrate on the liberation of the Sacred City from the Unspeakable Tyrant, no matter how dated or hackneyed the theme. I cannot *prove* that Nazarius was not briefed for the occasion, but I assume that a rhetor who rose to become a leading professor in the Schools of Bordeaux was capable of making a professional judgement of this kind without the assistance of the court.

Our Nazarius case has raised another question. What was the audience of our panegyrists? We know less than we would like, but for speeches delivered at the court of Trier we may assume the emperor, courtiers, senior officials, and palace bureaucrats...and frequently a greater public throng. The panegyrist of 311 specifically tells us (V(8)2.1) that the [94] emperor is present, his whole *amicorum...comitatus, et omnis imperii apparatus* ('the accompanying cohorts of friends, and all the apparatus of empire', i.e. all the imperial *apparatchiks*), 'and a whole host of men from practically every city [in Gaul], either on public missions or with private petitions'. The occasion was the Quinquennalia of 25 July 311. (The speaker had passed

---

[14] See Nixon (1981a) for a critique of his views.
[15] See Arnheim (1972), ch. 3; not undermined, in my opinion, by Novak (1979).

up an earlier opportunity to address the emperor in the vestibule of the palace on the grounds that the audience was inappropriately small.) Nazarius (1.1) speaks more vaguely of a throng (*coetus*), again for a Quinquennalia.

Oswyn Murray, in an interesting review of Johannes Straub's *Vom Herrscherideal in der Spätantike*, tilts against the line that the pane-gyrics have a 'publicizing function': talk of propaganda is inappropri-ate when it is a question of appealing to the converted; evidence for an 'immediate' (a cunningly chosen adjective!) impact on a wider public is scanty.[16] But this may not be enough to unseat his adversary. The fact that the audience on these occasions was not confined to the court itself is significant; it offers the possibility of a wider dissemina-tion of ideas and viewpoints, and rapidly, too, with the return of visitors to their respective *civitates* ('cities'). But I do not wish to seem to disagree with Murray; rather, I would direct our attention else-where, to a 'hidden audience', but more of this in a moment.

I wish now to revert to the question of how independent the panegyrists were of emperor and court. Can something be learned from the tone of the panegyrics? The corpus shows a complete range. On the one hand we have the confident panegyrist of 310 who has been around the court for a long time (VI(7)23.1), who can even contemplate extemporising in the presence of the emperor (were it not unbefitting to his age and the audience; for as he says, somewhat sententiously, 'he who extemporises before an emperor of the Roman people has no feeling for the greatness of the empire'), who can also put in a recommendation for his five sons and boast of his pupils in imperial service and private professions and, in closing, angle for a post as court orator. On the other hand, there are those who confess to nervousness at speaking at court. The panegyrist of 311, the local senator who thanks the emperor for tax remissions, vividly evokes a subject's feelings of awe in the presence of the *sacratissimus imperator* ('most sacred emperor').

> It is no small business to ask the emperor of the whole world for a favour for oneself, to put on a bold front before the aspect of such great majesty, to compose one's features, to shore up one's spirits, to think of the words, to utter them confidently, to know when to stop, to wait for a reply. (V(8)9.3)

[16] Murray (1966) 104.

But he delivers a fine speech which rather belies his pose, and this reminds us that our speakers are professionals; all (or nearly all) are or have been professors of rhetoric. Some, as we have seen above, have been called to court from the Schools; others, such as Eumenius, moved in the reverse direction. But whatever the nature of their experience at court or in the imperial administration one might expect them to be thoroughly conversant with 'the rules of the game' and to have a professional pride in their ability to compose an appropriate oration for any occasion. In other words, given the biographical data available, the apparent lack of novelty of the material—the absence of political 'news' (with the notable exception of the panegyric of 310)—and the unlikelihood of its uniqueness, one need not conclude that the imperial input in the panegyrics was very great at all.[17]

That, however, does not mean that the panegyrics were never 'instruments of propaganda'. But they were seldom instruments of propaganda in the crudest and most direct sense of the [95] phrase. Rather, they usually reflected imperial wishes in a more subtle way. For the Schools themselves were under imperial patronage. Upon the death of a distinguished *praeceptor* of the Maenian Schools in Autun, Constantius appointed as its new head, at a very handsome salary, Eumenius, *cuius eloquentiam et gravitatem morum ex actus nostri habemus administratione compertam* ('whose eloquence and seriousness of character we have ascertained from your administration of our affairs', IX(5)14.1). Let me emphasize that the initiative was taken by the emperor; Eumenius was ordered to exchange his secretarial

---

[17] Let me offer a further illustration, from XI(3). As we have seen above, its author 'Mamertinus' probably occupied an official post at the time. Here, if anywhere, we might expect obvious signs of imperial input. Now the centrepiece of the panegyrics is a description of the crossing of the Alps by the emperors Diocletian and Maximian, and their meeting at Milan (ch. 8–12). The orator discourses amusingly on the confusion arising when privileged subjects were confronted by the unaccustomed obligation to pay *adoratio* to two rulers of like status. But the meeting is described entirely from the viewpoint of the spectator; there is no hint that 'Mamertinus' was apprised of their counsels. If there were an announcement of an imperial programme policy, it certainly does not appear here. This is scarcely surprising. We can be sure that the main topic of conversation at the meeting was what to do about the rebel Carausius after the failure of Maximian's expedition of 289 against him (cf. X(2)12 with the silence of XI(3) about its fate and the revealing snippet in VIII(4)12.2). It were best for 'Mamertinus' to avoid the subject for the time being! In sum, deductions about imperial policy can be formed here from the panegyrics, but not as a result of any imperial announcements.

post at court for one at Autun: *qui [Constantius] honorem litterarum hac quoque dignatione cumulavit ut me filio potius meo ad pristina mea studia aditum molientum ipsum iusserit disciplinas artis oratoriae retractare* ... and so on ('he added to the prestige of letters as well as by this distinction, that when I myself was striving for an entry to my former studies, this time for my son, he ordered me to undertake anew the discipline of the art of rhetoric ... '). This solicitude for the education of the youth of Gaul—*merentur et Galli nostri ut eorum liberis, quorum vita in Augustodunensium oppido ingenuis artibus eruditu* ('Our Gauls, too, deserve that we should desire to make provision for the talents of their children, who are instructed in the liberal arts in the town of Autun ... ', 14.1)—was, of course, not entirely disinterested ... *et ipsi adulescentes, qui hilaro consensu meum Constanti Caesaris ex Italia revertentis suscepere comitatum, ut eorum indoli consulere cupiamus* (' ... and those youths, too, who cheerfully joined my retinue when I, Constantius Caesar, returned from Italy', 14.1).

     This imperial patronage of the Schools is scarcely surprising, for the Schools were the nursery or training ground for the imperial civil service, a recruiting ground for future officials and administrators. Another passage from Eumenius illustrates this very well. In the context of his appointment as *praeceptor moderatorque* Eumenius says that the emperors *litterarum* ... *habuere dilectum, neque aliter quam si equestri turmae uel cohorti praetoriae consulendum foret, quem potissimum praeficerent sui arbitrii esse duxerunt, ne hi quos ad spem omnium tribunalium aut interdum ad stipendia cognitionum sacrarum aut fortasse ad ipsa palatii magisteria provehi oporteret, veluti repentino nubilo in mediis adulescentiae fluctibus deprehensi, incerta dicendi signa sequerentur* ('held ... a levy of letters, and just as if they were providing for the command of a cavalry squadron or a praetorian cohort, they held it to be a matter for themselves to decide whom to put in charge in preference to all others, lest those who by rights had hopes of promotion to all the tribunals or on some occasions to service in the sacred (i.e., imperial) law courts, or perhaps even to the palace secretariats themselves, as if caught in a sudden cloud amidst the billows of youth, should pursue wavering standards of rhetoric' [or 'untrustworthy guides to eloquence'], IX(5)5.4). The Schools must have been especially important in Gaul where the recent location of the court at Trier will have created a great demand for educated men.[18] We have seen above how many imperial officials the panegyrist of 310 claimed to have trained. We should ask what the educational goals of the Schools were, and what was the nature of the training. I spoke before of a 'hidden audience' of the panegyrics. That audience was the youth of Gaul. Let me clarify my point by reminding you of the disparate nature of the Gallic corpus of panegyrics. It is a collection of panegyrics ranging in date (Pliny's excluded) from 289 to 389, united by no common political or historical theme. Indeed, it must be stressed that the speeches are patently untampered with, politically or religiously speaking. For example, there is no process of 'Constantinification', no attempt to revise the portrait of Maximian: he appears in various guises, now as brother and assistant of Diocletian (*Pan. Lat.* of [96] 289 and 291), now as promoter and patron of Constantine and Senior Augustus (in 307), and finally as traitorous villain (in 310). One might contrast Eusebius' *Ecclesiastical History* with its series of revisions. Or take the panegyrics of 313 and 321. In the former, Constantine is portrayed as the bold (indeed even brash) invader of Italy and aggressor against Maxentius, heedless alike of advice and entrails (XII(9)2.4). Nazarius, speaking in 321, portrays Maxentius as the aggressor, presumably in line with, if not compelled by, the current official view of the matter. Again, there is no attempt to suppress, or tone down, Constantine's Vision of Apollo, when that may have been regarded as inappropriate in many circles.

The collection of such a corpus of occasional speeches, some of very ephemeral and parochial interest, is at first glance surprising, and the motive for the compilation has naturally been seen as a literary one–these are examples of the best products of the Gallic Schools of rhetoric. I have no quarrel with this conclusion, but wish to draw attention to the very survival of these politically ephemeral pieces. The implication is that they were read and used as models in the Schools. Indeed, several of the panegyrists betray an awareness of the work of their predecessors, and borrow their phrases. Thus the

---

[18] This is not to discount pre-Tetrarchic Gaul as a centre of education. After all, Eumenius' grandfather, who was born in Athens and who had settled in Rome, left there and migrated to Autun, drawn by *amor doctrinae* ('love of learning'), in the days before the *Imperium Galliarum* ('Gallic Empire'). But Gaul's pre-eminence can be exaggerated; for example, Haarhoff (1920) 141 suggests without any trace of humour that perhaps the reason the emperors resided in Gaul in the fourth century was that, needing to mould public opinion, they selected the home of rhetoricians! Rather, Gallic pre-eminence was the consequence of imperial residence.

C. E. V. Nixon

panegyric of Eumenius (IX(5)) and that of 297 (VIII(4)) have parallels. This is not surprising, for their authors were contemporaries teaching at Autun.[19] More revealing is the fact that the panegyrist of 307 (VII(6)) borrows or adapts the phrase of ‘Mamertinus’ speeches delivered more than fifteen years before.[20] The panegyrist of 297 (VIII(4)) had already done the same,[21] and the panegyrist of 310 from Autun was perhaps to do so too.[22] The latter seems to draw upon the panegyric of 297 for information about Constantius’ campaigns between 293 and 296.[23] He certainly utilises Eumenius’ panegyric, especially at VI(7)22,[24] and, at times slavishly, the panegyric of 307.[25] Finally the panegyrist of 313 borrows several striking phrases from ‘Mamertinus’ and the panegyrist of 310.[26]

The inference is clear. Although this was not the primary intention of their authors, the influence of these panegyrics extended far beyond their immediate audience at the imperial court. It spread from Trier to Autun, into the Schools, and thence into the generations to come. Eumenius has some remarks, instructive in this context, to make on the educational goals of the Schools which Constantius was so eager to restore. In stressing the importance of restoring the School buildings themselves he points to their situation, ‘in the very path of our most invincible princes as they arrive here’ (IX(5)9.2), ‘as if between the very eyes of the city, between the Temple of Apollo and the Capitolium’ (9.3). ‘Assuredly, your Excellency [*vir perfectissime*; he addresses the governor of Lugdunensis], it is of importance to the fame which our great princes earn for their most frequent victories and triumphs *that the minds which are being carefully cultivated to sing their virtues* are honed not within private walls but

---

[19] See list above (nos. 2 and 3).   [20] Cf. Galletier (1952) 10–11.

[21] Klotz (1911a) 548–9; this speaker was (probably) from Autun, while ‘Mamertinus’ was probably from Trier.

[22] Klotz (1911a) 556–7 (alleged parallels not compelling).

[23] See Galletier (1952) 48.

[24] *quondam fraterno populi Romano nomine gloriatam* (‘once glorified by the fraternal name of the Roman people’, 22.4): cf. *olim fraterno populi Romano nomine gloriata* (‘glorified at one time by the fraternal name of the Roman people’, IX(5)4.1); *loca publica et templa* (‘public places and temples’, 22.4): cf.: *non templis modo ac locis publicis* (‘not only in temples and public places’, IX(5)4.2; *restitues* (‘you will restore’, 22.3): cf. *restitutionis* (‘restoration’ IX(5)4.1); *liberalitate* (‘generosity’ 22.4): *liberalitatis* (‘generosity’ IX(5)4.1); *sedemque iustitiae* (‘and the seat of justice’, 22.5): cf. *sedes ista iustitiae* (‘that seat of justice’, IX(5)1.2); and cf. Klotz (1911a) 557.

[25] Galletier (1952) 48; Klotz (1911a) 557–9.

[26] Klotz (1911a) 564–5.

in the public eye, and under the gaze of the city itself.'[27] The Schools of Gaul were in the service of the state. Not only did they provide the imperial government in Gaul with educated recruits, they inculcated the upper-class youth of Gaul with the right attitudes. The panegyrics had their part to play in this process. They were influential not only as rhetorical exemplars, but inevitably, in helping to form the political attitudes of the elite of Gallic youth who would go into public service, in affecting their sense of history, indeed in moulding their very historical knowledge. Brian Warmington has stressed the purely local and immediate nature of the 'propaganda' in the panegyrics.[28] The point is well worth making, but we must not neglect the wider and more enduring influence of these speeches, or underestimate their impact on the youth in the Schools of Gaul. [97]

The late Latin panegyrics are both manifestations of the political and intellectual control of the educated classes by the central government, and an important tool in the process of that political and intellectual control—that is in the education of youth.[29]

---

[27] For an example of the method, ibid., ch. 20 1–3: a geography lesson, complete with maps; the spirit of the lesson is in keeping with those of yesteryear, when our maps were painted red: 'Let the youth, moreover, see and gaze at every day in those porticos all lands and every sea and whatever cities, nations and tribes our most invincible princes are restoring in their piety, conquering by their valour, or holding fast by terror' (IX(5)20.2).

[28] Warmington (1974) reprinted below in chapter fifteen.

[29] Straub, writing in Germany in 1939 of the importance of the panegyrics in the 'formation of the political opinion of the young' (1939, repr. 1964) 148 comes closer to the mark than many.

11

Imagery in Panegyrics

Sabine MacCormack

The language of Late Antiquity was rich in images, and this was particularly so in the case of panegyrics. Certain parts of panegyrics describe an imperial tableau rather than events in historical narrative, and they describe facts as symbols rather than facts merely in themselves. Their words, as will be shown here, could be translated into images. In this, the panegyrics open up one aspect of the Classical perception of a harmony in the different arts. Earlier, Pliny, preceded by Cicero, among others, had explained the characteristics of literary styles in terms of light and shade as used by painters, and Quintilian matched the achievements and characteristics of particular orators with those of particular painters and sculptors.[1] Viewing the question from the angle of the visual arts, Philostratus said:[2]

> Whosoever scorns painting is unjust to truth; and he is also unjust to all the wisdom that has been bestowed upon poets—for poets and painters make equal contribution to our [178] knowledge of the deeds and the looks of heroes—and he withholds his praise from symmetry and proportion, whereby art partakes of reason.

The way in which some panegyrists made a contribution to such knowledge of 'the deeds of the heroes' consisted in their ability to expound imperial actions in terms that would evoke images, like the

---

[1] Cic. *Brut.* 63ff; cf. 141; 274 and *Orat.* 149; *Orat.* 3f, 7f, 36f, 65f, 73–4; *De or.* 3, 101; Quint. *Inst.* 12.10.1–12 (cf. Austin (1944) 17). A variety of points are made in these passages, showing a certain preoccupation with parallels in rhetoric and visual art, although no strict theory is worked out. Cf. the authors quoted by Lee (1940) 197ff.

[2] *Imagines* I preface (tr. Fairbanks, Loeb).

tableaux that have been referred to above. Panegyrists often described rather than narrated, and in their descriptions of actions used the methods of ekphrasis, as employed, for instance, by Philostratus and Procopius of Gaza in descriptions of works of art.[3] Such descriptions, initially perceived through the sense of hearing, in fact appealed to all the senses, but particularly to the eyes. This is also the case in those panegyrics which evoke images.

On the one hand, panegyrics bring to mind specific and simple images in imperial art and slogans on the coinage; on the other, they express themselves in such a way as to evoke mental pictures which can be matched with existing works of imperial art or an iconographic scheme which is familiar. This is the tableau, the scene in panegyric which is in fact a picture. Thus, Pliny's account of the deeds of Trajan, where division into 'scenes', so pronounced in later panegyrics, is incipient, can be paralleled in the iconographic schemes used on the coinage of the second century,[4] and in the attic of the arch of Beneventum, Iuppiter appears handing his *fulmen* ('thunderbolt') to Trajan, thereby leaving to the emperor the dominion of the earth, just as stated by Pliny.[5]

In Late Antiquity, imperial iconography, like panegyrics, became simpler, the images it used became fewer, and they were used more frequently, but often with great effectiveness. The message of imperial art, like the message of panegyrics, became more concise and compact. This factor in itself contributed to the more frequent correspondence of ideas in art and panegyric. Phrases in panegyric bring to mind images.

This is the case particularly in those panegyrics which above all were found to announce imperial programmes and policies in terms of symbols and pageants or tableaux, and which, at the same time, used a pagan idiom. Constantius, according to the panegyrist of 297, restored the prosperity of Gaul and Britain by his beneficent presence and is to be seen on medallions [179] greeted by a kneeling province—to be identified as Britain—whom he is about to raise.[6] The

---

[3] Friedländer (1912) esp. 83ff.

[4] e.g. *congiarium*, Pliny *Pan.* 25ff = *RIC* II pl.10, 177; buildings, Pliny *Pan.* 51ff = ibid. pl.9, 150 BASILICA ULPIA; pl.9, 153 FORUM TRAIAN; pl. 8, 146, and 11, 203 VIA TRAIANA . . . cf Toynbee (1944) 110–11; Hamberg (1945) 32ff.

[5] Pliny *Pan.* 80.4–5, but see Hamberg (1945) 64–7.

[6] Toynbee (1944) pl.8, 5; 6 (cf. pl. 6, 2) and pp. 174; 183; 195; the reverse legend of these medallions is PIETAS AUGG cf. *Pan. Lat.*XI(3)6 and MacCormack (1975)

coinage showed the emperor crowned by Victoria; the panegyrist of 310 visualized Constantine similarly crowned in a Gallic temple of Apollo. He also praised Constantine's beauty, resembling the beauty of Apollo, who in Late Antiquity was often identified with Sol. Thus the Ticinum medallion of 313 shows jugate busts of Sol and Constantine, and on the reverse is depicted a FELIX ADVENTUS AUGG NN, where the mounted emperor is preceded by Victoria holding high a wreath.[7] The emperor depicted on the coinage in the act of victory, crushing a barbarian with his foot, has a verbal parallel in Mamertinus' *gratiarum actio*[8], and another phrase of Mamertinus[9] is matched by a set of fourth-century coins showing the emperor standing in the prow of a ship. The origin of this type had been the third-century, ADVENTUS AUGUSTOR and TRAIECTUS AUG, but in the fourth century, legends were more general and the ship of state should not be excluded from the range of interpretation.[10]

Whether the coinage was deliberately used as an instrument of imperial propaganda is disputed.[11] What the parallels between coinage and panegyrics do make clear is that the former was used with a measure of planning to express ideas which were current at the time and to which, because of their appearance in both media, one can attribute some validity as expressions of imperial policy. Eusebius, characteristically, was aware of the possibilities of the coinage as a means of imperial advertising.[12] In the earlier fourth century, coinage and panegyric presented a uniform and coherent imperial programme. But the coherence of the two media began to disintegrate

160ff. On the Arras Medallion (Toynbee (1944) pl. 8, 4) and panegyric, cf. MacCormack (1972) 729.

[7] *Pan. Lat.* VI(7)21.4–6. On the coinage, e.g. *RIC* VII p. 368, Ticinum AD 316 RECTOR TOTIUS ORBIS, Constantine seated, holding zodiac, crowned by Victoria; *RIC* VII p. 474 Sirmium, AD 324 VICTORIA CONSTANTINI AUG, Victoria standing, crowning standing emperor. The Ticinum medallion, Toynbee (1944) pl. 17, 11, pp. 108–9.

[8] *Pan. Lat.* III(11)6.2. cf. Symm. *Orat.* 2.1, Cohen (1892) 51, no. 67 (Julian) VIRTUS AUG N, Julian in military dress, holding standard and laurel branch, placing foot on seated captive (cf. nos. 68–70); also no. 75, VIRTUS EXERC GALL, Julian in military dress holding captive by hair (cf. nos. 76–82); for Valentinian I, e.g. RIC IX, pl. 12, 2 = p. 218, 32; pl. 3, 6 = p. 14, 5.

[9] *Pan. Lat.* III(11)9.4.

[10] Kraft (1958) 170ff; 179–81, issues for Constans and Constantius II; pl. 12, 3; 9. The ship of state, e.g. *Pan. Lat.* X(2)4.2.

[11] Jones (1956) 14–16; Sutherland (1959) 46–53.

[12] *Vita Con.* 3.47; 4.15; 73. See also Schoenebeck (1939) 46.

in the latter part of the reign of Constantine; this corroborates what has been said about the panegyric of Nazarius, and the decreasing effectiveness of panegyric as a medium of imperial propaganda and communication in the later fourth century.[13]

So far, only simple images in art and panegyric have been mentioned. The tableau of the panegyric, like some works of imperial art, is, however, a complex image with many strands. The method of narrative in the relevant panegyric passages resembles the literary genre of ekphrasis: these passages are descriptive of a scene, a prospect, in the same way that Philostratus, John of Gaza and Paulus Silentiarius were descriptive. [180] They appeal to sight as much as to hearing, and the appeal to the sense of vision is often explicit in the wording of the panegyric, as it is for instance in the speech of 'Mamertinus' in 289, where he describes Maximian's entry on his consulship of 287[14]:

vidimus *te, Caesar, eodem die pro re publica et vota suscipere et coniunctim debere. quod enim optaveras in futurum, fecisti continuo transactum, ut mihi ipsa deorum auxilia quae precatus eras praevenisse videaris et quidquid illi promiserant ante fecisse.* vidimus *te, Caesar, eodem die et in clarissimo pacis habitu et in pulcherrimo virtutis ornatu.*

We have *seen* you, Caesar, taking up and fulfilling the vows for the state on the same day. For what you had desired for the future, that you performed yourself in the present, so that you were *seen* to anticipate the very aid of the gods for which you had prayed, and you achieved in advance what the gods had promised. We have *seen* you, Caesar, on the same day both in the most honoured attire of peace and in the most noble apparel of virtue (X(2)6.3).

The link between imperial art and panegyric could be an explicit one, although perhaps a commonplace: Pacatus exhorted artists to illustrate in their works the deeds of Theodosius, which he had described, rather than those of Liber and Hercules; Symmachus appealed to Zeuxis and followers of Apelles, and the panegyric of 307 contains, as part of the *laudes*, the ekphrasis of a wall painting in the palace of

---

[13] MacCormack (1975) 167 and 187.
[14] The emphasis on sight also in e.g. *Pan. Lat.* VIII(4)9. 1 *quis ... deus ... persuadere potuisset quod nunc vidimus et videmus, totis porticibus civitatum sedere captiva agmina* ('which god could have persuaded [us of] what we have now seen and see–captured cohorts sitting in all the porticoes of cities'); III(11)6.3.

Aquileia, which represented Fausta presenting a ceremonial helmet to Constantine as a betrothal gift.[15]

More effective, however, are those passages which, unlike the above, evoke themes such as *adventus*, which are commonly illustrated in imperial art and which were appropriate for various contexts. Here the orator could begin with a particular event or fact which, on the one hand, he could use to support a generalization, and on the other, could make into an image, a tableau, or several images. Generalization and image frequently coincided, for in Late Antiquity imperial art came to represent, like some panegyrics, less the historical identifiable event than general aspects of the emperor's rule and character.[16]

The panegyric of 297, as has been seen above, generalized [181] and universalized Tetrarchic dominion by drawing parallels between it and the order of nature. The rule of the four Tetrarchs was described as being matched symbolically in the order of nature by the four lights of the sky and other quaternities. The symbol of the four lights, like other Tetrarchic ideas, was still used in the early reign of Constantine. On the arch of Constantine, the representations of imperial deeds are framed by two medallions, showing, the one, Luna with Vesper, and the other, Sol with Lucifer.[17] Thus the imperial deeds were set into a cosmic context, as was still done in imperial and then in Christian art after the fourth century, for instance on the column base of Arcadius, which will be discussed below. The particular value of the panegyric of 297 consisted in making the very widely used and very general formulae of cosmic imperial dominion specifically relevant to the Tetrarchy by emphasizing the number four. In Constantinian and later imperial propaganda, on the other hand, the application of this symbol to reality had to be more general.

The panegyric of 289 discussed the rise to power of Diocletian and Maximian. Characteristically, here also, historical and dateable events were only referred to by implication, but were used as the starting point for imagery and generalization.[18]

trabeae vestrae triumphales et fasces consulares et sellae curules et haec obsequiorum stipatio et fulgor et illa lux divinum verticem claro orbe

---

[15] *Pan.Lat.* II(12)44.5, Symm. *Orat.* 3.5, *Pan. Lat.* VII(6)6.2–5.
[16] Kollwitz (1941) 58–62.   [17] *Pan. Lat.* VIII(4)4.
[18] *Pan. Lat.* X(2)3.2–4.1.

complectens vestrorum sunt ornamenta meritorum ...; *sed longe illa maiora sunt quae tu impartito tibi imperio vice gratiae rettulisti: admittere in animum tantae reipublicae curam et totius orbis fata suscipere et* ... *gentibus vivere et in tam arduo humanarum rerum stare fastigio, ex quo veluti terras omnes et maria despicias* ... *accipere innumerabiles undique nuntios, totidem mandata dimittere, de tot urbibus et nationibus et provinciis cogitare* ... *haec omnia cum a fratre optimo oblata susceperis, tu fecisti fortiter, ille sapienter.*

Your triumphal robes of state, your consular fasces, and your curule chairs, the glorious display of your subjects' allegiance, and that light which surrounds your divine head with a shining halo: these are the ornaments of your merits ...; but much greater are the benefits which you in turn have imparted on the empire which has been bestowed on you: your concern is the care of so great a commonwealth, and the destinies of the whole [182] world are your responsibility. ... You live for the nations and stand in that most exalted pinnacle of human affairs whence, as it were, you look down on all lands and seas. ... You receive messengers without number from all parts of the earth and send out as many orders, and countless cities, nations and provinces are the subjects of your consideration. ... All these tasks, which have been laid on you by your brother, you perform them with fortitude and he with wisdom.

The image here painted conveys the emperors enthroned high above all, surveying the world. Their role is not identical, however, for Diocletian, whose *parens* ('parent') is Iuppiter, acts *sapenter* ('wisely'), and Maximian, whose *parens* is Hercules, acts *fortiter* ('bravely'). This contrast was worked out throughout the Tetrarchic panegyrics.[19] The image of the emperor enthroned above all recurs in the panegyric of 307, where an attempt was made to preserve the ideology of the Tetrarchy for new circumstances. It is now, to use the vocabulary of 289, Maximian who acts *sapienter* ('wisely'), and Constantine, in the role of a Tetrarchic Caesar, who acts *fortiter* ('bravely').[20]

te pater [Maximian] ex ipso imperii vertice decet orbem prospicere communem caelestique nutu rebus humanis fata decernere, auspicia bellis gerendis dare, componendis pacibus leges imponere; te iuvenis [Constantine] indefessum ire per limites qua Romanum barbaris gentibus instat imperium, frequentes ad socerum victoriarum laureas mittere,

---

[19] *Pan. Lat.* X(2)4.1ff; cf 9.2, 13.3ff; XI(3)3, 7.6; IX(5)10.2.
[20] *Pan. Lat.* VII(6)14.1–2.

praecepta petere, effecta rescribere. ita eveniet ut et ambo consilium pectoris unius habeatis et uterque vires duorum.

Your role it is, Father [Maximian], to look out into the world which you both rule from the very summit of empire, and to decree the outcome of human undertakings by your celestial volition, to grant the auspices for wars which have to be undertaken, and to impose the terms when peace is to be concluded. And your role, young [Constantine] it is to traverse continuously the boundaries whereby the Roman empire is defended against barbarian nations, to send many laurels of victories to your father-in-law, to seek his instructions and to report to him when they have been performed. So it will come about that you both will work according to the counsels of one mind, yet you will each have the strength of two. [183]

In visual art the emperors enthroned *in vertice imperii* ('at the summit of empire'), *in tam arduo humanarum rerum fastigio* ('in that most exalted pinnacle of human affairs'), appear on the arch of Galerius, where Diocletian and Maximian are enthroned over the figures of earth and sky,[21] presiding over the other parts of the tableau, acting *sapienter* ('wisely'). On either side of them, the Caesars Galerius and Constantius, acting *fortiter* ('bravely') introduce conquered provinces to the enthroned emperors. The scene is framed by the Dioscuri, Oceanus and Tellus and other divinities, represented to convey the worldwide and eternal nature of Tetrarchic rule, which was also propagated in the panegyrics.[22]

An explicit interpretation of a historical event as a symbol, suitably introduced by a *praeteritio–transeo innumerabiles tuas tota Gallia pugnas et victorias* ('I pass over your countless battles and victories in all of Gaul', X(2)6.1)–occurs in the panegyric of 289. The matter under discussion was Maximian's consulship of 287, referred to above, which he entered upon in Trier.[23] On the day of the celebrations occurred a comparatively minor barbarian attack on Trier not recorded elsewhere, which Maximian repulsed. In itself the event was

---

[21] According to Seston (1946) 251, the emperors are enthroned over Pluto and Hecate, on the ground of their Mithraic devotion. I am doubtful of this interpretation, as it has no parallels in imperial art, whereas the emperor enthroned over the sky does, e.g. Euseb. *Vita Con.* 4.69. The motif was adopted in Christian art, e.g. on the sarcophagus of Junius Bassus, where the figure under the billowing veil can only be Coelus.

[22] Cf. Seston (1946) 252–3; *Pan. Lat.* XI(3)5–6, 14, 16; VIII(4)4, 20; IX(5)20.2.

[23] See p. 243.

of little significance, but it made an impression on the townspeople and it matched a common theme in imperial art and panegyric, the inter-relationship between imperial consulships and victory.[24] Thus, 'Mamertinus' made of it a symbol, an ekphrasis, something to be seen with the eyes, as he repeated himself. The themes of the episode are a correlation of Maximian's roles in peace and war, expressed by his wearing the consular *toga praetexta* and armour on the same day. His role in peace was fulfilled by his sacrifice to Iuppiter with the vows appropriate for imperial consulships, and his role in war by the engagement with the enemy.

Similar themes, victory and a religious observance, are joined together on the *Decennalia* base in the Roman Forum, which is part of a monument that was erected in 303 on the occasion of the *Vicennalia* ('twenty year anniversary') of Diocletian and Maximian and the *Decennalia* ('ten year anniversary') of Galerius and Constantius.[25] One side of the base, showing two Victories holding a shield inscribed CAESARUM DECENNALIA FELICITER ('Happily, the ten year anniversaries of the Caesars') over two crouching captives, the whole composition framed by two trophies, is devoted to imperial victoriousness, while the other three sides show the *suovetaurilia* ('sacrifice of sheep, pig and bull') in the presence of Mars, Roma and Sol, a civil ceremony, performed by a togate emperor. The performance of this sacrifice, one of the most ancient Roman religious rites, by [184] the emperor, has an antiquarian touch which also found expression in the panegyric of 289, where the legendary origins of Rome were recalled.[26]

A more integrated representation of the emperor's role in peace and war, of imperial consulship and victory, which in some senses is a better match to the panegyric, appears on the column base of Arcadius, to which I will return below.

Another tableau, where *adventus* and victory are intermingled, occurs in Mamertinus' *gratiarum actio* of 362. Some aspects of it have already been discussed in connection with the avoidance of issues not suitable for panegyrics, and in connection with parallels between individual phrases in panegyrics and iconographical schemes on the coinage. After stating, as has been seen, Julian's

[24] Cf. Alföldi (1935) 32ff; the themes of victory and imperial consulship are particularly clearly related to each other in Claudian's panegyrics on Honorius.
[25] Kähler (1964) 5ff; L'Orange (1938).   [26] X(2)1.1ff.

proclamation as Augustus by implication rather than expressly, Mamertinus went on to describe his welcome by the rejoicing populace
of the Danubian provinces in the current idiom of imperial advents.
He then contrasted the rejoicing of the Romans on one side of the
river and the abject submission of the barbarians on the other.[27]

*quae navigationis illius fuit pompa, cum dexteriorem incliti fluminis
ripam utriusque sexus, omnium ordinum, armatorum inermium perpe-
tuus ordo praetexerat, despiceretur ad laevam in miserabiles preces genu
nixa barbaria! omnes urbes quae Danuvium incolunt aditae, omnium
auditae decreta, levati status instaurataeque fortunae, innumerabilibus
barbaris data venia et munus pacis indultum.*

How glorious was our progress during that voyage, when the right bank
of the river was lined with an endless array of citizens of all ranks of
society, men and women, soldiers and civilians, while on the left bank
barbarians were to be seen sunken to their knees and uttering abject
entreaties! The emperor visited every city on the Danube, heard the
requests of all, raised their condition and restored their prosperity, and
granted pardon and the gift of peace to countless barbarians.

The *genu nixa barbaria* ('barbarians sunk to their knees') is a commonplace of imperial art.[28] It is more important that the image
presented by the passage as a whole appeared on the column base
of Arcadius. On the south side, Arcadius and Honorius were represented with a following [184] of court dignitaries, while, in the
register below, provinces wearing mural crowns made their offerings.
On the west side, the emperors, attended by soldiers, received the
submission of barbarians, shown in the register below with Victories
and a trophy.

The occasion of the erection of the column base was the expulsion
of Gainas and the consulship of Arcadius and Honorius in 402.[29]
Accordingly, on the east side, the emperors were shown togate as
consuls, attended by lictors, and, in the register below, by the senators
of Rome and Constantinople. In the bottom register were mourning
barbarians and piles of captured armour. This was an interpretation
in art of the themes of consulship and victory as described in the

---

[27] III(11)7.2ff.
[28] e.g. the column of Trajan, scene lxxv, left end, Hamberg (1945) pp. 111ff. pl. 20;
Kähler (1936) pl. 3 imitated on the bases of the arch of Constantine, L'Orange and
Gerkan (1939) 122, pl. 23; 125–6, pl. 29; 128–30, pl. 30.
[29] Kollwitz (1941) 27ff, 50ff; on the reliefs of the base, 33–58.

panegyric of 289. However, on the column base these themes were placed into a Christian, not a pagan or neutral context: the figurations of all three sides of the column base were dominated by the cross or Chi Rho, supported by angels or Victories, and framed by the old symbol of Sol and Luna.

By the later fourth century, imperial art achieved the fusion of Roman imperial traditions and Christian concepts of empire which panegyric failed to achieve. Imperial art became Christian, and continued to express itself in stylizations and universalizations, tableaux in other words, rather than in the conventions of narrative art, whereas panegyrics remained pagan or neutral and ceased employing tableaux as a means of expression. The panegyrics of Nazarius, Symmachus and Pacatus contain few images, and none that can be matched in imperial art, and they have no tableaux. This lessened their effectiveness as propaganda and as announcements of imperial programmes, quite apart from their content.

As has been shown above, the most successful panegyrics of Late Antiquity arose out of an interchange between court and schools in Gaul and out of imperial patronage. As a result, in the fourth century, Gaul was one of the centres of oratory in the West. The Gallic orators of the late third century developed techniques which made their panegyrics particularly effective: they spoke by allusion, implication, symbol, and they presented facts and events as images and tableaux. It is here that one can trace connections between imperial panegyrics and imperial art. [185]

From the point of view of imperial politics and propaganda, these connections and parallels show that the emperors were able to present a consistent, stable and continuous programme, which, because of its continuity, could be stylized and universalized and could be made to acquire symbolic meanings in art and rhetoric. The changes that occurred in the fourth century, especially after Julian, made it more difficult for panegyrists to use symbols and universalizations, partly because they—or at least those whose works survive—were too distant from the court, both physically and in outlook, and partly because imperial policies were too changeable for any fusion of art and panegyric to take place. From the point of view of the cultural history of the later empire, on the other hand, the parallels between art and panegyric illustrate a special sensitivity and skill on the part of the orators, for they succeeded in applying to the exposition of *res gestae* methods of description which had formerly been applied mainly to objects, in particular works of art. To achieve this, the orators utilized the genre of ekphrasis, description. Description, rather than narrative in the historical manner, was particularly suitable for panegyrics, the more so if it could evoke not only a visual experience in the imagination, but could also bring to mind actual works of imperial art and serve as a kind of commentary on them. However, the orators of the later fourth century returned to narrative in the historical manner: they spoke about facts and events rather than states of affairs and tableaux.

In verse panegyrics, on the other hand, images, personifications and divinities who also figured in late Roman and Byzantine art continued living a vigorous and picturesque existence: but verse panegyric was a different genre from prose panegyric, with different rules and conventions. Prose panegyrists under the Tetrarchy had created a specifically political and imperial imagery, which differed from the imagery of verse panegyric. Their expertise, the involvement of sight and hearing concurrently, was largely lost in the later fourth century. There occurred a change of awareness and ways of perception on the part of panegyrists, and perhaps their audiences. In the later fourth century, orators were not able or, perhaps, willing to convey emperor and empire as the theme that would absorb eyes and ears.

12

The Corpus of Latin Panegyrics from Late Antiquity: Problems of Imitation

E. Vereeke

Among the numerous studies devoted to the collection of Latin panegyrics from Late Antiquity there are a good fifteen which treat in various levels of detail the rhetorical methods used in the speeches. These studies have rarely been systematic. In some, technical problems of composition have only been touched upon for the occasion of a general presentation of the works in question, or by a chance stemming from works on authors engaged in a related literary genre;[1] others, more exclusively focused on rhetorical considerations, have either been limited to several speeches or to one alone.[2] [142] Finally, one finds very few philologists who, with tireless attention, have proposed to advance the methods of examination applied to the collection of eleven speeches, which with Pliny's panegyric to Trajan, constitute the corpus of the *Panegyrici Latini*.[3]

However, despite their different goals and wherever their contributions can claim to figure in a study devoted to analysis of panegyrical technique, all these critics without exception have had the same concern: to determine the place of Gallic orators in the history of a genre in which a good number of Greek and Latin authors shine. This

---

[1] Thus Boissier (1884), Pichon in a study of the world of the schools in Roman Gaul (1906a) 36–85, Pohlschmidt (1908), Parravicini (1909) and Cesareo (1936).

[2] Such as the articles of Klotz (1911a) and Mesk (1912), both limited to nine of the eleven speeches; and Schaefer (1914), and the following monographs, Grinda (1916), Gutzwiller (1942) and Lubbe (1955).

[3] Here, we only have the short thesis of Kehding (1899) and the two articles by Maguinness (1932) and (1933) to point out.

shared perspective has forced them to conduct a patient search for influences; now and then to produce lengthy articles on problems of imitation; and to speak of borrowings, models, prototypes. And so, certain philologists, convinced of the presence in the Gallic orators' speeches of rhetorical elements recommended by certain Greek rhetoricians, pronounce themselves persuaded that these orators had the precepts of Menander, or those of some other theoretician, before their eyes to compose their speeches.[4] For their part, other modern critics grappling with problems of comparable influences, underline reminiscences of Cicero or Pliny.[5] Faithfulness to precepts clearly defined by Greek rhetoricians or Greek rhetoric in general and influence from earlier Latin orators who were occasionally led by circumstances to make themselves panegyrists, [143] such are the two theses facing each other—and one could also say, such are the two limits of a dilemma between which the wisest have believed it good to make a choice.[6]

Studies of the panegyrics' plans, statements about their main themes, lists of the stylistic figures they used most often are the levels to which the problem of influences has been raised and determined, in a fashion which could be believed definitive in the reading of most recent works which turn back in their subject to the conclusions of critics like Kehding, Mesk or Boissier, often without any other verification.[7] Are these theories—some of them formulated over a century ago—defensible? Are there compelling reasons to speak so

---

[4] To stick to one or other example, we cite Kehding (1899) 5 who says of the author of X(2) and XI(3) 'we see that "Mamertinus" depends entirely on Menander'. Speaking of the same orator, Mesk (1912) 573 affirms 'This author therefore has a distinct schema before his eyes'; the schema in question equally being Menander's.

[5] Boissier (1884) 6 'the panegyrists copy the ingenious manner in which Pliny represents the actions of the emperor and draws out a whole topic for praise'; Pichon (1906a) 40 'the speech by which they are most directly inspired ... is the panegyric of Trajan by Pliny the Younger'; Maguinness (1932) 43 'These all derive a great deal via Pliny from such orations of Cicero as the *Pro lege Manilia*, *De Prov. Consularibus* and *Pro Marcello*'.

[6] More nuanced, Parravicini (1909) 41, envisages different schemas as much Latin as Greek, by which the panegyrists could have been inspired, but remains convinced that above all the panegyric by Pliny was the model for the later panegyrists.

[7] While referring to Kehding (1899), Pohlschmidt (1908) and Mesk (1912), in his edition Galletier (1949) 17 says of the author of X(2): '[He] is one of the better writers of the group of panegyrists ... It could easily be shown that he is full of the precepts of rhetoric and that he carefully follows the smallest rules which govern the anniversary panegyric or speech'. On the other hand, certain encyclopaedias have adopted the thesis of Boissier and Pichon.

categorically of models for Latin panegyrics? Can decisive arguments be found to privilege under this heading clearly identified Greek theoreticians at one time, Latin orators at another? Are these two theses irreconcilable as their supporters present them for thought, each one ignoring the other? And finally, why could Latin theoreticians or Greek orators also not have been able to influence the Gallic orators? It is with the design of proposing an answer to these questions that I have judged it useful for me in my turn to attend to the scholarship written on the subject. In the following pages I will first present the theories of philologists who have studied the relationships between the late Latin panegyrics and the precepts of Greek theory; in the second place I will study the theses of those who insist on the possible relationship between those same panegyrics and earlier Latin orators. [144] The objective of both parts will be a brief critical account in which I try to bring out the principal methods employed and conclusions obtained, while aiming to test the grounds of each.

The theory according to which the authors of the eleven panegyrics which detain us would have been inspired mainly by the precepts of Greek rhetoric goes back in its substance to Kehding's thesis, published in 1899.[8] In his short work, the author compares the speeches of the Gallic orators with the rules which Menander Rhetor (third century AD) airs in his *On Epideictic Speeches*.[9] Why this author precisely? Kehding explains: 'because the precepts of this author are practically the only ones to reach us'; however, he adds that 'before him, other rhetors could have given similar precepts.'[10] In Menander's work can be found a series of precepts to follow to compose the different types of set speech, and notably those to respect when making a eulogy of an emperor, in delivering a *basilikos logos*;[11] it is above all those latter rules which drew Kehding's attention. The advice Menander gives to compose a *basilikos logos* consists essentially of the presentation of a series of themes which the author ought to develop according to the following order:

1. *Introduction*, containing a statement of the difficulties that such a speech presents for the orator and an announcement of the subject to be discussed;

---

[8] Kehding (1899).   [9] 329ff.
[10] Kehding (1899) 4–5.   [11] 368–77.

2. *central section*, where the following points are to be spoken of in sequence:
   - the home country and nation of the person praised
   - their family
   - their birth
   - their nature
   - their education
   - their morals [145]
   - the actions they have accomplished
     - in war time
     - in peace time
   - their virtues (to which their actions will be attached)
   - courage
   - justice
   - wisdom
   - temperance
   - their good fortune
   - final comparison

3. *Peroration* where the Empire's general prosperity will be presented, and a prayer will be addressed to the gods.

Each of the points mentioned above is accompanied by a brief development intended to spare the orator any trouble in amplifying this schema.

Such are the precepts which, according to Kehding, can be found applied by the Gallic panegyrists. For proof, the philologist underlines in each speech a certain number of themes or methods mentioned by the Greek rhetor: in total, about sixty correspondences are wrought in this way. For Kehding, the possibility that these correspondences are an index of the panegyrists' fidelity to Menander's precepts is in no doubt.[12]

But I am not so sure, and for several reasons. To start with, in privileging Menander—while recognising that other rhetors before him could have written similar precepts—the German philologist seems to set very little value on the theories of Anaximenes, Aristotle, Dionysius of Halicarnassus or Theon: would the Gallic panegyrists

---

[12] For each panegyric there are found statements as distinct as 'we see that "Mamertinus" depends entirely on Menander' (1899, 5), 'he takes his thoughts from Menander' (6), 'I have found these instances expressed in imitation, from the precepts of Menander' (10).

have had easier access to the works of Menander? Can proof be found elsewhere of the influence of Greek rhetoric from the third and fourth centuries AD on the professors in the Schools in Gaul? What were the curricula at these Schools? Perhaps these questions are delicate, but they ought to have moved Kehding to greater caution. [146]. Next, since in my view a first step could have been to pose oneself the question whether the panegyrics present—at the level of an overall schema—from the introduction to the peroration a succession of themes proximate to Menander's, Kehding begins his work at the level of detailed correspondences by picking up in each speech the themes or methods recommended by the Greek rhetor. No classification system governs these comparisons, as if they had the same weight and that the same conclusions could be drawn from one coincidence as from several successive themes,[13] as from one such quite banal theme, such as one figure as unrevealing in my view as an instance of paronomasia or a comparison. Another error in method: in the presence of themes recommended by Menander and used by several panegyrists, the philologist never considers the possibility that—if there was any imitation—a Gallic orator could have been inspired by his predecessors. Systematically he concludes that each panegyrist followed the precepts of the Greek rhetor.[14] Finally, all these gaps contribute to give the impression that in his search for influences, Kehding misconceived a fundamental principle: the requisite necessity for a critique of serious authenticity to exercise a distinction between elements common to two works and elements peculiar to them. Only the latter could reveal direct influences (with which alone Kehding is occupied).

To verify this general impression, it seemed interesting to me to proceed to an enquiry that neither Kehding nor any of the others who have reprised his theory have made: to determine to what extent the correspondences highlighted between the panegyrics and the precepts of Menander could—or could not—also be there between the same panegyrics and other works. [147] To this effect I have taken several

---

[13] As is the case in X(2) where the home country, origins, infancy and education of the emperor are evoked before moving to his exploits, Kehding (1899) 5.

[14] Among other examples I note: the description of the site of military activities at IV(10)8 and VIII(4)19 which would have had as their model Menander Rhetor's *Basilikos Logos* 373, or the eulogy of imperial generosity recommended by Menander 373 and which is found at VIII(4)20, IX(5)9, X(2)8 and XII(9)21. Cf. Kehding (1899) 9–10, and 9, 10, 11, 15.

Greek and Latin authors earlier than the Gallic panegyrists, and whose works could grant a similar position to numerous comparisons: either that these authors had formulated rules of composition for eulogistic speeches, or that they themselves had practised the epideictic genre in the form of laudatory biography or of panegyric. Because the verification demands no well-determined criterion in selecting authors, I have taken particularly well-known works which span the fourth century BC to the second century AD. For the theoreticians of the genre, our choice has fallen on Anaximenes (fourth century BC) and Dionysius of Halicarnassus (first century BC), each the author of a *Techne Rhetorike*, Hermogenes (second century AD) the author of *Progymnusmata*, and on the Latin side, the *Rhetorica ad Herennium* (first century BC) and the *Institutes Oratoricae* of Quintilian (first century AD). As for eulogistic works, I have limited the study to the *Agesilaos* of Xenophon (fourth century BC), the *Evagoras* of Isocrates (fourth century BC), the *Agricola* of Tacitus (first century AD) and the *Panegyricus* of Pliny (second century AD). From the outset, I noticed that the themes identified by Kehding as common to the Gallic panegyrics and the *Basilikos Logos* of Menander belonged also for the main part to the works which we had considered.[15] The exercise clearly shows the critical excess testified by Kehding in his belief that he was right to speak of imitation. It remains to me now to examine whether later supporters of his theory were able to bring forward more convincing arguments in corroboration of his thesis.

In 1908 in a work dedicated to the orator Themistius (fourth century AD), W. Pohlschmidt in his turn credits the theory according to which the panegyrics had been composed according to the precepts of Greek rhetoric.[16] Conscious of certain gaps in Kehding's work—notably the fact that nowhere did his collected project include a comparative study—Pohlschmidt put side by side the plan proposed by Menander and those of the Gallic panegyrics, to which he added Pliny's. By introducing Pliny's speech here, it seems the author demonstrates his intention not to consider Menander's rules as the

---

[15] Besides, I am persuaded that one could easily obtain the same results by taking as reference points works other than the ones I chose. I have in mind, for example, the rhetorical treatises of Aristotle or of Theon, those of Cicero and those works which without being pure panegyrics, nonetheless contain laudatory sections of some importance, such as Cicero's *Pro Lege Manilia* or *Pro Marcello*. [The original article displays the findings of this exercise in tabular form.]

[16] Pohlschmidt (1908).

model by which the Gallic panegyrists would have been inspired directly, but as a legacy of earlier rules which could have influenced Pliny.[17] His study of the plans leads the philologist to the conclusion that they are practically identical: here, the emperor's life is recounted in chronological order; there his achievements are described to put his virtues in a good light (unless here his virtues are announced to have a structure into which to write his principal successes).[18] But we are entitled to ask—and this is an objection Pohlschmidt does not anticipate—if we can speak of fidelity to one single plan on the strength of such general, even banal coincidences. Is it necessary to resort to a whole series of influences to explain that the orators charged to praise a man would have taken a step as logical as that which consists of following the chronology of his life while insisting on his merits and actions? Without delaying any more on the plans, Pohlschmidt next raises a series of panegyrical themes which he declares to be inherited from Greek rhetoric ... since Menander recommends recourse there.[19] **[149]** The presence of this 'same plan' and 'same themes' in Themistius' speeches constitutes for him the proof that although he defends himself, this orator had recourse to collections of precepts. The thesis is possible, but in my view, insubstantially based.

In 1912 in an article titled 'On the technique of the Latin Panegyrists' in turn J. Mesk enumerated a whole series of themes recommended by Menander and employed by certain of the eleven panegyrists;[20] the bulk of his correspondences were reprises of Kehding and Pohlschmidt.[21] Mesk never says that Menander could have directly inspired the Gallic orators, but that the presence in their work of a good number of common themes is explained by reference to the precepts from Greek rhetoric of which Menander's small treatise is,

---

[17] Pohlschmidt is not explicit on this point.

[18] Pohlschmidt (1908) 49.

[19] Pohlschmidt (1908) 53ff: amongst these themes I note 'the emperor's conduct in war', 'the description of a battlefield', 'the victor's generosity', 'his virtues of forgiveness' etc.

[20] IV(10), III(11) and II(12) are excluded from the study.

[21] Contrary to the appearance of its title, this article is not a thorough study or research of analysis of panegyrical techniques. It takes its place in a long controversy which since Livineius and his edition of 1599 set at odds philologists who wanted to penetrate the anonymity behind which several of the authors of panegyrics were hidden. Following Klotz (1911) and Baehrens (1911), Mesk asserts in his article that Eumenius was not the author of speeches other than that of 298.

on one of many occasions, presented as the quintessence.[22] But as for Kehding, it is necessary to state that the points common to the panegyrics and the *Basilikos Logos*, noted by Mesk, can be found with great regularity in many Latin and Greek authors, be they theoreticians or orators.[23]

After Kehding, Pohlschmidt and Mesk, still more philologists could be cited who have spoken more or less consciously about the common ground in the composition of the Gallic panegyrics from Greek rhetoric via its theoreticians. For example, O. Schaefer devotes a whole chapter to this in his study of X(2) and XI(3);[24] F. Cesareo asserts [150] 'Pliny, like Eumenius later, applied the precepts of the rhetors which we know from Menander';[25] in his remarkable commentary on the panegyric of Julian by Menander, H. Gutzwiller draws many comparisons between such a paragraph of the Gallic orator's and a like precept of Menander.[26]

Having reached this stage in my paper, I would like to specify that it is not my intention to deny that Greek rhetoric could have left its imprint on the works of the Gallic orators who detain us; I intend only to underline the fact that in my opinion those who have wanted to demonstrate this common ground by studying several grand panegyrical themes and their manifestations have not succeeded and have likewise led into error those who have drawn on their conclusions. From the start, by privileging Menander in comparison with other rhetors (contemporaries or predecessors), Kehding suggested that this rhetor could have been used as a direct model by the Gallic orators. Next, by limiting their comparisons to Greek theoreticians of the genre—to writers of precepts only—most of the philologists cited above have completely misconceived the place which Greek *orators* who practised the genre of set speeches could have occupied in the tradition. Above all, I must insist on the fact that, centred exclusively on uncertain incidences from Greek rhetoric in Latin panegyrics, these same philologists have failed to raise the following questions: in the case of common ground from the Greek tradition, could these not have been indirect? Could this common ground not have been transmitted by *Latin* orators or theoreticians before the third or fourth centuries AD? Was the Latin tradition

---

[22] Mesk (1912) 572.   [23] [Table III in Vereeke's original article].
[24] Schaefer (1914) 17–31.
[25] Cesareo (1936) 124.   [26] Gutzwiller (1942) 92–9, 106, 166, 211.

materially different to the Greek? In sum, despite conclusions more sensible than Kehding's, and the reproaches that can be levelled against him, the returns of Pohlschmidt, Mesk and those who have followed them along the same path, interesting as they are, deliver no solution to the problem they posed. The correspondences they highlighted are undeniable, but they are situated in an enquiry which is incomplete: it only had Greek rhetoric, limited to its theoreticians— no, to Menander by himself, deemed to represent all the others—to view.

[151] Opposing the thesis of those who see in the Gallic panegyrics an application of the precepts from Greek rhetoric, there exists, we have said, another position itself defended since the end of the nineteenth century: its main thrust is to accentuate the Latin influences which could have left an imprint on these speeches. More concretely, the philologists who have subscribed to this movement see in Cicero or Pliny the precursors of the genre of Latin panegyric and the models for the later orators who practised it. Quite curiously, the first critics to have spoken of imitation of Cicero or Pliny by the panegyrists of the third and fourth centuries are also those to have employed the fewest arguments in the thesis' favour: thus Boissier, in review of a publication by Brandt, says without reservation, that the Gallic panegyrists imitated Pliny's *Panegyricus*.[27] No research has come to shore up this position by which its author seems to rally to an 'orthodox opinion' and to justify the position of the panegyric of Trajan at the head of the corpus of *Panegyrici Latini*.[28] The same groundless assertions can be found several years later in Pichon.[29] As for Parravicini, having insisted on the presence of a good number of encomiastic elements in Tacitus' *Agricola*, he likewise styles Pliny's *Panegyricus* as 'the most conspicuous working example of rhetorical

---

[27] Boissier (1884).

[28] Boissier (1884) 6–7, 'The orthodox opinion wants Pliny's speech to serve as a model to the others, and the editors of the panegyrics to have wished to have made this clear by the place they gave it in their collection . . . Brandt is not of this view . . . he insists they are, rather, the pupils of Cicero. It is this that is very difficult to accept. But if the panegyrists of the fourth century made speeches a little shorter than Pliny's, usually they reproduced his arrangements and general character. They imitate the ingenious manner in which he presents the actions of the prince and elaborate from it an entire subject of praise . . .'.

[29] Pichon (1906a) 40 'The speech by which they were most directly inspired, that which the compiler put at the head of the collection as if to place it under his patronage, is the panegyric of Trajan by Pliny the Younger'.

rules on this subject, which would serve as a model for later pane-gyrists'.[30]

[152] It was necessary to wait for Klotz's article in 1911 to find the first important comparative study between the Latin panegyrics and other earlier Latin works. Whatever is sometimes written, Klotz's purpose was not at all to study the relationship between the Gallic speeches and the precepts of rhetoric:[31] consequently, convinced by the evidence of a panegyrist[32] that when speaking in public the Gallic orators were striving to imitate the fluency of classical Latin authors, this philologist presented a whole series of parallels between expressions employed by Cicero, Sallust or Pliny on the one hand, and the panegyrists on the other. Across forty pages devoted to this research, Klotz is not concerned with laudatory method of itself; he seeks to show that the Gallic orators knew their Classics. The thesis is logical—we cannot see how these orators could have ignored such great masters. But we cannot fail to be struck by the poverty of the correspondences cited by Klotz... Must panegyrists have been inspired by Cicero to have recourse to expressions such as 'to contemplate in the mind', 'starting from that age', 'to divide into two', 'to deprive of light', 'to delight in joy', 'to miss these things out';[33] or to have recalled Pliny's *Panegyricus* when saying 'unique help', 'to

---

[30] Parravicini (1909).

[31] Thus Galletier (1949) lxix lists this article among the number of those to examine the question of the relationship between the panegyrists and the precepts of Greek rhetoric.

[32] XII(9)1.2 'I am well aware how inferior our abilities are to the Romans', since it is inborn in them to speak in Latin and fluently, but in us it is laboured, and if by chance we say something felicitous, our imitation derives from that source and font of eloquence'.

[33] Respectively Klotz (1911) 533 [XI(3)14.2: Cic. *Deiot.* 40], 541 [IX(5)1.1: Cic. *Man.* 1.1, *Div. In Caec.* 4], 542 [IX(5)3.4: Cic. *Cluent.* 1], 552 [VI(7)10.7: Cic. *Rosc. Am.* 63], 545 [VIII(4)19.1: Cic. *Phil.* 2.65], 562 [XII(9)4.4: Cic. *Deiot.* 15]. I could cite many examples of the same kind: for XI(3) alone, Klotz (532–4) presents no fewer than twenty parallels with Cicero, such as 5.3 'I do not mention . . . I do not say' and Cic. *Man.* 60 'I will not say . . . I will not mention', 10.2 'immediately the pastures and fields were deserted' and Cic. *Man.* 15 'the pastures are deserted, the cultivation of fields abandoned', 19.5 'you will decorate the rostra of the Roman field with new booty' and Cic. *Man.* 55 'decorated with naval booty and the fleets' spoils', 5.5 'but there are other greater things in your praises' and Cic. *Marc.* 6 'but there are other greater things', 3.2 'eternity preserves itself by its perpetual motion' and Cic. *Tusc.* 1.66 '(the mind) endowed with perpetual motion' and 10.4 'a clearer light spread through the whole of Italy' and Cic. *Nat. Deor.* 2.95 'with light spread through the whole sky'.

delight in rejoicing', 'to reform discipline'?[34] In short, I do not believe Klotz's study can be cited [153] in support of their thesis by those who claim to see the panegyrists' models in Cicero or Pliny.

In comparison with their predecessors, the two final studies dedicated to the methods used by Gallic panegyrists, those of Maguinness, offer appreciable progress in the sense that no longer is it simply a question of chosen themes or of statements presented without classification.[35] And so, Maguinness, who considers in his study the totality of Gallic panegyrics of the corpus, endeavours to underline the methods which, at various levels, had presided over their elaboration. For comparisons, for example, he highlights the different personages against whom the emperor is set: his predecessors (good or bad), mythological or legendary figures, natural phenomena.[36] Likewise, he devotes a number of pages to presenting the manner in which the panegyrists use antithesis and paradox: real inconsistencies, apparent or only verbal are presented and discussed with numerous examples.[37] These two very valuable articles contain no statements at all relating to the uncertain models for the panegyrics. In his first article, Maguinness declares in effect that as far as the substance, form and methods employed are concerned, the panegyrics derive, in large measure via Pliny, from the speeches of Cicero.[38] In his second article, he writes 'Here, as in almost every method we shall consider, Pliny points the way to his successors'.[39] For each method or theme he considers, it is not difficult for him to find 'prototypes' in the works of Cicero or in the panegyric of Trajan. Secure parallels are numerous and cannot be in doubt: nevertheless, they have nothing compelling, and to speak of a model, once again, is perhaps to rush the work. Comparisons, oppositions, *praeteriones*, [154] personifications, themes such as 'the speed of the *laudandus*', 'his altruism', 'his stimulating actions', 'the appeal to posterity'—these are commonplaces of the eloquence of set speeches. To be persuaded, it is enough to read Isocrates' *Evagoras*.[40]

---

[34] Respectively Klotz (1911) 535 [X(2)4.2: I(1)8.3], 550 [VII(6)14.4: I(1)89.1] and 554 [VI(7)2.2: I(1)53.1].

[35] Maguinness (1932) and (1933).

[36] Maguinness (1932) 45–53.

[37] Maguinness (1933) 118–26 [see below 266–75].

[38] Maguinness (1932) 43 cf. above n. 5.

[39] Maguinness (1933) 119 [see below 266].

[40] One reading of the *Evagoras* allows me to align the following references with the principle methods highlighted by Maguinness as shared by the panegyrists and Cicero or Pliny.

What conclusions can be drawn from examination of the main articles dedicated to the themes and methods used by the Gallic panegyrists? On the scheme of the supposed imitations, it must be recognised that if a good ten philologists have raised the question, the responses they have given are far from satisfactory: to my knowledge, nothing can prove in a plausible manner that the Gallic orators were inspired either by the precepts of Greek rhetoric or by the speeches of Cicero and Pliny. Happily aware of the alternative, the supporters of one or another theory have not judged it good to imagine the possible influence on the same panegyrics of Greek laudatory works or of earlier Latin precepts. Having tried to fill this gap, I think it possible to state that neither study is sufficient to come to a definitive answer. For that is the conclusion imposed by the business of my enquiry; we have a problem to which the actual state of our knowledge [155] does not allow us to offer any solution other than hypothetical. To explain the reasons for this powerlessness, I would like to begin by quoting de Saint-Denis who wrote in his study of Tacitus' *Agricola* 'Gudeman considers that in his short work, Tacitus has applied in anticipation the precepts of Hermogenes, Aphthonius, Theon and Menander; Cousin finds the plan of the *Agricola* in Quintilian's canvas. They are each right, because nothing resembles a panegyric more than another panegyric. If the addressees change, the same methods will be found, even if the eulogy is delivered in a poor rural cemetery by a panegyrist who has not studied rhetoric and who goes over as best he can the life of the deceased.'[41]

Comparisons – with persons worthy of eulogy, *Evag.* 34–8, 39, 65, 70.
– with persons worthy of blame, *Evag.* 25, 38.
– with a god, *Evag.* 29, 72.
Oppositions: *Evag.* 44, 45, 53, 59, 71 (of a verbal character, 7, 23, 25, 60).
Praeteritio: *Evag.* 21, 31.
Recourse to hypothesis: *Evag.* 33, 34, 38, 40.
Recourse to interrogation: *Evag.* 6, 12, 49, 69, 71.
Profession of sincerity: *Evag.* 21, 39, 66.
Appeal to posterity: *Evag.* 3, 76.
Theme of the speed of the *laudandus*: *Evag.* 30.
Theme of providence: *Evag.* 25, 42, 70.
Influence of the *laudandus* on others: *Evag.* 49, 50, 66.
Recourse to aphorism: *Evag.* 6, 27, 41–2.
Fictional kinship: *Evag.* 12.

[41] Saint-Denis (1941) 24.

Pretty much the same thing could be said for studies made of the Gallic panegyrics: the resemblances between the speeches are striking,[42] as are those the speeches share with the works which are eagerly named their models. But when proper reflection is taken, it is more tempting to be surprised that these panegyrics are so different. The orators who delivered them were in effect in practically identical situations: to offer a eulogy of their emperor. The duty to compose a speech on the same subject dictates that no opportunity should be missed to vaunt the person to be addressed. Then how could they not speak of his home country, and his origins, and not follow in chronological sequence the major stages of his life? How could they not speak of his virtues and achievements? Above all, how could they not amplify upon the subject?[43] A good number of methods common to the panegyrists are nothing other than a consequence of the material situation, so to speak, in which each orator found himself. A simple enumeration of facts, virtues, achievements, if they are genuine, does not allow the creation of a very long speech: it is necessary to recourse to [156] amplification, in which one of the most natural methods will be reference to others. An individual to be featured will be compared with personages known from elsewhere—with gods, natural elements—or opposed against rivals.[44] The same concern to improve by reference accounts for the number of purely verbal oppositions of character raised by Maguinness, or the habit the panegyrists have of making a statement after dwelling to deny its opposite or contradiction.[45]

The obligation to present the same realities, the same obligation to amplify them—these are already sufficient reasons to explain so many similarities between the panegyrics, between panegyrics and other laudatory works, and between this last type and the works of compilers. They practise a genre they had to teach. How could they have

---

[42] Cf. e.g. Klotz (1911) 548–9, 556–9, 564–5.

[43] Rather curiously, the term 'amplification' never appears (so to speak) in studies dedicated to the panegyrics.

[44] Whenever they have the chance, the panegyrists delight in putting in parallel the emperor and the tyrant who wanted to defeat him. In such a case, the tyrant is the object of a 'vituperation', a veritable negation of panegyric up to the slightest detail. Cf. VI(7)14–20, XII(9)14–18, IV(10)9–12, II(12)23–31.

[45] A hundred examples of this method could easily be found: VII(6)12.6 'I did not hand this over to you on loan, but forever: I do not take it back, but I look after it'.

ignored Greek and Latin rhetoric? Imbued themselves, they had the
power to imbue others; certain of them were not giving their first
speech of this genre,[46] and history does not tell us how many similar
speeches, delivered by their colleagues, they had occasion to hear, at a
time when panegyrics addressed to emperors were relatively frequent.[47] In these circumstances, to speak of imitation, of models
conscientiously followed, smacks of gambling.

[157] Is that to say that the research conducted by philologists that
we have quoted here has been useless? Certainly not, but it ought to
be used in a different perspective. In signalling so many correspondences between works of one single type, the majority of critics have
made several grand rules of the laudatory genre conspicuous to one
level—a thematic level. With Maguinness, there are more methods
underlying these themes which have been highlighted but the majority of these (comparisons, antitheses, paradoxes, recourse to hypothesis) are still presented one after the other. Much remains to discover,
which could be inscribed, in my opinion, with those already examined in a bigger synthesis than the one we work with—the art of
amplification in the genre of panegyric.

[46] 'Mamertinus' is the author of X(2) and XI(3) and he promises to deliver still
another at the time of Maximian's tenth imperial anniversary, XI(3)1.3.

[47] According to Jullian's estimations VIII (1926) 278, six per year had to be
delivered.

13

Locutions and Formulae of the Latin Panegyrists

W. S. Maguinness

In a paper published in *Hermathena* 47 (1932), I dealt with some methods of eulogy employed in the *Panegyrici Latini*. In that paper I confined my attention almost entirely to the subject-matter of the orations. The present article deals with the orators' methods of expression, the various devices of language in which their encomia find utterance, and the various tricks of rhetoric that they have inherited from their predecessors. We shall first consider methods of expression in the widest sense, passing from them to formulae of an essentially verbal character.

One of the weaknesses inseparable from the panegyrist's art is inconsistency, and this weakness, from which our authors are by no means immune, influences their expression in various ways. René Pichon, who refers to this tendency of the panegyrists in *Les Derniers Ecrivains Profanes* (65–7), says of them: 'The panegyrists are a little like official journalists who are always of the government's opinion, whichever government it is, who always take it upon themselves to justify the government, and whatever the cost, who get there by means of subtleties and recantations.' They are ever claiming the right to have it both ways, to deny what they have said in such a way that we shall believe, if it is to their convenience, both the statement and the denial. Sometimes they will attempt to veil their inconsistency by specious pleadings of a hair-splitting kind, anon, more bold, they will contradict themselves without apology or shame. Sometimes they employ phrases that imply a realization, or even contain a candid confession, [118] of such contradiction. Pliny, about to address to Trajan a twofold compliment involving a contradiction, declares: *iunxisti ac miscuisti res diuersissimas* ('you joined and combined most varied qualities', *Pan.* 24.1).[1] Such phrases as: *utrumque, Caesar Auguste, moderate* ('in both cases, Augustus Caesar, with moderation', *Pan.* 4.3), *utrumque recte* ('in both cases, correctly', *Pan.* 46.3) and expressions like: *accipe, imperator, ancipitem nostrorum sensuum confessionem* ('receive, emperor, a doubtful expression of our senses', VI(7)4.5) and *duplici fructu fruebantur* ('they enjoyed a double boon', XII(9)7.5) herald a similar compromise, or at least a reconciliation of statements containing some element of contrast.

I have used the word 'inconsistency' in a rather broad sense, to describe the ubiquitous tendency of the panegyrists to reconcile opposing actions or statements. But it is not to be understood that such reconciliation is always inconsistent in the strict sense. Just as contrasting actions may be right in contrary circumstances, so contrasting ideas and statements may be justified by the variety of circumstances. Having first endeavoured to examine instances of the latter kind separately, I found that the cases of what we may call 'self-contradiction' fell at least approximately into four classes, viz.:

(*a*) justifiable reconciliation of contrasting statements or ideas, and of seemingly inconsistent actions,

(*b*) instances of a simple desire for the juxtaposition of contrasted ideas, of the instinct for antithesis,

(*c*) real inconsistency or contradiction—the panegyrists' professional trick of 'having it both ways',

(*d*) contradiction or antithesis of a purely verbal nature.

It is hardly necessary to say that many instances could be referred to more than one of these categories. The word 'justifiable', for instance, implies a judgement that must often be personal. Yet they seem to provide a fairly accurate analysis of this method, and indeterminate cases are placed in the class of which they seem to be most characteristic. [119]

(a) Here, as in almost every method which we shall consider, Pliny points the way to his successors. The paradox *soli omnium contigit tibi ut pater patriae esses ante quam fieres* ('it happened that you alone

---

[1] *Cf.* II(12)2.2.

of all were father of the country before you became so', 21.3) is justified by the explanation *eras enim in animis in iudiciis nostris, nec publicae pietatis intererat quid vocarere* ('for you were in our minds and judgement, and it made no difference to public devotion what your title was', 21.3).[2] The people had received all their *congiarium* ('donation'), the soldiers only a part of their *donativum* ('largesse'). Pliny reconciles the contrast between these proceedings in a characteristic phrase *quamquam in hac quoque diversitate aequalitatis ratio servata est* ('although even in this difference, thought was given to fairness', 25.2), and proceeds with the cogent explanation, *aequati sunt enim populo milites eo quod partem, sed priores, populus militibus quod posterior sed totum statim accepit* ('for the soldiers were level with the people because they received a part [of their largesse], but first, while the people received their whole [donation] after the soldiers', 25.2). Again, the emperor's wife and sister had refused the title Augusta, offered by the senate, and Pliny declares *hoc magis dignae sunt quae in animis nostris et sint et habeantur Augustae, quia non vocantur* ('those who in our minds both are and are considered Augustae, are more deserving of this because they are not so named', 84.7).[3] It is obvious that the orator is making the best of both sides of the argument. They are praised for refusing to become Augustae, yet the title really belongs to them—because they have not got it! But behind the contradiction there lies an essential truth to justify it—that the honourable title is itself much less important than the respect and admiration of mankind. When Pacatus declares to Theodosius, regarding the motives of his speech, *quin et illud me impulit ad dicendum quod ut dicerem nullus adigebat* ('indeed the very fact that nobody was forcing me to speak compelled me to speak', II(12)2.2), he signifies in a similar way the truth that only voluntary eulogy is of value, adding, in the same manner *neminem magis laudari imperatorem decet quam quem minus necesse est* ('it is fitting to praise no emperor more than one who does not demand it', II(12)2.4). Later in the passage in which he makes the state rebuke Theodosius for his unwillingness to undertake the burden and responsibilities of empire, when summoned to the throne by Gratian, we find the [120] phrase: *imperium, quod ab imperatore defertur, tam*

---

[2] Cic. *De Sen.* 10.32.

[3] cf also 4.3, 10.6, 16 (where pacifism and militarism are reconciled according to variety of circumstances), 55.1–5, 65.1.

tibi nolle iam non licet quam uelle non licuit ('you are not now permitted to not want the imperial power passed on to you by an emperor, just as you were not permitted to want it', II(12)11.7), which is true of every heir or successor to a throne. When Mamertinus, thanking Julian for his consulship, says, *gratias tibi, gratias, imperator, si mereri me credidisti, et plures gratias, imperator, si tantum amasti ut me consulem faceres etiam non merentem* ('I give you thanks, emperor, thanks, if you believed me worthy, and more thanks, emperor, if you loved me so much that you appointed me consul even though unworthy', III(11)15.3), his attitude is neither noble nor consistent, and yet he would no doubt have *felt* thankful in either case. In praising the same emperor for having personally honoured the remains of his hostile predecessor, Constantius, the orator is commending a magnanimous action that is worthy of praise. But he cannot refrain from indicating the fusion of motives involved, in a phrase maintaining the emperor's right to opposite courses: *et memoria et obliuione mirabilis, oblitus inimici meminit heredis* ('admirable both when remembering and when forgetting, he forgot his enemy and remembered his heir', III(11)27.4). Finally, to quote one case from among many, an unknown panegyrist commends Constantine, as Pliny had already commended Trajan, for avoiding war when that was possible, and welcoming it gladly when challenged.[4]

(*b*) Some examples of this class could well be attributed to (*a*), but as a rule the opposition of ideas is less fundamental, is due simply to a fondness for the juxtaposition of dissimilar facts or notions. A few examples will suffice. Pliny, having stated that *imperatoris aduentu legatorum dignitas inumbratur* ('legates' dignity is overshadowed by the arrival of the emperor', 19.1), proceeds virtually to unsay what he has said, *tu tamen maior quidem omnibus eras, sed sine ullius deminutione maior* ('but you were greater than everyone but greater without diminishing anyone', 19.2). The banal explanation, *eandem auctoritatem praesente te quisque quam absente retinebat* ('everybody retained the same authority with you present as in your absence' 19.2) is less important to the orator than his self-contradictory *mot* (*Pan.* 19.1–2). The Nile, which, *inopina siccitate* ('with unexpected drought', 32.4) had deprived Egypt of its necessary floods, is urged

---

[4] XII(9)23.2. Cf. further II(12)15.3, IV(10)13.3, VI(7)3, VI(7)4.5, IX(5)12.2, X(2) 13.3, XI(3)13.5, XII(9)13.3, XII(9)16.

to make reparation in the future, *tanto* [121] *magis quia non exigimus* ('by all the more since we make no demands', 32.4) a piece of needless illogicality worthy of its context. Mamertinus is at pains to record the opposite impressions produced by the speed of Julian's march, *qui properationem illam contemplabitur, nihil egisse praeter viam imperatorem putabit; qui gestarum rerum multitudinem considerabit, properasse non credet* ('whoever contemplates that speed will think the emperor achieved nothing beyond the travel; whoever considers the number of achievements will not believe he hurried', III(11)7.3), a phrase reminiscent of Augustine's famous comment on Varro.[5] It is a simple desire for the proximity of contrasting ideas that makes Constantius' panegyrist close his speech by saying that he has good reason *et nunc desinendi et saepe dicendi* ('both in stopping now and in speaking often', VIII(4)21.3). Of a similar nature are the recurring references to the *oneness* of co-reigning emperors, such as *quamvis maiestatem regiam geminato numine augeatis, utilitatem imperii singularis consentiendo retinetis* ('although you increase the royal majesty by doubling the godhead, you retain the utility of a single empire by your unanimity', X(2)11.2). Likewise, of imperial partners unequal in age *intelligimus enim, sacratissimi principes, geminum vobis, quamvis dispares sitis aetatibus, inesse consensum* ('for we understand, most sacred emperors, that although you are different in age, you have a twin agreement', XI(3)7.7).[6]

(c) When Pliny claims, with regard to Trajan's banquets, *non ipsum tempus epularum tuarum, cum frugalitas contrahat, extendit humanitas?* ('when your frugality restricts the length of your feasts, doesn't your politeness extend it? 49.5), he is contradicting himself voluntarily (and needlessly, as the qualities mentioned, unlike the actions described by the verbs *contrahere* ('to restrict') and *extendere* ('to extend'), are not incompatible). When he says, *ingens, Caesar, et par gloria tua, sive fecerint istud postea principes sive non fecerint* ('This and your glory are equally great, Caesar, whether later emperors so behave or not', 64.3), or again *pietati senatus cum modestia principis felix speciosumque certamen, seu fuerit victa seu vicerit* ('the senate's devotion will be in happy and conspicuous competition with the emperor's modesty, whether it loses or wins', 79.4), he is simply

---

[5] *Civ. Dei.* 6.2.
[6] Cf. also *Pan.* 1.24.1, X(2)9.2, 11.1, XI(3)6.7, 14.3.

having it both ways.[7] Addressing the 'sainted Nerva' he declares *optimus ipse non timuisti eligere meliorem* ('as the best yourself you did not fear to elect a better man' 89.1), and later refers to the day *qui principem . . . dedit optimum, meliorem optimo genuit* ('which gave us the best emperor [and] gave birth to one better than the best', 92.4).[8] [122]

His complacent desire to make a point invites the obvious challenge. There is a delightful example of inconsistency in 88.7–8 of his speech. Speaking of Trajan's title, Optimus, he declares, *merito tibi ergo post ceteras appellationes haec est addita ut maior* ('deservedly therefore this was added after your other titles, because it was greater') and, a few lines further on, *ideoque ille parens hominum deorumque optimi prius nomine deinde maximi colitur* ('and so that father of men and gods is worshipped first by the name of Optimus then of Maximus'). On the question of Trajan's third consulship he performs a complete volte-face. In 56 and 57 the emperor is praised for accepting his second consulship, *quia princeps et pater deferebat* ('because an emperor and father bestowed it', 56.3) and refusing a third one shortly after the death of Nerva. But in 58 the tone begins to change, and we are prepared for the opening of 59: *sed iam tempus est te ipsi consulatui praestare ut maiorem eum suscipiendo gerendoque facias* ('but now it is the time to give yourself to the consulship, to make it greater by accepting and conducting it', 59.1) and the flood of specious reasons why the emperor should at last do what it was right not to do before.[9] But what is our astonishment, on passing on to chapter 60, to find that all the misplaced ingenuity of chapter 59 was a piece of retrospective dramatization, that Trajan had indeed in the end accepted a third consulship (as we know he did, in the latter half of AD 99, with Cornelius Fronto as his colleague)! We are now scarcely surprised to find the emperor urged, in chapter 78, to undertake a fourth consulship. In VI(7)12 the orator commends atrocities of Constantine, on which he dwells with a shocking delight. Yet soon the emperor is bidden to rejoice: *quod te talem Constantius Pius genuerit, talem siderum decreta formarint ut crudelis esse non possis* ('because Constantius Pius created you such, such did the decrees of

---

[7] 88.9 is similar.   [8] IV(10)4.1.

[9] Cf. II(12)11.7 where the imperial throne is in question, and the orator has a good reason for his assertion.

the stars form you, that you cannot be cruel', VI(7)14.4).[10] Contrary
tactics employed by Maximian against different tribes are equally
commended in a single chapter,[11] and only the most trivial reasons
are given, though cogent [123] ones may well have existed. The
unknown panegyrist of Constantine, whose oration comes last in
the series, provides a perfect example of this method in its most
insidious form. While Constantine is the *son* of Constantius Pius,
his enemy Maxentius is described as *Maximiani suppositus* ('Maximian's changeling'). The orator proceeds: *te, Constantine, paterna
pietas sequebatur, illum, ut falso generi non inuideamus, impietas.*
('Constantine, paternal piety followed you; him—not to grudge him
his false birth—impiety', XII(9)4.4).[12] Whether Maxentius is Maximian's true son or not, in either case his paternity is used as a ground
for attack. Nothing could be less consistent, or more unfair. Finally, it
is worthwhile to notice that in many of these cases the contradiction
is explained by some kind of conceit, often of a trivial or specious
character. One or two examples will suffice. Concerning the recipients
of Trajan's bounty it is said: *sciunt dari sibi quod nemini est ereptum,
locupletatisque tam multis pauperiorem esse factum principem tantum*
('they know that what is given to them has been snatched from
nobody, and that when so many have been made rich, only the
emperor has been made poorer'). But this remark, suggestive and
forceful as it is, is at once taken back in the words, *quamquam ne
hunc quidem* ('and not even the emperor') and the banal explanation
of the contradiction is this: *nam cuius est quidquid est omnium,
tantum ipse quantum omnes habet* ('for whoever has part of the
common weal owns as much as everyone', 27.4).[13] 'Mamertinus'
compares Maximian's action in crossing the Rhine to attack the
Germans with Scipio's invasion of Africa in the Second Punic War.
He asks the emperor if he had heard of Scipio's exploit. After all, one
could not assume in Maximian even a rudimentary knowledge of
history. However, it matters little: *hoc tu siue cognitum secutus es seu
te auctore fecisti, utrumque pulcherrimum est* ('whether you followed
something you knew or did it of your own accord—either way it is
most beautiful', X(2)8.3). This disarming impartiality is supported by

---

[10] The inconsistency is repeated in VI(7)20.1.
[11] X(2)5.2.
[12] Cf. also II(12)40.4, IV(10)26.2, XI(3)5.5.
[13] Cf. 46.2–3.

a series of epigrammatical remarks, introduced by the surprising assertion: *neque enim minorem laudem magnarum rerum aemuli quam ipsi merentur auctores* ('for those copying great deeds deserve no less praise than the authors themselves' X(2)8.4).

(*d*) When Pliny says, of Trajan and Nerva: *ita filius ac parens uno eodemque momento rem maximam* [124] *inuicem praestitistis: ille tibi imperium dedit, tu illi reddidisti* ('at one and the same instant, you exchanged the greatest gifts; he gave you power, you returned power to him', 6.4) he means to say that Trajan's accession to the throne as Nerva's partner confirmed the latter's position, which was at that time in jeopardy. He employs a phrase which implies a contradiction non-existent in the action described, a purely verbal antithesis. Similar is *augebat auctoritatem iubentis in summum discrimen auctoritas eius adducta, utque magis parendum imperanti putares, efficiebatur eo quod ab aliis minus parebatur* ('when brought into serious danger, his authority increased the authority of the man who gave the order, and so that you might think the order should be granted greater obedience, it came about that he received less obedience from others',10.1) where the same topic is discussed. The idea, which is in no real sense self-contradictory, could have been adequately conveyed without the antithetical form of expression. The glory Trajan earned by entering the city humbly on foot is described by the paradoxical expression: *te ad sidera tollit humus ista communis et confusa principis uestigia* ('that ground we share and the emperor's footprints mixed with our own lift you to the stars', 24.5). There is no inconsistency in the *fact* that his humility made him great. Pacatus claims that Theodosius *magis magisque uisus expetitur et, nouum dictu, praesens desideratur* ('sight of him is sought more and more and—new to relate—he is missed when he is present!', II(12)21.5). He merely means that the people can never see too much of their emperor, but produces a verbal contrast by the juxtaposition of *praesens* ('present') and *desideratur* ('is missed') which suggests a desire for something absent. Again, when he says, *qui uitae tuae sectam rationesque cognouerit, fidei incunctanter accedet nec abnuisse dubitabit imperium sic imperaturum* ('he who knows the path and principles of your life will believe it immediately and will not doubt that one going to rule in this way declined power', II(12)12.3) we have a mere trick of words. It is the same desire for the clash of opposing words that produces a phrase such as *o caelestem, imperator aeterne,*

pietatem tuam, quae tuum illum animum semper inuictum sola uicit
('o your heavenly piety, everlasting emperor, which alone has conquered that eternally unconquered mind of yours', VII(6)11.5).[14] The
statement itself is entirely consistent, but the author gives to its
expression a flavour of paradox.

What we have called the desire to have it both ways is likewise
responsible for a formula that can best be described as the 'unresolved
alternative.' The orator [125] suggests two or more possibilities, with
regard to which he declares himself to be undecided; whatever alternative the reader chooses to accept will further the author's purpose.
It is simply a way of saying two things at once. Syntactically the
formula generally takes the shape of a disjunctive question, direct or
dependent, but *seu . . . seu* ('either . . . or') is sometimes employed. We
may take first a few examples of the direct question. Pliny several
times asks which of two or more things, each excellent, is the most to
be admired: *initium laboris mirer an finem?* ('should I admire the
work's beginning or end?' 14.4). And again: *gestum consulatum mirer
an non receptum?* ('should I admire the consulship fulfilled or the one
refused?' 56.4) Or: *tuam uero magnanimitatem an modestiam an
benignitatem prius mirer?* ('Indeed, should I admire your magnanimity first, or your modesty, or your kindness?' 58.5). Similarly he
asks: *te magis mirer an improbem illos?* ('should I more admire you or
disapprove of them?' 71.2). Of his fellow townsmen declining to 'ask
for more', another orator demands: *o nos utrumne uerecundos ni-
mium dicam an satis gratos?* ('should I say we were too shy, or grateful
enough?' V(8)11.2). But the indirect question is much more common,
and is introduced by a large variety of phrases. *incertus* ('unsure') is
the commonest word so used. Pliny demands of Trajan: *quid isti
benignitati precer, nisi ut semper obliges obligeris incertumque facias
utrum magis expediat . . . debere tibi an praestitisse* ('what could I beg
of your kindness other than that you always commit to these mutual
obligations, and make it unclear whether it is better to be in your debt
or credit?' 60.7).[15] Pacatus says to Theodosius: *incertum meliores
uiros sapientia tua an fortuna quaesiuerit* ('it is unclear whether
your wisdom or fortune sought out better men', II(12)15.3), and
Nazarius describes Constantine's children as: *incerti (patrem)*

---

[14] Cf. also IV(10)13.4, V(8)5.6, VII(6)11.4.
[15] Cf. 92.5.

mirentur an diligant ('uncertain whether to admire or love their father', IV(10)4.3). But he betrays the purpose of the formula when he proceeds: *nisi quod necesse est utrumque permixte simul fieri* ('unless it must be that both happen together'). Pliny is equally significant when he says: *merito necne, neutram in partem decernere audemus* ('deservedly or not, we do not dare to decide', 91.4). *dubitare* ('to doubt') is a natural word to use in this connection.[16] So also is *nescio* ('I do not know'). Pliny had already employed it,[17] and 'Mamertinus' exclaims to Maximian: *illud malum... tua... nescio utrum magis fortitudine repressum sit an clementia mitigatum* ('I do not know whether that evil was more suppressed by your bravery or mitigated by your mercy', X(2)4.3). Pliny declares to Trajan the [126] elder: *cum eo qui adoptauit amicissime contendis pulchrius fuerit genuisse talem an elegisse* ('when you have a friendly contest with the one who adopted him, as to whether it was better to have fathered or chosen him', 89.2), and elsewhere we find, introducing the formula of the unresolved alternative, such expressions as: *me interrogo* ('I ask myself'), *ut plane in ambiguo sit* ('so that it is clearly moot') and *difficilis existimatio est* ('a decision is difficult').[18]

seu... seu ('either... or') is used in this way chiefly when the orator wishes to present a number of rival hypotheses on some philosophical or scientific topic, in such a way as to display his knowledge without having to decide on any one theory. Of such a decision, indeed, most of them, with the exception of Pliny, would have been incapable. In this way Pacatus sets forth the various theories on the relation between man's body and the indwelling soul,[19] and Constantine's panegyrist speculates (but with no result) on the nature of God: *summe rerum sator... siue in te quaedam uis mensque diuina est, qua toto infusa mundo omnibus miscearis elementis et... per te ipse mouearis, siue aliqua supra omne caelum potestas est qua hoc opus tuum... despicias, te, inquam, oramus...* ('greatest creator of things... whether in you there is a certain force and divine mind infused across the entire world [and] you mix with all the elements and... yourself move of your own accord, or you are some power above all of heaven from where you look down on this your work, I say, we beg of you...' XII(9)26.1). Similarly Constantius' panegyrist, displaying his knowledge of the various theories

---

[16] *Pan.* 84.1.   [17] *Pan.* 64.4.
[18] *Pan.* 64.2, II(12)6.2, IV(10)33.3.   [19] II(12)6.3.

propounded to explain the tides, but quite indifferent to their respective merits: *oceanus ille tanto libratus impetu, tanta mole consurgens, siue ulterioribus ut ferunt terris repulsus siue anhelitu quem respirat euectus seu quacumque alia ratione motus* . . . ('that ocean, balanced with such energy, rising with so great a mass, whether, as they say, driven back from more distant lands or carried by the breath it exhales or moved by some other reason . . .' VIII(4)6.4).[20]

The next formula we have to consider is that which substitutes for direct eulogy an affectation of censure or complaint. It is very common in the panegyrists, and is briefly indicated by Pichon.[21] It is worthwhile to notice certain characteristics of its use, which have not yet been pointed out. In the first place, it is not always the emperor, as we shall see, who is the object of this pretended censure. [127] Secondly, the complaint is sometimes directly expressed, sometimes merely hinted at or implied in the faintest manner. Thirdly, when it is addressed to the emperor, especially if it is expressed directly, the orator nearly always associates others with himself in the utterance of it, or even pronounces it as coming from other lips than his. Let us take first some examples of blame directly expressed, always remembering that it is an inverted form of eulogy. While Theodosius was conquering in the ends of the earth, Maximus established himself in Gaul. So Pacatus affects to chide the emperor: *nec tamen, imperator, existimes cuncta me ad aurium gratiam locuturum* ('but you should not think that everything I am going to say will please your ears'), continuing in the plural: *triumphis tuis Galli . . . irascimur* ('we Gauls are angered by your triumphs', II(12)23.1). 'Mamertinus' rebukes Maximian for his too intrepid courage, and speaks of *libertatem piae conquestionis* ('the liberty of a well intended complaint') which he attributes, not to himself alone, but also to his fellow citizens.[22] The author of the twelfth panegyric chides Constantine for the same fault, but on his own responsibility: *laudare me existimas, imperator, cuncta quae in illo proelio feceris? ego uero iterum queror* ('Emperor, do you think I am praising everything you did in that war? Indeed, I have a second complaint', XII(9)9.2).[23] But another panegyrist of

---

[20] See also III(11)1.2 where *sive . . . sive* is used just as *incertum . . . an* might have been used.

[21] (1906a) 64–5.

[22] XI(3)2.4. Cf. VII(6)9.1.

[23] Cf. VI(7)8.4. The earlier complaint was at 3.1–2.

the same emperor refers the censure to a hypothetical occasion, and gives it an imaginary mouthpiece: *si consilium alicuius amici callidioris admitteres, esset quod fortasse reprehenderet* ('if you were to accept the advice of a cleverer friend, perhaps there might be something he would criticize', V(8)10.3).

The author of the seventh speech, on the two occasions when he affects to blame the emperor, makes the state utter his complaint: *factum est enim, imperator aeterne, in quo uno querelam rei publicae paene meruisti* ('for this deed, everlasting emperor, was the one thing for which you almost deserved the state's complaint', VII(6)8.9) and again *Roma . . . queribunda clamauit: 'quousque hoc, Maximiane, patiar?'* ('Rome shouted in complaint 'How long must I suffer this, Maximian?'', 10.5–11.1).[24] As examples of censure not addressed to the emperor we may quote Pacatus' criticism of Fortune: *cui hoc nomine etiam succenseri potest quod quem sceptro et solio destinauerat* [128] *numquam indulgenter habuit* ('one could be angry [with Fortune] on these grounds—that she never cared indulgently for the man she had intended for the sceptre and throne', II(12)8.2); and Nazarius' reference to undesirable influences that had surrounded the youth of Constantine: *tibi quidem in erudiendo, imperator optime, non omnia proponebantur quae sequi uelles* ('indeed, in your upbringing, best of emperors, not everything presented to you was such that you would have wished to follow', IV (10)4.5).

When Pliny says to Trajan, in reference to his perhaps extravagant liberality: *interrogandus uideris satisne computaueris imperi reditus* ('you seem to need to be asked whether you have taken due thought for the empire's revenues', 41.1) he is gently hinting at a possible criticism, his real purpose being to emphasize the extent of the emperor's generosity. At 59.4, *quousque* ('how long?') conveys a hint of impatience, and the subsequent remark, *liceat experiri an aliquid superbiae tibi ille ipse secundus consulatus attulerit* ('let it be permitted to examine whether that second consulship itself has brought you some arrogance') implies a readiness on the people's part to criticize the emperor, *if* he should be found deserving of criticism. There is a suggestion of censure when a desire is expressed that Constantine's son shall not take the risks his father has taken: *sit aliquid quaesumus in quo te iterum nolit imitari* ('we beg there may

---

[24] Cf. II(12)11.3.

be some respect in which he does not wish to imitate you again', IV
(10)37.4). 'Mamertinus', likewise speaking in the plural, substitutes
for some such word as *improbabamus* ('we disapproved') the milder
expression, *pro amoris impatientia timebamus* ('out of love's impatience, we were fearful', XI(3)4.1). The speed and enthusiasm of
Constantine's army are exalted almost at the expense of the emperor
himself: *laborasti interdum ut quem ducebas sequereris exercitum*
('sometimes you laboured to follow the army you led', VI(7)18.5).[25]
Finally, there are a number of passages in which there is an implied
censure (not, of course, to be taken seriously) of the people, for
unrestrained expression of their sentiments towards the emperor.
Such are: *nullus cuiquam sui tuiue respectus: blandam tibi faciebat
iniuriam contumacia gaudiorum* ('nobody had any regard for themselves or you: the stubbornness of their rejoicing made the injury
flattering to you', II(12)37.3), *amoris nostri contumeliam feres* ('you
will tolerate the insubordination of our love', V(8)14.4) and *omnes
adorandi mora restiterunt duplicato pietatis officio contumaces* ('stubborn in the duplicated duty of piety, everyone stopped to extend their
adoration', XI(3)11.2).

[129] We have referred, in this connection, to a tendency of the
orators to make others the mouthpiece of their statements. This
tendency frequently finds expression in the formula known as 'prosopopoeia', or *personarum ficta inductio* ('the imaginary introduction
of characters') already affected in Cicero.[26] It is indeed used by the
panegyrists in several cases of pretended censure, as when the state

---

[25] Cf. 18.3 *tua, imperator, cura. . . . festinantibus paene non placuit* ('emperor,
your concern almost did not please [them] in their rush') Cf. also 20.4 (imitated in
II(12)44.2), where the words *di te uindicant et inuitum* ('the gods avenge you even
when you are unwilling') suggest that the emperor's intended clemency was a mistake.

[26] e.g. *Cat.* 1.7.18, 1.11.27; 4.9.18. It is worth while to quote Quintilian *Inst.* 9.2.29,
which admirably illustrates the panegyrists' use of this figure: *fictiones personarum,
quae προσωποποιίαι dicuntur . . . mire . . . cum uariant orationem tum excitant. his et
aduersariorum cogitationes uelut secum loquentium protrahimus . . . et nostros cum
aliis sermones et aliorum inter se credibiliter introducimus, et suadendo obiurgando
querendo laudando miserando personas idoneas damus. quin deducere deos in hoc
genere dicendi . . . concessum est. urbes etiam populique uocem accipiunt* ('the assumption of characters which is known as *prosopopeia* brings amazing variety and animation to the speech. By this we extend the thoughts of adversaries, as if talking to
themselves . . . and with credibility we introduce conversations between ourselves and
others, and between others, and by persuading, scolding, complaining, praising and
pitying, we give suitable characters. Indeed, it is permitted to introduce gods in this
type of speech. Even cities and people receive a voice').

expostulates with Theodosius, and Rome with Maximian,[27] or Constantine's officers rebuke his rashness in battle,[28] but it is common in other contexts as well. Sometimes the prosopopoeia consists of spoken words, sometimes of unuttered thoughts, and in both cases the *personae* ('characters') are extremely varied. In one speech we find an elaborate dialogue between Fortune and other abstractions,[29] in another a brief one between Jupiter and Maximian: *quid . . . putas tibi, Maximiane, Iouem . . . respondisse, cum tu . . . diceres 'recipe, Iuppiter, quod commodasti'? hoc profecto respondit 'non mutuum istud tibi tradidi, sed aeternum; non recipio, sed seruo.'* ('Maximian, what do you think Jupiter replied to you when you said "Take back, Jupiter, what you lent"? Certainly he replied as follows: "I did not hand this over to you as a loan, but for all time. I do not take it back, but I keep it safe", VII(6)12.6).[30] In another instance the speakers are Constantius' soldiers: *omnium . . . una uox et hortatio fuit 'Quid dubitamus? quid moramur? ipse iam soluit, iam prouehitur, iam fortasse peruenit . . . quid est quod timere possimus? Caesarem sequimur'* ('their voice and encouragement was unanimous—"why do we hesitate? Why do we delay? He himself is setting off, now he is being conveyed, now perhaps he is arriving . . . what is there we could fear? We are following Caesar"', VIII(4)14.5).[31] Enemies, again, are made to speak, a possibility that Quintilian had not overlooked. Thus Julian's former enemies in the state and Constantine's [130] barbarous foes are condemned out of their own mouths—the former by the malicious hypocrisy, the latter by the untimely arrogance, of the words they are made to speak.[32]

Sometimes the prosopopoeia consists of thoughts instead of spoken words: *cogitationes uelut secum loquentium* ('thoughts, as if talking to themselves') as Quintilian says. Pliny introduces such a prosopopoeia with the phrase: *nonne uobis . . . haec . . . (imperator) agitare secum uidetur* ('surely [the emperor] seems to you to think these things over', 67.8) and again, where the subjects are imaginary persons, with the words: *misera sed uera reputatio* ('a miserable but

---

[27] II(12)11.4, VII(6)11.1. Cf. Cic., *Cat.* 1.7.17–18, 1.11.27.
[28] XII(9)10.3. In *Pan.* 70.6, the censure is real, being directed against Trajan's predecessors.
[29] II(12)40.
[30] A god is also the speaker in III(11)13.3.
[31] Similarly XI(3)11.4, where the imaginary speakers are the members of a crowd.
[32] III(11)4.5–7, VI(7)21.2.

true reflection', 70.6). The despairing thoughts of the defeated and fleeing Maximus are introduced by the exclamation: *quotiens sibi ipsum putamus dixisse!* ('how often we imagine he spoke to himself!', II(12)38.2) and the orator Mamertinus records the following dialogue with himself: *tunc mecum 'Claudi Mamertine, non frustra hucusque uixisti. habes idoneum fidei ac industriae iudicem. memento in magno res tuas esse discrimine. scietur non meruisse te consulatum, si tibi non detulerit hic imperator'* ('Then I said to myself, "Claudius Mamertinus, you have not lived this long in vain. You have a suitable judge of your loyalty and hard work. Remember your affairs are under great judgement. It will be known that you did not deserve the consulship if this emperor does not bestow it on you"', III(11)17.4).

Before turning to formulae of a more purely verbal kind, it is worthwhile to notice an interesting locution by which the emperor is said to *make* men something that they would not otherwise be. It is in this spirit that Dante wrote:

per che si fa gentil ciò ch'ella mira
('whereby whatever she beholds grows gentle', *Vita Nuova* XXI)

Sometimes we are told that the emperor's presence or influence makes an orator of a man, renders him eloquent. Thus Constantius is told: *quamuis maxime orationi imparem parem facis, Caesar, auditor* ('although I am especially unequal to the speech, Caesar, as audience you render me equal to it', VIII(4)1.5) and Eumenius exclaims: *tantos principes unum hominem tanta laude decorare non est oratorem admonere, sed facere* ('to have such emperors honour one man with such great praise is not to remind him of his duties, but to make him an orator', IX(5)15.5).[33] Pliny had already said: *faciebas ergo, cum diceres,* [131] *optimos* ('therefore you made them excellent when you said so', 71.7) and a panegyrist of Constantine, speaking of the emperor's defeated and erstwhile degenerate foes, who are now brave soldiers in the victor's army, adds: *nec tamen id mirum uideri potest, cum qualemcumque militem fortissimum facias tuo, imperator, exemplo* ('but that cannot seem surprising, since you make any sort of soldier the bravest by your own example, emperor', XII(9)21.4).

When we come to discuss formulae of an essentially verbal nature, we find that one of the commonest is *praeteritio*, or *parasiopesis*. This

---

[33] The closing words of VI(7) are similar in spirit.

formula varies from the briefest mention of something on which the orator cannot or need not dwell to an exhaustive list of things which he emphasizes in pretending to omit.[34] This is the characteristically rhetorical use. *quid loquar rursus intimas Franciae nationes iam non ab his locis quae olim Romani inuaserant, sed a propriis . . . sedibus atque ab ultimis barbariae litoribus auulsas, ut in desertis Galliae regionibus conlocatae et pacem Romani imperii cultu iuuarent et arma dilectu? quid commemorem Lingonicam uictoriam etiam imperatoris ipsius uulnere gloriosam? quid Vindonissae campos hostium strage completos et adhuc ossibus opertos? quid immanem ex diuersis Germanorum populis multitudinem, quam duratus gelu Rhenus inlexerat ut . . . repente laxato flumine clauderetur,* etc. ('What will I say of those people from the interior of Francia, not now torn from those places which the Romans once invaded but from their native seats and the furthest shores of the barbarian world, so that, settled in deserted areas of Gaul, they help the peace of the Roman empire by farming and its army by signing up? Why should I recall the victory amongst the Lingones, famous for the wounding of the emperor himself? Why should I recall the plains of Vindonissa, filled with the slaughter of the enemy, and still covered with bones? Why should I recall the vast mass from the various German peoples which the Rhine enticed, hard with ice . . . to be shut off by the river's sudden thaw', VI(7) 6.2–4). It is obvious that the orator leaves nothing unsaid. Sometimes they seek to adorn the *praeteritio* by changing from one verb to another. Thus 'Mamertinus': *non commemoro*[35] . . . *rempublicam . . . liberatam, non dico . . . redisse prouincias, mitto*[36] . . . *dies festos uictoriis triumphisque celebratos, taceo*[37] *trophaea Germanica . . . , transeo*[38] *limitem Raetiae . . . promotum, omitto*[39] *Sarmatiae uastationem . . . illa quae armorum uestrorum terrore facta sunt . . . praetereo*[40] ('I do not mention that the state is liberated . . . I do not say that the provinces have returned . . . I pass over the festival days celebrated with victories and triumphs . . . I am silent about the German trophies . . . I pass over the fact that the boundary of Raetia was extended . . . I miss out the devastation of Sarmatia . . . and I pass by those things achieved through fear of your weapons', XI(3)5.3–4).[41]

---

[34] e.g. X(2)3.1, 6, 1.   [35] Cf. IV(10)30.1.
[36] Cf. III(11)6.1, 13, 2.   [37] Cf. II(12)41.4, III(11)22.2.
[38] Cf. VIII(4)2.1, X(2)6.1.   [39] Cf. X(2)3.1, XII(9)4.3.
[40] Cf. IV(10)27.1 and 3, 33. 7, VIII(4)9.5, X(2)1. 4.   [41] Cf. X(2)2.2–6.

This passage and the footnotes [132] on the several verbs illustrate the variety of the *uerba praetereundi* ('the lexicon of *praeteritio*'). Yet these are but a few of the words employed. Sometimes the orator makes great efforts to avoid any of the standard expressions, as, for example, in the following passage: *adoratae sint . . . Sarmaticae expeditiones . . . , dent ueniam trophaea Niliaca . . . , contenta sit uoce gloriae suae . . . ruina Carporum, reseruetur nuntiis . . . Mauris immissa uastatio: aliis haec . . . celebrabo temporibus* ('the Sarmatian expeditions were admired . . . may the Nile's trophies grant me pardon . . . may the ruin of the Carpi be content with a mention of its glory, may the devastation inflicted on the Moors be kept for messengers', VIII (4)5.1–2). Pacatus concludes an exhaustive description of the emperor's behaviour with the words: *horum haec linguis . . . laudentur qui . . . et dignius . . . et iustius poterunt praedicare* ('let these things be praised by the tongues of men who will be able to proclaim more worthily and justly', II(12)47.3–4). Among other expressions used we may cite the following: *nec in laudibus tuis ponam* ('I will not place amongst your praises . . .', *Pan.* 20.2), *non . . . oramus* ('we do not beg', *Pan.* 94.2), *differamus . . . quid memorem?* ('let us postpone . . . why should I mention?' IV(10)17.3–18.1),[42] *praetermittam* ('I will pass over', III(11)2.6),[43] *quid referam . . . sileantur* ('why should I speak . . . let them be silent', IV(10)8.3–4), *quid loquar?* ('why should I speak?' III(11)24.5).[44]

The figure of *praeteritio* implies that the orator has not said all that he might, and is thus comparable to another trick, favoured by most Greek and Latin orators, by which the speaker claims that he has not time enough for all he would wish to say. In each case there is a sort of indefinite multiplication of the praise that is actually uttered. The fifth chapter of Pacatus' speech, devoted to the praises of the elder Theodosius, is written in this strain. *nouam quandam patior ex copia difficultatem* ('I suffer a new difficulty—the mass of material', II(12) 5.1) the orator complains, and hints at the impossible digressions each topic would involve. When 'Mamertinus' concludes an account of Maximian's life and exploits with the words *sed qui uelit omnia ista complecti, saecula sibi optare debet et innumerabiles annos et quantam tu mereris aetatem* ('but anyone who wants to encompass all those things should wish for centuries for himself, for countless years

---

[42] Cf. III(11)3.1.   [43] Also at IV(10)29.1.
[44] Also at V(8)7.1, VI(7)5.4, XII(9)20.1. Cf. II(12)5. 2.

and for a lifetime as great as you deserve', X(2)2.7), he presents his successors with a form of expression of which they are not slow to avail themselves. Thus Constantius' panegyrist declaims *quibus* [133] *ego si omnibus immorari uelim, neque hic dies mihi totus neque proximus neque porro ceteri sat erunt* ('If I want to dwell on all these things, neither this day in its entirety nor the next nor all thereafter will be enough', VIII(4)4.4). An orator addressing Constantine is more moderate: *dies ante me deficiat quam oratio, si omnia patris tui facta uel hac breuitate percurram* ('the day would end before my speech if I ran through all your father's deeds, even briefly, VI(7) 7.1)[45] and Nazarius is content to say *uno hoc bello, si debitis laudibus immorari uacaret, dies integer conderetur* ('for this war alone, if there were opportunity to linger over the praises it deserves, a whole day would be taken up', IV(10)19.1).[46]

Paronomasia, sometimes called *adnominatio*, was a favourite proceeding of the Latin orators. It is often difficult to say whether what seems to be a play on words, or sounds, is intentional or not. But the examples quoted by Quintilian[47] suggest that he accepted a wide definition of the usage, and one need not hesitate to assert that it is fairly common in the *Panegyrici*. It will suffice to indicate a few cases in which there seems to be little or no doubt of the orators' intention, e.g. *cohonestatus ... beatus ... consecratus* ('honoured ... blessed ...

---

[45] I am indebted to my friend, Mr W. B. Anderson, Professor of Latin in the University of Manchester, for the following valuable reference. Cic., *Rosc. Am.*, XXXII.89 with Landgraf's note: *tempus te citius quam oratio deficeret* ('Time would fail you before the speech'). This formula is frequent in Greek and Roman orators; in Cicero cf. *Verr.* II.52 *nam me dies uox latera deficiant, si hoc nunc uociferari uelim* ('for the day, my voice, my lungs would fail if I wanted to express this now'); ibid. IV.59 *dies me citius defecerit quam nomina* ('the day would fail me sooner than the names') (followed by Ambros. *de Caïn et Abel*, I, 15); *Cael.* 29 *dies iam me deficiat si ... coner expromere* ('day would fail me now if I tried to express'; *Nat. Deor.* III.81, *dies deficiat si uelim numerare* ('day would fail if I wanted to enumerate'); *Tusc.* V.102, *dies deficiat, si uelim paupertatis causam defendere* ('day would fail if I wanted to defend poverty's case'), and in addition Kühner; Sall., *Iug.* 42.5 *de studiis partium et omnis ciuitatis moribus si ... parem disserere, tempus quam res maturius me deserat* ('if I prepared to speak about the interests of the factions and the customs of the whole state, my time would run out before my material'); Demos. *de cor.* 296 ἐπιλείψει με λέγονθ' ἡ ἡμέρα τὰ τῶν προδοτῶν ὀνόματα ('the day will leave me speaking the names of the traitors'); Isocrat. *Archidam.* 81, ἐπιλίποι δ' ἂν τὸ λοιπὸν μέρος τῆς ἡμέρας εἰ τὰς πλεονεξίας τὰς ἐσομένας λέγειν ἐπιχειρήσαιμεν ('if I tried to speak of all the greed to come, what is left of the day would fail').

[46] Cf. Pliny, 56.2. He may be taken literally.

[47] 9.3.66 ff. He gives numerous instances from Cicero.

exalted', II(12)20.2); *tecum fidem, secum perfidiam; tecum fas, secum nefas; tecum ius, secum iniuriam* ('trust on your side, treachery on his; right with you, wrong with him, justice with you, injustice with him', II(12)31.3); *limiti... decederet... militi... accederet* ('to leave the frontier... to add to the army', II(12)32.3); *honorem onere* ('the honour with the onus', III(11)1.4); *hominibus... moenibus... muneribus* ('with men... walls... gifts', VI(7)22.6); *fratre... matre* ('with brother... with mother', VII(6)11.4); *desinendi... dicendi* ('stopping... speaking', VIII(4)21.3); *potentia... eloquentia* ('power ... eloquence', IX(5)19.4);[48] [134] *uicissim nesciunt; sciunt... uicisse* ('in turn they do not know... they know [you] have conquered', XI (3)4.4); *inopia... copia* ('want... plenty', XI(3)15.3); *aemulandi... imitandi* ('rivalling... imitating', XII(9)1.5); *Pompeius... Pompeianus* (XII(9).8.1).

It is worthwhile to mention two forms of expression, united by the common quality of irony or sarcasm, and which we may call the formulae of the 'untenable hypothesis' and of 'contemptuous acquiescence'. In the former the orator adverts to some possibility that might be alleged in opposition to his statement, but which is mentioned in such a way that its absurdity shall at once strike the hearer. This proceeding is well known to readers of Cicero. To take an example at random, Cato, in the *De Senectute*, is made to say: *nisi forte ego uobis, qui et miles et tribunus et legatus et consul uersatus sum in uario genere bellorum, cessare nunc uideor, cum bella non gero* ('unless by chance I now seem to you to be doing nothing, since I'm not waging war—with my experience as a soldier, tribune, legate and consul in various types of war', 6, 18).[49] This construction of a negative condition is the commonest form of the locution. Pacatus entertains the possibility, but only to reject it, that Theodosius may have deteriorated since his accession: *nisi forte in te hodie aut pudicitiae remissior cultus aut minor sanguinis humani metus aut alienae rei maior est appetitus* ('unless by chance today your respect for modesty is more relaxed, or your dread of human blood is reduced, or your appetite for the wealth of others is greater', II(12)12.5).[50] So

---

[48] At IX(5)20.2 I do not think the reading *deuincunt... deuinciunt* can be upheld, see Maguinness (1933b).

[49] Cf. ibid. 10, 33. The possibility is not taken seriously, as it would be if *at* (*enim*) ('but', 'for') were used. Cf. ibid., 7, 21; 19, 68.

[50] Cf. 39.4.

Mamertinus, speaking of the indelible virtues of Julian: *nisi forte existimamus patientes uulnerum formas esse uirtutum* ('unless by chance we think forms of beauty suffer wounds', III(11)5.4).[51] Similarly Eumenius, referring to a letter from the emperors: *nisi forte Pythiados illius excellentem Socratis sapientiam uaticinatae aut magnificentius carmen uidetur aut uerius quam quod Iouii Herculiique pronuntiant* ('unless by chance the song of that Pythian prophecying Socrates' outstanding wisdom seems more magnificent or more true than the pronouncements of the Jovii and Herculii', IX(5)16.2).[52] *nisi vero* ('unless indeed', II(12)41.5) and *nisi si* ('unless if', X(2)12.2) are employed for the same purpose, and Pliny uses *quasi vero*: *alio me uocat numerosa gloria tua* . . . *quasi uero iam satis* [135] *ueneratus miratusque sim quod tantam pecuniam profudisti* ('your countless glory calls me elsewhere . . . as if indeed I have now adequately venerated and admired the fact that you have poured out such a sum of money', 28.1).[53] When the formula is not in the shape of a conditional clause, it may take such a form as the following: *at fortasse non eadem seueritate fiscum qua aerarium cohibes* ('but perhaps you do not control the fisc with the same severity as you do the treasury', 36.3) where the orator at once proceeds to demolish the supposition: *immo tanto maiore quanto plus tibi licere de tuo quam de publico credis* ('rather, you are more severe, in so far as you believe you have more licence with your own money than with the state's').We have seen that *scilicet* is similarly employed, and Nazarius says of Constantine's adversary: *dolis, credo, existimauit [te] decipi posse* ('I believe he thought [you] could be deceived with tricks', IV(10)11.4) and refutes the assumption by pointing to the emperor's vigilance and prudence.

The most interesting examples of 'contemptuous acquiescence' are those in which the orator refers to some tradition of history or legend, to which he flings a casual or disparaging assent, stating or implying that *he* has much greater things to tell. Nazarius is comparatively respectful: *equidem historiae non inuitus adsentior. . . . sed tamen illi qui hoc annalium monumentis inligauerunt verebantur ne aput posteros miraculi fides claudicaret. estote, o grauissimi auctores, de scriptorum religione securi: credimus facta qui maiora nunc sensimus.*

---

[51] The 'untenable hypothesis' is continued with the word *scilicet* ('of course').

[52] Cf. 18.3.

[53] With all the other expressions, except *nisi si* ('unless if'), the verb is in the indicative.

magnitudo principis nostri gestis ueterum fidem conciliat, sed miraculum detrahit ('Myself, I willingly agree with history.... But those who bound this in the historical record feared that posterity's faith in the miracle would waver. Rest assured in the sancitity of your writings, o most dignified authors; we, who have now seen greater things, believe in those deeds. Our emperor's greatness earns trust in the achievements of the ancients, but removes the miraculousness', IV(10)15.5–6). Pacatus, extolling Theodosius' native Spain, is more expressly disparaging towards the traditions of other lands: *scio fabulas poetarum auribus mulcendis repertas aliqua nonnullis gentibus attribuisse miracula. quae, ut sint uera, sunt singula; nec iam excutio ueritatem. sint, ut scribitur, Gargara prouentu laeta triticeo, Meuania memoretur armento, Campania censeatur monte Gaurano, Lydia praedicetur amne Pactolo; dum Hispaniae uni quidquid [ubique] laudatur adsurgat* ('I know the stories of poets, created to soothe the ear, attributed certain miracles to some peoples. Even supposing these miracles are true, they are isolated; I do not now explore their truth. As it is written, let Gargara be content with its wheat crop, let Mevania be known for its cattle, let Campania be renowned for Mt. Gaurus, let Lydia be proclaimed for the river Pactolus, providing that whatever is praised [everywhere] concedes inferiority to Spain alone', II(12)4.4). Elsewhere he delivers an open taunt: *eat nunc sui ostentatrix uetustas et illa innumeris litterarum uulgata* [136] *monimentis iactet exempla* ('Now let showy antiquity go and bandy the examples which are common in countless literary monuments', II(12)17.1) which he has probably derived from 'Mamertinus', *eant nunc rerum ueterum praedicatores et Hannibalem illum multis laboribus magnaque exercitus sui diminutione Alpes penetrasse mirentur* ('now let those who proclaim ancient subjects wonder that Hannibal crossed the Alps with much labour and great loss to his army', XI(3)9.4).[54]

When Quintilian inveighed against the rhetorical affectation of the clausula *esse uideatur* ('it seems to be'), his words would seem to have gone home.[55] In fact its avoidance is so marked in the speech of his pupil Pliny, and in the other panegyrics, that it was, we may conjecture, one of the things which students of rhetoric were taught to

---

[54] Cf. XII(9)23.1 where the same expression introduces the same formula in a quite different context.
[55] 10.2.18. Cf. also 9.4.73 (*'esse uideatur' iam nimis frequens* ('"it seems to be" is now too common').

avoid. But they obeyed in the letter and not in the spirit. The present subjunctive of *uideor* ('I seem') has other forms besides *uideatur*, and there are other infinitives than *esse* (and other parts of speech besides the infinitive), with which the same rhythmical effect may be produced. The orators frequently join *uideatur* with some infinitive other than *esse*, or with some part of speech other than the infinitive, to produce the rhythm—vvv-v either at the end of a sentence or before a medial pause; and they use *uideantur* ('they seem') *uideamur* ('we seem'), or *uidearis* ('you seem') in the same way, or with *esse*, to render the same effect. In either case *esse uideatur* is avoided. Most of the instances I have noted may be indicated without further comment. Those marked with an asterisk are not found at the end of a period.

uideatur: *Pan.* 2.1 (*potuisse uideatur*, 'he seems to have been able'); *Pan.* 56.2 (*laudasse uideatur*, 'he seems to have praised'); II(12)43.1 (*ordinata uideatur*, 'it seems ordained'); II(12)45.7 (*uictore uideatur*, 'he seems conquered by you'); VI(7)4.3 (*impressa uideatur*, 'it seems impressed'); XII(9)1.3 (*exaudita uideatur*, 'it seems heard').

uideantur: *Pan.* 25.1 (*esse uideantur*, 'they seem to be'); *Pan.* 51.3 (*commutata uideantur*, 'they seem changed'); *Pan.* 61.2 (*descendisse uideantur*, 'they seem to have descended'); *Pan.* 62.1 (*accepisse uideantur*, 'they seem to have accepted'); III(11)32.3 (*esse uideantur*, 'they seem to be') [137]; IV(10)19.2 (*esse uideantur*, 'they seem to be'); V(8)4.1 (*suauiora uideantur*, 'they seem sweeter'); X(2)11.6 (*prouenire uideantur*, 'they seem to advance').

uideamur: V(8)5.6 (*obtinuisse uideamur*, 'we seem to have obtained'); IX(5)12.2 (*adfectasse uideamur*, 'we seem to have pursued').

uidearis: *Pan.* 46.8 (*coegisse uidearis*, 'you seem to have forced'); X (2)6.3 (*praeuenisse uidearis*, 'you seem to have arrived before').

Sometimes one of these parts of the present subjunctive of *uideor* ('I seem') is so used for its own sake, where its introduction is not necessary to the construction or the sense. Thus, when Pacatus writes: *quin ita crebro historia decantata est magis ut ab isdem saepe dicta quam ut ab aliquo intermissa uideatur* ('indeed, history has declaimed it so frequently that it seems to have been said more often by the same people than omitted by anyone' II(12)33.2), the sense is the same as it would have been if he had written *intermissa sit* ('it has been omitted'). Nazarius similarly uses *uideatur* ('it seems') without adding anything to the sense: *perstringi haec satis est . . . ne pugna raptim*

gesta diutius narrata quam confecta uideatur ('It is enough to touch
upon these things . . . so that a battle completed quickly does not seem
longer in the telling than in the execution').[56] The author of VI(7)
twice uses *uideantur* ('they seem') without justification in an independent clause, to avoid the rhythm—vv–v—which *uidentur* ('they
seem') would have created: *iam omnia te uocare ad se templa uideantur* ('now all the temples seem to call you to them', VI(7)21.7), and a
little later: *quorum scaturigines leni tepore nebulosae adridere, Constantine, oculis tuis et osculis sese inserere uelle uideantur* ('Constantine, their spring waters, cloudy with gentle warmth, seem to smile, to
want to insert themselves in your eyes and lips' VI(7)22.1).

The panegyrists' habit of personification is one to which I have
referred in my previous paper.[57] I shall conclude this study with an
interesting form that personification frequently assumes in their
writings. This form consists of the use of a verbal noun in apposition
to a substantive describing an inanimate object, or, more frequently,
an abstraction. Nazarius is particularly fond of this usage, of which no
fewer than seven examples occur [138] in his single speech. In one
case the thing thus personified is a concrete object: *conciliatrices pacis
litteras* ('letters proposing peace', IV(10)24.6), in the other cases he is
dealing with abstract qualities: *virtutum opifex disciplina* ('training,
the creator of virtues', 4.2), *amor factorum commendator* ('love which
commends deeds', 4.3) *maiestas fandi ac nefandi discriminatrix* ('majesty which distinguishes between right and wrong', 7.4) *(concordiam)
pacis altricem* ('(concord) which nourishes peace', 10.2), *(historia)
ueri interpolatrix* ('(history) the furbisher of truth', 15.5), *species
luculenta non incitatrix licentiae . . . sed pudoris ornatrix* ('a splendid
appearance did not incite licence . . . but ornamented modesty', 34.1)
On two occasions rivers are personified in the same way: *populorum
altor Nilus . . . corporum durator Hister* ('the Nile which nourishes
peoples . . . the Danube which makes bodies hard', II(12)33.4) and
sancte Thybri, quondam hospitis monitor Aeneae ('sacred Tiber, once
an advisor to your guest Aeneas', XII(9)18.1).· Pacatus holds that:
intimos mentis adfectus proditor uultus enuntiat ('the betraying face

---

[56] IV(10)30.2. Cf. XI(3)13.5: *neque enim pars ulla terrarum maiestatis uestrae
praesentia caret, etiam cum ipsi abesse uideamini* ('for no corner of the earth lacks
the presence of your majesty, even when you yourselves seem to be absent') where
carere uidetur, etiam cum ipsi absitis ('seems to lack . . . even when you yourselves are
absent') would seem the natural way of expressing the idea.
[57] Maguinness (1932) 53–4.

announces the mind's inner emotions', II(12)37.2) but the nouns
employed in the locution are more often abstract: *contemptor ambi-
tionis et...potestatis domitor ac frenator animus* ('the mind which
despises ambition, which tames and reins in power', *Pan.* 55.9);
amplificatrix ueri uetustas ('antiquity which amplifies the truth',
II(12)8.5); *sui ostentatrix uetustas* ('showy antiquity', II(12)17.1);
caelestis spiritus (hominum) habitator ('heavenly spirit which lives
(within men)', VI(7)17.3).

14

Divine Insinuation in the *Panegyrici Latini*

Barbara Saylor Rodgers

Panegyrists and propagandists of the Late Empire insisted that there was a special relationship between sovereign and divinity; extravagant insistence seemed even to claim living deification for one ruler or another. When first-century emperors (Gaius, Nero, Domitian) displayed their megalomania even the ancients rejected their pretensions as soon as they safely could. One occasionally hears nowadays that reports of their dementia may have been exaggerated, that a later hostile tradition has inflated, if not invented, rumours of their mad masquerades. Third- and fourth-century emperors may not so easily be dismissed. In the first place, assertions of divinity by human beings are repugnant to modern minds, and recent students of ancient history have sought to reconcile their perception of an otherwise decent person, Diocletian for example, with this abhorrent aberration by arguing away the aberration. A second obstacle is the desire for order and consistency, although it requires considerable ingenuity to reduce the mass of conflicting evidence about the ruler-cult to a coherent system. Finally, one is struck by the absence of a conflict over the emperor's status in the fourth century: the concept of rule by divine grace became current so easily that it must not have had to supplant an idea of rule by divinity.

Since no whole can cohere unless its parts fit together, I have chosen to examine in this paper a small bit of evidence, eleven of the encomiastic orations known as the *Panegyrici Latini*.[1] The various

---

[1] There is one similar discussion, that of Béranger (1970). His brief review does not always do justice to the evidence in the *Panegyrici*, and I cannot agree with some

speeches, even those addressed to the same emperor, display no single, common theme, but they almost all reveal a measure of ambiguity. The development of the ruler-cult during the first three centuries of our era is not at issue here. The progression from *princeps* ('first citizen') to *dominus* ('lord') was not linear; the apparent excesses of Domitian almost required the apparent civility of Trajan. The notion of the emperor's superhuman stature insinuated itself slowly into the minds of men; it needed a century of turbulence and fear to settle itself in. When the night of the principate had passed, a figure emerged from the shadows of dawn: Diocletian, looking for all the world like an Eastern potentate. [70]

There were those in the fourth century who credited Diocletian with instigating emperor-worship (Aurelius Victor 39.4, Eutropius 9.26). But inflation had affected the imperial cult as well as the currency; one ought perhaps to claim that Diocletian attempted to restore soundness to both. He invented neither. Although Aurelian said that he was chosen by god to be emperor, on some of his coins (as on issues later under Probus and Carus) are the words *Dominus et Deus* ('lord and god'). No one denies that third-century emperors invoked sanctity of person as a defence against assassination, but whether Aurelian or anyone else wanted to be considered a god is open to doubt.[2]

The ruler-cult was unquestionably a political device, although politics and religion had united since early Republican times in the

of his conclusions. Liebeschuetz (1979) comments upon several of the *Panegyrici*: VIII (4), X(2), XI(3) (237–243), XII(9) (285–288), IV(10) (288–291), II(12) (301–302). The panegyrics (both these and others) are part of a grander whole in MacCormack (1981).

[2] Compare for example the opposing views of Kornemann (1901) 136 and Baynes (1935) 84. Baynes, and Nock (1930) 264, both find one piece of evidence conclusive against a view of emperor as god in the late third century: the story (in Müller, *FGH* 4.197) that Aurelian told his soldiers that god had chosen him emperor and fixed the length of his rule. The evidence of Aurelian's coins points to the opposite conclusion. See Dessau, *ILS* 585, 5687 for inscriptions, and *RIC* 5:1.264, 299 nos. 305–6; legends include IMP DEO ET DOMINO AVRELIANO AVG, DEO ET DOMINO NATO AVRELIANO AVG, SOL DOMINVS IMPERI ROMANI. Kubitschek (1915), however, denies any official authority to this coinage, all of which was minted at Serdica or Siscia. He attributes the legend *domino et deo* ('to lord and god') to the initiative of the workers at the mint. For relevant coinage of Probus and Carus see *RIC* 5:2.19, 109 no. 841, 114 no. 885 (DEO ET DOMINO PROBO INVICTO AVG); 133, 145 no. 96, 146 nos. 99–100 (DEO ET DOMINO CARO INVIC AVG, DEO ET DOMINO CARO AVG).

Pax Deorum ('the peace of the gods'). It is difficult to separate the two at any period. Apotheosis was not only a means of honouring dead rulers: an emperor with one or more divine ancestors enjoyed a powerful dynastic claim and appeared to be more than mortal. Septimius Severus employed this principle when he had himself adopted into the line of Marcus Aurelius; Constantine used Claudius Gothicus (*Pan. Lat.* VI(7)2.2.). Diocletian, on the other hand, found a divine parent in Jupiter himself.[3]

Ensslin has formulated three possibilities for the position of the emperor: he might be either a god, the agent of the divine spirit, or god's personally chosen ruler.[4] In any case, the emperor is more than a man. Although all three of these conceptions appear in some form in the *Panegyrici Latini*, the panegyrists most often resort to the first two ideas, and they often employ both in the same speech. [71]

I

As a preface to the examination of individual works, a look at the panegyrists' vocabulary[5] is tedious but necessary. In all of the *Panegyrici, divinus* ('divine') is the adjective which the orators most commonly use to describe things both celestial and imperial. It occurs far more often than *sacer* ('holy') or *sacratus* ('sacred') and their superlatives; *sacratissimus* ('most sacred'), for example, usually appears in the vocative, *sacratissime imperator* ('most sacred emperor'); *sacer* ('holy') having acquired an official meaning, was rendered encomiastically useless, although it does appear in the speeches.

---

[3] MacCormack (1981) 106–7 describes the departure under the Tetrarchs from dependence upon *consecratio*, and kinship with one's (now divine) predecessor: 'Death could add nothing'.

[4] Ensslin (1939) 387, (1943) 49–50 says that it does not matter which formulation came closest to the truth. MacCormack (1981)168–96 details the involvement of the divine in the election of an emperor.

[5] To which not all scholars attach equal weight. For example, Béranger (1970) 246–7 and nn. 33–4, cites the *TLL* definition (see n. 6) of *divinus = imperialis*, and assumes as well that the adjective 'more underlines subordination than identity'; cf. Herzog-Hauser (1924) 851.

divinus ('divine') often has this imperial connotation as well.[6] All of the orators use *divinus* to modify the emperor's mental attributes, other abstract nouns, and, occasionally, human beings. As a general rule, if one can substitute *sacer* for *divinus* without damage to the sense, *divinus* means 'imperial'. For example, *divinarum aurium aditus* ('approach to the divine ears', VIII(4)1.5) is a royal hearing.[7] Sometimes *divinus* stands for 'wonderful', or 'exceptional', equivalent to *praeclarus*: Fausta's beauty (VII(6)6.2) is one example, and *cuius umquam divinior felicitas fuit?* (III(11)27.1) may be translated, 'who ever had more incredible luck?'

divinus also pertains to the gods. One orator says *divina res* (X(2) 6.5) for 'sacrifice'. It is usually clear from the context what *divinus* means, for example at X(2)4.2, where it is said that Diocletian could not have restored the republic without help (*divinum modo ac ne id quidem unicum sufficeret auxilium* 'divine help, and not even that alone was enough'); Maximian played the part of Hercules helping Jupiter in his war against the giants. The transition from earthly problems to heavenly ones takes place within one sentence and the orator really means 'divine' in this instance.

The orators represent the emperors' power, or an emperor himself, with two abstract nouns, *divinitas* ('divinity') and *maiestas* ('majesty').[8] The author of VIII(4) is particularly fond of both words and frequently uses them as polite periphrases for *tu* or *vos* ('you') (e.g. 2.1, 5.3; but compare 2.3). On the other hand, Constantine's outward appearance is as beautiful as his divinity is certain (VI(7) 17.4). *divinitas* ('divinity') and *maiestas* ('majesty') like *divinus* ('divine'), retain at least two meanings, the original one of 'divinity' and 'majesty', and an imperial or formulaic meaning, which one can [72] represent either by the English expression 'your majesty', or by some

---

[6] *TLL* 5:1.7.1623, 34–71: *i. q. imperialis, regius, de vivo et consecrato principe, necnon de domo Augustorum* ('imperial, royal, about a live or dead emperor, particularly about the house of the Augusti').

[7] The lists in the appendix contain many examples from all the speeches, arranged in two categories, depending on whether the word modifies emperor or divinity. I have omitted the word *caelestis* ('heavenly') from consideration here, but included it in the appendix. It has about the same range of meaning as *divinus*, although it occurs infrequently, and its usage underwent the same changes.

[8] Cf. also *sanctitas* ('sanctity', XI(3)19.3) and Diocletian's *divina maiestas* ('divine majesty') (Dessau, *ILS* 627). Charlesworth (1936) has shown that by the end of the second century, *aeternitas* ('eternity') had also become an attribute of the emperor.

other suitable word such as *imperium* ('empire') (as at VII(6)3.2; see appendix for further examples).

Pliny employed the word *numen* ('godhead') exclusively (at least in the *Panegyricus*) for references to the divine: e.g. 1.4–5, 2.3, 33.4. The word retained this meaning in the third and fourth centuries; in the *Panegyrici* it usually means divinity or divine power; occasionally, the will of an emperor. Duncan Fishwick has rightly argued, against Pippidi and others, that the *numen* and the *genius* ('spirit') of the emperor are not identical.[9] I do not, however, agree with his conclusion that the attribution of a *numen* to the emperor was purely honorific.[10] The use of *numen* was flattery no more empty than any other of its sort.

The authors of the *Panegyrici* sometimes equate the emperor and his *numen* ('godhead'); the expressions *numen tuum* ('Your godhead') or *numen illius* ('his godhead') appear, like *divinitas* ('divinity') and *maiestas* ('majesty'), instead of *tu* ('you'), *ille* ('he').[11] One orator says that Maximian reports his actions to his colleague's *numen* (X(2) 9.1); when another speaks of a ship which carried the emperor's *numen*, he means the emperor's person (VIII(4)19.1). At other times *numen* is a divine attribute of the emperor, as at XI(3)10.4, when the emperors' *numen* shone forth from the Alps, or in a reference to their presence (*aures tanti numinis* 'the ears of such a godhead', VI(7)1.1).

The two categories may overlap. Does the speaker mean the emperor himself or the emperor's divine aspect when he says *veneratio numinis tui* ('veneration of your godhead', X(2)1.1)? *numen* is also used of an emperor no longer living (*divus* Claudius at VI(7)2.1).

Several of the orators call the gods *numina*, and in almost every case *numen* ('godhead') may be replaced by *deus* ('god'). For example, X(2)11.6 contains a reference to gods in general, IX(5)9.4 to Minerva and Apollo. At XI(3)14.2, though, Jupiter's *numen* is a separate aspect of the god. *numen* as it appears in the *Panegyrici* means any or all of the following: *(a)* godhead, divinity, divine power; applied to various deities and to emperors; *(b)* a god; *(c)* an emperor; replacing a pronoun or a proper name; sometimes formulaic cf. *divinitas* ('divinity') *maiestas* ('majesty').

---

[9] Fishwick (1969); Pippidi (1930) 136–7; cf. Pfister (1937) 1286–7.

[10] Fishwick (1969) 364–5; cf. Étienne (1958) 313.

[11] Schäfer (1914) 86–8.

In the appendix I have listed the places where the words *divinus, caelestis, divinitas, maiestas,* and *numen* appear in the *Panegyrici,* and I have indicated, perhaps arbitrarily in some instances, where *divinus* may be replaced by *sacer* or by *praeclarus* ('excellent'), where *divinitas, maiestas* and *numen* replace a pronoun. Although they appear in formulaic phrases, none of these words has become so [73] totally debased that it cannot be used of a deity. Sometimes the emperor is *invictus* ('unconquered') more often *invictissimus* ('most unconquered'), a further concession to devaluation. The emperor is sacred, most sacred, divine; he is majesty, divinity, deity. In terminology at least, the emperor has become one with his various aspects. One may still speak of the emperor's *maiestas, divinitas,* or *numen* as if these were distinct aspects of the ruler, who yet also becomes his *maiestas,* his *divinitas,* his *numen.* When it is possible to substitute a name, pronoun, or possessive adjective for any of these words, it is clear that the speaker has made no verbal distinction between human and divine. This lack of rigorous separation between emperor and the divinity gives rise to some peculiar expressions for empire, or for the process of becoming emperor. The author of VII(6) says that Maximian had *divinitas* ('imperial power') before Constantine (3.2). He also calls the beginning of Maximian's rule the *ortus* ('origin') of his *numen.*[12]

The lists in the appendix show that the equation of emperor and divinity, judged by terminology and the frequency of appearance, is more evident in the earlier speeches. Expressions such as 'your divinity', once in general use, may have lost some of their original meaning.[13] I say *may have* for there is also evidence that these words regained a certain force during the fourth century, as I shall show later on. Perhaps it is not a question of losing or regaining, but of staying the same.

I divide the *Panegyrici* into two groups, 'early' (V(8)–XI(3)) and 'late' (II(12), III(11), IV(10), XII(9)), although V(8) and XII(9) do not fit precisely into either group. The twelfth panegyric, delivered in 313, is a rich lode of equivocation. Various scholars have studied the panegyrics addressed to Constantine for evidence of change in his religious beliefs after 312; they discern a gradual development away

---

[12] Cf. VIII(4)2.2 *vestrae maiestatis ortus* ('the origin of your majesties').

[13] Liebeschuetz (1979) 238 n. 3 notes, 'such language had to become more extreme in order to compensate for the devaluation of the phraseology over centuries of use'.

from the outspoken paganism of the panegyric of 310, through a kind of philosophic, if somewhat confused, theology (313), to monotheism (321).[14] Since there is a space of only two years between the last 'early' speech (311) and the first 'late' one (313), 'pagan' and 'Christian' might seem to be more accurate designations. I avoid them because to place the speeches into such categories is misleading and is to make assumptions beyond what their evidence allows about the religious beliefs of the orators and of Constantine himself.

In the earlier panegyrics *divinus* refers to the emperor 37 times in 96 pages (approximately once every two and a half pages); to the gods, only seven times. In the last four [74] speeches the incidence is reversed, although not so disproportionately: 17 in 111 pages for the emperor—about once every six and a half pages—and 26 for the divinity. In addition, the gods have been replaced by one nameless god. *caelestis* appears rarely: it occurs 13 times in VI(7)–XI(3), 10 of which modify the emperor. The authors of V(8) and XII(9) do not use it. It shows up again 18 times in the three latest speeches and only once refers to the emperor.

In the earlier speeches the orators use *divinitas* only of the emperor, in the later ones, with two exceptions (both in *Pan.* XII(9) of 313), only of the deity. The use of *maiestas* is scanty in the later panegyrics, although that particular word has never been out of style.

Nazarius and Claudius Mamertinus never use *numen* of the emperor and each employs it only for the deity. Elsewhere its frequency and intent parallel that of the adjective *divinus*: 39 references to the emperor in V(8)–XI(3), eight to the gods; in II(12)–IV(10) and XII (9), six times for each. The author of XII(9) prefers *numen* as an attribute of the emperor (four times) and when he uses it of the deity he modifies it with *divinum* (cf. II(12)30.2, IV(10)7.3).

The orators' terminology has changed by the end of the fourth century. In the later panegyrics, especially in the last three, the speakers rarely attribute superhuman qualities to the emperor, and even *divinus*, that most common of adjectives, infrequently appears. One may also compare the ways in which Ausonius and Symmachus address late fourth-century emperors. Both reserve the word *deus* for the divinity; the ruler is *deo proximus* ('next to (the) god', Symm.

---

[14] See below on XII(9) and IV(10). For analyses of Constantine's religious development as discerned through the *Panegyrici*, see Pichon (1906a) 102–7; Maurice (1909); Liebeschuetz (1979) 281–91.

Orat. 1.18; Aus. *Gr. Act.* 5.21) or *deo similis* ('like (the) god', Symm. *Orat.* 1.1). The emperor is still 'your majesty'. To Ausonius, *numen* is the power of god; to Symmachus, who once calls Valentinian I *aeterne defensor* ('eternal defender' *Orat.* 2.27), *numen* can still describe the emperor (*quanto parcior vestri numinis cultus est quam deorum*, 'how much more sparing is your reverence than the gods", 2.32), although only twice in the extant orations and not as a term of direct address (at *Orat.* 1.22 Symmachus uses *tui numinis* 'of your godhead', instead of a possessive adjective). Once Valentinian's *consilia* ('plans') are *divina* 'divine' (Symm. *Orat.* 2.6) and Gratian's *auditorium* ('auditorium') is *sacrum* ('sacred'), (but that is the technical term: Aus. *Gr. Act.* 10.45). Ausonius (*Gr. Act.* 5.22) describes Gratian's *magnanimitas* ('magnanimity') as *caelestis* ('heavenly'), and Symmachus uses the same adjective (*Orat.* 3.5) of the *iudicium* ('decision') whereby the young man became emperor. One may note also Symmachus' use of the adjective *venerabilis* (*Orat.* 1.7, 2.18, 2.23, 3.11, 4.12; cf. Ausonius' *veneratio tua* ('your veneration') [*Gr. Act.* 1.3]). In the extant orations there is little to offend Christian ears besides the two instances of *numen* in Symmachus, and in Ausonius the phrase *divinitatis tuae... verba* ('your divinity's words', *Gr. Act.* 10.45).

Symmachus' *Relationes*, on the other hand, are filled with a variety of flattering formulations. In these official letters, *deus* is always, and *numen* occasionally, the divinity (cf. *deo proximus* ('next to (the) god') 14.3, 19.10); the emperor is (in descending order or frequency) *numen* ('godhead'), *clementia* ('mercy'), *aeternitas* ('eternity'), *perennitas* ('perpetuity'), *maiestas* ('majesty'), *mansuetudo* ('gentleness'), *serenitas* ('serenity'), *felicitas* ('good luck'). His attributes are *sacer* ('holy'), *divinus* ('divine'), [75]*venerabilis* ('venerable'), *caelestis* ('heavenly'), *aeternus* ('eternal'), *sacrosanctus* ('sacrosanct'). Almost without exception, these words belong to formulaic phrases and terms of address. They must reflect current epistolary correctness of form and demonstrate that bureaucratic convention is much slower than oratorical to change. Indeed, the expression 'your majesty' has endured almost two thousand years, although all the others have been given over. 'Majesty' ('biggerness') is something which monarchs unquestionably have in some sense, but they do not necessarily possess the rest. If *numen, aeternitas*, and similar words had been truly empty of meaning, one might find them yet in modern terminology.

II

Panegyric X(2) AD 289. Anonymous to Maximian.[15] Rome's birthday

In his opening words (1.1), the author of X(2) equates the honours of emperors and gods, but despite his mention of the rulers' divine paternity (2.3), he cares little for the gods. Maximian's education (2.4) suits a soldier-emperor—he spent his youth on the frontier, where the sounds of clashing arms drowned out his infant cries— but the orator twists the standard allusion: *finguntur haec de Iove, sed de te vera sunt, imperator* ('these things are made up about Jupiter, but about you they are true, Emperor', 2.5). He was probably not the first, and certainly not the last panegyrist to demote an Olympian.

The emperor himself is said to be a god more venerable than the invisible inhabitants of temples at Rome (*quanto tandem studio nos hic convenit [venerari], qui te praesentem intuemur deum toto quidem orbe victorem?*, 'finally with how much enthusiasm does it suit us to venerate here, who behold you the victor over the entire world as a manifest god?', 2.1).[16] Maximian's many services to Gaul prove that he is a god, or better: *quis deus tam insperatam salutem nobis attulisset, nisi tu adfuisses?* ('which god would have brought us such unhoped-for well-being, had you not been present? 5.1). When he returned triumphant from the field, his consular ceremony having been interrupted by a barbarian invasion, he filled Trier with joy and altars blazed with sacrifices to his *numen* ('godhead').[17] The emperor himself had fulfilled what he had asked of the gods earlier in the day, and again the gods had no part (6.3–4). [76] Once more the author

---

[15] Whether or not the same orator, one 'Mamertinus', wrote both Panegyrics X(2) and XI(3), I prefer to treat the two orations separately. In the first place, the identity of authorship cannot be proven beyond doubt; in the second, each effort is a literary unit and deserves to be treated as such.

[16] Nock has distinguished between the literal and figurative use of *deus*. He says (1928) 31 that you call someone a god 'either unreservedly or with reference to yourself, a *god to you.*' To the second category belong most of the examples from the Republican and Augustan periods (see his 31 n. 51). The instance here belongs to the first. *praesens deus* = θεός ἐπιφανής ('god present').

[17] See Price (1980) on sacrifice in the imperial cult, especially the conclusion (42) that the evidence precludes systematization. The emperor's position was often ambiguous, between men and gods; but occasionally the ruler was unquestionably treated in sacrificial matters as divine.

slights Jupiter to praise Maximian's *celeritas* ('speed').[18] Finally, at the end of the day, there were sacrifices thanking Maximian for delivering what he had asked of Jupiter in the morning (16.5).[19] Maximian, like Hercules, is known for his labours, while Diocletian accomplishes everything effortlessly. But whereas Diocletian, who seems not quite to measure up to his colleague in this speech, is equal to his father, Maximian has twice surpassed Jupiter himself.

Jupiter and Hercules frequently appear in this speech. One may object that Diocletian's assumption for himself and his colleague of the titles Jovius and Herculius indicates the emperors' subordinate relationship to the gods: Diocletian clearly wanted to claim divine protection for his person, if not actual divinity.[20] It is useless to ask to what extent his subjects pondered the theological implications of his cognomen. Diocletian had a human body, but he said that he was the son of Jupiter himself, not of a deified emperor. In this respect at least he departed from the practice of his predecessors.

Diocletian's motives aside, the real question is not whether the orator recognized other divine entities, but how he conceives of the emperor's relationship with these powers. In order to show that the emperors are responsible for their subordinates' accomplishments (11.5), the orator makes the analogy that although we seem to receive every benefit from various deities, all good really derives from Jupiter and Hercules: *sic omnibus pulcherrimis rebus . . . Diocletianus initium facit, tu tribuis effectum* ('in this way, in all most beautiful matters, Diocletian makes [the start], you grant the outcome', 11.6).[21] Here the two gods are the *summi auctores* ('highest agents'), greater than the other gods; the emperors are greater than other men. For the sake of the analogy, the speaker seems at first glance to have grouped the supreme powers into two different spheres, celestial and earthly. But the gods are not responsible solely for what happens in the heavens;

[18] It is strange that Liebeschuetz (1979) 238 and n. 5 has chosen section 6.4 as evidence of distinction between god and emperor.

[19] Cf. Ryberg (1955) 98 'The actual ritual of the imperial cult reappears in monumental art only when the reigning emperor receives offerings in his own person as a *praesens deus*, and when the worship of the living ruler finally displaces the old rites of the triumph and the payment of *vota* to the greater gods of the state'.

[20] With, for example, Baynes (1935) 84. But see MacCormack (1981) 169–72 for a very different conclusion.

[21] Galletier (1949) supplies *initium*. Mynors (1964) prints *Diocletianus † facit* and notes *alius aliud supplet* ('other scholars fill the lacuna variously').

they are the authors of *omnia commoda caelo terraque parta* ('all useful things produced in heaven and on land'). The emperors are the source of *omnes pulcherrimae res* ('all most beautiful things'). The speaker does not describe a separation of powers, but uses the gods as a literary device to prove his point.

Near the end of the speech, the orator turns again to the occasion of his panegyric. He speaks of the celebrations in Rome and imagines how much [77] more majestic the emperors' presence would make the city, *quae nunc sine dubio praesentiam vestri sibi fingit, aedes vestrorum numinum frequentando et* ... *invocando Statorem Iovem Herculemque Victorem* ('which now without doubt feigns your presence by frequenting the temples of your godheads and* ... *invoking Jupiter Stator and Hercules Victor', 13.4). Both here and in the next sentence, when the author reminds Maximian that Hercules derived the title Victor from a victory over pirates (13.5), Galletier translates *numen* 'divinité protectrice' ('protecting divinity'). One could argue that by *numen* the orator means 'godhead', a divine force emanating from Jupiter and Hercules in which the emperors partake, but in this speech there is no information about the emperors' powers which would warrant such an interpretation of this passage. Jupiter and Hercules are the 'parents' of the emperors. It is Herculius, though, *cui iam sic tempestatum opportunitas obsequatur* ('whom fair weather now thus follows') who will overcome the pirates (12.1–8). What is more, the Romans worship at the temples of Jupiter and Hercules only because the emperors are not there in person: they imagine the emperors' presence by worshipping the gods. Far from picturing the emperors as subordinates through whom the gods manifest themselves, this orator characterizes the gods as substitutes for the real thing. The Roman populace must be content with an approximation but the citizens of Trier may celebrate enthusiastically since the *deus* ('god') is actually *praesens* ('present').

Diocletian chose Jupiter and Hercules to symbolize his and Maximian's relationship to each other and to the gods.[22] The author of X (2) employs this imperial propaganda for his own purpose. Jupiter and Hercules are only symbols in his speech, useful for drawing analogies or for being compared unfavourably with the living

---

[22] These gods sometimes appear on coinage as something like servants, when Diocletian and Maximian sitting are shown being crowned by Jupiter and Hercules standing: Ensslin (1943) 39.

emperors. The gods play the role of stock figures in comparisons, like Alexander and real or mythical Roman heroes. One of the emperor's duties as Pontifex Maximus was to preserve the form of official Roman religion by offering sacrifice to the gods, as his predecessors had done. The orator represents Maximian performing these official functions, but he robs them of importance when he reveals the emperors as the real authors of the empire's well-being. Their subjects, therefore, owe them appropriate honors (6.5); the source of the greatest benefits to the provinces is the physical presence of the emperor himself (14.4–5).[23]

Panegyric XI(3) A.D. 291. Anonymous to Maximian. The emperor's birthday

The author of XI(3) commences with a standard reference to Maximian's divine parentage (2.4). He is interested in the emperors' restless energy, and [78] in the following section (3.1–8) their divine origin is prominent (*caelestis ille vestri generis conditor vel parens . . . vestri illi parentes . . . ille . . . Diocletiani auctor deus*[24]*parentes deos*, 'that heavenly founder or father of your family . . . those parents of yours . . . that god the founder of Diocletian . . . parent gods'). Diocletian and Maximian have inborn in them the flame of the divine mind; they are like their parents, who never rest and preserve their immortality by constant motion. Cicero had used his translation of Plato when he argued that the soul is immortal and that the gods open up the way to heaven for those who devote themselves to the state, but this speaker does not draw attention directly to the emperors' probable posthumous apotheosis when he describes their continual preoccupation with the empire.[25]

---

[23] This statement is as true as many another commonplace. The emperors' physical presence and personal interest were of real importance to the empire's inhabitants; the wheels of the administrative machine always turned very slowly, and often crookedly. The fifth panegyric shows that Constantine's visit to Autun resulted in immediate relief of some of the city's burden of taxation.

[24] Béranger (1970) 247 cites this phrase as an example of Diocletian's subordination to the god, but in this context *auctor* means that Jupiter is the progenitor of Diocletian's race: *TLL* 2.6. 1204, 58–9.

[25] In this connection it is interesting that within this same passage the orator says that Hercules was once a man. One might interpret this in two ways, either as a

At 6.1 the orator announces that he will dwell upon the emperors' *pietas* ('piety') and *felicitas* ('good luck') not their *res gestae* ('achievements'). The choice of *pietas* as a subject requires him to include the rulers' regard for the gods. The emperors increase the gods' honour both by the usual means (altars, statues, temples, money), but especially by adding their own names and images and by their example (6.1–2). The emperors' concern for each other, *id quod maxime deorum immortalium cum religione coniunctum est* ('that which is particularly joined with reverence of the immortal gods', 6.3), receives much longer treatment; their lack of selfishness proves their superiority to the rest of mankind; their immortal soul is greater than the empire itself (6.5).[26] As a result, the gods cannot divide their benefits between them (7.3). The orator seems to have demoted his rulers to the position of human recipients of divine favour, yet this sentence is but a traditional part of his description of their *pietas* ('piety') to which he has devoted more than a third of the speech.[27] It is also an argument for Maximian's equality to his senior colleague. The speaker insists upon the emperors' regard for each other: their *pietas* ('piety') gave them wings (8.3–4), their fiery and immortal minds do not perceive the delays to which bodies are liable (8.5). The climax of this portion of the speech is the conference at Milan. The emperors brought a *clarior lux* ('clearer light') to Italy with them; they are the source of a light so brilliant that it indicates the presence of a god (10.4–5). The orator imagines the joy and animation of the people of northern Italy: they worship the emperors [79] themselves, equated here with Jupiter and Hercules. The speaker ignores the official titles Jovius and Herculius: Diocletian and Maximian are gods in the flesh.[28]

---

compliment, with Hercules setting a precedent as a god who had lived among men, or as an allusion to the apotheosis of outstanding men and therefore an indirect hint that Maximian may still be a mortal. Cf. XI(3)6.4: *manifestum est ceterorum hominum animas esse humiles et caducas, vestras vero caelestes et sempiternas* ('it is clear that the souls of the rest of mankind are earthly and perishable, but indeed yours are heavenly and everlasting'). Do only emperors have immortal souls?

[26] The emperors seem in this passage to be independent powers: *vester vero immortalis animus omnibus opibus omnique fortuna atque ipso est maior imperio* ('indeed your immortal mind is greater than all riches and all fortune, even than the empire itself').

[27] Cf. 18.4, where *fortuna* ('Fortune') is the donor. But the orator has already said that the emperors' soul is greater than Fortune (see n. 26).

[28] *dis immortalibus laudes gratesque cantari, non opinione traditus sed conspicuus et praesens Iuppiter cominus invocari, non advena sed imperator Hercules adorari*

pietas ('piety') is the cause of the emperors' meeting in Milan; their ability to leave the empire's borders is proof of their *felicitas* ('good luck', 13.1–4): *neque enim pars ulla terrarum maiestatis vestrae praesentia caret, etiam cum ipsi abesse videamini* ('for no part of the world lacks your presence, even when you seem to be absent', 13.5). It is clear from his explanation of this statement that the orator separates the emperors' *maiestas* ('majesty') from their persons:[29]

> *itaque illud quod de vestro cecinit poeta Romanus Iove "Iovis omnia plena," id scilicet animo contemplatus, quamquam ipse Iuppiter summum caeli verticem teneat supra nubila supraque ventos sedens in luce perpetua, numen tamen eius ac mentem toto infusam esse mundo, id nunc ego de utroque vestrum audeo praedicare: ubicumque sitis, in unum licet palatium concesseritis, divinitatem vestram ubique versari, omnes terras omniaque maria plena esse vestri. quid enim mirum si, cum possit hic mundus Iovis esse plenus, possit et Herculis?*

> And so that which the Roman poet sang about your Jupiter, "Everything is full of Jupiter", of course bearing in his mind that although Jupiter himself holds the very utmost peak of heaven, sitting in perpetual light above the clouds and winds, however, his godhead and mind are infused throughout the whole world—it is that that I dare to proclaim about each of you: wherever you are, even if you retire into one palace, your divinity is in circulation everywhere, all lands and all seas are full of you. For what surprise is there if, when this world can be full of Jupiter, it can also be full of Hercules? 14.2–4

No matter where their bodies are, their *divinitas* ('divinity') is everywhere, just as Jupiter's *numen* ('godhead') and *mens* ('mind') fill the world. The god's and emperors' divine aspect is similar to the power of thought: an inseparable part of each individual which nevertheless, since it is not corporeal, is not bound by time and place. The orator has used his description of Jupiter in 14.2 to explain the emperors' power, and the final sentence of the analogy fulfils a twofold purpose, to equate the two emperors' capabilities and to unite again ruler and god: after *divinitatem vestram . . . vestri,* ('your divinity . . . you') *Iovis*

('they sing in praise and thanks to the immortal gods; not passed on by rumour, Jupiter is invoked, visible, present and close by; Hercules is adored not as a stranger but an emperor', 10.5). See Ensslin (1943) 49 and MacCormack (1981) 23–6 on this passage.

[29] Ausonius (*Gr. Act.* 1.5) treats the topic differently; Gratian's subjects are nowhere without reminders of his benefits. Cf. Symm. *Orat.* 1.1 on Valentinian's knowlege of his empire.

('Jupiter') and *Herculis* ('Hercules') stand for *Iovii* and *Herculii*. The main point of the final sentence is vindication of Maximian's status; the orator established earlier (10.5) the ruler-god equation with the words *praesens Iuppiter* ('present Jupiter') and *imperator Hercules* ('emperor Hercules').

Panegyric IX(5) A.D. 298. Eumenius to the provincial governor. Request to rebuild the Schools of Autun.

The ninth panegyric is valuable primarily as an example of how one speaks of the emperors when they are absent.[30] As a former *magister memoriae*, Eumenius has a fluent command of official terminology, although he prefers the superlatives *maximi* ('greatest'), *optimi* ('best'), *fortissimo* ('bravest') and *invictissimi* ('most unconquered') to *sacratissimi* ('most sacred'), and [80] his favourite expression is *tanti principes* ('such great emperors', 9.1, 13.1, 15.1 and 5).[31] He never equates the rulers with their divine parents; the emperors and Caesars are always Iovii and Herculii in his speech (cf. 8.1 and 3, 10.2, 16.2), and he is precise about family relationships. At 8.1 he calls Hercules Constantius' *avus* ('grandfather'). He carefully mentions all the rulers, distinguishing Augusti and Caesars; when he lists their accomplishments all over the empire he goes from east to west and back again, starting with the two Augusti, an arrangement which allows him simultaneously to observe imperial seniority (21.2). He takes pains, however, to describe the benefits deriving from the gods whose temples are situated near the Schools in Autun (9.3–10.3), as well as the mutual profit afforded by the association of Hercules with the Muses in the temple at Rome consecrated to them (7.3). Such descriptions advance the cause of literature and of education, the end of which is to prepare young men for positions in the imperial administration and to teach them how to rehearse the emperors' exploits. The gods are integral to his arguments, the emperors' divinity is not. The vocabulary of this former imperial official and his careful enunciation of the rulers' relationship with Jupiter, Hercules,

---

[30] Béranger (1970) 248.
[31] Note his frequent use of *sacer* ('holy' 9.5.4, 9.6.2, 9.11.1&2, 9.13.1&2, 9.16.4, 9.21.4) and *divinus* ('divine', see appendix).

each other, are fully in accord with official practice, and he adds no details of his own imagining to this formally correct presentation.

Panegyric VIII(4) A.D.298. Anonymous to Constantius. *dies imperii* ('an imperial anniversary'); recovery of a province

The author of the eighth panegyric is fond of representing the emperor and empire as a source of light. The sun must labour not to be outshone by the emperors' *maiestas* ('majesty', 2.2–3), the inhabitants of Britain, finally restored to life by the true light of the empire, regard Constantius as if he had just descended from heaven (19.1–2),[32] imperial rule is the source of light, and therefore of life, for Roman citizens (10.1). The orator asserts that the emperors oversee human affairs with more constancy than the sun and all the stars, since they alone, night and day, keep watch, by means both of their corporeal eyes and the eyes of their divine minds: *adeo, Caesar, vestra in orbem terrarum distributa beneficia prope plura sunt quam deorum* ('Thus, Caesar, your benefits distributed across the world are almost more than the gods", 4.3). To omit the adverb *prope* ('nearly') would exceed the bounds of propriety for this orator. He is more circumspect than the author(s) of X(2) and XI(3) when he compares the emperors with the gods: the people of Britain regard Constantius not as *deus* ('god'), but *ut caelo delapsus* ('as if fallen from the sky', 19.1). [81]

This orator uses inflated vocabulary more frequently than any other,[33] yet his words contain less substance than form. He gives to the emperor's *maiestas* ('majesty') a thunderbolt (13.1, 15.6), and identifies the emperors as superhuman powers when he says that the soldiers contemplated a victory derived from them: *non illi tunc vires, non humana robora, sed vestra numina cogitaverunt* ('they considered not your might, not your human strength but your godheads', 15.4). Only here does he use *numen* to indicate the emperors'

---

[32] [*Britanni*] *vera imperii luce recreati* ('[Britons] restored by the true light of the empire'). Cf. the words REDDITOR LVCIS AETERNAE ('restorer of eternal light') on the Arras Medallion (*RIC* 5:2 no. 430), which represents Constantius' arrival at London, and interpretation thereof in MacCormack (1981) 30–1.

[33] Unlike his predecessors, this orator prefers the vocative, *imperator invicte*, ('unconquered emperor') to other forms of address, e.g. *sacratissime* ('most sacred').

power, although in one other passage (13.2) he says that Constantius' *numen* was turned toward Britain. *numen* here is the mind or attention, like the watch which the emperors keep with their mind's eye (4.3).[34]

The author of the eighth speech rarely mentions the gods. Constantius has the unanimous will of the gods on his side, witness his victories (17.1). The orator does not think that even a god, addressing mankind directly, could have persuaded anyone before the event to believe the many benefits which men were soon to acquire from Diocletian and his colleagues (9.1). This sort of compliment is similar to those used in the tenth panegyric (e.g. X(2)2.5, 6.4). The implication may be that the gods were not helping the empire before Diocletian's accession: the orators sometimes attribute to god(s) a temporary (if inexplicable) lack of concern with human affairs (compare VIII(5)10.1–3; II(12)30.1; VII(6)9.1). What is more, a god's promises are weak substitutes for the emperors' performance.

The orator deals in a straightforward manner with Constantius' and his colleagues' considerable successes. There may be various reasons for his attitude: Constantius as a Caesar perhaps ought not to have been addressed as a fully fledged deity, yet the orator is speaking in the presence of the Caesar alone. Even if the same speaker might have addressed the question of Maximian's divinity with more obvious zeal, it would be rude to do so unless Maximian were there in person. The orator's consistent use of the second person plural indicates that he was mindful of other ears. Equally, his personal beliefs may be the cause of his devoting so little attention either to the emperors' divinity or to the gods. And MacCormack (1981, 27) observes the subordination in this speech of the themes of epiphany and divinity to the historical narrative.

Near the end of his panegyric, the speaker can think of no greater favour from the gods than that they allow the emperors' subjects and all their heirs forever to serve both the present emperors, whom he calls *perpetui parentes et domini generis humani* ('eternal parents and lords of the human race') and their offspring (20.1). His prayer, phrased in conventional terms, asks only for a series of good emperors. [82]

---

[34] At 4.2 *numen* means 'imperial power'; elsewhere it usually is equivalent to 'you' or to 'your majesty'.

The gods appear thrice in the speech, twice in conventional situations; the orator is more interested in the emperors and their accomplishments than in what kind of beings they are. Perhaps the emperors' divinity is an assumption which this speaker takes for granted. Perhaps divinity is of no importance. The orator's lack of interest in the gods implies that he does not expect anything from them. In any event, his comparatively restrained treatment makes all the more striking the excesses of the two earliest panegyrics.

Panegyric VII(6) A.D.307. Anonymous to Constantine and Maximian. Epithalamium (Constantine's marriage to Fausta)

The author of the seventh panegyric is, like Eumenius, a master of correct terminology, and more. He seems to have created a system of converting the emperors' attributes into synonyms for imperial power. He uses the world *maiestas* ('majesty') seven times, never as an epithet, always as an aspect of emperor or empire, and represents *imperium* in three different ways: *divinitas* ('divinity', 3.2), *sacrum istud fastigium divinae potestatis* ('that sacred peak of divine power', 6.1), *numen* ('godhead', 8.3). He does not use *divinitas*, *numen*, or the circumlocution of 6.1 anywhere else and almost seems to have introduced the terms solely for the purpose of definition. He carefully explains, too, the nature of immortality. The forethought of the *aeterni principes* ('eternal emperors') guarantees that Rome will be governed by successive generations of the same house (2.2); likewise, the immortality of the republic depends upon her citizens' producing children (2.3). Constantius himself has a special immortality beyond that of the other *divi* ('divines') because his son, who is like him in body and spirit, is emperor (14.5).[35] The orator has a purpose (the dynastic motif) and an occasion (a marriage) beyond that of definition for introducing these reasonings, but one can argue the value of marriage and child-rearing, one can justify Constantine's promotion to Augustus, without underscoring the emperors' mortality.

Like the authors of the tenth and eleventh panegyrics, this orator asserts that Maximian has proven his descent from Hercules (8.2); unlike them, he is always careful to separate divine and imperial

[35] Béranger (1970) 248: 'It is the conception of classical Rome'.

powers. He justifies Maximian's return from retirement; he speculates upon the divine purpose (7.5–6; 9.1; 10.1). Since Jupiter himself gave Maximian imperial power forever, the emperor should not have hesitated to take up the burden again: his inborn *maiestas* ('majesty') clung to him even while a private citizen (12.4–5). At this point the orator has compared the emperor's success in setting the state back on its course to Apollo's restoring the sun to its proper place in heaven (12.2–3).

Apart from the analogy between emperor and Apollo, there are two other places where Maximian's activities are likened to a god's. The orator describes his return to power as the point at which *omnibus spes salutis inluxit* ('hope of safety lit up everything', 12.7); the [83] turbulent conditions of the republic represent a spell of foul weather. If there are still any storms anywhere, he says, *necesse est tamen ad tuos nutus dilucescat et sileat* ('however, at your nod, it must dawn and fall silent', 12.8); a clever way of alluding to Maximian's troubles with Galerius. The orator's division of responsibilities between Maximian and Constantine suggests a position of godlike aloofness from human affairs for the senior ruler, although it indicates which emperor had the real power in Gaul (14.1).

This orator consistently represents the emperors as mortal recipients of divine favour. Coins issued under the Tetrarchy often project a similar image: the emperors receive their power directly from Jupiter.[36] The content of the sixth panegyric makes it clear that the practice of equating emperor and god had not gone out of fashion, yet the author of VII(6) not only avoids such an equation but even, in describing the hierarchy of divine and human power, denies it.

Panegyric VI(7) A.D.310. Anonymous to Constantine. Quinquennalia (and a request for Autun)

Imperium nascendo meruisti ('you deserved the empire, by your birth', 3.1): the gods, according to the author of the sixth panegyric, chose Constantine as emperor on the day he was born (3.1–4). Jupiter himself stretched forth his right hand to take Constantius from earth to heaven (7.3); Jupiter himself, the grantor of imperial power, sent *maiestas* ('majesty') on the wings of victory to Constantine (8.5), the

---

[36] RIC 6.283, 355, 358, 465, 531, 532, 580, 581, 621–2, 667, 670, 675, 690–1.

unanimous choice of all the gods (7.4–5). Even Constantine's arrival in Gaul was wonderful (7.5), as if Jupiter himself had sent him to earth.

The date of this speech is 310, the year in which Maximian, having tried unsuccessfully to wrest imperial power from both his son and his son-in-law, committed suicide. The author of this panegyric must support Constantine's claim to the title Augustus but he cannot mention the man who had granted that title three years before, nor the emperor who disputes it.[37] *divus* Claudius now makes his first appearance as ancestor of Constantine's house; Constantine is the only current ruler descended from two imperial forebears (2.1–5). The orator devotes slightly more than the first quarter of the speech to Constantine's antecedents;[38] he affirms both the dynastic principle and the divine support which Constantine enjoys. In this context, the gods have a definite place. No other orator devotes such long descriptive passages within [84] such a short space to justify the idea of rule by divine selection. But once he has made his point, he abandons it.

The orator finds Britain blessed above other places because Constantine became Caesar there, and he exclaims:

> *di boni, quid hoc est quod semper ex aliquo supremo fine mundi nova deum numina universo orbi colenda descendunt? sic Mercurius a Nilo cuius fluminis origo nescitur, sic Liber ab Indis prope consciis solis orientis deos se gentibus ostendere praesentes. sacratiora sunt profecto mediterraneis loca vicina caelo et inde propius a dis mittitur imperator ubi terra finitur.*

> Good gods, why is is it that new divine godheads, to be worshipped the world over always come down from some furthest limit of the world? So Mercury from the river Nile, whose source is unknown, so Liber from the Indies, almost privy to the rising sun, show themselves to mankind as present gods. Truly, places close to heaven are more sacred than the Mediterranean, and from there where the land ends, an emperor is sent more closely by the gods. (9.4–5)

---

[37] *ut enim ipsos immortales deos, quamquam universos animo colamus, interdum tamen in suo quemque templo ac sede veneramur, ita mihi fas esse duco omnium principum pietate meminisse, laudibus celebrare praesentem* ('for just as we venerate the very gods each in their own temple and home, although we worship them all in our mind, so too I think it right for me in my piety to make mention of all the emperors', VI(7)1.5).

[38] Constantine's illustrious family allows the orator to compose a longer section on his ancestors, real or adopted.

Although Constantine has been sent by the gods, he has now become a god himself, or, more precisely, a *dei numen* 'divine godhead'. That the creation of new gods is not without precedent supports the contention. The young emperor's appearance betrays his superhuman nature; he is a *pulchrum et caeleste miraculum* ('beautiful and heavenly miracle') whose *maiestas* ('majesty') invites the beholder's admiring gaze even while its splendour blinds him (17.1). Constantine is proof that one can form a just estimation, on the basis of physical beauty, of how great a heavenly spirit inhabits his body (17.3). His soldiers think he is a god, for his divinity is as sure as his outward form is beautiful (17.4).

It is hard to decide whether the vision of Apollo granted to Constantine is an invention or if it really happened, or the emperor thought it happened. The orator of 310, who wanted to magnify his ruler's power, has given modern scholars a passage provocative of endless discussion on the problem of Constantine's religious beliefs and political policy, not to mention the questions of responsibility and engineering.

A discussion of the vision is well beyond the scope of this paper;[39] Apollo represents a new divinity in Constantine's political life. Whoever he is, he has nothing to do with Hercules. Béranger's point (1970, 249) about the oration's Augustan overtones is well taken. Constantine's panegyrist proclaims a new order, a new Augustus, and by implication a sole guardian for the restored republic. Apollo here may be the same god as the one whom Augustus thanked for his victory at Actium, although Constantine's coinage from this period frequently displays the sun-god Sol Invictus.[40]

The author of VI(7), who is from Autun, observes that Constantine was so pleased with the encounter with the god that he made lavish donations to the [85] temple;[41] he hopes that Constantine might soon do the same for the temple of Apollo at Autun. He asks, *di immortales, quando illum dabitis diem, quo praesentissimus hic deus omni*

---

[39] See Saylor Rodgers (1980).

[40] The legends include SOLI COMITI AVG N and SOLI COMITI AVGG NN, SOLI COMITI CONSTANTINI AVG, SOLI INVICT COM DN, SOLI INVICTO, SOLI INVICTO AETERNO AVG, SOLI INVICTO COMITI, SOLI INVICTO COMITI DN: *RIC* 7.752–3. See also Halsberghe (1972) 167–9; Orange (1973) 344.

[41] *iam omnia te vocare ad se templa videantur* ('May all the temples seem to call you now', 21.7) whereas flowers spring up where Jupiter and Juno have lain, in the wake of Constantine's footsteps rise cities and temples (22.6).

*pace composita illos quoque Apollinis lucos et sacras aedes et anhela
fontium ora circumeat?* ('immortal gods, when will you grant that day
when, with complete peace established, this very present god may go
about those groves of Apollo too, and the sacred temples and the
steaming mouths of springs?' 22.1). Should Constantine visit Autun,
he would admire the temple of his *numen* ('godhead') in that city
(22.2). The orator has just referred to the emperor as *praesentissimus
hic deus* ('this very present god'): is the *numen* ('godhead') therefore
Constantine or Apollo? In the context, ambiguity may be deliberate.

Panegyric V(8) A.D. 311. Anonymous to Constantine.
Gratiarum actio for benefits conferred upon Autun

The fifth panegyric was delivered by a man sent from his native
Autun to thank Constantine for the emperor's kindnesses to that
city. The orator devotes the first half of the speech to Autun's merits
and its inhabitants' recent misfortunes, the second part to the help
which his countrymen received from the emperor. The speaker does
not stray far from his immediate subject and his praises relate directly
to Constantine's visit to Autun and naturally include a few remarks
on the nature of a benevolent prince.

The orator rightly insists that Constantine's entrance into the city
was the first sign of health for the citizens (7.6), but he ignores the
emperor's divine aspect, although he pays Constantine one curious
compliment, *quod pia mente conceperis statim voce declares* ('you
immediately declare by voice what you conceive in your pious
mind', 10.1). This swiftness of verbalization is like the speed with
which *divina illa mens* ('that divine mind') which rules the world,
accomplishes whatever it has decided to do. The emperor's word and
its accomplishment are the same. Constantine makes up to his citizens for whatever Terra and Jupiter withhold (13.6).

This speaker has really said nothing to indicate that Constantine is
a supernatural being. Constantine is, of course, the best of emperors,
whom the gods made prince for the benefit of his subjects (13.1). The
author of the fifth panegyric is, like Eumenius and the author of VII
(6), a man who prefers not to call his emperor a god. The occasion of
this speech, delivered in gratitude for favours granted, is not responsible for the lack of interest in the emperor's divinity and would not

have prevented a determined emperor-worshipper from praising the ruler in terms appropriate to a divine station.

Panegyric XII(9) A.D. 313. Anonymous to Constantine. Defeat of Maxentius

The author of XII(9) imagines the emperor acting by divine guidance, the human instrument of the deity's will. When he recalls the preparations for Constantine's campaign against Maxentius, he asserts that the god granted [86] Constantine a singular favour by revealing the divine will to him alone; Constantine had determined to march on Rome against everyone's advice and despite unfavourable auspices. *quisnam te deus, quae tam praesens hortata est maiestas?* ('which god, which majesty so present encouraged you?', 2.4) the orator asks, and later answers, *habes profecto aliquod cum illa mente divina, Constantine, secretum* ('indeed, you keep something in secret with that divine mind', 2.5). Constantine was plainly seeking a victory already promised by the divinity (3.3). The orator pretends to wonder at the emperor's temerity: *dic, quaeso, quid in consilio nisi divinum numen habuisti?* ('tell me, I ask, what did you have in your counsel if not a divine godhead?', 4.1). *divina praecepta* ('divine precepts') provided the basis of Constantine's faith, *superstitiosa maleficia* ('superstitious malpractice') of Maxentius' (4.4). Divine inspiration gave Constantine a solution to the problem of captured soldiers (11.4) while it deprived Maxentius of his senses (16.2).

Only one passage compares emperor and god: like the thunderbolts of god, the weapons of Constantine's soldiers *eadam sub numine tuo tela* ('the same weapons underneath your godhead') can distinguish between enemies and suppliants (13.2).[42] The comparison with the supreme deity (Jupiter? The orator calls him *mundi creator et dominus.*) is an isolated instance.[43]

Constantine is not, however, merely a servant of the divinity; he partakes of divine power himself. When the panegyrist speaks of the *divinum numen* ('divine godhead') counselling the emperor, he twice qualifies his statement: *an illa te ratio ducebat (sua enim cuique*

---

[42] Béranger (1970) 250 says of the *numen* in this speech, 'it only appears once'. See appendix.

[43] The panegyrist also compares Constantine favourably to the emperor's deified father (24.4–25.2).

prudentia deus est)?[44] ... *divino consilio, imperator, hoc est tuo* ('or did that reason guide you (for each person's own prudence is their god) ... by divine counsel—that is, your own, emperor', 4.2–5). The Roman senate dedicated a statue of a god to the emperor, and Italy had already sent a shield and a crown, both of gold: *debetur enim et saepe debebitur et divinitati simulacrum aureum et virtuti scutum et corona pietati* ('For, a golden likeness is owed to divinity and often will be, and a shield to virtue and a garland to piety', 25.4). *divinitas* ('divinity') like *virtus* ('virtue') and *pietas* ('piety') is an attribute of the emperor.[45] When the orator usurps the theme of Constantine's inability to stay at rest (*quisnam iste est tam continuus ardor? quae divinitas perpetuo vigens motu?* 'What is that eagerness, so ceaseless? What is this divinity, thriving with perpetual motion?', 22.1), he demonstrates that perpetual motion is indeed a divine aspect of the prince. But it is an aspect as well of the supreme being, the *summus rerum sator* ('supreme father of things') whom the orator asks to make Constantine [87] truly immortal.[46] Constantine has sons, yet this writer finds unsatisfactory the sort of immortality which the author of VII(6) had so carefully defined. Posterity will be truly happy, he says, if in addition to his imperial offspring, Constantine himself should remain forever the greatest emperor (26.2–5). Obscurity and inconsistency nearly overwhelm the assertion of immortality and divinity, but it remains.

---

[44] A Virgilian echo; *Aen.* 9.184–5; *dine hunc ardorem mentibus addunt,/Euryale, an sua cuique deus fit dira cupido?* ('do the gods add this ardour to minds, Euryalus, or is each man's grim desire his own god?').

[45] On golden statues see Nock (1930); Scott (1931). Many scholars agree that Constantine was represented with the attributes of a god, whether Apollo or Sol. See Alföldi (1948) 69, 132 n. 23; Maurice (1909) 172; Piganiol (1932) 67–8; Ligota (1963) 178–85. Barnes (1981) 46 and n. 16, supports Alföldi's view (1961) that the manuscript reading *dee* should be emended not to *dei* but to *deae*, and that the statue was of Victoria.

[46] Cf. expressions for god in Ausonius, *Gratiarum actio: aeterne omnium genitor*, ('eternal founder of everything', 18.80), *caeli et humani generis rector* ('controller of heaven and the human race', 4.20). In the present instance of the prayer form, the speaker does not refrain from speculation on the god's nature, but does not find a name; rather, he tries to ensure that the god will hear him by listing his possible forms instead of his epithets, and resumes, *te, inquam, oramus.* Cf. MacCormack (1981) 34–7. The orator has, at least, correctly reproduced the argument about eternal motion and immortality, unlike the author of XI(3). Compare also the description of the spirit in *Aen.* 6.724–51. On the eternity of the emperor, see Cumont (1896), Instinsky (1942).

Panegyric IV(10) A.D. 321. Nazarius to Constantine. Quinquennalia of the Caesars

Nazarius delivered his eulogy at Rome; Constantine was elsewhere. The orator never intimates that the emperor is a divine being, yet the consistent divine support which Constantine enjoys raises him high above the level of ordinary mortals (16.2).[47] Nazarius describes a ruler no less extraordinary than his 'divine' predecessors.

There is a copious stream of flattering asides and comparisons.[48] Constantine is greater than all other Roman emperors by as much as they themselves were greater than their subjects (1.1; cf. 15.3), and the army sent from heaven is honoured more by his use of it than he by its coming (14.4–6). Despite his superiority, Constantine is also more benevolent and more approachable than his predecessors. He tried without success to win over Maxentius by kindness (4.8–12). The *lux imperatoris* ('emperor's light') has undergone a healthy change from the blinding *fulgor* ('glitter') of other emperors (or of Constantine himself in earlier panegyrics); his *serenum lumen* ('serene light') invites contemplation (5.1–4).

Constantine's greatest glory is his spotless character, which is both proof of and justification for his having been chosen as the deity's favourite. This divine favour ensures the good of his subjects as well (2.6). Nazarius first establishes that god actually cares about the human race and its doings on earth (7.3); he often reiterates the principle. The deity sends Maxentius to his destruction (7.4, 27.5, 28.1), protects Constantine from harm, and helps him in all his endeavours (13.5, 16.2, 17.1), especially in the field (12.1, 14–15, 19.2–3, 29.1).[49] [88]

---

[47] Although his head (29.5) and even his person (35.3: *divinus princeps,* 'divine emperor') merit the adjective *divinus* ('divine').

[48] *erat quod tollere velles* ('there were things you would like to remove', Hor. *Sat.* 1.4.11) An example is his parenthetical comment, *cum dico proelia, significo victorias* ('when I say "battles", I mean "victories"', 19.4).

[49] *pietatem tuam texit* ('it protected your piety', 7.4); *summam illam maiestatem quae te circumplexa tueatur* ('that supreme majesty which surrounds and protects you', 16.1); *te per omnia subnixum deo vadere* ('that you walk through everything relying on [the] god', 18.4); *tu non intutior tempore quam deo tectior* 'you no more unguarded by the time than protected by [the] god', 26.1).

One of the highlights of this oration is Nazarius' two-page description of the heavenly army which suddenly appeared in Gaul to reinforce the emperor's ranks.[50] The orator cannot relate Constantine's military dispositions outside of Rome, for he does not know exactly where the celestial army fought, but assumes that it must have stood by wherever the emperor himself was (29.1). This is not the place to argue the relative merits of Nazarius' account against Lactantius', nor to try to trace the development of this legend to determine its significance for Constantine's religious convictions. The vision has a rhetorical purpose; if Nazarius had a religious bias he has kept it well hidden. The only hint he gives of his private beliefs is in his insistence upon divine interest and intervention in human affairs. If the orator's religious preference remains a mystery, pagan in ambiance though it may be, Constantine's own cannot be discovered by means of the evidence in this panegyric.[51] The deity appears in several guises; the author of XII(9) is equally reluctant to give god a name.[52] Nazarius shows that Constantine's greatness is upheld by divine power; the authors of V(8) and VII(6) do no less for their emperors, and no more. The speech was delivered at Rome; the orator's primarily pagan audience may be the most important factor governing Nazarius' interpretation of the divinity. Far more important than the views of either orator or emperor is the continued goodwill of the people of Italy and the West.[53] The apologetic elements interwoven into the description of the invasion of 312 hint broadly that the goodwill was valuable, especially when Constantine was contemplating the liberation of another sector of the world from the 'tyrant' Licinius.

---

[50] Reports of divine intervention in battle were common in the ancient world. See Pfister (1924). In the second chapter (Military Epiphanies) of *The Greek State at War* III, Pritchett (1979) cites examples taken from inscriptions as well as literary sources, and concludes that visions were not necessarily inventions made up after the event.

[51] Alföldi (1948) 70.

[52] *rerum arbiter deus* ('god, the arbiter of things', 7.3); *illa vis, illa maiestas fandi ac nefandi discriminatrix* ('that force, that majesty which distinguishes right from wrong', 7.4); *divinitas* ('divinity', 7.3, 13.5); *maiestas* ('majesty', 16.1, 19.2); *deus* ('god', 16.2 (bis), 18.4, 26.1, 28.1): the use of *deus* ('god') without qualification by *ille* ('that') or any other modifier is exactly the way a monotheist would describe the deity.

[53] See Alföldi (1948) 30–1, 75–81, 91, 134 n. 30, on Constantine's problems with Rome and attempts to maintain good relations with the inhabitants of the Eternal City.

Nazarius and the author of XII(9) are apparently monotheists, though a particular brand of monotheism cannot be definitely established for either. Consider the following description:

> *altissimum illum et cuncta potestate cohibentem deum, qui ditione perpetua divina atque humana moderatur, cum despiciat in terras* ...

> That highest god, who holds everything together in his power, who controls divine and human affairs with his perpetual authority, when he looks down on the lands ... (III(11)28.5) [89]

Hearing that a supreme being inhabits the heavens, a Christian can think of his own deity and a pagan of Jupiter. The words offend no one. Some examples already noted define the deity in no less nebulous terms:

> *spectat nos ex alto rerum arbiter deus, et quamvis humanae mentes profundos gerant cogitationum recessus, insinuat tamen sese totam scrutatura divinitas,* ...

> God, the arbiter of things looks down on us from on high, and although human minds keep deep recesses for their thoughts, however, the divinity insinuates itself completely when it is about to investigate. (IV(10).7.3)

> *summe rerum sator ... sive aliqua supra omne caelum potestas es quae hoc opus tuum ex altiore naturae arce despicias* ...

> Highest founder of matter ... if you are some power above the whole heaven that looks down upon this your work from nature's loftier citadel. (XII(9)26.1)

The third passage implies a creator god, the first two a moderator, but all three describe the most powerful divinity vaguely, namelessly. Yet half a century lay between the enunciation of the first and the third; the first belongs to the speech which Claudius Mamertinus delivered on the first day of January 362, in the presence of the emperor Julian. Orator and emperor were pagan, a large part of the audience Christian.[54]

---

[54] See Browning (1975) 160; MacCormack (1972) 734.

Panegyric III(11) A.D. 362. Claudius Mamertinus to Julian. *Gratiarum actio* for his consulship; successful outcome of a usurpation

Claudius Mamertinus, Nazarius, and the author of XII(9) all assert that the emperor has a very special relationship with the deity. For the sake of comparison, there follow a few passages from each speech:

> *perpetuam in te benignae maiestatis opem fluere* ('an everlasting wealth of kind majesty flows into you', IV(10)19.2)

> *caelesti ope salutem rei publicae propagatam* ('the state's well-being prolonged by heavenly wealth', III(11)27.4)[55]

> *caelestem in illo favorem* ('the heavenly favour to him', IV(10)2.6)

> *divino munere ... regnator est* ('he is ruler by divine gift', III(11)27.2)

> *quid in consilio nisi divinum numen habuisti?* ('tell me, I ask, what did you have in your counsel if not a divine godhead?' XII(9)4.1)

> *divino instinctu, quo regis omnia* ('by divine instinct, by which you rule everything', IV(10)17.1)

> *quacumque consilia eius gaudet formare divinitas* ('whatever divinity rejoices to shape his counsels', III(11)15.2)

> *non dubiam te, sed promissam divinitus petere victoriam* ('you seek no doubtful victory, but one divinely promised', XII(9)3.3)

> *venturae felicitatis eventum conscius divini animus praevidebat* ('the spirit which shares in the divine forsaw the outcome of future good luck',[56] III(11)14.6)

In one respect, Mamertinus is closer to the author of XII(9). As the last two sets of examples show, both stress the element of communication between emperor and god, whereas Nazarius' theme is the deity's protection of the emperor. Otherwise, Nazarius and Mamertinus show the greater affinity; the latter, unlike the author of XII(9), does not even suggest that Julian himself is divine.

There is one other difference between Julian and Constantine. Mamertinus judges Julian in terms of human beings. Nazarius says

---

[55] Cf. Symm. *negotiis tuis auxilio fuisse caelestes* ('the celestials were a help in your affairs', *Orat.* 2.23).

[56] Cf. Aus. *supremus ille imperii et consiliorum tuorum deus conscius et arbiter et auctor,* 'that supreme god and judge and founder, who shares in empire and your counsels', *Gr. Act.*18).

of Constantine, *nec* [90] *humanorum terminos curent qui semper divina meditantur* ('let those who always contemplate the divine not care for humans' limits', IV(10)2.6); Julian, too, is incapable of thinking merely human thoughts: *non potest quicquam abiectum et humile cogitare qui scit de se semper loquendum* ('he who knows he is always to be spoken of cannot think about anything abject and base', III(11) 31.2). Constantine's purity of soul both reveals and merits divine favour (IV(10)16.1–2); Julian's equal purity has as its aim immortality: *te . . . dirigere omnes opes et cogitationes tuas ad memoriam posteritatis aeternam* ('you direct all your resources and thoughts to posterity's eternal memory', III(11)31.1). Nazarius measures Constantine's greatness in terms of divine protection; Julian's immortality is that which men bestow. That is the Stoic ideal; it had been generations since a man of such sympathy for Republican forms had ascended the throne.

Other emperors have been likened to the sun, or emit a more or less blinding *fulgor* 'glitter' from their bodies or from their eyes (XII (9)19.6). Julian is like a star. Claudius Mamertinus calls him *quasi quoddam salutare humano generi sidus* ('as if some star that brings health to humankind', III(11)2.3),[57] rather than a source of the lifebringing *lux imperatoris* ('light of the emperor') and Julian's eyes flash with *sidereis ignibus* (III(11)6.4). The astrological orientation of III(11)2.3 avoids equating emperor and sun, and the qualifiers *quasi* ('as if') *quoddam* ('some') make the orator's metaphorical intention abundantly clear. Cicero was less restrained when he spoke of Pompey.

Thrice, Mamertinus does compare Julian with the gods, but two, if not all three, of the instances have no serious content. When he asks, *ecquis deus uno in anno multiplices fructus agro uni dedit?* ('Has any god given many harvests to one field in one year?', III(11)22.1), he does not mean that the fields are more productive or even, as at V(8) 13.6, that the emperor has lowered the taxes. The orator himself is the fertile field, bearing the fruits of three successive offices (III(11) 22.1–2) (cf. Aus. *dei munus imitaris* 'you copy the gift of god', *Gr. Act.* 5.22). Again, Mamertinus affects to despise the fruitfulness of the Blessed Isles:

---

[57] Compare Ammianus Marcellinus 21.10.2 (*ut sidus salutare*); Galletier (1955) 9 notes the similarity of expression. Cf. also 22.9.14, and see especially MacCormack (1981) 47–50.

*quantula ista sunt, si deum auctorem consideres, munera! nempe nobis
quoque, cum agrum non nostris manibus excolamus, haec illaborata
nascuntur. . . . provinciae, praefecturae, fasces sponte proveniunt.*

How small are those gifts, if you consider god their author! Although we
do not cultivate the the field with our own hands, surely these things are
born without labour for us as well. . . . provinces, prefectures, consulships, arrive spontaneously. (III(11)23.2–3)

The passage is a parody of other panegyrists' descriptions of utopias
and the golden age.

The third follows the reference quoted above to the nameless god
(III(11)28.5), who, when he gazes down upon earth, affects the elements by his facial expression, shakes the world at his nod, and in
gladness brings fair weather. It echoes the anonymous orator who
spoke before Constantine and Maximian in 307 (VII(6)12.7–8; above
under Panegyric VII(6)). Claudius Mamertinus employs the description in a way also familiar from Tetrarchic panegyrics. He says that
this is what 'poets relate' (*poetae ferunt*) of the god, and he believes
that it has been proven by a recent experience in the human sphere.
When Julian smiled upon [91] his consuls the crowd went mad
(III(11)29.1–3). This was not the last time that a panegyrist would
employ such a theme: see below on Panegyric II(12), and note 67. But
Mamertinus immediately retreats from what he has said and loses
himself in the joyful multitude to emerge as the honoured consul. It
was only a hint, and nearly lost amid the commotion. It may even be
another parody inserted for the amusement of his emperor, who was
himself an expert in the genre of encomiastic oratory.

Throughout the rest of the oration, the panegyrist restrains whatever impulse caused him to liken the emperor, however ambiguously,
to the supreme being. Although Julian receives divine guidance and
help, he himself never leaves the human realm, and his immortality
will be gained not even through apotheosis, but on human terms.
Claudius Mamertinus is the most careful of all the orators to represent the emperor as a human being; his concern extends even to the
avoidance of imperial terminology. He never mentions the emperor's
numen ('godhead'), *divinitas* ('divinity') or *maiestas* ('majesty'); *caelestis* ('heavenly') never refers to the emperor, although Nazarius
called Constantine's *prudentia* ('prudence') 'heavenly' (IV(10)9.3).
divinus ('divine') appears only three times; it modifies *munus* ('gift',
III(11)16.4), the favour bestowed upon the speaker, and two abstract

nouns *prudentia* ('prudence') and *felicitas* ('good luck'); Nazarius used the adjective twice as often, thrice of the emperor's person. Ammianus Marcellinus, although an historian, is more like a panegyrist than Mamertinus. The historian describes the appearance of Julian Augustus at Constantinople (*tamquam demissum aliquem . . . de caelo*, 'as if somebody dropped from heaven', 22.2.4) and at Antioch (*in speciem alicuius numinis votis excipitur*, 'he is received in prayer like a godhead', 22.9.14) as if he were an old hand at respectably moderate praising (compare Panegyric VIII(4)19.1). His summation of Julian's brief reign (22.9.1) also contains the requisite encomiastic elements (the horn of plenty, martial felicity).

One cannot know what combination of emperor, orator, and audience is responsible for Mamertinus' depiction of Julian, but one passage suggests that the orator is wary of the listeners' prejudices.[58] His cautious reference to the reinstatement of philosophy (III(11) 23.4–6) reads like a pagan apology, wherein philosophy is linked with *virtutes* ('virtues') (cf. III(11)19.3–21.5), literature, and the practical applications of stargazing. Mamertinus' genuine, if exaggerated, praise for Julian's accomplishments aside, in terms of the vocabulary of the ruler-cult, the speech might be called an anti-panegyric.

Public expressions of ideas about the emperor's relationship with the divinity seem to have undergone a transformation in little over sixty years, until finally the emperor himself has lost the trappings of divinity while he remains god's chosen ruler who can rely on heavenly support. In 381 Gratian [92] and Theodosius issued the first anti-pagan legislation since the reign of Constantius II; by 389, therefore, there should have been no question about acceptable convention.[59] One would not expect Pacatus, whatever his private convictions, to say that Jupiter had helped Theodosius to overcome Maximus.[60] This is not to say, however, that an orator must invoke Christ and all the saints. The time was not quite yet when bishops usurped the functions of rhetoricians and poets, but in view of the scanty evidence on

---

[58] Pichon (1906a) 135–6 explains that in the presence of the Christian senate, Mamertinus is silent about Julian's intended religious reforms. It was still too early in his reign to speak of that.

[59] *Codex Theodosianus* 16.10.7 banning sacrifices; 16.7.1 on apostates; see also 16.7.2 (AD 383).

[60] He mentions the ancient Romans laying the triumphal laurels in the lap of Jupiter Optimus Maximus (II(12)9.5), but it is part of a comparison between Theodosius and the ancient Romans.

Latin panegyric, changes had occurred. The gap of forty years between Nazarius and Claudius Mamertinus is frustrating; Symmachus
and Ausonius, however, are closer in tone to Mamertinus than to
anyone else. By the time it was Pacatus' turn, the rule was that there
was one god and that a very special human being was emperor.

Panegyric II(12) A.D. 389. Pacatus to Theodosius.
Defeat of the usurper Maximus

Pacatus says that the empire receives its share of divine aid through
the emperor (II(12)30.1–2). When Theodosius finally marched west
to put down the usurper, the divinity sped him on his way: *cur non
tuae publicaeque vindictae confessam aliquam immortalis dei curam
putemus adnisam?* ('why should we not think that some concern of
immortal god strove to avenge you and the state?' II(12)39.4).[61] In
both passages the orator is most interested in the empire and its
citizens, not in Theodosius: the emperor, as agent of the deity, has
restored the republic.

Pacatus also glorifies the emperor alone, apart from the deity, in a
series of images now tediously familiar. The *Romana lux* ('Roman
light') arose in the east when Theodosius became emperor and
restored life to the dying state (II(12)3.2–3); although it might have
been better had he received imperial power earlier, it really does not
matter: *parum interest quando coeperit quod terminum non habebit*
('it matters little when what will have no end began', 7.6).[62] The
emperor knows god's intentions (II(12)19.2)—he is not the first
emperor to have been so honoured—but when Pacatus describes
this process of secret-sharing he makes the emperor the deity's
partner (or vice versa).[63] It is only a small step from 'partnership

---

[61] See 39.4 and 5, where the orator justifies this claim.

[62] Cf. XII(9)26.5. I wonder, by the way, if Pacatus, if he was a Christian (see n. 68),
would have made a statement of this kind about eternity, even in a context of the
eternity of the emperor, not of God. Any Christian of this period should have been
sensitive to dogmatic questions. That which is eternal ought not to have a beginning,
but cf. Eusebius *LC* 6.3.

[63] *deo consorte* ('with god as a partner', II(12)6.4); *illi maiestatis tuae participi
deo . . . tibi aliqua vis divina subservit* 'that god who shares your majesty . . . some
divine strength serves you', II(12)18.4). Galletier remarks (1955) 116 'Note it is the
divinity which is in the emperor's service in the same way as it shares his majesty'.

with' to 'partaking of', or so it seems. Pacatus resurrects the idea of
perpetual motion and eternity:

> *gaudent profecto perpetuo divina motu et iugi agitatione se vegetat*
> *aeternitas et, quicquid homines vocamus laborem vestra natura est. ut*
> *indefessa vertigo caelum rotat, ut maria aestibus inquieta sunt, ut stare*
> *sol nescit, ita tu, imperator, continuatis negotiis et in suo quodam orbe*
> *redeuntibus semper exercitus es.*

Indeed, divine beings enjoy perpetual movement and eternity keeps
itself fresh with continuous activity and whatever we mortals call labour
is your nature. Just as a tireless revolution spins the heaven, just as the
seas are restless with the tides, just as the sun does not know how to
stand still, so you, Emperor, are always exercised by continual business
which returns in its own sort of cycle. (II(12)10.1)

The plural *vestra natura* ('your nature') contrasts with *homines*
('men'); it refers to *divina* ('divine'), *aeternitas* ('eternity'), *imperator*
(es) ('emperor/s').[64] The orator defines the emperor as someone who,
by nature, is different from human beings: Theodosius' incessant
movement is a natural phenomenon. The emperor is also a *numen*
('godhead'). A man who is refused an audience may at least be
consoled by having seen his ruler: *ferat tamen visi numinis conscien-*
tiam ('however, let him carry the awareness of the godhead he has
seen', II(12)21.2).[65] He has had, as it were, a glimpse of heaven.

Pacatus mentions the emperor's knowledge of heavenly secrets in a
context of philosophical speculation prompted by his admiration for
the emperor's physical beauty: *augustissima quaeque species pluri-*
mum creditur trahere de caelo ('each most august appearance is
thought accordingly to come from heaven', II(12)6.3; cf. VI(7)17.3).
The orator professes not to know whether the *divinus animus* ('divine
soul') chooses or creates a beautiful habitation for itself; Theodosius

Perhaps the *deus consors* ('the god as consort') is the divine *comes* ('companion')
under another name.

[64] Of these, Pacatus addresses only the emperor, and *vestra natura* ('your nature')
= *tibi eadem ac illis natura est* ('you and they have the same nature'). The plural
adjective happens also to give him a better clausula (-v- - -), but Pacatus did not write
vestra ('your') for the sake of the rhythm alone. The *vestra* may also embrace, as a
politeness, Valentinian II and Arcadius; it is still linked with *divina* ('divine') and
aeternitas ('eternity').

[65] Béranger (1970) 253, however, cites only 30.2 for the *numen* ('godhead') in this
speech.

shares this secret with the god. Pacatus states that he will say only what is intelligible to a man and proper for him to put into words:

> *talem esse debere qui gentibus adoratur, cui toto orbe terrarum privata vel publica vota redduntur, a quo petit navigaturus serenum, peregrinaturus reditum, pugnaturus auspicium.*

> Such a man ought he to be who is adored by nations, to whom across the whole world prayers are given in private and public, from whom the man about to set sail seeks a calm seas, the man about to travel a return, the man about to fight an omen. (II(12)6.4)

Here is an emperor of whom people are said to make requests which ought to be addressed to a god,[66] but Pacatus has so shamelessly copied from his predecessors that he gives Theodosius that title as well: *cedat his terris terra Cretensis parvi Iovis gloriata cunabulis et geminis Delos reptata numinibus et alumno Hercule nobiles Thebae. fidem constare nescimus auditis: deum dedit Hispania quem videmus* ('Let the land of Crete give way, made glorious by the cradle of the baby Jupiter, and Delos across which the twin godheads crawled, and noble Thebes with Hercules as a pupil. We do not know to trust what we have heard: Spain has given us a god to see', II(12)4.5).[67] That *deum dedit* ('has given a god') translates *Theodosium* ('Theodosius') [94] makes it no easier. The orator is careful to say that he cannot believe anything about these pagan gods, although Theodosius is a *deus praesens* ('present god') as well, for which *quem videmus* ('whom we see') is an equivalent. Pacatus has lifted the sentiment, including

---

[66] Liebeschuetz (1979) 302 finds the passage, 'which seems to imply full worship of the emperor', 'astonishing, coming from a Christian'. He characterizes it, however, as 'an expansion of a traditional theme', citing Pliny *Pan.* 4.4. The expansion is considerable; there is nothing like this statement in any of the other panegyrics. Pliny's description (*cuius dicione nutuque maria terrae, pax bella regerentur* ('at whose authority and nod, the seas, lands, peace and wars are ruled'—I do not know the source of Liebeschuetz's punctuation of this passage [comma after *pax*])—is of the commander-in-chief: Trajan rules the land and seas as head of the army and navy. He is not in charge of the weather.

[67] Compare *finguntur haec de Iove, sed de te vera sunt, imperator* ('these things are made up about Jupiter, but about you, Emperor, they are true', X(2)2.5); *non opinione traditus sed conspicuus et praesens Iuppiter* ('not passed on by rumour, but Jupiter is visible and present', XI(3)10.5; IV(10)15.1-7 (Castor and Pollux compared to the heavenly armies; imitated at II(12)39.4)). Lippold (1968) 245, reprinted below at 380 uses, the passage from panegyric II(12) as proof that the orator had doubts about the (pagan) gods' existence. The author(s) of X(2) and XI(3) must have had the same doubts. Denying or doubting the gods is still a compliment to the emperor's more present power.

the scepticism reserved for stories of the gods' infancy, directly from the tenth and eleventh panegyrics. Theodosius seems not to have minded the attribution. Perhaps he did not have to countenance it in person: the oration extends to 39 pages, a third again longer than Nazarius', and may have undergone expansion before publication. One may suppose that in Pacatus' audience were many sympathetic to pagan practices. As to the religious convictions of the orator himself, there is little agreement, although he advocates religious toleration.[68] One of Maximus' worst crimes was *religionis iniuria* ('crime of religion') to be partner to the persecution of the Priscillianists, in which the charge was *nimia religio et diligentius culta divinitas* ('excessive religion and a divinity too diligently worshipped', II(12)29.2). This is the only reference to Christianity in the speech. Twice Pacatus mentions other religious habits, turning toward the east to worship (*divinis rebus operantes* 'our conduct in divine rites' II(12)3.2)[69] and the description of Theodosius' reception by the city of Haemona (II(12)37.4). A crowd of the nobility poured forth: *conspicuos veste nivea senatores, reverendos municipali purpura flamines, insignes apicibus sacerdotes* ('senators conspicuous in their snow-white robes, cult-priests venerable in their civic purple, priests distinctive for their peaked hats')—the only things lacking are the *simulacra deorum* ('images of the gods').[70] The title of *flamen municipalis* ('municiple priest') remained an honorary one, like senator, for members of the upper class into the fifth century.[71] Pacatus says that the *nobiles* ('nobles') of Haemona support Theodosius. This statement has more political than theological importance, although the description of *nobiles* ('nobles') as *senators* ('senators'), *flamines* ('cult-priests') and *sacerdotes* ('priests') hints at Pacatus' sympathies.[72]

---

[68] For a variety of opinions, see Liebeschuetz (1979) 301 (Christian), Béranger (1970) 253 (possibly a Christian); Étienne (1962) 281 (tolerant, not a Christian); Pichon (1906a) 147 (neither Christian nor pagan in an obvious way; purposely vague); Galletier (1955) 51 (old-fashioned pagan); Ensslin (1943) 64 (pagan).

[69] Pichon (1906a) 147–8, dismisses this as insignificant. The expression *Vestale secretum* ('Vestal secret', 21.3) is a figure of speech. To 3.2 compare Ausonius *gratias ago: verum ita, ut apud deum fieri amat, sentiendo copiosius quam loquendo* ('I give thanks, indeed in such a way as is wont to happen with god—more fully in sentiment than in speaking', *Gr. Act.* 1.2)

[70] Cf. V(8)8.4 where, however, the orator does not mention priests.

[71] Hirschfeld (1913) 503–4.

[72] A *sacerdos*, unlike a *flamen*, was definitely a pagan priest: see Servius in *Ad Aen.* 2.863 and Isidore *Orig.* 19.30.5: *apex est pilleum sutile quod sacerdotes gentiles utebantur* ('an *apex* is a stitched hat which pagan priests use').

Pacatus assures Theodosius that the western provinces are loyal to him. Pacatus' countrymen in particular are glad that Maximus is finally dead (II(12)24.6). Pacatus seems to protest too much. Three years later Arbogast, having gotten rid of Valentinian II, set up Eugenius as emperor and invited the pagans to rally round their cause. Many of them did. [95]

Pacatus was not one of those who followed Eugenius in 392. After his performance in 389 he was promoted, to proconsul of Africa in 390 and in 393 to *Comes Rei Privatae* at Constantinople. Theodosius had found in Pacatus a loyal adherent; the emperor rewarded the man who called him a god, but the propaganda of the panegyric had little effect. Theodosius' acts and enactments as emperor far outweighed Pacatus' efforts to commend him to the Romans. After 390, no one could have doubted Theodosius' religious intentions. *nemo se hostiis polluat, nemo insontem victimam caedat, nemo delubra adeat, templa perlustret et mortali opere formata simulacra suspiciat, ne divinis atque humanis sanctionibus reus fiat* ('Nobody may pollute themselves with sacrifice, nobody slaughter an innocent victim, nobody enter a shrine, pass through temples and look up to icons formed by human hand or take part in divine or human sanctions', *Codex Theodosianus* 16.10.10 of 24 February 391. The language of his legislation against apostates in 16.7.4 of 11 May 391 is just as strong; compare 16.7.1 and 16.7.2 of 381 and 383).

Pacatus has given the Romans a view of the emperor with which they could sympathize. Theodosius is like the best rulers of tradition: *te ipsum qua...priscorum duritia ducum, castitate pontificum, consulum moderatione, petitorum comitate viventem* ('you yourself, alive with the hardiness of the leaders of old, the chasteness of priests, the moderation of consuls, the friendliness of political candidates', II(12) 20.5). The word *pontifex* ('priest') points to a particular religion only by the context. The orator feels that Brutus himself would approve of the present emperor. The words *prisci duces, pontifices, consules, petitores* ('leaders of old, priests, consuls, candidates') all recall the Republican period. But Pacatus includes more recent traditions as well: Theodosius is a *deus* ('god') even the Persian king worships him (II(12)22.5), scenes of his victories will decorate Roman temples (II(12)44.5), and his subjects pray to him for help. A. D. Nock feels that the emperor could not have appeared to anyone as a real divinity, for no one directed prayers to the ruler.[73] Pacatus says that people in

---

[73] Nock (1947) 104; (1952) 241; Fishwick (1969) 366.

various situations pray to the emperor.[74] Whether they really did or
not, the orator wants to say something that the Romans find comfor-
table and familiar. Whereas the Romans of the first and second
centuries were appalled by an emperor who so far broke with convention as to call himself *dominus et deus* ('master and god') by the
end of the fourth century tradition required this very appellation:
better *deus* ('god') than *Christianissimus princeps* ('most Christian
emperor').[75]

Pacatus owes many of the themes in his panegyric not only to his
being the latest in a long line of official orators. He has taken some of
his ideas particularly from the traditions of the earlier panegyrists,
who spoke before [96] Maximian and during the early reign of
Constantine.[76] The emperor's *numen* ('godhead') and *divinitas* ('divinity') do not intrude in the panegyrics of 321 and 362, and even
maiestas ('majesty') had all but disappeared. Pacatus, however, has
reinstated the *numen* ('godhead') and *maiestas* ('majesty') as attributes of the emperor.[77] The orator cannot, given the date of the
speech, emperor, and quantity of material, dwell on such themes;
their inclusion is enough.[78]

III

The men who praised the emperors had considerable freedom of
choice, and despite their 'modest' opinions of their own speaking
ability, they were not stupid provincials who understood little about

[74] Mention of soldiers asking for the emperor's *auspicium* ('guidance') makes the
other two kinds of request seem almost ordinary.

[75] Alföldi (1939) 194, observes, 'This theological transfiguration of the person of
the emperor and, even more so, his direct deification, had originally been in sharp
conflict with the old humanistic conceptions and, above all, with the mentality of the
senate. Now, however, the opposition of Christianity made the worship of the
emperor a part of the policy of the patriotic conservatives, and so it remained until
paganism had drawn its last breath'.

[76] *deus* ('god') X(2)2.1, VI(7)22.1; perpetual motion XI(3)3.1–8, XII(9)22.1–2;
vota ('prayers') X(2)6.5.

[77] *divinitas* ('divinity') strictly speaking, has disappeared, although Pacatus unites
divina ('divine beings'), *aeternitas* ('eternity'), and Theodosius at II(12)10.1.

[78] Theodosius' life supplies adequate material for the family, upbringing, deeds
and habits sections, not to mention the comparison by contrast with his enemy
Maximus: the apology, both for the Gauls and for Theodosius, is the essential element.

the emperor's policies. Neither were they summoned to the court to have their speeches dictated to them. While they were sure to give adequate coverage to the emperor's successes at home and in the field, and reproduced accurately enough the present emperor's version of his relationship with colleagues and would-be colleagues, the degree to which they magnified the emperor's person was left to the inclination of each speaker. The authors of II(12), VI(7), X(2) and XI(3) equate various emperors with gods and/or call an emperor *deus* ('god') without abandoning the themes of divine selection and the emperors' continued support of the official deities (in VI(7), X(2) and XI(3)). The language of the eighth panegyric assumes an imperial divinity which the speaker does not emphasize. Eumenius, Nazarius, and the authors of V(8) and VII(6) see the emperors as recipients of divine favour who enjoy a special relationship with the god(s). The emperors themselves drew attention to this favour on their coinage, but despite Nock's conclusion that the divine *comes* ('companion') is a protector, attached to the throne and not to the individual ruler, Diocletian and Constantine stressed their personal relationships with Jupiter and Sol respectively.[79] A relationship which develops into identity comes closest to the ideas about the emperors in Panegyrics VI(7), X(2) and XI(3), the three in which imperial divinity is best defined. This notion and that of rule by divine grace are worlds apart. The representation of an emperor's divinity, or the lack of it, and the degree to which an orator may or may not forget the mortality of the emperor, depended upon the orator himself as much as upon the circumstances and the emperor. One panegyrist preferred to dwell upon the [97] principle of divine selection and protection, another, to equate emperor and god.[80]

This variety in the panegyrics demonstrates that the rulers tolerated a wide range of opinions, but few agree as to whether this toleration was of belief or of disbelief: did any emperor want to be worshipped as a god? William Seston believes that the divinity was associated with the office,[81] and his theory is that Diocletian took over the Persian idea of kingship which receives divine support.[82] Perhaps

[79] Nock (1947).
[80] Fears (1977) 184, notes the political aspect of the theme of divine selection, which 'never became an indispensable element in imperial panegyrics'. The notion was most useful in fending off rival claimants or defending virtual usurpations.
[81] Seston (1950).
[82] Seston (1946) 225.

Persian theologians could have explained the difference between the actual king and the divine power behind the throne, but the usual Greek or Roman assertion was that the Persians worshipped their own kings. Two of the panegyrists show that this was what they considered the general belief. The orator of 289 says, *rex ille Persarum, numquam se ante dignatus hominem confiteri, fratri tuo supplicat* ('that king of the Persians, who never previously deigned to admit himself human, makes supplication to your brother', X(2) 10.6). A century later, Pacatus, in what must be conscious imitation, affirms: *denique ipse ille rex eius dedignatus antea confiteri hominem iam fatetur timorem et in his te colit templis in quibus colitur* ('finally that king himself who did not previously deign to admit himself human now confesses his fear and worships you in the very temples where he is worshipped', II(12)22.5). I cannot believe that Diocletian, of all his contemporaries, was able to understand the subtleties of Mazdaean theology so well that he adopted the Persian system in order to set his own government on a more reasonable foundation.[83] The author of XI(3) certainly did not understand the difference, if that was what Diocletian had in mind, for he says that he is speaking on the day on which Maximian's *immortalitatis origo* ('origin of immortality', XI(3)3.7) is celebrated. The occasion was the emperor's birthday, not his *dies imperii* ('anniversary of accession') and the orator affirms Maximian's divine nature when he says *cumque praeterea ingenitum illum vobis divinae mentis ardorem etiam earum quae primae vos suscepere regionum alacritas excitarit* ('and besides the liveliness of those regions which first raised you rouses that eagerness of divine mind which is inborn in you', XI(3)3.8); he goes on to speak of Illyricum and the emperor's military training. The orator says that the emperors were divine from birth.

Norman Baynes (1935) believes that Aurelian was the first emperor to stress the election of the emperor by god, and thus he hopes to demonstrate that there was no break between pagan and Christian ideas about the ruler's relationship with the divinity. But it is not necessary to deny, solely for the purpose of understanding the transition from paganism to Christianity, that any emperor of the third and early fourth centuries portrayed himself as god. Both ideas were

---

[83] Diocletian surprised one fourth-century (?) person merely by having quoted Virgil once (SHA [*Car.*] 30.13.3–4). If this anecdote is an invention of the author, his surprise is nonetheless plausible.

current during this period, both appear together in panegyrics [98] VI (7), X(2) and XI(3) (not to mention II(12)). Pagan orators often ignored or de-emphasized the notion of divine ruler, and most of their successors in the Christian period did the same. Finally, the beliefs of contemporaries and near contemporaries must count for something; that our understanding is superior is not the point.[84] The attitude of the eighth panegyrist may be indicative of a general tendency to exalt the emperor at the gods' expense:[85] in the end, the gods become less believable than ever. For three hundred years the empire's citizens had grown more and more accustomed to looking up to the emperor as the single most powerful potential in their lives. The emperors, through advertisement of their claims and powers, did their part in propagating the faith. Romans swore by the emperor's *genius* ('spirit') (or *numen*, 'godhead'), they honoured him in temples along with the gods, they became more submissive in the outward manifestations (e.g. the court ceremonial) of their relationship with the emperor, and—who knows?—some of them may even have prayed to him.[86] In the twentieth century, it is hard to imagine delivering a panegyric with a straight face. In the twentieth century, when it is unfashionable to believe in the possibility or efficacy of divine intervention, and when attempts by national governments to solve human problems appear futile, the phenomenon of divine rulership might find greater acceptance if one were to read *potestas* ('power') for *divinitas* ('divinity').[87]

Liebeschuetz (1979, 239–40) observes that miracles, or supernatural functions, were not expected of emperors. It was fortunate for a

---

[84] Fishwick (1969) 366, objects: 'If Jews or Christians chose martyrdom rather than compromise their faith by paying cult to the emperor, the theological error was on their part'. Liebeschuetz (1979) 239 argues from the silence of Lactantius against the importance of the ruler-cult. He notes the survival of the language and court etiquette under Christian rulers. But only some of the language survived: see above section I. Price (1980) 36–7 remarks upon the distinction between sacrifice to the gods and to the emperors, a lesser (but still acceptable) alternative. For other views, see Babut (1916); Mattingly (1952); Stern (1954). For ancient viewpoints, biased or exaggerated, see Aurelius Victor 33.30, 39.4, 41.5; Eutropius 9.26.

[85] See Charlesworth (1943); Burdeau (1964); MacCormack (1975b) for discussions of this development.

[86] MacMullen (1976) 35.

[87] See MacCormack (1981) 170–3.

few blind men of the first centuries after Christ that they were
unaware of their rulers' inability to cure them.[88] Miraculous actions
have great political value. In the third and fourth centuries, the
miracles required were less spectacular, for the benefit of individuals
only as members of a larger body: peace and prosperity had been
virtually unknown for some time. A reputation for controlling not
only the [99] forces of nature but even the barbarians might seem to
some to partake of the supernatural.

The fifth, seventh, and ninth panegyrics differ from the fourth and
twelfth in two ways: their combined incidence per page of the word
divinus ('divine') is greater, and their religious background is definitely pagan as opposed to vaguely monotheistic. Of the two later
panegyrists of Constantine, only Nazarius avoids equation of the
emperor with the deity as successfully as the author of VII(6), and
the monotheism apparent in panegyrics IV(10) and XII(9) cannot
definitely be attributed to the emperor alone. The author of X(2)
proclaimed Maximian's divine aspect to Jupiter's detriment, Claudius
Mamertinus emphasized Julian's humanity to the exclusion of any
notion of deity, Nazarius described in detail the relationship between
divine protector and divinely chosen ruler. Pacatus, like most of the
other panegyrists, found a middle ground. At one or more of the
many occasions graced by formal orations, the emperors, or their
advisors, chose or allowed all of these men to speak, and trusted them
to say appropriate things. Maximian, Constantine, and Theodosius
each heard a man call him a god. So far as anyone knows, none of
these three emperors found the epithet objectionable. Other men on
other occasions said other things, but one cannot always pay attention only to the others, or persuade oneself that because this exists,
that does not. There is no system and there never was. There is
circumstance, preference, and ambiguity.[89]

---

[88] Tacitus *Hist.* 4.81 and Suetonius *Vesp.* 7.2 both report that Vespasian sucess-
fully cured blindness: an auspicious beginning for the founder of a new dynasty. See
MacMullen (1976) 35–7, for further examples.

[89] I would like to thank the members of the Department of Religion at the
University of Vermont for their discussion of this topic at a colloquium in April
1983, and especially Professor Z. Philip Ambrose, who read an earlier version of this
paper and to whom I owe many suggestions for its improvement.

APPENDIX

Words for 'human' and 'divine' in panegyrics

Table 1. *caelestis*

	Emperor			God(s)
		Meaning		
Text	*caelestis*	*sacer*	*praeclarus*	
X(2)	14.5	–	–	–
XI(3)	6.4*	–	–	3.2
IX(5)	–	6.2, 13.1	–	–
VIII(4)	4.1	–	–	–
VII(6)	11.5	1.1, 3.3, 14.1	–	–
VI(7)	17.1	–	–	7.5, 17.3
V(8)	–	–	–	–
XII(9)	–	–	–	–
IV(10)	–	–	9.3	2.6, 14.2, 14.3, 14.4, 14.5, 19.2, 29.1
III(11)	–	–	–	10.1, 23.5, 23.6, 27.3, 27.5
II(12)	–	–	–	6.3 (bis), 19.2, 27.3, 39.5
Symm.*Orat.* 1–4	–	–	3.5	2.23, 2.26
Aus. *Gr. Act.*	–	–	5.22	–

* Combined with *sempiternus*.

Incidence in the *Panegyrici Latini*:	No. of Pages	Emperor	God(s)
Early [X(2), XI(3), VIII(4), IX(5),VII(6), VI(7), V(8)]	95.5	10	3
Late [II(12), III(11), IV(10), XII(9)]	110.5	1	17
II(12), III(11), IV(10)	91.5	1	17

Table 2. *divinus*

	Emperor			God(s)
		Meaning		
Text	*divinus*	*sacer*	*praeclarus*	
X(2)	2.3, 4.2, 10.1*, 14.1*	5.2 (bis), 8.2	–	1.1, 3.2, 6.5
XI(3)	8.3	5.1, 6.7, 9.5	4.4	3.8
IX(5)	8.2	3.2, 4.1, 6.2, 6.4, 13.1, 15.5, 16.1, 21.4	–	10.1
VIII(4)	1.1, 1.5, 4.3	2.2, 6.2, 7.2, 8.1	–	–
VII(6)	6.1	7.1	3.3, 6.2, 6.5	–
VI(7)	15.4	–	21.5	7.5
V(8)	11.5	1.3	–	10.2
XII(9)	4.5, 10.3	20.2, 26.5	–	2.5, 4.1, 4.4, 11.4, 16.2, 26.1
IV(10)	32.2, 34.2	3.3, 12.2, 29.5, 35.3	–	2.6, 7.3, 14.5, 14.6, 15.2, 15.3, 15.4, 17.1, 19.3
III(11)	–	21.3	16.4, 27.1	14.6, 27.2, 28.4, 28.5
II(12)	8.3†, 16.5†	47.3	3.6	3.2, 6.3, 10.1, 18.4, 30.2, 39.4, 39.5
Symm.*Orat.* 1–4	–	–	2.6	1.7
Aus.*Gr. Act.*	2.7†	–	–	1.5, 2.8

* Combined with *immortalis*. † Refers to the emperor's (deceased) father.

Incidence in the *Panegyrici Latini:*	No. of Pages	Emperor	God(s)
Early [X(2), XI(3), VIII(4), IX(5),VII(6), VI(7), V(8)]	95.5	37	7
Late [II(12), III(11), IV(10), XII(9)]	110.5	17	26
II(12), III(11), IV(10)	91.5	13	20

Table 3. *divinitas*

		Emperor		God(s)
Text	*divinitas*	Meaning pronoun	*imperium*	
X(2)	–	–	–	–
XI(3)	2.4, 14.3	–	–	–
IX(5)	–	–	–	–
VIII(4)	–	2.1, 8.4, 13.3, 15.2, 15.6	–	–
VII(6)	–	–	3.2	–
VI(7)	17.4	–	–	–
V(8)	–	–	–	–
XII(9)	22.1, 25.4	–	–	–
IV(10)	–	–	–	7.3, 13.5, 27.5
III(11)	–	–	–	7.2, 15.2, 28.4, 32.1
II(12)	–	–	–	29.2
Symm. *Orat.* 1–4	–	–	–	–
Aus. *Gr. Act.*	–	10.45	–	–

Incidence in *Panegyrici Latini*:	No. of Pages	Emperor	God(s)
Early [X(2), XI(3), VIII(4), IX(5),VII(6), VI(7), V(8)]	95.5	9	0
Late [II(12), III(11), IV(10), XII(9)]	110.5	2	8
II(12), III(11), IV(10)	91.5	0	8

Table 4. *maiestas*

		Emperor or Other Person		Rome/ Empire	God(s)
Text	*maiestas*	Meaning pronoun	*imperium*		
X(2)	1.3, 7.5, 11.2	–	–	14.3	–
XI(3)	2.1, 8.3, 9.2, 13.2, 13.5, 17.2	1.1, 5.2, 15.1	–	12.2	–
IX(5)	–	–	–	–	–
VIII(4)	2.3, 13.2, 15.6	1.1, 1.6, 2.2, 5.3, 6.4, 13.1, 19.1	–	–	4.1
VII(6)	3.2, 9.6, 11.4, 12.4	–	3.3, 7.2	10.5	–
VI(7)	1.4, 2.5, 8.5, 17.1	1.1, 21.1, 22.4	3.3	–	–
V(8)	9.3, 14.4	–	–	3.1	–
XII(9)	19.6	17.1	–	3.7, 15.1, 16.2	2.4
IV(10)	26.3	–	8.2	6.2	7.4, 16.1, 19.2

III(11)	24.4	–		–	–	–
II(12)	1.2, 18.4, 27.4	–		–	21.3	–
Symm. Orat. 1–4	1.5, 1.19, 2.32, 3.2, 4.12	1.10		–	1.15	–
Aus. Gr. Act.	1.1, 2.7	–		–	–	–

Incidence in the *Panegyrici Latini*:	No. of Pages	Emperor	God(s)	Rome
Early [X(2), XI(3), VIII(4), IX(5),VII(6), VI(7), V(8)]	95.5	38	1	4
Late [II(12), III(11), IV(10), XII(9)]	110.5	8	4	5
II(12), III(11), IV(10)	91.5	6	3	2

Table 5. *numen*

Text	Emperor				God(s)
	numen	Meaning pronoun	*imperium*		
X(2)	6.4, 11.2	1.1, 1.2, 3.1, 9.1, 13.5, 14.4	–		11.6, 13.4
XI(3)	1.2, 2.3, 3.8, 10.4, 11.1, 11.2, 17.4	–	–		14.2
IX(5)	–	8.1	–		7.3, 9.4 (bis), 10.1, 19.3
VIII(4)	13.2, 15.4	1.5, 5.4, 19.1, 21.3	4.2		–
VII(6)	–	–	8.3		–
VI(7)	1.1, 2.1, 2.5	1.4, 13.3, 14.1, 18.7, 22.6, 23.1, 23.3	–		9.4*, 22.2*
V(8)	–	1.3, 7.6, 9.1	–		–
XII(9)	–	1.1, 5.5, 13.2, 19.1	–		4.1
IV(10)	–	–	–		7.3
III(11)	–	–	–		3.2
II(12)	21.2	47.2	–		4.5, 21.1, 30.2
Symm. Orat. 1–4	2.32	1.22	–		2.21
Aus. Gr. Act.	–	–	–		9.43, 14.63

* These are listed under God(s), but both refer to the emperor Constantine. See narrative. They have been tallied under Emperor.

Incidence in the *Panegyrici Latini*:	No. of Pages	Emperor	God(s)
Early [X(2), XI(3), VIII(4), IX(5),VII(6), VI(7), V(8)]	95.5	39	8
Late [II(12), III(11), IV(10), XII(9)]	110.5	6	6
II(12), III(11), IV(10)	91.5	2	5

POSTSCRIPT

There has to my knowledge been no study of representation of the ruler-cult in the *Panegyrici Latini* appearing since 1986, although L'Huillier (1986), especially 545–561, addressed the question of divinity in the context of imperial representation, also using at times percentages in the texts, not of individual words but of attention given to whole concepts or different rulers. Rees (2002) takes attributes of divinity into account in his discussion of the earlier panegyrics. Mause (1994), esp. 32–3 and 220–25 incorporates the representation of emperors as divine, given the importance of his power, as a regular feature of late panegyric. Also touching upon the notions of associated divinity put forward by various panegyrists are Lassandro (2000), Kolb (2001), Clauss (2001 reprint). Studies of particular panegyrics include Enenkel (2000), who examines Panegyric 6, with its new interpretation of Constantine after the death of Maximian, and de Beer (2005), who notes that the treatment of Panegyrics V(8) and VI(7) in my original article can bear re-examination if one takes into account authorship and occasion, as different topics will necessitate different approaches to the emperor.

B. S. R.

15

Aspects of Constantinian Propaganda in the *Panegyrici Latini*

Brian Warmington

The *Panegyrici Latini* numbered VII(6) to IV(10), especially numbers VII(6), VI(7), and XII(9) are important sources for the period of Constantine's rise to power.[1] Naturally their limitations as evidence, given the nature of the panegyrical form and the refinements which generations of practitioners had made in the inherited stock of commonplaces, are well known to Constantinian specialists. This has not prevented some important conclusions from being drawn from them which would be important for our estimate of his aims and methods in the early part of his career if they could be substantiated. The object of this paper is to stress the misleading impression which can be obtained from a concentration on certain isolated themes such as a claim to rule by hereditary right rather than the Tetrarchic system, and to point out substantial differences of emphasis which exist between the messages of the panegyrists and those of the coin-age, another significant medium of propaganda.[2]

One reason for extreme caution in handling the panegyrics is a negative one—we have no comparable material about Constantine's rivals. If Constantine appears to make substantial propaganda claims through his panegyrists, he was certainly not the only contender to do so. For example, Maxentius unquestionably made use very explicitly

---

[1] [The numbering has been adjusted to conform with this volume's practice].

[2] A preliminary version was read at the Annual Meeting of the American Philological Association at St Louis on 30 December 1973. I owe much to discussion with Professor Alan Booth of Brock University.

in his coinage, with substantial emissions bearing the slogan CONSERVATORI URBIS SUAE ('to the preserver of his city'),[3] of his position as ruler of Rome—what [372] Groag called his 'national-Roman politics'[4] —and it is easy to imagine how his panegyrists could have handled the theme with suggestions implying his superiority to his rivals as holder of the imperial city. Again, as will be seen,[5] he made clear references on his coinage in 310 to his own hereditary claims, the same year that Constantine's panegyrist made the claim for his emperor. There is an assumption generally made that it was always Constantine who was particularly assertive in his claims in this period, but this need not be so. Similarly, the coinage of Licinius from 311 has been said to 'witness his assumption of the sanctions no less than the territories previously claimed by Galerius', that is to say, the senior Augustus.[6]

It is easily forgotten that the panegyrics are not proclamations for empire-wide distribution but ephemeral formalities, occasions for which would arise several times every year. Our collection contains only a few out of many; its core of five speeches seems to have been assembled at Autun in 312, partly to celebrate the efforts of Constantius and Constantine to restore the city to its former glory, partly to preserve examples of the talents of the speakers, four of whom appear to have been teachers of rhetoric there.[7] These speeches, with those added later, were preserved because they provided models for students (or practitioners) of rhetoric in the schools of Late Roman Gaul, not because they were historically significant documents. Only one of the panegyrics on Constantine was delivered at what was a relatively important political event—VII(6), on the marriage of Constantine to Fausta in 307. Nazarius' panegyric (IV(10)) given before the senate in 321 had perhaps the widest audience, but it may be significant that it has less specific to say of Constantine's actions than any of the others. These were all given before audiences in Gaul, probably at Trier; only V(8), strictly not a panegyric but a speech of thanks to Constantine for his visit to Autun[8] and the

---

[3] *RIC* VI, 293 (Ticinum), 324 (Aquileia), 371 (Roma).
[4] Groag (1930) 2457 ff.
[5] See n. 19.
[6] *RIC* VI, 507.
[7] See the demonstration in Galletier (1949) xi–xiv. IX(5) by Eumenius is precisely a speech of thanks to Constantius for restoring the Schools of Autun.
[8] But delivered at Trier; Galletier (1949) 77.

benefits which he had conferred on it, indicates the audience: the emperor in person, his councillors [373] (*amicorum comitatus,* 'accompanying colleagues') and high officials (*imperii apparatus,* 'offices of power') together with public delegations and private petitioners come to court from most of the cities of Gaul. There can be little doubt that the audiences of the rest of the panegyrics delivered in Gaul were similar. Thus the occasions and the audiences were intimately connected with the Gallic provinces in which Constantine passed the first six years of his reign. The naïve Gallic, or rather Gallo-Roman patriotism of the panegyrists is one of their best known features, and in their essentially local interest those on Constantine differ little from those on his father, or for that matter from those on Maximian, also delivered at Trier, and added to the initial collection later.[9]

The first panegyric to be considered, VII(6), was delivered in 307, probably at Trier at Constantine's marriage to Fausta and apparently after his acceptance of the rank of Augustus from Maximian, recently emerged from retirement. The point to be observed about this panegyric is that Maximian's position appears not just equal but superior to that of Constantine. It was natural in the circumstances of the marriage to Fausta that the idea of future succession in the Herculian line should arise, but the hereditary theme is muted. As far as Constantine himself is concerned, the panegyrist briefly refers to his father as the source of Constantine's power (*cum tibi pater imperium reliquisset,* 'when your father left you power' VII(6)5.3) but insists that he had refrained from using the title of Augustus till it had been bestowed on him by Maximian: *ipsum imperium hoc fore pulchrius iudicabas si id non hereditarium ex successione crevisses, sed virtutibus tuis debitum a summo imperatore meruisses* ('you judged this very power would be finer if you had not taken it as a legacy by inheritance, but had earned it from the greatest emperor as a desert for your virtues', VII(6)5.3). As for Maximian the orator found his abdication almost inexplicable—and indeed the uniqueness of the event must have cast him on his own resources, for he would have found no precedents in his models; it was due, he thought, primarily to his

---

[9] VIII(4) and IX(5) on Constantius, X(2) and XI(3) on Maximian. See below nn. 52 and 53 for the constant theme of the defence of the Rhine frontier which runs through the collection.

unquestioned loyalty[10] to Diocletian, but in fact the only justification for Diocletian's retirement would have been the succession of Maximian to sole power.[11] Strictly speaking, [374] perhaps, Maximian's retirement was a fiction; *non enim a te recessit imperium; et privatus licet dici velles, inhaesit tibi ingenita maiestas* ('for power did not leave you; and although you wanted to be known as retired, your inborn majesty clung to you', VII(6)12.4). The picture of the future roles of the two emperors given in the peroration is of Maximian giving orders and making laws while Constantine engages in untiring defence of the frontier sending back reports of his victories to his 'father'. This relationship corresponds to the relationship of an Augustus to a Caesar as envisaged by Diocletian—but Constantine was now an Augustus.

Constantine had to acquiesce in this public portrayal of his inferiority but he did nothing to help its realization.[12] In his coinage we see no more than due honour paid to Maximian on his emergence from retirement—and his second retirement after Carnuntum is quickly reflected. Further, the marriage was marked by only one very rare silver issue at Trier.[13] The panegyrist was speaking in the presence of the two emperors and the court where the higher status of the senior Augustus compared with the young Constantine, still (it seems) in his early twenties, could not be denied; but for all Maximian's energy shown in this affair, it was Constantine who was in control of the mints and who was able to play down his relationship to Maximian with the prudence he had already shown when he had contented himself with the title of Caesar reluctantly agreed to by Galerius.

The speaker of Panegyric VI(7), given at Trier some time in 310, had a more difficult task after the disgrace and death of Maximian. Attention has concentrated on two of his themes—hereditary succession and a vision Constantine is said to have had in which he was promised thirty years' rule by Apollo.[14] As regards the former theme, the panegyrist unveils the story that Constantine was descended from Claudius Gothicus and was thus the third emperor of his line. What distinguished him from his imperial colleagues, he argues, was that he

---

[10] *pietas fraterna* ('piety as a brother', VII(6)9.2). On the concept of brotherly harmony between Diocletian and Maximian, see X(2)13 and XI(3)6.

[11] VII(6)9.6.

[12] For the last years of Maximian, see Sydenham (1934).

[13] *RIC* VI, 216.

[14] e.g. Vogt (1960²) 149 ff.; Jones (1948) 65 ff.; Galletier (1952) 41 ff.

was born *imperator* ('emperor') and his actual promotion to the rank added nothing to his standing; in fact, *imperium nascendo meruisti* ('you deserved power by your birth', VI(7)3.1).[15] But this [375] does not mean that Constantine is claiming sole rule by hereditary right, and the orator in fact has it both ways; in spite of the claim that Constantine's elevation added nothing to his standing, and the obligatory reference to his choice by Divus Constantius and the approval of the other gods,[16] he devotes a substantial passage to the role of the army in 306, even bringing in the notorious commonplace of reluctance to take up the burden of empire.[17] He accepts the idea of a college of rulers (*concors et socia maiestas*, 'harmonious and shared majesty' VI(7)1.4) and envisages Diocletian (described as *divinum illum virum*, 'that divine man' VI(7)15.4) as being sustained in retirement by the new imperial college *quos scit ex sua stirpe crevisse* ('whom he knows to have grown from his own stock' VI(7) 15.5), that is, theoretical as opposed to natural descent. It was of course inevitable that after the death of Maximian, Constantine should seek to dissociate himself from him as far as he could, though it was not a constitutional necessity.[18] But the hereditary theme was double edged; Maxentius could do as well and his coinage in precisely this year honours DIVO MAXIMIANO PATRI ('to father, the deified Maximian'), DIVO CONSTANTIO COGNATO ('to the kindred deified Constantius'), and DIVO MAXIMIANO SOCERO ('to father-in-law, the deified Maximianus', i.e. Galerius).[19] In 311 even Maximinus Daia proclaimed himself the son of Divus Maximianus (Galerius).[20] All this testifies to the acceptability of the idea of (natural) hereditary succession, but not that it was special to Constantine. Indeed it is not even certain that he was the first to emphasize it; the coinage of Maxentius just referred to is dated by Sutherland to 310, and it could as easily have been before as after the panegyrist's claim.

Furthermore, the Claudius Gothicus motif does not appear on coinage till 317.[21] How can this be explained if the hereditary claim

---

[15] VI(7)2.2–3.1.
[16] VI(7)7.3–4, *sententia patris . . . omnium deorum sententia* ('the opinion of your father . . . all the gods' opinion').
[17] VI(7)8.2–5.
[18] So Straub (1939) 95. Cf. Jones (1964) 326.
[19] *RIC* VI, 346, 381 ff.; King (1959) 74.
[20] *RIC* VI, 682.
[21] *RIC* VII, 180, 252, 310, 394, 429, 502.

was so important, and if, as has been argued, the panegyrist's other story about the vision is reflected in the coinage with an increased emphasis on SOL INVICTUS ('unconquered sun')?[22] Surely because the claim when made in Gaul was of so limited an appeal: the significance of Claudius there some forty years after his death must have been negligible except [376] precisely at Autun, the city which bulks so large in the world of the Gallic panegyrists. Yet even there, Claudius was associated with failure, not success; the author of Panegyric V(8), given in 312, tells of the revolt of Autun against the usurper Victorinus and its appeal to Claudius *ad recuperandas Gallias* ('to recover Gaul', V(8)2.5 and 4.2). But he never came, and the city was sacked after a seven months' siege.[23] Hardly therefore an emperor of general appeal in Gaul. Indeed, his appearance on the coinage in 317, and in imperial titulature in the following decades,[24] must have been prompted by Constantine's acquisition in 316/7[25] of Illyricum where, if anywhere, Claudius might be remembered. The fact is that in 310 Constantine was in an embarrassing position not so much in his relations with the other rulers as in the eyes of general opinion in his own area. The execution (for this was presumably the truth about the end of Maximian) of a Senior Augustus, under whatever provocation, who had been for some twenty years the successful colleague of the prestigious Diocletian, with his own share of military success in Gaul, must have come as a profound shock. It is well known that the orator only tells the story of his plot after Constantine had indicated his personal approval,[26] and mentions his death in the obliquest possible manner.[27] Indeed, in discussing the affair, the orator contrasts Diocletian's honoured retirement with Maximian's restless discontent, and is not surprised that the man who had sworn an oath to Diocletian should also break faith

---

[22] See below, n. 33.

[23] Hanslik (1958).

[24] e.g. *ILS* 723, 725, 730, 732.

[25] The new date of the *bellum Cibalense*, 316, proposed by Bruun (1953) and (1961), is generally accepted; cf. *RIC* VII, 65 ff.

[26] *quemadmodum dicam adhuc ferme dubito et de nutu numinis tui exspecto consilium* ('still I almost hesitate at how to speak and I await advice from your godhead's nod', VI(7)14.1)

[27] Ingeniously put at VI(7)20.3–4 . . . *etiam non merentibus pepercisti. sed ignosce dicto, non omnia potes; di te vindicant et invitum* ('you even spared the undeserving . . . but excuse what I have said, you cannot manage everything; the gods avenge you even against your will'), with the comments of Galletier (1952) 40 and 71.

with Constantine.[28] For these reasons it was impossible to treat Maximian with the virulence shown by the orator of 313 (and by all other sources) towards Maxentius—and this worked to Constantine's benefit later, again in 317. He was able to 'rehabilitate' Maximian and the same series of coins which first honoured Divus Claudius also honoured Divus Maximianus, and henceforth he [377] appears sporadically in the titulature of Constantine's sons.[29] The message of the panegyrist of 310 is therefore one of reassurance in a difficult moment rather than the proclamation of an extensive new claim.

The vision of Constantine in a temple of Apollo[30] has been the subject of the most widely differing interpretations, ranging from that of Piganiol[31] who argued that it was the only 'real' vision of Constantine to that of Bidez, followed by Alföldi,[32] that the whole story is just a panegyrical invention—it occurs in the peroration where the story would form a fitting climax. In general it has been held to have had political overtones, as Constantine was now obliged, after the disgrace and death of Maximian, to seek some other divine support, preferably of wider appeal than that which the Jovian-Herculian system is supposed to have had, and has been associated with the greater prominence given to SOL INVICTUS ('unconquered sun') on Constantine's coinage from this date. Vogt, for example, put it that Constantine 'let his universal domination in space and endless time be ascribed to his relationship with Sol Apollo'.[33] But it is as well to realize that we have little to go on. Among other things we could be cautious about an easy identification of the relatively new and Oriental Sol Invictus with Apollo, in Gaul above all a god of healing

---

[28] VI(7)15.6.

[29] *RIC* VII, 180, 252, 310, 395, 429, 502; *ILS* 723, 725, 730, 732. The issues are all *aes* ('bronze') and rare but come from all Constantine's mints. Note that X(2) and XI (3), both on Maximian and delivered at Trier in 289 and 291, survived his disgrace and were added to the basic Constantian and Constantinian collection; Galletier (1949) xiv dates the addition 'a little time no doubt after the origin of the collection from Autun'. Perhaps therefore *c*.317—which was also the date at which Crispus took up residence in Gaul.

[30] VI(7)21.3–6. The temple visited by Constantine (presumably a fact) has been identified with that of Apollo Grannus at Grand (Vosges), Jullian vol. VII 107, Galletier (1952) 43, 44, and (1950).

[31] Piganiol (1932) 50.

[32] Alföldi (1948) 18.

[33] Vogt (1960²) 151.

and patron of sacred springs[34]—our panegyrist himself providing us with one of the many references.[35] The panegyrist makes only a literary or pseudo-philosophical reference (it appears) to the Apollo-Helios-Sol identification: *vidisti* [378] (sc. Constantine), *teque in illius specie recognovisti, cui totius mundi regna deberi vatum carmina divina cecinerunt* ('[Constantine], you saw and recognized yourself in his image, to whom the divine poems of bards have sung that the kingdoms of the whole world are owed', VI(7)21.5. Taken by itself this sentence would presumably be taken as referring to Jupiter; such are the pitfalls of the religious language of the panegyrists.) For the rest, the vision obviously shows Apollo in prophetic guise, and, still more, the panegyrist proceeded to a long passage inviting the emperor to visit another temple of Apollo, this one at Autun where precisely the centre of the cult was a warm spring.[36] Assuming that there was some change in Constantine's religious attitude, it is certain that the panegyrist does not tell us anything solid about what it was or on what level it was effective in Constantine's thinking, since he has presented his Apollo primarily in the form in which he was familiar to his Gallic audience.

His expression of the political consequences (if indeed it is one) is extremely brief, confined to the one sentence quoted above, where Constantine is said to have recognized himself in the features of the supreme deity. Surely this is very little. Vogt, who accepted the idea of a change in the emperor's religious outlook, was cautious about the immediate political consequences, and rightly so.[37] The significance of the increased emphasis on SOL INVICTUS ('unconquered sun') on Constantine's coins from 310 must be debatable since it is a question of degree. There are still plenty of issues with the previously popular Mars motif. Again, SOL INVICTUS ('unconquered sun') is popular in the mints of both Galerius and Maximinus Daia. It is only from 313 that the new motif becomes overwhelming (for a time) in Constantine's coinage. This leads to the conclusion that in 310 at least the religious motif had little significance as a support for political claims, nor can we assume that contemporaries in Gaul so viewed it.

---

[34] See Toutain (1917) 201–4, with references (not complete) to the cult of Apollo and his Gallic equivalents; 412 and 428 f. for their distribution.

[35] VI(7)21.7 and 22.1–3 (not in Toutain).

[36] VI(7)21.4–7.

[37] Vogt (1960[2]) 151.

Indeed, if we were to look for a really dominant religious theme on coinage before 313, it is to be found in Licinius' mints at Thessalonica and Heraclea, said by Sutherland to show 'unvaried Jupiter symbolism' and hence to witness Licinius' 'assumption of the sanctions no less than the territories claimed by Galerius'.[38] [379]

Panegyric XII(9), delivered in 313 at Trier, is largely devoted to Constantine's victory over Maxentius, and is a classic exposition of the theme of the triumph of a virtuous and legitimate ruler over a tyrannical usurper. It includes almost every known political commonplace in its vilification of Maxentius and in praise of Constantine for liberating Rome from oppression. Naturally there was nothing new in this sort of presentation, but its handling in other sources is of some interest. The theme of Constantine as the restorer of liberty is solidly represented in epigraphy in both Italy and Africa, and the inscriptions seem to be in a number sufficient to justify belief in a deliberate campaign; that on Constantine's arch in Rome is only the best known of many, the earliest of which is dated to 313.[39] The theme is also represented on Constantine's coinage from his original mints in Gaul and from Rome, but all the issues are rare, in contrast to the massive Maxentian issues CONSERVATORI URBIS SUAE ('to the preserver of his city'). To this slogan, Constantine's RESTITU-TORI ('to the restorer') or LIBERATORI URBIS SUAE ('to the liberator of his city') was the obvious if banal counterpart.[40] Whatever the real nature of Maxentius' reign, he had made much of his possession of the imperial capital and it was necessary for Constantine to make some sort of reply. It is well known that the panegyrist's view that Constantine attacked first was not the view of later Constantinian propaganda; Lactantius said that Maxentius was to blame, ostensibly to avenge his father, Nazarius that Constantine was driven to war by the provocations of Maxentius.[41] Actually, given the

---

[38] Above, n. 6. Nock (1947) concludes that Licinius' IOVI CONSERVATORI ('to Jupiter the preserver') and Constantine's SOLI INVICTO COMITI ('to unconquered sun, the companion') express an almost identical relationship between the emperor and the god.

[39] *ILS* 692 (Rome, dated 313), 694 (Rome), 687 (Ostia), 688–91 (African locations).

[40] *RIC* VI, 293 ff., 324, 371, 400 (Maxentius); 387 (Constantine) and variants from the Gallic mints, 235, 237, 165–6, 363 ff.

[41] Lact., *De mort.* 43.4; *Pan. Lat.* IV(10)9–13, and cf. Zosimus II. 14. Jones (1948) 74 believed that Maxentius struck the first blow.

propagandist nature of the theme of 'liberation from a tyrant', the panegyrist of 313 is not necessarily the more truthful, though his version seems the more probable.

The somewhat restrained note in the coinage may be due to Constantine's unwillingness at this point to alienate his new brother-in-law Licinius by emphasizing in such a public manner as a large emission his acquisition of territory originally destined for Licinius. It should be recalled that no source tells us under what circumstances Licinius agreed (if he did agree) that Constantine, not himself, should remove Maxentius in accordance with the plan of Carnuntum. It seems that the cautious [380] and defensive spirit which he always displayed had prevented him from attacking in the period 309–311, and the panegyrist's briefest of references, in connexion with Constantine's attack *quiescentibus cunctantibusque tunc imperii tui sociis* ('when your colleagues in power were relaxing and hesitant', XII(9)2.3) perhaps makes a fair point. It is, however, well known from the evidence of the panegyrists themselves that Maxentius had the bulk of his forces facing Licinius;[42] he could have been unaware of an agreement, but it remains a possibility that Constantine attacked without Licinius' knowledge while the latter was consolidating his hold on the Balkans after the events of 311, and left him with no choice but to accept a fait accompli.[43]

The defeat of Maxentius had further ramifications in the historiography of Constantine. It was notoriously of vital significance to the Christian view of the victory and conversion of Constantine found in Lactantius and Eusebius; in the brief accounts which survive from pagan sources of the later fourth and fifth centuries, Maxentius is also handled with uniform hostility, and in general Constantine's victory over him is viewed as a crucial point in his advance to sole rule.[44] In fact, of course, it was another twelve years before Constantine achieved sole power. Constantine had acquired Italy and the African provinces, but he had broken out of a confined area rather than broken through to supremacy. The very next year, Licinius received a much more substantial increase in strength when he defeated an

---

[42] XII(9)8–13, IV(10)25–7; the geography of the campaign has not been subject to panegyrical distortion. Cf. Anon. Val. 4.2.

[43] Vogt (1960²) 111 and Andreotti in De Ruggiero (1900) IV, 993, assume Licinius' agreement.

[44] Aur. Vict. *Caes.* 40; *Epit.* 40, 41; Eutrop. X.3–6; Zos. II.14 ff. Anon. Val. 4 and 5 is more balanced.

attack by Maximinus and thus added the whole of the East to his already substantial Pannonian and Balkan territories. This, together with their new relationship, was perhaps the reason why neither XII (9) nor IV(10) makes reference to the senate's designation of Constantine as *maximus* ('greatest'), thus designating him as the senior of the two Augusti; nor does the title appear on coinage till 315/6.[45] The explanation for the position of the Maxentian episode in pagan as well as Christian writers seems to lie in Constantine's subsequent success in dominating the historiography [381] of his own lifetime, and in constructing a picture which laid emphasis on the end of Maxentius. This ruler could easily be portrayed as a tyrannical usurper, and concentration on this theme would go some way to disguise the fact that Constantine had remained the colleague for some twelve years of a legitimate ruler of respectable qualities who could not be handled in history the same way as Maxentius. The middle decade of Constantine's reign is little known and to some extent this is because he successfully imposed the picture of his advance to sole rule as divinely inspired, effortless and swift.

It is in this respect that panegyric IV(10), delivered by Nazarius of Bordeaux in the senate in 321, is a disappointment, perhaps significantly so. The occasion was the *quinquennalia* ('fifth anniversary of accession') of the young Crispus and still younger Constantine II; the emperor himself was absent, and indeed had not been in Rome since the victory over Maxentius except for a brief stay in 315. The orator naturally has nothing but empty phrases to say on the actions of the two young Caesars and concentrates on Constantine. But he has little to add to what is in the other panegyrics—the campaigns in Gaul of 306–10 and 313, and—his main theme—the campaign against Maxentius. Since the rules of panegyric required that all attention be centred on the emperor to whom it was addressed[46] it is not surprising that there is no mention of Licinius, or for that matter the younger Licinius whose *quinquennalia* ('fifth anniversary of accession') fell on the same date as that of the sons of Constantine. It may be the case

---

[45] *senatus Constantino virtutis gratia primi nominis titulum decrevit quem sibi Maximinus vindicabat* ('the senate decreed the title of the first rank––which Maximinus claimed for himself––to Constantine because of his virtue', Lact. *De mort.* 44.11); *RIC* VII, 28.

[46] X(2) and XI(3), the panegyrics on Maximian, are exceptions, as they have much to say on Diocletian, but this is presumably because of the novelty of the situation.

that it was in precisely this year[47] that relations between the two rulers, which had been at any rate formally correct since the settlement of 317, began to deteriorate, but we cannot deduce anything from this panegyric. On the other hand it is notable that we hear nothing of Constantine's activities since 313 except a brief reference of a commonplace character to *novae leges* ('new laws', IV(10)38.4). It may be supposed that in the absence of the court the orator had no indicated line to follow and felt on safe ground in doing no more than rework the themes of the defence of the Rhine frontier and the defeat of Maxentius. One feature of his treatment of the latter has been found significant, namely its religiosity and [382] especially its several references to the *caelestis exercitus* ('heavenly army') fighting on Constantine's side.[48] This has been seen[49] as the culmination of Constantine's religious propaganda, which had begun with the vision in Apollo's temple, continued with the divine inspiration of his strategy against Maxentius and now reached a climax with the actual participation of a 'heavenly host' in the fighting, led by no less a person than his father Constantius.[50] Galletier's proposition is attractive (especially if the vision of 310 is regarded as mere panegyrical material, not representing any specific change in Constantine's religion), but on the whole the three aspects look more like variations on the commonplace of divine support. In Nazarius, the locale of the speech is perhaps important because he draws a deliberate comparison between the *caelestis exercitus* ('heavenly army') supporting Constantine and the appearance of the Dioscuri at Lake Regillus, one of the most cherished of Roman myths.[51] Concentration on the defeat of Maxentius would also no doubt have been at least as acceptable to the senatorial audience as anything else done by Constantine.

Finally, when all is said on these debatable points, it remains a fact that the chief theme of the *Panegyrici* is not any of those mentioned,

---

[47] Kornemann (1930) 127–8.
[48] IV(10)14 and 15; 19.2; 29.1.
[49] Galletier (1952) 155.
[50] VI(7)21 (temple of Apollo); XII(9)2.4 ff. (divine inspiration); IV(10)14.6 (Constantius as leader of the heavenly army).
[51] IV(10)15.2–7. This article has not attempted to deal with the problems, perhaps insoluble, of the religious vocabulary of XII(9) and IV(10)—i.e. in what degrees it is literary, pseudo-philosophical or plain evasive in the post-312 situation. In these and other passages Nazarius seems to reach new heights, or depths, of ambiguity.

but Constantine's defence of the Rhine frontier and his victories over the Germans. The defence of the Rhine had indeed been of vital concern to the panegyrists of Maximian and Constantius as well.[52] In the case of Constantine they are mentioned in VII(6), when they had hardly begun, and are treated at some length in panegyrics VI(7), XII(9), and IV(10).[53] The most sensational single event, the capture and death in the amphitheatre of the two kings Ascaric and Merogaisus is mentioned by three panegyrists;[54] it appears to have already occurred by [383] early 307, but campaigns certainly continued for several more years. So important was the defence of the frontier in the eyes of the panegyrists that the speaker of XII(9) in 313 claims that the withdrawal of troops from the frontier did not endanger it, though in fact he himself reveals that this was not true and that Constantine had to return to the Rhine in a hurry after his meeting with Licinius at Milan early in 313.[55] The successful outcome of the series of campaigns from 306 to 309 or 310 are celebrated on coinage of 310 with the legends FRANCIA and ALEMANNIA.[56] It may be that the campaigns were not so extensive as the panegyrists try to make us believe; the repetition of the death of the two kings, which had occurred at the start of the campaigns, and the lack of much other concrete information look suspicious. But there is no reason to doubt that Constantine successfully maintained the relative improvement in stability along the Rhine and in this was succeeding to his father's role, and the role expected of him by the panegyrists. It is well known that they combine in a somewhat naïve way a 'Roman' with a 'Gallic' patriotism,[57] and appear to have viewed Constantine, as they did Constantius, as 'their' emperor. As for Constantine's coinage, this is not substantially Gallic in tone, but according to Sutherland, commenting on the issues from Trier (the most productive mint) from 306 to 312, 'Coinage in all metals, taken as a whole, gives overwhelmingly strong emphasis to Constantine himself: the issues for his

---

[52] X(2)5–8.10; VIII(4)8 and 9; 18; 20.
[53] VII(6)4; VI(7)10 ff. and 31; XII(9)21–4; IV(10)16–18. The exploits of Constantius are recalled in VI(7)4 ff. and XII(9)24.
[54] VII(6)4.2 (unnamed); VI(7)10.2 and 11.5; IV(10)16.5.
[55] 2.6–3.3 (Rhine defence maintained); 21.5 (rapid return to Rhine).
[56] *RIC* VI, 160.
[57] The whole group bears witness to this. Cf. especially V(8)2–7 and (inevitably) XII(9).

colleagues are little more than bare courtesy coinage.'[58] If true—and the whole matter is rather subjective, requiring comparison with the volume of analogous coins from the mints of Constantine's colleagues, and their attitudes to each other—we may see the importance attached by Constantine to securing loyalty to his own person, if not to the intensely self-centred, self-admiring side of his personality. It must also not be forgotten that in spite of his recognition by Galerius, his position vis-à-vis Maxentius can hardly have seemed overwhelming at any stage, given the collapse of the attempts by both Severus and Galerius to remove him.

It would seem therefore that neither the panegyrics nor the coinage [384] of Constantine in the early part of his career give much support for the idea of a young man gripped from the start by a driving ambition for sole rule.[59] We may of course believe that he was, in which case the message of the contemporary sources for the years 306–13 shows an underestimated aspect of Constantine—his prudence and circumspection. Perhaps he was consciously building up during these years an army of a new type,[60] the basis of the future *comitatenses*, ready to strike swiftly when ready; but then, his victory over Maxentius was followed by another decade of shared rule with Licinius, including the indecisive war of 317. Constantine, in short, may be compared in several respects not so much with Caesar as with Augustus;[61] not only in his youth when launched into power, but also in his diplomatic adroitness, his cautious assessment of political and military realities, and his largely successful manipulation of his own image.

---

[58] *RIC* VI, 159.

[59] Best formulated by Jones (1964) 78. Aur. Vict. *Caes.* 40.2 is the most explicit source: *iam tum a puero ingens potensque animus ardore imperitandi agitabatur* ('right from childhood his great and able mind was preoccupied with a desire to rule').

[60] So van Berchem (1952) 108.

[61] Vogt (1960²) 141.

16

The Panegyric of Claudius Mamertinus on the Emperor Julian*

Roger Blockley

The verdict in Pauly-Wissowa[1] upon the low historical worth of the panegyric of Claudius Mamertinus on the Emperor Julian has hardly been upheld by the later studies of Pichon, Gutzwiller, and Galletier.[2] These scholars have shown that the speech is, on the one hand, a personal statement of Mamertinus' gratitude to Julian, but, on the other, a well thought out and carefully written work with a dual political purpose—first, by praising Julian's achievements as Caesar and by contrasting his virtues with the failings of his predecessors to remove the stigma of usurpation and to suggest that he is a true emperor; secondly, to present, as it were, a manifesto, an outline of Julian's programme for the future.

The analysis of the speech both as propaganda and as a political document of some importance can be taken further. I propose to add to this analysis by arguing that: (1) the desire to contrast in detail the characters of Julian and of Constantius as rulers strongly influences the tone and content of the speech, and the characters themselves

* Acknowledgements are due to Mr W. R. Chalmers of the Department of Classics, Nottingham University, and to Dr A. Fotiou of the Department of Classics, Carleton University, Ottawa, who read an earlier draft of this paper and commented upon it for me.
[1] Gensel (1899).
[2] Pichon (1906a) 116 ff.; Gutzwiller (1942) 81ff.; Galletier (1955) 7–9. Barabino (1965), in her ch. 6, *'Il programma politico'* ('The political programme' 49–61), adds little new that is relevant to the present paper. She is primarily concerned to set the speech in its historical context.

which emerge are very similar to the portraits in Ammianus and Libanius; (2) not only is the religious question treated in a very circumspect manner because of the time and place of the delivery of the panegyric, but also the fact that Julian's military exploits in [438] Gaul are almost ignored is to be explained by similar considerations. Mamertinus does not often attack Constantius directly, preferring rather to censure the vices of the recent past.[3] But that the deceased emperor is the primary target of such censure is clear from the nature of the charges made and from a comparison with direct attacks, especially of Ammianus and Libanius. This policy of refraining from open attacks upon Constantius was Julian's own[4] and was dictated by caution, since, when the new emperor had declared war upon his predecessor, he soon found himself facing considerable opposition, not only in the East[5] but also in areas of the West.[6] Certainly to some extent affection for Constantius seems to have out-lasted the reign of Julian.[7]

Mamertinus states that the reign of Constantius was marked by a bad choice of officials. When Julian arrived in Gaul as Caesar (winter AD 355–6) he found much of the land ravaged by the German invaders (III(11)3.1; 4.1), whom he easily crushed in one battle (4.3). Far more formidable were the 'wicked brigands who were called governors' (4.2), who devastated the parts which were safe from the Germans, insulting, injuring, and torturing the inhabitants, allowing to escape only those who could pay a bribe and creating such a desperate state of affairs that people longed for the barbarians to come as saviours (ibid.). When Julian strove to mend their vices, they retaliated by arousing the jealousy of Constantius against him (4.3–7).

Later Mamertinus broadens his attack. The majority of office holders had achieved their positions through sycophancy [439] and bribery, especially of the women and eunuchs who had the emperor's ear. Then they went off to plunder their provinces in order to

---

[3] e.g. III(11)19.3–20.4 referring to *paulo ante* ('a little earlier'). This is noted by Pichon (1906a) 118 ff. and Gutzwiller (1942) 83.

[4] See especially Julian, *Ep.*, 9 (ed. Wright); *Misopogon*, 357B; Ammianus, 21.16.20; Libanius, *Or.* 18.120.

[5] Especially in Constantinople and Antioch; Sievers (1868) 86 ff.

[6] e.g. in Italy (Ammianus, 20.9.1; 21.10.7; 11.2–3) and Africa (Ammianus 21.7.2; cf. III(11)14.5). Cf. Dagron, (1968) 69 n. 202.

[7] Ammianus 26.7.10.

subsidise their own further advancement (19.3–5). The emphasis of the reign was upon the amassing of wealth; military service and legal or oratorical skill counted for nothing (20.1–3; cf. 17.3). Thus the cities fell into ruin (cf. 7–9); and Mamertinus himself, when *comes sacrarum largitionum* ('count of sacred treasury') found the provinces wasted and the soldiers unpaid (1.4).

A similar, gloomy picture is painted by Libanius and confirmed in points by Ammianus. The former alleges widespread sale of offices and pillaging of subjects and whole cities, especially by eunuchs, notaries, and *agentes in rebus* ('state agents');[8] and he echoes the claim made by Mamertinus that the captives of the barbarians were as well off as those who remained in Gaul.[9] Ammianus notes the extortion of the tax collectors;[10] the fiscal abuses which Julian had to correct in Gaul;[11] the plotting at the court of Constantius which aroused the jealousy of the emperor against Julian (17.11.1; cf. 9.7); the corruption of Constantius' eunuchs,[12] who, he says, together with the emperor's wives, had excessive influence over him (21.16.16; cf. 20.2.4) and whose favours were vigorously sought (18.3.3). Julian himself accuses his predecessor of personal avarice (*Misopogon*, 357B).

Mamertinus further censures the orientalizing court which was cultivated by Constantine I and his sons,[13] with its pomp and magnificence and stylized ceremonial. The attack is twofold. First, the enormous numbers of servants, the lavish and luxurious feasts, and the extensive use of marble and gold in the decoration of the palace occasioned excessive expenditure [440] and added to the financial misery (11). Secondly, the arrogance of the courtiers who controlled access to and influenced the emperor forced those who sought advancement to grovel at their knees and to recognize that favours given were not as a result of benevolence or judgement but of

---

[8] Libanius, *Or.* 18.130–45. On the low quality of Constantius' officials in Gaul see Julian, *Ep. ad Ath.* 281D–82D.

[9] Libanius, *Or.* 18.35.

[10] Ammianus 21.16.17 (cf. 16.5.14; 17.3); Julian, *Ep. ad Ath.*, 280A.

[11] 18.1.1–2 (cf. 24.3. 4).

[12] 14.11.3; 15.2.10; 18.5.4. This particularly reflects Julian's personal hatred of Eusebius (cf. *Ep. ad Ath.*, 274A-B).

[13] The court style of Constantine I and Constantius II is praised by their panegyrists, Eusebius and Themistius: Straub (1939) 168 ff.

misericordia ('pity', 20.4), an idea especially associated with the absolutist regime, implying as it does the unfettered power of the giver.

Such charges are repeated by Ammianus and Libanius,[14] the former also accusing Constantius of personal arrogance.[15] The strong distaste which the pro-Julian sources feel for the court of Constantius is itself a reflection of the policy of Julian, who reacted away from the absolutist orientalizing monarchy of his predecessors and back towards the traditional notion of the emperor as a constitutional ruler[16] and with it a simpler style of court life.

Finally Mamertinus notes the jealousy of Constantius, which, he says, was aroused against Julian by the corrupt officials whom he had angered in Gaul (4.3–7) and which, according to the panegyrist, could only be assuaged if the Caesar would acquiesce in the *status quo* and allow the provinces to be destroyed by the greed of their governors (5.1–3). This the virtue of Julian would not permit him to do (5.4); and when Constantius called in the barbarians against him (6.1), he invaded Illyricum to the joy of all the cities through which he passed (6.2–7.3).[17]

The jealousy and suspicion of Constantius is a commonplace in all hostile sources.[18] But more interesting is Mamertinus' treatment of Julian's usurpation, in that he does not actually [441] mention the circumstances in which the Caesar was declared Augustus. Ammianus, Libanius, and Julian himself are at great pains to explain the act, stressing that the new emperor was elevated by the soldiers against his own will[19]—which was certainly the official version.[20] The motives of the troops are variously described: anger that Constantius, jealous of Julian, was withdrawing the Gallic troops to the East (an action

---

[14] Ammianus 15.5.18 and 27; 16.10.2 and 10–2 (contrast 21.16.7); 19.12.16; etc. Libanius, *Or.* 18.130 ff.

[15] 15.1.3; 5.35; 12.68; 17.4.12; 20.8.2.

[16] Cf. Dvornik (1966) vol. 2, 659 ff.

[17] The joy of the cities is overstated. Julian had not left Dacia when he received the news of the death of Constantius (Ammianus 22.1.3). For opposition to Julian in the West see above, n. 6.

[18] Libanius *Or.* 18.90; 12.43 and 57; Julian *Ep. ad Ath.*, 272A (Constantius' jealousy of Gallus), 274D, 277D; Ammianus 14.5.2 and 4; 9.2; 11.4; 15.3.9; 16.7.1; 19.12.5; etc.; Eunapius fr. 14.4; Zosimus 3.8.6.

[19] Libanius *Or.* 18.95 ff.; 12.58; 13.33–4; Julian *Ep. ad Ath.*, 283A-B; Ammianus 20.4.2 ff.; 8.5–10. Also Zosimus, 3.9.

[20] Petit (1956) 480.

which, it is claimed, broke Julian's promise to the auxiliaries at least that they would not have to cross the Alps, and which would render Gaul defenceless);[21] desire to make their successful leader more than a Caesar;[22] or the fulfilment of God's will.[23] The version of Mamertinus ignores the claim that Julian was forced to usurp and implies that he himself actually took the decision to revolt, which is probably nearer to the truth.[24] There was a lapse of time between Julian's usurpation and his invasion of Constantius' territory, during which negotiations took place.[25] By ignoring the act of usurpation Mamertinus can suppress this interval and imply that Julian was finally aroused to action by Constantius' incitement of the barbarians to attack him (a move which is noted by other pro-Julian sources, but which is usually placed after the usurpation).[26] Thus justice [442] is placed wholly on the side of the usurper who is presented as the saviour of the empire from the corruption of Constantius' regime.[27]

Julian's advance along the Danube and into the Balkans is described by Mamertinus as a triumphal procession. As he sailed down the river the right bank was lined by the provincials who turned out to greet him, the left by the barbarians who begged for mercy and received it.[28] The cities which he visited were given freedom and hope and revived by immunities, privileges, and money (7, 3; 8, 3–4). Mamertinus describes the ruinous state of the towns (9) and pictures

---

[21] See above n. 19.

[22] Libanius *Or.* 13.33–4 (cf. Ammianus, 20.8.7; 16.12.64).

[23] Libanius *Or.* 12.58. On the circumstances contributing to the different interpretations in Libanius see Petit (1956) 479–81.

[24] Cf. Müller-Seidel (1955).

[25] Ammianus 20.8–10.

[26] Libanius, *Or.* 18.107–8; Julian *Ep. ad Ath.*, 286A; Ammianus 21.3.4–5 (stressing that it was only a rumour). Constantius is also said to have called the barbarians in against Magnentius: Libanius, *Or.* 18.33; Zosimus, 2.53.4. Gutzwiller (1942) 125 is wrong to cite Socrates 3.1 and Sozomen 5.2 as evidence to confirm the pro-Julian claims that Constantius summoned the barbarians against Julian. Since in these Christian writers the claim of the Germans that they obeyed Constantius is made before the battle of Strassburg, it clearly refers to the earlier summons against Magnentius. Thus there is no Christian evidence that the Germans were summoned against Julian. (For other arguments that the charge is genuine see Thompson (1943)).

[27] Mamertinus mentions in passing (27.4) that Constantius named Julian as his heir. Ammianus (21.15.2 and 5) treats this as a rumour; but in 21.2.1 he indicates that the messengers who reported the Emperor's death to Julian announced it as a fact.

[28] 7.2–3. This clemency to the barbarians is noted a number of times by Ammianus, e.g. 16.12.65, 17.8.4–5, 10.4.

them and their lands renewed by the benefactions of Julian (10).[29] All of this is a rather overdone reflection of a genuine concern of Julian to lower taxation and to revive the cities.[30]

Mamertinus claims that this reverse flow of wealth to the cities is made possible by Julian's personal parsimony (10.2–3). *tam severe parcus in semet* ('so severely sparing towards himself', 12.1), he rejects the luxury of Constantius' court,[31] preferring to eat only when necessary and taking the food of a common soldier out of any chance vessel (11). He labours with his troops (6.4) and by his own energy eases the burden of his officials (12.1 and 3; cf. 7.1). In short, Julian is a slave to the liberty of his people. The toil and the battles which he endures, the continence and justice which he imposes upon himself would have terrified usurpers [443] such as Nepotianus and Silvanus, who looked forward to a life of dissipation (13.3). This appeal to the commonplace that a tyrant (= usurper) is a man full of vices (which is, of course, the regular view of the failed usurper in the late Roman Empire) reinforces what is implied in the whole speech, that Julian, because he is virtuous, cannot be a tyrant.[32]

As usual the other friendly sources advertise Julian's moderation in eating, his general temperance,[33] and his willingness to undertake toil.[34] Ammianus says that after his elevation to Caesar, Julian *murmurans querulis vocibus saepe audiebatur: nihil se plus assecutum, quam ut occupatior interiret* ('was often heard murmuring in a tone of complaint that he had achieved nothing more than that he would end his life more busy', 15.8.20).

According to Mamertinus (and in this he is supported by Libanius),[35] not only does Julian help both cities and individuals by his generosity, but he has also improved the general condition of the provinces through his appointment of good officials.[36] In contrast with Constantius he rejects servility and wealth as a recommendation

---

[29] Cf. III(11)14, where Julian is said to have eased a famine at Rome.

[30] See Libanius, *Or*. 18.23; 146–8; 163; 193; 13, 44; Ammianus 17.3.5–6; 9, 11; 18.1.1–2; 21.5.8; Julian *Misopogon*, 365B; 367C–371B (cf. *Or*. I, 42D–43A).

[31] See especially Libanius, *Or*. 18, 130 and Ammianus 22.4.

[32] Cf. Gutzwiller (1942) 84; Barabino (1965) 60.

[33] Libanius *Or*. 18.174–81; 13.44; 12.94–5; 17.27; Ammianus 15.8.10; 16.5.1–5; 21.9.2; 24.4.27; 25.2.2; etc. (cf. Julian, *Misopogon*, 340B–42A; 345C–D; 354B–C; *Or*. I, 11A–B).

[34] Libanius *Or*. 18.174–6; 276 (cf. Julian *Ep. ad Them*. 259B–D; *Or*. II, 87D–88A).

[35] Libanius *Or*. 18.194; 13.43 (cf. Julian *Or*. II, 90C–91D).

[36] Menander Rhetor, *Basilikos Logos* 375 makes this one of the regular categories of praise of an emperor.

for office and friendship, demanding instead honesty and hard work. The official will be judged by his service and the possession of four virtues, *iustitia* ('justice'), *fortitude* ('bravery'), *temperantia* ('temperance'), *prudentia* ('prudence') (17.3–4; 21; cf. 25.1–2; 26.4–5).[37] This new breed of administrator is characterized as *hominum genus*...
rude (ut urbanis istis videtur), parum come, subrusticum ('a type of man, rough (as it seems to those urbane men), too obliging, rustic', 21.2)—obviously a reference to the untidy appearance of the emperor himself,[38] rather than to any intellectual awkwardness. Julian looks for skill in war, oratory, and legal science in his [444] officials (23.3–5), and during his reign the study of philosophy and the liberal arts, which lapsed under Constantius,[39] has revived (23.4). Julian and Ammianus,[40] and other pagans of the fourth century,[41] lay great stress upon the importance of education and its value as a means of inculcating virtue.

Julian is generous not only to the cities and citizens of the empire, but also to his friends. This generosity which Mamertinus praises (12.2–3), and other sources confirm,[42] made him a prey to the greed of unscrupulous men, as Gregory Nazianzen alleges and Libanius admits.[43] Julian made a special effort to cultivate *civilitas* ('fellow citizen status') towards his officials and, as far as possible, towards people in general,[44] a virtue which is claimed for him by Mamertinus more strongly and at greater length than any other (12; 28–9; 30), reflecting not only the contrast with the ceremonious remoteness of

---

[37] These are listed as the four royal virtues by Menander *Basilikos Logos* 373. III (11)5.4, ascribes to Julian *aequitas* ('fairness'), *temperantia* ('temperance'), *fortitude* ('bravery') *and providentia* ('foresight') (cf. Ammianus, 25.4.1–10; Libanius *Or.* 18.281).

[38] Cf. Julian *Misopogon*, 338B–339D.

[39] Constantius gave offence to those who had enjoyed the traditional classical education by selecting persons without this background for administrative positions; Festugière (1959) 92–4; Dagron (1968) 71–2.

[40] Julian *In Galileos*, 229D–E (cf. Downey (1957)). Ammianus 29.2.18 (cf. 16.7.5; 17.3.31; 29.1.42).

[41] e.g. Themistius *Or.* XI, 143C–46C. Aurelius Victor (Den Boer (1968) 258). The *SHA* (Syme (1968) 126).

[42] Ammianus 25.4.15; Eutropius 10.16; John of Antioch, fr. 180.

[43] Gregory Nazianzen *Or.*, 4.44 and 72; 5.19. Libanius *Or.*, 18. 200–3.

[44] Ammianus 25.4.7; Libanius *Or.*, 18.154; 189–92; 12.82. In *Or.* 18.155–6 Libanius praises Julian for rushing from the senate house to greet the philosopher Maximus (cf. Eunapius, *Vit. Soph.*, 476 ff.), an action which Ammianus (22.7. 3–4) condemns as cheap popularity seeking.

Constantius, but also the need felt by the new regime to calm the fears which had been engendered by the hostile propaganda of Constantius and which must have lingered in the East.[45]

Nevertheless Julian's care for people was genuine and is illustrated, far better than by Mamertinus, in the report of Ammianus that upon his death bed the emperor refused to [445] mourn himself, but grieved deeply over the loss of his Master of the Offices, Anatolius (25.3.21). In the opinion of many, including Ammianus, Julian at times carried his *civilitas* ('fellow citizen status') too far and his behaviour degenerated into mere popularity seeking,[46] an interpretation which, according to Ammianus (22.7.1), was placed by many upon the action of the emperor, praised by Mamertinus (30.2), of proceeding on foot to the inauguration of the consuls for 362.

Although such behaviour on the part of Julian was conditioned by the conscious reaction away from the remoteness and pomp of the court of Constantius, it had one very salutary effect, as Mamertinus notes (26.1–3). Since the officials could be open and honest towards Julian, the servility and deceit of the court of the previous regime was swept away. This *libertas* ('freedom') is stressed by Ammianus in his account of Julian's reign; and throughout his history he makes it one of the central virtues of a good official to correct boldly and openly the errors of his master.[47]

These are the major traits of the regimes of Constantius and Julian which are discussed by Mamertinus. His proposition is that during the reign of Constantius the state suffered financial ruin as a result of the corruption of its administrators and the lavish court, and that the despotic emperor himself was a prey to jealousy and to the intrigues of his servile courtiers. On the other hand, Julian is generous both to the cities and to his friends; he chooses his officials wisely; and is as unsparing of himself as he is affable towards others. Thus the panegyrist builds up a contrast between the characters of the regimes of the two rulers and (in accordance with the practice of the age, which ascribed the vices and virtues of a regime to its head) of the rulers themselves.

---

[45] Cf. 14.6 where Mamertinus claims that Julian refused to intercept Constantinople's corn supply.

[46] Ammianus 22.7.3–4; 25.4.18; Eutropius, 10.16; Anon., *Epit. de Caes.* 43.7; John of Antioch, fr. 180; Zonaras, 13.13.

[47] Ammianus 16.7.6; 22.7.2; 10.3; 25.4.16 (cf. 16.8.7; 27.6.14; 7.10; etc.).

The virtues ascribed to Julian, affability, honesty, care in the choice of officials, and public and private liberality (virtues which were associated with the Hellenistic king in his role as *euergetes*, 'benefactor'), appear regularly in the works on kingship [446] and the panegyrics of the fourth century and earlier.

On the other hand, the praise for the revival of the cities reflects the philosophy of the opposition to the regime of Constantius which bemoaned the increasingly bureaucratic centralization of the age and the consequent decrease in the prestige and the power of the local city governments in the East.[48] Thus too Julian's deference towards the senate of Constantinople contrasts with Constantius who, according to Libanius, never entered it.[49]

The contrasting details of character, even though, as Barabino says,[50] they are probably more than mere *topoi*, are nevertheless, in the manner in which they are used by Mamertinus, of the nature of pro-Julian propaganda. This is clear not only from Mamertinus' speech itself, but also from the use of the same details of character by Julian in his *Letter to the Athenians* and elsewhere and by Libanius in his *Epitaphios*. More interesting is the appearance in Ammianus' *History* of similar characterizations.[51] Galletier has suggested, from a comparison of certain passages of Ammianus and Mamertinus, that the former had read the latter.[52] Most I do not find convincing; but in one passage there is striking verbal similarity. Mamertinus, 2, 3, describes Julian as *quasi quoddam salutare humano genere sidus* ('like some star that brings health to the human race') and Ammianus, 21.10.2, calls him *sidus salutare* ('a health-bringing star'; also 22.9.14). Since such panegyrics were popular and widely read,[53] it is quite likely that Ammianus had seen that of Mamertinus. This is not to suggest that the historian modelled his account of Julian's career up to 362 upon the version of the panegyrist; his description, for instance, of Julian's revolt differs. Nevertheless the possibility that he knew this (and other) pro-Julian propaganda, together with the

---

[48] Cf. Dagron (1968) 47 ff.
[49] Libanius *Or.*, 18. 154; cf. Pichon (1906a) 138.
[50] (1965) 58–9.
[51] The fact that Ammianus draws a contrast between Constantius and Julian has been noted by a number of scholars, e.g. Jannaccone (1960) 39; Di Spigno (1962) 456 ff.
[52] (1955) 9, nn. 4 and 5.
[53] Straub (1939) 146–53.

striking similarity of detail in the characterizations [447] of Julian and Constantius, suggests that here Ammianus was strongly influenced by such propaganda and must be used with caution. As important as the positive aspects of Mamertinus' propaganda are his omissions. He says little either on religious or military matters. In religion he was probably pagan, but his solitary reference, to the god of the old poets (28.5), is vague and hardly provocative. As the commentators have noted,[54] this reticence reflected the official policy of the moment, caution.[55] When Mamertinus delivered his speech, in early January 362, Julian had already openly professed his paganism and had probably issued his edicts for the restoration of the worship of the old gods and toleration for all creeds and recalled the Christians exiled by Constantius.[56] But the edicts can only have been in force for a short while, with little or no time to have taken effect. Thus the emperor and his supporters could not as yet have had an opportunity to evaluate their reception in the markedly Christian city of Constantinople, which Julian had only entered on 11 December 361.[57]

The treatment of the religious problem is what one might expect for the date of delivery. Apparently more surprising is the lack of interest in Julian's military exploits, upon which there is nothing beyond a short account of the expedition along the Danube and into the Balkans against Constantius. Yet Julian's success in Gaul ranks as one of his major achievements, and in general military exploits form one of the most important ingredients of panegyric. Ammianus, Libanius, and Julian himself devote much space to the Gallic campaigns,[58] whereas [448] Mamertinus, who notes that they have already been well publicized in the East (3.1), dismisses the fighting of a number of years against the Germans with the words, *una acie Germania universa deleta est, uno proelio debellatum* ('all of Germany was destroyed in one battle; in one engagement the war was decided', 4.3). This, of course, is itself good panegyric insofar as the ease of this difficult exploit serves to emphasize its brilliance; and the

---

[54] Gutzwiller (1942) 23–4; Pichon (1906a) 135; Galletier (1955) 5; Barabino (1965) 60.

[55] Certainly while Constantius was still alive Julian had only cautiously practised his paganism (Ammianus 21.5.1; Eunapius, *Vit. Soph.*, 476 ff.).

[56] Ammianus 22.5; Ensslin (1923) 110.

[57] Ammianus 22.2.4.

[58] Libanius *Or.* 18.42–83; 13.30–2; Julian *Ep. ad Ath.* 278D–28IC; Ammianus 16.2–4; 11–2; 17.1–2; 8–10; 18.2. If Zosimus 3.3–8 is an accurate reflection of Eunapius, then the latter also stressed Julian's military exploits in Gaul.

personal nature of the *actio gratiarum* ('thanksgiving') might be thought to account for the lack of stress laid upon military matters by Mamertinus, whose career seems to have been a civil one. But there are two positive reasons for playing down this aspect of Julian's success. First, Julian's triumphs in the West were the triumphs of the western army, and as such would have been of little interest to the people of Constantinople. To flaunt them might have aroused the jealousy of the eastern forces which Julian had only lately taken over, which had recently been preparing to fight him, and which could not have been happy at the presence of the victorious western army in the vicinity of the capital.[59]

Secondly, when Mamertinus was delivering his speech, the trials of the civilian officials of Constantius were taking place at Chalcedon.[60] Julian, for personal and political reasons, was allowing the military to use these trials to attack the civilian officials of the dead emperor;[61] and since in this way he was making his peace with the soldiery, at the cost of some unjust condemnations (especially of the wholly blameless Ursulus, who had been a good friend to Julian but who had incurred the wrath of the troops by his criticism of the great expenditure upon the army and its ineffectiveness against the Persians[62]), there was no need to use the speech of Mamertinus towards this purpose; although Mamertinus is careful to note that the emperor does have the support of the military (24.5–7). Better [449] to use it to justify the condemnations of some of the accused against the protests which were to arise and which had perhaps already begun.[63] Thus in attacking the regime of Constantius, Mamertinus concentrates on civil affairs and especially the alleged crimes of the civilian officials, which (in Gaul at least) are stressed by contrasting the ease of the campaign against the Germans with the difficulty of the fight against the corrupt governors.

---

[59] The division between the generals of the two armies never completely healed, and reopened after the death of Julian as the two sides supported their own candidates for emperor (Ammianus 25.5.2).

[60] Ammianus 22.3. Ensslin (1923) 116–18, argues that the trials began in the second half of Dec. 361 and continued into Feb. 362.

[61] For the argument for this interpretation of the trials at Chalcedon see the appendix to the original article.

[62] Ammianus 22.3.7–9; 20.11.5.

[63] Ammianus 22.3.4, 7–8 and 10. Taurus, one of those considered to have been unjustly punished, was condemned during his own consulship (i.e. before the end of Dec. 361).

17

The Ideal of the Ruler and Attachment to Tradition in Pacatus' Panegyric

Adolf Lippold

The orator and poet Latinus Pacatus Drepanius was from Bordeaux or its close vicinity.[1] He belonged to the circle of friends of his countryman Ausonius,[2] and enjoyed friendly relations with Q. Aurelius Symmachus.[3] In the summer of 389 in Rome, he delivered a panegyric to the emperor Theodosius.[4] Probably in recognition of this act, the orator was appointed *proconsul Africae*.[5] It is possible that he became *comes rerum privatarum* ('count of the private estates') in 392/3, but this is not firmly established.[6] We also have no means of

[1] Sid. Apoll. *Ep.* 8.11 refers to Aginium (cf. Stroheker (1948) 197 n. 271). Pacatus (2.1) on the other hand, suggests a location near the coast: cf. Baehrens (1921) 445; Galletier (1955) 48.

[2] Cf. Aus. [Schenkl] 20, 23, 27 1; 4.10 and 13.21.

[3] Pacatus is established to be the addressee of *Epist.* 9.61 and 64 (two letters of recommendation) and 8.12, and assumed (e.g. by Seeck (1883) 193 and Hanslik (1942) 2058 to be that of 8.11 and 9.72. Seeck (1883) dates 8.11–2 to 397, on the basis of the remark *nam mei quoque corporis vigor post infirmam valetudinem coepit adsurgere* ('for the strength of my body began to increase after my weak health', 11), which would fit well with the *vita* ('life') of Symmachus. Even if this argument is held to be compelling, however, it can scarcely be said to establish the orator Pacatus as addressee of the letter.

[4] Theodosius arrived in Rome on 13 June 389, and left the city again on 1 September—Mommsen (1892) 245 and 298; Marcellinus Comes = Mommsen (1894) 62.

[5] Cf. *Cod Theod.* 9.2.4 for 4 February 390; Auson. 20 and 27 1.

[6] *Cod Theod.* 9.42.13 for 12 June (or 12 January; cf. Seeck (1919) 134.8 and 282.1) 393: *Drepanio comiti rerum privatarum* ('for Drepanius, a count of the private estates'); a *comes rerum privatarum* ('count of the private estates') named Drepanius was also already in office during the lifetime of Valentinian II: *Cod. Iust.*

knowing whether, as Seeck assumed, he was still alive in 397.[7] The occasion for Pacatus' speech before emperor and senate in Rome was the victory gained by Theodosius over the usurper Maximus in 388. Maximus, having been proclaimed emperor by the army in Britain at the beginning of 383, and become master of Britain, Gaul and Spain shortly after the assassination of Gratian (25 August 383), had at first been recognized, or at the very least tolerated, by Valentinian II and Theodosius.[8] [229] Theodosius did not proceed in strength against Maximus until after the latter had gone so far as to drive Valentinian from Italy in 387.[9] While it can scarcely be said that Theodosius welcomed or even favoured the revolt of Maximus, whom he probably knew, but to whom he was not, as rumour had it, related,[10] at the time the usurpation succeeded he had no resources available for a western campaign,[11] nor does it appear that he was asked for aid in the crisis, and it may be that he hoped that an arrangement could be made with Maximus the good Catholic.[12] Pacatus gives considerable space in his speech to portraying not only the struggle against

11.67.1—according to Seeck (1919) 134 to be dated between 23 February and 15 May 392. Identification of the *comes rerum privatarum* ('count of the private estates') with the panegyrist of 389 is pure speculation.

   [7] Assumed by Seeck (1883) purely on the grounds of Symmachus, *Ep.* 8.11 f; but cf. above, n. 3.

   [8] On the immediate commencement of negotiations with Maximus by Valentinian II or his advisers, cf. Ensslin (1930) 2548; Piganiol (1947) 241. Theodosius did not comply with Maximus' desire for recognition (Zos. 4.37) until, in the summer of 384 on a journey through Upper Italy, he became convinced that the situation could not for the present be altered; cf. Ensslin (1930) 2549 and (1948a) 2111; Stein (1959) 202. It is virtually impossible to determine whether Maximus was recognized formally or merely de facto.

   [9] Ensslin (1930) 2552–3.

   [10] On Maximus' appeal to kinship with Theodosius, and rumours to that effect, cf. Pacatus 24 and 31; Zos. IV 35 (cf. Ensslin (1930) 2546). Among those who speak of an understanding between Theodosius and Maximus are Seeck (1913) 168–9; Solari (1934) 165–6; Hartke (1951) 230 n. 2; Fortina (1953) 258 n. 25; but none are able to attest to it by reference to sources.

   [11] Contrary to Pacatus II(12)23.1, Theodosius led no far-flung campaigns at the time of Maximus' usurpation; but the following should be borne in mind: (1) even the *foedus* ('treaty') concluded with the Goths in Thrace in the autumn of 382 did not yet enable any troops to be withdrawn from that region; (2) the position on the eastern border was by no means resolved in early 383; (3) Theodosius may not have heard of the usurpation until it was already too late to intervene effectively (cf. Ensslin (1930) 2547); and, (4) scarcely anyone could have foreseen that Gratian's power would disintegrate so quickly.

   [12] On Maximus' Catholicism cf. Sulpicius Severus, *Chron.* 2.49–50, *Coll. Avell.* nos. 39–40 = *Günther*(1895–8) 88–91, Theodoret 5.14; cf. Ensslin (1930) 2550–2.

Maximus, but also the suffering of Gaul under his regime (chs. 23 ff.). In his attempt to explain the long hiatus between the usurpation and Theodosius' intervention, Pacatus is also not entirely uncritical.[13] In pursuing his actual main theme, praise of the emperor, Pacatus provides the outline of an ideal of the ruler. In so doing, he takes up the schema presented in the *Basilikos Logos* of the third-century rhetorician Menander,[14] along with various speeches included in the *Panegyrici Latini* corpus.[15] **[230]** Even though such commentators as Rudolf Hanslik thought Pacatus' lack of original ideas undeniable,[16] the ideal of the ruler presented by him deserves general recognition thanks to some variant insights it presents in relation to other authors.[17] Pacatus tells his audience[18] to envisage that the discussion as to who would have been capable of taking on the guidance of Rome's fate in such a critical situation as existed upon Theodosius' assumption of rule is pertinent *in quodam orbis terrarum comitio* ('in a certain meeting of the world' 3.5, cf. 3.1 ff.).[19] *nonne is omnium suffragiis hominum tributim centuriatimque legeretur, cui felix patria, cui domus clara, cui forma divina, cui aetas integra, cui militarium civiliumque rerum usus contigisset?* ('surely he would be elected by the votes of all men by tribe and century, whose home country was blessed, whose house famous, whose physique divine, in the prime of life, experienced in military and civilian matters', 3.6). The standpoint presented in this sentence defines the tenor of the rest of the speech (cf. 4.1), and conforms with Menander's guidelines.

---

[13] Cf. II(12)23.1 (and above n. 11), according to which Theodosius fought with extraordinary success in the East *c*.383 (cf. 22.2–3), and 32, where Pacatus states that the war against Maximus was as painstakingly prepared as if it had been against a really serious opponent (particularly critical is 32.1).

[14] Cf. Grinda (1916) 23; on Menander's schema, Bursian (1882), Straub (1939) 153ff; Gutzwiller (1942) 92ff.

[15] Grinda (1916); Galletier (195) 59–60; Hanslik (1942) 2059.

[16] Hanslik (1942).

[17] For the ideal of rule in Late Antiquity, cf. besides Straub (1939) especially Wickert (1954) and Rubin, (1960) 127 ff.

[18] It must be borne in mind completely that we do not have the speech given in 389 verbatim before us; but there is nothing to indicate any drastic revision.

[19] It is evident that *orbis terrarum* ('world of countries') should here be identified with *imperium Romanum* ('Roman empire'); similarly in II(12)6.4 and 20.5, and for *orbis* ('world') in 21.1. On the other hand, *orbis noster* ('our world') in 22.2 (cf. 3.5 and 14.2) is clearly not conterminous with *orbis terrarum*. Finally, in 4.3 we find Spain described as *velut alter orbis* ('like another world'), and in 39.2 *alius orbis* ('another world') in the sense of a part of the empire. Contemporaries of Pacatus used *orbis* in a similar variety of ways; cf. Vogt (1942) 200–1 (cf. also Demandt (1963) 25).

What is striking here, however, is the way Pacatus delineates the *consensus universorum* ('universal consent') which was stressed in nearly all speeches to emperors.[20] The picture of the election of the *princeps* ('emperor') begun in 3.5 is further described as an election by the people, similar to that of Republican officials. The passage viewed in isolation opens Pacatus to the accusation of making a constitutionally incorrect statement, or not even knowing that the emperor was never elected by the people.[21] Upon closer perusal, however, it becomes clear that Pacatus' statement in 3.1–2 was perhaps intentionally incorrect, in order to give his speech what I should like to call a 'Republican gloss'.[22]

In the context of the fourth chapter, concerned with the praise of Spain, Theodosius' home country,[23] Pacatus refers to the fact that, prior [231] to Theodosius, the emperors Trajan and Hadrian also came from Spain (4.5). He does not bestow either emperor with a particular epithet. The fact that no greater emphasis is given to Trajan elsewhere in the speech either is remarkable, in that the tale of Theodosius' direct descent from this emperor, who had acquired exemplary status in the fourth century more than ever before, may already have been widespread *c.*389;[24] it may perhaps be explained by the circumstance that reminiscences of earlier emperors are in any case not numerous in the speech. Central to the *domus clara* ('famous house') section is the figure of Theodosius' father, who had risen to the rank of *magister equitum praesentalis* ('master of the horse in presence') and so to the highest ranks of society.[25] Pacatus, of course, knew the value the emperor placed on honouring his father, who had

---

[20] We find a more 'usual' form of the *consensus universorum* ('universal consent', cf. Wickert (1954) 2264–9) in II(12)31.2.

[21] II(12)6; on 3.6 cf. Grinda (1916) 22.

[22] Cf. 1.4; 5.4 (see also n. 25); 7.2 ff; 9.5 ff; 20.3 ff.

[23] Cf. Grinda (1916) 23–4 and esp. Galletier (1930); the special knowledge shining through the topical conventions is perhaps based on Pacatus' own experience; on close contacts between Bordeaux and Aquitainia and Spain *c.*389 cf. e.g. Sulpicius Severus, *Chron.* 2.47 and 49, as well as Stroheker (1965) 68; Étienne (1966). *cedat . . .* ('let it give way', 5) intimates how Spain surpasses other countries; on this particular formula in panegyric literature cf. Curtius (1954²) 171.

[24] Cf. esp. [Aur. Vict.] *Epitome* 48.1; *Them. Or.* 34. 450 and contorniate coins in Rome; cf. Wickert (1954) 2153; also Alföldi (1943); Radnoti-Alföldi (1963) 68 (but cf. below n. 76).

[25] Along with other high imperial officials, military commanders belonged to the rank of *illustres* ('distinguished') from 372 at the latest (cf. *Cod. Theod.* 6.7.1, 9.1, 14.1 and 22.4 for 372).

been condemned to death by Valentinian I in the autumn of 375, probably as a victim of court intrigue.[26] He regarded the elder Theodosius as a man who, thanks to divine providence, united all the virtues (5.3), and who could have laid claim to no end of victorious epithets, if such had still been the custom at his time.[27] *o digna imperatore nobilitas eius esse filium principem, qui princeps esse debuerit*... ('o nobility worthy of an emperor, for the ruler to be the son of a man who ought to have been ruler', 6.2) exclaims the panegyrist to his audience. Lothar Wickert thinks that 'this *nobilitas* of one called to rule is 'not to be understood in the social sense'. 'Thus', [232] Wickert goes on, 'the conception that an emperor who does not have the legitimacy of dynastic descent must at least be noble in the sense of old Roman conceptions of rank, having been lost in the third century, still has not regained full validity in the fourth, either in political reality or in theory'.[28]

Contrary to Wickert's surmise, however, Pacatus by no means dismisses the emperor's *domus clara* ('famous house') with a single mention (in 3.6). He not only praises the deeds, good fortune, qualities of character and imposing physical stature of Theodosius the father (chs. 5–6), but goes on (31.1) to stress once more that Theodosius is the son of a *triumphalis vir* ('triumphal man') and heir to a *nobilissima familia* ('most noble family'). Pacatus appears indeed to understand *nobilitas* ('nobility') in an entirely social sense. Over and above what has already been mentioned, this is indicated by the comparison he makes between the Emperor's *pater divinus* ('divine

---

[26] Testimony in Ensslin (1934) 1944; cf. also the Ephesus relief in Miltner (1958) 104–5 (fig. 90) and (1959) 270–1. Although I think it possible that the sentence was not carried out until the beginning of 376, I would concur with Ensslin (1934) and Alföldi (1952) 9, that the signature on it was Valentinian's (neither Fortina (1953) 43, nor Waas (1965) 112–3 et al. has produced any convincing grounds for believing that the responsibility was Gratian's). While the thesis taken up again by Demandt (1963) 64 ff., that Ammianus' favourable picture of the elder Theodosius was influenced by political pressure on that historian, is not capable of precise confirmation, there is, however, no denying that reverence for the emperor played a role here (cf. also n. 124).

[27] 5.4; as in 3.5–6, here too Pacatus certainly knows that a *privatus* ('private individual') could not assume the title of a victor (cf. Grinda (1916) 30; Galletier (1955) 73 n. 1), but, rather than use the constitutionally correct expression, prefers to hark back to a Republican form of words. He wishes to compare Theodosius, or his father, with heroes of the past, and at the same time say that the Emperor, or his father, surpasses even those colossi.

[28] Wickert (1954) 2199 and 2200.

father') in his function of bringing up his son to be a capable soldier, and the adoptive father of the younger Africanus, as well as the fathers of Alexander and Hannibal (8.3–5). It appears to me that the reference to *nobilitas* ('nobility') in the old Roman sense then becomes manifestly clear in 9.5, where, in respect of Theodosius' enforced retirement to his Spanish estates (cf. n. 49), Pacatus affirms *sic agrestes Curii, sic veteres Coruncani, sic nomina reverenda Fabricii, cum indutiae bella suspenderant, inter aratra vivebant*... ('thus the rustic Curii and Coruncani of old and the Fabricii – names to be revered—when truces had ended war, used to live amongst their ploughs', II(12)9.5). Theodosius the emperor, who could well be conceived to have been elected after the manner of the old Roman magistrates, is from a *domus clara* ('famous house'); he belongs to the *nobilitas* ('nobility'), not only, under the theory presented by Pacatus, according to the concept of nobility prevailing at the time, but according to the conception of a *nobilis* ('noble') current in the good old days of the third and second centuries BC.

Only very briefly, and rather for form's sake, does Pacatus linger over the point of *forma divina* ('divine physique', 7.1). Of more interest, again, are his remarks concerning achievement of the principate at the right age. Having himself seen Gratian elevated to Augustus in 367 at the age of eight, Valentinian II in 375 at the age of four, and Arcadius in 383 at not yet six years old, Pacatus could not have doubted that Theodosius would likewise appoint his second son Honorius, born in 384,[29] and he was, of course, entirely aware of the difficult problem he was accosting.[30] It is therefore not surprising that he should have introduced his remarks on *aetas integra* ('the prime of life') with [233] a carefully formulated question: *an vero quicquam putamus in imperii tui declaratione praeteritum, cum ductam esse rationem ipsorum etiam videamus annorum?* ('Indeed do we think anything was passed over in your proclamation as emperor, when we

---

[29] Theodosius took the boy with him to Rome, probably in order to present him as future ruler; cf. *Cons. Const.* or *Cons. Ital.* = Mommsen (1892) 245 and 298; contrary to the account in *Chron. Pasch.*, Honorius was elevated to Augustus not in 389, but only in 393.

[30] On the problem of *principes pueri* ('boy emperors') cf. Straub (1952) 75 ff.; Wickert (1954) 2208 ff.; Ruggini (1963). In the following, the problem of criticism of the child emperors and the dating of the *Historia Augusta* is intentionally omitted, as, notwithstanding researches to date, renewed, specific investigation is probably required.

see that even the calculation of your years was taken into consideration', 7.2). Thus he does not make a display of indignation at the fact
that many rulers were not of suitable age,[31] but gives unconcealed
expression to his satisfaction that Theodosius himself conforms ideally to requirements in this respect. His justification appears typical:
cuius quidem rei tanta fuit cura maioribus ut non solum in amplissi-
mis magistratibus adipiscendis, sed in praeturis quoque aut aedilitati-
bus capessendis aetas spectata sit petitorum nec quisquam tantum
valuerit nobilitate vel gratia vel pecunia qui annos comitiali lege
praescriptos festinatis honoribus occuparit ('Our ancestors' concern
for this matter was so great that not only in securing the grandest
magistracies but also in acquiring praetorships and aedileships, the
age of the candidates was taken into account, and nobody's nobility,
favour or money was so strong that he could hold offices in advance
of the ages prescribed by electoral law', 7.2). Grinda (1916, 33) and
Galletier (1955, 74 n. 3) see here a reference to the *lex Villia annalis*.
In view of our uncertain knowledge of this law, however, it appears
preferable to believe that Pacatus was thinking not so much of a
particular law, as of the outcome of a long process of attempts to
determine the official career structure.[32]

Pacatus sees the justification of the *cura maiorum* ('ancestors'
concern') in respect of the appropriate age for office-bearers in the
fact that even men of great ability are exposed to the enticements of
youth,[33] and he then points out (7.4) that even the most famous
Romans—*Sullas, Catulos, Scipiones loquor* ('I speak of the Sullas,
Catuli, Scipiones'[34])—at times succumbed to *luxuria* ('luxury').[35]

---

[31] Cf. the overview in Wickert (1954) 2137 ff.

[32] Cf. Rögler (1962); Lippold (1963) 110–11.

[33] 7.3; on *illo tamen adulescentiae lubrico* ('but on that slippery path of youth')
Hartke (1951) 222 n. 4 refers to Ambrose, *De obitu Valentiniani* 46. Ambrose,
evidently wishing to defend Valentinian II against possible suspicions, refrains from
making direct reference to Pacatus' speech, but instead points to parallel cases where
the question of the temptations of youth was discussed at this period of very youthful
emperors. Only a few years earlier, Ambrose himself had been critical of child
emperors, expressly mentioning *adulationes atque delicias, quae teneris inolitae aeta-*
tibus vel acre ingenium enervare consuerunt ('flatteries and charms which once
implanted in tender years were used to enervate even a keen character', *Exameron*
5.68; cf. Ruggini (1963) 73–4).

[34] As, e.g. in 1.4 and 9.5, the plural is used hyperbolically, although in each case
only one bearer of the particular name may be indicated; in 7.4, Pacatus is probably
referring back to Val. Max. 6.9; cf. Grinda (1916) 34.

[35] 7.3–4 is reminiscent of Cic. *Cael.* 28; cf. Grinda (1916) 34.

Theodosius combines in one and the same person *virtus iuvenum* ('virtue of young men') and *maturitas seniorum* ('maturity of old men').[36] Finally, Pacatus thinks (7.6) that Theodosius should perhaps have taken power earlier, [234] so that he could have reigned longer; but the hope of a long life to come will remedy this defect.

Generally speaking, the unmistakable message of chapter seven is that Theodosius came to head the state at an ideal time, and that his predecessors' concern in respect of the appropriate ages for magistrates was very useful. Homage to the reigning emperor is leavened with an idealization of Republican conditions. Unlike Hartke (1951, 219), I can see in 7.6 no suggestion that Pacatus had 'something else lying prepared in his desk', that is, an address designed to be given to a very youthful Augustus, similar to Symmachus' *laudatio* to Gratian in 369 (*Oratio* 3). It is striking that Hartke does not cite the conclusion of 7.6, *parum interest quando coeperit quod terminum non habebit* ('it is of little interest when what will have no end began') where limits are imposed on the regret expressed at the beginning. All who had ears to hear it must have interpreted Pacatus' emphasis on hope for the prince's long life (surely a common component of the panegyrist's oratorical armoury), especially at this point in the speech, as an aspiration that Theodosius would go on living long enough for Valentinian, Arcadius and Honorius to reach the age necessary for them to rule on their own account. Accordingly too, Pacatus' remark, *scimus quidem nihil umquam novandum, cum Romanum imperium aut tuum futurum sit aut tuorum* ('indeed we know nothing need ever be renewed, since the Roman empire will either be yours or your family's', 45.3) does not signify a coming to terms with the rule of youthful emperors: he is affirming his belief in the enduring rule of Theodosius and his heirs. Pacatus is able with equanimity to describe the sons as the hope of the empire[37] because, in 389, he can count on 15 to 20 more years of life for Theodosius, who, as he stresses, had no connection to the imperial house when he arrived at the principate.[38]

---

[36] 7.5. In *Pan. Lat.* VII(6)13.5 it is held to be Rome's good fortune that, through the common rule of Constantine and Maximian, it can rely on *virtus iuvenis* ('a youth's virtue') and *maturitas senioris* (an older man's maturity'); cf. Grinda (1916); Hartke (1951) 149.

[37] *filii, geminae illae spes oculique rei publicae* ('sons those twin hopes and eyes of the state', 16.4).

[38] in addition: *nam et eras a familia imperatoris alienus* ('for you were even unrelated to the emperor's family', 12.1).

Pacatus states how little suited, in his opinion, a minor would be as emperor, when, in depicting the position at the beginning of 379, he has *res publica* ('the state') say: *principum senior in tanta bella non sufficit,*[39] *alter, etsi futurus sit aliquando fortissimus, adhuc tamen parvus est* ('the older prince is not up to so many wars, the other— even if one day he will be most brave—for now is still a youngster', 11.5). Although, in all this, he shows a certain reverence for Valentinianus II, who was born in 371 and was still reigning in 389, at the same time he says that a seven- to eight-year-old boy is not suitable for rule.[40] [235]

We learn in chapter eight what is required to make emperors' sons into truly capable rulers. The theme here is that, to sons they love, fathers are particularly strict, and that Theodosius is accordingly so suited to assume rule because his father took him on various campaigns, and by such hard schooling gave him the opportunity to prove his worth.[41] It must be said that, if these remarks were intended as an encouragement to Theodosius to habituate his own sons to a military life, they remained ineffective. Some ten years later, Synesius of Cyrene reminded the emperor Arcadius in strong terms, but actually in a spirit of resignation, of the soldierly merits of his father, and urged him to imitate Theodosius' glorious example.[42] Scepticism in

---

[39] A similar thought occurs in 3.5. While this does not necessarily represent a belittling of Gratian, it is striking that neither here nor in other mentions (e.g. 24.4 and 28.5) is he lavished with praise. Only in 42.3 do we find the epithet *venerabilis* ('venerable'). It is not Gratian, Theodosius' *auctor imperii* ('source of power') but Theodosius' father who is described in 16.5 as *felicitatis publicae auctor* ('the founder of public good fortune').

[40] That Valentinian, who, after all, reigned as senior Augustus in 389 (cf. Ensslin (1948b) 2225) is mentioned only here and in 3.5, and there too neither by name nor in his function as Augustus, might, on the one hand, signify a certain annoyance felt in Gaul over the fact that, as recently as early 387, Valentinian had continued to maintain good relations with Maximus (cf. Ensslin (1948b) 2222–3), and, on the other, an acknowledgement of the de facto situation in giving prominence to Theodosius as overall ruler of the empire. In any event, Pacatus' treatment of Valentinian II shows that the absence of any positive comment on Valentinian II by Ammianus tells us nothing in itself about the date of Ammianus' work (cf. however, *contra*, Hartke (1951) 72 n. 1).

[41] 8.2–5; Grinda (1916) 35–6 interprets 3–5 too one-sidedly suggesting that the emperor should be placed above heroes of the past. In my opinion, Pacatus' concern is rather to emphasize the exemplary collaboration of father and son.

[42] *Peri Basileias* 4–5. On this speech, which should be dated to *c*.399, cf. Straub (1952) 94; Lacombrade (1951). It must be said that the unreserved tone taken towards Arcadius causes Ensslin (1955) 266 to doubt whether the speech was delivered in this form. It is surely not by chance that Ammianus Marcellinus *c*.390 celebrates the

respect of the *principes pueri* ('boy emperors') may, finally, have been behind Pacatus' reminder, in a detailed section on *amicitia* ('friendship') as a virtue of rulers (16–17), that Theodosius had bestowed the highest possible honour, the consulate, on many of his friends before his sons.[43] As, apart from 389, Theodosius never had more than one consulship at his disposal, was himself consul in 380 and 389, and appointed Arcadius for 383 and Honorius for 386, the gesture towards his friends had not been quite so noble as the speaker makes out. But it was, perhaps, precisely because the role Theodosius intended for his sons was already so clearly evident, that Pacatus was less concerned with the actual state of affairs than with the opportunity presented here to show the emperor, in a flattering way, how ideal the speaker held it to be that the highest honours should be granted on account of merit and not birth.[44]

Pacatus indicates Theodosius' military prowess prior to his elevation to emperor by the campaigns upon which he accompanied his father,[45] [236] and his victorious undertakings against the Sarmatians after his appointment as *magister equitum et peditum* ('master of cavalry and infantry') in 378.[46] Theodosius shared all his soldiers' hardships, distinguished himself personally in battle, and proved himself a clever commander, thus fulfilling the ideal of *andreia* ('bravery') even before assuming power.[47] Pacatus sees Theodosius' temporary retirement into private life in 375–6, compelled by internal political enemies, as proof of the concealed nature of Fortuna's plans: in this way, he was given the opportunity to show evidence of his abilities in the civil sphere.[48] The remarks concerning the extensive rural and urban works carried out by Theodosius at that time (9.3) are not accompanied by concrete data, and show clear signs of panegyric exaggeration. In reality, the life led by Theodosius on his Spanish

---

emperor Julian for bearing everything in common with his soldiers (16.12.41; 17.1.2; 24.4.4); Ammianus (27.6.12) also has Valentinian I advising his eldest son to take all burdens upon himself (cf. Demandt (1963) 44).

[43] 16.4–5, cf. 17.2.

[44] Theodosius' regard for performance is particularly emphasized in 15.2.

[45] Ch. 8, cf. Ensslin (1934) 1938ff.; cf. n. 42 and n. 76.

[46] 10.2–3, cf. Theodoret 5. 5–6; Pacatus evidently overlooked the victory won by Theodosius over the Sarmatians as *dux Moesiae* ('general of Moesia') in 374 (see Stein (1959) I 182).

[47] On this component of Menander's schema cf. Straub (1939)155.

[48] See Ensslin (1953) 6; on *fortuna* ('good fortune') cf. n. 120.

Adolf Lippold

estates before being recalled to court in 378 may have been largely politically inactive.[49] The importance of this passage for the image of Theodosius as an ideal ruler lies mainly in the way his activities during his enforced idleness are compared with those of honourable *consulares* and *triumphatores* of ancient times, who, after their victories, returned to hard toil on the land, before being recalled from the plough to serve a consulship or dictatorate.[50] Whether Pacatus found his references to Curii, Coruncanii and Fabricii in Cicero[51], or knew them from some other source, what is important is that the panegyrist continually compares his hero with these men as figures exemplary of Rome's impecunious and unsophisticated past,[52] and that he wishes to evoke that association, so that his hearers are reminded of these people by Theodosius. It is also worthy of note that Pacatus mentions here the laying of the laurel in the lap of Jupiter, which formed part of the ceremonial of [237] the celebration on the Capitol that concluded a triumph.[53] Once Pacatus has established in such detail why the qualifications for the assumption of the principate were ideally fulfilled in Theodosius, in chapters 11 and 12 he concerns himself at some length with Theodosius' *refutatio imperii* ('refutation of power'). The panegyric appreciation of the *refutatio*, which belonged to good etiquette from time immemorial, uses the traditional phraseology that was in general use.[54]

The list of rulers' virtues mentioned in the first part of the speech is expanded many times over from chapter 12 onwards. Easy to distinguish is the way Pacatus gives particular weight to individual points. Once elevated *princeps* ('emperor') and thus become *pater* ('father')

---

[49] Cf. Grinda (1916) 37; Ensslin (1953). The extensive estate remained in the family's possession after 379; see Stroheker (1965) 73; in 72 n. 1 Stroheker refers to remains of 4th- and 5th-cent. Roman villas in Spain.

[50] As attested in *TLL* II 400, 64 ff.; on the emergence of the romanticized conception of earlier Roman history of the 1st century BC cf. also Lippold (1963) 33ff. and 89.

[51] Grinda (1916) 39.

[52] Notwithstanding the use of the plural form (cf. n. 34), only the most celebrated members of the families mentioned may be meant: M. Curius Dentatus, consul I 290; C. Fabricius Luscinus, consul I 282; Ti. Coruncanius, consul 280. On their particular mention, cf. e.g. Cic. *Cat.* 15 and 43; Val. Max. 4.3.5–6; A. Gell. 1.10.1.

[53] 9.5 cf. Ehlers (1939) 510; Grinda (1916) indicates correctly in respect of 9.6 that the *tunica palmata* ('tunics with embroidered palm-leafs') probably formed part of the official attire of consuls only from the 2nd century AD onwards; central in this context, however, is the reference to Republican manners (cf. n. 22).

[54] Cf. generally Straub (1939) 62 ff.; Béranger (1948); Wickert (1954) 2258 ff.

and *dominus* ('master'),[55] Theodosius retains the good traits he already possessed previously.[56] He remains true to the laws, and, unlike bad rulers, does not exploit the opportunity to live *legibus solutus* ('exempt from the laws').[57] The emperor does not merely eliminate vice, but also takes the trouble to remedy the faults of others (13.1). In the pursuit of his *cura* ('concern'),[58] he strives to harm no one. Rather than threatening use of the law, he seeks to achieve his purpose through example,[59] applying *censura* ('censure') first at court, and applying constraints to the luxury brought there from the East.[60] [238] He himself lives modestly, demonstrating the virtue of *parsimonia* ('thrift').[61] This is not the only part of the speech where reference is made to tolerance as a characteristic of the ideal ruler. Very important in this respect is also chapter 29, in which Pacatus speaks of Maximus' persecution of the Priscillianists in Gaul. The following brief remarks may serve to clarify how tricky a theme is being touched upon here, and why the speaker mentions neither Priscillian himself or any of his followers, nor, apart from Maximus, any of the persecutors by name. After the Priscillianists had been declared to be heretics at a synod of Spanish and Aquitanian bishops in 380, their opponents also enacted against them a rescript of the

---

[55] 11.7; 12.2; 13.3. On the use of *dominus* ('master') with reference to the emperor in a positive sense cf. Wickert (1954) 2132; Béranger (1953) 63.

[56] Cf. Plin. *Pan.* 24.2; Claudius Mamertinus III(11)27.1–3; Them. *Or.* 5.66–7. See Gutzwiller (1942) 214–5.

[57] 12.4–6; thus, as in Them. *Or.* 16.212d (from 383), the idea that the emperor stands as such above the written law.

[58] As before in 11.6 (cf. Grinda (1916) 42; Galletier (1955) 79.1), the reference here is probably to Augustus' *cura morum* ('care for morals').

[59] Cf. 13.3–4; 14.4; 15.1. A variant on this kind of praise is when Sozom. *Hist. eccl.* 7.12 remarks in respect of the emperor's religious policy that, although he promulgated laws incurring legal penalties, he did not execute such penalties, and rejoiced at voluntary conversion to the true faith.

[60] 13.2 (*censura* = 'severity in moral judgement'). Owing to the topological character of the passage, I concur with Hartke (1940) 90 n. 5 against Grinda (1916) 44 in not seeing 13.2 in connection with contemporary efforts to renew the *censura*, touched upon in a non-extant speech by Symmachus (*De censura non restituenda*—mentioned esp. in Symmachus, *Ep.* 4.29 and 5.9). Against Hartke's attempt (1940) 85 ff. to use this speech by Symmachus, together with SHA *Val.* 5.4 (according to which Valerian rejected the *censura* offered him prior to his elevation as emperor) for his dating of SHA to 394–5 (Hartke presents an unconvincing defence in (1951) 287ff.), I concur with Ensslin (1942) 256–7 (similarly Straub (1952) 100–1).

[61] 13.3–4; 14.2 and 4; 20.5—on the strong dependence of 13–4 on III(11)11, cf. Grinda (1916) 43–4 and Gutzwiller (1942) 154 ff.

emperor Gratian.[62] Both Damasus of Rome and Ambrose of Milan then rejected Priscillian's pleas for help. Condemned again in 384 at a synod at Bordeaux, thus in Pacatus's homeland, Priscillian appealed to Maximus. The trial having by now been arranged, Martin of Tours attempted to prevent it.[63] At the urging of a number of bishops, however, it took place at the end of 384/beginning of 385. Priscillian and some of his followers were condemned to death, and further excesses followed against Priscillianists. A synod at Trier in 386 approved the measures taken by the emperor,[64] and in 389 the Priscillianists, described as Manichaeans, were still held to be heretics, thus, according to Theodosius' legislation, a community banned by statute.[65] It is undeniable, at least according to the testimony of Sulpicius Severus (cf. n. 62), that the radicalization of the course embarked upon by Gratian, and, basically, only further pursued by Maximus,[66] originated from Gallic and [239] Spanish bishops, and that the majority of the Gallic episcopate in particular enjoyed a good understanding with Maximus.

As an *exemplum* ('example') of the excesses under Maximus, Pacatus chooses the proceedings against the wife of a poet,[67] accused, it seems, of *nimia religio* ('excessive religion') and *diligentius culta divinitas* ('worshipping a divinity too diligently'). At 29.3, Pacatus

---

[62] Main sources on the Priscillian struggle: Sulpicius Severus, *Chron.* 2.46 ff.; *Dial.* 2 =(3)11–2; Prosper Aquit., *Chron.* 1187 = Mommsen (1892) 462; Hydatius, *Chron.* for 385 and 387 = Mommsen (1894) 15—see Ensslin (1930) 2550–1; Caspar (1930) 217–8; *Priscillian* and *Priscillianismus* in Höfer and Rahner (1957–65); Vollmann (1965).

[63] Martin was probably above all against the intervention of the secular power; his general relationship with Maximus was, on the whole, good. Cf. Sulpicius Severus, *Vita S. Mart.* 20; *Dial.* 2(III) 11–2.

[64] *Coll. Avell.* no. 40 = Günther (1895–8) 90–1 too offers no sufficient evidence for Siricius of Rome's having protested against Priscillian's condemnation (another view is in Höfer and Rahner (1957–65).

[65] It is remarkable that, *c.*390 in Callecia (Gallaecia), Theodosius' home province, all but one of the bishops were followers of Priscillian (cf. Fliche and Martin vol. III (1947) 468). A few days after his entry into Rome (cf. n. 4), thus shortly before Pacatus delivered his speech, Theodosius had issued a severe edict against the Manicheans (*Cod. Theod.* 16.5.18 of 17 June 389 to the city prefects of Rome). Theodosius had already taken harsh measures against various communities characterized as Manichean (as well as actual Manicheans) earlier on (e.g. *Cod. Theod.* 16.5.9 for 31 March 382 and 16.5.11 for 25 July 383).

[66] Neither does Maximus appear to have been the first to appreciate the possibility of enhancing state finances by confiscating the goods of many followers of Priscillian.

[67] Euchrotia, the wife or widow of Attius Tiro Delphidius; Sulpicius Severus, *Chron.* 48.2–3; 51.3; Prosper Aquit. *Chron.* 1187.

speaks of *accusator sacerdos* ('an accuser—a priest'), and *hoc dela-
torum genus qui nominibus antistes re vera autem satellites atque adeo
carnifices* ('this type of informer, who were priests by name, but in
reality henchmen and executioners'), addressing his strictures in all
severity against the clergy too, although for him, of course, Maximus
is the main culprit.[68] Nothing, finally, could be clearer than his
remark: *hos*—'those cruel tormentors'—*ille Falaris in amicis habebat,
hi in oculis eius atque in osculis erant* ('that Phalaris had among his
friends, these were the apple of his eye, his bosom friends', 29.4).[69]
Galletier (1955, 58) is right to stress that Pacatus' standpoint is one of
tolerance and humanity in respect of the proceedings against the
Priscillianists. I would add, in amplification of Galletier, that in
denouncing the tyrant's intolerance, Pacatus is exhorting the emperor
to be tolerant, and declaring this trait to be a component of the ideal
of the ruler.[70]

   A particular aspect of Theodosius' renown, according to Pacatus, is
that he has made *amicitia* ('friendship') up to now not fully appre-
ciated as a virtue worthy of a ruler, so to speak court-capable, and is
himself a living exemplar of it (16–17). The emperor, who lives such a
disciplined life and has such an extraordinary esteem for friendship,
often shows himself in public, and is easily accessible.[71] To the fore
among the virtues extolled by Pacatus, besides *clementia* ('clemency')
which he stresses particularly in respect of the victory over Maximus,[72] **[240]** are *fortitudo* ('bravery'), *humanitas* ('humanity'), and

---

[68] The highly respected men who died under Maximus according to 25.1 may also
have been prominent Priscillianists.

[69] 29.4; parallels for the mention of Phalaris as *exemplum crudelitatis* ('example
of cruelty') in Late Antiquity include *SHA, Max.* 8.5 and Claudian, *Carm.* 3.253
(= *in Rufinum* I); further references in Lenschau (1937) 1651.

[70] Cf. also 36.3, according to which Theodosius treated Maximus' soldiers *liber-
aliter* ('generously'). In 389 it could still be hoped that Theodosius would be amenable
to such exhortations.

[71] 21.2–3; the emperor's affability is also stressed in 17.4 and 47.3 (cf. Them. *Or.*
15.190; Zos. 4.27–8; Anon. *Epit. De Caes.* 48.9). Such a demeanour may have been
possible with the army, and also occasionally elsewhere; but, when Theodosius was
residing in Constantinople, Thessalonica or Milan, he may have lived in the kind of
seclusion, regulated by tight ceremonial, that had long been normal for emperors (cf.
n. 81).

[72] Cf. 31.3; 43.4; 44.2–3; 45.4. In contrast, in ch. 46 Pacatus remembers the terrors
of the civil wars of the last decades of the Republic. When the circumstances were not
familiar to him, he could find material in Val. Max., or inspiration in the anonymous
panegyric to Constantine the Great (*Pan. Lat.* XII(9)20.3); for there too it is shown
that the civil war of the emperor to be lauded should be assessed quite differently from

sapientia ('wisdom') or *prudentia* ('prudence').[73] Among those that he leaves unmentioned—and this appears to me characteristic of Pacatus' religious attitude—is *humilitas* ('humility') which is given such prominence by Ambrose.[74] The panegyrist then further highlights Theodosius' qualities by repeatedly referring to the vices of Maximus and of bad rulers in general. *crudelitas* ('cruelty'), *libido* ('lust'), and *cupiditas* ('desire') are the main targets for his censure.[75]

In the context of a fictional speech by a personified Res Publica ('State') on the subject of Theodosius' *refutatio imperii* ('refutation of power'), Pacatus presents a 'catalogue' of good rulers: *quod cum me Nerva tranquillus, amor generis humani Titus, pietate memorabilis Antoninus teneret, cum moribus Augustus ornaret, legibus Hadrianus imbueret, finibus Traianus augeret, parum mihi videbar beata quia non eram tua?* ('because when gentle Nerva, the love of the human race, [and] Antoninus, memorable for his piety, held me, when Augustus decorated me with customs, Hadrian imbued me with laws, Trajan extended my borders, did I seem to myself too little blessed because I was not yours?', 11.6).[76] Apart from this meagre

earlier civil wars, owing to the victor's behaviour (cf. Grinda (1916) 76–7; Ensslin (1942) 264). It should be noted that Pacatus includes Caesar in his critique (1), and remembers the great victims (Cicero, Cato, Pompey) of that age of terror. As Ensslin (1942) correctly stresses, 46 shows in any event that Theodosius heard of comparisons with the victors of other civil wars on at least one occasion (cf. also [Aur. Vict.], *Epit.* 48.12, which relates how Theodosius often displayed his outrage over Cinna, Marius and Sulla, and August. *Civ. Dei.* 5.26, where Cinna, Marius and Sulla too are contrasted with the mild Theodosius), and, against Hartke (1940) 156, (1951) 52, Theodosius did not need the accounts of emperors' mildness towards the sons and followers of usurpers in the *Historia Augusta* to be moved to similar behaviour towards the followers of Eugenius in 394. *clementia* ('clemency') which, from all evidence, was actually displayed by Theodosius, and for which he was universally celebrated (see Lippold (1973)), was indeed one of the most important components of the ideal of the ruler in the Imperial period (cf. Wickert (1954))!

[73] Cf. 6.2; 7.1; 15.3; 16.5; 18.3; 20.2 and 5–6; 22.1; 40.3; 45.4.

[74] Ambrose *De obitu Theodosii* 12; 28; 34; cf. August. *Civ. Dei.* 5.26; Theodoret, *Hist. eccl.* 5.18.

[75] 12.4; 14.1; 20.3–5; 24.6; 29.3; 31.3.

[76] Radnoti-Alföldi (1963) fundamentally misunderstands the passage when she writes 'Pacatus becomes impolite to the point of antagonism against his emperor, for Theodosius does not shine with military virtues. The complaining Dea Roma herself contrasts him with Trajan in his guise as enlarger of the empire'. But Pacatus does not have Res Publica (not Dea Roma!) complain that Theodosius has in some way failed in his external policy: he has her give expression to her sorrow at Theodosius' hesitation in taking up the reins of power. Reference to chapters 8 and 22–3 should suffice here to demonstrate that it is precisely in Pacatus' speech that Theodosius'

praise, Pacatus' remarks about earlier emperors are, in accordance with panegyric tradition, and perhaps also with the thinking of contemporary aristocratic [241] circles,[77] almost without exception critical[78] and anonymous.[79] It may be seen as natural that Pacatus should begin his criticism of earlier emperors where the main foci of his praise for his own master lie. Thus, in connection with Theodosius' 'election', he complains that many a pretender has bought the legions in order to win the throne (12.1). With praise for Theodosius' economical housekeeping is linked blame that luxury has penetrated from the East through the foibles of some of his predecessors (13.2), that the means to pay for lavish banqueting have often been extorted from the provinces, and that individual courses of such meals— *cuiusdam retro principis* ('some emperor of old', 14.3)—have cost 100 million sesterces.[80] Despite the assurance *quos loquar notum est* ('it is known of whom I speak', 21.3), we no longer have any way of knowing which *principes* ('emperors') they were who, unlike Theodosius, remained shut up and inaccessible in their palaces.[81] A further criticism Pacatus makes is that none before Theodosius counted friendship among the highest virtues of rulers, and that *humanitas* ('humanity') was so seldom shown by emperors before this time.[82]

military prowess (which I see no convincing reason to doubt) is emphasized, and no question left as to his ability to protect and even expand the empire. On Titus cf. e.g. Suet. *Tit.* 1; Aur. Vict. 10.6; on Nerva, Martial *Epig.* 5.28 and 8.70.

[77] Apart from Pliny's panegyric, none of the other speeches included in the *Panegyrici Latini* collection mentions Titus, Trajan and Hadrian. Demandt (1963) 135 points out that, unlike Ammianus, authors close to the Roman senate, such as Symmachus, Claudian and Rutilius Namatianus, produce either no examples at all or scarcely any worthy of celebration from the history of the Imperial period.

[78] Exceptions are 4.5; 27.4 and 33.3.

[79] 16.1, where, among other things, it is stated *optimus ille ditabat, non etiam diligebat* ('the best of emperors gave away his money, but not his love'), also belongs to this category, for, even if the passage can be related to Trajan, who, admittedly, did receive the epithet *Optimus*, his actual name is not mentioned. Of Theodosius' coregents, only Arcadius is mentioned (11.4): on Valentinian cf. n. 40.

[80] Examples of emperors in respect of whom similarly high expenditure on feasting is reported are Caligula (Sen. *Helv.* 10.4), Vitellius (Suet. *Vit.* 13) and Heliogabalus (*SHA* v. *Heliogab.* 17); there seems no way of telling which emperor Pacatus was thinking of here.

[81] The isolation of the emperor from his subjects, which had been normal from the early Imperial period, and become ever stronger, was a matter of course in the second half of the fourth cent.; cf. e.g. Them. *Or.* 1. 2; 11. 170 and Synesius, *Peri Basileias* 16 (further references in Alföldi (1934) 101 ff.; Gutzwiller (1942) [cf. n. 14] 260).

[82] 16.1 and 20.2; indirect criticism too in 22.3.

Perusal of Pacatus' assessment of earlier emperors reveals that it is primarily to personalities and institutions of Rome's Republican age that the panegyrist looks to draw his picture of the ideal ruler. Pacatus sees *Catones et Tullos et Hortensios omnesque illos oratores* ('Catos and Ciceros and Hortensiuses and all those orators', 1.4) as his own great models,[83] and, besides the strictures already mentioned, goes on to remark that Theodosius prepared for the war against Maximus[84] **[242]** with similar care to that devoted in former times to the wars against Pyrrhus, Hannibal and Perseus,[85] and that, in the very force of memory he displayed in that endeavour, he towered above such men as Hortensius, Lucullus and Caesar.[86] Finally, chapter 20.3 ff. is also significant in this connection. Here, Pacatus speaks of the ancestors, who, because *superbia* ('arrogance') and the other associated vices of King Tarquinius were even less bearable to them than *servitus* ('slavery'), were eventually compelled *post bellatores Tullos Numasque sacrificos et Romulos conditores regnum usque ad nomen odisse* ('after the Tulluses the warriors, and the sacrificing Numas, and the Romuluses the founders, to hate monarchy even to its name', 20.3). If Brutus, *illae Romanae libertatis adsertor, regii nominis... osor* ('champion of that Roman liberty, hater of the name of king', 20.5), had known the age of Theodosius, he would have seen that *dignitas* ('dignity') and *libertas Romana* ('Roman freedom') were more in evidence under this emperor than under himself as consul, and he would have been for the removal only of Tarquinius, not of the *regnum* ('monarchy'). Cicero[87] himself talks of its not being the monarchy itself but the depravity of its incumbents that led to its rejection, and positive use of *regnum* ('monarchy') is then entirely

---

[83] cf. n. 34.

[84] His elevation is compared in 23.1–2 with slave uprisings during the final century of the Republic. Referring to Florus 2.7.9, 8.3 and 12, Grinda (1916) 54 remarks correctly that Pacatus refers to the slave uprising that broke out in Sicily in 104 and the revolt of Spartacus. On the equation Theodosius = master, Maximus = slave, cf. esp. 30.5 and 31.1.

[85] 32.1; cf. n. 13.

[86] 18.3; Hortensius and Lucullus are not otherwise mentioned at all in *Pan. Lat.*; Caesar is mentioned occasionally, but not for his good memory.

[87] Grinda (1916) 49–50 refers to Cic. *Leg.* 3.7.15 and *Rep.* 2.30.52. On Cicero's contradictory attitude to the monarchy, and his dependence on the particular context when taking up a position, cf. Klein (1962), esp. 81–3 on Tarquinius Superbus. Classen (1965) has reiterated that positions were rarely taken up in the Republic against the monarchy as such, but frequently against Tarquinius Superbus.

usual from the early Imperial period onwards.[88] The thought that Brutus would have lived happily under the ruling *princeps* ('emperor') of the time also occurs long before Pacatus.[89] It is, however, noteworthy and at the same time typical that, for Pacatus, Theodosius' rule is now not only the equal of the good monarchy embodied by Romulus, Numa, and Tullus: the panegyrist represents the *regnum* ('kingdom') of Theodosius as being more or less imbued with Republican elements, here emphasizing that the emperor lives in public and in private *consulum moderatione, petitorum comitate* ('with consuls' moderation and candidates' friendliness', 20.5).[90] [243]

Theodosius' rule brings *felicitas* ('good luck'),[91] *securitas* ('security'), and *libertas* ('freedom').[92] That the freedom achieved for the entire empire by the defeat of Maximus is, of course, not freedom in the Republican sense, that what is meant is only freedom from tyrannical rule, is shown by the fact that, for Pacatus as for his contemporaries in general, the *princeps* ('emperor')[93] is also *dominus* ('master', cf. n. 55), into whose *servitus* ('slavery') one even enters voluntarily.[94] The empire[95] is secure thanks to the emperor's victories

---

[88] Instances in Wickert (1954) 2111 ff.; complemented by Suerbaum (1961) 284 ff. (also 216 ff. and 238 ff.). *regnum* ('monarchy') also occurs in a sense similar to 20.6 in 12.2 and 12.4; against Wickert (1954) 2126, it appears to me that there is no suggestion of an unfavourable use of the word *rex* ('king') here, for the target of 12.4 is not *regna*, but those who, unlike Theodosius, who has now become *invitus princeps* ('an unwilling emperor', cf. 12.1), *avide regna desiderent* ('let them covet kingdoms'). Pacatus is, on the whole, very restrained in his use of *regna, rex* and similar terms.

[89] Cf. e.g. Martial 11.5.9 ff: Claudian *Carm.* 17.163–5 does not depend on Pacatus (as, notwithstanding, intimated in Grinda (1916) 50 and Galletier (1955) 87 n. 3), but on Martial. In Martial and Claudian, the message is not associated with Brutus' having been *Romanae libertatis adsertor* ('champion of Roman liberty').

[90] Of further interest is that *Numa sacrificus* ('Numa sacrificing') is mentioned among the good kings, and, according to 20.5, the exemplary traits of Theodosius included living *castitate pontificum* ('with the chasteness of chief-priests'): from the context, this cannot refer to any Christian priests (cf. on Pacatus' religion).

[91] Cf. 1.2; 3.1; 16.5; 19.3.

[92] Cf. 1.2; 2.2–4; 19.3; 20.6; 33.5; 45.1 and 3; 46.4. On the link between *securitas* ('security') and *libertas* ('liberty') in the Imperial period cf. Wickert (1954) 1096–7; Walser (1955) 364–6.

[93] After *imperator* ('emperor') as chosen form of address (19 times; and three times *imperator Auguste* ('emperor Augustus')), *princeps* ('prince') is the term Pacatus uses most frequently for the ruler (c.20 times). On the use of *imperator* as a form of address to emperors being celebrated in the *Panegyrici Latini*, cf. Schaefer (1914) 81–6.

[94] 37.4; cf. also 20.3, where, for the ancestors, *servitus* ('slavery') is said to have been easier to bear than *superbia* ('arrogance').

[95] The empire is referred to most frequently—c.15 times—as *res publica*; cf. n. 19 on *orbis* ('earth') and n. 88 on *regnum* ('kingdom').

over its enemies in the East, and over the barbarians in the lower Danube (22–3). Pacatus' formulations are those that had been in normal use for centuries to express Rome's victorious prowess against the barbarians.[96] Thanks, however, to the high proportion of barbarians in the army that was victorious in the struggle against Maximus, the triumph over the barbarians celebrated only in 386 in Constantinople,[97] and the freedom from external attack enjoyed in the West too *c.*389, Pacatus' audience may not have perceived it only as extravagant praise, all too familiar to their ears, or propaganda inspired from on high,[98] when he said that the barbarians, when they were not serving in the army or cultivating Roman fields, were now fully dependent on Rome.[99] Like Themistius in his favourable assessment of the treaty with the Goths in 382, Pacatus personally may not have been motivated merely by panegyric intent, but also by genuine hope.[100] [244]

So far, our interpretation of the ideal of monarchy sketched by Pacatus has no more than touched upon one substantial aspect, that of religion. As we now pursue the question of the way in which the panegyrist's portrayal endows the emperor with such outstanding traits, lifting him above the level of ordinary mortals, we will at the same time also turn our attention to the question of Pacatus' own religion. The fact that various answers have been mooted[101] is a result of the intellectual and politico-religious situation at the end of the fourth century, a period in which so many people were uncertain in their religious conceptions, and often motivated by opportunistic considerations. The same situation has given rise to differences of

[96] Cf. e.g. Hartke (1940) 82 ff.

[97] *Chron. Const.* for 386 = Mommsen (1892) 245; Marcellinus Comes = Mommsen (1894) 62; see Kollwitz (1941) 64; Velkov (1961) 60.

[98] In this connection, cf. in the imagery and legends on Theodosius' coinage, which was subject to little change over his reign (cf. *RIC* 9. 39), the legend VIRTUS EXERCITI ('virtue of the army', [*sic*!]; also in the West the legend VIRTUS EXERCITUS, 'virtue of the army', of earlier vintage), in combination with the image of a standing emperor, holding in his hands the *labarum* ('standard') and *globus* ('globe'), his left foot resting on a captive (e.g. 197.24; 233.83; 243.25).

[99] 22.3–4; 32.3–5; 33.

[100] *Them. Or.* 18.222a; on the treaty of 382 with the Goths see Stein (1959) I 194; Lippold (1973).

[101] Among those who describe him as a pagan are Güldenpenning in Güldenpenning and Ifland (1878) 17; Seeck (1913) 227 with reference to 3.2; 4.2; 10.1 and 21.1; Stein (1959) 530; as a Christian, if only in a purely formal sense, and opportunistically motivated: Grinda (1916) 50.

opinion in respect of the religious beliefs of such figures as the usurper Eugenius and the poet Claudian. They, too, may, on the basis of formal arguments, be characterized as Christians, although, as determined on the basis of their deeds or writings, their associations with Christianity are non-existent or at most lukewarm.[102]

In 4.5, Pacatus apostrophizes the emperor Theodosius with the phrase *deum dedit Hispania quem videmus* ('Spain gave us a god we look upon'). Now, it is true that, up to the summer of 389, the emperor had not yet undertaken any particularly severe measures against non-Christians, and had, indeed, entrusted many such with high office or leading military roles, but he may already have been regarded as *imperator christianissimus* ('most Christian emperor'). On the basis of the titles of other emperors of the fourth century, Grinda (1916, 27) opines: 'Here again, it is not possible to arrive at any conclusion as to Pacatus' religious stance'. Pichon (1906a, 148 n. 3), rightly describes Pacatus' apostrophe as a 'simple formula of official politeness'. No more does Grinda allow himself to be shaken from his conception of Pacatus as a Christian by the passage 6.3–4, referring to the emperor's divinity, or, for example, by *sed cum.....* *ad contuendum te (sc. principem) adorandumque properassem* ('when I had rushed to see and adore you (emperor)', 2.1), or by the clear distancing of the emperor from other men in 10.1.[103] In the later fourth century, in fact, [245] *adoratio* ('adoration') of Christian emperors became possible without reservation even for Christians. The forms of reverence for the Christian emperor by God's grace and for the divine emperor were very similar, and Theodosius himself placed much value on such reverence for his person and his house, or at the very least for the imperial monarchy in general.[104]

---

[102] In the case of Claudian, the short poem *de Salvatore* (*Carm. min.* 32), if by him, may be seen as evidence of nominal Christianity (thus Schmid (1957) 162–3); but, on the basis of the spirit of most of his works, Claudian should rather be characterized, with Orosius (*Adv. Pag.* VII 35.21) as *paganus pervicacissimus* ('most stubborn pagan') or, with Augustine (*Civ. Dei.* 5.26), as *a Christi nomine alienus* ('a foreigner to the name of Christ'). On Eugenius cf. Straub (1966).

[103] Galletier (1955) 50–1 cites 6.4 in particular against Pichon as evidence that Pacatus still truly adhered to the ruler-cult. Pichon's interpretation of 4.5 is shared by Burdeau (1964), 16–7: although Burdeau has then (17 n. 3) to give a highly ingenious interpretation of 6.3–4, in order to deny that cult reverence of the emperor is at least discernible in Pacatus.

[104] Cf. Ensslin (1943) esp. 68–9 and 75.

If, however, that very phrase cited above from 4.5 is placed in its textual context, and if closer attention is given to 6.3–4, it becomes evident that reverence for the emperor, irrespective of its common basis, could be given various forms of expression according to the subject's own religious conception. At the end of his eulogy to Spain, Pacatus says: *cedat his terris terra Cretensis parvi Iovis gloriata cunabulis et geminis Delos reptata numinibus et alumno Hercule nobiles Thebae. fidem constare nescimus auditis: deum dedit Hispania quem videmus* ('Let the land of Crete give way to the land [of Spain], glorious for the cradle of Jupiter, and Delos, crawled upon by the twin godheads, and Thebes, noble for its pupil, Hercules. We do not know to put our trust in hearsay: Spain has given us a god to look at', 4.5). Pacatus' gist here seems to be that only in the case of Spain can it be said with certainty that it is the home of a god, whereas no such certainty is possible in the cases of Crete, Delos and Thebes. In any event, I can see no grounds for assuming that the speaker also wishes to cast doubt on the existence of Jupiter, Apollo, Artemis and Hercules. The cult of Hercules, regarded as the model of the ideal ruler, was still alive *c*.390;[105] in 394, it is likely that portraits of Hercules adorned the standards of Eugenius' army, and a statue of Jupiter is supposed to have been erected behind the lines of the Eugenians:[106] so there is a possibility that the divinities in 4.5 were not purely by chance.[107] Just like Jupiter and Hercules, such divinities as Victoria and the Dioscuri are entirely real phenomena for Pacatus. This emerges from remarks in 39.1 and 39.4, where we hear that painters and poets were right to represent Victoria with wings,[108] and that, just as the Dioscuri (Castores) once brought news of the victory

---

[105] Cf. Derichs (1950) 115–6; Bloch (1945) 201 ff.

[106] Cf. Theodoret 5.26 (see Straub (1966) 870) and August. *Civ. Dei.* 5.26.

[107] Hercules figures frequently on the contorniates minted in the latter part of the fourth cent. in Rome, as do, if more rarely, Jupiter, the Dioscuri, Apollo, and (more often on coins originating, according to Alföldi, between 395 and 410) Victoria (cf. Alföldi (1943)). Feasts of Jupiter, Apollo, Diana, Castor/Pollux, and Hercules are still listed in the calendar for 354 CE (Philocalus). For the enduring importance of Apollo in the second half of the fourth cent., one need only consider the bases of statues of Valentinian I and Valens at Delphi (see Vatin (1962) 238–9). On Jupiter, Hercules, and Apollo in the *Panegyrici*, cf. Burdeau (1964) 13–4.

[108] Against Grinda (1916) 70, I do not have the temerity to decide whether this is a reference to the image of Victoria removed from the Curia on the orders of Gratian.

over Perseus [246] to Rome with incredible speed,[109] now in the case
of the battle against Maximus an 'immortal divinity' (*immortalis
deus*) expedited the march of Theodosius.[110]

According to 22.5, the Persian king had Theodosius worshipped in
the temples in which he himself was worshipped, and the inclusion of
the Roman emperor in a non-Christian pantheon is, so to speak,
further underlined by 6.3–4 and some other passages. In 6.3, in the
context of a brief meditation where he seeks support from the panegyric of 310, or from his own knowledge of the ideas of Plotinus, who
was so influential in the fourth century, Pacatus refers to explanations
of the way divine attributes can pass to humans,[111] but then he
remarks: *tibi istud soli pateat, imperator, cum deo consorte secretum.*
illud dicam quod intellixisse hominem et dixisse fas est: talem esse
debere qui gentibus adoratur, cui toto orbe terrarum privata vel pub-
lica vota redduntur, a quo petit navigaturus serenum, peregrinaturus
reditum, pugnaturus auspicium ('Let that secret be disclosed to you
alone, emperor, with the god who is your consort. I shall say what it is
right for man to understand and say: that such he ought to be who is
adored by peoples, to whom private and public prayers are given
throughout the whole world, from whom calm weather is sought by
the man about to sail, a homecoming by the man about to travel, a
good omen by the man about to fight', 6.4). Galletier (1955, 51) is in
my opinion correct in thinking this definition of imperial divinity
incompatible with even a decidedly tepid Christianity. It is remarkable that Grinda (1916, 31), in respect of *deus consors* ('the god who is
your consort') does not immediately cite 18.4, where Pacatus, in
praising the emperor's remarkable memory, interpolates the question: *utrum tamen ipse te admones an, ut illi maiestatis tuae participi*
deo feruntur adsistere fata cum tabulis, sic tibi aliqua vis divina
subservit, quae quod dixeris scribat et suggerrat? ('But do you remind
yourself or, just as the Fates are said to sit at their writing tablets with
that god who shares in your majesty, thus does some divine force
serve you, writing down and noting what you have said?'). Just as, in

---

[109] Pacatus may here be referring to Val. Max. 1.8.1 or Florus 1.28.14f, cf. Grinda
(1916) 71; on the currency of the representation of the Dioscuri as messengers of
victory c.390 cf. Amm. Marc. 28.4.11.

[110] As *Castores* agrees with *immortalis deus* ('immortal god'), *immortalis deus*,
contrary to Galletier (1955), is not to be translated as '*the* immortal God' (or 'the
Godhead'); the conception of divine aid is further elaborated in 5.

[111] VI(7)17.3, cf. Grinda (1916) 31; Galletier (1955) 78.

6.3, a god is *consors* ('consort') of the emperor, so in 18.4 one is the emperor's *particeps* ('partner'). Here, in so many words, it is proposed that there is a god who partakes in the emperor's majesty: a blasphemy, even for a merely formal Christian.[112] According to Pacatus, this participating divinity is attended by *fata cum tabulis* ('the Fates at their writing tablets'). The way Pacatus describes their function, these *fata* ('Fates') are unlikely to be the same as those mentioned only in Tertullian *De anima*. 39.2, which were appealed to on the last day of a child's first week of life. It can also not be established whether the writing divinities represented on Etruscan sarcophagi are a parallel phenomenon.[113] Of central import in this context is the fact that Pacatus knows a tradition that ascribed the *fata cum tabulis* ('Fates at their tables') a [247] particular function, and that he offers a concept that is not foreign to the Roman/pagan religion.[114]

It would also be wrong to associate any specific statement as to Pacatus' religious beliefs with *privata vel publica vota reddentur* ('to whom private and public prayers are given') and *auspicium* ('good omen') in 6.4, viewed in isolation. Christian emperors, too, tolerated *privata vel publica vota* ('private and public prayers') and *auspicium* ('good omen') here needs mean nothing more than 'success'.[115] We should, however, remember that an attentive listener would still have fresh in his mind not only 4.5 but also the beginning of 3: *det igitur mihi sermonis huius auspicium ille felicitatis publicae auspex dies qui te primus inauguravit imperio* ('Therefore, let that auspicious day of public happiness which first inaugurated your rule grant me an omen for this speech'). Admittedly, this may again, echoing Grinda (1916, 21), be characterized as a set formula used by panegyrists; but in none of the parallels that can be cited[116] is the reference to *augurium/ auspicium* ('beginning/omen') so sustained. The impression that, in 3.1, Pacatus is perhaps nevertheless inspired by his circle of non-Christian acquaintanceship in the city of Rome is reinforced by further reading of the third chapter. Little as 3.1 and 3.2 alone reveal

---

[112] On 6.3 and 18.4 cf. also 19.2, which tells of the emperor's being *conscius caelestis arcani et naturalium depositorum* ('aware of the heavenly mystery and natural secrets').

[113] The only reference for *fatum* 'fate' here is Eisenhut (1967).

[114] Further instances of *fatum* 'fate' in Pacatus are 3.5; 11.4; 15.3; 24.1 and 27.3; but these passages allow of no conclusion as to Pacatus' religious orientation.

[115] Straub's translation (German: *Erfolg*) in (1939) 157.

[116] VI(7)2.3; VIII(4)2.2; IX(5)2.2.

about Pacatus' religious sense, seen in combination they permit the conclusion that, like such passages as 4.5 and 6.3–4, they are spoken by a man who, at the very least, has not yet become accustomed to a Christian mode of expression.[117]

When Pacatus speaks in 4.2 of the *supremus ille rerum fabricator* ('that supreme creator of things'), and in 21.1 of the *summum numen* ('the highest godhead'), these expressions permit of an *interpretatio Christiana* ('Christian interpretation')[118] but *summum numen* ('the highest godhead') in 21.1 can very well also mean the emperor, or the supreme divinity apart from whom other gods also exist.[119] *fortuna* ('good luck') plays an [248] extraordinary role in Pacatus. An extensive discussion (40–42) is devoted to the contribution made by *fortuna* to the emperor's victory. According to Pacatus, *fortuna* was needed in order to give full effect to Theodosius' victories on the battlefield, and bring about the enemy's downfall. Here and in other places,[120] on the one hand *fortuna* is no more than fate, but, on the other, one has the impression that, for Pacatus, it or she is a force like Tyche, something in which one believes, for which one hopes, which

---

[117] Of a 'pagan' flavour are e.g. also 9.5; *aliquod Vestale secretum* ('some Vestal secret', 21.3); *tandem in nos* (i.e. the West) *oculos deus* (here neither clearly pagan nor Christian) *retulit et bonis orientis intentus ad mala nostra respexit et hunc sacerrimo capiti obiecit furorem ut foedus abrumpere, ius fetiale violare, bellum edicere non timeret* ('finally god turned his eyes towards us, and intent on the prosperity of the East, he looked back to our evils and inspired this madness in the most cursed head that he did not fear to break treaties, violate fetial law and declare war', 30.1). Striking here is, on the one hand, that Pacatus speaks without qualification of a *foedus* ('treaty') between the emperors and Maximus, and, on the other (at the same time illustrating his 'antiquating' tendency), that he accuses Maximus of having infringed against the *ius fetiale* 'fetial law' (*fetiales*, of whom the emperor was always one, existed into the Severan period; cf. Latte (1960) 124 n. 1); 37.4.

[118] Cf. also *deus* ('god', 30.1) (see n. 112). In 21.2, Pacatus uses *numen* ('godhead') to characterize the emperor, a usage that also occurs not only in Symmachus, but also in laws of Theodosius (*Cod. Iust.* 12.50.9 for 383; see Ensslin (1943) 76). In 30.2, it is as if the *res publica* ('state') manifests itself as *numen divinum* ('divine godhead').

[119] Pacatus speaks of the necessity, when visiting great cities, of first viewing *sacras aedes et dicata numini summo delubra* ('sacred temples and shrines dedicated to the supreme divinity', 21.1). Now, a possible meaning of *aedes sacra* ('sacred temple') is 'church'; although, however, we have no evidence (cf. *TLL s.v. delubrum*) for *delubrum* = 'church', we have ample evidence for *delubrum* = 'site of the imperial cult' (e.g. Plin. *NH* 35.91; Tac. *Ann.* 4.37).

[120] 9.1; 15.3; 16.2; 23.2. On *fortuna/Fortuna* in Pacatus, cf. the important role played by Tyche for Libanius, according to his autobiography first published in 374, but much revised between 380 and 392 (*Or.* 1; see Festugière (1965) 626–8); on *fortuna* in the fourth cent. see also Burdeau (1964) 12–3.

one fears. In this prominence given to *fortuna/Fortuna* perhaps lies the panegyrist's true confession. To sum up, we may say that Pacatus believes in the divinity of the emperor, and that he speaks about it in a way that would seem alien to a Christian. He does not expressly doubt the existence of the old gods, but, as was true for most of his 'pagan' contemporaries, a real, intimate relationship to those gods is no longer detectable. According to the testimony of his speech, Pacatus is not a convinced believer in any cult save veneration of the emperor. He believes in the power of Fortuna, and he expects tolerance from Theodosius, the *princeps* ('emperor') who guarantees the well-being and security of the *res publica* ('state').

Just as we saw Pacatus' ideal of the ruler characterized by reminiscences of Roman tradition, so the non-Christian tone of his characterization of the superhuman status of the emperor is also engendered by a consciousness of tradition. Alongside such thinking, which perhaps resulted from a genuine interest in history, Pacatus expresses the conviction that his own time will remain alive in the memory of posterity.[121] He is confident that his speech will have a strong influence on future accounts of the events he is depicting (47.6). Consciousness of Rome's past, discernible as a tendency in Pacatus, was evident in many of his contemporaries, whether they were now convinced Christians,[122] remained true to the tenets of 'pagan' religions,[123] or were indifferent in respect of religion; [249] they did not, however, always combine the trait with the optimistic view of the present that comes naturally to a panegyrist. The tradition regarding the historical interests of the emperor Theodosius fits well with the

---

[121] Cf. 12.3; 44.4–6; 45.1. When, in 44.4–5, Pacatus advises the *pii vates* ('pious poets') to leave aside well-worn themes (such as the deeds of Hercules, Liber's Indian triumphs, and battles between giants), and to write about present-day events, going on to say ... *his fora, his templa decorentur* ... (' ... let fora, let temples, be decorated with these ... '), we are entitled to ask those who doubt Pacatus' paganism whether they know of triumphal paintings in fourth-century churches.

[122] These should include, to judge by their careers, such figures as Augustine, Orosius, and Prudentius, besides Ambrose and others.

[123] The remarks of Paschoud (1965) 215 ff., although they certainly oversimplify the issues, and in part are too much concerned with formalities, are to my mind timely in warning against a view that gives too much emphasis to genuinely religious motivations in the spiritual attitude of Symmachus and his pagan friends. Also bound up in the pagan tradition was Naucellius (lit. in Mariotti (1962) 411–5), a writer in the classical style who was acquainted with Symmachus, and has become better known only in recent times.

zeitgeist discernible here.[124] Theodosius was evidently favourably disposed to historical studies. He had a high regard for Virius Nicomachus Flavianus, who, although his adversary, dedicated his *Annales* to the emperor;[125] Ammianus Marcellinus produced his historical work during Theodosius' reign,[126] and Vegetius was perhaps inspired by him[127] to write his memoir of Rome's glorious past, the *Epitoma rei militaris*.[128] Pacatus showed fitting reverence not only to the emperor, but also to the senate and the city of Rome,[129] and could assume that his audience enjoyed some familiarity with examples from history.[130] [250] It is precisely in the ideal of the ruler

---

[124] [Aur. Vict.] *Epit.* 48.11–2. If, previously in 48.9, the writer has remarked of Theodosius *simplicia ingenia aeque diligere, erudita mirari, sed innoxia* ('he loved simple intellects equally, admired the educated if harmless'), it is scarcely possible, with Thompson (1947) 110, to extrapolate from this a suggestion that Theodosius took particular care to see that writers adjusted their politics to his liking. Thompson requires his interpretation to support the thesis that Ammianus' positive picture of Theodosius' father should be attributed to pressure from the emperor (cf. above n. 26). An interest in history on Theodosius' part is given further support by Them. *Or.* 17.215a, and the emperor's speech in Claudian, *Carm.* 8 (*De IV cons. Hon.*) 396ff. (cf. *inter al.* Hartke (1940) 144 n. 1, and Thompson (1947)).

[125] Cf. Dessau *ILS* 2947; Ambrose, *De obitu Theodosii* 4; Flavianus (Lippold (1967)) had been called to court by Theodosius *c.*383 as *quaestor sacri palatii* ('quaestor of the sacred palace') and in 390 was appointed *praefectus praetorio Italiae, Illyrici et Africae* ('Praetorian prefect of Italy, Illyricum and Africa').

[126] In order to avoid any possible misunderstandings, it should be emphasized that I do not believe Ammianus to have been encouraged in his undertaking by Theodosius, and that, to my mind, the question of relations between the historian and the emperor has not up to now progressed beyond hypothetical assumptions (cf. n. 26 and n. 124).

[127] Cf. Mazzarino in Gianelli and Mazzarino (1956) 488–9 and 542–3; Neumann (1965).

[128] Also relevant is the advancement of the historian Sextus Aurelius Victor to city prefect of Rome by Theodosius in 388–9 (see Chastagnol (1962) 232–3). Against Seeck (1905) 151; Petit (1955) 305 et al., the identification of the *praefectus praetorio Orientis* of 380–1 and consul of 387 Eutropius with the historian of the same name appears to me incapable of proof.

[129] Cf. 1.2 ff.; 45.7; 47.1 and 5. When Pacatus speaks in 1.2 of *maiestas utriusque* ('the majesty of each', i.e. of the emperor and the city of Rome), this is perhaps less, as intimated by Grinda (1916) 18 in reminiscence of the *maiestas populi Romani* ('the majesty of the Roman people') than in emphasis of the dignity of the city, significant just at this period, when *maiestas* was increasingly becoming the official attribute of the ruler (cf. *TLL* VIII *s.v. maiestas* 155–6).

[130] Cf. e.g. the excursions of Ammianus, who enjoyed great success *c.*390 in giving lectures on the Roman nobility in 14.6 and 28.6 from his work or drafts of his work (cf. Lib. *Ep.* 1063 F = 983 W for 392).

reflected in such examples that we are able to discern the panegyrist's intimate association with historiographical activities that were becoming so clearly visible in pagan aristocratic society in the city of Rome *c.*390,[131] and it was in that society that Pacatus' close intellectual kinship lay.

[131] Cf. in this regard the thorough account by Hartke (1940) 116 ff.; (1951) 52 ff.). I must, however, confess that I am unable to endorse the conclusions he draws as to the date of the *Scriptores Historiae Augustae* (cf. above n. 60 and n. 72). Against Hartke, adherents both of a 'Julian' and of a 'post-Theodosian' date for *SHA* could find support for their theories here. Complementary to Hartke is, e.g. Bloch (1945).

Bibliography

Adam, T., *Clementia Principis. Der Einfluss hellenistischer Fürstenspiegel auf den Versuch einer rechtlichen Fundierung des Principats durch Seneca* (Stuttgart, 1970).

Adams, J. N., *The Regional Diversification of Latin, 200 BC–AD 600* (Cambridge, 2007).

Ahl, F., *Lucan. An Introduction* (Ithaca, NY, 1976).

—— 'The Art of Safe Criticism in Greece and Rome', *American Journal of Philology* 105 (1984), 174–208.

Alexander, W. H., 'The Professoriate in Imperial Gaul (297 AD)', *Proceedings and Transactions of the Royal Society of Canada* 3rd ser. 38 (1944), 37–57.

Aldus, C., *Plinii Secundi Novocomensis Epistolarum libri decem et Panegyricus* (Venice, 1508).

Alföldi, A., 'Die Ausgestaltung des monarchischen Zeremoniells am römischen Kaiserhofe', *Römische Mitteilungen* 49 (1934), 3–118.

—— 'Insignien und Tracht der Römischen Kaiser', *Römische Mitteilungen* 50 (1935), 1–171.

—— 'The crisis of the Empire (AD 249–270)', *Cambridge Ancient History* 12 (1939), 165–231.

—— *Die Kontorniaten* (Budapest, 1943).

—— *The Conversion of Constantine and Pagan Rome* (Oxford, 1948).

—— *A Conflict of Ideas in the Late Roman Empire. The Clash between the Senate and Valentinian I* (Oxford, 1952).

Alföldi, M. R., '*signum dei*. Die Kaiserzeitlichen Vorfahren des Reichsapfels', *Jahrbuch für Numismatik und Geldgeschichte* 11 (1961), 19–32.

Allain, A., *Pline le Jeune et ses Héritiers* 3 vols. (Paris, 1901–1902).

Allen, G. B., *Pliny the Younger. Selected Letters* (Oxford, 1915).

Alvarez, E., *Los Panegiricos de Corippo* (Universidad de Santiago de Compostela, 1972).

Amat, J., *Bucoliques/Calpurnius Siculus; Éloge de Pison/Pseudo-Calpurnius* (Paris, 1991).

Amman, R., 'De Corippo priorum poetarum latinorum imitatore', diss., Keil, 1885.

Anderson, W. B., *Sidonius* 2 vols (London, 1936, 1965).

André, J.-M., 'Les *Ludi scaenici* et la politique des spectacles au début de l'ère antonine' in *Actes du IXe Congrès de l'Association Guillaume Budé*, i (Paris, 1975), 468–79.

Andreotti R. 'Recenti contribute alla cronologia costantiniana', *Latomus* 33 (1964), 537–55.

Andrews, J. U., *Concordantia in Flavii Corippi Iohannida* (Olms, 1993).

Antès, S., *Corippe. Éloge de l'empereur Justin II* (Paris, 1981).

Armisen-Marchetti, M. 'Pline le Jeune et le sublime' *Revue des Etudes Latines* 68 (1990), 88–98.

Arnheim, M. T. W., *The Senatorial Aristocracy in the Later Roman Empire* (Oxford, 1972).

Arntzen, I., *Latini Pacati Drepanii Panegyricus et al.* (Amsterdam, 1753).

Asche, U., 'Roms Weltherrshaftsidee und Aussenpolitik in der Spätantike im Spiegel der Panegyrici Latini', diss., Bonn, 1983.

Athanassiadi-Fowden P., *Julian and Hellenism. An Intellectual Biography* (Oxford, 1981).

Aubrion, E., 'Pline le Jeune et la rhétorique de l'affirmation', *Latomus* 34 (1975), 90–130.

Austin, R. G., 'Quintilian on painting and statuary', *Classical Quarterly* 38 (1944), 17–26.

——*Quintiliani Institutionis Oratoriae Liber XII* (Oxford, 1972).

Babut, E.-Ch., 'L'Adoration des empereurs et les origines de la persecution de Dioclétien', *Revue Historique* 123 (1916), 225–52.

Baehrens, A., 'Kritische Bemerkungen zu den lateinischen Panegyristen', *Rheinisches Museum für Philologie* 27 (1872), 215–25.

——*XII Panegyrici Latini* (Leipzig, 1874).

——'Zur Handschriftenkunde der lateinischen *Panegyrici*', *Rheinisches Museum für Philologie* 30 (1875), 463–5.

——*Poetae Latini Minores* v (Leipzig, 1883).

Baehrens, W. A., *Panegyricorum Latinorum Editionis Novae Praefatio Maior accedit Plinii Panegyricus exemplar editionis* (Groningen, 1910).

——*XII Panegyrici Latini* (Leipzig, 1911).

——'Zur quaestio Eumeniana', *Rheinisches Museum für Philologie* 67 (1912), 312–16.

——'Pacatus', *Hermes* 56 (1921), 443–5.

——'Bericht über die Literatur zu einigen wichtigen römischen Schriftstellern des 3. und 4. Jahrhunderts aus den Jahren 1910/11–1924, II *Panegyrici Latini*', *Bursians Jahrbuch für Altertumskunde* 203 (1925), 90–112.

Baglivi, N., 'Pan. Lat. XII(9) 26.5. Attualità ideologica e problemi interpretativi', *Orpheus* 5 (1984), 32–67.

——'A proposito di impero, imperatori, e *Panegyrici Latini*', *Vichiana* 4 (2002), 107–15.

Baldus, H. R., 'Theodosius der Grosse und die Revolte des Magnus Maximus', *Chiron* 14 (1984), 175–92.

Baldwin, B., 'The career of Corippus', *Classical Quarterly* 28 (1978), 372–6.

—— 'Tacitus, the *Panegyrici Latini* and the *Historia Augusta*', *Eranos* 78 (1980), 175–8.

Bannister, M. 'Heroic Hierarchies: Classical models for panegyrics in seventeenth-century France' *International Journal of the Classical Tradition* 8 (2001), 38–59.

Barabino, G., *Claudio Mamertino, Il Panegirico dell'imperatore Guiliano* (Genoa, 1965).

Barbu-Moravová, M., 'Trajan as an Ideal Ruler in Pliny's *Panegyric*', *Graecolatina Pragensia* 18 (2000), 7–18.

Barchiesi, A., 'Poetry, Praise and Patronage: Simonides in Book 4 of Horace's *Odes*', *Classical Antiquity* 15 (1996), 5–47.

—— 'The Uniqueness of the *Carmen saeculare* and Its Tradition' in Woodman, T. and D. Feeney (eds.) *Traditions and Contexts in the Poetry of Horace* (Cambridge, 2002), 107–23.

Bardon, H., *Les Empereurs et les lettres latines d'Auguste à Hadrian* (Paris, 1940).

Barner, G., *Comparantur inter se Graeci de regentium hominum virtutibus auctores* (Marburg, 1889).

Barnes, T. D. 'Publilius Optatianus Porfyrius', *American Journal of Philology* 96 (1975), 173–86.

—— 'Imperial Campaigns AD 285–311', *Phoenix* 30 (1976), 174–93.

—— *Constantine and Eusebius* (Cambridge, MA, 1981).

—— *The New Empire of Diocletian and Constantine* (Cambridge, MA, 1982).

—— 'Emperors, Panegyrics, Prefects, Provinces and Palaces (284–317)', *Journal of Roman Archaeology* 9 (1996), 532–52.

Barr, W., *Claudian's Panegyric on the Fourth Consulate of Honorius* (Liverpool, 1981).

Bartsch, S., *Actors in the Audience. Theatricality and Doublespeak from Nero to Hadrian* (Harvard, 1994).

Bastien, P., 'Multiples d'or, *adventus* et Panégyriques de Constance Chlore', *Bulletin Cercel Etudes Numismatiques* 15 (1978), 1–6.

Baudrillard, J., *Simulacres et simulations* (Paris, 1981).

Baynes, N. H., review of Vogt, J. and E. Kornemann, *Römische Geschichte* (Leipzig, 1933) *Journal of Roman Studies* 25 (1935), 81–7.

Beard, M., J. North, and S. Price, *Religions of Rome* 2 vols (Cambridge, 1998).

Beaujeu, J., *La Religion romaine à l'apogée de l'Empire* (Paris, 1955).

—— review of Mynors (1964), *Revue des Etudes Latines* 43 (1965), 565–7.

Beeson, C. H., 'Isidore's *Institutionum Disciplinae* and Pliny the Younger', *Classical Philology* 8 (1913), 93–8.

Belloni, G. G., 'La bellezza divinazzante nei panegirici e nei retratti monetali di Costantino', *Contributi dell'Instituto di Storia Antica* 7 (1981), 213–22.

Bennett, J., *Trajan. Optimus Princeps. A Life and Times* (London, 1997).

390 *Bibliography*

Béranger, J., 'Le Refus du pouvoir. Recherches sur l'aspect idéologique du principat', *Museum Helveticum* 5 (1948), 178–96.

—— *Recherches sur l'aspect idéologique du principat* (Basle, 1953).

—— 'L'Expression de la divinité dans *Les Panégyriques Latins*', *Museum Helveticum* 27 (1970), 242–54.

Bernhardy, G., *Grundriss der römischen Litteratur* (Braunschweig, 1872).

Beroaldus, P. C., *Plinii Iunioris Epistolae et Panegyricus* (Venice, 1501).

Berriman, A. and M. Todd, 'A Very Roman Coup: the Hidden War of Imperial Succession, AD 96–8', *Historia* 50 (2001), 312–31.

Bidez, J., *La Vie de l'empereur Julien* (Paris, 1930).

Binns, J. W., *Latin Literature of the Fourth Century* (London, 1974).

Birley, A. R., *Hadrian, the Restless Emperor* (London, 1997).

—— *Onomasticon to the young Pliny. Letters and Panegyric* (Munich, 2001).

Bitschofsky, R., *De C. Sollii Apollinaris Sidonii studiis Statianis* (Vienna, 1881).

Bloch, H., 'A New Document of the Last Pagan Revival in the West, 393–394 AD', *Harvard Theological Review* 38 (1945), 199–244 = A. Momigliano (ed.) *The Conflict between Paganism and Christianity* (Oxford, 1963), 193–218.

Blockley, R. C., 'The Panegyric of Claudius Mamertinus on the Emperor Julian', *American Journal of Philology* 93 (1972), 437–50.

Bodelòn, S., 'Merobaudes. Un poeta de la Betica en la corte de Ravenna', *Memorias de historia antigua* 19–20 (1998–9), 343–68.

Boissier, G., 'Les Rhétors Gaulois du IVe siècle', review of A. Baehrens (1874) and Brandt (1882), *Journal des Savants* (January 1884), 5–18, and 125–40.

Bonaria, M., 'Echi Lucanei in *Panegyrici Latini* IV(10)29.5', *Latomus* 17 (1958), 497–9.

Bonjour, M., 'Personnification, allégorie et prosopopée dans les *Panégyriques* de Sidoine Apollinaire', *Vichiana* 11 (1982), 5–17.

Bonner, S. F., *Roman Declamation* (Liverpool, 1969).

—— *Education in Ancient Rome* (Berkeley, 1977).

Born, L. K., 'The Perfect Prince According to the Latin Panegyrists', *American Journal of Philology* 55 (1934), 20–35.

Borsa, M. 'Correspondence of Humphrey, Duke of Gloucester and Pier Candido Decembri', *English Historical Review* 19 (1904), 509–25.

Bowersock, G., *Julian the Apostate* (London, 1978).

Brandt, S., *Eumenius und die ihm zugeschriebenen Reden* (Fribourg, 1882).

Braund, S. M. 'Paradigms of Power: Roman emperors in Roman satire' in Cameron, K. (ed.) *Humour and History* (Oxford, 1993), 56–69.

—— 'The Solitary Feast: A contradiction in terms?', *Bulletin of the Institute of Classical Studies* 41 (1996), 37–52.

—— 'Praise and Protreptic in Early Imperial Panegyric', in Whitby, M. (ed.) *The Propaganda of Power: the Role of Panegyric in Late Antiquity* (Leiden, 1998), 53–76.

—— *Seneca: De Clementia* (Oxford, 2009).

Brodka, D., 'Die Idee der *Roma aeterna* in den Kaiserpanegyriken des Sidonius Apollinaris', *Classica Cracoviensia* 3 (1997), 121–8.

—— 'Die Weltherrschaftstopik in den Kaiserpanegyriken des Sidonius Apollinaris', *Eos* 85 (1998), 81–90.

Brosch, P. 'Zur Präsentation der Tetrarchie in den Panegyrici Latini' in *Die Tetrarchie. Ein neues Regierungssystem und seine mediale Präsentation* (Zakmira-Schriften 3) (Wiesbaden, 2006) 83–101.

Browning, R., *The Emperor Julian* (London, 1975).

Brunt, P. A., 'Lex de Imperio Vespasiani', *Journal of Roman Studies* 67 (1977), 95–116.

—— 'Divine Elements in the Imperial Office', review of Fears (1977), *Journal of Roman Studies* 69 (1979), 168–75.

—— *Roman Imperial Themes* (Oxford, 1990).

Bruun, P., *The Constantinian Coinage of Arelate* (Helsinki, 1953).

—— *Studies in Constantinian Chronology* (New York, 1961).

Bruyère, R. T., 'Tacitus and Pliny's *Panegyricus*', *Classical Philology* 49 (1954), 161–79.

Bruzzone, A., *Concordantia in Flavium Merobaudem* (Hildesheim, 1998).

—— *Panegirico in versi. Flavio Merobaude* (Rome, 1999).

Burckhardt, J., *Die Zeit Constantins des Grossen* (Basle, 1853).

Burdeau, F., 'L'Empereur d'après les *Panégyriques Latins*', in Burdeau, F., N. Charbonnel, and M. Humbert (eds.) *Aspects de l'Empire Romain* (Paris, 1964) 1–60.

Burgess, T. C., *Epideictic Literature* (Chicago, 1902, repr. 1980).

Burkhard, C., 'de perfecti tertiae personae pluralis formis in *(e)runt* et *ere* exeuntibus, qui in *Panegyrici Latini* inveniuntur' *Wiener Studien* 8 (1886), 170–2.

—— 'de particulae *deinde (dein)* apud Plinium ceterosque XI Panegyristas usu', *Wiener Studien* 25 (1903), 160–1.

Bursian, C. 'Der Rhetor Menandros und seine Schriften', *Bayerische Akademie der Wissenschaft* 16.3 (1882), 1–152.

Cairns, F., *Generic Composition in Greek and Roman Poetry* (Edinburgh, 1972).

Cameron, Alan *Claudian. Poetry and Propaganda at the Court of Honorius* (Oxford, 1970).

—— 'Claudian' in Binns, J. W. (ed.) *Latin Literature of the Fourth Century* (London, 1974a), 134–59.

—— 'The Date of Priscian's *De Laude Anastasii*', *Greek, Roman and Byzantine Studies* 15 (1974b), 313–16.

——*Circus Factions: Blues and Greens at Rome and Byzantium* (Oxford, 1976).

——*Callimachus and his Critics* (Princeton, 1995).

——'Claudian Revisited' in Consolino, F. E. (ed.) *Letteratura e propaganda nell' occidente latino da Augusto ai regni romanobarbarici* (Rome, 2000), 127–44.

Cameron, Averil, *Flavius Cresconius Corippus. In Laudem Iustini Augusti minoris* (London, 1976).

——'The Career of Corippus Again', *Classical Quarterly* 30 (1980), 534–9.

——'Education and Literary Culture' in Cameron, Averil and P. Garnsey (eds.) *Cambridge Ancient History* 13 (1998), 665–707.

Caplan, H. 'The Latin Panegyrics of the Empire', *Quarterly Journal of Speech Education* 10 (1924), 41–52, repr. in *Of Eloquence* (Ithaca and London, 1970) 26–39.

Carey, C., 'Epideictic Oratory' in Worthington, I. (ed.) *A Companion to Greek Rhetoric* (London, 2007), 236–52.

Casey, P. J., *Carausius and Allectus: The British Usurpers* (London, 1994).

Caspar, E., *Geschichte des Papstums* 2 vols (Tübingen, 1930, repr. 1933).

Castello, G., 'Il pensiero politico religioso di Constantino alla luce dei panegirici', *Atti Accademia Romanistica Constantiniana, I Covegno Internazionale* (Perugia, 1975), 49–117.

Castagna, L. and Lefevre, E. *Plinius der Jüngere und seine Zeit* (Munich-Leipzig, 2003).

Castritius, H., *Studien zu Maximinus Daia* (Kallmünz, 1969).

Catanaeus, J. M., *C. Plinii Caecilii Secundi Epistolae et Panegyricus* (Milan, 1506; Paris 1533).

Cecconi, G., '*Delicata Felicitas*: osservazaioni sull'ideologia imperiale della vittoria attraverso le fonti letterarie', *Clio* 27 (1991), 5–29.

Cesareo, E., *La poesia di Calpurnio Siculo* (Palermo, 1931).

——*Il panegirico nella poesia latina* (Palermo, 1936).

Chadwick, N. K., *Poetry and Letters in Early Christian Gaul* (London, 1955).

Chambers, H. E., 'Exempla virtutis in Themistius and the Latin Panegyrists' diss., Bloomington, 1968.

Champlin, E., *Fronto and Antonine Rome* (Cambridge, MA, 1980).

——'The History and Date of Calpurnius', *Philologus* 130 (1986), 104–12.

——'The Life and Times of Calpurnius Piso', *Museum Helveticum* 46 (1989), 101–24.

Charlesworth, M. P., '*Providentia* and *aeternitas*', *Harvard Theological Review* 29 (1936), 107–32.

——'The virtues of the Roman Emperor: Propaganda and the creation of belief', *Proceedings of the British Academy* 23 (1937), 105–38.

——'*Pietas* and *victoria*; the Emperor and the citizen', *Journal of Roman Studies* 33 (1943), 1–10.

Charlet, J.-L., *Claudien* 2 vols (Paris, 1991 repr. 2001).

—— 'Aesthetic Trends in Late Latin Poetry (325–410)', *Philologus* 132 (1988), 74–85.

Chastagnol, A., *Les Fastes de la préfecture de Rome* (Paris, 1962).

—— 'L'Evolution politique du règne de Dioclétien', *Antiquité Tardive* 2 (1994), 23–31.

Chauvot, A., *Panégyriques de l'empereur Anastase I. Procope de Gaza, Priscien de Cesaree* (Bonn, 1986).

Christiansen, P. G., *The Use of Images by Claudius Claudianus* (Paris, 1969).

—— A Concordance to Claudianus (Hildesheim, 1988).

—— and J. E. Holland, *Concordantia in Sidonii Apollinaris carmina* (Hildesheim, 1993).

Christol, M., 'Panégyriques et revers monétaires: l'empereur, Rome et les provinciaux à la fin du IIIe siècle', *Dialogues d'Histoire Anciennes* 2 (1976), 421–34, 442–3.

—— 'Littérature et numismatique: l'avènement de Dioclétien et la théologie du pouvoir impérial dans les dernières décennies du IIIe siècle', in Bastien, P., F. Dumas, H. Huvelin, and C. Morrisson (eds.) *Mélanges de numismatique, d'archéologie et d'histoire offerts à Jean Lefaurie* (Paris, 1980), 83–91.

—— 'La pieté des Tétrarques: une retractatio' in *Romanité et cité chrétienne. Permanances et mutations, intégratio et exclusion du 1er au 6e s., Mélanges en l'honneur d'Yvette Duval* (Paris, 2000), 219–31.

Chruzander, C. G., 'De elocutione panegyricorum veterum Gallicanorum quaestiones', diss., Upsala, 1897.

Cizek, E., *L'Epoque de Trajan: Circonstances politiques et problèmes idéologiques*, tr. Caius Frantescu (Paris, 1983).

Clark, G. and T. Rajak (eds.) *Philosophy and Power in the Graeco-Roman World* (Oxford, 2002).

Clarke, M. L., *Rhetoric at Rome: A Historical Survey* (London, 1996).

Classen, C. J., 'Die Königszeit im Spiegel der Literatur der römischen Republik', *Historia* 14 (1965), 385–403.

Clauss, M., *Kaiser und Gott. Herrscherkult im römischen Reich* (Leipzig, repr. 2001).

Clover, F. M., *Flavius Merobaudes. A translation and historical commentary* (Philadelphia, 1971a).

—— 'Toward an Understanding of Merobaudes' *Panegyrici*', *Historia* 20 (1971b), 354–67.

—— 'The Return of Merobaudes', review of Bruzzone (1999), *Classical Review* 54 (2004), 130–1.

Cohen, H., *Description historique des monnaies frappées sous l'empire romain* 8 (Graz, 1892).

Coffey, M., 'Turnus and Juvenal', *Bulletin of the Institute of Classical Studies* 26 (1979), 88–94.

Coleman, K. M., 'The Emperor Domitian and Literature', *Aufstieg und Niedergang der römischen Welt* II.32.5 (1986), 3087–115.

——*Statius Silvae IV* (Oxford, 1998a).

——'Martial Book 8 and the Politics of AD 93', *Papers of the Liverpool Latin Seminar* 10 (1998b), 337–57.

Colton, R. E., *Some Literary Influences on Sidonius Apollinaris* (Amsterdam, 2000).

Condorelli, S., *L'esametro dei Panegirici di Sidonio Apollinare* (Naples, 2001).

Corcoran, S., *The Empire of the Tetrarchs: Imperial Pronouncements and Government AD 284–324* (Oxford, 1996, repr. 2000).

Cotton, H. M. and A. Yakobson, '*Arcanum Imperii*: The Powers of Augustus', in Clark. G. and T. Rajak (eds.) *Philosophy and Power in the Graeco-Roman World* (Oxford, 2002), 193–209.

Courtney, E., *The Fragmentary Latin Poets* (Oxford, 1959).

Covino, R., 'The *laudatio funebris* as a Vehicle for Praise and Admonition' in Covino, R. and C. J. Smith (eds.) *Praise and Blame in Roman Republican Rhetoric* (Swansea, 2011) 69–82.

Covino, R. and C. J. Smith (eds.) *Praise and Blame in Roman Republican Rhetoric* (Swansea, 2011).

Coyne, P., *Priscian of Caesarea's De Laude Anastasii imperatoris* (Lewiston, 1991).

Cullhed, M., *Conservator Urbis Suae. Studies in the Politics and Propaganda of the Emperor Maxentius* (Stockholm, 1994).

Cumont, F., 'L'éternité des empereurs Romains', *Rev. d'hist et de littér. relig.* 1 (1896), 435–52.

Curtius, E. R., *Europäische Literatur und lateinisches Mittelalter* (Bern, 1954).

Cuspinianus, J., *Panegyrici variorum auctorum* (Vienna, 1513).

Dagron, G., 'L'Empire romain de l'Orient au IVme siècle et les traditions politiques de l'hellénisme', *Travaux et Memoires* 3 (1968), 1–242.

Dalzell, A., 'Asinius Pollio and the Introduction of Public Recitation at Rome' *Hermathena* 86 (1955), 20–8.

Damon, C., *Tacitus, Histories Book 1* (Cambridge, 2003).

Davies, C., 'Poetry in the Circle of Messalla', *Greece & Rome* 20 (1973), 25–35.

de Beer, S., 'The Panegyrical *Inventio*. A Rhetorical Analysis of *Panegyricus Latinus* V(8)', in Enenkel, K. and I. L. Pfeijffer (eds.) *The Manipulative Mode. Political Propaganda in Antiquity: A Collection of Case Studies* (Leiden, 2005), 295–317.

Del Chicca, F., *Q. Aurelii Symmachi Laudatio in Valentinianum seniorem Augustum prior* (Rome, 1984).

——'La struttura retorica del panegirico latino tardo imperiale in prosa. Teoria e prassi', *Annali della Facolta di Lettere e Filosofia dell' università di Cagliari* 6 (1985), 79–113.

Delatte, L., *Les Traités de la royauté d'Ecphante, Diotogène et Sthenidas* (Liège, 1942).

D'Elia, S., 'Ricerche sui Panigirici di Mamertino a Massimiano', *Annali della Facolta di Lettere e Filosofia dell' università di Napoli* 9 (Universita di Napoli 1960/1), 121–391.

Demandt, A., 'Zeitkritik und Geschichtsbild im Werk Ammians', diss., Marburg, 1963.

Den Boer, W. 'Rome à travers trois auteurs du quatrième siècle', *Mnemosyne* 21 (1968), 254–88.

Derichs, W., 'Herakles' diss., Cologne, 1950.

Dessau, H., *Inscriptiones Latinae Selectae*, 5 vols (Berlin, 1892–1906).

De Ruggiero, E., *Dizionario Epigrafico di Antichità Romane* (Rome, 1900).

De Trizio, M. S., 'Un' eco vergiliana del *Panegirico* di Mamertino del 289 d. C', *Invigilata Lucernis* 27 (2005), 155–68.

—— 'Echi ciceroniani nel *Panegirici* di Mamertino per l'imperatore Massimiano', *Invigilata Lucernis* 28 (2006), 61–74.

—— 'La propaganda della *Concordia Augustorum* nei *Panegyrici* di Mamertino', *Classica et Christiana* 2 (2007), 133–46.

—— *Panegirico di Mamertino per Massimiano e Diocleziano (Panegyrici Latini 2[10])* (Bari, 2009).

Dewar, M., 'Laying It on with a Trowel. The proem to Lucan and related texts', *Classical Quarterly* 44 (1994), 199–211.

—— *Claudian. Panegyricus de sexto consulatu Honorii Augusti* (Oxford, 1996).

Di Brazzano, S., *Laus Pisonis* (Pisa, 2004).

Diggle, J. and Goodyear, F. R. D., *Flavii Cresconii Corippi Iohannidos seu De Bellis Libycis Libri VIII* (Cambridge, 1970).

Di Spigno, C., 'Studi su Ammiano Marcellino: il regno di Constanzo II', *Helikon* 2 (1962), 442–64.

Doblhofer, E., *Die Augustuspanegyrik des Horaz in formalhistorischer Sicht* (Heidelberg, 1966).

Dolan, F. M., 'Fear of Simulation: Life, Death and Democracy in Postwar America', *Massachusetts Review* 32.1 (1991), 61–75.

Dominik, W. and J. Hall (eds.) *A Handbook of Roman Rhetoric* (London, 2007).

D'Ors, A., *Plinio el Joven. Panegírico de Traiano* (Madrid, 1955).

Dowling, M. B., *Clemency and Cruelty in the Roman World* (Ann Arbor, 2006).

Downey, G., 'The Emperor Julian and the Schools', *Classical Journal* 53 (1957), 97–103.

Du Quesnay, I. M. Le M., 'Vergil's Fourth *Eclogue*', *Papers of the Liverpool Latin Seminar* 1 (1976), 25–99.

Due, O. S., 'An Essay on Lucan', *Classica et Mediaevalia* 23 (1967), 68–132.

Durry, M., *Pline le Jeune. Panégyrique de Trajan* (Paris, 1938).

—— *Letters X et Panegyricus. Pline le Jeune* (Paris, 1947).

—— 'laudatio funebris et rhétorique', *Revue Philologique* 16 (1942), 105–14.

Dvornik, F., *Early Christian and Byzantine Political Philosophy* 2 vols (Washington DC, 1966).

Dyer, R. R., 'Rhetoric and Intention in Cicero's *Pro Marcello*', *Journal of Roman Studies* 80 (1990), 17–30.

Eck, W., 'An Emperor is Made: Senatorial politics and Trajan's adoption by Nerva in 97', in Clark, G. and T. Rajak (eds.) *Philosophy and Power in the Graeco-Roman World* (Oxford, 2002) 210–26.

Ehlers, W. 'triumphus', *Real-Encyclopädie d. klassischen Altertumswissenschaft* 7.1 (1939), 493–511.

—— 'Epische Kunst in Coripps *Johannis*', *Philologus* 124 (1980), 109–35.

Eichholz, D. E., 'Constantius Chlorus' invasion of Britain', *Journal of Roman Studies* 43 (1953), 41–6.

Eisenhut, W., 'fatum', *Der Kleine Pauly* 2 (1967), 520–1.

Elefante, M., *Velleius Paterculus. ad M. Vinicium consulem libri duo* (Hildesheim, 1997).

Elliot, T. G., 'The Language of Constantine's Propaganda', *Transactions of the American Philological Association* 120 (1990), 349–53.

Ellul, J., *Propaganda: the formation of men's attitudes*, tr. K. Kellen and J. Lerner. (New York, 1968).

Enenkel, K., 'Panegyrische Geschichtsmythologisierung und Propaganda: Zur Interpretation des *Panegyricus Latinus* VI(7)', *Hermes* 128 (2000), 91–126.

—— 'Suetons Augustus-vita und Plinius' *Panegyricus*', *Wiener Studien* 116 (2003), 155–71.

—— and I. L. Pfeiffer (eds.) *The Manipulative Mode. Political Propaganda in Antiquity. A Collection of Case Studies* (Leiden, 2005).

Ensslin, W., 'Kaiser Julians Gesetzgebungswerk und Reichsverwaltung', *Klio* 18 (1923), 104–99.

—— 'Magnus Maximus', *Real-Encyclopädie d. klassischen Altertumswissenschaft* 14 (1930), 2546–55.

—— 'Flavius Theodosius', *Real-Encyclopädie d. klassischen Altertumswissenschaft* 5A (1934), 1937–45.

—— 'The Reforms of Diocletian' in Cook, S. A. et al. (eds.) *Cambridge Ancient History* 12 (1939), 383–408.

—— review of Hartke (1940) *Gnomon* 18 (1942), 248–67.

—— *Gottkaiser und Kaiser von Gottes Gnaden* (Munich, 1943).

—— 'Valens', *Real-Encyclopädie d. klassischen Altertumswissenschaft* 7 (1948a), 2096–148.

—— 'Valentinian II', *Real-Encyclopädie d. klassischen Altertumswissenschaft* 7 (1948b) 2204–32.

—— *Die Religionspolitik des Kaisers Theodosius des Grossen* (Munich, 1953).

—— review of Lacombre, C., *Le Discours sur la Royauté de Synésios de Cyrène à l'empereur Arcadios* (Paris, 1951), *Deutsche Literaturzeitung für Kritik der internationalen Wissenschaft* 75 (1954), 263–7.

Estefania Alvarez, D. N., *Los panegyricos de Corippo* (Universidad de Santiago de Compostela, 1972).

—— 'El panegírico poético latino a partir de Augusto: algunas calas', *Myrtia* 13 (1998), 151–75.

Étienne, R., *Le culte impérial dans la péninsule ibérique d'Auguste à Dioclétien* (Paris, 1958).

—— *Bordeaux Antique* (Bordeaux, 1962).

—— 'Ausone et l'Espagne', in *Mélanges Carcopino* (Paris, 1966), 319–32.

Eyssenhardt, Fr. 'Lectiones panegyricae' *Prog. D Friedrichs Werderschen Gymnasiums* (Berlin, 1867).

Fantham, E., *Roman Literary Culture. From Cicero to Apuleius* (Baltimore, 1996).

—— 'Two Levels of Orality in the Genesis of Pliny's *Panegyricus*' in Mackay, E. A. (ed.) *Signs of Orality. The oral tradition and its influence in the Greek and Roman world* (Leiden, 1999), 221–37.

Fargues, P., *Claudien. Études sur sa poésie et sons temps* (Paris, 1933).

—— *Claudien, Panegyricus de quarto consulatu Honorii Augusti* (Aix-en-Provence, 1939).

Faure, E., 'Notes sur le *Panégyrique VIII*', *Byzantion* 31 (1961a) 1–41.

—— 'Etude de la capitation de Dioclétien d'après le Panégyrique VIII' in *Varia. Etudes de droit romain, Institut de droit roman de l'Université de Paris* 4 (1961b) 1–153.

Fears, J. R., *Princeps A Diis Electus: The Divine Election of the Emperor as a Political Concept at Rome* (Rome, 1977).

—— 'The Cult of Jupiter and Roman Imperial Ideology', *Aufstieg und Niedergang der römischen Welt* II.17.1. (1981), 3–141.

—— 'The Cult of Virtues and Roman Imperial Ideology', *Aufstieg und Niedergang der römischen Welt* II.17.2 (1981), 736–826.

Fedeli, P., 'Il *Panegirico* di Plinio nella critica moderna', *Aufstieg und Niedergang der römischen Welt* II.33.1 (1989), 387–514.

Festugière, A.-J., *Antioche paienne et chrétienne* (Paris, 1959).

—— 'L'autobiographie de Libanius', *Revue des Études Grecques* 78 (1965), 622–34.

Feurstein, D., *Aufbau und Argumentation im Plinianischen Panegyricus* (Innsbruck, 1979).

Fishwick, D., '*genius* and *numen*', *Harvard Theological Review* 62 (1969), 356–67.

Fitzgerald, W., *Martial. The World of the Epigram* (Chicago, 2007).

Flach, D., 'Die Dichtung im frühkaiserzeitlichen Befriedungsprozess', *Klio* 54 (1972), 157–70.

Flasar, M., 'orbis quadrifariam duplici discretus Oceano', in Srejovic, D. (ed.) *The Age of the Tetrarchs* (Belgrade, 1995), 115–25.

Fliche, A. and V. Martin (eds.) *Histoire de l'église* 21 vols (Paris, 1942–64).

Flower, H. I., *Ancestor Masks and Aristocratic Power in Roman Culture* (Oxford, 1996).

Fo, A., *Studi sulla tecnica poetica di Claudiano* (Catania, 1982).

Formisano, M., 'Speculum principis, speculum oratoris: alcune considerazioni sui *Panegyrici Latini* come genere letterario' in Castagna, L. and C. Riboldi (eds.) *Amicitiae templa serena*. Vita e Pensiero (Milan, 2008) 581–99.

Fortina, M., *Graziano* (Turin, 1953).

Fowler, R., 'Anti-language in Fiction', in *Literature as Social Discourse: The Practice of Linguistic Criticism* (London, 1981).

Fox, M., 'Imagining the Emperor', review of Mause (1994), *Classical Review* 46 (1996), 255–6.

Fraenkel, E., *Horace* (Oxford, 1957).

Franzi, M., 'La propaganda costantiniana e la teoria di legittimazione del potere nei *Panegyrici Latini*', *Atti della Accademia delle Scienze di Torino* 115 (1981), 25–37.

Friedländer, P., *Johannes von Gaza und Paulus Silentiarius* (Leipzig, 1912).

Galletier, E., 'L'éloge de l'Espagne dans le panégyrique de Theodose par Pacatus' in *Mélanges Paul Thomas* (Bruges, 1930), 327–34.

—— *Panégyriques Latins* 3 vols (Paris, 1949, 1952, 1955).

—— 'La mort de Maximien d'après le panégyrique de 310 et la vision de Constantin au temple d'Apollon', *Revue des Études Anciennes* 52 (1950), 288–99.

—— review of Lubbe (1955), *Révue de Philologie* 31 (1957), 332–3.

Gamberini, F., *Stylistic Theory and Practice in Pliny the Younger* (Hildesheim, 1983).

García Ruiz, M. P., 'Función retórica y significado politico de la *gratiarum actio (Claudii) Mamertini de consulatu suo Iuliano Imperatori*' in Alonso del Real, C., M. P. García Ruiz, A. Sanchez-Ostiz, and J. B. Torres Guerra (eds.) *Urbs Aeterna* (Pamplona, 2003) 461–80.

—— '*quasi quoddam salutare sidus* (Pan. Lat. III (11) 2.3): el tópico y su contexto histórico', in Calderón Dorda, E., A. Morales Ortiz, and M. Valverde Sánchez (eds.), *Koinòs lógos. Homenaje al profesor José García López* (Murcia, 2006a), 293–304.

—— *Claudio Mamertino Panegírico (gratiarum actio) al emperador Juliano* (Pamplona, 2006b).

—— 'The Evolution of the Political Image of Emperor Julian through Consular Speeches: Mamertinus' *Pan. Lat.* III(11) and Libanius *Or.* XII', *Minerva* 21 (2008a), 137–53.

—— 'Una lectura de la *gratiarum actio* de Claudio Mamertino a la luz de los primeros escritos de Juliano', *Emerita* 76 (2008b), 443–64.

Garthwaite, J., 'The Panegyrics of Domitian in Martial Book 9', *Ramus* 22 (1993), 78–102.

Gennaro, S., *Da Claudiano a Merobaude. Aspetti della poesia cristiana di Merobaude* (Catania, 1959).

Gensel, P., 'Claudius Mamertinus', *Real-Encyclopädie d. klassischen Altertumswisenschaft* 3 (1899), 2730–1.

George, J. W., *Venantius Fortunatus: A Poet in Merovingian Gaul* (Oxford, 1992).

—— *Venantius Fortunatus: Personal and Political Poems* (Liverpool, 1996).

—— 'Venantius Fortunatus: Panegyric in Merovingian Gaul' in Whitby, M. (ed.) *The Propaganda of Power: the Role of Panegyric in Late Antiquity* (Leiden, 1998), 225–46.

Gérard, J., *Juvénal et la réalité contemporaine* (Paris, 1976).

Geyssen, J. W., *Imperial Panegyric in Statius. A Literary Commentary on Silvae 1.1* (New York, 1996).

Giancotti, F., 'Il De Clementia', *Rendiconti della classe di scienze morali, storiche e filologiche dell' Accademia dei Lincei* 8th ser. 9 (1954), 587–609.

Gianelli, G. and S. Mazzarino, *Trattato di Storia Romana* 2 vols (Rome, 1956).

Gianotti, F. F., 'Il principe e il retore: Classicismo come consenso in età imperiale', *Sigma* 12 (1979), 67–83.

Giarratano, C., *Calpurnii et Nemesiani Bucolica* (1943, repr. Turin, 1973).

Gibbon, E., *The History of the Decline and Fall of the Roman Empire* 6 vols (London, 1776–88).

Gibson, B. J. 'Unending Praise: Pliny and Ending Panegyric' in Berry, D. and A. Erskine (eds.) *Form and Function in Roman Oratory* (Cambridge, 2010), 122–36.

—— 'Contemporary Contexts', in Roche, P. (ed.) *Pliny's Praise. The Panegyricus in the Roman World* (Cambridge, 2011) 104–24.

—— and R. D. Rees (eds.) *Pliny the Younger in Late Antiquity* (forthcoming).

Giovannini, A., 'Pline et les délateurs de Domitian' in *Opposition et résistances à l'empire d'Auguste à Trajan. Entretiens sur l'Antiquité Classique* 33 (Geneva, 1987), 219–48.

Glover, T. R., *Life and Letters in the Fourth Century* (Cambridge, 1901).

Goffman, E., 'The Nature of Deference and Demeanour' in *Interaction Ritual. Essays on Face-to-face Behaviour* (New York, 1967), 47–95.

—— *Strategic Interaction* (Philadelphia, 1969).

Goodenough, E. R., 'The Political Philosophy of Hellenistic Kingship' *Yale Classical Studies* 1 (1928), 58–102.

Gonzales, J., (ed.) *Trajano. Emperador de Roma* (Rome, 2000).

Goodyear, F. R. D., 'History and Biography' in Kenney, E. J and W. V. Clausen (eds.) *Cambridge History of Classical Literature* II. *Latin Literature* (Cambridge, 1982), 639–66.

Gotoff, H. G., *Cicero's Caesarian Speeches* (Chapel Hill, 1993).

Götze, R., *Quaestiones Eumenianae* (Halle, 1892).

Gowing, A. M., *Empire and Memory* (Cambridge, 2005).

Gradel, I., *Emperor Worship and Roman Religion* (Oxford, 2002).

Grainger, J. D., *Nerva and the Roman Succession Crisis* AD *96–99* (London, 2003).

Green, R. P. H., *The Works of Ausonius* (Oxford, 1991).

Green, S. J., '(No) Arms and a Man: The Imperial Pretender, the Opportunistic Poet, and the *Laus Pisonis*', *CQ* 60 (2010), 497–523.

Grégoire, H., 'La 'conversion' de Constantin' *Rev. Univ. Brux.* 36 (1931), 231–72.

Griffin, M. T., *Seneca: A Philosopher in Politics* (Oxford, 1976).

——*Nero: The End of a Dynasty* (London, 1984).

——'*Clementia* after Caesar: From Politics to Philosophy' in Cairns, F. and E. Fantham (eds.) *Caesar against Liberty? Perspectives on his Autocracy. Papers of the Langford Latin Seminar* 11 (2003) 157–82.

Grimal, P., *Sénèque ou la conscience de l'Empire* (Paris, 1978).

Grinda, F., 'der Panegyrikus des Pakatus auf Kaiser Theodosius', diss., Strasbourg, 1916.

Groag, E., 'Maxentius', *Real-Encyclopädie d. klassischen Altertumswissenschaft* 14.2 (1930), 2417–84.

Gruber, J.1, 'Typologisches Argumentieren in der lateinischen Panegyrik' in Czapla, B. (ed.) *Vir bonus dicendi peritus. Festschrift A. Weische* (Wiesbaden, 1997) 129–34.

Grünewald, T., *Constantinus Maximus Augustus. Herrschaftspropaganda in der zeitgenössischen Überlieferung* (Stuttgart, 1990).

Gruterus, I., *XII Panegyrici veteres* (Frankfurt, 1607).

Gruzelier, C. E., 'Claudian. Court poet as artist', *Ramus* 19 (1990), 89–108.

Guillemin, A.-M., *Letters I–IX. Pline le Jeune* 3 vols (Paris, 1927–47).

——'La critique littéraire au Ier siècle de l'empire', *Revue des Etudes Latines* 6 (1928), 136–80.

Güldenpenning, A. and J. Ifland, *Der Kaiser Theodosius der Grosse* (Halle, 1878).

Güngerich, R., 'Tacitus' *Dialogus* und der *Panegyricus* des Plinius' in H. Erbse (ed.) *Festschrift für Bruno Snell zum 60* (Munich, 1956), 145–52.

Günther, O., *Epistulae imperatorum pontificum aliorum* (CSEL 35) 2 vols (Vienna, 1895–8).

Gutzwiller, H., *Die Neujahrsrede des Konsuls Mamertinus vor dem Kaizer Julian* (Basle, 1942).

Haarhoff, T. J., *Schools of Gaul*, (Oxford, 1920; Johannesburg, 1958).

Häfele, U., *Historiche Interpretationem zum Panegyricus des jüngeren Plinius* (Freiburg, 1958).

Hägg, T. and P. Rousseau (eds.) *Greek Biography and Panegyric in Late Antiquity* (Berkeley, 2000).

Hall, J. B., *Claudianus. Carmina* (Leipzig, 1985).

Halliday, M. A. K., 'Anti-languages' in *Language as Social Semiotic* (London, 1978) 164–82.

Halsberghe, G. H., *The Cult of Sol Invictus* (Leiden, 1972).

Hamberg, P. G., *Studies in Roman Imperial Art* (Copenhagen, 1945).

Hammond, M., 'Pliny the Younger's Views on Government', *Harvard Studies in Classical Philology* 49 (1938), 115–40.

Hanslik, R., 'Pacatus', *Real-Encyclopädie d. klassischen Altertumswisenschaft* 18.2 (1942), 2058–60.

——'Victorinus', *Real-Encyclopädie d. klassischen Altertumswisenschaft* 8.A2 (1958), 2074–9.

——'M. Ulpius Traianus' in *Real-Encyclopädie d. klassischen Altertumswisenschaft Supp.* 10 (1965), 1035–102.

Hanson, R. P. C., 'The Circumstances Attending the Death of the Emperor Flavius Valerius Severus in 306 or 307', *Hermathena* 118 (1974), 59–68.

Hardie, A., *Statius and the Silvae: Poets, Patrons and Epideixis in the Graeco-Roman World* (Liverpool, 1983).

Harries, J. D., *Sidonius Apollinaris and the Fall of Rome* AD 407–485 (Oxford, 1994).

Harrison, G. T., 'The Verse Panegyrics of Sidonius Apollinaris. Poetry and Society in Late Antique Gaul', diss., Stanford, 1983.

Hartke, W., *Geschichte und Politik im spätantiken Rom* (Klio Supp. 45, 1940).

——*Römische Kinderkaiser* (Berlin, 1951).

Hartman, J. J., 'de Domitiano imperatore et de poeta Statio', *Mnemosyne* 44 (1916), 338–73.

Heath, M., *Menander. A Rhetor in Context* (Oxford, 2004).

Heldmann, K., *Antike Theorien über Entwicklung und Verfall der Redekunst* (Munich, 1982).

Henderson, J. G., 'Lucan/The Word at War', *Ramus* 16 (1987), 122–64.

——'Tacitus/The World in Pieces', *Ramus* 18 (1989), 167–210.

——*Fighting for Rome: Poets and Caesars, History and Civil War* (Cambridge, 1998).

——'Down the Pan: historical exemplarity in the *Panegyricus*', in Roche, P. (ed.) *Pliny's Praise. The Panegyricus in the Roman World* (Cambridge, 2011), 142–74.

Hendrickson, G. L., 'The Peripatetic Mean of Style and the Three Stylistic Characters', *American Journal of Philology* 25 (1904), 125–46.

Herrmann, P., *Der Römische Kaisereid* (Göttingen, 1968).

Heuvel, H., 'de inimicitiarum quae inter Martialem et Statium fuisse dicuntur indiciis', *Mnemosyne* 4 (1937), 299–330.

Herzog-Hauser, G., 'Kaiserkult', *Real-Encyclopädie d. klassischen Altertumswisenschaft* Suppl. 4 (1924), 806–53.

Hirschfeld, O., *Kleine Schriften* (Berlin, 1913).

Hofacker, C., 'de clausulis C. Caecilii Plinii Secundi', diss., Bonn, 1903.

Höfer, J. and K. Rahner (eds.) *Lexikon für Theologie und Kirche* 10 vols (Freiburg, 1957–65).

Hoffer, S. E., *The Anxieties of Pliny the Younger* (Atlanta, 1999).

—— 'Divine Comedy? Accession Propaganda in Pliny, *Epistles* 10.1–2 and the *Panegyric*', *Journal of Roman Studies* 96 (2006), 73–87.

Hofmann, H., 'Überlegungen zu einer Theorie der nichtchristlichen Epik der lateinischen Spätantike', *Philologus* 132 (1988), 101–59.

Hollis, A. S., *Fragments of Roman Poetry c.60 BC–AD 20* (Oxford, 2007).

Hostein, A., 'Panégyrique et revers monétaire: l'*amplexus* entre la cité et l'empereur' in *Hypothèses 2002: travaux de l'Ecole doctorale d'Histoire del'Université Paris 1* (Panthéon-Sorbonne, 2003) 249–60.

—— 'Le corpus des *Panegyrici Latini* dans deux ouvrages récents', review of Lassandro and Micunco (2000) and Rees (2002), *Antiquité Tardive* 12 (2004), 373–85.

Howell, P., *Martial* (London, 2009).

Hunt, E. D., review of MacCormack (1981), *Classical Review* 33 (1983), 83–6.

Hutchinson, G., 'Politics and the Sublime in the *Panegyricus*' in Roche, P. (ed.) *Pliny's Praise. The* Panegyricus *in the Roman World* (Cambridge, 2011), 125–41.

Innes, D. C., 'The *Panegyricus* and Rhetorical Theory' in Roche, P. (ed.) *Pliny's Praise. The* Panegyricus *in the Roman World* (Cambridge, 2011), 67–84.

Instinsky, H. U., 'Kaiser und Ewigkeit', *Hermes* 77 (1942), 313–55.

Jal, P., *La Guerre civile à Rome* (Paris, 1963).

Jannaccone, S., *Ammiano Marcellino* (Naples, 1960).

Janson, T., *Concordance to the Latin Panegyrics* (Hildesheim and New York, 1979).

—— 'Notes on the *Panegyrici Latini*', *Classical Philology* 79 (1984), 15–27.

Johnson, T., *Symposium of Praise. Horace returns to Lyric in Odes IV* (Madison, 2004).

Johnson, W. R., *Momentary Monsters: Lucan and his Heroes* (Ithaca, NY, 1987).

Jones, A. H. M., *Constantine and the Conversion of Europe* (London, 1948).

—— 'Numismatics and History' in Carson, R. A. G. and C. H. V. Sutherland (eds.) *Essays in Roman Coinage presented to Harold Mattingly* (Oxford, 1956), 13–33.

—— *The Later Roman Empire 284-602: A Social, Economic and Administrative Survey* 3 vols (Oxford, 1964).

Jones, C. P., *The Roman World of Dio Chrysostom* (Cambridge, MA and London, 1978).

Jullian, C., *Histoire de la Gaule* 8 vols (Paris, 1909-1926).

Kaerst, J., *Studien zur Entwicklung und theoretischen Begründung der Monarchie im Altertum* (Munich, 1898).

Kähler, H., *Zwei sockel eines triumphbogens im Boboligarten zu Florenz* (Berlin, 1936).

—— *Das Fünfsäulendenkmal für die Tetrarchen auf dem Forum Romanum* (Cologne, 1964).

Kehding, O., 'De panegyricis latinis capita quattuor', diss., Marburg, 1897.

Keil, H., *Editio Maior Gaii Plinii Secundii* (Leipzig, 1870).

Kelly, G. and L. Grig (eds.) *Two Romes. Rome and Constantinople in Late Antiquity* (Oxford, 2012).

Kennedy, G., *The Art of Persuasion in Greece* (Princeton, 1963).

—— *The Art of Rhetoric in the Roman World* (Princeton, 1972).

Kienast, D. 'Nerva und das Kaisertum Trajans', *Historia* 17 (1968), 51-71.

Kierdorf, W., *Laudatio funebris. Interpretationem und Untersuchungen zur Entwicklung der römischen Leichenrede* (Meisenheim am Glan: Beiträge zur klassischen Philologie 106, 1980).

Kilian, B., 'Der Panegyrist Eumenius' diss., Würzburg, 1868-9.

King, C. E., 'The Maxentian Mints', *Numismatic Chronicle* 19 (1959), 47-78.

Klein, R., 'Königtum und Königszeit bei Cicero' diss., Erlangen, 1962.

Klose, O., *Die beiden an Maximianus Augustus gerichteten Panegyrici Latini* (Salzburg ,1895).

Klotz, A., 'Studien zu den *Panegyrici Latini*', *Rheinisches Museum für Philologie* 66 (1911a), 513-72.

—— review of W. A. Baehrens (1911b) in *Berliner Philologische Wochenschrift* 31 (1911), 42-9.

—— review of Stadler (1912) in *Berliner Philologische Wochenschrift* 33 (1913), 744-50.

Kluge, E., *Publilii Optatiani Porfyrii Carmina* (Leipzig, 1926).

Kolb, F., *Diokletian und die Erste Tetrarchie: Improvisation oder Experiment in der Organization monarchischer Herrschaft?* (Berlin, 1987).

—— *Herrscherideologie in der Spätantike* (Berlin, 2001).

—— '*praesens deus*. Kaiser und Gott unter die Tetrarchie' in Demandt, A., A. Goltz, and H. Schlnage-Schöningen (eds.) *Diokletian und die Tetrarchie* (Berlin, 2004), 27-37.

Kollwitz, J., *Oströmische Plastik der theoosianishen Zeit* (Berlin, 1941).

Kornemann, E., 'Zur Geschichte der antiken Herrscherkulte', *Klio* 1 (1901), 51-146.

404   Bibliography

—— *Doppelprinzipat und Reichsteilung im Imperium Romanum* (Leipzig, 1930).

Kraft, K., 'Die Taten der Kaiser Constans und Constantius II', *Jhb. F. Numismatik und Geldgeschichte* 9 (1958), 141–86.

Kronenberg, A. I., 'ad *Panegyricos Latinos*', *Classical Quarterly* 6 (1912), 204.

Kubitschek, W., '*Dominus et Deus* auf Münzen Aurelians', *Numimatische Zeitschr.* 8 (1915), 167–78.

Kukula, R. C., *Plinius Minor. Opera* (Leipzig, 1923).

Kühn, W. C., *Plini Caecilii Secundi Panegyricus Traiano imperatori dictus* (Darmstadt, 1985).

Kühner, R., *Tusculanae Disputationes* (Jena, 1829).

Kuhoff, W., *Diokletian und die Epoche der Tetrarchie* (Frankfurt, 2001).

La Bua, G., '*Laus deorum* e strutture inniche nei Panegirici latini di etá imperiale' *Rhetorica* 27 (2009), 142–58.

—— 'Patronage and Education in Third-century Gaul: Eumenius' Panegyric for the Restoration of the Schools', *Journal of Late Antiquity* 3 (2010), 300–15.

Lacombrade, C., *Le Discours sur la royauté de Synesios de Cyrène à l'empereur Arcadius* (Paris, 1951).

Lagioia, A., 'L'*epifania* di Giuliano in Illiria e il Palladio (*Pan. Lat.* III(11) 6.4)', *Invigilata Lucernis* 26 (2004), 123–37.

Landgraf, G., *Kommentar zu Ciceros Rede pro Sex. Roscio Amerino* (Leipzig, 1914).

La Penna, A., *Orazio e l'ideologia del principato* (Florence, 1963).

Lassandro, D., 'I manoscritti HNA nella tradizione dei Panegyrici Latini', *Bollettino del Comitato per la preparazione della Edizione Nazionale dei classici Greci e Latini* 15 (1967), 55–97.

—— 'Batavica o Bagaudica Rebellio? (A proposito di *Pan. Lat.* V 4.1 e VIII 4.2)', *Giornale italiano di filologia* 25 (1973), 300–8.

—— 'La rappresentazione del monde barbarico nell'oratoria encomiastica del IV secolo d. C.', *Invigilata Lucernis* 2 (1980), 191–205.

—— 'La demonizzazione del nemico politico nei Panegyrici Latini', *Contributi dell'Instituto di Storia Antica dell'Univ. del Sacro Cruore*, Milan 7 (1981), 237–49.

—— 'Le rivolte bagaudiche nelle fonti tardo-romane e medievali; aspetti e problemi (con appendice di testi)', *Invigilata Lucernis* 3–4 (1981–2), 57–110.

—— 'L'integrazione romano-barbarica nei Panegyrici Latini', *Contributi dell'Instituto di Storia Antica dell'Univ. del Sacro Cruore*, Milan 12 (1986), 153–9.

—— 'Il limes renano nei Panegyrici Latini', *Contributi dell'Instituto di Storia Antica dell'Univ. del Sacro Cruore*, Milan 13 (1987a), 295–300.

——'Pan. Lat. X(2)4 ed un gruppo statuario del Museo di Metz', *Invigilata Lucernis* 9 (1987b), 77–87.

——'terra mater frugum. Da Orazio ai *Panegirici Latini*' in Fedeli, P. (ed.) *Orazio in Colloquio* (Venosa, 1988) 123–8.

——'Inventario dei manoscritti dei *Panegyrici Latini*', *Invigilata Lucernis* 10 (1988), 107–200.

——'Bibliografia dei *Panegyrici Latini*', *Invigilata Lucernis* 11 (1989), 219–59.

——*XII Panegyrici Latini* (Paravia, 1992a).

——'*Aedui, fratres populi Romani* in margine ai *Panegirici Gallici*', *Contributi dell' Instituto di Storia Antica* 18 (1992b), 261–5.

——'Oriente e Occidente nei *Panegirici Latini*' in Conca, F., I. Gualandri, and G. Lozza (eds.) *Politica, Cultura e Religione nell'Impero Romano (secoli IV-V) tra Oriente e Occidente* (Naples, 1992c), 219–25.

——'Sulla traduzione dei testi storici' in Amata, B. (ed.) *Cultura e lingue classiche* (Rome, 1993), 569–77.

——'Storia e ideologia nei Panegirici Latini' in Criniti N. (ed.) *Sermione mansion. Società e cultura della Cisalpina tra tarda Antichità e alto Medioevo* (Brescia, 1995), 111–21.

——'La riva sinistra del Danubio e la *gratiarum actio* di Claudio Mamertino all'imperatore Giuliano (362d.C.)', *Studia Antiqua et Archaeologica* 5 (1998), 175–88.

——*Sacratissimus Imperator. L'immagine del princeps nell' oratoria tardoantica* (Bari, 2000).

——'Il *concentus omnium laudum* in honore dell'imperator nel *Panegirico* di Plinio e nei *Panegirici Latini*' in Castagna, L. and E. Lefevre (eds.) *Plinius der Jüngere und seine Zeit* (Munich-Leipzig, 2003), 245–55.

——and R. Diviccaro, 'Rassegna generale di studi sui *XII Panegyrici Latini*', *Bollettino di studi latini* 28 (1998), 132–204.

——and G. Micunco, *Panegirici Latini* (Turin, 2000).

Latte, K., *Römische Religionsgeschichte* (Munich, 1960).

Leach, E. W., 'The Politics of Self-presentation: Pliny's *Letters* and Roman portrait sculpture', *Classical Antiquity* 9 (1990), 14–49.

Leadbetter, W., '*patrimonium indivisum*? The Empire of Diocletian and Maximian, 285–289', *Chiron* 28 (1998), 213–28.

——'Best of Brothers. Fraternal Imagery in Panegyrics on Maximian Herculius', *Classical Philology* 99 (2004), 257–66.

——*Galerius and the Will of Diocletian* (London, 2009).

Lee, R. W., '*ut picture poesis*. The Humanistic Theory of Painting', *Art Bulletin* 22 (1940), 197–269.

Lehner, J., *Poesie und Politik in Claudians Panegyrikus auf des vierte Konsulat des Kaisers Honorius* (Königstein, 1984).

Lenschau, T., 'Phalaris', *Real-Encyclopädie d. klassischen Altertumswissenschaft* 19 (1937), 1649–52.

Leo, F., *Venantius Fortunatus. Opera Poetica* (Monumenta Germaniae Historica. Auctores Antiquissimi 4) (Berlin, 1881).

Levene, D. S., 'God and Man in the Classical Latin Panegyric', *Proceedings of the Cambridge Philological Society* 43 (1997), 66–103.

Levi, M. A., 'La campagna di Costantino nell'Italia settentrionale', *Bolletino storico-bibliografico subalpino* 36 (1934), 1–10.

Levick, B. M. 'Imperial Control of the Elections in the Early Principate', *Historia* 16 (1967), 207–30.

Levitan, W. 'Dancing at the End of the Rope: Optatian Porfyry and the field of Roman verse', *Transactions of the American Philological Association* 115 (1985), 245–69.

Levy, H. L., 'Themes of Encomium and Invective in Claudian', *Transactions of the American Philological Association* 89 (1958), 336–47.

L' Huillier, M-C., 'A propos de l'étude des *Panégyriques* et des revers monetaires, quelques remarques sur 'idéologie au Bas-Empire', *Dialogues d'histoire ancienne* 2 (1976), 435–42.

—— 'La figure de l'empereur et les vertus impériales. Crise et modèle d'identité dans les *Panégyriques Latins*', in *Les grandes figures religieuses, fonctionnement pratique et symbolique dans l'antiquité*, Besançon, 25–26 avril 1984 *Ann. Litter. de l'Univ. de Besançon* (1986) 529–82.

—— *L'Empire des mots. Orateurs gaulois et empereurs romans 3e et 4e siècles* (Paris, 1992).

Liebeschuetz, J. H. G. W., *Continuity and Change in Roman Religion* (Oxford, 1979).

—— 'Religion in the *Panegyrici Latini*' in *From Diocletian to the Arab Conquest* (Aldershot, 1990) 389–98, repr. from F. Paschke (ed.) *Uberlieferungsgeschichtliche Untersuchungen* (Berlin, 1981).

Lieu, S. N. C. (ed.) *The Emperor Julian. Panegyric and Polemic* (Liverpool, 1989).

Ligota, C., 'Constantiana', *Journal of the Warburg and Courtauld Institute* 26 (1963), 178–92.

Lippold, A., *Consules. Untersuchungen zur Geschichte des romischen Konsulates von 264 bis 201 v. Chr.* (Bonn, 1963).

—— 'Flavianus 2', *Der Kleine Pauly* 2 (1967), 567–8.

—— 'Herrscherideal und Traditionsverbundenheit im Panegyricus des Pacatus', *Historia* 17 (1968a), 228–50.

—— *Theodosius der Grosse und seine Zeit* (Munich 1968b, 1980).

—— 'Theodosius', *Real-Encyclopädie d. klassischen Altertumswisenschaft* Supp. 13 (1973), 837–961.

—— 'Constantius Caesar, Sieger über die Germanen-Nachfahre des Claudius Gothicus?' *Chiron* 11 (1981), 347–69.

Lipsius, *Iusti Lipsi Dissertatiuncula Apud Principes: Item C. Plini Panegyricus Liber Traiano Dictus. Cum eiusdem Lipsi perpetuo Commentario* (Antwerp, 1600).

Livineius, J., *XII Panegyrici veteres* (Antwerp, 1599).

Lockwood, R., *The Reader's Figure: Epideictic Rhetoric in Plato, Aristotle, Bossuet, Racine and Pascal* (Geneva, 1996).

Lolli, M., 'La *celeritas principis* fra tattica militare e necessità politica nei *Panegyrici Latini*', *Latomus* 58 (1999), 620–5.

Lomas, F. J., 'Propaganda y ideología. La imagen de la realeza en los *Panegíricos Latinos*' in Candau Morón, J. M., F. Gascó, and A. Ramírez de Verger (eds.) *La imagen de la realeza en la Antigüedad* (Madrid, 1988), 141–63.

L'Orange, H. P., 'Eine tetrarchisches Ehrenmal auf dem Forum Romanum', *Römische Mitteilung* 53 (1938), 1–38.

—— and A. von Gerkan, *Der spätantike Bilderschmuck am Konstantinsbogen* (Berlin 1939)

—— *Likeness and Icon. Selected Studies in Classical and Early Mediaeval Art* (Odense, 1973).

Loraux, N., *The Invention of Athens: The funeral oration in the classical city* (tr. A. Sheridan (Cambridge, MA and London, 1986).

Lovejoy, A. O. 'Milton and the Paradox of the Fortunate Fall', *English Literary History* 4 (1937), 161–79.

Lovino, A. 'Su alcune affinità tra il *Panegirico* per Theodosio di Pacato Drepanio e il *de Obitu Theodosii* di St. Ambrogio', *Vetera Christianorum* 26 (1989), 371–6.

Lowe, E. A., *Codices Latini Antiquores. A Palaeographical Guide to Latin Manuscripts Prior to the Ninth Century* iii (Oxford, 1938).

Loyen, A., *Recherches Historiques sur les Panégyriques de Sidoine Apollinaire* (Paris, 1942, repr. 1967).

—— *Sidoine Apollinaire* 3 vols (Paris, 1960).

Lubbe, W. J. G., *Incerti Panegyricus Constantino Augusto dictus* (Leiden, 1955).

—— 'De codice Clujensi qui nunc dicitur (olim Blajensi) 168', *Mnemosyne* 10 (1957), 247.

Luetjohann, C., *Gai Solli Apolloniaris Sidonii epistulae et carmina* (Monumenta Germaniae Historica. Auctores Antiquissimi 8) (Berlin, 1887).

Lunn-Rockliffe, S., 'Commemorating the Usurper Magnus Maximus: Ekphrasis, Poetry and History in Pacatus' Panegyric of Theodosius', *Journal of Late Antiquity* 3 (2010), 316–36.

MacCormack, S., 'Change and Continuity in Late Antiquity: the ceremony of *adventus*', *Historia* 21 (1972), 721–52.

—— 'Latin Prose Panegyrics' in Dorey T. A. (ed.) *Empire and Aftermath, Silver Latin II* (London, 1975a), 143–205.

—— 'Roma, Constantinopolis, the Emperor, and His *genius*', *Classical Quarterly* 69 (1975b), 131–50.

—— 'Latin Prose Panegyrics: Tradition and discontinuity in the later Roman empire', *Revue des Études Augustiniennes* 22 (1976), 29–77.

—— *Art and Ceremony in Late Antiquity* (Berkeley, 1981).

MacCormick, M., *Eternal Victory. Triumphal Rulership in Late Antiquity, Byzantium and the Early Mediaeval West* (Cambridge, 1986).

MacMullen, R., *Constantine* (New York, 1971).

—— *Roman Government's Response to Crisis* (New Haven, 1976).

Maguinness, W. S., 'Some Methods of the Latin Panegyrists', *Hermathena* 47 (1932), 42–61.

—— 'Locutions and Formulae of the Latin Panegyrists', *Hermathena* 48 (1933a), 117–38.

—— 'Two Notes on the *Panegyrici Latini*', *Classical Review* 47 (1933b), 219–20.

—— 'The Gerundive as Future Participle Passive in the *Panegyrici Latini*', *Classical Quarterly* 29 (1935), 45–7.

—— 'Eumenius of Autun', *Greece & Rome* 21 (1952), 97–103.

—— review of Mynors (1964), *Classical Review* 16 (1966), 65–6.

Malaspina, E., *De Clementia. Libri Duo* (Turin, 2001).

Malcovati, E., *Plinio il Giovane. Il Panegirico di Traiano* (Florence, 1952).

Malissard, A., 'Tacite et le théâtre ou la mort en scène' in Bländsdorf, J. (ed.) *Theater und Gesellschaft im Imperium Romanum* (Tübingen, 1990) 213–22.

Manolaraki, E., 'Political and Rhetorical Seascapes in Pliny's *Panegyricus*' *Classical Philology* 103 (2008), 374–94.

Manuwald, G., 'Republican and Imperial Panegyric in Rome. Ciceronian Praise as a Step Towards Pliny's *Panegyricus*' in Roche, P. (ed.) *Pliny's Praise. The* Panegyricus *in the Roman World* (Cambridge, 2011), 85–103.

Mariotti, S., 'Naucellinus' *Real-Encyclopädie d. klassischen Altertumswissenschaft Suppl.* 9 (1962), 411–5.

Marrou, H.-I., *Histoire de l'éducation dans l'antiquité* (Paris, 1948).

Marsili, A., *Discorso di Eumenio per la restaurazione delle scuole di Autun* (Pisa, 1965).

Martindale, C. A., 'The Politician Lucan', *Greece & Rome* 31 (1984), 64–79.

Matthews, J. F., *Western Aristocracies and Imperial Court* AD *364–425* (Oxford, 1975).

Mattingly, H., *Coins of the Roman Empire in the British Museum* iii (Nerva–Trajan) (London, 1950).

—— 'Jovius and Herculius', *Harvard Theological Review* 45 (1952), 131–4.

Maurice, J., 'Les Discourses des *Panegyrici Latini* et l'évolution religieuse sous le règne de Constantin' *Comp. Rendus Acad. Inscri. Bell. Lettr.* (Paris, 1909) 165–79.

Mause, M., *Die Darstellung des Kaisers in der Lateinischen Panegyrik* (Stuttgart, 1994).

Mazza, M., 'Merobaude. Poesia e politica nella tarda antichità' in *La Poesia Tardoantica* (Messina, 1984), 379–430.

McCrum, M. and A. G. Woodhead, *Select Documents of the Principates of the Flavian Emperors, AD 68–96* (Cambridge, 1966).

Merrill, E. T., *Selected Letters of Pliny the Younger* (London, 1903).

Mesk, J., 'Die Überarbeitung des plinianischen *Panegyricus* auf Traian' *Wiener Studien* 32 (1910), 238–60.

——'Zur Quellenanalyse des Plinianischen *Panegyricus*', *Wiener Studien* 33 (1911), 71–100.

——'Zur Technik der Lateinischen Panegyriker', *Rheinisches Museum für Philologie* 67 (1912), 569–90.

Messina, M. G., 'Il Panegirico di Costantino del 312 e alcuni aspetti fiscali delai Gallia del IV secolo', *Index* 9 (1980), 41–77.

Méthy, N., 'Eloge, rhétorique et propaganda politique sous le Haut-Empire. L'example du *Panégyrique* de Trajan', *Mélanges d'Archéologie et d'histoire de l'École francaise de Rome* 112 (2000), 365–411.

Migne, J.-P., *Patrologia Graeca* multiple vols (Paris, 1856–8).

Miltner, F., *Ephesos* (Vienna, 1958).

——'Vorläufiger Bericht über die Ausgrabungen in Ephesos', *Jahreshefte des Österreichischen Archäologischen Instituto* 44 (1959), 243–314.

Mohr, P., *C. Sollius Apollinaris Sidonius* (Leipzig, 1985).

Moles, J., 'The Kingship Orations of Dio Chrysostom', *Papers of the Liverpool Latin Seminar* 6 (1990), 297–375.

Molin, M., 'Le *Panégyrique* de Trajan: éloquence d'apparat ou programme politique néo-stoïcien?' *Latomus* 48 (1989), 785–97.

——review of Lassandro (1992) *Latomus* 55 (1996), 450–1.

Mommsen, T. 'Zur Lebensgeschichte des jüngeren Plinius', *Hermes* 3 (1868–69), 31–139.

——*Chronica Minora* i (Monumenta Germaniae Historica. Auctores Antiquissimi 9) (Berlin, 1892).

——*Chronica Minora* ii (Monumenta Germaniae Historica. Auctores Antiquissimi 11) (Berlin, 1894).

Moreau, J., 'Sur la vision de Constantin', *Real-Encyclopädie d. klassischen Altertumswisenschaft* 55 (1953), 307–33.

Morford, M. P. O., 'How Tacitus Defined Liberty', *Aufstieg und Niedergang der römischen Welt* II.33.5 (1991), 3420–49.

——'*iubes esse liberos*. Pliny's *Panegyricus* and Liberty', *American Journal of Philology* 113 (1992), 575–93.

Mullaney, S., *The Place of the Stage: Licence, Play and Power in Renaissance England* (Chicago, 1988).

Müller, C. et al. *Fragmenta historicorum graecorum* 5 vols (Paris, 1841–72).

Müller, M., 'De Apollinaris Sidonii Latinitate', diss., Halle, 1888.

Müller-Rettig, B., *Der Panegyricus des Jahres 310 auf Konstantin den Grossen* (Stuttgart, 1990).

——*Panegyrici Latini. Lobreden auf römische Kaiser* i (Darmstadt, 2008).

——*Panegyrici Latini. Lobreden auf römische Kaiser* ii (Darmstadt, forthcoming).

Müller-Seidel, I., 'Die Usurpation Julians des Abtrünnigen im Lichte seiner Germanenpolitik', *Historische Zeitschrift* 180 (1955), 225–44.

Murdoch, A., *The Last Pagan. Julian the Apostate and the Death of the Ancient World* (Stroud, 2003).

Murgia, C. E., 'The Date of Tacitus' *Dialogus*', *Harvard Studies in Classical Philology* 84 (1980), 99–125.

Murray, O., 'Sailing to Byzantium', review of Straub (1939, 1964), *Classical Review* 80 (1966), 102–5.

——'Philosophy and Monarchy in the Hellenistic World' in Rajak, T., S. Pearce, J. K. Aitken, and J. Dines (eds.), *Jewish Perspectives on Hellenistic Rulers* (Berkeley, 2007), 13–28.

Mynors, R. A. B., *XII Panegyrici Latini* (Oxford, 1964).

Namia, G., 'Appunti per una nuova lettura dello *Panegyricus Messallae*', *Vichiana* 4 (1975), 22–59.

Nauta, R. R., *Poetry for Patrons: Literary Communication in the Age of Domitian* (Leiden, 2002).

Neumann, A. R., 'Vegetius', *Real-Encyclopädie d. klassischen Altertumswissenschaft Supp.* 10 (1965), 992–1020.

Nissen, T., 'Historisches Epos und Panegyrikos in der Spätantike', *Hermes* 75 (1940), 298–325.

Nixon, C. E. V., 'The Occasion and Date of Panegyric VIII(V) and the Celebration of Constantine's *quinquennalia*' *Antichthon* 14 (1980), 157–69.

——'The "Epiphany" of the Tetrarchs? An Examination of Mamertinus' Panegyric of 291', *Transactions of the American Philological Association* 111 (1981a), 157–66.

——'The Panegyric of 307 and Maximian's Visits to Rome', *Phoenix* 35 (1981b), 70–6.

——'Latin Panegyric in the Tetrarchic and Constantinian period' in Croke, B. and E. M. Emmett (eds.) *History and Historians in Late Antiquity* (Sydney, 1983) 88–99.

——'The Use of the Past by the Gallic Panegyrists' in Clarke, G. (ed.) *Reading the Past in Late Antiquity* (New South Wales, 1990), 1–36.

——'*Constantinus oriens Imperator*: Propaganda and Panegyric. On Reading Panegyric 7 (307)', *Historia* 42 (1993), 229–46.

——review of L'Huillier (1992), *Journal of Roman Studies* 84 (1994), 293–4.

——and Saylor Rodgers, B., *In Praise of Later Roman Emperors. The Pane-gyrici Latini*. Introduction, translation and historical commentary, with the Latin text of R. A. B. Mynors (Berkeley, 1994).

Nock, A. D., '*A Diis Electa*: A Chapter in the Religious History of the Third Century', *Harvard Theological Review* 23 (1930), 251–74.

——'Notes on the Ruler-cult I-IV', *Journal of Hellenic Studies* 48 (1928), 21–43.

——'Σύνναος θεός', *Harvard Studies in Classical Philology* 41 (1930), 1–62.

——'The Emperor's Divine *comes*', *Journal of Roman Studies* 37 (1947), 102–16.

——'The Roman Army and the Religious Year', *Harvard Theological Review* 45 (1952), 186–252.

Noreña, C. 'The Communication of the Emperor's Virtues', *Journal of Roman Studies* 91 (2001), 146–68.

——'Self-fashioning in the *Panegyricus*', in Roche, P. (ed.) *Pliny's Praise. The Panegyricus in the Roman World* (Cambridge, 2011), 29–44.

North, H. F., 'Canons and Hierarchies of the Cardinal Virtues in Greek and Latin Literature' in Wallach, L. (ed.) *The Classical Tradition (Studies in Honor of A. Caplan)* (Ithaca, NY, 1966) 165–83.

Novak, D. M., 'Constantine and the Senate: an early phase of the Christia-nisation of the Roman aristocracy', *Ancient Society* 10 (1979), 271–310.

Novák, R., 'In Panegyricos Latinos studia gramatica et critica', *České Museum Filologické* 7 (1901), 161–200, 241–83.

Oberhelman, S. M. and R. G. Hall, 'A New Statistical Analysis of Accentual Prose Rhythms in Imperial Latin Authors', *Classical Philology* 79 (1984), 114–30.

——'Meter in Accentual Clausulae of Late Imperial Latin Prose', *Classical Philology* 80 (1985), 214–27.

Oberhelman, S. M., 'The *cursus* in Late Imperial Latin Prose: A Reconsidera-tion of Methodology', *Classical Philology* 83 (1988a), 136–49.

——'The History and Development of the *cursus mixtus* in Latin Literature', *Classical Quarterly* 38 (1988b), 228–42.

——*Prose Rhythm in Latin Literature of the Roman Empire–First Century BC to Fourth Century AD* (Lampeter, 2003).

Odahl, C. M., 'A pagan's reaction to Constantine's conversion. Religious references in the Trier panegyric of AD 313' *Ancient World* 21 (1990), 45–63.

——*Constantine and the Christian Empire* (London, 2004).

Orentzel, A. E., 'Pliny and Domitian', *Classical Bulletin* 56 (1980), 49–51.

Pabst, A., *Quintus Aurelius Symmachus: Reden* (Darmstadt, 1989).

Paladini, M. L., 'La *gratiarum actio* dei consoli in Roma attraverso la testimonianza di Plinio il giovane', *Historia* 10 (1961), 356–74.

Paladini, V. and P. Fedeli, *Panegyrici Latini* (Rome, 1976).

Palanque, J.-R., *Histoire du Bas Empire* 2 vols (Paris, 1949–1959).

Paredi, A., *La Biblioteca del Pizzolpasso* (Milan, 1961).

Paribeni, R., *Optimus princeps: saggio sulla storia e sui tempi dell'imperatore Traiano* (Messina, 1927).

Parravicini, A., *Studio di retorica sulle opere di Claudio Claudiano* (Milan, 1905).

——*I panegyrici di Claudiano e i panegirici latini* (Milan, 1909).

Partsch, J., *Corippi Libri qui supersunt* (Monumenta Germaniae Historica. Auctores Antiquissimi 3.2) (Berlin, 1879).

Pascal, P., 'The *Institutionum disciplinae* of Isidore of Seville', *Traditio* 13 (1957), 425–31.

Paschoud, F., 'Réflexions sur l'ideal religieux de Symmaque', *Historia* 14 (1965), 215–35.

——'Les *Panégyriques latins* et l'*histoire Auguste*: quelques réflexions' in Defosse, P. (ed.) *Hommages à Carl Deroux* (Collection Latomus, ii, *Prose et Linguistique, Médecine*, 2002), 347–56.

Pasqualini, A., *Massimiano Herculius. Per un'interpretazione della figura e dell'opera* (Rome, 1979).

Passerini, A., 'Osservazioni su alcuni punti della storia di Diocleziano e Massimiano', *Acme* 1 (1948), 131–94.

Pellegrin, E., 'Manuscrits d'auteurs latins de l'epoque classique conservés dans les bibliothèques publiques de Suède', *Bulletin d'Information de l'Institut de Recherche et d'Histoire des Textes* 4 (1955), 18–20.

Perassi, C. 'Ideologia e prassi imperiali: *Panegirici Latini*, monete e medaglioni' in Kluge, B. and B. Weisser (eds.) *XII Internationaler Numismatischer Kongress Berlin 1997 Akten-Proceedings 2* (Berlin, 2000), 830–9.

Perelli, R. 'Panegirici e propaganda' in Mazzoli, G. and F. Gasti (eds.) *Prospettive sul tardoantico. Atti del Convegno di Pavia* (Como, 1999), 143–9.

Pernot, L., 'Les Topoi de l'éloge chez Ménandre le rhéteur', *Revue des Études grecques* 99 (1986), 3–53.

——La Rhétorique de l'éloge dans le monde gréco-romain (Paris, 1993).

Petit, P., *Libanius* (Paris, 1955).

——'Recherches sur la publication et la diffusion des discours de Libanius', *Historia* 5 (1956), 479–509.

Pfeiffer, R., *History of Classical Scholarship 1300 to 1850* (Oxford, 1976).

Pfister, F. 'Epiphanie', *Real-Encyclopädie d. klassischen Altertumswissenschaft* *Suppl.* 4 (1924), 277–323.

——'numen', *Real-Encyclopädie d. klassischen Altertumswissenschaft* 17.2 (1937), 1273–96.

Pichon, R., *Les Derniers Ecrivains Profanes* (Paris, 1906a).

—— 'L'Origine du recueil des *Panegyrici Latini*', *Real-Encyclopädie d. klassischen Altertumswissenschaft* 8 (1906b), 229–49, also published in (1906a) 270–91.

—— 'La Politique de Constantin d'après les *Panegyrici Latini*', *Comptes rendus de l'Académie des Inscriptions et Belles-lettres* 50 (1906c), 289–97.

Picone, G., *L'eloquenza di Plinio*. *Teoria e Prassi* (Palermo, 1978).

Piganiol, A., *L'Empereur Constantin* (Paris, 1932).

—— 'La Capitatio de Dioclétian', *Revue Historique* 176 (1935), 1–13.

—— *Histoire Romaine* IV.2 (Paris, 1947).

Pippidi, D. M., 'Compte-Rendu des séances', *Revue des Etudes Latines* 8 (1930), 136–8.

Pitkäranta, R., review of Gamberini (1983), *Gnomon* 59 (1987), 357–9.

Plass, P., *Wit and the Writing of History. The Rhetoric of Historiography in Imperial Rome* (Madison, 1988).

Platnauer, M., *Claudian* 2 vols (London, 1922).

Pohlschmidt, W., *Quaestiones Themistianae* (Münster, 1908).

Polara, J., *Publilii Optatiani Porfyrii Carmina* (Turin, 1973).

Porter, S.E., (ed.) *Handbook of Classical Rhetoric in the Hellenistic Period (330 BCE–CE 400)* (Leiden, 1997).

Portmann, W., *Geschichte in der spätantiken Panegyrik* (Frankfurt, 1988).

Previale, L., 'Teoria e prassi del panegirico bizantino', *Emerita* 17 (1949), 72–105 and 18 (1950), 340–66.

Price, S. R. F., 'Between Man and God: Sacrifice in the Roman Imperial Cult', *Journal of Roman Studies* 70 (1980), 28–43.

Pritchett, W. K., *The Greek State at War* III (Berkeley, 1979).

Purser, L. C., 'Notes on the *Panegyrici Latini*', *Hermathena* 46 (1931), 16–30.

Puteolanus, F., (Milan 1476 or 1482; Venice 1499).

Putnam, M. C. J., *Artifices of Eternity. Horace's Fourth Book of Odes* (Ithaca, NY, 1986).

—— *Horace's* Carmen Saeculare: *Ritual Magic and the Poet's Art* (New Haven, 2000).

Radice, B., *The Letters of the Younger Pliny* (Harmondsworth, 1963).

—— 'Pliny and the *Panegyricus*', *Greece & Rome* 15 (1968), 166–72.

—— *Pliny. Letters and Panegyricus* 2 vols (London, 1969).

Radnoti-Alföldi, M., *Die constantinische Goldprägung* (Mainz, 1963).

Ramage, E. S., 'Velleius Paterculus 2.126.2–3 and the Panegyric Tradition', *Classical Antiquity* 1 (1982), 266–71.

—— 'Juvenal and the Establishment', *ANRW* II.33.1 (1989), 640–707.

Ramelli, I., 'Il concetto di *res publica* nei panegirici latini dell'età imperiale', *Rendiconti Istituto Lombardo* 133 (1999), 177–97.

Ramirez de Verger, A., *Flavio Cresconio Coripo El Panegírico de Justino II* (Seville, 1985).

Rawson, E., *Roman Culture and Society: Collected Papers* (Oxford, 1991).

Rees, R. D., 'The Private Lives of Public Figures in Latin Prose Panegyric', in Whitby, M. (ed.) *The Propaganda of Power: the Role of Panegyric in Late Antiquity* (Leiden, 1998), 77–101.

—— 'To Be and Not To Be; Pliny's paradoxical Trajan', *Bulletin of the Institute of Classical Studies* 45 (2001), 149–68.

—— *Layers of Loyalty in Latin Panegyric* AD *289–307* (Oxford, 2002).

—— 'Talking to the Tetrarchs; the dynamics of vocative address' in Deroux, C. (ed.) *Studies in Latin Literature and Roman History XI* (*Collection Latomus* 272) (Brussels, 2003), 447–92.

—— 'Praising in Prose; Vergil in the Panegyrics' in Rees, R. D. (ed.) *Romane memento; Vergil in the Fourth Century* (London, 2004), 33–46.

—— (ed.) *Romane memento; Vergil in the Fourth Century* (London, 2004).

—— 'The Emperors' New Names. Diocletian Jovius and Maximian Herculius' in Rawlings, L. and H. Bowden (eds.) *Herakles/Hercules in the Ancient World* (Swansea, 2005), 223–39.

—— 'Latin panegyric' in Dominik, W. and J. Hall (eds.) *A Handbook of Roman Rhetoric* (London, 2007), 136–48.

—— 'Form and Function of Narrative in Roman Panegyrical Oratory' in Berry, D. and A. Erskine (eds.) *Form and Function in Roman Oratory* (Cambridge, 2010a), 105–21.

—— 'Words of Praise', *Millenium* 7 (2010b), 9–28.

—— 'The Whole Truth? *Laudationes* in the Courtroom' in Covino, R. and C. J. Smith (eds.) *Praise and Blame in Roman Republican Rhetoric* (Swansea, 2011a), 83–98.

—— 'Afterwords of Praise. The ancient afterlife of Pliny's *Panegyricus*' in Roche, P. (ed.) *Pliny's Praise. The* Panegyricus *in the Roman World* (Cambridge, 2011b), 175–88.

—— 'Bright Lights, Big City. Rome and the *Panegyrici Latini*' in Kelly, G. and L. Grig (eds.) *Rome and Constantinople in Late Antiquity* (Oxford, 2012).

Reeve, M. D., 'The Addressee of the *Laus Pisonis*' *Illinois Classical Studies* 9 (1984), 42–8.

Ricciotti, G., *Giuliano l'Apostato* (Milan, 1962).

Rimell, V., *Martial's Rome. Empire and the Ideology of Epigram* (Cambridge, 2008).

Robert, L., 'Les Inscriptions de Thessalonique' *Revue Philologique* 48 (1974), 180–246.

Roberts, M., *The Jeweled Style. Poetry and Poetics in Late Antiquity* (Cornell, 1989).

—— *The Humblest Sparrow. The Poetry of Venantius Fortunatus* (Ann Arbor, 2009).

Roche, P. A., 'The Public Image of Trajan's Family', *Classical Philology* 97 (2002), 41–60.

—— 'The *Panegyricus* and the Monuments of Rome' in Roche, P. (ed.) *Pliny's Praise. The* Panegyricus *in the Roman World* (Cambridge, 2011a), 45–66.
—— (ed.) *Pliny's Praise. The* Panegyricus *in the Roman World* (Cambridge, 2011b).

Rodgers, D. A., *Contested Truths: Keywords in American Politics since Independence* (New York, 1987).

Rodríguez Gervás, M. J., 'Las virtudes del emperador Constantino', *Studia Historica. Historia Antigua* 2–3 (1984–5), 239–47.

—— 'Constantino en los panegíricos', *Studia Zamorensia* 7 (1986), 423–8.

—— *Propaganda Política y opinión Pública en los Panegíricos Latinos del Bajo Imperio* (Salamanca, 1991).

Rögler, G., 'Die *lex Villia Annalis*', *Klio* 40 (1962), 76–123.

Roller, M. B., *Constructing Autocracy: Aristocrats and Emperors in Julio-Claudian Rome* (Princeton, 2001).

Romano, D., *Claudiano* (Palermo, 1958).

—— 'Per una nuova interpretazione del *Panegirico latino* in onore dell'imperatore', *Annali del Liceo classico G. Garibaldi di Palermo* 2 (1965), 327–38.

—— *L'ultimo epos latino. Interpretazione della Iohanis di Corippo* (Palermo, 1968).

—— *In Laudem Iustini* (Palermo, 1970).

Römer, F., 'Kenntnis und Imitation des plinianischen *Panegyricus* bei italienischen Humanisten' *Grazer Beitrage* 16 (1989), 271–89.

Ronning, C., *Herrscherpanegyrik unter Trajan und Konstantin* (Tübingen, 2007).

Rosati, G., 'Luxury and Love: the encomium as aestheticisation of power in Flavian poetry' in Nauta, R. R., H.-J. Van Dam, and J. J. L. Smolenaars (eds.) *Flavian Poetry* (Leiden, 2006), 41–58.

Roueché, C., 'Acclamations in the Later Roman Empire: New evidence from Aphrodisias', *Journal of Roman Studies* 74 (1984), 181–99.

Rubin, B., *Das Zeitalter Justinians* i (Berlin, 1960).

Rudd, N., *Themes in Roman Satire* (London, 1986).

Ruehl, H., *De XII Panegyricis Latinis Propaedeumata* (Greifswald, 1868).

Ruggini, L., 'Il vescovo Ambrogio e la *Historia Augusta*; attualità di un topos politico-letterario' in *Atti del colloquio Patavino sulla Historia Augusta* (Padua, 1963), 67–79.

Rundle, D., '"Not so much praise as precept": Erasmus, panegyric, and the Renaissance art of teaching princes' in Too Y.L. and N. Livingstone (eds.) *Pedagogy and Power. Rhetorics of classical learning* (Cambridge, 1998), 148–69.

Russell, D. A. and N. G. Wilson, *Menander Rhetor* (Oxford, 1981).

Russell, D. A., 'The Panegyrists and Their Teachers' in Whitby, M. (ed.) *The Propaganda of Power: the role of panegyric in Late Antiquity* (Leiden, 1998), 17–50.

Ryan, F. X., 'Pacatus on the Mnemonic Capabilities of Republican Political Figures' *Leeds International Classical Studies* 8 (2009), 1–5.

Ryberg, I. S., *Rites of the State Religion in Roman Art* (Rome, 1955).

——'Clupeus Virtutis' in Wallach, L. (ed.) *The Classical Tradition (Studies in Honor of A. Caplan)* (Ithaca, NY, 1966), 232–8.

Sabbadini, R. 'Spogli Ambrosiani latini' *Studi italiani di filologia classica* 11 (1903), 165–385.

——*Carteggio di Giovanni Aurispa* (Rome, 1931).

Sabbah, G. 'De la rhétorique à la communication politique: les *Panégyriques Latins*', *Bulletin de l'Association Guillaume Budé* 4 (1984), 363–88.

Sachs, A., *De quattuor panegyricis qui ab Eumenio scripti esse dicuntur* (Halle, 1885).

Saint-Denis, E., 'Qu'est-ce que l'*Agricola* de Tacite ?', *Les Études classiques* 10 (1941), 14–30.

Saylor Rodgers, B. S., 'Constantine's Pagan Vision', *Byzantion* 50 (1980), 259–78.

——'Divine Insinuation in the *Panegyrici Latini*', *Historia* 35 (1986), 69–104.

——'The Metamorphosis of Constantine', *Classical Quarterly* 39 (1989a), 233–46.

——'Eumenius of Augustodunum', *Ancient Society* 20 (1989b), 249–66.

Schaefer, O., *Die beiden Panegyrici des Mamertinus und die Geschichte des Kaisers Maximianus Herculius* (Strasburg, 1914).

Schanz, M. 'Zu den lateinischen Panegyriken', *Rheinisches Museum für Philologie* 44 (1889), 480.

Schenkl, C., '*Lectiones Panegyricae*', *Wiener Studien* 3 (1881), 118–30.

——*Magni Ausoni opuscula* (Monumenta Germaniae Historica. Auctores Antiquissimi 5.2) (Berlin, 1883).

Schetter, W., review of Mynors (1964), *Gnomon* 39 (1967), 500–507, repr. in *Kaiserzeit und Spätantike. Kleine Schriften 1957–1992* (Stuttgart, 1994), 184–92.

Schindler, C., 'Tradition–Transformation–Innovation: Claudians Panegyriken und das Epos' in Ehlers, W.-W., F. Felgentreu, and S. Wheeler (eds.) *Aetas Claudianea* (Leipzig, 2004), 16–37.

——*Per carmina laudes. Untersuchungen zur spätantiken Verspanegyrik von Claudian bis Coripp* (Berlin, 2009).

Schmid, W., 'Claudianus', *Reallexicon für Antike und Christentum* 3 (Stuttgart 1957), 152–69.

Schmidt, P. L., *Politik und Dichtung in der Panegyrik Claudians* (Constanz, 1976).

Schoenebeck, H., *von Beiträge zur Religionspolitik des Maxentius und Constantin* (Leipzig, 1939; 1962).

Schoonhoven, H., 'The *Panegyricus Messallae*: date and relation with *Catalepton* 9', *Aufstieg und Niedergang der römischen Welt* II.30.3 (1983), 1681–707.

Schowalter, D. N., *The Emperor and the Gods. Images from the Time of Trajan* (Minneapolis, 1993).

Schuster, M., *Epistularum libri novem: epistularum ad Traianum liber, panegyricus* (Leipzig, 1958).

Schwarz, C., *C. Plinii Caecilii Panegyricus Caesari imp. Nervae Traiano Aug. Secundi dictus* (Nuremberg, 1746).

Scott, J. C., *Domination and the Arts of Resistance: Hidden Transcripts* (New Haven, 1990).

Scott, K., 'The Significance of Statues in Precious Metals', *Transactions of the American Philological Association* 62 (1931), 101–23.

—— 'The Elder and Younger Pliny on Emperor Worship', *Transactions of the American Philological Association* 63 (1932), 156–65.

—— 'Statius' Adulation of Domitian', *American Journal of Philology* 54 (1933), 247–9.

—— *The Imperial Cult under the Flavians* (Stuttgart and Berlin, 1936).

Scourfield, J. H. D., (ed.) *Texts & Culture in Late Antiquity. Inheritance, Authority and Change* (Swansea, 2007).

Seager, R., 'Some Imperial Virtues in the Latin Prose Panegyrics. The Demands of Propaganda and the Dynamics of Literary Composition', in Cairns, F. (ed.) *Papers of the Liverpool Latin Seminar* 4 (1983), 129–65.

Seeck, O., *Q. Aurelii Symmachi quae supersunt* (Monumenta Germaniae Historica. Auctores Antiquissimi 6.1) (Berlin, 1883).

—— 'Studien zur Geschichte Diocletians und Constantins, I. Die Reden des Eumenius', *Neue Jahrbücher für Philologie und Pädagogik* 137 (1888) 713–28.

—— *Die Briefe des Libanius* (Leipzig, 1905).

—— 'Eumenius' in *Real-Encyclopädie d. klassischen Altertumswisenschaft* 6 (1909), 1105–114.

—— *Geschichte des Untergangs der antiken Welt* v (Berlin, 1913).

—— *Regesten der Kaiser und Pipste für die Jahre 311 bis 476 n. Chr.* (Stuttgart, 1919).

Seelentag, G., *Taten und Tugenden Traians* (Stuttgart, 2004).

Semple, W. H., 'quaestiones exegeticae Sidonianae' (Cambridge, 1930), 1–116.

Seston, W., *Dioclétien et la Tétrarchie* (Paris, 1946).

—— 'Jovius et Herculius ou 'l'épiphanie' des Tétrarques', *Historia* 1 (1950), 257–66.

Shea, G. W., *The Iohannis or De Bellis Libycis of Flavius Cresconius Corippus* (Lampeter, 1998).

Shelton, J. A., 'Pliny's *Letter* 3.11: Rhetoric and autobiography', *Classica et Mediaevalia* 38 (1987), 121–39.

Sherwin-White, A. N., *The Letters of Pliny* (Oxford, 1966).

——*Fifty Letters of Pliny* (Oxford, 1967).

——'Pliny, the Man and his Letters', *Greece & Rome* 16 (1969), 76–90.

Shiel, N., *The Episode of Carausius and Allectus. The Literary and Numismatic Evidence* (Oxford, 1977).

Shochat, Y., 'The Change in the Roman Religion at the Time of the Emperor Trajan', *Latomus* 44 (1985), 317–36.

Shotter, D. C. A., 'Tacitus' View of Emperors and the Principate', *Aufstieg und Niedergang der römischen Welt* II.33.5 (1991), 3263–361.

Sievers, G., *Das Leben des Libanius* (Berlin, 1868).

Simon, W., *Claudiani Panegyricus de Consulatu Manlii Theodori* (Berlin, 1975).

Simpson, C. J., '*Laeti* in Northern Gaul. A Note on *Pan. Lat.* VIII 21', *Latomus* 36 (1977), 169–70.

Smith, R. R. R., 'The Public Image of Licinius I', *Journal of Roman Studies* 87 (1997), 170–202.

Solari, A., 'L'*alibi* di Theodosio nella opposizione antidinastica', *Klio* 27 (1934), 165–8.

——'L'antistoricismo nell' attivita letteraria di Plinio', *Rend. Accad. Naz. Lincei, Classe Sc. Mor. Stor. Filol.* 5 (1950), 457–62.

Solmsen, F., 'Demetrius *peri hermeneias* und sein Peripatetisches Quellenmaterial', *Hermes* 66 (1931), 241–67.

——'The Aristotelian Tradition in Ancient Rhetoric', *American Journal of Philology* 62 (1941), 35–50, 169–90.

Sordi, M., 'I rapporti fra Ambrogio e il panegirista Pacato', *Rend. Ist. Lomb. Sc. Lett* 122 (1988), 93–100.

Soverini, P., 'Imperio e imperatori nell'opera di Plinio il Giovane: aspetti e problemi del rapporto con Domiziano e Traiano', *Aufstieg und Niedergang der römischen Welt* 33.1 (1989), 515–54.

Spagnuola Vigorita, T., *execranda pernicies. Delatori e fisco nell' età di Costantino* (Naples, 1984).

Spengler, L., *Rhetores Graeci* (Leipzig, 1856).

Stache, U. J., *In laudem Iustini Augusti minoris* (Berlin, 1976).

Stacey, P., *Roman Monarchy and the Renaissance Prince* (Cambridge, 2007).

Stadler, A., Die Autoren der anonymen gallischen Panegyrici, diss. Munich, 1912.

Stein, E., *Histoire du Bas Empire* 2 vols. French edition by J.-R. Palanque (Paris, 1959).

Stern, H., 'Remarks on the '*Adoratio*' under Diocletian', *Journal of the Warburg Institute* 17 (1954), 184–9.

Stevens, C. E., *Sidonius Apollinaris and His Age* (Oxford, 1933).

Stevenson, T. R., 'The Ideal Benefactor and the Father Analogy in Greek and Roman Thought' *Classical Quarterly* 42 (1992), 421–36.

Storch, R. H., 'The *XII Panegyrici Latini* and the Perfect Prince' *Acta Classica* 15 (1972), 71–6.

Strack, P. L., *Untersuchungen zur römischen Reichsprägung des zweiten Jahrhunderts I* (Stuttgart, 1931).

Straub, J., 'Eugenius', *Reallexicon für Antike und Christentum* 5 (Stuttgart, 1966) 860–77.

——*Vom Herrscherideal in der Spatantike* (Stuttgart, 1939; repr. 1964).

——*Studien zur Historia Augusta* (Bern, 1952).

——'Konstantins Verzicht auf den Gang zum Kapitol', *Historia* 4 (1955), 297–313.

Strobel, K., 'Zu zeitgeschichtlichen Aspeketen im Panegyricus des jüngeren Plinius: Trajan–imperator invictus und novum ad principatum iter' in Knape, J. and K. Strobel (eds.) *Zur Deutung von Geschichte in Antike und Mittelalter* (Bamberg, 1985), 9–112.

Stroheker, K. F., *Der senatorische Adel im spätantiken Gallien* (Tübingen, 1948).

——*Spanische Senatoren der spätrömischen und westgotischen Zeit, Germanentum und Spätantike* (Stuttgart-Zurich, 1965).

Strömberg, E., 'ad codicem Upsaliensem qui Panegyricos Latinos continet', *Eranos* 2 (1897), 46–7.

——*Studia in Panegyricos veteres* Latinos (Upsala, 1902).

Strong, D. E., *Roman Art* (Harmondsworth, 1976).

Struthers, L. B., 'The Rhetorical Structure of the Encomia of Claudius Claudianus', *Harvard Studies in Classical Philology* 30 (1919), 49–87.

Styka, J., *Sydoniusz Apollinaris I Kultura Literacka w Galii v wiekn* (Krakow, 2008).

Suerbaum, W., *Vom antiken zum frühmittelalterlichen Staatsbegriff* (Munster, 1961).

Suster, G., 'Notizia e classificazione dei codici contenenti il *Panegyrico* di Plinio a Traiano', *Rivista di Filologia* 16 (1888), 504–51.

——'De Plinio Ciceronis imitatore' *Rivista di filologia e di istruzione classica* 18 (1890), 74–86.

Sutherland, C. H. V., 'The Intelligibility of Roman Coin Types' *Journal of Roman Studies* 49 (1959), 46–55.

Sydenham, E. A., 'The Vicissitudes of Maximian after His Abdication', *Numismatic Chronicle* 14 (1934), 141–67.

Syme, R., review of Durry (1938) *Journal of Roman Studies* 28 (1938), 217–24.

420   Bibliography

—— The Roman Revolution (Oxford, 1939).

—— Tacitus (Oxford, 1958a).

—— 'Consulates in Absence' Journal of Roman Studies 48 (1958b), 1–9.

—— Ammianus and the Historia Augusta (Oxford, 1968).

Szelest, H., 'Domitian und Martial', Eos 62 (1974), 105–14.

Taegert, W., Claudius Claudianus: Panegyricus dictus Olybrio et Probino consulibus (Munich, 1988).

Talbert, R. J. A., The Senate of Imperial Rome (Princeton, 1984).

Tandoi, V., 'Giovenale e il mecenatismo a Roman fra I e II secolo', Atene e Roma 13 (1968), 125–45.

Tantillo, I., 'L'ideologia imperiale fra centro e perfiferia. A proposito di un elogio di Costantino di Augusta Traiana', Rivista di filologia e di istruzione classica 127 (1999), 73–95.

Teurfs, C. and Didderen, J.-C., Corippe. La Iohannide ou sur les Guerres de Libye (Paris, 2007).

Thiele, G., 'Die Poesie unter Domitian', Hermes 51 (1916), 233–60.

Thomas, K., 'Cuspinians Panegirikerausgabe', Rheinisches Museum für Philologie 122 (1979), 338–43.

Thompson, E. A., 'Three Notes on Julian in 361 AD', Hermathena 62 (1943), 83–8.

—— Ammianus Marcellinus (Cambridge, 1947).

Tillemont, Histoire des Empereurs IV (Brussels, 1732).

Tommasi Moreschini, Ch. O. Flavius Cresconius Corippus. Iohannidos Liber III (Florence, 2001).

Toutain, J., Les Cultes paiens dans l'empire romain III (Paris, 1917).

Toynbee, J. M. C., Roman Medallions (New York, 1944).

Tränkle, H., Appendix Tibulliana (Berlin, 1990).

Traube, L. in Mommsen, T. (ed.) Cassiodori Senatoris Variae (Monumenta Germaniae Historica. Auctores Antiquissimi 12) (Berlin, 1894).

Trisoglio, F., 'Le idee politiche di Plinio il Giovane e di Dione Crisostomo' Il Pensiero Politico 5 (1972), 3–43.

—— Plinio Cecilio Secondo. Opere 2 vols (Turin, 1973).

Turcan, R., 'Images solaires dans le Panégyrique VI', in Renard, M. and R. Schilling (eds.) Hommages à Jean Bayet (Brussels, 1964), 697–706.

Turcan-Verkerk, A.-M., Un Poète latin chrétien redécouvert: Latinius Pacatus Drepanius, panégyriste de Théodose (Brussels, 2003).

Usener, H. and L. Radermacher (eds.) Opuscula 2 [Opera VI] (Stuttgart, 1965).

Valpy, A. J., Panegyrici Veteres (London, 1828).

Van Berchem, D., L'Armée de Dioclétien et la réforme constantinienne (Paris, 1952).

Van Den Hout, M. P. J., A Commentary on the Letters of M. Cornelius Fronto (Leiden, 1999).

Van Sickle, C. E., 'Eumenius and the Schools of Autun' *American Journal of Philology* 55 (1934), 236–43.

Vatin, C., 'Les Empereurs du 4ième siècle à Delphes', *Bulletin de Correspondance Hellénique* 86 (1962), 229–41.

Velkov, V., 'Ein Beitrag zum Aufenthalt des Kaisers Theodosios I' *Eunomia* 5 (1961), 49–65.

Verdière, R., 'L'Auteur du *Panegyricus Messallae* tibullien', *Latomus* 13 (1954), 56–64.

Veyne, P., 'Lisibilité des images, propaganda et apparat monarchique dans l'empire romain', *Revue Historique* 621 (2002), 3–30.

Vereeke, E., 'Le Corpus des *Panégyriques Latins* de l'époque tardive: problèmes d'imitation', *L'Antiquité Classique* 44 (1975), 141–60.

Vielberg, M., *Pflichten, Werte, Ideale* (Stuttgart, 1987).

Vinchesi, M. A., *Flavii Cresconii Corippi Iohannidos liber primus* (Naples, 1983).

Vogel, F., *Magni Felicis Ennodi Opera* (Monumenta Germaniae Historica. Auctores Antiquissimi 7) (Berlin, 1885).

Vogt, J., *Vom Reichsgedanken der Römer* (Leipzig, 1942).

——*Constantin der Grosse und sein Jahrhundert* (Munich, 1960).

Vollmann, B., *Studien zum Priszillianismus* (St. Ottilien, 1965).

Vollmer, F., *Laudationum funebrium Romanorum historiae et reliquiarum editio* (Leipzig, 1891).

Vollmer, F., *Flavii Merobaudis reliquiae. Blossii Aemelii Dracontii carmina. Eugeni Toletani Episcopi carmina et epistulae* (Monumenta Germaniae Historica. Auctores Antiquissimi 14) (Berlin, 1905).

Waas, M., 'Germanen im römischen Dienst im vierten Jahrhundert', diss., Bonn, 1965.

Wallace-Hadrill, A., 'The Emperor and His Virtues', *Historia* 30 (1981), 298–323.

——'*Civilis Princeps*: Between Citizen and King', *Journal of Roman Studies* 72 (1982), 32–48.

——*Suetonius* (London, 1983).

Walser, G., 'Der Kaiser als *Vindex libertatis*' *Historia* 4 (1955), 353–67.

Ware, C. 'Claudian, Vergil and the Two Battles of Frigidus' in Rees, R. D. (ed.) *Romane memento; Vergil in the Fourth Century* (London, 2004), 155–71.

Ware, C., *The Epic World of Claudian* (forthcoming).

Warmington, B. H., 'Aspects of Constantinian Propaganda in the *Panegyrici Latini*', *Transactions of the American Philological Association* 104 (1974), 371–84.

Waters, K. H., 'The Character of Domitian', *Phoenix* 18 (1964), 49–77.

——'*Traianus Domitiani Continuator*', *American Journal of Philology* 90 (1969), 385–404.

—— 'Juvenal and the Reign of Trajan', *Antichthon* 4 (1970), 62–77.

Watson, L., Sidonius Apollinaris. Carmina 1 and 2 diss., London, 1997.

—— 'Representing the Past, Redefining the Future: Sidonius Apollinaris' Panegyrics of Avitus and Anthemius' in Whitby, M. (ed.) *The Propaganda of Power: the Role of Panegyric in Late Antiquity* (Leiden, 1998), 177–98.

Weinstock, S., *Divus Iulius* (Oxford, 1971).

Welzel, E., 'De Claudiani et Corippi sermone epico', diss., Breslau, 1908.

Wheeler, S., 'More Roman than the Romans of Rome: Virgilian (self-)fashioning in Claudian's *Panegyric for the Consuls Olybrius and Probinus*' in Scourfield, J. H. D. (ed.) *Texts & Culture in Late Antiquity. Inheritance, Authority and Change* (Swansea, 2007), 97–133.

Whigham, F., *Ambition and Privilege: the Social Tropes of Elizabethan Courtesy Theory* (Berkeley, 1984).

Whitby, M., (ed.) *The Propaganda of Power. The Role of Panegyric in Late Antiquity* (Leiden, 1998).

White, P., *Promised Verse: Poets in the Society of Augustan Rome* (Cambridge MA, 1993).

Whitmarsh, T., *Greek Literature and the Roman Empire* (Oxford, 2001).

Whittaker, C. R., '*agri deserti*' in M. I. Finley (ed.) *Studies in Roman Property* (Cambridge, 1976), 137–65.

Wickert, L., '*princeps*', *Real-Encyclopädie d. klassischen Altertumswisenschaft* 22 (1954), 1998–2296.

Wilfried, E., *Die Laudes Honorii Claudians. Die Beispiele poetischer Konsulatpanegyrik im Vergleich* (Regensbourg, 1987).

Wilamowitz-Moellendorff, U. von, *History of Classical Scholarship*, tr. A. Harris (London, 1982).

Williams, G., *Change and Decline. Roman Literature in the Early Empire* (Berkeley, 1978).

Winterbottom, M., '*Concedat laurea linguae*', review of Paladini and Fedeli (1976) *Classical Review* 29 (1979), 234–5.

—— 'Panegyrici Latini' in L. D. Reynolds (ed.) *Texts and Transmission. A Survey of the Latin Classics* (Oxford, 1983), 289.

—— review of Lassandro (1992), *Gnomon* 67 (1995), 560–1.

Wirszubski, C., *Libertas as a Political Idea at Rome during the Late Republic and Early Principate* (Cambridge, 1950).

Wiseman, T. P., 'Calpurnius Siculus and the Claudian Civil War', *Journal of Roman Studies* 72 (1982), 57–67.

Wistrand, E., 'A Note on the *geminus natalis* of Emperor Maximian', *Eranos* 62 (1964), 131–45.

Woodman, A. J., *Velleius Paterculus. The Tiberian Narrative (2.94–131)* (Cambridge, 1977).

Worthington, I., (ed.) *A Companion to Greek Rhetoric* (London, 2007).

Woytek, E., 'Der *Panegyricus* des Plinius: Sein Verhältnis zum *Dialogus* und den *Historiae* des Tacitus und seine absolute Datierung', *Wiener Studien* 119 (2006), 115–56.

Zarini, V., *Berbères ou barbares? Recherches sur le livre second de la Iohannide de Corippe* (Paris 1997a).

—— 'Poésie officielle et arts figurés au siècle de Justinien: images de pouvoir dans la *Iohannide* de Corippe', *Revue des Etudes Latine* 75 (1997b), 219–40.

—— *Rhétorique, poétique, spiritualité: la technique épique de Corippe dans la Iohannide* (Turnhout, 2003).

Zetzel, J. E. G., *Cicero: De Re Publica, selections* (Cambridge, 1995).

Ziegler, K., 'Panegyrikos', *Real-Encyclopädie d. klassischen Altertumswissenschaft* 18.2 (1949), 559–81.

Acknowledgements

It is my pleasure to record my thanks to authors and publishers for permission to reproduce work originally published elsewhere, as follows:

R. A. B. Mynors, 'Preface' (*XII Panegyrici Latini*, Oxford 1964, pp. v–xi).

R. Pichon, 'L'origine du recueil des *Panegyrici Latini*' (Appendix 1 in *Les Derniers Ecrivains Profanes* (Paris 1906) 270–91) (= *REA* 8 (1906) 229–49).

B. Radice, 'Pliny and the Panegyricus' (*G&R* 15 (1968) 166–72).

S. Morton Braund, 'Praise and protreptic in early imperial panegyric' in M. Whitby (ed.) *The Propaganda of Power. The Role of Panegyric in Late Antiquity* (Brill: Mnemosyne Supplements 183, 1998) 53–76.

E. Fantham, 'Two levels of orality in the genesis of Pliny's *Panegyricus*' in E. A. Mackay (ed.) *Signs of Orality. The oral tradition and its influence in the Greek and Roman world* (Brill: Mnemosyne Supplements 188, 1999) 221–37.

M. P. O. Morford, '*iubes esse liberos*. Pliny's *Panegyricus* and liberty' (*AJP* 113 (1992) 575–93).

S. Bartsch, 'The Art of Sincerity. Pliny's *Panegyricus*' from *Actors in the Audience. Theatricality and Doublespeak from Nero to Hadrian* (Harvard 1994) 148–87.

S. Hoffer, 'Divine Comedy? Accession propaganda in Pliny, *Epistles* 10.1-2 and the *Panegyric*' (*JRS* 96 (2006) 73–87).

C. E. V. Nixon, 'Latin Panegyric in the Tetrarchic and Constantinian period' in B. Croke and A. M. Emmett *History and Historians in Late Antiquity* (Sydney 1983) 88–99.

S. MacCormack from 'Latin Prose Panegyrics' in T. A. Dorey (ed.) *Empire and Aftermath II* (London 1975) 143–205, pp. 177–86.

E. Vereeke, 'The corpus of Latin Panegyrics from Late Antiquity: Problems of imitation' (*L'Antiquité Classique* 44 (1975) 141–60).

W. S. Maguinness, 'Locutions and Formulae of the Latin Panegyrists', (*Hermathena* 48 (1933) 117–138).

B. Saylor Rodgers, 'Divine insinuation in the *Panegyrici Latini*' (*Historia* 35 (1986) 69–104).

B. H. Warmington, 'Aspects of Constantinian Propaganda in the *Panegyrici Latini*' (*TAPA* 104 (1974) 371–84).

R. Blockley, 'The Panegyric of Claudius Mamertinus on the Emperor Julian' (*AJP* 93 (1972) 437–50).

A. Lippold, 'Herrscherideal und Traditionsverbundenheit im Panegyricus des Pacatus' (*Historia* 17 (1968) 228–50).

Index